The Old-House Journal

Restoration Manual No. 11

The 1986 Yearbook

The Old-House Journal

Restoration Manual No. 11

The 1986 Yearbook

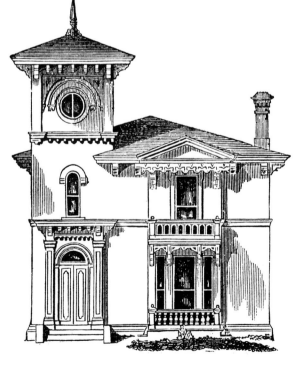

Contents

→

PREFACE

Restoration Vs. Renovation

An old house brings with it some responsibilities along with its joys. A house that has survived the ravages of years and previous owners is now part of our cultural history. The following guidelines are offered for the consideration of those who have just bought — or are about to buy — an old house.

First of all, you have to be clear on your purpose — do you intend to restore your house, or do you only want to renovate it? A restoration involves putting the house back into a state that resembles its condition in an earlier period. Renovation means just putting the house back into sound mechanical condition without regard to any particular style. Restoration vs. renovation is a basic design decision.

Whichever course you select, there's one rule to keep in mind: Don't destroy detail. Removal of architectural detail should be regarded as a cultural high crime. Detail represents labor and craftsmanship which, because of today's economics, is an irreplaceable resource. Detail, both interior and exterior, is what distinguishes most old houses from the cardboard boxes of modern builders. By preserving detail, you are not only conserving a cultural resource, but also insuring the long-term market value of the house. The restoration of damaged or neglected detail is well within the capabilities of most home craftspersons; the basic ingredients are time and patience.

Don't do anything that can't be undone. Nothing lasts forever — everything you do to a house today will have to be re-done by somebody (maybe you) at a later date. So each project should be undertaken with the idea, "How can this be renewed in the future?"

Be wary of period changes. There's no way to transform a big old Victorian into a cute little colonial. Learn as much as you can about the period in which your house was built, and then try to keep your modifications consistent with the concept of the builders.

Old houses are a fragile resource. They're a responsibility and a commitment — and a considerable amount of work. They're also one of the greatest sources of pride and satisfaction a homeowner can experience.

The Editors

A word on page numbers. . . .

In 1986, The Old-House Journal began running paid advertisements. We've deleted the ads from this Yearbook, and so had to come up with a new sequence of page numbers — the italic numbers at the upper corner of each page. It is these italic page numbers which are referred to in the Table of Contents. But in order to preserve the cross-referencing information in the 1986 Index (which will be incorporated into a future revision of the Cumulative Index), we've retained the <u>original issue page numbers</u> — the bold numbers at the lower corner of each page. It is these original page numbers which are referred to in the Index.

What?!
No More Holes?

SO HERE'S the expanded OHJ we promised. We're exhilirated by the changes -- and we can't imagine anybody complaining about the color cover, expanded editorial, our new features on post-Victorian and vernacular houses, or the appropriate advertising from old-house companies.

WE CAN IMAGINE one complaint, however. The holes are gone. We know how attached most of you are to those three little holes that let you keep your OHJs in a ring binder. (It's how we keep our back copies here in the office, too.) Most magazines don't have holes, and for them it's not a big deal. But since a lot of people consider OHJ more a working tool than a magazine, keeping them organized and accessible is paramount.

PLEASE don't get upset! We have two answers to the problem -- you get to choose. We've made arrangements with the Jesse Jones Box Company to provide customized storage for your OHJs. You can order a slipcase -- a box that holds a year's worth of issues. Or you can order a large binder that holds each issue in place with a wire. (That way they stay in the binder and you can open them flat to read.) We have some here already, and HONEST! they're very classy ...deep maroon with the OHJ logo in gold. To tell you the truth, they're much nicer than the brown binders were.

Why'd We Do It?

IN THE THIRTEEN YEARS that we've been publishing, preservation has grown from almost an occult subject into a mainstream concern. We've wanted to expand our editorial coverage for a long time. But subscription revenue, not advertising, has been our only source of income--and there's a limit on how much you can charge subscribers for a periodical. To give you more, we'd have had to charge a lot more, and that would mean losing some readers. Not a happy thought.

THE RESTORATION-products market grew tremendously during this past decade, too. Our first Buyer's Guide Catalog listed 303 companies; the current Catalog lists 1,416. This proliferation of products has been outstripping our ability to report on them all in OHJ. By giving advertisers access to pages, we provide additional product information for you, and find a way to pay for extra editorial.

A HEALTHY PUBLICATION always changes. If it doesn't, it's pretending that the field it covers hasn't changed, either. And that's certainly not the case in preservation!

What's New?

WE'VE GOT a new feature on the back cover. (Remuddling fans take note: It hasn't disappeared, just moved to the last page in the issue.) In the feature on Vernacular Houses, we'll cover folk houses, builders' houses, regional types -- those houses that make up most of American architecture, but that don't fit neatly into academic categories of style.

THE COVERS themselves are new. Four-color! Yes, it's more expensive. But it's pretty

and gives us a chance to show some subjects in color instead of black-and-white. And it may attract potential subscribers, too.

THE OTHER NEWS is our regular feature on post-Victorian houses. Most of our articles apply to all old houses, of course, and we'll continue to do articles about early and Victorian houses. But, for a while, we want to call special attention to houses built after 1900. Until very recently, these houses have been preservation orphans.

LOOK FORWARD to articles on post-Victorian fence designs, mail-order interiors, furniture built-ins, Bungalow backyards, kitchens and baths....

But We Loved OHJ As It Was!

YEAH...SO DID WE. That's why we haven't changed it in any radical way. Look closely at this issue and you'll find that it's really just more of what you've always expected: useful information about doing good work, and preserving what we've inherited.

Patricia Poore
Clem Labine

GOSSIP & MISCELLANY

FIRST, thank you so much to everybody who called about my editorial in the December issue! It was gratifying to get that kind of response (and commiseration). Please read the "counterpoint" letter I got from ex-staffer and current contributing editor Walter Jowers. (on p. 6)

LATE FLASH: Our office manager (who's recently been pressed into service as advertising production coordinator) Tricia Martin gave birth to a baby boy on December 19. Congratulations, John and Tricia (and please, Tricia, hurry back).

WE GO into the new year with some additions to OHJ staff. Eve Kahn joins the editorial team. And our favorite (and first) Advertising Director is W. Robert Boris, who lives in Hingham, Massachusetts. Eve's desk is already a mess and Bob calls twice a day, so I guess they both hit the deck running!

Patricia

When this photo was taken, nobody had told editor Poore and publisher Labine how much work the new OHJ would be!

Letters

"Wiring" Responses

Dear Editor,

The recent article on routing wiring was good -- and I know you were assuming some electrical knowledge on the part of the reader -- but you should have made it clear that only BX armored cable should be used as shown, <u>never</u> Romex.

-- <u>Andy Wallace</u>
New Lisbon, N.Y.

Dear Editor,

The OHJ article "Routing Wiring" was most informative, and I could not help wishing I'd read it before learning those little tricks the hard way. A couple more tips:
● When fishing through walls or ceilings, I find a small mirror very handy. Used in conjunction with a light source (penlight or light from another hole), it allows me to look inside the framing cavity without making more than a relatively small opening. I use a mirror -- not unlike a dentist's -- which is about 1-1/2 inches in diameter and connected to a slender handle with a swivel joint. Available in most tool stores.
● Sometimes an old laundry chute serves as a convenient electrical chase, especially in multi-story buildings. Check the codes if the chute is still in use, and take precautions so that your skivvies don't get hung up between floors.

-- Kevin M. Clark
West St. Paul, Minn.

Dear Editors:

As a part-time remodeller, I read with some interest your article "Routing Wiring" in the October 1985 issue. The drawings were great and most of the advice beneficial.

But as a Master Electrician with some years in the trade, I must warn against a few of these suggestions. Anyone attempting to run their own wiring should at least read the relevant articles in the 1984 National Electric Code -- I suggest especially Article 300-4 and (for nonmetallic-sheathed cable) Article 336 or (for armored cable) Article 333. Some people groan at the word "codes," but informed workmen know how they save lives and property. The numbers in parentheses are the relevant articles for the following:

VENTILATION SHAFTS: You cannot run "Romex," as nonmetallic (plastic) sheathed cable is called in the trade; nor can you run BX (armored cable) in any ventshaft or duct space if the cable runs the long dimension of such a space. (Cables may pass across duct spaces.) (300-22)

DUMBWAITERS: Neither Romex nor BX can be run in Dumbwaiter or elevator shafts. (336-3, 333-6)

VOIDS NEXT TO CHIMNEYS: Unless the chimney is permanently disabled so that a later owner can't use it either, it's a bad idea. Not only is the ambient temperature around a working fireplace too hot for household wiring, but the chance of even the mildest chimney fire makes <u>any</u> wiring a bad bet next to chimneys. (336-2)

On the other hand, here are some tips for routing wiring that I've used successfully:
● Wrapping the end of the fishtape that holds your cable with cheap electrical tape makes a smoother "head" to pull through holes; on tough pulls, slicking up your cable with wire lubricant makes an easier pull and helps protect the cables from abrasion.
● An 8-in. or 10-in. length of fixture-hanging chain ("jack-chain") is the best tool for fishing through single walls (i.e., no fireblocks and no insulation). In the attic, drill down through the top plate and drop your chain down ... connect your wire and pull it back up! An "inspection mirror," available at hardware or auto-parts stores, helps in finding obstructions, guiding drillbits, etc.

Finally, a tool I've had some success with (though it takes some practice!) is a long, semi-flexible drillbit called a "D'versiBIT." It can drill through some fireblocks and bottom and top plates from the <u>outlet opening</u> itself (the hole you cut for your switch or receptacle). One feature is a swivel-hook that lets you tie on your cable and then back the bit (and attached cable) through the hole just drilled. They can be obtained from Diversified Mfg. & Mktg. Co., 1086 Gant Road, Graham, NC 27253. (919) 227-7012.

-- Pat Rowe, Rowe Electric
Dallas, Tex.

A Window Wonder

Dear OHJ:

The enclosed photo may interest you. This house is not remuddled, but stands very much as originally built.

(Probably the only change is the balustrade around the porch.) The one window is obviously the main point of interest, for I have never seen one like it before. The house is brick, but if you look carefully you can see a stone arch and border around that window. Personally, I don't like the window, but I think it's an interesting variation. The house is in Johnstown, Pennsylvania.

-- Don H. Berkebile
Mercersburg, Pa.

Concrete-Block Mould

Dear Patricia,

It all started with a bicycle trip in Frank Perdue country, along the eastern shore of Maryland. Remembering Randall Cotton's articles on ornamental concrete block, my eye went immediately to the foundations of the small post-war farmhouses and mobile homes we passed. Rock-faced concrete block! But wait ... some of them were rusting. I soon realized that I was seeing metal siding panels imitating concrete block (which imitated stone).

At a restoration products show a month later, I met the Quitno family, owners of W.F. Norman, the steel-ceilings company. I asked whether they

Letters

still made the stone-faced metal siding, they said yes, we got to talking -- and came up with an alternative way to cast new blocks.

Those metal panels are casting moulds all set to go! If you have to duplicate the rock-faced blocks, the back-side of a pressed-metal panel can be used instead of a latex mould. You still have to build a wood form (as shown on page 204 of the November 1984

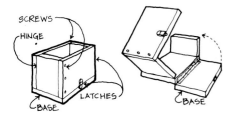

WOOD FORM FOR MOULD

OHJ), but the time-consuming part -- making the mould -- would be done for you. (You'll have to make a latex mould to duplicate fancy-faced blocks.)

-- Ron Pilling
Baltimore, Md.

[Sounds reasonable. See "Ornamental Concrete Block Houses," Oct. 1984 OHJ, and "Repairing Ornamental Concrete Block," Nov. 1984. -- ed.]

"Real Men . . ."

Dear Patty,

I just got my December issue and read your editorial about going barefoot. I was inspired to write this reply. Let's call it ...

Real Men Don't Mind Toxic Dust

I don't want to finish work on my old house. I don't look forward to the day that I put the last coat of varnish on the floor of my living room (which is now my workshop). When that day comes, I'll be expected to put all my tools in the basement and just take them out when the toaster breaks or the lawn mower needs a tune-up. I'll be Dagwood. Pfaw!

Living on a jobsite is fine

with me. I like the way a house looks before the walls are finished -- when it's all studs and wires and pipes inside. It's like living in my own giant Erector set. Building (or restoring) your own house is widely known to be one of the Great Male Fantasies -- right up there with sailing alone around the world, or having your own band or restaurant.

I like the work, too. When I'm working on the house, I get to destroy things I don't like and create things I do like. Climb up and down unfinished stairs. Fight wasps from laddertops. Throw rocks at pigeons. Conquest and Adventure!

And then there's the camaraderie. At lunchtime I go out on the porch with the subcontractors and we scarf a plate of ribs, down a gallon of iced tea, pick our teeth with pocketknives, and tell lies. Life just doesn't get any better than this.

I don't see the dirt and clutter as a problem. I see it as an opportunity to slip the bonds of tidiness. In this house, I don't have to wipe my feet or put away my toys. (My tools are strewn just the way I like them.) I can even leave a bathtub ring -- hey, it's just gonna come back tomorrow.

But there's no justice. As long as the house is under construction, I'll get plenty of "attaboys," as the neighbors come by, wander through the mess, and tell me how wonderful it's all going to be. Think I'll hear a word of praise once the place is all finished and decorated down to the last doily? Nooo.... That's when they'll all ooh and aah and tell my wife Brenda what a wonderful job she's done with the place.

And what do I have to look forward to the day the house is finished? I'll have to move furniture, hang pictures on the wall, wipe up spills, make sure there's a coaster under my glass.... What kind of life is that?

Of course, I'll try to stretch out the work on this

house indefinitely. But if I ever do (gulp, shudder) finish the place, maybe I can convince Brenda that too much equity in a house is no good. We should sell this one, take the profit, get liquid, buy another wrecked house. A really big (and bad) one this time -- one that I can't possibly finish before I'm sans teeth, sans hair, sans power drill.

-- Walter Jowers
Nashville, Tenn.

Time Well Spent

Dear Old-House Journal,

I am in the most enviable position of having quit my job to devote full time to restoring our 1905 Colonial Revival, while my wife supports me and the house.

Prior to resigning, I made copies of the time sheets used at work. At the end of each day, I fill out the numbers of hours put in and the task undertaken. Thus I have some idea of the time it takes to do a job.

For instance, in our bedroom it took:
40 hours to strip 4 coats of paint from all doors and mouldings;
14 hours to remove four layers of wallpaper;
7 hours to make repairs to the closet;
5 hours to repair the ceiling;
20 hours to sand the parquet floors;
21 hours for painting and wallpapering.

That's 107 hours total for the restoration of one room.

With friends who live in prefabricated houses built for them by teams of hired workers, it helps forestall the stupid remarks like: "You've been working on the house for four years now! Haven't you got it finished yet?" or "It must be great to be retired and putter all day."

I also suggest that people keep swatches of their old wallpapers.

-- Robert E. Law
Amenia, N.Y.

Old~House Living ...

A Century Of Memories

by Charles Stetter

OUR OLD HOUSE in Central Mine, Michigan, owes its existence, indirectly, to Douglas Houghton, Michigan's first state geologist. In 1841 Houghton reported finding deposits of copper and iron in the upper peninsula of the four-year-old state. That report triggered a rush by many in quest of adventure and fortune. Townsites developed around the mines, and Central Mine opened in 1854, ten years after the first settlers had arrived to dwell among the Chippewa Indians.

RICH IN COPPER, Central Mine made a profit in its first year and continued to do so throughout its 44-year lifetime. The mining company built the town: houses for its employees, schools, stores, churches. The small log and clapboard homes built for the miners were in the heart of the town; the more elaborate homes of the officials were at the outskirts.

THE MINE CLOSED in 1898 and the population moved on to other towns where work was available. A few families had summer homes in Central, but most of the buildings were vacant and decaying. We arrived at Central to spend our summers in 1925, when I was six years old. We lived in one of the miner's homes, and would have wonderful family gatherings every year.

BECAUSE FEW PEOPLE lived in Central at the time, the whole town was a playground for my cousins and me. We were taught early on to avoid the place of greatest danger: the shaft house that covered a 2000-ft.-deep pit. But we were free to roam through the doctor's office, where bottles of medicine still lined dusty shelves, and to explore the old school, a grand building with fish-scale shingles, a mansard roof, and 20 dormers.

IFOUND THE HOUSE we now own during an explor-. ation one fall day in 1934. My two cousins and I saw this abandoned house with a sagging front porch. We climbed through one of the broken windows and began our tour of inspection. Doors opened off both sides of the dining room. We took the one to our left, which led to the back parlor, Murescoed a horrible shade of pink. We went through the archway to the front parlor that still had Victorian wallpaper with a gold scroll design and a 12-in. border. The windows in this room were long, almost floor to ceiling. The kitchen opened off the other side of the dining room. It was 20 feet long, and the end near the dining room was narrower because of a pantry. We discovered a wood shed just beyond the kitchen, and an indoor privy with three holes: two for adults, one for a child.

WE FOUND FOUR BEDROOMS upstairs; two were quite small, but the others were grand. In the back bedroom, an entire wall was panelled with pine, concealing a back stairway and a built-in wardrobe which were on either side of the chimney. The master bedroom in the front of the house had a built-in wardrobe, too, and floor-to-ceiling windows.

The author, flanked by his cousins, in a (light-struck) photo taken in Central Mine in 1925.

WE WERE BESIDE OURSELVES with excitement. We had to get our parents to see it, and somehow we had to have it! It took two more weekends to persuade our parents to look at it, but finally their curiosity got the better of them, and they let us conduct them through "our house." They were as excited by the house as we were, and by the time of their second tour, they were deciding where the furniture would go. They immediately made arrangements to lease the house from the mining company.

ARMED WITH BROOMS and dustpans, we made our first trip to the house on May 10, 1935. I can be precise about the date because on that day we began keeping a log in which we recorded every visit to the house, along with all the events that transpired there for the next 50 years. But restoration was the farthest thing from our minds as we began tearing down the old wallpaper, patching plaster, and replacing the 50 missing window panes. We were in the middle of the Depression, and our solution to the decorating problem was simple: We whitewashed every room. We furnished it with cast-offs from our home in Calumet; in the dining room we installed a cast-iron woodstove that had been in my father's boyhood home back in the 1890s.

OUR EXTENDED FAMILY enjoyed many summers at our house in Central until World War II began, and my cousins and I joined the service. Gasoline rationing kept others from making the 600-mile trip from the Detroit area, and the house suffered years of neglect. The end of the War brought us to a crossroads: The house was still under lease from the mining company, and some family members were reluctant to spend money on it, even though it needed to be repaired. But my parents and I remained loyal to Central, and we undertook the repairs at our own expense.

RESTORATION took place almost imperceptibly -- certainly not consciously. In 1946 we rebuilt the front porch, doing the work ourselves, exercising care not to alter its appearance in any way. We found the original shutters in the caretaker's storehouse and rehung them. We also hired a stone mason to rebuild a corner of the foundation which had fallen away.

It looks like a 19th-century kitchen, but ... concealed in the 'woodbox' at left is an electric stove; the refrigerator is kept in an adjoining room (right through that louvered door).

THE FIRST SPECIFIC REFERENCE to "restoration" is the log entry for August 20, 1958: "Visitors were Mr. and Mrs. E.G. Magnuson and Mr. and Mrs. Herbert Hanson of Chicago. Mr. Hanson was much impressed, as an architect, with the construction of the house. All were greatly pleased with it and with our plans for restoration." From time to time we showed the house to the tourists passing through town. Looking at our home through their eyes, we saw a historic dwelling, rather than just an old house in a copper-mining ghost town. So we embarked on the restoration project, agreeing that Mother would have the last word on furnishing the rooms; Dad would be responsible for painting, wallpapering, and refinishing the furniture. I became the historian, taping interviews with old-timers, and haunting libraries, archives, and historic collections.

Left: The restful porch of Yesteryear House. *Below:* Originally, the porch had a board-and-batten roof. "The entire front porch was rebuilt in 1947, but it leaked badly. Dad covered it with roll roofing and replaced the batten strips, so it would look as it was intended to look."

The framed picture on the dresser is a photo of Edith Robert when she was 14. Four years after, in 1894, she stepped out of that bedroom window, climbed down a ladder, and eloped.

CIRCUMSTANTIAL EVIDENCE suggests that the first occupants of our house was the George H. Satterlee family. (We have a New Testament, dated 1869, that belonged to his daughter Jennie.) But it was the Robert family who left their mark on Central and on the house during their residency from 1875 to 1906. I was fortunate to locate John F. Robert's granddaughter, Ethel Crase Smith, who gave me considerable insight into the Roberts' background and personality.

THE FIRST John F. Robert was a French Huguenot, a colonel who arrived on our shores with Lafayette to fight in the American Revolution. After the war he acquired an estate on the Hudson River, just north of New York City. The John F. Robert of Central Mine was from a later generation that lived in Yonkers, New York. They were in the banking business, but John didn't care much for banking. What he enjoyed was the New York social life, and it was at a party in New York that he met Henrietta Brunn (Etta, as she was known to her friends), who was destined to be his wife.

CENTRAL MINE, like most midwestern mining operations, had its main office in New York City. John accepted a job as clerk for the mine, and moved to Central in 1875. The dining room window still bears witness to his arrival: Cut into the glass, presumably with a diamond, is the inscription "J.F.R. 1875." Etta followed as soon as their infant daughter Edith could safely make the journey.

MR. AND MRS. ROBERT were reserved and aloof, and did not socialize with the miners. Edith was just the opposite, lively and friendly, and as she matured, her parents exerted considerable effort to keep her from forming any romantic alliances with the youths of Central Mine. They intended to send Edith to New York to be properly educated and introduced into society. Despite their efforts, Edith fell in love with Frank Crase, an apprentice machinist who was nine years her senior. Crase earned the undisguised hostility of Edith's parents, and it was with great satisfaction that Mr. Robert brought to the dinner table the news of Crase's plans to move "out West." Edith was not dismayed, and her parents assumed that the affair had ended. However, on the night of August 20, 1894, Frank placed a ladder outside Edith's bedroom window, and the 18-year old girl quietly slipped out of the house. A closed carriage took them to Calumet, where they were married before boarding a train for Butte, Montana. Mr. Robert tried to overtake them, but failed.

RELATIONS between Edith and her parents were cool until the birth of her first child, Fred. Edith told them of the news and asked if she could come visit with her family. Her parents forgave them and celebrated the return with a lawn party to which everyone was invited -- a most uncharacteristic gesture for them. Ethel, the Crases' second child, was born not long after.

This photograph was taken in August of 1876, either by John F. Robert or at his behest.

WHILE I RESEARCHED the history, the restoration went forward. A glance at the log reveals that the front halls were covered with antique Brussels carpeting salvaged from the superintendent's house. In 1959, a carpenter rebuilt the front porch and installed a new ceiling in the dining room.

WE WANTED to restore the house accurately, but made a few mistakes. In 1966 we painted the house pea green with white trim, instead of its original olive green with red trim. Indoors, we still have to replace the dining room's inappropriate wallpaper (spinning wheels and butter churns!).

Above: The front parlor of Yesteryear House: "Friends frequently gave us beautiful items of furniture and china that had been in their family for years. It reached a point where entering the house was tantamount to turning the clock back to the days when the mine worked." *Right:* A 1970 photo of the author's mother, wearing an 1880s wedding dress of brown satin and cut velvet. "She's holding an etiquette book of the 1880s, with a foreword written by Mrs. Grover Cleveland."

WE BUILT AN ADDITION onto the house in 1963, constructed entirely of lumber salvaged from the superintendent's house. It accommodates the family while tours are conducted. Formal tours began in 1962; that first year, over 1500 people visited "Yesteryear House," as Mother renamed it.

WE WANTED Yesteryear House to remain as it was in Victorian times; the problem was our need for modern conveniences during the four months of the year when we lived there. When electricity came to Central Mine in 1967, we had the company bring it in through the rear and wire only a few areas in the house: the basement, the new sunroom in the addition, the bathroom, one outlet in the kitchen, and two on the second floor.

THAT SAME YEAR, we drilled a 167-ft. well, eliminating the need to carry water from the spring. A bathroom was added to the new addition; it was off limits to tourists, but nevertheless we installed a free-standing bathtub with claw-and-ball feet and a brown marble lavatory. The water also enabled us to install a small steam furnace, fueled by propane gas, which heats three radiators (antiques salvaged from the superintendent's house).

MOTHER OBJECTED to cooking on the cast-iron range with a hot-water reservoir at one end, although it was perfect for the old kitchen and gleamed under a coat of stove polish. To satisfy both her and the need for historical accuracy, we installed an apartment-sized electric stove, then had a cabinetmaker build a false wood box over it. We hid the refrigerator from view by building an alcove for it in the new addition.

WE CONVERTED the large bedroom over the kitchen into a library; the room is heated by an 1880 Detroit Jewel stove. The other bedrooms were papered with appropriate wallpaper patterns. In Edith's bedroom, visitors will find her portrait on the dresser. In the master bedroom, Etta's gloves are on display, as is John's cigarette holder. The entire house is furnished with Victoriana, from hand-worked linen towels down to the collection of milk glass. They came from a variety of sources: friends, churches, schools, antique shops.

OUR HOME is in the Central Mine Historic District, which is listed in the National Register; it's also in the Historic American Buildings Survey. We received a commendation in 1976 from the American Association for State and Local History, for our work in preserving the house and the heritage of Keweenaw Peninsula.

WE HAVE BEEN RICHLY REWARDED for the effort we put into the house. Tourists often express their admiration of the house. (One youngster walked through the rooms in awe and finally turned to his mother and exclaimed, "This is just like Gunsmoke, Mom!") But old houses have a way of outlasting their owners. Dad passed away in 1980 and Mother, at 90, is confined to a nursing home. With my advancing age and without a family member to carry on, the future of our old house is uncertain. I am, therefore, actively seeking a purchaser for the house and its furnishings, to assure its continued preservation and development as a historic site. If someone out there would like to take the reins from me and drive on into the future, please contact me at 216 Pewabic St., Laurium, Michigan 49913, or call (906) 337-4251. I have every confidence that a transfer to the right 'driver' will enable Yesteryear House to survive another 130 years.

TROUBLESHOOTING OLD WINDOWS

What To Do With
Neglected Double-Hung Windows

by Bill O'Donnell

THIS ARTICLE IS NOT for the real-estate developer who buys a derelict (or not-so-derelict) old building and begins by gutting plaster and replacing all the neglected windows. It is meant for the individual owner -- you who recognized that your windows were in terrible shape from the day you moved in, but who haven't tackled them yet because so many things seem to be wrong with them. We're going to troubleshoot together. As we go from one common window problem to the next, it will become apparent that the repair techniques are exceedingly simple (if labor-intensive).

WINDOWS GET into bad shape because they're subject to exterior weathering and because they have moving parts. Old windows are easy to fix because they're very simple -- just two counterweighted sashes running in a slot -- and because they're made of wood, the easiest building material to renew.

THE DEVELOPER or commercial owner will learn something from this article, too. As long as you can get the workers in place to do the simple carpentry and painting that's usually needed, window rehabilitation is often less expensive, less disruptive, and more in character than window replacement.

AS YOU READ about the problems, refer to the large illustration of a typical double-hung window on page 19. Better yet, belly-up to one of your own windows, where everything described is tangibly illustrated.

TAKE A LITTLE TIME to watch the problem window in action. If the lower sash sticks a little, you may be able to fix it by just moving the stop moulding out a bit. If the sash is loose, maybe repositioning the stop closer will do the trick. (Pry off the stop moulding carefully. If it does split, similar stock can be purchased at a lumberyard.) Above all, don't jump to conclusions and plane the living daylights out of the sash to keep it from binding. If you didn't understand exactly what was causing the binding, you might be left with the same problem and a loose sash that's had too much wood removed. Look first for easy-to-fix troubles like loose hardware, paint-encrusted sash chains, misplaced stops, or improperly-installed weatherstripping.

Trouble With
Immovable Sash

EVERY OLD HOUSE HAS window sash that binds up or is just plain stuck. It's usually caused by excessive paint layers between the sash and the parting bead or stop. The solution may be as simple as carefully removing and repositioning the window stop. At worst, you'll have to remove some of the paint buildup. Following are the steps to take if the window is...

PAINTED SHUT:

DON'T USE A SCREWDRIVER to break the paint film that's keeping your windows stuck! It will permanently damage the wood. Use the right tools -- and a little patience.

FIRST, USE A RAZOR KNIFE to cut the paint film between the sash and jamb. Then gently work a wide-blade putty knife between the stops and sash all the way around the window. Even once the paint film is broken, you'll have to apply some force to free the window (because of the paint buildup between the sash and stops). Insert the putty knife between one end of the sash and the sill. Work a flat prybar under the putty knife, and place a scrap of wood under the prybar to protect the window frame. Pry (apply leverage) one side of the window at a time until it's free. If it resists, go back to working the putty knife around the window and try again.

SWOLLEN OR WARPED:

ANOTHER REASON FOR unbudging windows is warpage or swelling of the wood sash. If an isolated part of the sash has had all the paint rubbed off it, you probably have a case of warping. Check the surface for trueness with a straight edge. Plane bowed areas of

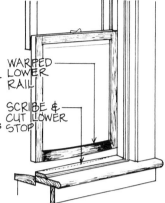

the sash after you've removed the paint. (Severe warping may require replacement sash.)

YOU CAN PLANE swollen sash so it runs smoothly. But remember that even a well-maintained window swells up in humid weather. If it's very humid, some minor resistance is acceptable; the window will run effortlessly once the weather is drier. If the window was improperly (or not recently) painted, the sash may have patches of bare wood which have swollen from recent exposure to rainwater. Allow the wood to dry -- and shrink back to its natural size -- before you begin planing away any material.

STICKING OR BINDING:

IF THE WINDOWS are operable but difficult to open and close, a little lubrication may be all they need. Scrape excess paint off the inside of the stop, off both sides of the parting bead, and off the stiles. After you repaint, wax the mating surfaces with a bar of paraffin, then reinstall the sash.

Prying open a stuck top sash.

Trouble With
Loose & Broken Glass

REMOVING WHAT'S LEFT of the putty on a neglected window is usually no problem -- you can just about pick it out with your fingers. If the putty still has good bond, soften it up with paint stripper. Use a thick, methylene-chloride-based stripper; it will stay on the putty long enough to soften it without dripping all over the rest of the window. If glass is missing or has been removed, you can also use a heat gun or a soldering iron to soften hard glazing compound.

WHEN THE PUTTY IS gone, pull out the glazing points and remove the pane of glass. Wear heavy-duty work gloves and goggles when handling glass. Thoroughly clean debris out of the groove. While the glass is out, prime any bare wood on the muntins or sash with a mixture of linseed oil and turpentine. This improves the bond between the wood and new glazing compound.

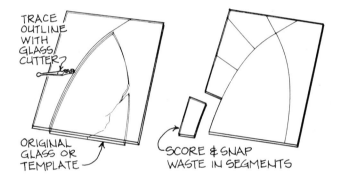

CUTTING REPLACEMENT PANES of glass isn't difficult, but it does require some practice -- especially with curved pieces. If you're not sure of yourself, refine your technique by practicing cutting on an unusable piece of glass. Straight pieces are easy: Use a straight edge as a guide, and just score the piece with one firm, even stroke of a sharp glass cutter dipped in oil. Then tap along the line to break it off. Plastic glass-cutter's pliers can also be used to break the glass with a quick, downward snap. Cut the piece ever-so-slightly smaller than the window opening.

CURVED PIECES are trickier. Making a template out of Masonite or cardboard is easier than scoring the piece freehand. Gradual curves can be broken off in one piece, but extreme curves will have to be made by removing one small section at a time, as illustrated above.

PLACE THE NEW PANE in the window and secure it with several glazing points. Roll some glazing putty between your hands to form a bead, and press it in place along the edge of the glass. Smooth into a triangular shape with a flexible putty knife. It'll take a little practice to run an even bead that clears the glazing points.

Trouble With
Counterweights & Cords

IF YOU'RE STILL HAVING sash problems after removing excess paint from your windows, check the counterweights and sash cords. For some of the fixes prescribed here, you have to gain access to the weight pocket. Most window frames have an access panel at the bottom of the jamb. If your window doesn't have an access panel, carefully remove the inside window trim. The first thing to check is that the weights move freely through the pocket without obstruction. Badly placed nails or screws may have to be removed from the casing.

PULLEY PROBLEMS:

THE MOST FREQUENT PROBLEM with sash cords is a frozen pulley. When a pulley isn't turning freely, you have to apply more force to open

the window, in order to overcome the friction between the sash cord and pulley. Tie off the sash cord and remove the pulley -- it's usually held with two finishing nails or small screws. Dip the pulley in a bath of chemical paint stripper to remove all traces of paint. Straighten dents in the pulley with a pair of pliers. Apply some oil to the pulley before reinstallation, to ensure free spinning.

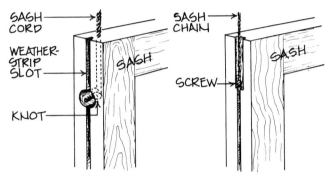

PAINT-ENCRUSTED SASH CHAINS:

ANOTHER common problem with old windows. On many windows there's an access panel to the weight pocket at the bottom of the jamb. Unscrew the chain from the sash and tie a string to the end. Remove the access plate and let the weight drop to the bottom of the pocket. Disconnect the chain from the weight and pull it out from the top. Bathe the chain in a water-rinsable paint stripper until the paint has softened. Rinse thoroughly, dry, and apply a little WD 40 or other non-staining lubricant to keep the chain flexible.

BROKEN SASH CORDS:

ROPE CORDS can be fixed in much the same manner. Tie a small weight to one end of the replacement cord and feed it down to the weight. Temporarily attach the other end of the cord to the sash, and test the window before cutting to final length. When the lower sash is all the way open, the weight should be close to the bottom of the pocket without "bottoming out" -- there should always be tension on the cord.

Frozen pulleys like this one can be fixed by removing excess paint.

Counterweights are easily accessed through a panel in the jamb.

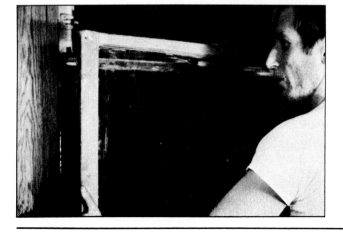

All illustrations by Jonathan Poore

Disassembly

The diagram on the facing page shows the construction of a typical double-hung window. To disassemble it, remove the stops; lift the bottom sash out; unscrew the sash cords from the window. Tie a knot in the cord to keep it from falling into the weight pocket. (If it's a sash chain, place a small finishing nail through one link to hold it in position while the sash is out.) To remove the parting bead, carefully pry it out, starting at the sill and working your way up to the bottom of the upper sash. Then lower the upper sash and pry from the top down. Lift out the upper sash, and secure the cords as you did with the lower ones. (See OHJ, June 1985 for tips on removing trim.) ➡

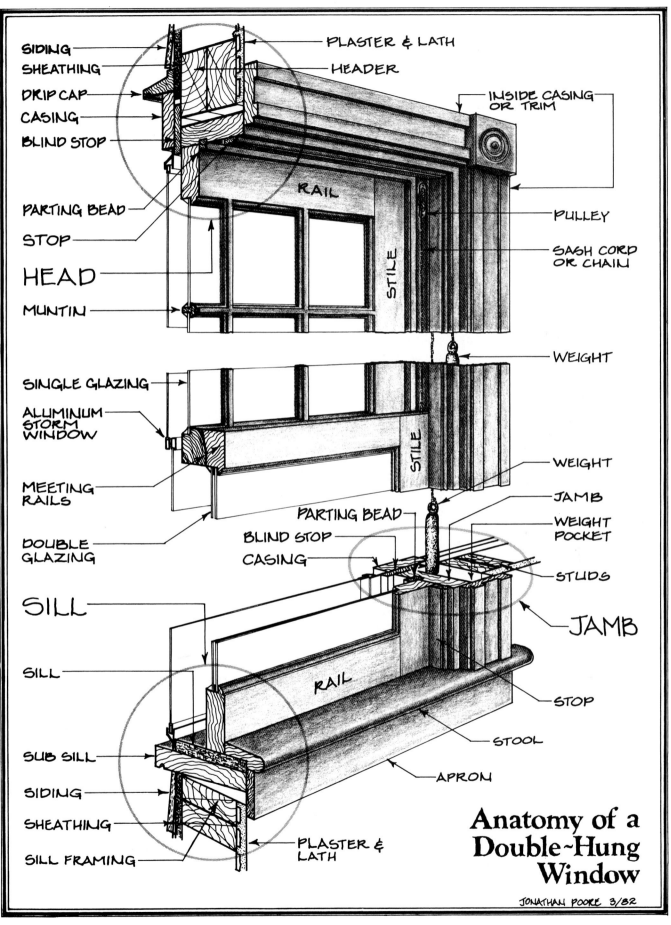

SIDING
SHEATHING
DRIP CAP
CASING
BLIND STOP

PLASTER & LATH
HEADER

INSIDE CASING
OR TRIM

PARTING BEAD
STOP
HEAD
MUNTIN

RAIL

STILE

PULLEY

SASH CORD
OR CHAIN

WEIGHT

SINGLE GLAZING
ALUMINUM
STORM
WINDOW

MEETING
RAILS

DOUBLE
GLAZING

STILE

WEIGHT

JAMB

WEIGHT
POCKET

PARTING BEAD
BLIND STOP
CASING

STUDS

SILL

JAMB

SILL

RAIL

STOP

STOOL

SUB SILL
SIDING
SHEATHING
SILL FRAMING

APRON

PLASTER &
LATH

Anatomy of a Double~Hung Window

JONATHAN POORE 3/82

Stripping Windows

Neglected windows won't have paint buildup on the outside. More likely, you'll find bare and weathered wood. The inside of the window will be another story. Generations' worth of cosmetic painting leaves windows covered with hopelessly thick paint buildup. The thick paint obscures architectural detail and makes the sash bind. To make the window run more smoothly, you can just scrape or spot-strip the worst areas. But if you want to "start fresh" and remove all the paint, here are some window stripping tips:

● Use heat on the sill, runs, stops, parting beads, and window casing, but don't use the heat gun on window sash unless you remove the glass first. Glass will break if the heat gun is pointed at it.

● Use chemicals on the window sash. A thick, methylene-chloride-based product is best (Zip-Strip, Bix Tuff Job, and Rock Miracle are typical brand names). Apply a heavy coat of stripper and wait 20-30 minutes before scraping. If the chemical starts to dry out, throw some more on. Scrape the loosened paint off with a putty knife. Clean up with more stripper and steel wool or brass brushes. Once the paint is off, use denatured alcohol (or another solvent) and steel wool to remove sticky residue.

● Dip-stripping is another option if you have many windows to strip. But beware — dipping removes old putty. This is good if you want to reglaze, not so good if you want to save the old glass. Take out the glass before bringing your windows to the strip shop. And don't let them dip your windows in lye: Caustics raise the grain, loosen glued joints and, if not properly neutralized, may cause failure of the new paint.

Allow the wood to dry thoroughly before priming (this may take a few days). Seal bare wood with linseed oil or an alkyd primer as described on page 21.

Trouble With
Wood Rot

IF YOUR WINDOWS have been left unpainted for years, chances are the wood has rotted to some extent. Lucky for old-house owners that wood is so repairable. It can be patched, filled, consolidated, and selectively replaced using simple, relatively inexpensive techniques. (By contrast, if one element of a new vinyl-clad aluminum window fails, it's very difficult to fix without replacing the entire assembly.)

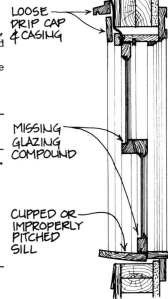

IMPROPER FLASHING

LOOSE DRIP CAP & CASING

MISSING GLAZING COMPOUND

CUPPED OR IMPROPERLY PITCHED SILL

BEFORE REPLACING or repairing rotted wood, figure out what caused the rot. If the sill pitches in towards the window, for instance, it's trapping water against the lower sash. Unflashed openings above the window allow water in, as does missing or deteriorated glazing putty. Be sure to correct these problems before repairs are made.

PATCHING TECHNIQUES:

PATCHING ROTTED WOOD is easy once you've chosen the right product. Standard wood fillers are good for very small areas and nail holes, but less effective on large areas. Auto-body fillers will make a neat patch, but tend not to last very long because the filler won't expand and contract with the wood. Once the filler shrinks or pops, water collects under it, causing further deterioration unseen.

EPOXY CONSOLIDANTS AND FILLERS are best for patching rotted areas of exterior wood. True, they're more expensive, but unlike other fillers, they form a superior bond with the wood and expand and contract with it. Consolidants like Abatron's Abocast 8101-4 are low-viscosity liquids that penetrate deteriorated wood fibers. When dry, the consolidant strengthens the wood and prevents further decay. Epoxy fillers like Abatron's Woodepox-1 mix to the consistency of glazing compound. Use them to replace "rotted-out" sections after consolidating the surrounding wood.

CHISEL OUT unsound wood around the area to be patched. Wherever possible, undercut the hole you've created. Before mixing any filler, be certain the area is free of any paint, dirt, or loose splinters -- such debris interferes with proper bonding. Mix the patching material according to manufacturer's directions and work it thoroughly into the hole; don't leave any voids or air pockets. As the filler begins to harden, scrape off excess with a sharp putty knife. Leave the patch to dry, raised slightly above the surrounding area. After the patch is thoroughly dry, sand it flush and smooth. Wear a dust mask when sanding fillers.

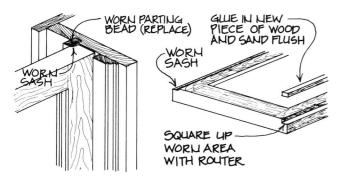

Replacing Worn Areas

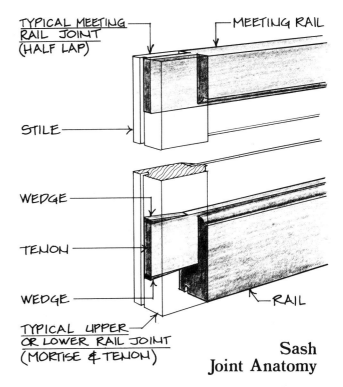

Sash Joint Anatomy

LARGER AREAS (a section of the window sill, for example) can be patched using a carpenter's "dutchman." Carefully saw out unsound wood. Square off the area to be patched, and cut a new piece of wood to the exact dimensions of the hole. Use wood of the same species and make sure the grain runs in the same direction. Glue or screw the patch in place, fill the joints after the glue has dried, and sand the patch smooth. After you paint, the patch will be nearly invisible.

HERE'S A TRICK that saves the new paint job on even severely weathered wood: Seal it with linseed oil before priming. Mix boiled linseed oil and paint thinner 50/50, and liberally brush it onto the wood. Allow it to dry for 24 hours, then repeat the process. Very weathered wood requires a third application. Allow three days for the oil to dry before sanding and priming.

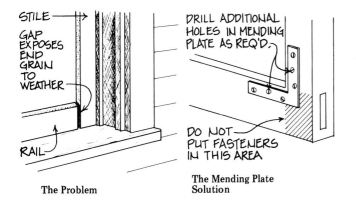

The Problem

The Mending Plate Solution

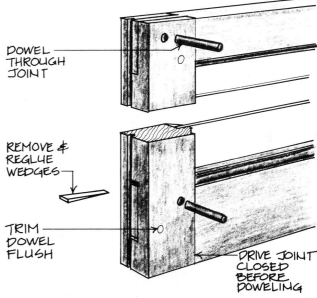

Sash Joint Repairs

SEPARATED JOINTS:

AN OLD WINDOW frequently starts to separate at glued joints. Worse, delicate pieces such as muntins may be nearly or completely rotted through. These problems usually don't require complete disassembly and rebuilding of the affected window. There are several low-tech, inexpensive measures you can take to stabilize the window and arrest further decay.

THE JOINTS OF the stiles and meeting rail in the upper sash are usually first to separate. (Nobody ever paints the meeting rail, and a lot of condensation runs down the upper window panes.) If the window isn't a focal point at eye level, simply reattach the separated stiles and rails with a metal mending plate -- from the street, no one will notice your time-saving trick. If you're really fussy,

chisel out a small mortise for the plate: Once you've screwed it in place, the plate will be flush with the rest of the window and nearly invisible after it's painted.

IF THE WINDOW is a real attention-grabber, reattach the loose pieces using more traditional woodworking practices. Reglue mortise-and-tenon joints and drive a small wedge next to the tenon. Resecure half-lap joints by drilling a hole through both pieces and inserting a glued dowel. Clamp the joint together while it dries.

Trouble With
Draftiness

WHEN THE WINDOWS are functioning properly, they'll be less drafty. If you've
got them running smoothly but snugly in
their channels, if they close all the way and
have no gaping holes or broken glass, then
they're already pretty tight. But there are
several additional steps you can take to improve their energy efficiency. The following
inexpensive suggestions all address infiltration. Even windows
with storm sash become
much more efficient if
these steps are taken.

CAULKING:

SEAL AROUND THE WINDOW
casing with a paintable
caulk -- a tremendous
amount of air can pass
behind the window trim.
Most folks caulk around
the visible points where the trim meets plaster, for appearance. But also check above the
top of the window casing, and below the apron:
There's almost always a gaping hole in these
locations.

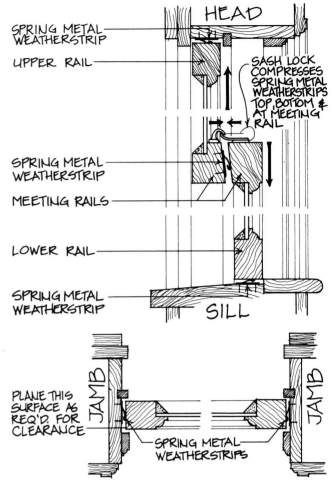

FILL GAPS WITH PLASTER AND/OR CAULK

SASH LOCKS:

SASH LOCKS DO MORE than discourage burglars.
Install new ones if necessary, or strip paint
off the ones you have and adjust them so they
close completely and snugly. Sash locks
greatly reduce infiltration by pulling the
meeting rails together and holding the window
tightly closed.

WEATHERSTRIPPING:

THERE ARE COUNTLESS VARIETIES of weatherstripping materials being offered to an increasingly energy-conscious market. Adhesive-backed
plastic springs, metal-backed felt, adhesive-
backed strips of felt, tubular gaskets... the
list goes on. Although some of these products
do have suitable applications, they generally
have the disadvantage of being too conspicuous
(ugly), wearing out too fast, or not forming a
complete seal. For a double-hung window, we
recommend you use either integral-metal or
spring-metal weatherstripping.

If your windows already have integral weatherstrip, be
certain to scrape them free of paint buildup. If the grooves
are full of paint, the window won't close completely.

SPRING-METAL:

SPRING-METAL WEATHERSTRIPPING is installed in
the sash runs, between meeting rails, and
along the head and sill of your windows.
Spring-metal requires no complex carpentry to
install -- you just nail it in place. It
works as well as integral weatherstrip, but
won't hold up as long.

INTEGRAL WEATHERSTRIPPING:

MANY OLD WINDOWS will already have some weatherstripping in place. Integral metal weatherstrip is perhaps the most common -- and the
best. If you don't already have it and want
to install it, the basic procedure is as
follows:

YOU REMOVE THE LOWER SASH and cut a slot
(usually 7/16" deep) down the length of the
lower rail both stiles. (Read the instructions included with the weatherstrip before
you begin.) You can rout the sash with a
radial arm saw, table saw, or router; if you
don't have any of these tools, a local woodworker will cut these channels for you -- for
a price, of course. Channel the upper sash
through the top rail and both stiles.

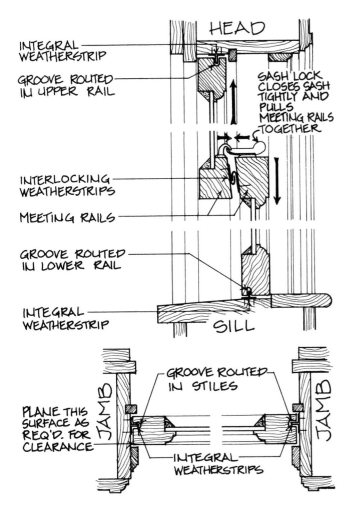

INTEGRAL WEATHERSTRIP

GROOVE ROUTED IN UPPER RAIL

HEAD

SASH LOCK CLOSES SASH TIGHTLY AND PULLS MEETING RAILS TOGETHER

INTERLOCKING WEATHERSTRIPS

MEETING RAILS

GROOVE ROUTED IN LOWER RAIL

INTEGRAL WEATHERSTRIP

SILL

GROOVE ROUTED IN STILES

JAMB   JAMB

PLANE THIS SURFACE AS REQ'D. FOR CLEARANCE

INTEGRAL WEATHERSTRIPS

THEN YOU INSTALL the metal strips in the jamb, head, and sash. You'll have to cut the strips so that they leave a gap at the pulleys. Don't attach the weatherstripping with more than just a couple of nails until you test them for fit with the window reinstalled; you'll probably have to make some minor adjustments before securing the strips.

FINALLY, ATTACH interlocking weatherstripping to the meeting rails, reinstall the sash, and test for fit. Work the sash up and down to be sure they run smoothly. Make certain they close all the way, and that the weatherstrip at the meeting rails locks snugly. Integral weatherstripping is often called carpenter-installed weatherstrip -- you can often find carpenters who are old hands at this.

OTHER OPTIONS:

YOU NEEDN'T ALWAYS go through the trouble of installing integral metal weatherstripping. If you use the window only for ventilation in warmer months, weathersealing can be as simple as shoving a little Mortite or other temporary roll-type caulking between the moving parts of your window. If the window never gets used, you can even caulk it shut permanently with an acrylic latex caulk (of course, this makes for additional work the next time you have to clean or paint the window). Some people caulk only the upper sash, to leave the lower sash operable.

And Finally
The Paint Job

HAD THEY BEEN properly maintained, your windows wouldn't have been such a mess. After spending time working on them, you'll want them protected from the elements. The simplest and most important step is to keep them correctly painted inside and out.

PAINT ALL THE PARTS with an alkyd primer. Be sure to cover every surface, especially where bare wood is exposed. Follow with two coats of a high-quality latex or oil/alkyd finish paint, preferably from the same manufacturer as the primer. The correct window-painting procedure is as follows:

1) REMOVE ALL HARDWARE from the window -- including curtain hardware, sash locks, and handles. Not only will this make painting faster and easier, but it will also prevent drips and buildup on and around these fittings.

2) SCRAPE THE WINDOWS with a single edge razor blade <u>before</u> painting, to remove previous painting errors. Reverse the sash, and begin by painting the lower half of the upper sash. As you paint the rails, stiles, and muntins, run the paint slightly up onto the glass. If you just slop paint all over everything and then scrape the glass later, you'll break the paint seal where the glass meets wood -- permitting condensation to soak into the sash, leading to future window problems.

RUN THIN EVEN BEAD OF PAINT ONTO GLASS TO SEAL OUT MOISTURE

3) CLOSE THE WINDOWS, and finish painting the sash. Don't put the paint on so heavily that it drips between the sash and jamb; that just causes paint buildup again. Work from the sash to the jamb to the casing to the apron. Don't paint the sash cords or chains; they must remain flexible. Pull them out of your way and paint behind them.

4) WHEN THE PAINT is almost dry, but still slightly tacky, open and close the window to break the paint seal. It's a lot easier now than it will be after the paint sets hard. 🏠

WEATHERSTRIPPING SUPPLIERS

Spring metal and integral metal weatherstripping aren't found in every neighborhood hardware store. These products are normally sold through contractors and large building supply warehouses. If you plan to do the work yourself and can't find the materials locally, call or write one of the companies listed below. They'll supply the name of a dealer or contractor who uses their products in your area.

Accurate Metal Weatherstrip
725 South Fulton Ave. Dept. OHJ
Mount Vernon, NY 10550
(914) 668-6042

Pemko Company
Box 3780 Dept. OHJ
Ventura, CA 93006
(805) 642-2600

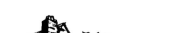

To open our new section on post-Victorian houses:
A review of some common styles of that era. Following this
is an article describing the renovation
of a typical turn-of-the-century bedroom hall.

POST-VICTORIAN HOUSES are the most familiar old houses in America. Nationwide sales of pattern books, mail-order houses, and building products made it possible for the same style (in fact, the same house) to be built in New York State and in Illinois. Post-Victorian houses are abundant. You'll recognize them on the West Coast and the East, in semi-rural areas and in towns that have become cities, in revival neighborhoods and in unchanging ethnic ones. And because these houses were often built speculatively in a development area, they're found in harmonious neighborhoods -- each an unassuming architectural tapestry where the landscaper's saplings have since grown into shade trees, and the shingles and stones have acquired an agreeable patina.

THE RESIDENT of a post-Victorian house doesn't have to alter his lifestyle (or the house) very much. Preservation is easier even for non-purists. For example, it's hard to live with the servants' basement kitchen in an 1860s house, or the trunk room (but no

Prairie Style

closets) in an 1880s house. People raised in the 20th century even have trouble adapting to the small rooms and dozens of doors in a Victorian house.

THESE HOUSES, though, are different. For the most part, they were built with kitchens and bathrooms in the "modern" places. They have closets. The plans are more open, sunporches abound, buildings were designed for central heat . . . in short, these houses are more comfortable and convenient than we old-house addicts have any right to expect.

HOUSES of the early 20th century are as diverse as those of the Victorian period. An easy way to begin categorizing the styles is to recognize two very different philosophical streams of the time. On the one hand, the first stirrings of the modern movement were seen in the buildings associated with the Prairie School, The Craftsman magazine, and the builders' updated versions of American vernacular house forms. We might call this philosophical stream "Utilitarian."

ON THE OTHER HAND, many houses of the period are decidedly nostalgic, looking not forward but back. Such houses are romantic revivals, meant to recall historical associations. If we call this stream "Romantic," there are two major branches: American Revivals and English Revivals. America's colonial architecture was revived (sometimes in hardly recognizable form) in Federal and Georgian Revival, Neo-Colonial, Spanish and Dutch Colonial Revival houses. English romantic styles included all the variations of what we call Tudor: half-timbered, folk cottage, English manor house.

LET'S LOOK first at the "new" architecture. The Prairie School has been recognized and studied for decades. It was a well articulated style that flourished in the Midwest. (Chicago was the capital of modern architecture during this period.)

THE IMPACT of buildings and books of the Chicago architects (of whom Frank Lloyd Wright is the most well known) cannot be overstated. Their influence is felt in domestic building to this day: They championed suburbia and were arguably the grandfathers of the ubiquitous ranch house. But it's important to keep in mind that the number of houses actually built by these first-generation thinkers is small.

The American Foursquare

Their influence on the minor architects and the builders of the period is what's significant. Spec houses all over the country clearly show Prairie-School influence. Look for an emphasis on the horizontal: broad, low

Basic Homestead

eaves, long porches, Roman brick, bands of windows.

THE HOUSE at the bottom of the previous page might be called the architectural mascot of the post-Victorian period. It's the American Foursquare. Popular all across the country in thousands of variations, it was

Tri-Gabled Ell

economical, homey, and adaptable. The boxlike shape and hipped roof accommodate the most room for the least money. The basic Foursquare is simple, honest, substantial, and practical. And the basic Foursquare could be modified for each customer. With a change in window style, porch detail, or cladding material, the American Foursquare became Classical, Colonial Revival, "artistic," or Prairie style.

THE HOMESTEAD house types (above) were vernacular descendants of common American house forms of the past. The basic Homestead is very much an updated version of the rural Greek Revival house. The entrance on the gable end and truncated cornice returns suggest the temple form.

by Patricia Poore
drawings by Leo Blackman; logo drawing by Larry Jones

A FAMILIAR and homey variation is the Homestead with a tri-gabled ell shape. Either leg of the ell can be longer, and often a porch is tucked into the space formed by the two legs. Porch ornamentation varies according to time and region. The tri-gabled version is particularly common in New England and the Midwest.

"CRAFTSMAN" is a style name used today to describe those modern houses that embodied the tenets of Gustav Stickley and other architects, writers, and critics. Strictly speaking, only those houses published in The

Craftsman magazine (1901-1916) are Craftsman houses. But countless houses of the period between 1905 and 1925 have obvious, Craftsman-inspired details.

Craftsman Cottage

THERE IS a truly American house style associated with the Craftsman movement: the Bungalow. The work of many Bungalow architects was published in the magazine, including the ultimate Bungalows of Charles and Henry Greene. But the Bungalow spread far beyond Craftsman philosophy. During the 1920s, many thousands of builders' bungalows went up, with details ranging from Japanesque to the less appropriate colonial.

THE TRUE BUNGALOW is a one-storey, picturesque house (not necessarily small), usually with a low-pitched roof and a pergola, verandah, or generous porch. "Natural" construction materials such as fieldstone, stained shingles, and earth-colored stucco were common. Builders of the period would have called the house pictured below a semi-Bungalow, because it has one-and-a-half storeys.

Bungalow Style

ROMANTIC REVIVAL houses fell into two major streams: American Colonial Revival, and Old English. The majority of Colonial Revival houses harkened back to the original colonies, so they were based on English forms. This is a big, diverse country, however. The Dutch Colonial Revival and the Spanish Colonial Revival were on their way during this period, too. They started as regional revivals, but by the '20s builders were selling modest Spanish Revival houses in New Jersey, and architects were designing academically correct Georgian Revival houses on the West Coast.

"free Colonials" were built than were true revival versions. We call them Neo-Colonial, to signify that they are something new.

PERHAPS THE MOST ROMANTIC, associative houses were built in the English styles. Generally referred to as Tudor Revival, all are loosely based on medieval prototypes. Early examples, built between the 1890s and 1910 or so, were generally architect-designed and grander than later versions. These earlier models can claim style names like Elizabethan or Jacobean because their detailing more closely follows medieval buildings from those periods of English history. Later Tudor Revival houses are often recognized as such only by their typical Old English details, which may be grafted onto an all-purpose builder's plan. Half-timbering (generally applied over the stucco cladding and not in any way structural) is common, as is a steeply pitched roof with very little eave overhang at the gables. Windows are small casements, tall and usually grouped. Chimneys are prominent and sometimes elaborate. Models from the '20s and '30s are most often brick-clad.

Federal Revival

Neo-Colonial

THE DUTCH COLONIAL is readily identified by its gambrel roof. Unlike the originals, revival versions often have long shed dormers to increase second-floor space. Spanish Revival houses are almost always stucco (or adobe in the Southwest), and have Mediterranean details such as punched windows, rounded arches, and clay tile roofs.

WHAT ABOUT those odd hybrids that seem to have Colonial details grafted onto a Victorian or Foursquare plan? These are houses that would never have existed in the Colonies or during the Federal period. Many more of these

English Cottage

Spanish Colonial Revival

Dutch Colonial Revival

Tudor Revival

SMALLER ENGLISH COTTAGE style houses are picturesque and quaint, their prototypes being the rural masonry farmhouses of England rather than the larger timber-framed buildings. Some have rolled eaves suggestive of thatch. The English Country house or manor is more sophisticated, a stylized rendering of English vernacular forms.

MAKING A HALLWAY LIVABLE
by Patricia Poore

URN-OF-THE-CENTURY houses often have hallways as long, dim, and boring as this one. Our back bedroom hallway was lit by one overhead fixture on a pull-chain. (Electricity was still a wonderful new thing when this house was built; it didn't have to be used <u>well</u> to be appreciated.) The finish coat of plaster was delaminating from the brown coat in large sections. Decades ago, someone tried to solve the problem by slathering a lime-based stucco texture finish over one-third of the wall area; now it too was failing. That rough texture, plus the aqua paint over everything, did a good job of absorbing what little light there was. Plaster repair and a paint job were obvious fixes. But an update of the clumsy lighting plan was what <u>really</u> improved this hall.

MOST OF the plaster repair was standard for an old house. But the ugly texture finish was a bear. It was falling off in places, yet it held fast in other areas. The solution was to use a one-inch "combat chisel" -- a sturdy old wood chisel no longer good enough for carpentry. It's small and sharp enough to find all the loose areas and really get under the texture finish. (Wide scrapers did not work.) After many hours of scraping, we were left with a "relief map" of scraped plaster and tenacious texture finish. The answer: three quick skim coats of joint compound. (Go in one direction with the first coat, perpendicular to that with the second, and back to the original direction for the third.) The walls were thoroughly washed with clear water before skimming to remove traces of lime.

THREE-WAY SWITCHES that allow lights to be turned on from either end of the hall were installed. An odd condition suggested another lighting improvement. We had the electrician install a fluorescent fixture long-ways in the plumbing riser niche. Then we hid both riser and lamp behind a plasterboard baffle. It's a deceptively simple but elegant solution. The riser is gone from view,

The finished hallway — well lit to the end.

Before: The single overhead bulb created hot spots on both the ceiling and interior window. Little light reached the bedroom door.

Here's graphic proof that you should never repair plaster until the electricians leave. Indirect light has already been installed.

and indirect light illuminates dumbwaiter and bedroom door. The "dead end" is banished.

WE GOT RID of the harsh overhead light and installed sconces along one wall. These give off a more diffuse, asymmetrical light -- much more pleasant and interesting than the old spot-lit effect. Because there is original wall-sconce lighting in other areas of the house, I don't think our change is out of character. A cue for the sconces' design was taken from the house, too -- the oak stairway and dining room woodwork are clearly Craftsman-inspired, and Japanesque sconces fit right in with that period.

BEAUTIFUL ANTIQUE fixtures and authentic reproductions are available, especially Mission-style brass sconces. But this is a back hall. With many more projects to go, we hadn't the inclination to spend lots of time and money on these sconces. Also, the hallway is very narrow and very plain, so we wanted unassuming fixtures that hug the wall. The easiest solution was to build them.

WE STARTED with one-bulb socket fixtures from the local lighting store. These didn't have to be pretty or expensive, just safe. Each sconce consists of an upper and lower horizontal wood baffle around a little box. We used 5/4-in. birch, ripped on a table saw to 1/2-in. and 1/4 in. (Using

Here goes the first skim coat of joint compound. The photos above show a "textured" corner, before and after.

View from rear bedroom: the riser before it was enclosed, and dumbwaiter we reopened.

The naked riser before we added a fluorescent fixture and Sheetrock baffle.

Indirect light comes from this riser niche in this photo taken from bedroom end of the hall.

cherry or another hardwood would make these fixtures fine furniture quality). Mitre joints in the small boxes at top and bottom are glued and nailed. The larger pieces have glued lap joints. Upper and lower members are joined vertically at the corners with hardware-store birch dowels.

THE SHADE is rice paper, which you can buy at a well-stocked artist's supply store. We picked a highly textured, pale tan paper. The parchment-color paper (rather than white) makes the fixtures look older -- and more Craftsman than sushi-bar. The paper is wrapped tightly around the rear dowels and glued to itself with Elmer's glue. Masking tape held the paper in place while the glue dried.

OUR PAINT SCHEME is a simple two-color one for now, pending decoration of the rest of the house (which we'll get to around the year 2003). For now, here's some advice:

PRIME repaired surfaces as soon as possible. This "evens out" the space so you can better see remaining problems, test your lighting plans, and so on. After priming, it's time to caulk around trim, too: You can see the cracks. Look at the primed surfaces with fixtures in place -- raking light shows up plaster imperfections you may have overlooked (or hoped wouldn't show).

ORCHESTRATE lighting and paint color; they create a mutual effect. A paint chip won't tell you what the color will look like in a room. After you have your lighting in place, buy a small amount of the color you think you want and paint a section of wall or ceiling. (Put up the fixtures temporarily, if you need to, to see the effect.) A color that seems brilliant may wash out; a color you hoped was a subtle, greyed hue might be more intense than you bargained for; a cozy tan can turn to pasty flesh. It all depends on the quality and location of light, and the surfaces that the light is bouncing off.

ALSO, YOU MIGHT have to shade or tint a color for part of the job. For example, we had to darken the paint color in the pocket created by the riser wall just to make it match the rest of the walls, because the line of light washed it out.

ABOVE ALL, do not feel like a failure if you don't get the color right the first time. It happens to all of us. (That's why you didn't buy six gallons of a custom color up front, right?)

ALTHOUGH our specific solutions may not fit conditions in your house, the principles are food for thought. Indirect lighting can be used in lots of places besides a pipe chase -- say, atop a breakfront or behind the cornice on kitchen cabinets. And even if you don't like the looks of our sconce, its basic design is worth noting: Really, it's just a fancy shade mounted over an inexpensive fixture -- one that already had UL approval. 🏛

The sconces might be called Craftsman-Japanesque.

Sconces were made up of simple wood parts and rice paper, mounted over inexpensive store-bought fixtures.

Tricks Of The Trades

by Joseph V. Scaduto   illustrations by the author

AS A GENERAL CONTRACTOR, I work with all types of tradespeople, and I'm frequently surprised by the various "tricks of the trade" they employ. When I express amazement at some of their ingenious solutions, they'll give me a look of "what's with you?" They seem to freely pass these tricks amongst themselves, but the information seldom finds its way into print. Maybe people in the building trades are like magicians, sworn never to give away their tricks. Well, if that's true, somebody should have told me, because I just can't resist the urge to pass on a few of them.

Jeeves, Draw My Baath . . .
And Fetch The Caulking Gun

WHAT'S THE MAJOR CAUSE of tile and wallboard failure in bathrooms? Water penetration, of course. Once the seal between the tile and the tub is broken, water can penetrate; over a period of time, it will cause tiles to fall off walls, and plaster or wallboard to crumble. Wait too long and the wall studs and floor joists could be damaged.

HOW DO YOU PREVENT these failures? Most people would say, "just caulk up the space between the tub and the wall." That's correct, but you must keep in mind the difference between an empty tub and one that has both a person and water in it. The difference is hundreds of pounds; enough pressure to cause the tub to move away from the wall -- not enough movement to see, but enough to break the seal of caulking compound.

ANY "OLD-TIME" TILESETTER can give you the solution to this problem: Apply the caulk while the tub is full of water -- preferably with you in the tub. (Silicone rubber tub-and-tile caulk is best.) The idea is to caulk the tub while it is at its lowest point. After the caulk has set, drain the tub. Any further movement will not adversely affect the caulking because the seal was applied while the gap was at its widest.

A Lead Pipe Cinch

MANY BUILDINGS still have lead water lines running from the street to the basement. Lead from these pipes leaches into the water -- a known health hazard. Still, many people haven't yet replaced their lead pipes. Some don't even know they have lead pipes, until one breaks during a hard freeze (which guarantees you can't get a plumber for weeks). And even if you could get a plumber, the ground might be frozen too hard to allow you to dig up the whole pipe.

I WAS IN such a predicament during a recent blizzard. Fortunately, my plumber associate came down to the basement, looked over the situation, and immediately corrected it this way: He just took a hammer and gently tapped the leaking area of the pipe, forming the surrounding soft lead into a self-sealing patch. I stress that the tapping was gentle. He emphasized that this was just a temporary repair and that the entire line should be replaced as soon as possible. His temporary repair lasted for 18 months....

When An Irresistible Force
Meets An Immovable Object,
The Irresistible Force Wins

ANYONE WHO HAS ever tried to take apart old galvanized plumbing knows that sometimes a threaded pipe joint will simply refuse to move. In such cases, my plumbing associate says, "Think positive. If the pipes won't move, persuade them."

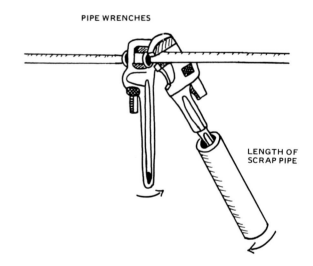

PIPE WRENCHES

LENGTH OF SCRAP PIPE

ONCE WE HAD an 18-inch pipe wrench on an unyielding pipe. Our best effort failed to move it, and I was ready to give up. But not my associate; he took a length of scrap pipe and fitted it onto the handle of the wrench. The 18-inch wrench was transformed into a giant 30-inch wrench, and the stubborn joint, of course, gave in. The one thing you have to be aware of when using "pipe persuaders" is this:

Make sure you can hold the opposing wrench fast against the force of the oversized wrench. (You might have to put a length of pipe over both wrenches.) You don't want one wrench to overpower the other -- you could take apart more plumbing than you want to.

Lube The Gutters, Please

IF YOU HAVE WOOD GUTTERS, you probably know that replacing a section of rotted gutter is an expensive proposition -- expensive enough to make you want to properly maintain your existing wood gutters. The conventional wisdom of wood-gutter maintenance says to clean the gutters once a year and oil them with linseed oil. This is not entirely adequate.

FIRST, YOU SHOULD clean the gutters at least twice a year (spring and fall), especially if you have many trees near your house that drop buds, catkins, and leaves into your gutters. Second, my wood-gutter specialist tells me that the linseed oil used on the gutters should be thinned with turpentine. A mixture of 75% linseed oil and 25% turpentine is best. Linseed oil alone will just sit on the wood instead of penetrating it. The turpentine allows the oil to penetrate into the wood, providing better protection.

The Dreaded Ice Dam

IF YOU LIVE IN AN AREA that gets heavy snow accumulations, you should be aware of the ice-dam problem: Ice from intermittent melting builds up at the eaves; melting snow runs down until it hits this ice "dam," and then accumulated water seeps up behind roof shingles and runs into the house, where it soaks insulation, damages plaster, and rots framing members.

HERE'S THE SOLUTION to the ice-dam problem: When you re-roof, install a 3-ft. strip of 90-lb. roll roofing along the eaves of the house, then install shingles over the roll roofing. Water usually won't back up on the roof more than three feet, even if there is an ice dam. (As an alternative to roll roofing, you can install a 3-ft.-wide roll of sheet metal -- copper or terne-coated stainless are best.)

PROPER ATTIC INSULATION and ventilation are also important in preventing the formation of ice dams -- especially in old houses where the original insulation and ventilation have been changed, or were inadequate originally. Your local heating utility probably has good information on insulation and ventilation specifications for your area.

The Suction Solution

SEVERAL YEARS AGO, when I was learning the heating business, I would go out on troubleshooting calls with a top-notch heating man. I learned more from watching him than I ever did from any heating manuals. We were riding in his truck one day when we received an emergency call from his office. A homeowner had tried to remove the oil filter from his oil tank, but had broken off the shutoff valve.

WE FOUND the embarrassed homeowner in his basement. He had jammed a plug into the hole of the oil tank to stem the flow of oil. My friend looked at the tank and then at the homeowner, and started mumbling to himself. I wondered how in heaven's name will he repair the shutoff valve when the tank was still three-quarters full?

MY FRIEND ASKED me jokingly, "Okay Joe, how are you going to replace the valve without losing any oil?" The only thing that I could think of was to completely drain the tank of oil and then repair the valve. His answer was, "Nah, that's too much work. Let's do it the easy way."

AND EASY IT WAS. It seems that this problem is fairly common, and my friend had done this type of repair many times before. The first thing he did was go outside and pop off the cap to the oil-tank vent pipe. He then took his industrial vacuum cleaner and hooked up the hose to the exposed vent pipe. I was given the honor of plugging in the vac.

WITH THE VACUUM SWITCHED ON, we went back down to the basement. He walked over to the tank and removed the temporary plug. I expected oil to come running out, but none did. My friend explained that the vacuum created within the tank prevented the oil from leaking out. He quickly replaced the broken valve and said, "Now wasn't that easy!" I guess anything is easy, if you know what you're doing.

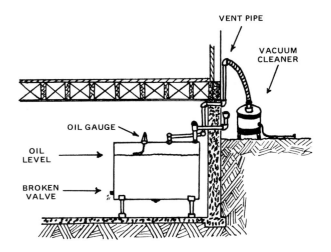

A Word Of Caution

THESE TRICKS are simple and easily applied, but you should use caution and common sense before employing any unfamiliar process. This is particularly true when you're repairing leaking water lines or working on an oil tank. If you're not sure whether or not your "trick" will work, call in an expert. But even if you do have to call in professionals, you might have the chance to show them some "tricks of the trade."

Reading The Old House

The Romanesque Revival -- A.K.A. Richardsonian Romanesque

BY JAMES C. MASSEY & SHIRLEY MAXWELL

CONICAL ROOF

MASSIVE CHIMNEY

TALL HIPPED ROOF

QUEEN ANNE MULTI-STOREY BAY FOR PICTURESQUE EFFECT — NOTE SMALL PANES & DECORATIVE PANELS

FLAT OR JACK ARCH LINTEL

WINDOW IN CHIMNEY WITH ARCHED TRANSOM

ROCK FACE ASHLAR BASE

CIRCULAR TOWER WITH ARCADED WINDOWS

ORNAMENTAL SCROLL FRIEZE

TRIPLE PEDIMENTED DORMER

RECESSED PORCH

CHECKER WORK

ANIMAL-HEAD ORNAMENT

ENTRANCE PORCH WITH MASSIVE ROUND ARCH

SOURCE: *AMERICAN ARCHITECT* JUNE 23, 1888

TYPICAL FEATURES: ROMANESQUE STYLE SOFTENED BY QUEEN ANNE DETAILS; MASSIVE ARCH ENTRY, MASSIVE ASYMMETRICAL COMPOSITION, CORNER CIRCULAR TOWER OR TURRET.

IF ANY SINGLE architectural style characterizes urban neighborhoods built within the last decades of the 19th century, surely it is the Romanesque Revival. Just as Gothic seemed "the only proper style" for country and suburban residences in the 1850s, the Romanesque Revival expressed the worldly outlook and solid prosperity of the city's growing middle and upper classes in the 1880s. Indeed, Romanesque dwellings usually had clients -- and architects -- as substantial as the buildings themselves.

LIKE THE GOTHIC, the Romanesque Revival had its origins in medieval Europe, particularly in the churches of England, France, and Germany. But while the soaring spires and pointed arches of Gothic structures aim for the heavens, Romanesque buildings clung determinedly to the earth, firmly anchored by squat, round arches and heavy masonry. Their thick, fortress-like walls and forbidding corner towers rebuff the encroaching city. Not for them the wide, welcoming verandahs of the Queen Anne and the Eastlake!

IN THE UNITED STATES, the style took root in the 1850s, in important public buildings like James Renwick's castle-like design for the Smithsonian Institution, and churches such as John Notman's Holy Trinity in Philadelphia.

Stylistic variants were often named for the regions from which their features were drawn: English Norman, Italian Lombard, German, Burgundian, Auvernesque -- each a variation on a theme. Then, in the late-19th century, the style fell into the hands of an architectural genius, Henry Hobson Richardson. His influence, although brief, was so profound that American Romanesque Revival became, once and for all, "Richardsonian Romanesque."

> "... dignity and strength, calmness and repose ... could only be obtained by the most carefully studied proportion of parts and masses, by the greatest simplicity of form and treatment, — for grandeur is always characterized by simplicity, — and by unity of design, to obtain which I used one consistent treatment around the whole structure, interior and exterior."
> – *H.H. Richardson, 1883*

AT FIRST, Richardson used the style only in public buildings and churches; his Trinity Church in Boston remains the major example. Later, in a remarkable architectural transference, he adapted the monumental forms to the needs of the Victorian city residence, such as the John Hay and Henry Adams houses in

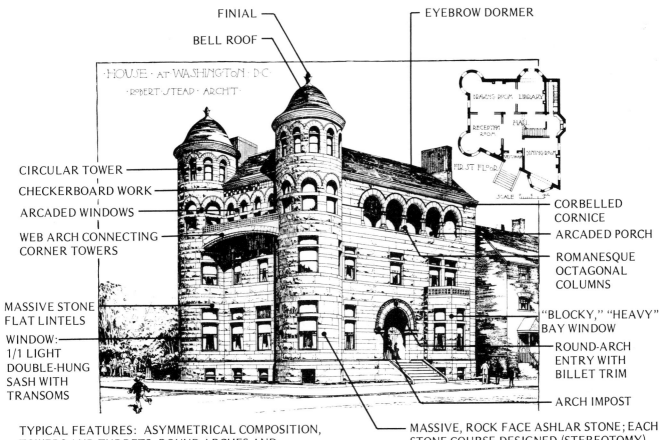

FINIAL —

BELL ROOF —

EYEBROW DORMER —

·HOUSE· AT· WASHINGTON· DC·
·ROBERT· STEAD· ARCH'T·

CIRCULAR TOWER —

CHECKERBOARD WORK —

ARCADED WINDOWS —

WEB ARCH CONNECTING CORNER TOWERS —

MASSIVE STONE FLAT LINTELS

WINDOW: 1/1 LIGHT DOUBLE-HUNG SASH WITH TRANSOMS —

CORBELLED CORNICE

ARCADED PORCH

ROMANESQUE OCTAGONAL COLUMNS

"BLOCKY," "HEAVY" BAY WINDOW

ROUND-ARCH ENTRY WITH BILLET TRIM

ARCH IMPOST

TYPICAL FEATURES: ASYMMETRICAL COMPOSITION, TOWERS AND TURRETS, ROUND ARCHES AND ARCH ARCADES, ROCK FACE ASHLAR STONE.

MASSIVE, ROCK FACE ASHLAR STONE; EACH STONE COURSE DESIGNED (STEREOTOMY)

SOURCE: *AMERICAN ARCHITECT* MARCH 24, 1888

Washington (1884) and Chicago's Glessner House (1885 -- certainly one of America's finest town houses).

FROM RICHARDSON, the style spread quickly to other architects and areas. His followers included his successors in his architectural firm, Shepley, Rutan and Coolidge; other notables were Ware and Van Brunt, John Wellborn Root, James H. Windrim and Thomas F. Schneider. The style was used for all types of buildings, particularly in the newer building areas of midwestern cities.

ROMANESQUE REVIVAL BUILDINGS are nearly always of masonry construction, preferably in rugged, rock-faced stone with heavy, intertwining decorative forms. Mixtures of stone, which might include granite and brownstone, were chosen for color and effect. Brick walls with stone or terra-cotta trim are also common. The mood is generally dark and ponderous, often even gloomy or pretentious to the modern eye. There are few examples in wood, although there is a resemblance to the Shingle Style, in which Richardson also worked.

ALMOST OBLIGATORY in Romanesque Revival buildings are strongly emphasized round-arch open-

ings, often in a large entrance or an arcade. If there is no arch, there must at least be a heavy stone lintel. Rounded corner towers are also nearly ubiquitous.

ORNAMENT is varied and dramatic, as bold and basic as the style itself. In addition to linear decorations on arches, doorways, and belt courses, there is a wealth of figurative ornamentation drawn from original sources, with a wonderfully literal nomenclature: beak, cable, chevron, roll, nailhead, dogtooth, cat's-head, billets, scallops, lozenges.

FEW OF THE ARCHITECTS who adopted the style handled it as well as Richardson. An inventive utilizer of "stereotomy" (the science and art of stonecutting), he carefully planned the size and placement of every stone before construction. Less-talented imitators favored picturesque, asymmetrical forms that were based more on a hodge-podge of motifs than on the coherent overall composition exhibited by Richardson's designs. A penchant for "quaintness" lead to bartizans without and inglenooks within. The style was rarely pure in its execution, and houses of the period were often warmed somewhat by Queen Anne elements.

AFTER RICHARDSON'S DEATH IN 1885, Romanesque forms quickly gave way to the picturesque pleasures and human scale of Queen Anne and Shingle styles, and by the turn of the century Americans were building cozy suburban bungalows -- a dizzying change in only 20 years!

Inside A Romanesque Masterpiece

In 1885, when H. H. Richardson planned a Chicago home for John J. Glessner, he not only outraged Glessner's neighbors — he also revolutionized the way architects laid out domestic interiors.

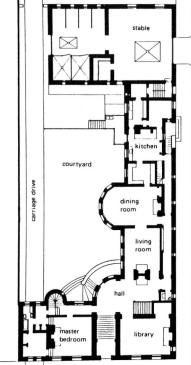

The heavy beams, dark panelling, and massive fireplace in the entrance hall suggest the great hall of a medieval castle. The balustrade on the main stair has four baluster patterns — one of each on each step — an idea borrowed from early American homes. (Late in Mr. Glessner's life, he still vividly recalled that the balusters had cost $1 each.) The Glessners used this space as a "living hall," and had it more extensively furnished and carpeted than it is today.

The library, as it looked in the Glessner era. Dark wood, imposing beams, and a king-size chimney piece create a serene refuge. Above the bookcases, a blue glaze over yellow paint was used to produce brilliant green walls. Many of the gas and electric fixtures, wallpapers, curtains, and carpets in the house came from (William) Morris & Co., London.

ALTHOUGH the Glessner House is severe and fortress-like on the outside (which greatly upset the neighbors), the warm oak interior creates a homey, sheltered environment that still captures the spirit of the Glessner family.

INSTEAD OF THE STREET, Richardson's revolutionary plan focused the house on the landscaped courtyard -- where there were numerous ample windows and curving towers and bays. Because the Glessners entertained frequently and on a large scale, Richardson planned interior circulation with great care. All major rooms have at least two doorways, allowing the house to comfortably accommodate 100 or more guests. With so much traffic through the house, the Glessner family appreciated the extra soundproofing that Richardson had specified.

Special thanks to Elaine Harrington, curator of Glessner House. One-hour tours of the house (1800 South Prairie Ave., Chicago) take place at 12, 1, 2, and 3 p.m., Tues. through Sun. $4. Tel. (312) 326-1393.

Restoration Products

Reviewed by Larry Jones

Midget Louvers

Does wood deterioration and/or paint failure plague your house? You can eliminate a lot of problems by venting enclosed spaces, from the foundation crawlspace to the attic and cornice. The vents should be in inconspicuous locations, so as not to detract from the building; they also have to be of sufficient size to ventilate properly.

The round Midget louvers come in diameters from 1 to 6 in. and are simple to install. Drill or cut a hole into the surface to be vented and simply tap the round louver into place. No nails or screws are required because the louvers are slotted for tension and swedged for anchorage. The aluminum louvers come in two main styles: the #LD Midget with insect screen (for interior use or for areas where there's no danger of rain blowing in); the regular Midget with screen and louvered deflector.

With these louvers you can ventilate everything from soffits to the cavities of damp basement cinder-block walls; they're especially handy for venting newel posts and columns. Be sure not to paint over the louvers -- you'll stop them up. And size the vents accordingly, because the louvered deflectors reduce the area of the vent and amount of air that can pass through it. The regular aluminum louvers sell for $5.56 per dozen for the 1-in. size; most sizes can be found locally at paint and hardware dealers. For more information write Midget Louver Co., Dept. OHJ, 800 Main Ave., Rt. #7, Norwalk, CT 06852. (203) 866-2342.

Classic Hardware

In case you're unfamiliar with Garrett Wade's excellent Woodworking Tools Catalog, now is a good time to order the new 1986 edition ($3). They also have a fine little catalog called Classic Hardware. Most of the hardware is North American or British, is solid brass and reflects a considerable amount of hand labor. Many are authentic for period furniture, and could be considered original rather than reproduction because they're made from 100-year-old casting and forging moulds.

All of these pieces are pictured actual size in the catalog -- you can trace or cut out the photos to see how the hardware will look with your furniture. You will also find a handy hardware primer in the front and back of the catalog. The bulk of the catalog consists of pulls, knobs, and hinges of every size and shape. But there are also a lot of pieces that we haven't seen available before, such as a forged chest chain with mounting tips, which would work perfectly for transom windows. There's a very nice selection of high-quality brass picture hooks, braided-brass picture wire, and plate rings for hanging pictures from picture rails. The prices range from $.85 to $32. To get your copy of Classic Hardware, send $1 to Garrett Wade Co., Dept. OHJ, 161 Ave. of the Americas, New York, NY 10013. (212) 807-1757.

For Stove & Hearth

Have a stove, range, or fireplace -- antique or modern -- that you want to keep safe, efficient, and attractive? Then you'll be glad to hear about Temproof, a new line of maintenance and repair products from United Gilsonite Laboratories. There's furnace cement, stove polish (paste and liquid), 1200-degree stove paint, fireplace mortar (black, buff, and grey), stove-gasket cement, chimney treatment, gasket-replacement kits, stove thermometers, and self-serve spools of bulk fiberglass gasketing. And all these materials -- which can be darn hard to find locally -- are conveniently packaged in small containers, so you don't end up with leftover. Especially for old equipment: The furnace cement allows you to seal up cracks and seams; the stove-gasket cement makes antique stoves more airtight. Products are available from hardware and paint centers nation-wide. For more information write Temproof, UGL, Dept. OHJ, P.O. Box 70, Scranton, PA 18501. (800) UGL-LABS.

Border Paper

Here's something a little different: a new 9-in. wide, Icanthus-leaf-design, trompe l'oeil, fabric-backed border paper. The matte-finish vinyl paper mimics a cast-plaster frieze border with subtle shading for depth, and comes in beige, grey, and taupe. It sells for $4.95 per yard (5-yard minimum), plus $3.50 shipping and handling. Samples are free by writing Metrostyle, Dept. OHJ, 1634 Norman Way 8, Madison, WI 53705.

Restoration Products

Heat Shield for Stoves

Fire codes usually require
wood- and coal-burning stoves
to be a certain minimum distance from things that burn,
such as walls and floors. And
so the stoves take up a lot of
space which could be used for
other furniture. But if you
use the Durock Tile Backer
Board between a stove or
heater and a combustible wall
surface, you'll have the same
level of safety and more usable space within the room:
You can reduce the clearance
by two-thirds to a minimum of
12 in. The Backer Board has
been listed by Underwriters
Laboratories (UL) as a fire-
resistant heat-shield for use
with UL-listed, solid-fuel-
type room heaters and fireplace stoves. It comes in
three sizes: 3x4-ft., 3x5-ft.,
and 3x6-ft. It's asbestos-
free, easy to cut with hand
tools, installed dry, and can
be covered with non-flammable
products such as tile, plaster, slate, or stone. Durock
is available at building supply dealers nationwide. Write
for a free illustrated brochure with installation
details from the Durabond Division of USG Industries,
Inc., Dept. OHJ, 101 S. Wacker
Dr., Chicago, IL 60606.

Fireplace Surrounds

If you're building or restoring a fireplace you might want
to consider a decorative fire
surround and summer cover.
Nostalgia offers five styles
reproduced from Savannah originals in either cast iron or
aluminum. The iron nautical
cover and surround, pictured,
is $144.65 plus shipping.
Send $2.50 for a catalog from
Nostalgia Architectural Antiques, Dept. OHJ, 307 Stiles
Ave., Savannah, GA 31401.
(912) 232-2324.

Reproduction Clocks

Cumberland General Store has a
collection of four clocks,
three of which are reproductions of original designs.
Each clock is imported with a
keywound movement that counts
the hours and strikes on the
half hour. Our favorite is
the Patti model, originally
produced in 1860 by the E.N.
Welch Co. This 29-lb. mantel
clock is made of solid walnut
and has a cast brass pendulum
and two side windows; its
nicely turned features include
a top rail and four ornate
columns. It sells for $198
plus shipping.
    All the clocks in this line
would look good in any old
house: the Danbury mantel/
shelf clock of 1890 by Seth
Thomas, with hand-carved floral designs, $280; the 1903
Stationmaster wall clock by
Sessions, with a silkscreened
railroad station on its glass
door, $249; the Railroad
Regulator, a recreation of a
typical turn-of-the-century
railroad wall clock, with solid brass movement, $269.
Shipping and handling charges
are F.O.B. from Crossville,
Tenn. Send $3.75 for the Wish
& Want Book (a catalog jam-
packed with practical "old-
time" items for home or farm)
from Cumberland General Store,
Dept. OHJ, Route 3,
Crossville, TN 38555.
(615) 484-8481.

High-Performance Caulk

Sikaflex Multi-Caulk may be
the answer for those places on
your old house where conventional caulks fail. The one-
part polyurethane is a caulk/
adhesive with a high bond
strength; it clings tightly to
wood, metal, plastic, masonry,
tile, and other materials.
Apply it whenever the surface
is above freezing. Use your
fingertip, dipped in diluted
soapy water, for tooling before it skins over; then immediately apply paint or stain
(paint will slow its curing
rate). The caulk can be sanded when cured. (Belt sanding
is best; rotary sanders can
pull the caulk loose.) The
caulk stays permanently flexible, allowing for expansion
and contraction even when
bonded to dissimilar materials, such as wood and galvanized metal. It should work
well for porch floorboard
joints, wood trim and siding
seams, door and window trim,
and masonry joints; it's not
advised for tub and shower
joints, or to replace missing
pieces of wood. It's reversible, so old Sikaflex joints
can be cleaned out and new
Sikaflex or other caulks can
be effectively applied.

This new consumer-grade
caulk has a longer shelf life
and is easier to apply with a
caulking gun than the marine
and commercial grades of Sikaflex; otherwise there's no
difference. It's the first
polyurethane caulk to be
available to homeowners from
home centers and hardware
stores, and comes in Terratone
Bronze, Midnight Black, Snow-
flake White, D.C. Tan, Dark
Bronze, and Limestone Gray.
Each 10.3-fl.-oz. cartridge
sells for around $4, and will
seal a 1/4-x-1/4-in. joint
that's 24 linear feet long.
For a free brochure write or
call Sika Corporation, Retail
Sales Division, Dept. OHJ, 210
River St., Hackensack, NJ
07601. (201) 933-8800.

Restoration Products

Wood Terrace Doors

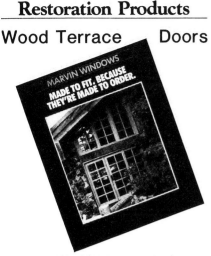

Are you stuck with some crummy old aluminum sliding doors, perhaps in an addition? If so, Marvin Windows has a new solution: the Marvin Terrace Door, a patio-type door of non-fingerjointed lumber. Made from deep-treated Ponderosa pine, these hinged or sliding doors can be ordered in a variety of sizes, including 5-ft. and 6-ft. retro sizes, and 8-ft. heights. We especially like the authentic, individually glazed, divided-light option -- no cheap, pop-in plastic muntin-bar grids here! It's available with either single or insulated-tempered glass. The doors can be ordered with or without the standard Marvin lock system; their foam-filled weather-stripping along the Lexan header and jam eliminates air infiltration. Also available is energy-saving Low E glass, removable double glazing, leaded-glass panels, and a storm-and-screen combination. And there's Marvin's Retro-Glide Patio Door, a wood slider that's designed to fit into existing metal door openings.

For more information on these and other products contact Marvin Windows, Dept. OHJ, Warroad, MN 56763. (800) 346-5128.

Thermal Window Shades

For those wanting to make their own thermal window shades, Rockland Industries makes insulated drapery materials that are sold in many departmant stores and fabric shops. The Wonderful Window Shade System is a new line of window based on shades made of DuPont Dacron Hollowfil II, Mylar, Roc-lon Thermalsuede, and a polyurethane moisture barrier. Once covered with your decorative fabric, the shade is mounted on the window with an ingenious plastic track system of snap tape and glides, which allows removal and reinstallation of the window covering, and lets it operate vertically or horizontally (handy for sliding doors). The shade systems are available in Roman, ballroom, and Austrian shades, or traditional draperies. For flush-mounted shades that provide an air-tight seal around your windows, try Roc-lon Magnetic Tape.

You can sew-it-yourself with prepackaged kits (or by-the-yard through fabric outlets). Ready-made kits are available from home centers and department stores. Made-to-measure shades, for odd size windows, can be ordered through your decorator or Roc-lon service center. Custom-made shades and draperies are available through decorators or home-furnishing dealers. A ready-made insulated Roman shade, complete with track, 36-in.-x-36-in., sells for about $49.95; the same shade for an 84-in.-x-84-in. patio door is around $129.95. For free color brochures of these products and a listing of the dealers nearest you, write Rockland Industries, Inc., Thermal Products Division, Dept. OHJ, P.O. Box 17293, Baltimore, MD 21203. (301) 522-2505.

Insulating Shades

Good insulating window shades do more than reduce drafts and make the house warmer in winter: They save you money on summer air-conditioning. You can make your own shades for any window in your old house in about two hours -- providing you know how to sew and you follow the step-by-step instructions in the Sensible Warmshade booklet from the Jasmine Company. The $3 booklet contains complete illustrated instructions, a materials list, and buying information. The company also sells many of the necessary materials for making the shades, such as insulating fabric and magnetic-edge tape. For a free brochure write the Jasmine Co., Dept. OHJ, P.O. Box 7304, Denver, CO 80207. (303) 399-2150.

Restorer's Notebook

Quarter-Round Compromise

QUARTER-ROUND SHOE MOULDING solves a real problem: It closes the gap between the baseboard and the floor, cutting down on air leakage. However, the disadvantage is that it doesn't really belong in an old house (as we nit-pickers remind ourselves). Also, quarter-round keeps furniture farther from the wall than we would like to have it. So before I began painting the baseboards and working on the floors in my house, I removed the quarter-round than had been added. Afterwards, I bought brown latex caulk and ran it around all of my baseboards, and then touched it up with baseboard paint.

      -- Charles W. Wilson, Mechanicsburg, Pa.

How To Sop The Slime

HERE'S A TIP on removing old varnish from interior woodwork. Use a liquid-type stripper applied with #1 steel wool pads (if you tear the pads into quarters they'll go a lot further). After rubbing with steel wool, allow the stripper to work for a minute longer, then apply more stripper. Wipe the mess off with old horsehair carpet pads cut into 3-in. squares. That crummy old padding works great for sopping up the slime. These pads are still available, and they're cheap.

      -- Ken Runyan, Elgin, Ill.

A Brand New (Mortar) Bag

HERE'S A HELPFUL HINT I'd like to pass along to the readers of The Old-House Journal. When pointing brick, take a heavy plastic bag and cut a 1/2-in. hole in one corner. Mix the mortar very fine and slightly wet. Pour the mortar into the bag and twist the top closed. Squeeze the bag, and the mortar comes out as if you were using a caulk gun.

      -- Dennis Quesnel of Tait Roofing
      Moorestown, N.J.

Instant Patina

A LOT OF THE MOULDING in our house was changed or destroyed, and we've had to use new wood for replacements that match the existing mouldings. The problem was getting the new wood to match old wood that had been stripped and refinished. The old wood always seemed to take on a more golden tone, even though we stained and finished both with the same materials.

    The best way I've found to match the new to the old is to use orange shellac as the first finish coat on the new wood (after it's been stained with the same stain as the old wood). Two coats are usually needed to make sure the entire area is covered. Then, once the shellac is dry, both the new and old wood can be top-coated with varnish -- make sure not to top-coat with polyurethane, which is incompatible with shellac.

If the shellac seems <u>too</u> orange (different brands vary in "orangeness"), it can be mixed with white shellac or toned down with aniline dye. (I've used brown aniline dye mixed with orange shellac to give a more yellow appearance.) You may have to experiment to get a good match; if it isn't right at first, the shellac can be easily stripped off with denatured alcohol.

      -- Terri Peterson, St. Paul, Minn.

Patching Plaster Mouldings

THE PLASTER CEILING MOULDINGS in my parlor were chipped and had several small 1-in. sections missing. I tried patching them with plaster of paris, but found that the plaster set too quickly and dried to a rough surface that was difficult to sand and shape.

    As an experiment, I tried making patches with drywall joint compound. Success! I could shape the material easily with my fingers in most cases; other times I used a putty knife. Joint  compound shrinks when it dries, and so I had to make several applications. But this wasn't a problem.

    After the defects were brought up to level, I smoothed the patches by "sanding" them with a damp sponge.

      -- Fredericka Wales, Chicago, Ill.

Saved By Spar Varnish

I'VE DISCOVERED a superior finish for trim that was originally finished with shellac. Spar varnish -- designed for marine use -- is extremely tough, and absolutely impervious to water. When used to finish baseboards and window surrounds, it gives an appearance that is indistinguishable from the original shellac, but can withstand misdirected rain and plant waterings. Shellac, on the other hand, sustains white spotting when exposed to water.

    In addition to their water resistance, quality spar varnishes also have a sun screen. This keeps wood exposed to direct sunlight from bleaching out. The sun screen also keeps the varnish from peeling off sun-drenched woodwork the way polyurethanes do.

      -- Ned Ford, Cincinnati, Ohio

Tips To Share? Do you have any hints or short cuts that might help other old-house owners? We'll pay $15 for any short how-to items that are used in this "Restorer's Notebook" column. Write to Notebook Editor, The Old-House Journal, 69A Seventh Avenue, Brooklyn, NY 11217.

opinion...
Remuddling

SUBSCRIBER Charles W. Wilson of Mechanicsburg, Pa., sent us these photos, which were taken in 1864 and 1984: "Incredible as it may seem, these photos are of the same house. But the present owners should not be made to shoulder all the blame -- this house has had a long history of abuse. It was bought by my great-grandfather in 1864 for $14,000. In 1876 my ancestor had it moved onto an adjoining lot. (Because of its size, it had to be cut up and carried in five parts, then reattached.) He rented out the house but retained the wing on the right as his office. Around the turn of the century, the house was sold to two families, and it has remained a duplex ever since."

Photos from a grant winner: Sign of a triumph for The Gifford Park Association, which was instrumental in bringing Neighborhood Housing Services to Elgin; right, an 1886 house in the historic district on which the Association has worked for six years (and more to come).

Attention Preservation Groups:
The 1985 OHJ Grant Winners

IS YOUR NEIGHBORHOOD GROUP looking for ways to raise money? Then you might want to do what 145 other preservation groups did last year: enroll in OHJ's Revenue-Sharing Program. In 1985 these 145 groups split $24,000 in revenue-sharing and grant funds from OHJ.

THE REVENUE-SHARING PLAN lets preservation groups offer members and neighbors OHJ subscriptions at a discount. And each group keeps half of all the money it collects.

TO FURTHER ENRICH the program, OHJ awards six $1,000 grants to participating groups. The six 1985 grant winners are:

Gifford Park Association, Elgin, Ill.

Cityside, Wilmington, Del.

Valentine Neighborhood Assn., Kansas City, Missouri

Roxbury Highland Historical Society, Roxbury, Mass.

Park Slope Civic Council, Brooklyn, N.Y.

West End Community Assn., Milwaukee, Wisc.

THE FIRST $1,000 GRANT goes to the organization that signs up the most OHJ subscribers; in 1985 it was the Gifford Park Association. The other five

grants are determined by a drawing -- this year presided over by Michael Lynch, the Historic Sites Restoration Coordinator at the New York State Historic Preservation Office.

SINCE THE PROGRAM's beginning, OHJ has funneled $102,000 to preservation groups. The money has supported such varied activities as conducting a neighborhood architectural survey, funding a preservation workshop, beginning a home maintenance program for senior citizens, printing a community brochure, and moving a historic building.

UNDER ITS energetic president Dan Miller, Gifford Park has been participating in the OHJ Revenue-Sharing Program for

Michael Lynch of the Albany SHPO pulls 5 winners out of the hat held by editor Poore.

several years and has thus added almost $5,000 to its treasury. Dan, a long-time OHJ reader and occasional contributor, apparently can recommend OHJ to his neighbors in a most convincing fashion.

DAN TELLS US that the OHJ money raised this year is going into the organization's house purchase/rehab fund. The group is putting the money together with a grant from the city -- plus the promise of a bank loan -- to buy a house to restore and resell. The goal is to create a revolving fund that will continually buy, fix up, and resell run-down neighborhood houses.

OHJ's REVENUE-SHARING Program started a few years ago when we realized we were spending a small fortune on postage to solicit new subscriptions. Rather than give all that money to the Post Office, we felt we'd rather divert the money to preservation groups that help us find subscribers.

MORE THAN $25,000 has been allocated for Revenue-Sharing in 1986. If your group would like to participate, contact:

Barbara Bouton
The Old-House Journal
69A Seventh Avenue
Brooklyn, NY 11217
(718) 636-4514

...and congratulations to the winners!

Letters

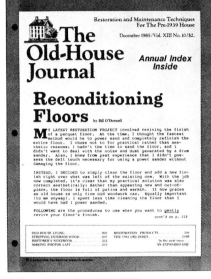

Before: December 1985 OHJ

After: Jan. — Feb. 1986 OHJ

shouldn't a thirteen-year-old publication. Congratulations on your new facelift. It looks great, and we wish you the best of luck.
-- Gary Cooke of C & H Roofing
Sioux Falls, S.D.

To the editor:
I just want to tell you how disappointed I am with your new format. You've sold us out! The stuff you've added isn't even any good -- you ought to change your name to Schlock Restorer's News. OHJ used to have value to collectors, but it's lost that now. It's become another so-what magazine. I can already see it going downhill.
I don't understand why you've increased your overhead like this. You're going to be in bad shape come renewal time; I'm not going to renew, and I'll bet most other old readers feel the same.
-- Ben Johnson
Staten Island, N.Y.

[We're sorry you feel that way. -- OHJ staffers]

Comments on Format Change

Dear Friends:
As a ten-year subscriber to your publication, I thought you may like to hear some of my thoughts regarding OHJ's new format.
When I first subscribed, I recall reading the Old-House Living section and thinking, "My God, there are people out there who are going through the same thing as I am." I've felt like part of an exclusive network ever since. So it's understandable that I felt a bit nostalgic and saddened when I saw the slick color cover. Times change, though, and restoring old houses has become more of a mainstream endeavor. After so many years of sharing information with one another, we've become a more sophisticated audience, and I think it's good that your new format reflects that change.
I found the ads somewhat distracting (it makes the pages busier than when you had 100% editorial), but I understand the need for advertising and I'm sure I'll get used to them. Just be sure to continue to keep shoddy products off your pages.
Overall, I think it's a change for the better. There's more OHJ to read each month, and the editorial quality is still excellent.

I have just one question: What do you expect me to do with all these three-ring binders?
-- Jim Boone
Springfield, Mass.

Dear OHJ:
It was a daring move to unload a new format on a bunch of fussy subscribers who scorn the remuddling of old classics. But the country's premier preservation publication did a tasteful renovation on its first new issue. Of course, rehabilitating an old magazine is something we'd expect you to do with considerable care and sensitivity. A close look at the issue bears out what Patricia Poore promised in her editorial comments. No radical changes, just more of what we've always expected. OHJ is still, "Useful information about doing good work and preserving what we've inherited."
As a regular OHJ Catalog advertiser, we are very pleased to get the chance to reach more readers more often. Your readership certainly can't complain about receiving more product information in each issue -- even if it takes the form of advertising.
After all, if a sagging porch roof needs a little help after sixty years, why

Dear OHJ:
We were a little afraid that the new format would make OHJ look too much like every other magazine. After reading the Jan./Feb. issue, however, it's clear that you have kept the integrity of the old "newsletter." The ads are informative in their own right; they're all related products -- no cigarette or perfume advertising. We appreciate that.
The introduction to the new section on post-Victorian houses was wonderful, but it just whet our appetites (we're hungry for more). Keep up the good work as always!
-- Susan & Cliff Goldthwaite
Teaneck, N.J.

Can I Dip?

Dear Ms. Poore:
Regarding "Stripping Paint from Exterior Wood" [December 1985 OHJ]: Do you have new information which leads you to recommend chemically dipping shutters? OHJ has consistently, both editorially

and through readers, warned against dipping shutters due to the residue problem. Now, after ten years, you change your tune. Please explain in more detail since I have 17 pairs of blistered wood shutters waiting for restoration.
-- Barbara N. Flagg
Bellport, N.Y.

[When shutters (or any other exterior wood pieces) are dip-stripped in lye or other strong caustic, the wood absorbs some of the chemical. If not completely neutralized by an acid wash and rinsing, the wood will continue to "bleed" lye, and the new paint or varnish will fail. Unfortunately, neutralization is often neglected or rushed, and it's tricky even when the operator attempts to do a good job.

Earlier warnings about not dipping exterior wood apply to wood stripped in lye (or potassium hydroxide or tri-sodium phosphate). Most dip-strip shops use a strong caustic for heavy paint buildup, so it's important to be aware of the problem.

However, dipping shutters in a methylene-chloride-based stripper saves a lot of time over hand-stripping each slat. You can do this your-self by making a shallow dip-tank. The article did make the distinction between sol-vent strippers and caustic strippers, but not specifi-cally in regard to shutter-stripping. Sorry for the confusion. -- P. Poore]

Outside Admiration

Dear Friends,
I have never done a lick of work on an old house, but I follow the detailed in-structions of every issue word for word. It pleases me to be able to follow and un-derstand these instructions. Perhaps I am destined to be a future old-house owner.

I especially enjoyed the article "Caveat Emptor," by Greg Jackson [Old-House Living, December 1985 OHJ]. Such humor could only come from (1) the love of old houses (which is crazy to begin with); (2) the ability to continue with a project you love-hate -- because you love it.

If a large bank account or twelve skilled craftsmen and a dental pick were all that

Letters

were required, I might try it myself. I think it also requires love, dedication, and a great sense of humor. Go to it. I envy you.
-- Elaine Don-Batalla
San Lorenzo, Cal.

S.A.D. Electricians

People:
In today's Chicago Sun-Times I read a reprint from your Journal on the subject of mechanical doorbells [August-September 1985 OHJ]. My father was an old-time electrical contractor. He started in 1898. At one time, when Albany Park was being subdivided on the northwest side of Chicago, he got a contract from Mike Faherty to install bells in 42 homes. There were no lights installed; they thought gas was more reli-able. The bells were powered by wet batteries. Sometimes they quit functioning and people called the electrician to come out in his horse-drawn cart. He'd go over the connections and when the owner wasn't looking, he'd surreptitiously take a small wooden stick and stir up the sal ammoniac in the wet-battery jar. This restored power and the bells worked. The electricians were given the name "Sal-Ammoniac Dis-turbers" by those in the know.
-- Leonard W. Johnson
Des Plaines, Ill.

Mind Readers?

Dear Friends,
I was pleased to see the Bungalow issue last May. I live in a 1925 Bungalow, but many people think my house is practically new. (I feel like a stepchild among owners of pre-1900 homes. Like old money, old houses sometimes breed snobbery.) OHJ, though, has always been a good friend. I have many problems common to owners of much older houses: stripping paint, finding hard-ware that isn't plastic and aluminum, dealing with unimag-inative contractors ("Lady, you can't do that"), trying to heat and cool the house sanely.

We've been amazed more times than I can tell you at

what OHJ brings. Just as we're trying to figure out windows, along comes a special issue on windows. We'll be talking about Venetian blinds, and the mailman brings OHJ's Venetian-blind issue. We'll be wondering about the plumb-ing or electricity, and OHJ runs an article discussing just that. It's uncanny! You must be reading our minds.
-- Catherine Hayes
Mobile, Ala.

[Thanks for the compliment. If it seems like we're reading your mind, it must be because we're old-house people our-selves! Please note our new regular feature: Post-Victor-ian Houses. -- ed.]

Asbestos Hazards

To the editor:
I've been remodelling old houses here in Houston for the past few years, and I've come across enough toxic substances to wipe out an army. I know you're concerned about these.

The one that worries me the most, however, is asbestos. Removing shingles from houses releases this deadly stuff, and I've found it many times as insulation on hot-air ducts in attics -- flaking off. I'm not an expert on asbestos, and I don't even know if anyone has done extensive epidemio-logical research on the health risks of domestic asbestos, but it seems that urban pio-neers should be aware of the killer waiting for them in their attic or basement. I'm an avid reader of your fine publication, and look forward to many years of old-house enlightenment from it.
-- George P. Szontagh
Houston, Texas

[We're preparing an article on inspection and removal of do-mestic asbestos; readers' com-ments and experience are eagerly sought. By the way, the Safe Buildings Alliance warns that unnecessary removal of asbestos can be more haz-ardous than leaving it in place. "Risk is posed by the presence of airborne asbestos -- not by the presence of as-bestos-containing materials," says SBA's John Welch. -- ed.]

Old-House Living ...

FRIENDS AND FAMILY DESERTED ME
A Twenty-Year Struggle In Brownville, Nebraska

by Donald J. Gappa

1966: MOVING THROUGH the tangle of tall grass and weeds, the real-estate agent and I discovered wild roses and peonies, irises and tiger lilies. Like the dilapidated but still dignified house that stood behind them, the flowers defied neglect and mistreatment, and hinted at the charm and elegance of earlier days.

AND LIKE EVERYTHING else I'd seen that day, they seemed to be conspiring to win my heart. I'd come to Brownville, Nebraska, simply to attend the annual antique flea market. But I found myself captivated by the warm sunshine, the autumn leaves, the tables of antiques lining both sides of the main street, the friendly local people and especially the mellow, old, red-brick homes. Then before I knew it a friend was introducing me to the real-estate lady.

SHE SHOWED ME four houses in all, and we had to make our way through shoulder-high weeds to look at each one. She came equipped with a can of insect spray so we could enter one of them through a swarm of wasps.

ALL FOUR were interesting, but the one we stood before was fascinating -- time had treated it terribly, and its sorry state intrigued me. The flat top of the hipped roof looked cropped, as if something were missing; a curious second-storey door on the south side suggested a porch had once stood underneath; window frames and doors were grey after many paintless years. Recent repairs to the eaves

of the roof had destroyed the ornamental roof brackets; only bare spots in the paint marked the places they had occupied. During roof repair the twin chimneys had also been removed; and, as if all the humiliating removals had not been sufficient, two "additions" constituted a final insult: a coat of aluminum paint and a bright blue, asphalt-shingle roof.

WE ENTERED the magnificent kitchen first. The 15x25-foot room was littered with junk furniture, dirt and debris. Wallpaper hung in tattered strips from the walls, and a single dead, naked light bulb dangled from a long cord in the center of the lumpy ceiling. But the room was redeemed by many things, besides its size. Sunlight was streaming through three big windows in the foot-thick walls; there was a large, ornate wall shelf and a built-in china closet.

BEHIND A BOARD WALL a narrow, winding stairway led up. At the top of the worn stairs lay a formal dining room complete with mantel and woodwork, eleven-and-a-half foot ceilings and transoms over all the doors. Beyond the dining room was a formal parlor with another mantel, woodwork even more elaborate, and the same high ceilings. Even the gaudy plastic drapes on the windows could not compromise the grace and dignity of that fine old room.

I WENT TO HAVE COFFEE and "think it over." I was back in half an hour with a deposit, and back again two days later with a down payment. From that moment my life was never the same.

ABOVE: This is the eastern half of the enormous kitchen, with the built-in china closet & wall shelf over the sink that intrigued the author. Behind the vertical boards (in back of the stove) lies the narrow, winding staircase that leads to the dining room.

BELOW: In the western end of the kitchen is a sunlit sitting area which is a favorite gathering place.

All interior photos are by Cliff Beuterbaugh.

FRIENDS AND FAMILY deserted me; they refused to leave the comforts of Omaha for the dust, insects, well water and slow pace of Brownville. I started working alone on weekends. First to go was the aluminum paint. Sandblasting would damage the soft brick, so I took a brick to Omaha and had paint mixed to match its color. While I was busy painting, an electrician was rewiring the entire house. Adding plumbing and central heating, which frequently presents serious problems for old-house restorers, was relatively easy in this case. The house had a large unfurnished area behind the kitchen, which now contains the bathroom and all heat-

ing and plumbing equipment. No structural or aesthetic compromises had to be made for these updates.

THE FIRST ROOM I restored was the kitchen. Five 9x12 sheets of linoleum had accumulated at each end of the room, and grey paint covered the gap between the stacks. The wide pine boards underneath needed some patching, but otherwise required only stripping of the paint. The floor is now varnished with a clear finish that brings out its mellow glow.

I PULLED A LITTLE piece of wallpaper from the ceiling and a whole 6x12-foot section of ceiling came crashing down, along with a dormant beehive and hundreds of its deceased inhabitants. The plaster had been removed long ago, and the many layers of wallpaper that were pasted to cardboard just couldn't hold any more.

UPSTAIRS THERE WAS more damage to undo. An entire wall had been removed between two bedrooms. Holes in the plaster had been stuffed with rags and then papered over. The plaster on one dining room wall was replaced with concrete, causing both the wall and the floor beneath it to sag. The beautiful woodwork in the dining room, including a walnut balustrade and mantel, had been painted white, presumably when the room was used as a kitchen.

AS THE YEARS PASSED the work continued and the house blossomed. I made new friends and had plenty of help and encouragement. Family members visited more frequently and stayed longer. Interior work was done mostly in the winter, exterior and yard work in the summer. Some projects were pretty routine, like stripping woodwork and re-roofing. But others I found especially exciting, like restoring the missing porch and cupola.

I LOOKED for old pictures of the house for years and talked to old-timers, trying to find out what the missing porch had looked like and what, if anything, had stood on top of the roof. No one had any pictures and no one could remember. After much frustration I decided to do an interpretive restoration based on similar houses in the region. Reconstructing the porch did not prove difficult; I created a design based on a remnant of post and railing removed from another old house in town, and then built the porch myself.

LEFT: In the refurbished dining room, note the walnut balustrade, mantel, and door. The fireplace was never intended to function, but rather to provide an ornate frame for the stove.

BELOW: Here's the same room during renovation. White paint covers the woodwork, chunks of plaster have fallen from some of the walls, and the fireplace wall is stripped to bare lath.

BOTTOM: This is a photo of the rear elevation, after restoration. Like many of the houses in Brownville, the building is accessible from the ground on both levels. The cupola, chimneys, and brackets were missing when the author first saw the house in 1966.

BUT THE "TOP" REMAINED a tantalizing mystery until one afternoon in 1981. I received a call from the Brownville Historical Society, and was excited to learn that in a box of items recently donated to the museum, they'd found an old painting of my neighbor's house which showed mine in the background, sporting a cupola! The "painting" turned out to be a tinted photograph, whose paint obscured the architectural details of the cupola. But at least there was evidence that there had been one. The Nebraska State Historical Society was unable to remove the paint from the photo, so I completed my own cupola design patterned heavily after one in Hannibal, Missouri, which I felt best suited the size and style of my house.

THE DAY THE TIN and tarpaper were removed from the flat top of the roof marked the realization of a fifteen-year goal. At last I was actually replacing the cupola I was sure the house once had. But even as I worked I felt a slight twinge of uncertainty -- maybe there was no cupola under the paint in that picture! Well, old pictures may lie, but old houses don't. There, beneath layers of tin and tarpaper, lay the crudely hacked-off stumps of the four full-dimension posts that had risen beyond the roof to form the corners of the original cupola!

The House's Past

MY HOUSE'S FIRST OWNER, I. S. Nace, settled in Brownville after serving in the Union Army in the Civil War. He operated a general store and owned both rental property and farmland. With his wife Mary, he raised two sons and two daughters, and by 1871 they were prosperous enough to build themselves a fine new home (now my fine old one). As their resources and family continued to grow, they were able to build a second and larger brick Italianate house in 1885 (a structure whose cupola, by the way, now sits in a clump of weeds in its backyard). They then rented out their older home.

MR. NACE DIED in 1890, and the family sold the 1871 house for use as a parsonage. During the Great Depression, the stairway was closed and the house used as a duplex, with one family living upstairs and another downstairs. It changed hands many times during the years following, and was deserted by the time I first saw it on that warm fall day in 1966.

LEFT: No, this isn't a period photograph, but a modern one that illustrates the sensitivity of the interior restoration. The woodwork is original to the room; furnishings were collected by the author over the years.

BELOW: This one is the author's favorite photo of the house. The front porch was missing when he first saw the place. He replaced it, basing it on period designs and a section of post and beam removed from another old house in town.

MY INTENTION WAS always to return the house to its original appearance, inside and out. All the rooms, doors, windows, and so on are exactly as they would have been the day the house was finished 115 years ago. The rooms are used for the purpose for which they were intended. All decorating and furnishings are typical of what might have been in the house at that time. I never tried to change the house or force it to be something it was not; I let it show me how to enjoy it, and it has shown me how comfortable, rewarding and fascinating old houses, old things, and old ways can be.

Twenty Years Of Love

THIS FALL I'll be celebrating my twentieth year of old-house living. I loved it the day I started, and I still love it. I love sitting by the fire in the evening, snuggling down in bed under the antique patchwork quilt; I love having breakfast with friends in that magnificent sunny kitchen, drinking holiday toasts in the dining room, listening to someone play the organ in the parlor, hosting tours of the house, sitting on the porch swing on hot summer evenings with the crickets, waking in the night to hear a whippoorwill, or walking among the flowers that color the yard from May to September.

BUT MY OLD HOUSE isn't only nostalgic. It's also down-to-earth 1986 living, with the thunder of a teenager's rock and roll, the banter of mid-winter poker games, tennis shoes carelessly discarded in front of the kitchen woodstove, a motorcycle parked at the hitching stone where I. S. Nace once tied his horses. The house connects the past with the present. It gives me a sense of balance and perspective; it is an island of stability in a relatively unstable world.

THE OTHER DAY I realized that the kitchen needs new wallpaper. It was the first room I papered twenty years ago, and it occurred to me that we have come full circle, my old house and I. At some point, we passed from "restor-

ing" to "restored." I never noticed when it happened, because I was having too much fun -- living in the house and working on it. I used to wonder what I would do when I finished restoring it, and now I know. I'll just keep right on having fun -- living in it and working on it.

Worth Writing For

Here are some notable catalogs and publications that have turned up in the OHJ mailbox lately.

Wood Window Literature

Need replacement wooden windows? This millshop specializes in stock and custom windows in Ponderosa pine. Also, custom wood storms & screens, and a replacement kit for double-hung sash. Literature $2.50 from: D.V.H. Co., Dept. OHJ, 15 S.W. 3rd Ave., Gainesville, FL 32607.

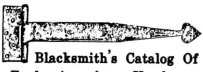

Blacksmith's Catalog Of Early American Hardware

Here are ideal replacement items for houses built before 1850 -- and for Colonial Revival homes that require an authentic finishing touch. Hand-forged thumblatches, bar sets, mortise locksets, pintle hinges, hinge plates, T-, H-, and HL-hinges, iron door knockers, hooks, bootscrapers, shutterdogs, cabinet & cupboard hinges, candle sconces, and porcelain knobs are all available in this handsome 26-page brochure. Catalog $3 from: Williamsburg Blacksmiths, Dept. OHJ, 1 Buttonshop Rd., Williamsburg, MA 01096.

Guidelines For Re-Wiring

This well-illustrated 102-page softcover volume contains a comprehensive guide to historic wiring and lighting systems, along with down-to-earth suggestions for cost-effective re-wiring and lighting design during rehabilitation. A truly unique reference. It's $10.95 from: AFC/Nortek, Dept. OHJ, 55 Samuel Barnet Blvd., New Bedford, MA 02745.

Catalog Of House Parts

Exquisite Cirecast bronze Victorian hardware (cast by the expensive lost wax process), solid brass door hardware, porcelain door knobs, solid brass mailboxes, mech-

anical doorbells, Victorian lighting fixtures, old-style Chicago faucets, Victorian bath accessories, real marble reproduction mantels, and old-fashioned wood corner beads are just some of the items shown. Catalog is $2 from: Crawford's Old-House Store, 301 McCall St., Rm. 86, Waukesha, WI 53186.

Old-Fashioned Wish Book

Looking for kitchen items like your grandmother had? Old-style kerosene lamps? An 1890s top hat? A straight razor kit? Good sturdy farm tools? Victorian hardware & furniture? All this and thousands more items are found in the 256-page "Wish & Want Book." It's a truly extraordinary collection of well-made, usable items -- mostly from the pre-electric era. Catalog $3.75

from: Cumberland General Store, Route 3, Dept. OH86, Crossville, TN 38555.

Wood Mantels Brochure

Softwood mantels in classical designs -- suitable for painted or stained finishes -- fit very well into early 19th century and Colonial Revival houses. A 20-page brochure shows 26 designs and provides complete measuring instructions. "Wood Mantel Pieces" is $2 from: Readybuilt Products, 1701 McHenry St., Dept. OHJ, Baltimore, MD 21223.

Dumbwaiter Specifications

Did somebody remove the dumbwaiter from your building? Hand-powered dumbwaiters are still made; the design hasn't changed much from the 19th century. Free brochure (Cat. No. 983) giving measurements and specifications is available from: Vincent Whitney Co., P.O. Box 335, Dept. OHJ, Sausalito, CA 94966.

THE HAND RUBBED FINISH

It's easy to create a superbly smooth finish on interior woodwork and furniture

by Larry Jones

ONCE YOU'VE TAKEN the time and trouble to strip paint or blackened varnish from a piece of furniture, a neglected mantel, or several hundred feet of fine wood trim, you don't want to skimp on the finish. You've coped with the unexpected time and backbreaking labor that surface preparation demanded, so you don't mind putting in a little extra effort to apply the perfect finishing touch.

WHY NOT TRY a hand-rubbed finish? There's no comparison to the silky smooth, rich luster achieved from the basic finishing techniques explained here. With the right materials and techniques, you can rub out a finish to a dull luster or a super gloss.

IF YOU'VE GROWN ACCUSTOMED to throwing a couple of coats of polyurethane over your freshly-stripped woodwork, hand-rubbed finishing is probably not for you. Hand rubbing is a labor-intensive refinishing method best suited for fine woodwork. It's especially appropriate for pieces that have broad, flat surfaces that exaggerate minor imperfections in the finish.

The Basic Process

RUBBING IS LIKE SANDING in that you create finer and finer scratches going with the wood grain until you've arrived at the finish you want. Each time you rub the finish, you remove ever-finer imperfections. When we speak of gloss in this article, we're talking about smoothness as well as reflectivity. A thick coat of polyurethane hastily applied in a dusty room will reflect a lot of light, but close inspection will reveal bumps, bubbles, bristles and brush marks.

EACH COAT APPLIED in a hand-rubbed finish is sanded, or "rubbed," until it is smooth and level. The idea is to eliminate brushmarks, pimples, and debris. The abrasives should be fine enough so that the scratches do not show through the next coat of finish. Successive coats are applied and rubbed down until a sufficient thickness is built-up (three to six coats is typical). The final coat is leveled and then rubbed with pumice or rottenstone and oil to achieve the desired gloss.

Preparation

SMOOTH SURFACES PRODUCE smooth finishes. Paste wood fillers, such as Behlen's Por-O-Lac, help you produce smooth-as-glass finishes on open-pored woods like oak, ash, and mahogany. (Don't confuse fine wood fillers with wood putties and doughs.) Tinted fillers are mixed to the consistency of cream and brushed into the bare wood pores. Burnish off the excess by rubbing across the grain. Then sand smooth with #220 grit or finer abrasive paper. Allow to dry for 48 hours before finishing.

DON'T MAKE MORE WORK for yourself by starting with a coarser grade of paper than necessary. Use a sanding block to avoid creating wavy

A thick cork block makes an excellent applicator for wood filler. It forces the filler deep into open pores and doesn't pull it out on the backstroke.

surfaces and rounded edges. Don't rely too heavily on fillers, stains, and top coats to hide sanding irregularities.

PRACTICALLY ANY gloss varnish, lacquer, shellac, or enamel can be rubbed down to get the surface sheen you want. It's best to select a product specifically designed for rubbing. (Behlen's 4 Hour Rubbing Varnish, McCloskey's Hour Varnish, and McCloskey's Bar Top Varnish are three examples. For more information on finishing products, see Restoration Products on page 92.)

APPLY THE FINISH carefully. No matter what material you choose to apply, how fine your brush is, or how well you dust the surface, there's bound to be some imperfections in the finish. Neat work habits and careful application will minimize these nuisances. Don't do this work while any demolition or construction is going on -- you want the environment to be as dust-free as possible. As for the remaining imperfections: Rub them out!

YOU CAN QUICKLY ACHIEVE a relatively smooth finished surface by avoiding between-coats rubbing. Apply a minimum of three coats of varnish and allow each to dry hard (some varnishes may take 48 hours or more to dry completely). Then, rub out the top layer only.

DON'T USE THIS ABBREVIATED METHOD on an especially fine piece, though. Building up coats with no intermediate rubbing may trap hard, sharp grit in the finish coats. Rubbing the top coat may cause this foreign material to pull out of the finish -- imparting deep

scratches. If you do use this method (for less-than-outstanding woodwork), keep one thing in mind: The cleaner your equipment and environment, the better the results.

IF THE QUALITY of the final finish is very important, you may wish to lightly sand out each coat of varnish (after the second one). Be sure each coat is completely dry before applying another. Expert wood finishers use this technique to build one layer on top of another, producing flawlessly smooth finishes. Each sanding removes the dust and other surface irregularities that settle into the varnish as it dries. For the greatest depth and luster, apply four or more coats of varnish and lightly sand before rubbing. Highly visible or heavily used surfaces may need more coats than less noticeable areas.

Sanding The Initial Coats

MOST TRADITIONAL hand-rubbed finishes are initially smoothed out with garnet, silicon carbide, or aluminum oxide wet-or-dry sandpaper and oil to produce a dull matte finish.

RUB LIGHTLY with dry #220 or finer sandpaper on the first primer/sealer coat. For subsequent coats, try #280 or #320 with oil. For top coats that are fairly smooth, start with #400 wet-or-dry sandpaper and move up to #600. Dip the sandpaper into oil periodically. Between-coat sanding with oil will leave a residue. Clean up with benzine before applying the next coat.

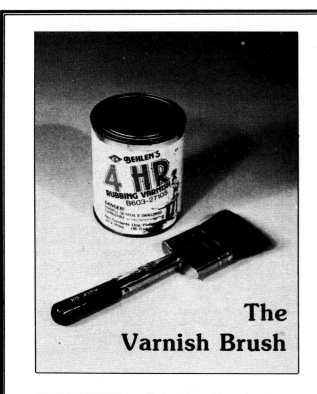

The Varnish Brush

FINE BRUSHES are the best buy. There is no economy in cheap or neglected brushes. For lacquer, varnish, shellac, or enamel, soft hair brushes such as Ox,

Fitch, or Badger are best. Don't use your varnish brush for other coatings — dried pieces of paint will contaminate your finish.

Keep your brushes clean. To reduce the chances of getting loose bristles in your work, gently tap the brush against the palm of your hand (never hit it against a hard surface — you'll ruin the brush setting). Twirl the brush rapidly back and forth between your palms, and vigorously run your fingers through it several times. Work clean varnish into the brush by dipping and wiping off a few times.

Break-in a varnish brush by using it for undercoats only. Never use your brush sideways or poke and jab with it. If you're doing a lot of varnishing, store the brush, fully submerged, in a container of exterior spar varnish. Keep the brush suspended in the varnish (with a wire or rod) — never allow the bristles to touch the bottom of the container. Keep the container tightly sealed.

When your project is complete, clean your brush immediately. Wipe out the excess varnish, then work the bristles while submerged in benzine. Follow with a washing in turpentine. Clean shellac brushes in denatured alcohol, and lacquer brushes in lacquer thinner. Shake or gently squeeze out excess solvent and allow the brush to dry. Fold blotter or brown wrapping paper over the ends of the bristles to maintain shape during storage.

A sanding block ensures even rubbing during the initial wet-sanding stage. Here, the refinisher is using mineral spirits and fine wet-or-dry sandpaper. Mineral spirits won't raise the grain, and it cleans the paper better than water. Grocery-store baking tins make a convenient container for the lubricant.

Above: Apply the pumice evenly over the entire surface. Try to put on enough pumice to do the whole area at once. Adding more pumice may produce dull spots in the finish. *Below:* Oil and pumice are being rubbed across the finish with a dense felt rubbing block. Blocks like this one make it easy to apply uniform rubbing pressure.

SANDING GRIT can't be rubbed out of a varnished surface without damaging the finish, so be careful to remove all the grit before you apply the next coat. Keep the paper clean (if you drop it on the floor, get another piece).

YOU MIGHT TRY using a newly-developed 1200-grit wet-or-dry sandpaper. On smooth surfaces you can produce practically the same quality of rubbed finish as that obtained with pumice. These super-fine sandpapers are available from woodwork supply dealers.

Flowing On The Finish

DON'T SHAKE, stir, or strain varnish: You'll create air bubbles that will mar the finish. Dip the brush into the varnish about 2/3 of the bristle length. Gently tap off the excess on the inside of the container. With a little practice, you'll develop a feel for loading the brush with just enough varnish to avoid drips.

Flow on the finish slowly and smoothly in the direction of the grain. Avoid flexing the brush. After laying on each brushload, go back and cross-brush it into the surface. Finish off with a final smoothing using only the tips of the bristles. Overlap and repeat this process in the next area.

Complete one section at a time with a uniform coat. Use breaks in the surface, such as seams, edges, and mouldings, as starting and stopping points. Look for drips, sags, and runs as soon as you finish each section. Use raking light to spot "holidays" (skipped places). Carefully brush out "fatty runners" (varnish that collects along edges). Avoid fat edges by applying the finish first at the center and working toward the edges. Before the finish begins to set up, give the entire surface a final brushing with a fairly dry brush using long, light strokes extending past the edges.

YOU CAN USE WATER as the lubricant on varnish, enamel, and lacquer, but water will damage shellac finishes. The process is the same as with oil rubbing. The paper will cut into and remove the finish faster with water, so be careful. Use a damp chamois for clean-up and drying. Don't let water stand on the finish.

STAINLESS STEEL OR BRONZE WOOL are also good for rubbing down finishes, provided you use the right grade. (Regular steel wool may leave splinters that will rust under the new finish, and discolor the piece.) Grades 2/0 (00) and 3/0 are a good choice for a satin finish; 4/0 will add more sheen. Don't use coarser grades; they'll scratch the wood. Steel wool can be rubbed dry, or used with a light mineral oil to soften the cutting action and reduce dust particles. Always rub with the grain. Steel wool pads disintegrate fairly quickly and have to be turned over periodically to expose fresh cutting fibers.

Rubbing With Pumice And Rottenstone

PUMICE IS PRODUCED by grinding volcanic ash into various grades of coarseness. Pumice powder is a white, fine-grain, hard abrasive that resembles flour.

A natural-bristle toothbrush is ideal for intricate details.

While they work great for flat surfaces, felt blocks won't conform to rounded shapes — use a thin scrap of felt instead. For vertical surfaces like this chair spindle, dip the felt into lubricant, then coat it with a thin layer of pumice. Again, coat with enough pumice to do the whole piece.

PUMICE IS IDEAL for amateur use because it cuts the finish slowly. It can be used alone or with rottenstone, depending on the finish you want. Rottenstone (also known as tripoli powder) is a very fine, ash-grey abrasive that comes in only one grade. Pumice is used first because it's coarser. Think of rottenstone as a final polishing agent to be used where you want super gloss. Both of these abrasives are inexpensive (about $1.25 per pound). You can find them at most paint and hardware stores, but don't be surprised if they're on a dusty back shelf, and nobody in the place knows what they're used for. For small projects, 1/2 pound may be all you'll need.

ALTHOUGH PUMICE is available in solid bricks, powder is most useful for rubbing finishes. It's available in course (1F), medium (2F), fine (3F), and extra fine (4F). For most jobs the 2F to 4F grades are adequate. Some stores sell pumice in medium and fine grades only. Try the fine grade first. Take great care to keep foreign matter out of the powders (sift the abrasives before use).

LUBRICANTS MUST BE USED with pumice stone and rottenstone, or else the heat generated by rubbing friction will damage the finish. To repeat, water can be used on varnish, lacquer, and enamel finishes, but will cloud water-sensitive shellac. Water and pumice cut a finish down very quickly, so work carefully. Adding

a little soap to the water helps slow the cutting action of the pumice -- giving you greater control. Unlike oil, water won't leave behind a residue.

OIL IS A GOOD lubricant for use on all finishes. It's especially suited for intricate decorations where it's very easy to rub through the finish. Paraffin oil (a clear mineral oil with wax content) is the most commonly used and the easiest to find. It can cause some finishes to cloud or turn white, so test in an inconspicuous location first.

The Rubbing Pad

FOR THE SMOOTHEST FINISHES and fastest cutting, felt pads are best. (Old cotton rags and the like trap abrasive in the weave.) You can make your own felt rubbing pad from an old felt hat, but for the smoothest "felting down" of a surface, buy several hard felt blocks from a woodworking supply house. The blocks or pads are made specifically for rubbing finishes. They can be ordered in thicknesses of 1/4 in. to 1/2 in., in sizes from 3x5 to 6x5 in. These dense felt blocks make it easier to apply uniform rubbing pressure and improve the cutting action of the abrasive. Cut the pads into smaller pieces for rubbing intricate mouldings and carvings.

OTHER GOOD MINERAL OIL lubricants include white neutra oil (the stuff used in lemon-oil furniture polishes) and light sewing-machine oil. Still another option is white non-blooming rubbing oil; it too is a high-grade mineral oil, but it doesn't leave behind the white film common with other oils.

BEGIN BY SPRINKLING pumice and lubricant over flat horizontal surfaces. Prewet the felt pad (see "The Rubbing Pad") before you start by dipping it into lubricant. Rub back and forth with the grain. It's easier to rub one small area at a time. Overlap your strokes and the areas you work. Don't rub any more than you have to -- you may cut through the finish. Check your progress often by wiping away the residue and examining the surface under a strong light.

BE CAREFUL when working near edges. The finish is thinnest here, and there's a tendency to apply more pressure. Avoid using felt rubbing pads for rounded surfaces like turnings and chair legs. The pressure of the pad on a small area will cut through the finish. Use small pieces of felt cut from an old hat instead -- they're thinner and will conform to the surface.

ON REALLY INTRICATE carvings, use a short-bristle brush to rub the abrasive. Keep the bristles clean. A natural-bristle toothbrush is great for small places. Dip the brush in lubricant, then into the pumice. Again, watch your progress, especially at the edges.

WHEN ALL THE SANDING marks in the finish have been removed, clean up the residue by carefully rubbing with soft cloths. Fine abrasive residue will be stuck in the grain, corners, and carvings. Clean with a stiff, fine bristle brush dampened with benzine. Follow up with a soft, benzine-moistened cloth. Wipe the entire surface to remove any oil that remains on the finish. To clean surfaces rubbed with water, soften the dry pumice residue with a damp sponge. Rub the surface in the direction of the grain with a soft chamois to remove excess water and residue.

IF YOU WISH TO produce a high gloss or super-polished finish, then there's one final step. Allow the surface to dry for 24 hours before polishing with rottenstone. The process is identical to rubbing with pumice. Make sure the surface is clean (dust free), and use a different felt pad than was used for the pumice. When you reach the sheen you want, clean the surface, and you're ready to wax.

RUBBING COMPOUNDS, developed for automotive finishes, also work well on wood finishes. Compounds come premixed, with abrasives and lubricant combined. Rubbing compound corresponds to pumice; polishing compound, to rottenstone. Both are used in exactly the same manner. Clean rubbing pads often, to prevent dried abrasive from scratching the finish.

THE THICKNESS OF compounds make them handy for vertical surfaces, but their residue is sometimes hard to remove. Compounds made specifically for woodworking come in colors that match the wood, making the residue less noticeable. Compounds sell for about $2.50 to $3.00 a can.

PROTECT YOUR FINE FINISH. Waxes protect the finish from wear, enhance the colors of wood, and make dusting easier. A good quality carnauba furniture wax is the only kind to consider. The more carnauba in the wax, the harder it will be, and the better the shine you'll get. Purchase a wax that dries neutral or get one that comes pretinted to match your wood. (S.W. Gibbia's book Wood Finishing and Refinishing explains how to make and tint several good paste waxes.) Avoid abrasive polishing waxes; your rubbing has eliminated the need for further polishing!

A TACK-CLOTH picks up dust, lint, grit, and other foreign matter from whatever surface you're getting ready to finish. To make one, all you need is soft cheesecloth or clean, soft linen. Avoid coarse materials, synthetics, and fabrics with hems or stitching — they may scratch. Shake a few drops of varnish into the rag and work it around until it's good and sticky — a little goes a long way. That's all it takes!

Gently wipe the surface with a tack-cloth after each sanding, before the first coat of finish, and between coats. Add a little more varnish periodically to spruce it up; you'll be surprised at how much dirt it can hold! Store your tack rags in an airtight container to avoid spontaneous combustion. When you do throw them out, soak them in water first, and dispose of them out of the house.

Never use silicone-impregnated dust cloths: Once the silicone gets on the surface, finishes won't adhere. Wolf Paints and other finish suppliers stock a wide variety of ready-made tack-cloths in every degree of tackiness. They're sold by the amount of resinous material they contain; a 50% tack-cloth contains resin that's equal to half the dry weight of the cloth. They're reusable and won't catch on fire. Find them at woodworking supply dealers, paint stores, and automotive paint distributors.

TEXTURED PLASTER FINISHES
HOW-TO TECHNIQUES

by Walter Jowers

MILLIONS OF YEARS AGO a large, tailless, knuckle-dragging ape strained to pull itself upright, hand over hand, balanced against the muddy wall of a damp cave. The creature stood, walked out of the cave, and emerged into the light, leaving its palmprints on the cave wall as evidence of the miracle: The Dawn of Man! The Dawn of Textured Wall Finish!

SINCE THEN, plaster of one type or another has been troweled, brushed, stippled, or hand-patted onto the walls of almost every type of building. In fact, textured finishes are so widespread, and the techniques for producing them so diverse, that it is almost impossible to pin down exactly which wall finishes are appropriate for which houses. These decorative finishes were especially fashionable, though, during the period circa 1915-1935; they were often used in the bungalows, cottages, foursquares, and English and Colonial Revival houses of the period. Then again, there are areas of the country where not a single house from this period has a textured wall finish -- it all depended on prevailing regional tastes and the skills of local craftsmen.

NOT ALL of the textured finishes from this period were done in the finish coat of plaster. Commercially available "plastic paint" products were also used to produce these effects. Similar products are available today; they are generically called "wall texture," "texture paint," or even (rather humbly) joint compound. One of these products, Textone (manufactured by United States Gypsum), was sold as a plastic paint in the 1920s, and is still sold today in premixed form. Early Textone came in powder form, and had to be site-mixed with water and/or sand. The modern product comes pre-mixed in four different formulations: a smooth texture, a sand texture, and two coarser textures. The Muralo company markets a dry powder product, Mural-Tex, that must be mixed with warm water to form texture paint. Several other paint companies currently make texture-paint products; these products vary from one region to another.

IF YOU WANT TO FIX a textured wall that is in disrepair, the first step is to patch any holes in the wall. The textured finish can be worked into a coat of finish plaster or a coat (or two) of texture paint; either of these materials must be applied over a sound substrate. A sound substrate in this case means a wall that is properly patched with patching plaster or joint compound, sanded smooth, and sealed with shellac or latex paint.

THE SECOND STEP is to make a choice: Do you want to site-mix plaster, or use a pre-mixed texture paint? If the area to be repaired is large, plaster will be less costly but more hassle (dust, leftover plaster to discard). If the damaged area is small, the cost (and hassle) differential is negligible. Either material should give satisfactory results.

ONCE THE WALL IS READY for texturing, the repair-person needs to get ready. Practice making the desired texture pattern on a piece of gypsum wallboard before you work on the wall. When you have the hang of it, try it on a section of the damaged wall. If the texture looks wrong, don't let it dry -- scrape the unsuccessful texture off the wall with a putty knife and start again.

Finishes On Parade

THE FINISHES shown on the next two pages were popular during the 1915-1930 era, but they were by no means the only popular period finishes. These descriptions and illustrations depict the tools and methods traditionally employed to produce textured wall finishes. Once you're familiar with them, you should be able to match the wall finish in your old house.

The walls and ceiling of this room have been finished with a Holland plaster wall texture, a finish which is shown in detail in Illus. 1 on the next page.

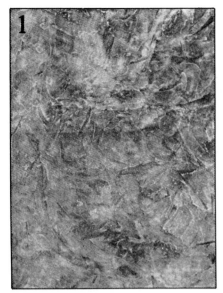
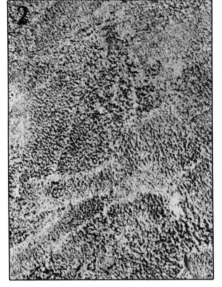

HOLLAND PLASTER -- (Illus. 1) Named after the historic textures in old Dutch houses, this finish is suitable for formal or informal rooms. Generally, in a smaller room, the effect would be understated; in a larger room, exaggerated.

THE PLASTER (or texture paint) is applied with a trowel, but the raised and rough edges left by the trowel are retained, giving the appearance of torn edges of paper. One popular treatment: Tint the texture material a cream color, then apply a medium-dark stain overglaze, and lightly sand the high spots to reveal streaks of the base color.

EARLY COLONIAL PLASTER -- (Illus. 2) This is a sand finish, most easily produced with a commercial sand-texture paint.

THE TEXTURE is produced by brushing on the paint in a "thick and thin" manner, then going over the partially-set material in all directions with a bricklayer's small pointing trowel. Then immediately stipple the surface with a whisk broom, and smooth up the high points again with the trowel.

ITALIAN PLASTER FINISH -- (Illus. 3) Plaster or texture paint can be used to produce this finish. The material is brushed on with a large paintbrush, then randomly stippled with a stippling brush. After the plaster or paint becomes tacky, brush in random semicircles with a short-bristled paintbrush. As soon as the material has set enough to hold its shape, lightly skim the surface with a plasterer's steel trowel. Glaze topcoats were often used with this finish.

IMITATION BRICK/STONE/TILE -- (Illus. 4) These finishes are usually done in plaster. Brick finishes are done with colored plaster; stone finishes often have colors brushed into the wet plaster to simulate natural grain. Brick textures are simulated by wire brushing; rough stone textures are produced by laying on plaster in crude, irregular gobs, then brushing out the roughest spots with a coarse brush. Imitation tile or smooth stone is worked into smooth plaster.

A "MORTAR JOINT" EFFECT can be achieved by applying the finish plaster coat over a dry coat of contrasting-color plaster, and then

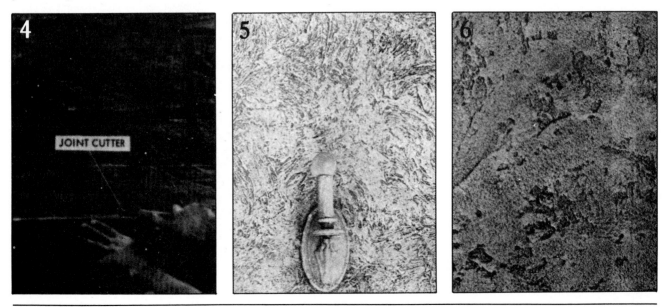

JOINT CUTTER

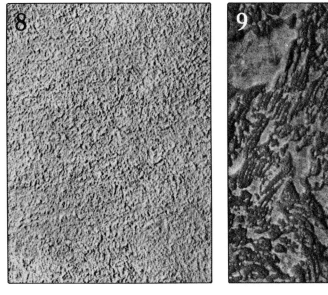

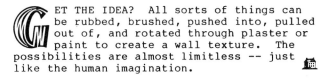

cutting the "joints" with an old screwdriver, using a level as a guide. The sharp edges produced by the cutter are lightly brushed out.

BRUSH FINISHES -- The finish in Illus. 5 is created by applying a thick coat of texture paint, then brushing the material in tight semicircles with a short-bristled brush. After the material has set enough to hold its shape, a plasterer's trowel is pressed into the paint, pulled out a little, then shifted to one side to drag the material.

THE FINISH in Illus. 6 is produced by roughening a thick coat of texture paint with a stipple brush, then pulling the material up into points with a plasterer's trowel, pushing it in and quickly pulling it out. The trowel is then used to randomly smooth down some rough edges.

THE VERY ROUGH brushed texture shown in Illus. 7 is suitable only for large rooms. A thick coat of texture paint is stippled with a stippling brush, then whisk-broomed into

large semicircles. At the end of each semicircular stroke, the whisk broom is pulled away sharply. After the material dries, use sandpaper to knock off the sharp points.

STIPPLED FINISHES -- Stippling brushes, wadded paper, or sponges can be used to create many subtle and striking effects. Illus. 8 shows a finish produced by daubing a texture paint with a stippling brush. Illus. 9 is a wall finish created by stippling texture paint with a sponge.

HAND FINISHES -- Illus. 10 shows a wall finish produced by hand-daubing plaster into place. The finish in Illus. 11 is done by pressing hands into texture paint, then pulling them straight back. Illus. 12 shows a wall covered with fingerprints.

GET THE IDEA? All sorts of things can be rubbed, brushed, pushed into, pulled out of, and rotated through plaster or paint to create a wall texture. The possibilities are almost limitless -- just like the human imagination.

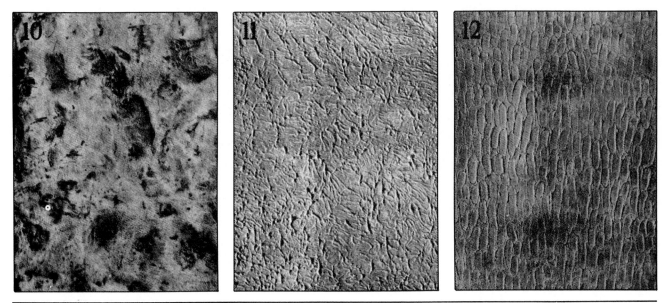

Fences & Gates

by John Crosby Freeman
detail drawings by Jonathan Poore

VICTORIAN examples of fence designs can be found in the reprinted patternbooks of Sloan, Bicknell, Comstock, Cummings and Miller, Palliser, and Barber. (Especially if you adapt their designs for porch and balcony railings to fences). But documentation of post-Victorian fences is relatively rare. Here are five designs from William Radford's Architectural Details of 1921.

FOR AN INTRODUCTION to building a fence that won't rot, refer to "The Best Way to Build a Fence," pp. 101-103 in the June 1983 issue of OHJ. These heavily illustrated pages are full of specific tips on materials to use, building and anchoring posts, designing rails to shed water, and fastening pickets. See also "No-Sag Garden Gates," p. 125 in the July 1983 issue.

IT'S HARD TO IMAGINE a post-Victorian house for which none of these designs would be appropriate. Do note, however, that these are tidy, finished fences -- if you want a rustic one for a stone-and-shingle bungalow, look elsewhere. These fences would look best painted, not stained or unfinished. (Fence number 3, perhaps, could go either way.)

(Note: The original drawings that follow are not consistent in scale from one to the next. Also, we added the grey tint to make them easier to read.)

FENCE NUMBER ONE was probably intended to be seen as a Mission design with its X-braces amidst the pickets and the severity of the rhythm at the top. To get the effect you see here, leave the same space between pickets as the pickets are wide. The fence as drawn would stand 5-1/2 to 6 feet tall.

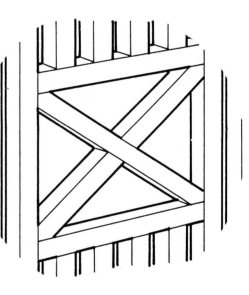

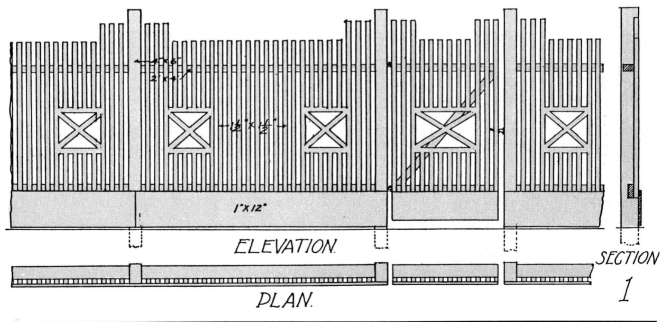

ELEVATION.

PLAN.

SECTION

1

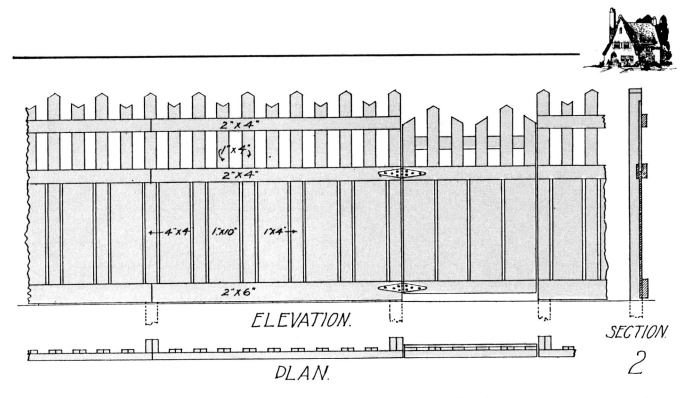

ELEVATION.

PLAN.

SECTION.

2

SOME COMMENTS: The 1x12 board at the bottom is very large to be so close to the ground -- warping or splitting might occur. Try a 1x8. The gate might look better if its "window" were also square, rather than rectangular. All of the gate designs -- and this one in particular -- would be improved by replacing the wood diagonal brace with a metal cable and turnbuckle, which would be less visually disruptive.

NUMBER 2 evokes the picket fence but deflects it with a clever wave effect at the top. The V-cuts of the shorter pickets, incidentally, are the other half of the taller pickets. The wide boards of the bottom provide the

privacy essential in populated suburban settings. Each tall picket (every other one) extends down between the wide boards to the bottom of the fence, knitting the top and bottom together. The 4x4 posts, too, are the same width as the pickets so that the overall rhythm is unbroken. (Note that the top of the posts have been cut to match pickets.) The fence stands about 6 feet tall as drawn.

FENCE NUMBER 3 is the easiest to build and plain enough for the country -- or stylishly severe enough for a suburban bungalow. A rhythm of 5 squares by 7 squares between posts would be more lively, I think, than the 5 x 8 shown. The fence is 4-1/2 feet tall.

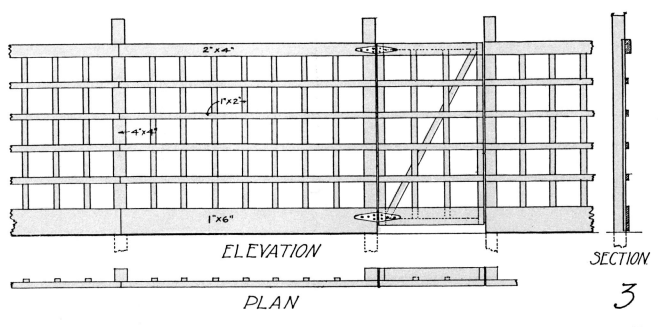

ELEVATION

PLAN

SECTION

3

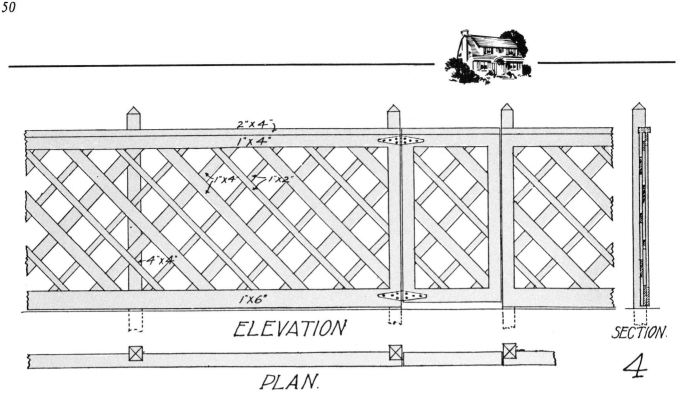

2"x4")

1"x4"

1"x4"   1"x2"

4"x4"

1"x6"

ELEVATION

SECTION.

4

PLAN.

FENCE NUMBER 4 is a basket-weave effect made interesting by alternating 1x4 strips with narrower 1x2s. (As drawn, it's 5-1/2 to 6 feet tall.) One improvement would be to position the post at the apex of two strips (instead of annoyingly off-center as it appears in the documentary drawing). See the small drawing below.

THIS DESIGN begs for manipulation. Variations might be made by moving the horizontal rails (top and bottom) to control their intersection with the basket-weave. Another suggestion: Shorten the posts so that they aren't higher than the top rail.

A MORE SERIOUS WEAKNESS of the design as it was drawn is that the rear diagonal slats do not have adequate fastening at top and bottom (there's a gap between those slats and the apron in front). The only way to fasten,

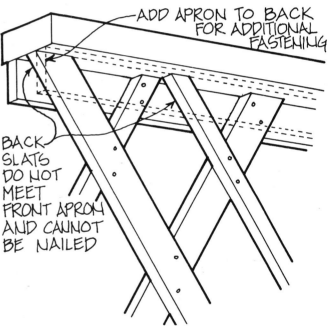

ADD APRON TO BACK FOR ADDITIONAL FASTENING

BACK SLATS DO NOT MEET FRONT APRON AND CANNOT BE NAILED

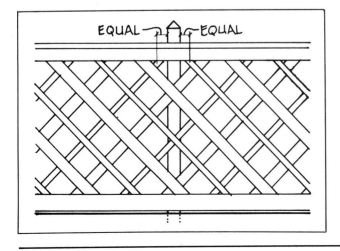

EQUAL   EQUAL

therefore, would be to toe-nail into the cap -- and the slats still would not be fastened at the bottom. One suggestion, shown above, is to add rear aprons at top and bottom. This would allow all slats to be nailed to a continuous apron.

NOTE THAT the face board of the frame is in front of the post and very close to it. Water and dampness could become trapped between them -- in an area where the sun won't shine. Solution: Allow the front slats to pass between the trim board and the post to act as a 3/4-inch spacer.

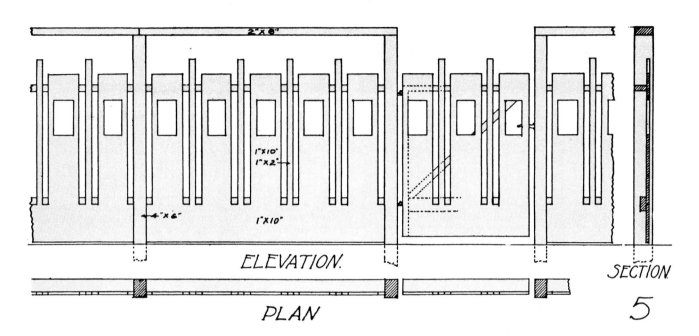

ELEVATION.

PLAN

SECTION

5

FENCE NUMBER 5 is the most stylish of all, its rhythm and cut-out rectangles evoking the designs of the Prairie School. It's an uncommon design for an uncommon post-Victorian house; such an unusual design is perhaps best reserved for a house of similar character and period. (The fence is about 4 feet high at the pickets; 5 feet overall.)

READ THE DRAWING to get some sense of the complexity of this screen-in-a-frame design. The 2x4 rail passing behind the fence near the bottom gives a layered, three-dimensional effect. The 2x4 passing behind at the top is a critical design element as well; note its calculated position midway between the top of the vertical 1x10s and the cut-out windows. Structural elements are planned as part of the overall geometry and design -- they're not merely braces and nailers.

THIS DESIGN requires extra work to build -- and has some details that make it extra vulnerable to weathering. Some suggestions: The horizontal 1x10 is a large piece of wood over a long span, minimally braced by a 2x4 rail at its top edge. To minimize warping, use only well dried wood. Keep it clear of the ground, and be sure the area drains well. Make five wide slats between posts the maximum span (as shown). Where the 2x4 lower rail meets the butted joint between the vertical and horizontal 1x10s, water may stand. So treat the end grain of the vertical 1x10s with a water-repellent preservative, prime it, and caulk the joint (front and back) before painting. Keep this fence maintained -- it's a lot of work to replace a "picket."

ALL OF THE DESIGNS shown could be adapted for different heights. Just be sure to draw your variation to scale -- to check that proportions look right -- before you cut any wood.

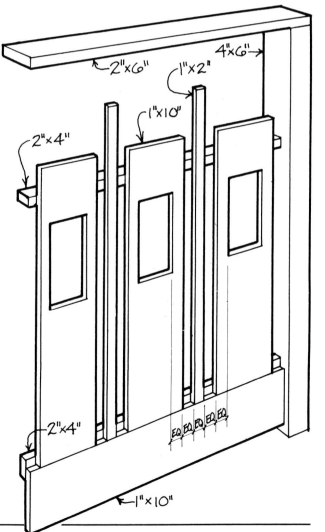

ART DECO REVIVAL

BY LARRY JONES

THE REINTRODUCTION OF HIGH-STYLE MODERNE FURNITURE

BACK IN THE LATE '60s, David Bell could be found combing California flea markets in search of his favorite furniture style: Art Nouveau. Finding that good pieces were both highly sought after and expensive, he turned his attention to the Moderne furniture of the '30s and '40s. "At the time I didn't know that what I'd found was called Art Deco or Streamlined Moderne," David recounts. "All I knew was that the public had no interest in it then, and truly high-style pieces could be had real cheap."

NO SMALL TASK! He chose only the most popular and prized original pieces for reproduction. He recalls, "With my red and black chair, a classic 1935 Streamline design, I visited 52 tubing benders in the L.A. area before I finally found one who was willing to bend the quantity and quality I needed."

ALTHOUGH DAVID'S furniture is almost identical to the originals, he made some improvements in materials. For instance, he substituted hardwood for pine in his chair and sofa frames;

This Egyptian-styled Art Deco leather chair is boldly enhanced by a stepped profile.

You'll find form & function in this 1934 magazine rack made from birch plywood.

NEW YORK GALLERIES and antique dealers are credited with stimulating the revival of interest in the sleek furnishings of the period. What began as a hobby for David soon became a business. By the time he opened shop in 1973, prices for Art Deco furniture were already rising; they soon doubled. By 1977 or '78, even major auction houses were getting into the act. Since furnishings and decorative arts in this period were produced for a relatively short -- and lean -- period from the Depression to World War II, demand for them began to outstrip supply. So David polled his customers to see if they would consider purchasing accurate reproductions. The response was so positive he started looking for suppliers. Royal Chrome, a major manufacturer in the '30s and '40s of dinettes, had gone out of business, and most of the other original manufacturers had moved on to other products. David decided to set up his own shop to produce pieces of exactly the same design and construction as the originals.

all springs are of the no-sag type. Believe it or not, Naugahyde was the original upholstery material -- and as luck would have it, Uniroyal, the manufacturer, still makes the same red that they've offered for forty years. A pink Naugahyde really sets off several pieces in the line; it's the exact same color and material Uniroyal created for furniture of the period. (The factory now makes the pink exclusively for use in David's furniture.)

WE WERE ASTONISHED and excited by the variety of pieces that David's company has painstakingly brought back. There are chairs, ottomans, couches and convertible chairs, a day bed, dining table, coffee table and even a 1934 magazine rack. Robust geometric designs rendered in iron, steel, and glass appear in a firescreen, indoor-outdoor table and chairs, and several coffee tables. There are also many high-style lounge sets; one particularly attractive collection, c. 1935, consists of a matching chair, ottoman, loveseat and sofa.

Below: The sleek designs of this 1938 trio, consisting of a club chair, ottoman, and sofa, are set off with original pink-and-black, two-tone upholstery, chrome arms and trim.
Lower Right: These tubular chrome chairs from 1939 sport the bold styling of richly rounded shapes and a strong horizontal emphasis.

One of our favorites in the collection is this classic 1935 "Streamline Moderne" club chair with two-tone red and black upholstery, grey piping, and tubular chrome arms.

TO FULLY APPRECIATE the wonderful, sculptural shapes and color combinations, you must see the full color catalog ($3). There are 37 pieces in the collection, with more being added regularly. Most of the furniture can be ordered with your choice of Naugahyde, 100% wool fabric, leather, or (on some pieces) even calfskin. Yardage required for each piece is listed in the catalog, so you can cover frames with your own material if you prefer. Standard cushion construction is high-quality foam wrapped in Kodel, but innerspring or down cushions are available on special order.

WITH GOOD ORIGINAL pieces now found in museums or at high prices in galleries, we were glad to note that David's reproductions are priced competitively with other new furniture of similar quality. As with most high-style reproductions, these pieces should appreciate in value. Write or call Jazz Art Deco Revival Interiors, 8113 Melrose Ave., Dept. OHJ, Los Angeles, CA 90046. (213) 655-1104.

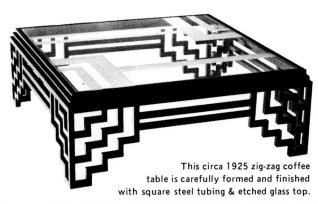

This circa 1925 zig-zag coffee table is carefully formed and finished with square steel tubing & etched glass top.

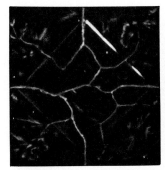

COLLECTING VICTORIAN EMBOSSED CERAMIC TILE

by Susan Warren Lanman

H, THE JOYS of Victorian excess! Decorative plaster mouldings, intricate parquet flooring, hand-painted wallpapers, beautifully crafted woodwork.... Those of us who appreciate high-Victorian decor will go to great lengths to repair or replace these distinctive elements. Now, add another one to your list: Victorian ceramic tiles.

CERAMIC TILE was an important decorative element in this country from 1876 right up until the First World War. At the height of their production, there was a virtually infinite variety of styles and patterns to choose from. Repeating geometric or floral tile motifs graced even modest fireplaces of the period. Truly ostentatious mantels and hearths combined several patterns, often incorporating polychromed tiles. Alas, tastes change, and these ornate ceramics gradually faded into oblivion.

TODAY, however, there is renewed interest in this "lost" art form. Large quantities of salvaged Victorian ceramic tiles can be found at antique shops and the showrooms of dealers specializing in architectural elements. With a lot of footwork and a little knowledge, you can recreate or restore a fireplace, or collect tiles for use in the kitchen or bathroom.

A LITTLE BIT OF HISTORY

THE PHILADELPHIA Centennial Exposition of 1876 stimulated American interest in ceramic tiles. Earlier in the nineteenth century, the English had developed the clay dust process for mechanically producing stamped designs of uniform size on tile. They'd been marketing these embossed tiles as well as smooth transfer-printed tile in America for some time. The English displays in Philadelphia were designed to bolster an already lucrative market.

WHILE THE BRITISH displays in Philadelphia did increase demand for tiles, it also spawned a domestic tile industry. The British soon lost most of the American market. Between 1875 and 1879, five art tile manufacturers began production: American Encaustic Tile Co., Zanesville, Ohio; J. & J.G. Low Co., Chelsea, Mass.; Star Encaustic Co., Pittsburgh, Pa., Wheatly Pottery Co., Cincinnati, Ohio; and the United States Encaustic Tile Works, Indianapolis, Ind.

MANY OF THE EARLY companies employed foreign-trained craftsmen and ceramic technicians. England and Germany provided many skilled craftsmen whose talents enabled the early American companies to produce tiles that equaled those manufactured overseas. Eventually, American-trained artists replaced the foreigners, and some, like John G. Low, developed uniquely American decorative ideas and manufacturing processes.

HOW THEY WERE MADE

VICTORIAN MAJOLICA or impressed tiles were produced by forcing clay in its plastic state into frames shaping the tile. A relief pattern or die providing the design was placed on the bottom of the frame. The tile was then pressed in the frame, removed, cleaned, dried, and fired. The fired tile, called a bisque, was then dipped in a colored glaze which accentuated the relief design by lending a deeper hue to depressed areas and lighter shades to raised ones.

BUFF, SALMON, GREY, red, chocolate, and black, known as the "plain colors," were the cheapest to produce. (So it's not surprising that those are the colors most often found by today's collectors.) White was twice as expensive, and blue three times as expensive as the plain colors. Sometimes a tile was treated with several glazes to produce a polychrome effect. Tube line tiles, those produced with small raised seams of clay separating and defining the pictorial area, were colored with separate glazes inserted in each design area.

THE MOST COMMON tiles were six by six inches, designed to be used as a set. They were found most frequently in fireplace mantels and furniture. Sometimes a modeler chose to create six by twelve inch or six by eighteen inch tiles for inclusion as fireplace inserts. Occasionally, extremely large tiles were produced (The Trent Tile Company produced a twelve by twenty-four inch tile in 1893).

SIX-INCH TILES were primarily used in fireplace surrounds. The most common design is each tile bearing a self-contained pattern. Subjects were usually geometric or floral. Tiles used in fireplace mantels were often linked by two special corner tiles functioning to turn the pattern. Seventeen tiles

Trent Tile Company

Trent Tile Co.

These two vertical runs demonstrate the variety of styles.

made a complete set for a fireplace: five for each side, five across the top, and two corner tiles. The most elaborate designs pictured a single theme in each set of five tiles; subjects might include bouquets, pastoral scenes, or classical figures. Another popular scheme was to use facing male and female profiles for the corners, with the other tiles complementing the profile tiles.

Corner tiles unite the pattern.

WHAT TO LOOK FOR

MANY OF THE BEST tiles reflect the special artistic style of their modelers. For example, Ferdinand Mersman and Clem Barnhorn of the Cambridge Art Tile Works were known for their superb figure designs and panels. Arthur Osborne of J. & J.G. Low was famous for his oversized tiles done with the wet clay process. These tiles were produced by packing wetter-than-normal clay into plaster moulds. When the plaster drew out enough moisture, the tiles were removed from the moulds and the detail was reworked. This process allowed for larger and more intricately executed designs.

PROVIDENTIAL Tile Works employed Isaac Broome as chief modeler until 1893, and he was succeeded by Scott Callowhill. Their most popular designs included hunting scenes of stags, sportsmen, and dogs worked on six by twelve or six by eighteen inch panels. Adaptations of famous paintings by Callowhill in the same size format were also popular.

THE TRENT TILE Company hired William Wood Gallimore (who had trained in France, England, and Ireland) in 1886. Gallimore is famous for his delightful designs featuring boys and cupids. These figures romp across a variety of ingenious and fanciful tiles.

RUTH M. WINTERBOTHAM was chief modeler for the United States Encaustic Tile Works in Indianapolis, and became extremely well known for her allegorical figures. One of her most popular designs was a three-section mantel surround depicting Dawn, Midday, and Twilight.

TILE MODELERS WERE sensitive to changing tastes in design, and these changes are reflected in their work. The owner of an 1850s Italianate would do well to choose tiles with cabbage roses and cupids. Owners of a turn-of-the-century Classical Revival should seek tiles that depict classical figures. If you're uncertain about style, pick the simple floral and geometric designs that appear throughout the period -- they're safe choices.

MANY PERIOD TILES exhibit hair-line cracks called crazing. Crazing occurred shortly after the tiles were set, possibly as a result of contact with moisture from the portland cement they were set in. Crazing is perfectly authentic and will not affect the value of the tiles, but care should be taken to avoid further crazing. Don't scrub your tiles under running water; use mild soap and a damp cloth.

TILES -- especially complete sets and runs -- are becoming increasingly expensive. If you buy a complete run, make sure the tiles are of the same set. The manufacturer's name is often stamped on the back, although it may not appear on each tile in the set. Generally, a set of tiles with a single pictorial theme is more valuable than single-matched tiles with corner turns. Oversized tiles, six by twelve or six by eighteen inches, are rare and more expensive than standard tiles. Profiles, heads, and historic figures will also cost more. The box listing major tile companies of the past will help you choose and date tiles.

THOSE INTERESTED in additional information should consult <u>Victorian Ceramic Tiles</u>, by Julian Barnard, published by Mayflower Books. The book contains valuable and detailed information on both English and American manufacturers and their tiles. It has recently been re-issued as part of Christie's International Collectors Series, and lists for $14.95.

Notable Companies of the Period

American Encaustic Tiling Co., Zanesville, Ohio. 1875-1936. By the '30s, had become the largest tiling company in the world. Herman Mueller became chief modeler in 1886; tiles bearing his mark were produced until 1893. Production of souvenir plaques — eagerly sought by collectors today — began in 1892.

Beaver Falls Art Tile Co., Beaver Falls, Pa. Est. 1887 by F.W. Walker. Initially specialized in tile for solid wall decoration, but by 1893 they were also producing portrait tiles and panel runs.

J. & J.G. Low, Chelsea, Mass. 1877-1893. John G. Low studied art in France, then returned to form a partnership with his father John. Developed a number of new manufacturing processes and design ideas. The name was changed to J.G. & J.F. Low in 1883 when the elder John retired, and John G.'s son joined the firm.

Mosaic Tile Co., Zanesville, Ohio. 1894-1967. One of the largest tile companies; employed over 1,200 people in the 1930s. Founded by Herman Mueller and Karl Langerback, the firm produced a complete line of architectural tiles. Also produced a number of commemorative tiles and plaques.

Old Bridge Enamelled Brick & Tile Co., Old Bridge, N.J. 1890-1927. Founded by William C. Rivers. Produced some of the finest enamelled colors and vitreous glazes of the period.

Robertson Art Tile Co., Morrisville, Pa. Est. 1890. Founded by George Robertson to produce plain enamelled wall tile. Hugh Robertson began modeling embossed tiles.

United States Encaustic Tile Works, Indianapolis, Ind. 1877-1932. One of the larger firms, they produced a full range of interior architectural tiles.

MY CASE HISTORY

Above: The author's study fireplace, complete with the full set of tiles she was fortunate enough to find at a local dealer.

Left: Detail of one of the vertical runs.

WHEN WE PURCHASED our 1888 Queen Anne it was in need of complete restoration. The existing fireplaces needed rebuilding and major tile replacement. I was disappointed that so little of the original tile remained, because I am an avid collector. Over the years, I'd acquired a full set of Trent six by six inch face tiles in a rich blue; the color and design were perfect for the parlor. We still needed face tile for the remaining fireplaces and enough small tile for two hearth pads, though. I was going to have to find complete sets.

I CAREFULLY SEARCHED all the antique shops and salvage yards in town. (Dealers often keep tile in hidden corners or the basement, so ask at each shop if you don't see any sitting out.) Persistence and an educated eye pay off: I found a complete set of A.E.T. face tiles depicting two bowls of day lilies merging into scattered blossoms. When I discovered them they were caked with paint and portland cement, and I assumed that they were two odd lots of tile. As I carefully scratched off a bit of paint on several tiles and examined the glaze, it began to dawn on me how the pattern

The tiles incorporated into this vanity splashback were leftovers from the bedroom fireplace (pictured at left).

The parlor fireplace — with its "compromise" pad.

fitted together. Figuring out tile runs is a little like working a jigsaw puzzle. The dealer parted with them for three dollars per tile, and I went home to begin cleaning them. I used a very mild paint remover, and then soaked the portland cement in water, (without submerging the tile itself), until the cement was soft enough to scrape free.

MY NEXT FIND was more commonplace. I happened upon a shop that had a large batch of six by six inch repeat tiles (probably removed from a large fireplace with a double row of tile). It was enough for the bedroom fireplace and the splashback of the vanity in the master bathroom. The double use of the same pattern added a nice note of continuity to the two rooms.

THE HEARTH PAD in the study was intact, but we were still faced with replacing two pads in other rooms. Each pad required approximately eighteen square feet of tile -- a formidable challenge. Historically, hearth tile rarely matched face tile, but it was compatible in color. Hearth tile was usually smaller, of assorted shapes, and laid to form separate patterns. Antique dealers generally do not bother with such smaller pieces -- salvage and wrecking yards are generally the best source for it. I was able to put together one pad of assorted tile from just such sources.

THE PARLOR PAD was a different story. We had waited a year to get a good mason sensitive to historic structures. He was due to arrive in just three weeks and I still hadn't any suitable tile. I purchased some good quality, modern glazed tile in blue and brown, and laid it in a historical checkerboard pattern. The new tile has the correct face proportions, but is half the thickness of original tile. Of course, with the tile set, its depth is not discernible. When all the tiles were finally in place, and the mantels reinstalled, the rooms assumed a new richness. 🏠

Ask OHJ

How To Nail Wood Siding

Q: WHAT'S THE BEST WAY to nail wood siding? Recently, I had to reside a section of my house with 6" wood siding. I had previously applied siding by nailing through the bottom of the clapboard so that the nail will also grab the board below. This is the way all the carpenters I've known did it. But the yardman where I got the lumber told me not to do it that way. He said I should nail higher up on the board so the nail doesn't penetrate the underlying clapboard. I looked it up in a government publication, and they agreed with the yardman. So that's how I did it, but I felt like I was wrong the whole time. What does OHJ recommend?

-- Patrick Kee, Ida Grove, Iowa

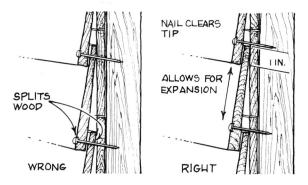

NAIL CLEARS TIP

ALLOWS FOR EXPANSION

SPLITS WOOD

WRONG   RIGHT

A: THE YARDMAN WAS CORRECT. If you nail through the top of the underlying clapboard, you're likely to split the wood. One row of nails along the center of each clapboard is sufficient to hold it in place, and is less likely to split the wood.

In The Grip Of Goop

Q: THE ROUND PORTICO ROOF of our Queen Anne house has built-in gutters. They were originally lined with metal, but over the years someone applied a very thick (and uneven) coating of black roofing compound to the inside of the gutters. Now water spills over the front edge of the gutters, causing the paint on the house to peel.

Roofers in our area want no part of repairing the gutters, and they seem perplexed about how to install new gutters in an arc to fit our round roof. Can we repair the old gutters? If not, how can we find someone to install a new lining?

-- Anne Wilson, Louisville, Ky.

A: YOU ARE PLAGUED by an extreme case of The Dreaded Black Goop Non-Solution. At one time, your gutter probably had a leaky joint that somebody patched with roofing compound. One thing led to another, and what once was a gutter became a shallow tar pit. Leaks in metal gutters should be repaired with soldered sheet metal patches.

It's too late for soldered patches now, though. Metal has to be very clean before it can be soldered, and you'll never get all that roofing compound out of your gutters. The best solution is to re-line the gutters with copper, terne-coated stainless steel, or galvanized steel with soldered (NOT caulked) joints -- a job for a sheet-metal worker.

Many roofing companies don't do sheet-metal work these days, so your best bet is to deal with a sheet-metal contractor -- one who is experienced in architectural sheet-metal work.

Red-Cedar Requirements

Q: I HOPE YOU CAN ANSWER a couple of questions regarding some roofing work we're having done on our house:
1) The roof is red cedar, and the gutters are copper. What type of circles, brackets, and clips should be used to support the gutters, and why?
2) What type of preservative should be applied to the roof, and how should it be applied?

-- Carol Schramek, Erdenheim, Pa.

A: FIRST OF ALL, copper is not the best material for a gutter if you have a red cedar roof: Red cedar is rich in tannic acid. Over the years, normal precipitation and weathering will cause some of this weak acid to leach out of the shingles, accelerating corrosion of the gutters. If you do use copper gutters, all the hardware that contacts them should also be copper to avoid galvanic corrosion.

Cedar is naturally rot-resistant, so you needn't feel compelled to use a preservative. Many readers have reported favorable results with CWF -- a clear water-resistant preservative manufactured by the Flood Company. CWF can be sprayed on and it contains no penta, so it's not as dangerous as other WRPs. Your shingles will still grey and weather, but this product will slow the process and your roof will retain its color longer.

Calcimine-Paint Source

Q: SEVERAL AREAS in our ca. 1870 farmhouse were painted with calcimine paint. As nothing will stick to calcimine but calcimine, I would rather repaint with the original material if possible. Is anyone currently manufacturing calcimine paint? If so, where can I find it?

-- Gregory Furness, Crown Point, N.Y.

A: THE JOHNSON PAINT COMPANY of Boston has agreed to ship hard-to-find calcimine to OHJ subscribers upon receipt of a written order and payment (no CODs). Call for current prices and shipping costs before ordering -- (617) 536-4838.

Calcimine won't stick to a previous layer of calcimine, just as latex paint won't. Regardless of what paint you decide to use, the existing layer of calcimine will have to be washed off. This may seem to be a nuisance, but at least you won't have to worry about paint buildup obscuring architectural detail. Just scrub the old calcimine off with sponges and hot water -- the hotter the better. A few tablespoonfuls of TSP mixed with the water will speed up the process.

Chinking, Daubing, & You

Q: WHAT IS A GOOD MIX for plastering over the chinking (external) between the logs of a log house? Proper appearance is of course important, but durability and adherence are of greater concern. On old cabins, the chinking looks light tan, which probably means a lot of sand (plus aging). Modern mixes look too grey, suggesting too much cement. That old buff color blends so nicely with the logs.
— Don H. Berkebile, Mercersburg, Pa.

A: WE SENT Mr. Berkebile's letter to Douglass Reed, a preservation consultant with a special interest in log structures (Preservation Associates, Inc., 207 S. Potomac St., Hagerstown, MD 21740). Here's his reply:

Mr. Berkebile's reference to "plastering over the chinking" deserves a bit of background clarification first. The plastering is actually termed daubing, and historically had about as many mixes and ingredients as the inventive minds of the builders could conceive. Daubing is the mix that was applied over some form, or matrix, to close the interstices between horizontally-laid wall logs of a log-frame structure. The matrix is commonly called chinking and, as with the daubing, was made from a wide variety of materials; wood and stone were the most common. (I've seen bones, bricks, and bedposts used as chinking.)

Illustration by Madelaine Thatcher from *The American House*, Harper & Row

In renovation today, everyone tends to worry more about how the daubing will look rather than its mechanical properties. Elasticity is most important. Even more so than appropriate mortar for old brick, the appropriate mortar (daubing) between the logs must be soft enough so that when the logs inevitably expand and contract with the changes in temperature and moisture, the sides of the logs will not be worn and rubbed into oblivion. A hard daubing mix will cause the logs to chafe, and collect and hold moisture, which will accelerate deterioration. To make matters worse, most of this destructive action takes place out of sight. The damage often doesn't show until the logs are in advanced states of decay.

I'm greatly concerned with getting as soft a mix for the daubing as possible. If the log frame is to be exposed to the weather, the mix has to be stronger than one used on a structure that will be sided and protected from the elements.

Basically, we tend to work along the same lines as restoration masons. The brick-mortar mix recommended for soft historic brick isn't much different from the basic starting-mix for daubing:

> 1/2 to 1-1/2 parts mason's hydrated lime
> 1 part white portland cement
> 4 to 6 parts tan-colored sand

The rule of thumb is never to use more than 20% by volume portland to the rest of the ingredients. (The ratios between the portland, lime, and sand should vary according to such things as the color and sharpness of the sand, whether the daubing will be exposed or covered, the dryness of the logs, the humidity, and wind and sunlight exposure on the newly applied daubing.)

It's always recommended that sample mixtures of at least 3 or 4 variations of the ingredients be prepared. Each sample should be spread 1/2 inch thick in the bottom of an 8-in. throw-away pie pan. Allow the samples to dry for 3 days. When they've cured, check for drying cracks: Too much lime in combination with different sands and brands of portland cement can result in surface drying cracks. Drying cracks are commonly found in daubing; they're unsightly but tend not to be deep or problematic. They can be avoided by playing around with the amount of lime in the daubing mix, and by keeping the mix moist and out of direct sunlight while it's setting up.

You'll also want to test the samples for strength. A 1/2-in.-thick sample firmly held in both hands should not crumble into pieces, but it should break in half without a great deal of strain. If the sample won't break in half, the mix is far too rich in cement. If the mix crumbles, it's too sandy.

Another reason for the daubing samples is to check the color. Color is determined by the sand, because the other two ingredients are white — and should not be altered by additive dyes. You can get the best-looking sand by going to a large river shoreline and gathering the sand in buckets. Pick an area where the currents are swift, or go to a river after a period of flooding: The sandy deposits are more likely to be free of silt. Select a sandy deposit that is as clean as possible.

Riverbed sand deposits are the best for their aggregate makeup and elasticity. However, if several tons of sand are needed, it can be very costly and time-consuming to gather sand in this manner. We have on occasion mixed riverbed sand with store-bought, washed bank sand; the results were quite acceptable.

If you have no source for riverbed sand, regular sand will do fine. Don't look at one sandyard pile and assume that's all that's available in the area. Different commercial building supply outfits may purchase sand from different quarries, so go look at different piles before choosing.

Let me add a few cautions. Daubing should be applied so that it is tucked under the log — about 1/2 inch set back from the face. It should angle to the forward edge of the log below, flush with the face of the log. The finish of the daubing should be smooth and level. This slight angle and smooth finish increase water repellency, which is very important to the longevity of log walls. It is also the most appropriate finish historically.

General interest questions from subscribers will be answered in print. The Editors can't promise to reply to all questions personally—but we try. Send your questions with sketches or photos to Questions Editor, The Old-House Journal, 69A Seventh Avenue, Brooklyn, NY 11217.

Restoration Products

reviewed by Larry Jones

WOOD FINISHING PRODUCTS & SUPPLIERS

Refer to "The Hand Rubbed Finish," page 70.

Behlen's Finishes

Behlen's has long been known as the most complete line of high-quality wood-finishing supplies. The products are sold under the Behlen's name through professional woodworking catalogs and suppliers, and under the Mohawk label to consumers. Especially handy for rubbed finishes are their 4-Hour Rubbing Varnish, which can be rubbed to any sheen desired; Rockhard Table Top Varnish, which resists abrasion and chemicals; Water White Restoration Varnish; Deluxing Compound, a one-step polish and wax. Also: paste wood filler; Wood-Lube rubbing compound; ultra-fine buffing paste for final top-coat rubbing; rubbing compound, in colors and tintable; Rub Cut Oil, with fine chemical abrasives and rubbing oils for use with sandpaper or pumice; Flat Lube for water and steel-wool rubbing; Fitch and Badger brushes; cork and felt rubbing blocks; paint removers; lacquers; shellacs; tack cloths; woodworking and upholstery tools. For a catalog write Mohawk Finishing Products, Dept. OHJ, Rt. 30 North, Amsterdam, NY 12010. (518) 843-1380.

The Woodworkers Store

The Woodworkers Store has a $2 catalog loaded with wood products, specialty cabinet hardware, finishing supplies, and tool books. For wood finishing, they sell cork sanding blocks; Norton rubber sanding blocks; a fine Porter Cable Speed-Bloc Finishing Sander; Disolv Wood Refinisher for varnish, shellac, and lacquer; tintable Wood-Kote Paste Wood Filler; felt rubbing blocks; McCloskey varnishes; Watco Danish Oil Stains; stains from Minwax, Tungseal, Beverlee's, Tru-Tone Aniline Colors, and Wood-kote; Behlen's shellacs. The Woodworkers Store, 21801 Industrial Blvd., Dept. OHJ, Rogers, MN 55374. (612) 428-4101.

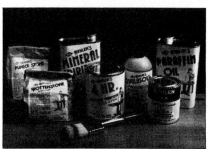

Garrett Wade Co.

The Garrett Wade Co. Catalog is a legend in woodworking circles: It's more like an information-packed cabinetmaker's book than a catalog of supplies. (And the introduction to their finishes section offers plenty of good tips.) They carry all of the Behlen finishing products; tack cloth; long-lasting English steel wool; brushing lacquers; Behlen's Rockhard Violin Varnish; 4-Hour Rubbing natural-resin oil varnish; paraffin rubbing oil; rubbing blocks; steel and bronze wool pads; pumice and rottenstone; French Polishing Cloth; Rapid Lak Beeswax Polish, and bulk waxes so you can make your own; Hamilton brushes; Behlen Badger Hair Brushes for flowing on finishes; and an excellent book selection. Catalog is $3 from Garrett Wade Co., 161 Avenue of The Americas, Dept. OHJ, New York, NY 10013. (800) 221-2942.

Daly's Wood Finishing

Daly's manufactures a line of high-quality wood-finishing products, including Benite Clear wood sealer for varnishes; Penlac sealer for use with lacquers; Paste Wood Filler; BenMatte Clear Danish Tung Oil Finish; BenMatte Stain; Sea-Fin Teak Oil, excellent for maintaining varnished surfaces such as floors and exterior doors; varnish; QuickFin, a pre-coat for varnish; stain removers; brass wire brushes. Wood Finishing Class Notes booklet is $2 ppd.; the catalog is free. Daly's Wood Finishing Products, 3525 Stone Way North, Dept. OHJ, Seattle, WA 98103. (206) 633-4276.

Wolf Paints

If every town had a Wolf's Paints and Wallpapers store, restoring old houses would be a whole lot simpler. Wolf's has been the source in New York for hard-to-find finishes and supplies since 1869. It's one of those wonderful places that has everything and knows everything; you can get their catalog for $2. Steve Wolf carries abrasives of all types; sanding blocks; pumice and rottenstone; rubbing compound; Behlen's wood finishes; super-quality paint, varnish, and specialty brushes made in England by Hamilton; brushkeepers for handy storage and cleaning of brushes; Mira-Spin paintbrush cleaners; DeVilbiss spray equipment; paraffin and neutra rubbing oils; Benjamin Moore One-Hour Varnish and Impervo Floor and Trim Varnish; McCloskey Varnishes; shellacs; lacquers; tack rags; for cold weather, painter's mittens; steel wool; heavy duty paint respirators for paint, lacquer, and enamel organic vapors and mists. Wolf Paints and Wallpapers, 771 Ninth Ave., Dept. OHJ, New York, NY 10019. (212) 245-7777.

Coastal Trade

Epifanes produces a variety of professional paint brushes and high-quality marine finishes. Epifanes Rubbed Effect Varnish gives a satin finish and can be rubbed out. Also sold: Epifanes Gloss Varnish for exterior protection; Epifanes Teak & Tropical Wood Finish; Stunt Oil (which increases working time of paints and varnishes). They also sell Italian round, oval, and elliptical black Chinese Boarbristle paint brushes of unusual quality. For more information contact Coastal Trade, Inc., 601 S. Andrews Avenue, Dept. OHJ, Fort Lauderdale, FL 33301. (305) 467-8325.

Flood Products

An excellent, two-part, clear finish is Deks Olje #1 and #2, manufactured by the Flood Co. A marine finish originally designed to withstand the harsh weathering and abrasion which wooden boats encounter, Deks Olje is a long-lasting finish for varnished surfaces on old houses, such as floors on interiors and porches. First you let the unfinished wood soak up all the Deks Olje #1 it can take, and wipe off the excess. If you just want a non-slip, matte-finish, oiled look that resists water and stains, you can stop here; but for a smoother finish with a deeper look and additional protection, apply Deks Olje #2. Two to four coats, sanded in between, will produce a tough, long-lasting finish. After it dries, you can lightly rub out the glossy top coat to get the sheen you want. The finished surface can be washed with soap and water; it won't turn dark with age, and can easily be touched up in the future. For a satin finish on the top coats without rubbing, try applying 2 to 3 coats of Deks Olje #1 and #2 mixed equally.

For hand-rubbed and other finishes, interior and exterior, another Flood product we've found very useful is Penetrol. This conditioner can be mixed with oil-based paints or varnishes to make materials spread easier, with greater, more uniform flow and coverage. Particularly useful with varnishes, Penetrol will make your brushmarks disappear (especially where you have overlaps). Used alone, it dries to a stainable matte finish with no buildup, and can be mixed 50/50 with varnishes such as McCloskey's; it also produces a good finish when mixed with 10 to 15% with a stain. For free information on these and other Flood products useful for old houses, write The Flood Co., 1213 Barlow Rd., Dept. OHJ, Hudson, OH 44236. (800) 321-3444.

Restoration Products

McCloskey Varnishes

For 130 years, McCloskey has produced a full line of quality varnishes, stains, wood preservatives, and polyurethanes. They have varnishes for every need, including Bar-Top Varnish which resists alcohol and detergents; Hour Varnish, excellent for rubbing; Man-O-War Spar Varnish, a flexible finish for outdoor use; Heirloom Varnish for fine woodwork and furniture; Quick Dry Varnish for sealing and undercoating; Stain Controller & Wood Sealer base coat for even staining; Tung Oil Finish for a penetrating finish; Gymseal Floor Finish, a tung-oil product with greater durability than polyurethane; Dura-Fame Polyurethane Varnish. Products are available nationwide; the catalog is free. McCloskey Varnish Co., 7600 State Road, Dept. OHJ, Philadelphia, PA 19136. (215) 624-4400.

Constantine's

Constantine's has produced lumber and sold woodworking supplies since 1812. All the products listed are available in their current catalog ($1). For paint and varnish removal, there's a brush with fine brass bristles; McCloskey's varnishes; polishing compound; tack rags; Antiquax, a high-quality English furniture wax; Butcher's Boston Polish Wax; rubber sanding blocks; felt rubbing pads; White Non-Blooming Rubbing Oil, which doesn't leave a white film; Hope's refinishing products; rottenstone and pumice powder; extra-fine, 1200-grit finishing paper; Constant Lacquer; Alcoholproof Rubbing Varnish, a tough, polyurethane-based finish; Behlen's shellac; Watco Danish Oil; woodworking tools and hardware. Constantine, 2050 Eastchester Rd., Dept. OHJ, Bronx, NY 10461. (800) 223-8087.

Woodcraft Supply

Since 1928, Woodcraft Supply has been around with quality woodworking tools, finishing materials, cabinet hardware, and books. They sell Goddard's Cabinetmaker's Wax; Renaissance Wax for antiques; Patina Rub Set for revitalizing old varnish and other finishes; steel wool in economical contractor-size reels; Lochwood's Aniline Dyes; tack cloth; Traditional Dusting Brush, ideal for removing dust from finishing woodwork; shellac sticks and burn-in knives for filling; abrasive cords and strips; Watco Danish Oil products; pumice and rottenstone rubbing abrasives. For a free catalog, write Woodcraft, P.O. Box 4000, Dept. OHJ, Woburn, MA 01888. (800) 225-1153.

Wood Finishing Supply

Wood Finishing Supply offers a wide variety of finishing supplies through its mail order catalog ($2.50). They sell all of Behlen's finishing products. Also, they offer the Perdue 3002, a black Chinese Hog bristle brush that's designed for rubbing out carvings and mouldings, and for removing excess filler, pumice stone, and dust from carvings and mouldings on furniture and cabinets. They offer fine Lorient, Dunnet, and Leith brushes for flowing on shellacs, varnishes, and lacquers. Also available are beautifully built Stuhr single- and double-pad sanding and rubbing machines. These all-metal, air-powered, professional tools come with rubber pads for sanding and felt pads for use with rubbing mediums. The tools can be used with water or rubbing oils and are ideal for sanding and rubbing large flat areas. Wood Finishing Supply Co., Inc., Dept. OHJ, 1267 Mary Dr., Macedon, NY 14502. (315) 986-4517.

New Faux-Finish Papers

Manuscreens' "Architectural
Effects" is a new collection
of high-quality ceiling papers, architectural friezes,
and faux textures. They've
combined Neo-Classical details
with the natural finishes of
marble, stone, brick, moire,
sandblast (a natural finish?),
crackle effect, strie, and
silk. The first part of the
two-part collection are 65
small-scale, textured, natural
faux effects. The second part
has larger-scale faux effects
in the form of ornamental
mouldings, soffits, dados,
ceiling papers, and borders.

All the patterns are screen-
printed paper, backed with
vinyl. They're available in
custom colorways, and the textured natural effects are designed to coordinate with the
architectural details.

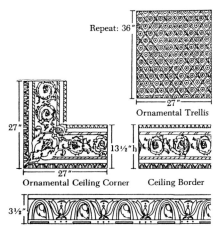

Repeat: 36"

27"

Ornamental Trellis

27"

13½"h

Ornamental Ceiling Corner

Ceiling Border

27"

3½"

Egg & Dart Border

These papers could be ideal
in situations where professionally painted faux finishes
are too expensive or just
unavailable. They're sold to
the trade only, so there's no
brochure; have your interior
designer or local wallpaper
dealer secure samples and
check on the prices for you.
Manuscreens, 20 Horizon Blvd.,
Dept. OHJ, S. Hackensack, NJ
07606.

New Styles of Anaglypta & Lincrusta

Crown Decorative Products
Ltd., the English firm that
reintroduced the embossed
wallcoverings Anaglypta, Supaglypta, and Lincrusta (first
produced in the 1870s and
'80s), have discovered more
old rollers in their basement.
The result, we're glad to say,
is four Lincrusta patterns and
one Supaglypta pattern, all
produced from turn-of-the-century embossing cylinders.
(Crown holds the copyright on
the words "Anaglypta" and
"Lincrusta.") You really have
to see samples of the new
patterns to fully appreciate
the extraordinary quality of
their rich relief and delicate
designs. Here at OHJ, after
we unwrapped some samples of
the new styles, we hung them
up on our display board;
nearly everyone who ventures
into our office stops to examine them. (One person even
tried to cut off a swatch!)
Two styles of 10-inch Lincrusta friezes (#s 1957 &
1958) cost $42.50 each; an in-
teresting low-relief Lincrusta
wall pattern (# 1589) and a
Lincrusta wall-and-ceiling
pattern (# 1956) sell for $85
per double roll. The Supaglypta (# RD 160) is a heavy
embossed paper suitable for
wall or ceiling, and sells for
$25 per double roll. Shipping
is extra. Paper hangers will
have no trouble mounting the
Crown products, if they follow
the instructions.
Order the color catalog
first ($2 ppd.) - it comes
with samples. If you think
you're interested in the products, get the pattern book
($15 ppd.) which contains
larger samples of all the
available styles. You can

also order the recommended ad-
hesive, Shur-Stik 111 (Shur-
Stik 66 for Lincrusta). Order
a catalog from the dealer
nearest you. LOUISVILLE, KY:
Bentley Brothers (800) 824-
4777. DENVER, CO: Mile Hi
Crown (303) 777-2099.
FULLERTON, CA: Classic
Ceilings, (714) 526-8062. NEW
YORK CITY: Norton Blumenthal,
Inc. (212) 752-2535.

Solarium Patio Door

The E.A. Nord Company has a
new pre-hung, ready to drop-
in, all-wood, hinged patio-
door system called Solarium.
Made from prime-quality Western hemlock, it's said to be
30% more energy efficient than
the aluminum sliders it's designed to replace. The door
system is sized to fit all
standard openings and is highly leak resistant. Features
include a choice of 1/2-in.
clear insulated glass; Solar
Bronze or Solar Grey glass;
grill assemblies; treated and
prefinished oak sill; wide-
applied brick moulding; sill,
header and brick mould gaskets; self-adjusting frame;
upper drip cap; and complete
kerf-installed foam compression weatherstripping around
doors and frame. Any size and
style lock can be used on the
door system. For a color brochure send $.25 to E.A. Nord
Co., P.O. Box 1187, Everett,
WA 98206. (206) 259-9292.

Restoration Products

NEW: Urns–Cornices–Finials–Balusters in W.F. Norman's Architectural Sheet Metal Line

NEW: 20 Woodworking Videotapes

Most OHJ readers know about the fine pressed-metal ceilings, roofing, storefronts, building cornices, marquees, and awnings which W.F. Norman has been producing from its turn-of-the-century dies since 1898. But with their two recent acquisitions, they should become the nation's leading supplier of period-style, architectural sheet-metal products. They purchased the Architectural Sheet Metal Products Division of Kenneth Lynch & Sons, Inc., and Triangle Metal Spinning of Long Island City, New York.

Kenneth Lynch & Sons is one of the country's most respected and well-known makers of architectural metal ornament. W.F. Norman acquired their vast line, formerly owned and developed by the equally well-respected firm of Miller & Doing (who had operated in Brooklyn since 1892, until Lynch took it over in 1973).

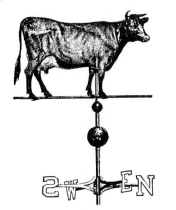

W.F. Norman has purchased the mill, machinery, and equipment in Sterling, Conn., and will offer the products under their own name. But Kenneth Lynch & Sons will stay in business, producing large street clocks, cast-lead and cast-stone planters, fountains, garden-

related items, and their outstanding wrought-iron work.

If your building is missing some or all of its pressed-metal ornament, W.F. Norman can probably supply whatever you need, from a missing urn to a complete decorative cornice. With the acquisition of the metal-spinning plant, they can even produce balls, finials, and turned balusters. Pressed-metal details often can be successfully substituted for missing pieces that originally were made from wood or compo -- and they're usually lighter and easier to keep painted. There's pressed-metal ceilings, keystones, capitals, gargoyles, pinnacles, brackets, festoons, weathervanes, panel ornaments, and hundreds of other decorative pieces. And they're manufactured just as they were in the last century, by the "rope-drop stamping" process. This old technique actually hammers out, rather than stamps, decorative sheet metal. W.F. Norman has taken great pains to preserve the old drop hammers and the skills needed to operate them. (The drop hammers from Kenneth Lynch & Sons will be moved to the W.F. Norman facilities in Missouri.)

The Kenneth Lynch & Sons catalog, a treasure of decorative pressed-metal work, is now relabelled W.F. Norman; it's available for $2.50, and all of the pressed-metal items listed are in production. Also available, for $3, is their ceiling catalog #350. W.F. Norman Corp., Dept. OHJ, P.O. Box 323, Nevada, MO 64772. (800) 641-4038.

Woodworker's Supply of New Mexico now sells 20 new VHS woodworking videotapes. They range in price from $39.95 to $69.95 (depending on length), but by putting up a deposit equal to the purchase price, you can rent any one for 30 days, for only $19.90; the difference is refunded when you return the undamaged tape, or you can purchase the tape and just keep it. The videos are like attending woodworking seminars -- it's a great way to learn skills and techniques from master woodworkers.

Since we've been discussing wood finishing in this issue, we decided to review the video "Wood Finishing With Frank Klausz." Produced by Fine Woodworking magazine, it runs 110 minutes and costs $59.90. There's so much info packed in that to get it down in notes, you'd have to watch it three times. So why not buy a book? Well, books have advantages too. But with a tape, you can observe the nuances of a craftsman at work. A third-generation professional cabinetmaker, trained in Hungary, Frank Klausz specializes in antique reproduction and restoration. In the video, he explains secrets he's learned over his 20-year career -- the subtle tips and techniques which make a big difference in the way tools perform and finishes come out.

Available videos cover: basic tools, dovetailing, finishing and polishing, radial-arm saw joinery, drill-press expertise, table-saw expertise, bowl turning, hinging, clamping and screwing, mortise-and-tenon joints and making and using planes. The Woodworker's Supply catalog lists them all, and it's free for the asking; just write Woodworker's Supply of New Mexico, Dept. OHJ, 5604 Alameda N.E., Albuquerque, NM 87113. (505) 821-0500.

opinion...
Remuddling

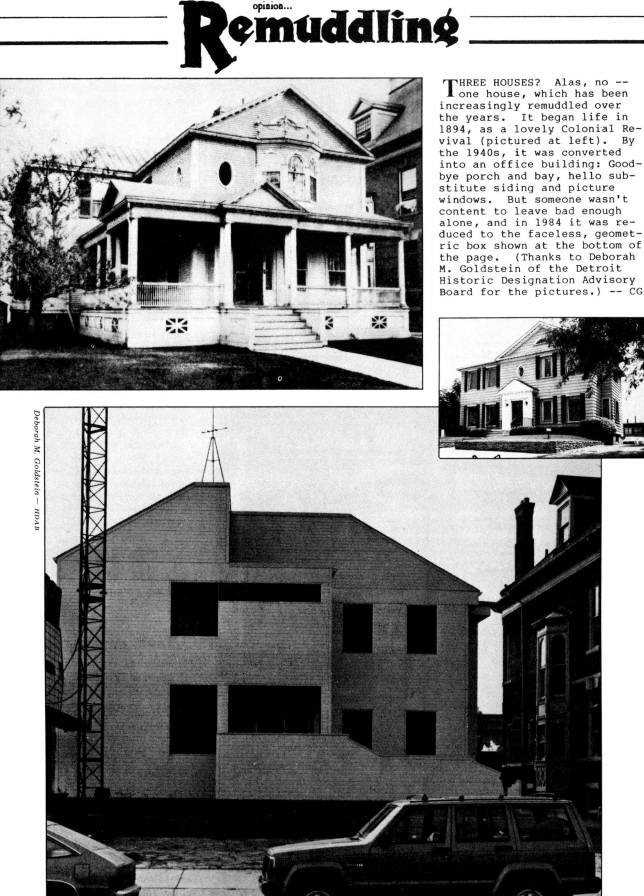

Boston Historical Collection, Detroit Public Library

Deborah M. Goldstein — HDAB

D.M.G.

THREE HOUSES? Alas, no -- one house, which has been increasingly remuddled over the years. It began life in 1894, as a lovely Colonial Revival (pictured at left). By the 1940s, it was converted into an office building: Goodbye porch and bay, hello substitute siding and picture windows. But someone wasn't content to leave bad enough alone, and in 1984 it was reduced to the faceless, geometric box shown at the bottom of the page. (Thanks to Deborah M. Goldstein of the Detroit Historic Designation Advisory Board for the pictures.) -- CG

Real Houses, Real Places
"VERNACULAR"

Dear OHJ,

I enjoy your new back-cover feature. The houses (so far) are wonderfully gritty -- no cute over-restoration here, just the Real McCoy! They've got history written all over them.

I wonder, though, what you mean by "vernacular." Is it their preserved, unrestored character that makes them vernacular? Or do you mean vernacular in the sense of "local"?

-- Larry Pendergast
Portland, Oregon

GOOD QUESTION! "Vernacular," when applied to buildings, has a lot of different (but related) meanings. Let's start with the dictionary definitions* of the word. Then I'll share some quotes on the vernacular as applied to architecture.

VERNACULAR -- from the Latin vernaculus: belonging to homeborn slaves; domestic, native, indigenous. From verna: a homeborn slave.

as an adjective:
1. using the native language of a country or place (as a writer).

California

2. commonly spoken by the people of a particular country or place; said of a language or dialect: often distinguished from literary.
3. of or in the native language.
4. native to a country -- "the vernacular arts of Brittany."
5. peculiar to a particular locality -- "a vernacular disease."

* from Webster's New Collegiate Dictionary, © 1977 by G. & C. Merriam Co., and Webster's New Twentieth Century Dictionary, unabridged second edition, © 1971 by The World Publishing Company.

as a noun:
1. the native speech, language, or dialect of a country or place.
2. the common, everyday language of ordinary people in a particular locality.
3. the shop talk or idiom of a profession or trade.
4. the mode or expression of a group or class.

ALL OF THESE definitions are important to developing a sense of the word as it applies to architecture. A few illustrative quotes follow.

Virginia

(on vernacular Victorian): "Vernacular architecture tends to reiterate local forms, adapting them to changing conditions over a long period of time. For economy, a compact plan is the rule. Hence, an agglutinative character results from the addition of service units and successive enlargements."
-- Carole Rifkind in A Field Guide to American Architecture (p. 66)

"The England of the early years of the 19th century was a country of the vernacular, local speech, local customs, local products all combining with one another to provide communities, each of which had individual style and methods .... The artisans and craftsmen over many years became skilled in the use of local material.... Buildings and building materials closely reflected this regionalism....
--Jack Bowyer in Vernacular Building Conservation (p. 4)

"Folk houses, sometimes called vernacular buildings, are

those built by an individual who lacked specific training, but who was 'guided by a series of conventions built up in his locality, paying little attention to what may be fashionable on an international scale' [R.W. Brunskill, Illustrated Handbook]. Tradition determines the size, shape, and methods and materials of construction.
-- Allen G. Noble in Wood, Brick, and Stone (p. 107)

"The products of folk architecture are not derived from the drafting tables of professional architects, but instead from the collective memory of a people. These buildings.... are based not on

Texas

blueprints but on mental images that change little from one generation to the next.... Folk buildings are extensions of the people and the region .... Do not look to folk architecture for refined artistic genius or revolutionary design. Seek in it instead the traditional, the conservative, the functional. Expect from it ... expression of traditional culture."
-- Terry G. Jordan in Texas Log Buildings (p. 3)

YOU MIGHT SAY that vernacular architectural types are like regional accents. English is spoken all over the country, but Alabama sure sounds different from Maine. Same with architectural dialects.

THE BACK COVER OF OHJ is sort of our consciousness-raising department -- first with Remuddling, now with Vernacular Houses. We've got three new goals: to acknowledge the vast number of houses that aren't the excellent "examples"; to draw attention to the rich variations in regional domestic architecture; to increase understanding of American architecture by showing pictures of real houses that don't "fit" into academic style categories.

Patricia Poore

Letters

As we anticipated, most of the letters we've been getting have been in reference to our change in format. The Letters department will continue to be a regular feature in OHJ. Your comments on previous articles are much appreciated.

Clean with Care

Dear Patricia:

In your December 1985 article, "Making Photos Last," you show before and after pictures of a daguerreotype. The upper caption refers to "layers of tarnish" on the picture which, in the lower photo, have been removed after "a careful cleaning." Parenthetically, the caption writer says, "Unfortunately, you can't clean away the scratches."

This item may suggest to the unknowing that a rare and valuable daguerreotype can be restored by an amateur. In most cases, an inexpert cleaning will at least introduce scratches and may well result in the total obliteration of the image. Any kind of friction will rub off the image. Owners of a daguerreotype should consult with their local museums or schools of photography as to the methods of cleaning. One such method is offered in Beaumont Newhall's authoritative The Daguerreotype in America. This book should be available in most public libraries and is available in a Dover reprint for $7.95. It's a wonderful book to read, even if you don't own a daguerreotype.

-- Everett Ortner
Brooklyn, N.Y.

[Dover's address: 31 E. Second Street, Mineola, N.Y. 11501]

Thanks for the Memories

Dear Mrs. Poore:

I enjoyed reading the article about you and Clem Labine in the most recent issue of Historic Preservation [February 1986]. I, too, had wondered if you were married (to each other), and I'm glad to have the mystery cleared up.

Needless to say, I was happy and proud to open my January-February issue of The Old-House Journal and find my article in print (A Century of Memories). Several of my family members and friends, who were familiar with the house and our restoration, expressed their approval at the way it was handled. I have heard from two people who have congratulated me on it. One was a minister from Illinois, and the other a former local resident now living in Nebraska. Both are subscribers to OHJ.

I just wanted to tell you how much I enjoyed sharing our restoration with you and how proud I was to have it appear in print. Once again, I can't tell you how much I appreciate your interest in our old house at Central. It's given my morale a big boost. I can't think of a better way to begin a new year unless it would be to write the book I have been promising to write about Central for many years.

Also, I LOVE the new format and I'm happy that my article appeared in the first issue to use it. It was an excellent move, I believe.

-- Charles Stetter
Laurium, Mich.

Toasting the New Format

Dear Friends,

The February 1986 issue has just arrived, and although I was initially 'put off' by the slick appearance, I am very happy to see the familiar pages inside. And I guess I will have to buy some binders -- it will take a while to get used to no holes. Whatever you do, please don't stray too far from your present format; I would hate to have to look at something that resembled "House and Garden" when what I really want is help repairing my peeling ceilings! Thanks for such a great magazine.

-- Mary-Louise Eggimann
Worcester, Mass.

Dear OHJ:

I really enjoyed the latest issue. My first reaction was, "Where's Remuddling?" I calmed down when I found it inside the back cover, though. The vernacular architecture section that took Remuddling's place on the back cover is great. It gives us a better, more educated view of the diversity of domestic American architecture. Patricia & Clem's editorial was warm and honest -- it reassured us that there would be no major changes inside the covers.

The color cover should increase circulation through newsstand sales -- that's important because it means your message of sensitive rehabilitation will get to more people. And the introduction of color advertising gives us at Bradbury and Bradbury the opportunity to display our new patterns to a wide audience (at a very reasonable cost).

Congratulations on a job well done. We wish you the very best.

-- Joni Monnich
(a former OHJ editor)
Bradbury & Bradbury Wallpapers
Benicia, Cal.

Dear OHJ:

Love your new look. Thanks for featuring us common house folks [referring to new Vernacular Houses section]. My house started out in 1880 as a Gothic Revival. Then there were large additions added in 1909 and 1920. Now it's sort of a Gothic Crafted Bungle -- but still lovable.

-- William Lugenbuhl
Bluffton, Ohio

Dear OHJ:

I don't know anyone who knows OHJ who doesn't like it a lot. It's always been a highly personal Journal, as much enjoyed for its personality as treasured for its content. I am an architect involved with restoration and traditional design. I know no other source for practical information as rich and comprehensive as OHJ, and of course, it's entertaining.

However the importance of a magazine may be measured, this one may rank in the megaunits. Its impact on our nation's domestic environment must be enormous.

Letters

In light of that, however, I must confess a little disappointment with the new image. Of course I miss the little holes, the no-nonsense paper stock, the quick-fit format, the frugal shirt-sleeved whimsey, in short, all those components of OHJ personality for which readers have an affectionate regard.

I see much of that special tonality is still there, and I will certainly continue to enjoy my subscription. Indeed, by now it's almost indispensable. But to these old eyes, it now looks a lot like many other magazines. I do resent, though perhaps not for long, having to leaf through so much familiar advertising to get to the heart of OHJ. Nonetheless, I wish it well. It has provided so much support to me for so long -- I will always be a fan.

-- Alvin Holm, AIA
Philadelphia, Pa.

Dear OHJ Friends:
Congratulations on your new format. The cover looks great, and the articles remain informative and interesting. Your success is a tribute to the talent and creativity of your founders and staff.

-- Preston Maynard
New Haven Preservation Trust
New Haven, Conn.

Dear Patricia,
I do like the advertising in the Journal. It is really helpful to readers. We really love the magazine and hope your new style will expand the readership even more. I see it as an important goal to upgrade the public knowledge of restoration -- so that more buildings will be saved (and done right!). Keep up the good work.

-- Beth Maxwell Boyle
Mayville, N.Y.

Dear Mrs. Poore/Mr. Labine:
The new Old-House Journal format is quite exciting! A perfect balance has been struck between the familiar and celebrated OHJ format and the introduction of color and advertisements.

As a merchant specializing in Victorian Revival products, I am especially excited by the opportunity to advertise my goods in OHJ. The OHJ readership has always been a responsive and strong market -- both from notices of new products included in editorial copy, and from the yearly OHJ Catalog. Now, at last, the inclusion of advertisements in the monthly Journal will allow us to bring notice of our products and services to OHJ readers on a regular basis.

Congratulations and best wishes for continued success.

-- John Burrows
J.R. Burrows & Co., Boston

Dear OHJ:
Keep up the good work! You're looking better than ever!

-- Larry A. Reed
State Historical Society of Wisconsin, Madison

Mr. Labine:
All I can say is great! Having been an OHJ subscriber for many years, I was stunned when I received the Jan./Feb. issue in the mailbox ten minutes ago. It is obvious that hard work and perseverence wins out in the end. My personal congratulation for an excellent issue.

-- Bruce Strachan
Bedford, Ohio

Dear OHJ:
When the latest issue came the other day and I saw the glossy cover, I thought, "Oh no! They've gone yuppie! All is lost."

However, even the quickest of glances at the inside would be enough to restore one's faith, and as you reassure us on page 2, not only is all not lost, but much is gained.

So congratulations on the new look, expanded pages, advertising, etc. Long may you prosper.

No, there are no more holes, but I'm just as glad. I always thought they were a pain anyway.

-- Ted Smith
Chatham, Mass.

Dear Ms. Poore & Mr. Labine:
I love the new format of The Old-House Journal! The color cover is beautiful. I enjoyed reading your editorial and the articles on post-Victorian and vernacular houses. Thanks for making OHJ even better!

-- Marcy Werner
Coral Gables, Fla.

Some Aren't Pleased

Dear OHJ:
Yeah, and you talk about remuddling!! I don't like it! I don't care for it! It means greater expense -- passed along to subscribers no doubt!

I own a 14-room Victorian, and I often refer to the old Old-House Journal. In looseleaf and notebook form, it was so easy to use!

What good is another magazine?! Should I pile them up, or throw them away to get rid of the magazine clutter?

No thank you! Change back, or I'm afraid this is a longtime subscriber lost. I'm sure that house-bugs like myself feel the same. Forget the new! Give us the old! That's what made you!

-- Lavern H. Pangborn
Sioux City, Iowa

Dear Mr. Labine,
All your reasons for the new format are obviously valid. Your publication was excellent, but it has totally lost its charm -- it looks like just another magazine on the outside. All magazines have four-color covers, now OHJ looks just like the rest.

I suspect my opinion has little company, but if the expense of color gets too much, I'd be pleased if you went back to the old paper and just used a heavier weight for the cover.

The printing business, I am aware, has so many problems. I hope the new format sells more OHJs, even if it isn't attractive to me.

-- Becky Anderson
Brattleboro, Vt.

Undecided

Dear Friends,
Don't know if I like the "new" Old-House Journal... I'll tell you later.

-- M. Higgins
New Plymouth, Ohio

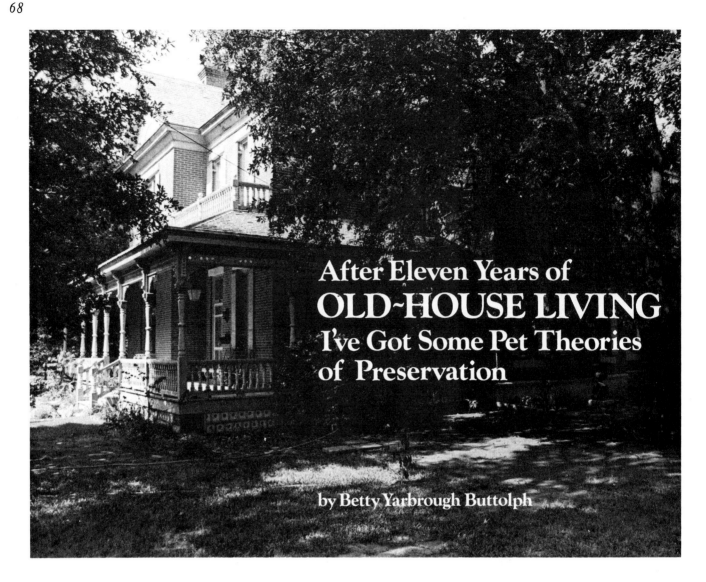

After Eleven Years of OLD-HOUSE LIVING I've Got Some Pet Theories of Preservation

by Betty Yarbrough Buttolph

1 MARRY SOMEONE who thinks he or she wants an old house. Personally, I'm blessed with a husband who's sensitive to my needs. He gives me wonderful presents, like a mini-chainsaw that's suitable for a 54-year-old woman who weighs 107 pounds. I also have my own blow-torch, trowel, electric hedge clippers, and more. And people always get a good laugh out of the monstrous yellow wheelbarrow that I gave him -- mainly because it has his monogram on it. (I have unlimited use of that, too.) A corollary here is: "Keep a sense of humor in your marriage when fixing up an old house, or else you'll kill each other."

2 "NOT THIS YEAR." That's his favorite answer to repair requests. Sometimes, being a little poor can actually be a good thing. There's so much to do on an old house and when there isn't much money to do it with, the house breathes a sigh of relief; when you rush into things, you make mistakes. Another corollary: "When in doubt, don't."

3 DO NOT DO ANYTHING to an old house that cannot be reversed. You've probably heard that before, but it bears repeating. You are only the caretaker of the house, not a permanent fixture, no matter how long you think

your family will live there.

4 EDUCATE YOURSELF and do it yourself. Chances are you know or can learn more about proper preservation techniques than any worker you hire. If done "professionally," the smallest change or repair will cost three times what you expect, and even then it may not look right. Often the "experts" don't know what they're doing until you tell them.

5 IT HELPS to stay away from home a lot; that way you don't worry or get depressed. We travel a lot, and we also entertain a lot. When we come home and are having guests that night, I just ignore the mess. I plant some chrysanthemums from the local Safeway around the house and hand people a drink when they walk in the door. If the house is interesting, nobody notices if it's not clean and neat.

6 TALK TO THE OLD FOLKS who wander by the house. Although you have to take their stories with a grain of salt, sometimes these people come up with an actual fact. They'll also reassure you that you're doing great things by restoring an old house. And you'll have made a new friend as well.

This is the earliest photo of the house, taken circa 1895. The two children in front are most likely Judge Davis's children, Owen and Sarah. The iron fence, alas, is gone.

7 PAY ATTENTION to detail -- it's what makes your old house special. And it can sometimes help you solve puzzles that would challenge Sherlock Holmes. Not that I'm slow, but it took me years to notice a different plinth block, a different glass doorknob; to see that the door in the servants' quarters really went in the dining room.

MY HUSBAND DICK and I like to say that our house -- the one that taught us all these lessons -- found _us_. In 1974, we were settled in California with our two children, content in the three-bedroom government quarters the Marines supplied for us. He had no plans to retire, and we weren't intending to leave the West Coast -- let alone return to my hometown of Gainesville, Texas (about 70 miles from Dallas).

BUT THEN my mother called one day to tell us "the Davis place" was for sale, and to ask, would we be interested? Would we! I'd last seen the Davis home the year before on New Year's Eve; we'd stopped briefly at a party there. Before that I hadn't been inside since 1950, when the mistress of the house -- the daughter of the first owner, Judge Davis -- lent me some antique dresses that had been part of her trousseau, so I could dress up for Gainesville's centennial. I dimly recalled a high-ceilinged parlor full of antiques and packing boxes.

MY HUSBAND SAID, "Go look at it. If you like it, we'll buy it." (That's how we do things in this family: on impulse.) By that night I was in Gainesville, and my husband followed the next afternoon. And in a few days' time everything was in motion for us to purchase the 1891 red-brick Queen Anne.

WE'D BEEN COLLECTING antiques for years, but with all the traveling and transferring we'd done, we'd never thought of owning an antique house. Fortunately I'd amassed a large enough collection of Oriental rugs that we could cover all the floors in our expansive new home. Assisted by the pieces that came with the house -- armoires, a William and Mary chair, a grandfather clock -- we managed to fill the place. Some things, like the original shutters and

This stained glass window stands between two contemporary paintings, above an antique sofa.

items from the Davis collection that had been sold off, turned up later. That's how things happen to me: If I want something I just wait, and it turns up. That includes things (like this house) that I didn't even know I wanted!

A FEW IRREVERSIBLE CRIMES had been committed on the building (see rule 3). The same family had owned it since its construction and had kept it basically unchanged, but they'd added an elevator, closed in the rear porches and, worst of all, installed aluminum windows. Also the bricks had been repointed improperly. What once looked like a solid brick wall now has too-wide mortar joints. See what I mean about the "experts" (rule 4)! Luckily they left the back and porch walls alone.

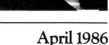

No trace remains today of the broken bits of stained glass that dot the gable in this circa 1915 photo. Note the vines growing up the porch trellises (which are bare in the older picture shown on page 114).

or even high school education). He went on to serve as Texas Senator for six years and argued cases before the Supreme Court; he also drafted the Gainesville city charter and was elected mayor at age 81.

DAVIS BUILT several of the fine red brick buildings that typify Gainesville's historic architecture. (Some of those older buildings have been torn down, by the way, and I don't know how the pigeons that lived in them knew which house to haunt, but somehow they all found their way here!) He built his own house at the corner of Denton, Dodson, and, of course, Davis Streets.

ONE (THANKFULLY REVERSIBLE) "improvement" was the peppermint-green paint job. A little detective work (see rule 7) told me what the original colors had been; traces of them were left on a porch door upstairs and on a pair of shutters I found in the attic. So, aided by a painter who worked by the hour, we undid the crime.

AS WE WORKED on the house, we also learned a great deal about its first owner, Judge W. O. Davis, a well-known lawyer and statesman. After serving in the Confederate Army, he arrived in the tiny town of Gainesville in 1870. When the town became the headquarters of the western Texas cattle industry, Davis built up a law practice (despite his lack of a college

THE OLDER FOLKS have told us many things about him (see rule 6), one story being that he was a cattleman. I don't like to tell half-truths, so I'll say only what I've been able to verify. (His granddaughter has been a very reliable source.) Like us, Davis was an avid gardener. That's why there's a bathroom in the brick outbuilding (which is not, as people mistakenly told us, the servants' quarters). We also know people that played with the Judge when they were children. He would wait in the garden for them; they remember sitting with him on the verandah.

WE'VE KEPT THE INTERIOR, structurally, as Judge Davis would have known it in 1891. The plaster, covered with canvas, has a few bumps and bubbles, but we didn't want to damage the ornate woodwork by installing Sheet-rock. And we like to say that the wrinkles in the plaster are like those on a beautiful woman: They show character.

OUR DECOR, however, might surprise him. It's what you'd call eclectic. The Davis's William and Mary chair looks great with my Chinese and Japanese lacquer collection; the kitchen is blue and white and decorated with pieces of Imari china. On the walls we hung our contemporary paintings. The house is not a Victorian showplace -- you can tell a modern family lives there -- but our collection is one you couldn't replace in any store. I like to say my pieces fit in so well because they were so fine to begin with.

Here's a close-up of the front (east) facade.

Looking through the open arch over the entrance hall, note the many old light fixtures.

eight years to get a Texas Historical Marker for the house, ten years to get it in the National Register, and about the same to open the pass-through from the pantry to the dining room and to disguise the dishwasher with discarded Victorian lumber I hauled home in Dick's monogrammed wheelbarrow. The house is still far from perfect. The aluminum windows remain, but nobody except me and the National Register knows they're there.

REMEMBER, WHERE ELSE but in an old house can your kids have their own fireplaces in their bedrooms? Where else can you have bathrooms bigger than your kids' college dorm rooms, room for a real slumber party or a wedding reception on the verandah? I've even got the oldest stove in Cooke County. Good thing, too: If I had a new one Dick might expect me to cook!

The author would like to thank Libby Barker for her help editing this manuscript.

THE "VIBES" of the place are good. The lights flicker when I put up the 11-foot Christmas tree and during house tours, but that's about it. And during the first week we lived there, my husband was jumping out of bed all night because I said I "heard things." But the house soon calmed down; it must have decided we were "o.k."

OH, I ALMOST FORGOT rule number eight: Do not despair. Just sharpen your chainsaw and get out your drill and read your Old-House Journal. As for me it took

The southern elevation, with its paired brick chimneys and roof-peak finial, shows how the bricks have been awkwardly repointed — originally, the mortar lines were nearly invisible.

SHINGLE SIDING REPAIR

by Gordon Bock

FROM NEW ENGLAND Salt Box to California Queen Anne, part of the charm of many an older house is the wood shingle siding that covers the outside. Excellent as an exterior covering, shingles also have a visual appeal that's hard to duplicate. The Victorians manufactured them in a stupendous array of geometric patterns, and even the square-butted shingle or shake has the warmth and interest of wood's natural texture.

WITH A MINIMUM of maintenance, cedar shingles can have a lifespan of over seventy years. Too often, a few areas of storm or water damage, or changes in the sizes of windows and doors, spell the end for a whole wall of shingles because the owner thinks repairs can't be made without disturbing all the siding and making a mess. In fact, part of the excellence of wood shingles is that they can be removed and repaired individually if the right tools are used.

How They're Made & Applied

WOOD SHINGLES are manufactured from clear, knot-free trees. Cedar is the most common source, but oak, redwood, and cypress have also been used. Shingles are machine-sawn into tapered boards of different lengths (16, 18, and 24 inches) and sorted by quality into four grades. Number one shingles have no sapwood, are completely clear, and are all edge-grained. Number two shingles are generally applied as finish shingles with reduced weather tolerances from number one. Grades three and four are generally used only as undercoursing. Shakes, the rough and more textured variety, are hand split with a froe, then sawn in half to get flat, regular backs. Originally, all shingles were hand-split.

A BUNDLE OF SHINGLES covers approximately twenty-five square feet (enough for a minor repair). You'll most frequently encounter shingles or shakes being sold by the square, though. A square is enough to cover one hundred square feet (four bundles). Prices reflect type of wood and grade, length of shingles, and of course, the quantity of your purchase.

SHINGLE SIDING is nailed on from the bottom up in straight rows (courses). There are two methods for nailing -- single course and double course. In single-course siding (the traditional nailing method), the shingles are spaced so that each covers roughly half of the one nailed below it. Nails are spaced one inch up from the bottom edge of the next course to go on, so that the next course will conceal the nails of the previous course.

IN DOUBLE-COURSE siding, two layers of shingles are applied in each course; #1 grade on top, and a lesser grade (usually #3) underneath. Since two layers of shingles are used, the spacing or exposure between the courses

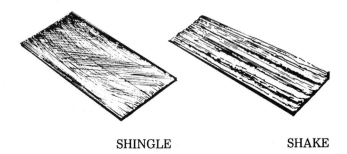

SHINGLE   SHAKE

Single-Course Siding

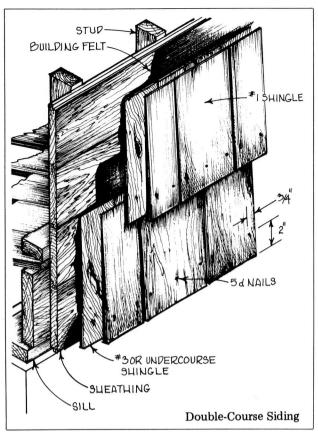

STUD

BUILDING FELT

#1 SHINGLE

3/4"

2"

5d NAILS

#3 OR UNDERCOURSE SHINGLE

SHEATHING

SILL

Double-Course Siding

can be much wider (typically 14 inches on 18-inch shingles). This method reduces cost because fewer finish shingles have to be used (the undercourse shingles are inexpensive). It also provides deeper shadow lines. The outer course is nailed with its butt edge one-half inch below that of the undercourse. Nails remain visible on the outer shingles because there is too little overlap to conceal them.

Removing Shingles

WHAT THIS MEANS for repairs and changes is that as you remove individual shingles, there will be some nails that you can't reach from the outside on double-course siding, and you will be unable to reach any nails on single-course siding. So how do you remove shingles without disrupting adjacent courses? If you need only remove a few shingles, simply split each shingle out with a hammer and chisel. Position the chisel about three-quarters of an inch in from the sides -- the most likely location for nails. Once they're split, pull out the shingles in pieces from around the

Removing a damaged shingle is easy (if you don't plan to reuse it). Simply split the shingle with a hammer and chisel — then pull the pieces out from around the nails.

Use a shingle puller to...   Snag a nail...   And hammer it out.

nails. Occasionally, there's a third nail in the middle of wide shingles. Remove any accessible nails that remain in the sheathing.

IF YOU MUST remove many shingles, it's best to invest in a shingle puller. This tool has a long, thin blade allowing it to slide under an existing shingle. Two hooks at one end are designed to snag nails. It first appeared in New England where shingles have long been popular. It's not the type of item you're likely to find at your local hardware store, but it can be purchased directly from the manufacturer. Call or write for catalog: C. Drew Company, P.O. Box 125, Maple Street, Kingston, MA 02364. (617) 585-2537.

WORK THE PULLER up under a shingle and maneuver it to the edge of the shingle (where you suspect there's a nail), then tap down on the puller handle with a hammer. Once you snag a nail, a few hard whacks will pull it out of the sheathing. Move over to the other nail and repeat the process. The shingle will fall right out, nails and all. It works like a charm.

Installation

REPLACING SHINGLES is easy once the damaged ones have been removed. First, check the exposed building paper and wooden sheathing for deterioration. Patch and repair as necessary. Buy appropriate shingles (see companies that supply fancy-cut shingles on page 122), and prime front and back if the house is painted. If the shingles are to be left unpainted, consider using a water-repellent preservative like Cuprinol Clear. This will retard weathering, causing the

shingles to retain their color longer -- so it will take longer for the patch to blend with the surrounding shingles. Nail back in place with waterproof nails. Don't drive the nails too deeply, or you may split the shingle. Copper (except with red cedar) or bronze nails are best, but aluminum or hot-dipped, zinc-coated nails will pass. Don't use plain steel or electro-coated nails; they'll stain the siding, and eventually fail. Red cedar is rich in tannic acid and will corrode copper nails.

IF MORE THAN ONE course of shingles has been removed in an area, reinstall as with new work, using either the single-course or double-course method to match the existing work. Shingles come in random widths, and are laid (very generally) big, small, big, small. Make sure the joints between the shingles are not in line from course to course, or else water will run in (allow at least a one and one-half inch offset). When it's time to install the last shingle in a course, you'll first have to fit it to size with a saw or plane. A utility knife is useful for cutting shingles along their grain. Keep a coping saw handy for fitting around obstacles like pipes and vents.

THE LAST COURSE between new and old work has to be a compromise: Because of limited space under the old shingles, and nails that might be left behind, you may have to trim individual shingles, and you will have to face-nail all the shingles in this course. In double-course siding, tap the undercourse up behind the existing work (it will usually will fit full length). If the shingles hit nails or bind before they're all the way into position, they'll have to be trimmed at the top by the

The last shingle in a course must be custom fit.

Above: Shingles in the final course may not fit full length. Trim the top by the distance the shingle sticks out at the bottom. *Below:* One way to keep the course line straight.

distance they stick out from the bottom. Once they fit, nail as usual. The upper course of shingles may have to be trimmed in the same manner. Don't be tempted to whack the shingles in full length if they start to bind. A hidden nail will split the shingle after only a couple of blows. The final course in single-course siding is face-nailed as well -- it's the only way to secure them without disturbing the course above. Face-nailing is also required when nailing the last course under an eave or window.

Larger Jobs

IF YOU MUST REPLACE more than a couple of square feet of shingles, be sure to keep the lines of the courses straight (so the patch blends with the old work). In new construction a chalkline is usually snapped across the previous course to indicate where the butts of the next course should go. For repair work, it's easier to tack a length of light, straight lumber right up against the butts of the shingles on either side of the patch (a taught string stretched between nails can also be used). This ensures each course will be laid in a straight line. For siding that has a one up, one down course line, tack the lumber against the bottom-most shingles, then use a piece of scrap of the right thickness (usually one-half inch) to help position each "up" shingle.

ADDING VENTS AND WINDOWS to a shingled wall, or changing their sizes or locations, provokes much concern and worry. It needn't; the

secret to a good job is accurate measurement and keeping shingle cutting to a minimum. Most clothes-dryer vents and exhaust-fan ports have round ducting to go through the wall, and are designed to fit over all types of siding. Drill a pilot hole from inside the house, then work carefully with a drill and holesaw, or by hand with a keyhole saw, to cut through shingle and sheathing at the same time. Once the vent is in place, caulk it right to the

siding. Small vents, of course, are best located on a single shingle. On larger units, slip some flashing under the course above the vent, and caulk directly to the vent housing.

ADDING A WINDOW should not disrupt neighboring courses either. For a new window, drill pilot holes through to the outside. Cut out the sheathing and siding <u>after</u> the structural carpentry in the wall has been completed from the inside. Insert the window for fit, and mark the shingles for trimming. Resecure cut sheathing to new framing members and re-nail any cut shingles to the sheathing. Flash and install the window according to standard building practices. If the heavy carpentry is all done from inside the house, the finished job should need no new shingling. Larger windows can be accommodated the same way. Removing a window or changing to a smaller one will, of course, require patching with new shingles.

Matching Shingles

IF YOU ARE making a small repair or alteration on a house with unpainted, weathered shingles, and don't want to wait for new shingles to age, consider swapping new for old somewhere else on the building. Steal some old shingles from an inconspicuous spot at the back of the house, along the foundation, or off the garage. You have to be patient to remove shingles intact, but with a shingle puller it can be done. Pick ones that have plenty of life left in them and have weathered to the same appearance as the ones they will replace.

TO DUPLICATE PATTERNED or fancy-cut shingles, small quantities can be cut by hand -- if the shape is not too complex. Fancy-cuts are all the same width, and must be installed accurately to ensure precise repetition of the pattern. Fancy-cuts are more expensive than square shingles. They're sold by the bundle; one bundle covers approximately twenty-five square feet.

Replacing all of the siding on a building is more than a day's work. It makes sense to repair damaged shingles immediately.

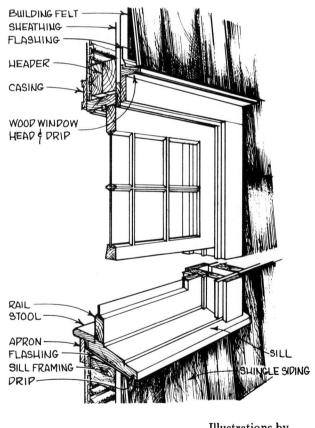

Illustrations by
Larry Jones

LATE VICTORIAN DINING ROOMS

Wherein the Author provides rare insight
into the Social History of the Dining Room,
followed by rare insight into what's
Practical Today.

by John Crosby Freeman

Executive Director, The American Life Foundation
Architectural Historian

WITH FEW EXCEPTIONS, it is possible to do what you want with late Victorian rooms and call them Queen Anne. When jewelers are shown an odd stone mixed with many different minerals, they call it agate. Queen Anne is the agate of Victorian design.

TODAY, the splendor of the Victorian Queen Anne is most often celebrated in restored parlors. (See "The Queen Anne Parlor," OHJ Nov. 1985.) In its own time, however, the dining room was of far greater social importance, a judgment that survives in the higher value we give to a dinner invitation over one for cocktails. Even so, there are two barriers to our re-entering the lifestyle of Queen Anne dining rooms: servants and sexism.

SERVANTS: The typical Queen Anne house required at least one female servant. She lived and worked via the back stairway -- which is the sole surviving clue that Queen Anne houses were designed as much for servants as for the ladies they served. The "girl" -- stereotyped by popular writers of the day as Betty, Bridget, or Beulah -- made the ideal Queen Anne lifestyle possible. Yet she was more often a dream though one could afford her. Reality was the "vanishing servant" gone elsewhere for a buck-a-week extra or "a sudden marriage with some dumb suitor just as invitations had been sent for an important dinner." (Thomas Beer in The Mauve Decade, 1926.)

MEN WHO WROTE for ladies' magazines (the Phil Donahues of late Victorian society) did so in the class security of emigrant-crowded Eastern cities like Boston, New York, Philadelphia. Readers inland could only romanticize about Queen Anne living in "the metropolis," and took cold comfort in one writer's lament about servant-trouble being "such a mean tragedy in so many women's lives."

SEXISM: A simple-minded sexism in late Victorian interiors was partly a reaction to the feminism and women's suffrage issues of the day. The simple formula was to hand over the parlor to the wife and reserve the dining room for the husband. Parlors were associated with the female-dominated boudoirs and salons of 18th-century France and England. Male superiority in the dining room was much older.

LANDSEER'S famous "Stag at Bay" (today the logo for a Connecticut insurance company) was a popular painting for Victorian dining rooms, because it symbolized man's ancient role as hunter/provider...though commuting office workers dragged home a pay envelope instead of a slaughtered stag or boar.

New-Style Dining Rooms

CLARENCE COOK'S House Beautiful, first published in 1877 as a recycling of articles he had written for "Scribner's" magazine, was one of the gospels of the Queen Anne lifestyle. Written by a New York bachelor for an exclusive female audience, he disapproved of the old Victorian sexist formula here described:

"We were taught that dining-rooms ought to be fitted out with dark hangings and furniture, dark paper, dark stuffs, and the rest. They eat up a ruinous quantity of light, and the principal meal of the day is almost always nowadays served at a time when we must employ artificial light."

COOK SAID that it ought, rather, "to be a cheerful, bright-looking room" positioned for the morning sun. This is curious because he then launches an attack on the American family breakfast. Along with "early rising for its own sake" he said "there never was a greater humbug." What he really means is that breakfast in common lacks class: "Nobody needs [it] except day-laborers" and a light snack is "plenty for people who live by their brains to work on till twelve o'clock."

BECAUSE WE in the late 20th century have followed Cook's advice on breakfast, forget the morning sun for your Queen Anne dining

From <u>Modern Dwellings</u> by Henry Hudson Holly, 1878. This illustration was recycled from his 1876 series in "Harper's Monthly," which Holly credits with bringing the Queen Anne house style to America from England. Holly was, however, an unreconstructed sexist when it came to dining-rooms. He said they "should be treated in dark colors." Here are the Eastlake "lumps" that Cook complained about.

One neat detail is how the two lowest horizontal bands in the portieres line up with the chair-rail and moulding above the baseboard. If the traditional white table-cloth is not for you, take Holly's suggestion: He preferred a cream tint for the unpatterned area. *[A reprint of this book is available from OHJ; please see the Order Form in this issue.]*

room and locate it on the shady side of your house. You'll place your contemporary "breakfast nook" to face the morning.

THE GENDER of your dining room is a real issue. Strangely, it is unlikely still that a wife or sister has ever carved the meat in the dining room. Does visible male presence stop with the carving -- or shall the room go on to look like a fine men's club? Your choice.

THE ABSENCE of servants requires buffets, small parties, and family-style service. But please -- don't do a Yuppie dinner in your Queen Anne dining room. It is ridiculous to get decked out in formal attire, load the table with gourmet food, only to leap up and hit the deck between courses, clattering off soiled crockery and lugging back the next round of "cuisine." If you have the money to spend, spend some more on a servant hired for the evening, or cater the whole thing.

I SUSPECT most of you are more like me: too much house, too much taste, too little cash ...The Old-House Poor who have come to depend upon The Old-House Journal to learn how to cope. With that in mind, here are my personal recommendations for spending a limited amount of money to re-create a Queen Anne dining room. The principle to follow is this: Don't spend so much on your dining room that you can't afford to feed your friends in it. (Those who would be offended by your limitations aren't your friends.)

The Floor

SATISFY EXPECTATIONS of a hardwood border. Elaborate parquet is not necessary but still possible. Straight boards mitred at the corners are fine, or they could end in a parquet corner-block. Do the rest in 3/4-in. plywood which will be hidden by the carpet. A modern reproduction of an oriental (inexpensive in man-made fibers) is good enough because the table and chairs keep it in shadow

and the table-cloth will hide most of it. Feet and chair-legs will wear it out and butterfingers will stain it. Come to think of it, get a dark one instead of a light one.

Wall Treatments

EXCEPT FOR HIS OWN hand-screened papers, there is no substitute for Bruce Bradbury's articles about late Victorian wall and ceiling decoration (OHJ October 1983 and August-Sept. 1984). Although the division of wall (dado, fill, frieze, etc.) tended to be the same throughout the Queen Anne, there were many, many combinations of wood, paper, cloth, paint, and stencils. Here is one suggestion from Cook:

From Clarence Cook's <u>House Beautiful</u>, 1877. The original caption read, "He can do little who can't do this" — the shallow breast is faked, the mantel-shelf is a board on brackets, an odd lot of Dutch tiles provides decoration. The classical bust on the pedestal is Clytie in her Nightie.

[Mr. Freeman is being familiar with Clytemnestra. — ed.]

From <u>Decoration and Furniture of Town Houses</u> (1881) by London architect Robert W. Edis. The Queen Anne is served up with competing dishes in this room: 17th-century chairs and chandelier, 18th-century swag frieze. The decorated door, sunflower and-irons, and Morris Willow wallpaper are Aesthetic. The frieze is emphasized by the unusual absence of a dado.

Over-scaled parts energized the Queen Anne interior. The over-mantel crowds the wall, breaks into the frieze, masquerades as a back-board to the altar of the home — the hearth. In place of a crucifix stands an Oriental vase in an arched and mirrored shrine that lends a Baroque magic to the room. ART is the religion of the room, and the room itself is the chief work of art. That's why the other art — prints and paintings — look out of place.

...black walnut wainscotting with oiled and shellacked panels of white pine which yellowed rapidly; the panels could have been stained Venetian red and shellacked. The wall above was papered with a pale lemon-yellow ground with a figure containing dark green and red. A small room, the low ceiling was papered with a blue-grey ground bearing a figure in a darker shade of the ground. The cornice was a wood moulding 3 inches on the wall and 2 inches on the ceiling, painted black and red with a narrow moulding of gold, less than 1/2-inch wide, running directly under it. "The effect of this room was equally pleasant by daylight or lamplight."

Lighting

PEOPLE EXPECT a chandelier. Avoid the temptation, especially if it will compromise the food beneath it. Even a rheostat and fake candle bulbs give off too harsh a light. Small sidelights are best for electric illumination. The best and cheapest light is candlelight. Wall sconces are nice but not necessary. Candelabra are pretty but extravagant. Candlesticks on the table in glass, brass, or silver are the smart choice. Simple glass ones are perfectly adequate -- after all, one looks at the candle and not the stick once it is lit. I prefer brass to silver because it is warmer, cheaper, and usually lacquered to minimize tarnishing.

CANDLES UNITE with a white table-cloth in summoning up deep and powerful associations of the sacramental meal. Gilded details on furniture and in wallpaper are lost in stronger lighting, but candles bring them to life. Candles make a place magical by obscuring details and warming surfaces. Candles make people relax... no wonder they are chosen for seduction.

COOK'S WISH that "gas will someday be superseded by something better" was prophetic. And his campaign for candlelit dining rooms succeeded beyond his wildest dreams. By the time electric lighting dominated American interiors in the 1920s, candle forms had acquired so much class that most electric lights were made in their image. Note that kerosene, which is what real people used to light their rooms during Queen Anne times, is beneath the contempt of a snob like Cook.

The Table

COOK WASN'T CRAZY about extension dining tables. He called them a "puzzle designers have been beating their brains over for the last fifty years." He said they were badly designed and didn't work easily. I suspect he was against them, common objects that they were, because they lacked class. If you find one you like at the right price, fine. If not, consider making your own table.

The Victorians had a love/hate relationship with the extension table. Love that convenience. Hate that look. *(from* House Beautiful, *1877)*

DURING THE TIME your guests are present the table will be completely covered with a white table-cloth. Who is to know or care what is underneath? As with the carpet, even the most surreptitious exploration by a guest betrays bad breeding and is rude.

A sketch by George DuMaurier. The caption tells us the ladies have not withdrawn from the dining room after dinner, but remain as the port is passed. (We're also reminded that Victorian gentlemen were not necessarily undersexed.) Note decorative features: great lamps over the table and on the sideboard, the proper use of a screen in front of the open door.

I like this illustration because it reminds us that dining rooms are used primarily at night. The best detail is the floral pieces; similar examples in other illustrations look ridiculous because the people are missing. People at the table fill the gap and establish scale. In order not to block the diners' views of each other, floral sprays would have to be paltry affairs on the plane of the table; raised up like this, they can be glorious! Imagine their fragrance as the heat of the evening rose through them.

POST-PRANDIAL STUDIES

FAIR HOSTESS (*passing the wine*).—"I hope you admire this decanter, Admiral?"
GALLANT ADMIRAL.—"Ah! it's not the vessel I am admiring. . . ."
FAIR HOSTESS.—"I suppose it's the *port?*"
GALLANT ADMIRAL.—"Oh, no; it's the pilot."

MAKE A SERIES of square table-tops of plywood, frames of dimensional clear pine, and store-bought legs. Line up as many as you need for your party. At other times, they can be used as utility tables or kept covered with a table-cloth. Cook said to make the top project "well over the frame, so that there is no danger of knocking one's knees against the table-leg in sitting down -- one of the minor miseries of life."

IF YOU ARE so cramped for space and money that you are being forced into a small parlor and a small dining room, consider making one big, double-duty parlor/dining room. There was ample Victorian precedent both rural and urban. The key is a convertible settle/table. His example is shown open against a wood wainscot and chair-rail, and reveals where to put the upholstery. (It ignores his own dictum to provide ample top projection.) American country-furniture fans will recognize the form as a hutch/table designed for double-duty in a country kitchen. A pair of them would provide flexibility.

Chairs

IN THOSE SPRAWLING antique shops, look for them upstairs or out back. The Queen Anne period was so open-minded about styles that anything would be proper except cold contemporary, frank modern, or High Victorian Baroque and Rococo and subsequent Phooey-Louis. Colonial Revival, which begins with the Queen Anne, is proper. It doesn't matter if it is good or bad since they didn't seem to know the difference. The same is true of other neo-classical styles such as Louis XVI, Hepplewhite, Sheraton, or vernacular Windsor. Consider Country Empire -- made from early Victorian times through the 1930s, when it became better known as "Early American."

ORIENTAL VICTORIAN in ebonized wood, or latter-day import-shop Oriental, is proper for those exploring exotic aspects of the Queen Anne. Remember that a chair's function is to be sat upon rather than looked at: Let them be sturdy, well-proportioned for people, and of the proper height for your table.

Sideboard

THE BEST THING about dining rooms, said Cook, was "that they have so little furniture in them! The dining-table, the chairs, and a sideboard are all the pieces we must have." A sideboard is the only piece of Victorian furniture that is still priced close to its utility value. If you don't get one, you will have to provide the storage and serving surface with other furniture. A chest of drawers might be found for storage and serving. Find a small table with or without a gateleg extension. A tea-cart or shelves on wheels would be helpful.

BUT -- these are alternatives only if you can't find a late Victorian or Colonial Revival sideboard, and there are plenty of them around. Avoid golden oak: Real or fake mahogany, cherry, and ebony were the Queen Anne wood finishes of choice. Walnut was associated with old-fashioned High Victorian furniture. The other woods lacked class, especially ash: "the coldest, most unsympathetic, most inartistic of woods," said Cook.

From <u>The Practical Cabinet-Maker</u>, a popular British handbook of the 1880s. Late Victorians were either mix or match — free-thinkers or fascists. (All of their rooms look "the same" to us because they look "Late Victorian.") There was more than one Late Victorian — this is the "match" variety carried to the extreme of custom built-ins, a fascist interior which presages the "modern" design of the early 20th century (which was fascist, too, although that's a nasty word to throw at the good guys of the post-Victorian period). Socially they were free, but when it came to design, they liked their sticks tightly bundled.

See how the galleries on the door, sideboard and front wall line up, and how those on the over-mantel, windows, and back wall line up. Whoever designed this, liked his decor to fly in formation!

Table-Cloth

IT MUST BE WHITE...the only absolute in Victorian dining. (Holly suggests cream; period photos show that the advice of the tastemakers was often ignored.)

China

"THE ONLY PLACE where I am content to see [white china] is on the table of a hotel or restaurant, because there I want ware which tells me at a glance it has been properly washed. But in my friend's house, or in my own, I wish to take the proprieties for granted, and to have my eyes play the epicure, not the pedagogue. And they can never be pleased with the look of a table that has no color in its decoration."

AH, THE UBIQUITOUS white French porcelain of Cook's day. There was and still is plenty of late Victorian transfer-printed French porcelain available at antique shops -- for a fraction of the cost of its modern, department-store equivalent. There is no law that

says you must have china "of the period" or that it must match. Cook suggests the collection of what we might call today a "heritage set." Remember that it was common at all levels to have separate tea china and dessert china. As long as you avoid collectible potteries, all old china is a bargain today. Antique dealers get sets of family china when they buy estates, and are glad for you to take it off their hands.

IF YOU MUST buy new, go to the import shop and get some blue-and-white. This was the great cliche of Queen Anne dining rooms. Whatever you do, avoid buying a name:

"Go by what is pretty, or rich, or effective, and if on turning up your tea-cup or its saucer you should find a famous potter's name written on it, thank the gods that they made you poetical, and gave you a pair of eyes of your own for what is pretty."

QUEEN ANNE dining rooms require decisions. If you want to maintain traditional Victorian maleness, the dark Eastlake furniture "lumps" despised by Cook are the furniture for you, along with Prussian textiles and wall treatments. If you want to feminize it, follow Cook and other leaders of the Queen Anne. Go for either an exotic in-house museum setting or a textbook environment of simplicity and subdued ornament.

EVER SINCE the Queen Anne raised the issue, we have agonized over simplicity and ornament. The best thing about Queen Anne is that it was at the crossroads between High Victorian ornament (all historical ornament is good and more is better) and Post Victorian ornament (no historical ornament is good and less is more). In retrospect, Clarence Cook was a sane voice when he stated:

"We are not strong enough in our own taste to be able to relish plain surfaces without panels, edges without mouldings, and a pleasingness, generally, that depends on good proportions and nice finish. Ornament is a thing to be desired, but to be desired it must be good, and it must be in its place."

The Queen Anne unleashed an army of lady decorators. And just like the army, they tended to paint anything that stood still. Decorating mirrors was one of the ugliest things they did; decorating door panels was one of the most charming. A bit cute for parlors, where they often appeared, they are really more appropriate for dining-rooms, to bring a bit of the outdoors inside. They would be visible only when the room was in use and the door shut. *(from Woman's Handiwork in Modern Homes (1881), by Constance Cary Harrison)*

POST-VICTORIAN HOUSES

Landscape & Gardens

by Scott G. Kunst

REACTING AGAINST INDUSTRIALISM and the machined excesses of Queen Anne styling, early-20th-century homeowners turned to an architecture that evoked a simpler, stabler, more humane way of life. Be it Four-square, Bungalow, Craftsman, Colonial Revival, Cotswold Cottage, Mission, Prairie, or Tudor Revival, this new architecture spoke of simplicity, honesty, natural materials, and fine craftsmanship. So too, post-Victorian gardens turned away from elaborately artificial designs and bright, exotic plants in favor of simpler home landscapes based on those of medieval England and colonial America.

SEVERAL GUIDING PRINCIPLES were at work in these gardens. Most important was to reunite people with nature. Accordingly, the open spaces in the Arts and Crafts interior continued into the garden. Banks of windows and French doors to the outside were popular, as were sun porches, sleeping porches, and broad front porches. Terraces, pergolas, and foundation plantings also linked house and garden.

Linking House And Garden

FOUNDATION PLANTINGS were relatively new during the post-Victorian era, and were frequently recommended as a way to "settle" the house in its grounds. Made up of shrubs, small trees, flowers, and groundcover planted at the base of the house, foundation planting has become a convention of 20th-century landscaping. For most pre-1890 houses, however, foundation planting is anachronistic. Even during the post-Victorian era, garden writers were busy explaining and promoting it, while most gardeners left their foundations relatively open or simply planted flowers there. Dense, evergreen planting became popular even later. In re-creating a post-Victorian landscape, then, keep the foundation planting simple and sparse, perhaps transferring some later plantings elsewhere.

PERGOLAS are long, open arbors, Italian-inspired but distinctly Arts and Crafts. Frequently attached to the house as a porch, they served as a mid-step between built and natural spaces. They also served as walkways into the garden or as a background and retreat at the end of the yard. Modern reproductions often look flimsy and out-of-scale because of the slender lumber used. So 'think thick' when reconstructing; use high-quality cedar or redwood for a durable pergola that weathers to a natural patina. (For more information, see "The Perennial Pergola," April 1984 OHJ.)

PERGOLAS WERE MEANT FOR VINES, and vines were popular throughout the post-Victorian garden. Besides providing shade, privacy, and vertical interest in small spaces, vines helped integrate house and site in a naturalistic way. Vines were grown on pergolas; up chimneys, walls, and fences; on arches over doors and gates; and on lots of trellises. Bungalow trellises were usually sturdy, simple grids with an "X" or two for decoration. Many good examples survive to model reproductions after.

IN HIGH-STYLE HOUSES of Bungalow, Mission, and the English Revival styles, courtyards and terraces were important features. Eventually, no American backyard was complete without a patio. The "room for outdoor living" has been a guiding concept in 20th-century landscape design, and post-Victorian gardeners were among the first to embrace it. Enclosed, a terrace became a Spanish courtyard; with a stone balustrade, it was Italian. Frank Lloyd Wright's terraces were outflung projections of his houses, whereas Arts and Crafts terraces were often pergola-ed or "sunken" (set below lawn level). Flagstone, especially in local stone, was the favorite paving for Bungalows; brick, gravel, and concrete were also popular.

Ladies' Home Journal, 1915

A border of flowers mirrors the foundation plantings in this early-20th-century garden.

Scott G. Kunst

Foundation plantings, trellises, and window box all serve to unite this house with nature.

OUTDOOR FURNITURE made the post-Victorian outdoor rooms truly livable. Most popular and most in tune with the Arts and Crafts spirit was rustic furniture made of willow, hickory saplings, or unpeeled logs. Adirondack chairs and other wooden furniture with a colonial or hand-crafted look were also common. Carved stone benches added a formal note, while porch swings, lawn swings, and hammocks continued to be well loved.

WHAT HAS COME to be called "container garden-ing" also softened the transition from inside to out. For the colonial or cottage look, garden writers recommended window boxes. Large pots were more common, set on terraces, stone walls, and porches. Favorite materials included carved stone, cast concrete, Italian terra cotta, and (especially) glazed pottery. Victorian cast-iron urns, however, were defi-nitely out of vogue. For the true craftsman, magazines featured "how-to" articles on making

The Craftsman, 1914

Here's an Arts and Crafts dream come true: a pergola-ed patio (covered with vines), plus table, chairs, & hammock — a room without walls, where indoors and outdoors are one.

rustic planters from twigs and bark, or cement and small stones. Many good examples of this craft survive.

"This might be used as an outdoor living room and furnished with tea table, chairs, ham-mocks, and rugs." — *The Craftsman*, 1904. This bungalow courtyard facing the water is a beautiful example of a house that integrates the indoors and the outdoors.

Open Grounds

THE FLOW OF SPACE from inside to outside continued throughout post-Victorian grounds, embodying a second principle of Arts and Crafts gardening: openness. The abundance of beds, shrubs, and ornaments which cluttered Victorian lawns were banished in favor of the "open center" plan still so common today. Although parts of the grounds might be given over to small, specialized gardens, an open flow was maintained through-out the whole. Plantings were simplified and generally clustered along the foundation and boundaries.

PROPERTY LINES were opened up to an unprecedented extent. In fact, a lack of fencing is one of the hallmarks of the post-Victorian home land-scape. Although no fence at all might be the most appro-priate choice for your house,

The House Beautiful, 1921

To quote *The House Beautiful*, "What is more pleasant than to dangle one's feet from such a wall?" (Note the small pool at lower left.)

Ladies' Home Journal, 1923

Not stone but a smartly trimmed hedge serves as a fence for this charming Dutch Colonial Revival.

a few fence styles were typical of the early 20th century. (See "Post-Victorian Fences," March 1986 OHJ, for five designs.)

OPEN LATTICEWORK FENCES were more a decorative background for plants than a protective barrier. As such, latticework was considered friendly and modern; classical associations gave it added value. Although latticework was rarely used across the front of a yard, free-standing latticework panels were used as trellisses and screens throughout the garden.

PAINTED THE TRADITIONAL WHITE or in soft colors that harmonized with the house, simple picket fences were appreciated because they were old fashioned. Low masonry walls were often recommended to echo the stone or brick-work of a Bungalow, and further unite house and site. Woven-wire (the predecessor of chain-link) made a handy, low-maintenance fence not always restricted to backyards.

A HEDGE made the most neighborly and natural of all fences. In England, hedges had a long tradition, but they were never widely popular in America until the early 20th century. For the more formal Colonial Revival and Tudor Revival styles, tightly sheared hedges were the rule, usually in privet, yew, barberry, or boxwood. For Bungalows and more relaxed styles, unclipped, informal hedges were recommended, usually of flowering shrubs such as spirea, mock-orange, and rosa rugosa. (Hedges were also used to separate garden "rooms" -- more on these below.)

ENGLISH ARTIST AND REFORMER William Morris once said, "Have nothing in your house that you do not know to be useful, or believe to be beautiful." Combining utility and beauty was indeed a cornerstone of the Arts and Crafts aesthetic. Not surprisingly, the gardens used utilitarian plants in ornamental ways. Currants and gooseberries might be used as hedges, dwarf fruit trees could replace magnolias, and pergolas were

often planted with grape vines. Some writers even recommended putting the vegetable garden in front of the house, as was common in English village gardens. In his magazine The Craftsman, Gustav Stickley argued that vegetables harmonized with the Craftsman spirit and that "a properly kept vegetable garden is in its way as beautiful as a flower garden."

The front yard of this house boasts both a flower-lined path and a utilitarian vegetable garden.

Brick piers and simple wooden pickets do the honors for this English Cottage residence.

A circular brick path sets off this herb garden from the rest of the landscaped grounds.

HERBS, well loved by both Arts and Crafts and Colonial Revival gardeners, were another expression of utilitarian beauty. Herb gardens were usually laid out in symmetrical beds -- often separated by brick paths and edged with boxwood, lavender, or pinks -- and frequently featured a sundial or other old-fashioned ornament. Although some herbs were actually used in cooking or potpourri, most were chosen for beauty, fragrance, or nostalgia.

CARPET BEDDING and elaborate Victorian gardens had been labor-intensive and, by Arts and Crafts standards, wasteful. Therefore, just as the simplified Arts and Crafts interiors were touted as labor-saving and freeing, so too the new Arts and Crafts gardens were designed to reduce outdoor drudgery. Gardens for working people, Stickley wrote, should "require the minimum amount of care and stand the maximum amount of neglect."

THAT'S "LOW MAINTENANCE" in modern parlance (although these gardens were still far from maintenance free). The open-center plan made mowing easier; fence care was often eliminated; and tough, dependable perennials and shrubs reduced the need for digging, spraying, and general coddling. The popularity of low-maintenance groundcovers began during the post-Victorian era, with ivy, myrtle, ajuga, and variegated goutweed common. The extensive, ornamental use of mulch, however, is a much later development. To mulch a re-created post-Victorian garden, use unobtrusive material such as cocoa-bean hulls or a "dust mulch" of regularly cultivated soil.

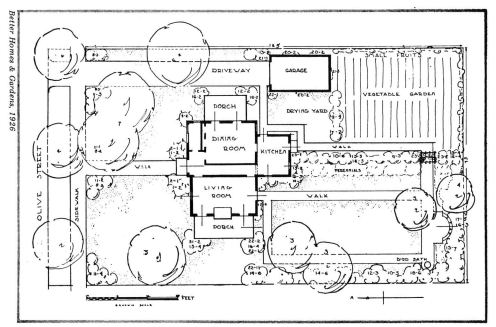

This drawing demonstrates several characteristics of Arts and Crafts landscaping, such as the foundation plantings, perennial border, and vegetable garden — there's even a birdbath!

THE QUESTION facing early-20th-century gardeners was "formal or informal?" On the one hand, the informal nature of the Bungalow suggested a similarly informal garden plan; the highly influential Japanese gardens were naturalistic and irregular. Informal landscapes also took less upkeep. On the other hand, period designers looked back fondly to medieval and colonial gardens, where well ordered symmetries were the rule, and most post-Victorian English gardens were classically ordered. Besides saving space, neatly rectilinear plans also contrasted with the romantic curves of high-Victorian landscapes.

A Spectrum Of Possibilities

Recreating a period garden begins with respecting what you have inherited. If you own a post-Victorian garden, chances are some of the following plants still persist in it — cherish them and add more. Most of these are easy to grow and readily available by mail, if not locally. (See "Seed Sources" in the April 1985 OHJ, p. 69, as well as p. 142 in this issue.)

CLEMATIS *(VINES)*

HYDRANGEA PANICULATA GRANDIFLORA
(SHRUBS)

JAPANESE ANEMONE *(PERENNIALS)*

SHRUBS

arbor vitae
barberry
deutzia
Hydrangea arborescens
   ('Hills of Snow')
Kerria japonica
lilac
mock orange
rosa rugosa &
   other roses
rose-of-Sharon
spirea (Thunberg's,
   Van Houtte, prunifolis)
weigela

WILD FLOWERS

American columbine
bee balm (Monarda)
crane's-bill geranium
ferns
Solomon's seal
trillium
violets
Virginia bluebells
   (Mertensia virginica)

ANNUALS

alyssum
asters
bachelor's buttons
cosmos
dahlia
forget-me-not

herbs
johnny-jump-up
   (Viola tricolor)
snapdragons
tall zinnias

VINES

bittersweet
Boston ivy
cinnamon vine
   (Dioscorea batatas)
clematis
Dutchman's pipe
   (Aristolochia)
grapes
morning glory
climbing roses
Virginia creeper
wisteria

ROCK GARDEN

Alyssum saxatile
   (basket of gold)
creeping phlox
   (Phlox subulata)
hens-and-chicks,
   stonecrop, &
   other hardy
   succulents
scilla & other small
   spring bulbs
snow-in-summer
   (Cerastium
   tomentosum)
wild flowers

GREY FOLIAGE

artemesia (wormwood,
   southernwood, etc.)
dusty miller
lamb's ears
   (wooly betony)
lavender
pinks (plumarius,
   allwoodii, etc.)

PERENNIALS

achillea
chrysanthemum
columbine
daylily
delphinium
foxglove
golden glow
   (Rudbeckia laciniata)
herbs
hollyhock
hosta
iris, including Japanese
   and Siberian
Japanese anemone
Madonna & Regal lilies
New York &
   New England asters
Oriental & Iceland
   poppies
peonies
phlox (tall)
red-hot poker
   (kniphofia)
sweet William

WEIGELA ROSEA *(SHRUBS)*

More Craftsman Homes, 1912

The Craftsman, 1914

This Long Island house showcases several Arts and Crafts features: pergola, a change in level, Italian-inspired pots.

An ornamental pond beautifully complements the rustic gazebo and arbor (with flagstone path) of this old garden.

ANOTHER FORMAL INFLUENCE was the classic Italian garden, much loved by Arts and Crafts designers in England. Italian gardens were "architectural," with their spaces delineated by low balustrades, straight paved paths, and changes in level -- an especially popular recommendation for early-20th-century gardens. Stone, brick, and concrete retaining walls cropped up everywhere, and every stylish front walk now managed to include a couple of steps, perhaps flanked by large pots with simple topiary. Along with water and statuary, large pots were important accents in the Italian garden, all formally designed and placed.

AN INFORMAL, Japanese-inspired Greene & Greene landscape, then, might be diametrically different from a high-style, highly formal Georgian Revival or Italian garden, but most Bungalow gardens were created by ordinary people. It was common, therefore, to see both approaches combined in a Bungalow landscape. Rectilinear concrete paths might outline an essentially informal planting, for example, or an otherwise informal backyard might be highlighted by a small, formal rose garden.

Other Garden Rooms

NOT ONLY could formal and informal be combined, but stylish gardens also featured an eclectic array of specialized little gardens, sometimes conceived as garden "rooms." Five favorites were rock, water, rose, wild, and Japanese gardens.

ALTHOUGH "ARTIFICIAL ROCKWORK" had been popular throughout the 19th century, rock gardens as we know them were developed around the turn of the century, to showcase exotic alpine plants coming into England from plant explorations around the world. For most gardeners, however, rock gardens were simply an unusual, naturalistic way to garden with low-growing plants such as dwarf iris, sedum, and creeping phlox. In gardens with a fashionable variety of levels, rock gardens often covered the banks in between.

LILY PONDS AND ORNAMENTAL POOLS -- in both formal and informal designs -- were also very popular, inspired in part by Italian gardens. Stone fountains and well-heads added an elegant touch, or you could handcraft a rocky waterfall; but Victorian cast iron, of course, was shunned.

A CLASSIC FLOWER, the rose was well loved by Arts and Crafts designers. Morris designed with it, and Stickley published whole articles about it. Climbing roses and simple "species" roses best fit the Bungalow spirit, but more than one garden writer recommended modern hybrids around an old-fashioned sundial. Stickley even suggested tree roses or "standards," saying their formality was "not too strong to harmonize with a Craftsman house."

WITH THEIR EMPHASIS on natural simplicity, it's not surprising that Arts and Crafts proponents advocated wild gardens. Plants included both local and exotic wildflowers, and design was based on natural models or a blurring of the distinctions between the garden and the wild. In the Midwest, "Prairie Landscaping" was promoted, while gardeners in wooded regions favored dogwood, trillium, ferns, and other woodland natives. Naturalizing spring bulbs, such as daffodils, in the lawn or woods was also highly recommended.

WILD GARDENS often included birdbaths and birdhouses, and both were used throughout the Bungalow garden. Bird-watching and feeding became popular hobbies during this period, and birds had a special appeal to the Arts and Crafts gardener. Stickley featured articles on attracting birds, pointing out that they were beautiful, wild, useful (all those insects!), and vanishing in the onrush of modern civilization.

STARTING ON THE WEST COAST, Japanese gardens became fashionable at the turn of the century. Archways and stone lanterns were popular features, as were miniature scenes worked out in boulders and dwarf plants. Frequently these gardens were more picturesque than authentic. Japanese plants were also used throughout the garden, including flowering cherries and crabs, Japanese irises and peonies, dwarf pines, and hosta.

The Craftsman, 1914

This handsome bungalow, with its "porches for outdoor living and sleeping," was designed by Gustav Stickley. (Note the birdhouse above the pergola.)

The English Perennial Border

A ROCK GARDEN might be a nice touch, but the hallmark of the Arts and Crafts garden -- and every fashionable garden in the early 20th century -- was the English perennial border. A reaction against Victorian carpet bedding, the perennial border was inspired by the informal, traditional gardens of the English countryside. Carpet bedding had depended on bright, exotic, ever-blooming annuals, whereas these "cottage gardens" emphasized softly colored, hardy, old-fashioned or wild flowers in an ever-changing succession of bloom. Instead of cookie-cutter shapes and elaborate pattern-work, the perennial border was laid out in simple beds -- frequently long "borders" -- with flowers mingled in naturalistic drifts and cloud-shapes.

Scott G. Kunst

Ladies' Home Journal, 1915

This grouping of rocks and pond has been artfully designed to re-create a forest scene.

Wrapped in vines, this birdbath becomes simply another natural element within an early-20th-century garden.

The English Flower Garden, 1883

This engraving shows part of William Robinson's own garden, "in rose and pink time ... The garden is, in fact, as it should always be — a living room ... it is by far the best way to have the real flower garden, where all our precious flowers are, in close relation to the house, so that we can enjoy and see and gather our flowers in the most direct way."

ENGLISHMAN William Robinson first championed and tirelessly promoted the cottage garden, and he's credited by Henry Mitchell with having "invented gardening as we (the civilized) know it." His greatest book, The English Flower Garden, went through 16 printings between 1883 and 1956, and has recently been reissued. Equally influential was Gertrude Jekyll, who gained modest acclaim for her embroidery and craftwork before becoming in her later years the world's most sought-after "garden artist." (Jekyll's books are also newly available again.)

NATURE WAS A TOUCHSTONE for Robinson and Jekyll. They insisted on respecting plants individually, rather than reducing them to mere blobs of color. They valued the natural change brought to the garden by the perennials' short season of bloom. They blurred the boundaries between garden and woods or meadow, and eschewed over-developed hybrids in favor of simpler plants.

COLOR WAS TO BE USED harmoniously, Jekyll wrote, as in nature. Warm colors were grouped together; cool colors were contrasted. Her own large perennial border (which measured 14 by 200 feet) began with "flowers of tender and cool coloring -- palest pink, blue, white, and palest yellow -- followed by stronger yellow, and passing on to deep orange and rich mahogany, and so coming to a culminating glory of the strongest scarlet tempered with rich but softer reds," before ebbing gradually back to the other end and "a quiet harmony of lavender and purple and tender pink." The whole was softened and tied together by grey and silver foliage plants.

JEKYLL'S COLOR THEORY was a hit with American garden writers, and popular magazines featured plans that promised a full season of ever-changing, always harmonious bloom with plenty of stylish grey and silver foliage. Single-season or single-color gardens -- a June garden, for example, or a blue garden -- were also recommended. Stickley published plans for entire home landscapes geared to a single season and one or two colors that harmonized with the house and roof colors, but -- like his totally "unified" interiors -- this was probably too extreme for most people. A mixed perennial border, however, would be an important and pleasurable feature of any re-created post-Victorian garden.

WHAT DIDN'T the post-Victorian garden have? No decks, no plastic hanging pots, no split-rail fences, no yellow rhododendrons, and no (alas!) impatiens. But you don't have to give up all that to re-create or restore your own garden. Period gardening, like decorating with antiques, is rarely a museum-level affair. It blends old and new, finding creative solutions that meet modern needs while maintaining the look and spirit of an earlier age.

RESPECT THE GARDEN you've inherited; consider period solutions before jumping to modern conventions; keep in mind OHJ's maxim, "To thine own style be true"; and you, too, can have a comfortably contemporary garden that also flatters your old house and harmonizes with the Simplicity, Utility, and natural Beauty of the post-Victorian spirit.

Good Books

Gardening In America

Gardening In America examines the changes in styles and designs of gardens, tracing their development up through the turn of the century. Selected garden and landscape plans are illustrated, as are period garden furniture, implements, fountains, and statuary. The bibliography alone is worth the $9.95 (plus $2 shipping) cost of the book. For a copy write the Margaret Woodbury Strong Museum, Dept. OHJ, One Manhattan Square, Rochester, NY 14607. (716) 263-2700.

Courtesy of the Margaret Woodbury Strong Museum

Herb Garden Design

Seven years in the making, Herb Garden Design contains 51 plans created by landscape architects and members of the Herb Society of America. The beautifully drafted plans can be easily adapted to suit your needs -- large or small, formal or informal. Garden designs are grouped by their level of difficulty, specialty, degree of maintenance, historic interest, and educational purposes. Included in the book are: a 1730s colonial herb garden; a Shaker garden; a garden for an 1850s smokehouse; a children's garden; a moonlight herb garden; even a plan for the smallest rowhouse backyards.

You don't have to be a gardener to use this book; every detail is covered in step-by-step fashion, down to how to draw plans and measure sites. Each easy-to-understand plan is accompanied by details and dimensions, a commentary, and a plant list; decorative elements, paths, hedges, and fences are also shown. They even tell you how many plants are needed! The book also has a listing of common and botanical plant names, plus a handy glossary and bibliography. Herb Garden Design comes in paperback for $15.95 (clothbound, $30) plus $1.50 for postage from University Press of New England, Dept. OHJ, 3 Lebanon St., Hanover, NH 03755. (603) 646-3349.

Garden Statuary

Fauns And Fountains: American Garden Statuary, 1890-1930 is a one-of-a-kind catalog that accompanied a 1985 exhibition of outstanding garden statuary (assembled by the Parrish Art Museum of Southampton, New York). Prior to the exhibition and this booklet, information on this "sideline in American art and architecture" was hard to find.

This 76-page book should be useful to anyone landscaping a country home built between 1900 and 1930. For your copy, send $15.00 plus $3 handling to The Parrish Art Museum, Dept. OHJ, Southampton, NY 11968. (512) 283-2118.

Landscaping Handbook

If you're planning any sort of landscaping around your old house, you should consult The Harrowsmith Landscaping Handbook. It deals with such landscape basics as: planning, energy conservation, using indigenous trees and shrubs, ground covers, flowers, shrubbery, hedges and vines, trees, cold-climate planting. Each chapter is written by a specialist in the field. The handbook has an array of interesting early photos and planting schemes; there's also a glossary of terms, a listing of various plant types, and mail-order sources. The Harrowsmith Landscaping Handbook sells for $17.95 plus $1 shipping from Harrowsmith, The Creamery, Dept. OHJ, Charlotte, VT 05445. (800) 343-3350.

The English Flower Garden

In 1883, William Robinson wrote The English Flower Garden, one of the most important and influential of all garden books. His principles revolutionized gardening in England and America; arguing for the simple cottage garden over artificial, highly formal plans, he pioneered the natural plantings of perennials and wildflowers, which we still favor today.

If you're interested in period-style garden of a less formal nature for your house (1880-1940), you'll find a fine resource in this readable, well illustrated book. Updated for this edition, it has 290 pages of text, plus a 430-page dictionary full of descriptions, planting advice, and lore. This hardcover sells for $35 ppd. from Kraus Reprints & Periodicals, Dept. OHJ, Route 100, Millwood, NY 10546. (914) 762-2200.

Garden Sourcebook

The House of Boughs, A Sourcebook Of Garden Designs, Structures, And Suppliers is a detailed compendium of sundials, sculptures, outdoor furniture, period fences, gazebos, summer houses, topiary, and more.

There's a brief history of gardening through the ages and a good list of scholarly books on the subject. Most importantly, the book lists suppliers who can furnish many of the items that illustrate the text. This hardbound book sells for $35 plus shipping; to order your copy, contact Customer Service, Viking Penguin, Dept. OHJ, 299 Murray Hill Parkway, E. Rutherford, NJ 07073. (201) 933-1460.

Gardening Bookstore

With nearly 600 publications, Capability's Books has one of the most complete selections of landscape and gardening books around. They sell books on perennial gardens, historic flowers, cottage gardens, restoring and recreating period gardens, building stone walls, garden ornament, 19th-century glasshouses & wintergardens, and much more.

Got a computer? Here's something really special: This store sells Ortho's Computerized Gardening Program ($49.95). Just give it your zip code and ask whatever you need to know: The information it gives will be tailored to your region.

The catalog is free to OHJ readers. Write Capability's Books, P.O. Box 114, Dept. 86-OHJ, Highway 46, Deer Park, WI 54007. (715) 269-5346.

Dress Your Yard In Blue

by Dennis W. Brezina

THE INCREASINGLY RARE "Blew Robin" (as it was known in colonial times) was once common to orchards and pastures. If your house has a large yard, and you live in an outlying suburb, a small town or village, or a rural area, you have a good chance of attracting a bluebird family. If you succeed, the bird that "carries the sky on his back," may well return to raise one or more broods year after year; in the Southern United States, it may loyally remain near the nesting site all year round. All you have to do is build a bluebird-nesting box, mount it on a tree, post, or pipe, and monitor the box.

AS YOU CAN SEE from the diagram, it's easy to build a box that will appeal to this cavity-nesting bird. Select a short length of No. 3 pine wood or a small sheet of 3/4"-thick exterior plywood; use aluminum or galvanized nails, 1-3/4" long, with roughened shanks.

THE ENTRANCE HOLE should be between 1-7/16" and 1-1/2" in diameter. A larger-size hole will invite the pesty starling, one of the bluebird's main competitors for increasingly limited nesting sites. A hole no larger than 1-1/2" can also accommodate the House Sparrow, the bluebird's other major rival. (If your box has a movable top, you can remove a sparrow's nest as soon as it's built.)

TO KEEP OUT THE RAIN, the roof should slope toward the front of the box and overhang the entrance hole, which should face away from the prevailing winds. (A perch is not advised, as it will attract unwanted birds.) Drill several small ventilation holes near the top of the box, and saw off 3/8" from each corner of the floor for drainage. Painting is unnecessary.

LOCATE THE BOX on your lawn (or orchard, pasture, park land, or golf course), preferably in a rural or semi-rural habitat. Keep boxes away from thick fence rows or woods, to discourage wrens from taking over. The bluebird has a strong territorial imperative, so put out two or more boxes only if they can be placed at least 75 to 100 yards apart.

FASTEN THE BOX to the trunk of an isolated tree or fence post, with vines and other vegetation turned away. The box is easy to monitor and clean out if it's mounted 3 to 5 feet above the ground. For the most protection against predators, mount it on top of a 6- or 7-foot iron pipe sunk into the ground. A pipe flange secured to the bottom of the box can be screwed onto the threaded end of the pipe. Coat the pipe with axle grease to prevent raccoons, possums, and snakes from climbing up and eating the eggs or young. The box should face a shrub or tree that's no more than 50 feet away, so the baby bluebirds, when they're ready to fledge, have a good chance to end their first flight safely above the ground.

IF YOU'D LIKE to observe the birds, place the box within 20 feet of your kitchen or den window. If the box has a movable top, you can open it and watch the progress of the bluebird family (or maybe an equally fascinating family of chickadees or titmice). Boxes can be set out from early February (South) to early March (North). After the female approves her mate's choice of a site, the pair will skillfully weave a fragile nest of soft grass. One blue egg (rarely, white) is laid each day for five to six days. Incubation starts after the last egg is laid and lasts 13 to 14 days. Once hatched, the baby bluebirds grow rapidly and are ready to fly in 15 to 20 days. After the young have fledged, you can clean out the old nest in anticipation of another nesting attempt within a week or two.

FOR MORE INFORMATION on building bluebird-nesting boxes, and on ordering either an assembled box or a do-it-yourself kit, write the North American Bluebird Society, Box 6295, Silver Spring, MD 20906. (Please include 50¢ and S.A.S.E.) You can join the Society and learn about the many conservation and education activities it promotes in its efforts to increase the population of Eastern, Western, and Mountain Bluebirds. Include yourself among the bluebird's friends, who have placed tens of thousands of boxes throughout the continent. After all, "The bird with feathers of blue (may be) waiting for you, back in your old backyard."

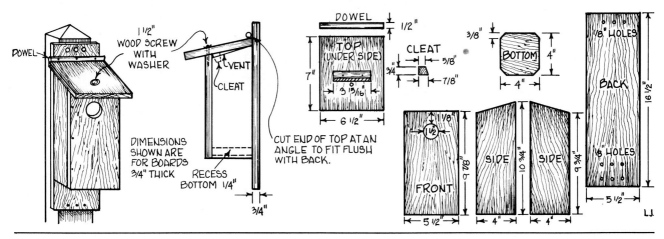

Restoration Products

At long last: Scalamandre by Mail Order!

A Scalamandre employee is shown reproducing one of eight silk tassels for the Old Merchants House in New York. The original tassel is shown on the left.

Chances are, the decorative curtain tie-backs, tassels, braids, and other high-quality trimmings you've seen in restored museum-house interiors were either original or handmade by Scalamandre.

Ordinarily, their outstanding collections are available to you only if you're working with an interior designer or architect. But now, you can call up one of their Silk Surplus outlets yourself.

Scalamandre has long been know in preservation circles as the firm capable of duplicating just about any wall covering, rug, trimming or textile. Their historical reproductions are often produced in quantities large enough to make them reasonably affordable. Assuming you don't have a specific sample (called a document) that has to be duplicated exactly, you can realize considerable savings by dealing with the Silk Surplus outlets. These stores, the exclusive dealers for Scalamandre close-outs, offer fabrics and trimmings (often from discontinued lines). There are four stores, all in the New York area; they sell directly to the public and are happy to accept mail orders. Call (718) 361-8500 for the address and phone number of one of the outlets; then call up the outlet and tell them what you need. They'll send samples of what's available, and after you decide what you want, call them back (they accept credit-card orders). That's all there is to it.

For the most exact hand-woven reproductions, Scalamandre has re-created two 18th-century hand-trimmings looms, worked by master weavers.

A massive amount of hand labor goes into their tassels and woven trimmings, eloquently testifying to Scalamandre's dedication to craft. There are about 20 craftspeople at their factory who hand-sew tassels, sometimes taking several days to complete each one. Tassel prices range from around $70 to hundreds of dollars. They also have about 30 hand-loom weavers that can duplicate almost any trimming. Scalamandre has offices, open only to the trade, in most major U.S. cities.

Stone Restoration

Fleur Palau and Adrienne Collins are two sculptors who have established Pietra Dura, a stone-restoration company that specializes in historic buildings and monuments. They are personally involved on every project, working with an array of skilled sculptors and craftspeople. They strive to retool rather than introduce foreign patching materials onto a building's surface.

Their work, which is of a very high caliber, includes: retooling or recarving existing mouldings and bas-relief motifs in stone; honing worn or spalling surfaces in stone and precast work; re-creating lost mouldings and missing decorative elements in the original material (stone, wood, clay, color-matched mortar, polymer concrete); installation of stone dutchmen; matching textural finishes in stone or mortar; mould-making

and casting; precast work in mortar, polymer concrete, and cast stone; gilding. Call if you'd like to discuss a project, or send $1 for their brochure. Pietra Dura Restoration, Inc., 340 East 6th St., Dept. OHJ, New York, NY 10003. (212) 260-3702 or 260-6187.

Chimney–Lining System

About five years ago, a chimney-lining system called Solid/Flue was introduced in the States by American Chimney Lining Systems. The English have used it for the last 25 years to install one-piece, continuous masonry liners in deteriorated, damaged, and unlined chimneys. A trained installer cleans the chimney and inserts an inflated rubber-tube former in the flue (centering it a minimum 3/4 in. on all sides). The openings at the bottom are sealed off, and a special concrete mix is poured around the former. After a day or so, the mix sets up and the former is deflated and removed -- and the flue is relined without changing the chimney's appearance. (Naturally, it's not quite this simple. Your firebox may require rebuilding, or you may need to install a damper sys-

tem. And of course, the chimney must be structurally sound and the mortar joints in good repair before installing the new cement lining -- see "Relining Your Chimney Flue" in the September 1982 OHJ.)

Solid/Flue is said to strengthen the chimney system, insulate the old masonry from high heat, provide a hotter and cleaner flue, and withstand a 2100-degree chimney fire. The lining is estimated to have a minimum life of 60 years. But bear in mind that it's not reversible: Once it's bonded to the old masonry, it can't be removed -- or easily repaired, should cracks develop or the concrete begin to disintegrate.

Currently, the company's most ambitious project is the relining of 15 to 20 chimneys per year for the next three to five years on Mackinaw Island, Michigan. We saw a videotape of the work there: They're relining just about every type of chimney. There are trained Solid/Flue installers now in 17 states; to learn more about the system, write or call Doug LaFleur at American Chimney Lining Systems, Solid/Flue, 9797 Clyde Park SW, Dept. OHJ, Byron Center, MI 49315. (616) 878-3577.

Bar Keepers Friend

Mrs. E.P. Hollenbach of Oyster Bay, New York, turned us on to Bar Keepers Friend. It's a great old product, a scouring powder that really works. It removes rust stains and lime deposits almost instantly. Bar Keepers Friend has been around since 1882; it must have earned the friendship of saloon keepers, because it works beautifully on brass, porcelain, copper, stainless steel, and chrome. I tried it on a rust-stained bathtub, and was amazed at how quickly and completely it removed the stains. (It also works as a poultice for really difficult stains.) Its main ingredient is oxalic acid, so remember to wear gloves when using it.

Its abrasives are less harsh than those in Ajax or Comet, but it's a stronger product than Bon Ami: Before cleaning antique fixtures, test it first to make sure it won't etch the surface.

If you can't find Bar Keepers Friend at your grocery or hardware store, write the company for your nearest dealer: SerVaas Laboratories, Inc., Dept. OHJ, P.O. Box 7008, Indianapolis, IN 46207. (317) 636-7760.

Victorian Ice Cream

Victorian Ices & Ice Cream is a great little book for anyone who likes homemade ice cream. The Metropolitan Museum of Art has taken an 1885 book of 117 unusual and tasty recipes and updated them for modern kitchens. The book is loaded with turn-of-the-century photographs and illustrations of ice cream moulds, soda fountains, spas, and life on the front porch. It's number DO-901K and sells for $7.95 plus $2 postage from the Metropolitan Museum of Art, Special Services Dept., Dept. OHJ, Middle Village, NY 11381. (516) 794-6270.

Snow Guards & Copper Gutters

Michael Mullane is a roofer, the owner of Round Oak Metal Specialties Co., and a long-time OHJ subscriber. When he found that he couldn't buy snow guards or hooks for less than $14 each, he decided to make his own. Improving on a design his grandfather installed on slate roofs some 60 years ago, Michael had a local foundry cast the head in bronze (cast-iron leaves rust stains). The snow guard hooks into place by sliding up under the slate -- you can attach it without removing any slates. Best of all, these high-quality snow guards sell for only $6.50 (with instructions).

Michael also makes beautiful -- and unusually strong -- copper gutters in any size or shape. The one pictured has a sturdy reinforcing bar along its outside edge; twisted hangers are attached to the bar with brass bolts. (The twist forces water running down the hanger to drip into the gutter.) Copper roofing (flat, locked, standing seam), ice belts, ridge and valley flashing for slate roofs, flashing, and accessories are also available. For a free brochure, contact Round Oak Metal Specialties, P.O. Box 108, Dept. OHJ, Hudson, MA 01749. (617) 568-0597.

Heirloom Garden Seed & Early Plant Varieties

We've compiled the following list of firms because many OHJ readers have written us asking for mail-order nurseries and seed companies which offer trees, shrubs, flowers, and vegetables appropriate for period gardens and landscapes. Just keep in mind that these companies aren't consultants for period plantings; do the research yourself, and then approach the firms with your needs.

Due to evolution, not all plants can be expected to look as they did a century ago; their names may be the same, but they may no longer be true to type. Also, many older varieties of plants and seeds have been replaced by newer, genetically engineered, dis- ease-resistant, vigorous-grow- ing hybrids. But quite a few heirloom seeds are still available. Planting these will yield vegetables and flowers which look just like their 19th-century ancestors.

Barnhaven Primroses and Rare Flower Seeds from North Gardens
16785 Harrison
Livonia, MI 48154
(313) 422-0747
Hardy cyclamens, ferns, and early primroses.

Bittersweet Hill Nurseries
Route 424 and Governor's Bridge Road
Davidsonville, MD 21035
(301) 798-0231
Plants and herbs common to the 18th and 19th century; free listing.

Bluestone Perennials
7211 Middle Ridge Rd.
Madison, Ohio 44057
(216) 428-1327
Their free catalog lists over 400 flowering perennials potted for shipping.

Botanic Garden Seed Company
9 Wyckoff St.
Brooklyn, NY 11201
(718) 624-8839
Sells wildflower seed blended to your region by zip code.

Bountiful Ridge Nurseries
P.O. Box 250
Princess Anne, MD 21853
(800) 638-9356
Their free catalog offers 60 varieties of peach trees, dwarf and semi-dwarf fruit trees (ideal for city gar- dens), apricots, almonds, nectarines, apples, and more.

Catnip Acres Farm
Christian St.
Oxford, CT 06483
(203) 888-5649
Culinary and medicinal herbs and other aromatic plant seeds; 22 types of lavender; scented geraniums; 17 types of jasmine; and even three kinds of catnip. Catalog, $1.

Comstock, Ferre & Co.
263 Main St., P.O. Box 125
Wethersfield, CT 06109
Heirloom vegetable seeds.

Faith Mountain Herbs
P.O. Box 199
Sperryville, VA 22740
(703) 987-8824
Specializes in herb seeds and Everlast flowers (grown since the 1800s for making dried- flower arrangements). Also offers classes on period gar- dening and flower arranging.

Farmer Seed and Nursery Co.
Faribault, MN 55021
Heirloom vegetable seed.

Heirloom Vegetable Garden
Department of Vegetable Crops
Cornell University
Ithaca, NY 14853
Roger Kline and associates at Cornell have produced a useful 28-page book entitled The Heirloom Vegetable Garden. It describes 36 antique vegetable varieties, 19th-century crop histories, preparation tips, and recipes, taken from period garden books; it's $3. Also they offer two heirloom garden kits: the small kit (for 10-x- 15-ft. gardens) contains 22 varieties of heirloom seeds, and costs $8; the large kit (for 10-x-30-ft. gardens) con- tains 36 varieties, and costs $12. Kits come with the book.

Joseph Harris Co.
Moreton Farm
Rochester, NY 14624
Heirloom vegetable seed.

Mellinger's
2310 W. South Range Rd.
North Lima, OH 44452
Heirloom vegetable seeds.

Native Plants, Inc.
P.O. Box 177
1697 West 2100 North
Lehi, UT 84042
(801) 768-4422
Sells special wildflower seed mixes tailored for specific regions of the country. Free price sheet.

Nichols Garden Nursery
1190 North Pacific Hwy.
Albany, OR 97321
Heirloom vegetable seeds and plants.

L.L. Olds Seed Co.
P.O. Box 7790
Madison, WI 53791
Heirloom vegetable seeds.

Roses of Yesterday and Today
802 Brown's Valley Rd.
Watsonville, CA 95076
(408) 724-3537
Old and rare as well as modern varieties of roses are shipped dormant and bare-rooted. Catalog, $2.

Seed Savers Exchange
c/o Kent Whealy
203 Rural Ave.
Decorah, IA 52101
This non-profit organization is dedicated to saving endan- gered vegetable varieties from being lost. For a $10 member- ship fee, you get a 200-page winter yearbook listing old and heirloom types of vege- tables. Members trade among themselves or can purchase seed from other members.

R.H. Shumway, Seedman
628 Cedar St.
Rockford, IL 61101
Heirloom vegetable seeds.

Southmeadow Fruit Gardens
Lakeside, Michigan 49116
Rare, unusual, and early fruit varieties. Catalog is $8 -- and packed with interesting descriptions, illustrations, and historical detail.

Stokes Seeds
1236 Stokes Building
Buffalo, NY 14240
Their free catalog lists over 1600 vegetables, flowers seeds, and accessories. Many heirloom varieties.

Restorer's Notebook

Lacquer Soup

RECENTLY, I purchased an English tea kettle that came with advice on how to remove the plastic-looking lacquer which had been applied to it. The procedure was less trouble than using paint stripper, and worked not only on the teapot, but also on some lacquered brass hardware of mine.

Immerse the brass in a solution of 4 tablespoons baking soda per quart of water. Make enough to fully immerse the objects to be stripped, bring the solution to a boil, and drop them in. You'll find that even the most stubborn lacquer will usually come off within 15 minutes. Then all you have to do is rinse off the items with water.

What I like best about this technique is that I can do it on the kitchen stove, with no bother from noxious fumes or dangerous chemicals. (One caution: If you're removing the lacquer from copper pots and pans, you must protect the tinned interior surfaces by filling them with water before immersing them into the solution.)

-- Rebecca Frackenpohl, Muncie, Ind.

Roller Wrap

HERE'S A TIP passed on to me by a large, professional painting shop. New paint-roller sleeves, regardless of the length of their nap, will shed a few fibers when used for the first time. That can mar a finish. To reduce this problem, they wrap each new roller sleeve with two-inch-wide masking tape and then pull it off immediately. That removes most of the loose fibers that may have ended up stuck in the finish.

-- Steve Wolf of Wolf Paints
New York, N.Y.

Housebroken Chemicals

IF YOU'VE EVER used chemicals to strip interior woodwork, you know what a godawful mess drools down onto the floor. Kraft paper and newspapers keep the slime from damaging your floor, but you still have to walk through the stuff while you're stripping.

I solve this problem with clay cat litter (don't use the type with deodorants). Simply sprinkle litter on top of the newspapers at the junction between wall and floor. As the chemical stripper and softened paint spill onto the floor, the cat litter soaks up most of the fluids, and keeps the mess from sticking to your masking materials. After about a half hour, the stuff can be swept up and disposed of; less mess and less hassle.

Clay litter also makes a great absorptive material for a variety of poultices. I've used it with different solvents to remove stains from porcelain, marble, and cement. Best of all, it's really cheap.

-- Melissa Faust, San Francisco, Cal.

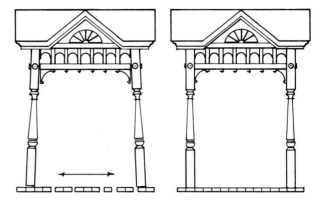

Pipe Down

RESTORING our Victorian porch included the need to straighten out our leaning posts. A sledge hammer probably would have done the trick, but may have left the posts a little worse for wear. I chose instead to use several of my woodworking pipe clamps (they can be coupled to make a clamp of any length). I protected the posts from the clamp with a couple of pieces of scrap lumber, then tightened it up to pull the posts together. If the posts won't budge, take some pressure off them by carefully lifting the roof with a car jack and 2X4. The pipe clamps also came in handy for pulling together the loose tongue-and-groove porch floor.

-- Dan Miller, Elgin, Ill.

Varnishing Tip

IF YOU'VE EVER had to varnish a large surface like a door or a floor, you know how difficult it is to keep the "wet edge" wet. Lap marks, created where your brush goes through tacky varnish, can ruin your finish. Well, there is a simple way to slow down the drying time of your varnish.

Cool the can of varnish to about 55 degrees (any cooler and it may get too stiff to brush smoothly). If the varnish is cool, the solvents will evaporate more slowly, and the wet edge will remain so longer. On an especially warm day, keep the can of varnish in a makeshift ice bucket.

-- Karen Narsiffe of Coastal Trade, Inc.
Fort Lauderdale, Fla.

Tips To Share? Do you have any hints or short cuts that might help other old-house owners? We'll pay $15 for any short how-to items that are used in this "Restorer's Notebook" column. Write to Notebook Editor, The Old-House Journal, 69A Seventh Avenue, Brooklyn, NY 11217.

opinion...
Remuddling

Whatnot-Shelf Housing

UNFORTUNATELY, this isn't a trick photo; someone has actually plopped a bloc of apartments on top of these rowhouses. (With the current real-estate situation in many American cities, we may see a lot more greedy, cynical remuddling ... as a way to squeeze extra rent money out of a piece of property.) Subscriber Albert M. Coffey, Jr., submitted what he calls "this blight upon a fine old Back Bay Boston street scene." And indeed, it isn't just this group of rowhouses which has been compromised; in the picture at left, you can see how the character of the entire neighborhood is distorted by this bizarre addition. Remuddling has sunk to an all-time low -- or rather, risen to a new height -- in Massachusetts. -- CG

Funnier Than Fiction

I GUESSED what "The Money Pit" must be about before I saw the promos. We own one (a money pit), so I knew.

A BUNCH OF US went to see the movie on the night it opened. Would a dog-eared copy of OHJ turn up next to the bed or sharing space with Reader's Digest on the back of a toilet? (It didn't.) Well, it wasn't a great movie. A missed opportunity came when the writers decided the old-house owners would hire contractors for everything. Contractors can be a hoot, but real craziness starts when you try to do it yourself. The other problem was that the film's pratfalls were exaggerated (a staircase collapses all at once; an oven ejects a turkey out the window). Exaggeration and slapstick are unnecessary and somehow they missed the point.

I WISH I knew how to make movies. Think of what you could do with material like this:

Scene 1:
Mother Cleans House

Nice young couple [guess who?] buy old house in city; house has received no maintenance in exactly 42 years. Looks okay, but filthy. Her mom says, "I'm going to come stay for a long weekend and help you fix it up." (Mom and Dad's last three houses were 14, four, and three years old at time of purchase.) Daughter (me) and son-in-law (Jonathan) are grateful for help. (Maybe Mom will scrape grease off kitchen range!) But we hope she won't be disappointed when we're still not ready to hang cafe curtains on Sunday night.

Mom arrives and is pleasantly surprised. Bless her heart, she looks beyond dirty aqua paint and peeling ceiling and sees spaciousness, old-house character. "Just like those '30s movies where Claudette Colbert comes down the staircase and through the French doors!" [Mom has been living in ranch houses too long.]

We set to work cleaning kitchen, scrubbing away with Top Job [cuts anything]; suddenly, panic in her voice. I turn radio down and ask what's wrong. "The walls are coming off!" she says with horror and embarrassment, as if she'd broken some fine china. Scrubbing has brought crumbly plaster right off masonry wall.

I show no surprise, but definite amusement. "Ma, that always happens -- you don't just clean an old house when you move in. It'll get a lot worse before it gets better." Mom says, "Maybe we shouldn't, uh, clean it anymore until Dad sees it." (Dad has some heavy bread invested in the downpayment, you see.)

Scene 2:
Design by Moonlight

[Background: Much of the plaster in dining room had already come down by itself -- it was a bad job from day one, right on exterior masonry without furring and lath, had water damage, was texture-finished in the '20s. Only way to get to a sound substrate is to demolish and replace with a three-coat plaster job on metal lath. The old-house couple are over their heads now and hire plasterers.]

One crisis after another: crew has to know where to install nailers for the wall battens

The formal dining room

before the plastering starts -- tomorrow. We haven't designed room yet. After long day at office and long night at house, crisis dawns on Jonathan.

I'm in bed, trying to fall asleep in house still full of activity (it's only 1 A.M.-- thought I'd turn in early). Jonathan comes in and puts on lights. "Come downstairs with me; we have to talk about

where the battens go." I whine, "Do we have to do this now? I can't think straight." "Well, the guys are coming at 7:30 in the morning..."

Find shoes (even slippers are out), tromp downstairs. Mere few hours ago room was in thick cloud of demolition dust. Scene is cataclysmic: plaster debris covers floor, walls are naked structure of bare brick, wood lath. Debris crunches underfoot; we stand ankle-deep in rubble, photo-floodlamps light two bare walls. We measure and discuss aesthetic impact of various panel widths. Use plasterers' coal shovels and broom handles as make-believe battens. "Move it a few inches to the left." Crunch, crunch. (They're removing our dining room walls with coal shovels! How much did we pay for this house?!)

Scene 3:
It's Raining

Ate supper out after 10 P.M. [my stomach thinks I changed time zones]. Home around 12:30. In the dark (no lights remain on most of first floor), Jonathan opens kitchen door and fumbles for switch. We're talking, he walks half-asleep into kitchen. "HEY!"

It's raining... we have a swimming pool in our kitchen. The plaster ceiling, already bad, bulges. We try to fix problem with carefully chosen four-letter words; it just keeps raining.

Only thing to do is take down ceiling. Plaster comes down without any dust -- like wet mud. 75-year-old construction debris comes down too: bricks, broken tile, chunks of cement. Problem is a burst elbow in cold-water supply pipe to rear bathroom upstairs.

So here's the count: no living room, no dining room, no kitchen ceiling, no rear bathroom. Bad enough, but there's more: Demolition is due to start on the only remaining bathroom tomorrow.

I didn't make any of this up. If Mr. Spielberg wants to make a sequel, he can ask me. (Or you, right?)

Patricia Poore

Letters

More "Painted Ladies" Sought

Dear Patricia,

Michael Larsen and I are planning a second book about exterior color schemes. We're looking for leads on beautifully painted houses that should be photographed for the book. Would you put the following query to your readers?

For a sequel to Painted Ladies: San Francisco's Resplendent Victorians, the authors seek photos or information about Victorian homes, businesses, and bed-and-breakfasts around the country, painted in three or more colors.
The authors would like to hear from homeowners, preservationists, color designers, painters, architects, and architectural photographers. Send a color photo (and a stamped envelope if you want it back) to: Larsen/Pomada, 1029 Jones Street, San Francisco, CA 94109. (415) 673-0939.

Thanks.

-- Elizabeth Pomada
San Francisco, Ca.

Burning Sensation

Dear Editors:

You asked for feedback on exterior stripping (Dec. 1985 OHJ). For 6 years I stared at my 1910 clapboard farmhouse, its peeling paint looking more like a "before" ad for an aluminum siding company. It was 1976 and our country was celebrating its 200th birthday and we were celebrating the birth of our son. So with an abundance of patriotic perse   ance (& a lack of experience), I decided to single-handedly strip and repaint our two-storey, six-bedroom house.

From past projects on the farm, I had acquired scaffolding, sturdy wooden 40-ft. ladders, ladder jacks, and assorted planks, giving me a good start on the basics. To begin with, I chose a Sears electric heat plate. Its design with the handle mounted

perpendicular to the plate, made it less tiring to use than the horizontal handle. (It did, however, require periodic maintenance.) To power the unit I used two 50-foot, #12, 3-wire extension cords. Using an old painting dropcloth to catch the hot paint droppings proved to be a mistake. It caught on fire and was immediately replaced with a heavy welding curtain and a side order of five gallons of water.

Definitely -- complete one section right through to painting before starting on a new area. The only exception: If the weather didn't permit painting, I'd get a jump on burning off a new section.

Without some form of entertainment, I never could have completed the work. Dancing

Sheldon Shaver on the lookout for dancing girls.

girls first entered my mind, but my wife took a dim view of that. So I hooked up my old reel-to-reel tape recorder and played back classical and early jazz recordings and programming. Listening to radio talk shows is another option that eases the pain.

TOP 10 TOOLS & PROCEDURES:
1) Heat Plate
2) #12, 3-wire Milwaukee Electric Tool extension cord
3) 3-in. scraper with off-set handle
4) #3010, 1-in. Red Devil Scraper (perfect for corners and underneath siding)
5) 50-grit 3M open-coat sandpaper
6) Wipe clean; vacuum around windows.
7) Sand nail heads -- prime with aluminum paint.
8) Primer: Oil-base Dutch Boy #010

9) Apply two finish coats Dutch Boy Super Latex.
10) Wear non-slip footwear.
Unlike some of the restoration projects that may exceed $100,000, mine was completed on a shoestring budget. Consider these additional facts: A) I also restored seven outbuildings; B) My regular job required up to 700 hours (annual) overtime; C) If you live and breathe restoration ONLY, anyone can do it.

It took six years to complete (Wisconsin weather wasn't always accommodating), burning off and repainting the cedar siding (2-1/2 inches to the weather exposure). The results were excellent and it was well worth the time and effort. However, I wouldn't do it again ... but then, I won't have to.

-- Sheldon Shaver
West Bend, Wisc.

Pier Pressure

Dear OHJ:

Six months ago we completed rehabbing a late 19th-century two-storey vernacular farmhouse in northeast Georgia. In it, extra consideration and expense were given to preserving one of its most distinctive features -- the fieldstone piers the house rests on. Today, our independent insurance agent informed us that no company he is aware of will underwrite our homeowner's policy because, "no underpinning presents a fire hazard."

Virtually all historic rural houses (grand and modest) in this area were constructed on brick or stone piers to keep them dry and well ventilated. Most foundations have been infilled by now, but we are determined to preserve this regional characteristic in our home. Where can I go for homeowner's insurance without being penalized?

-- Sara Glickman
Athens, Ga.

[Holy cow! We haven't heard this one before. Are there other readers who've had this problem and solved it (with persuasion or a different insurance company)? -- ed.]

Letters

Clapboard Controversy

Dear OHJ,

I am not in the habit of writing letters; however, I must call you on this one.

"Ask OHJ" in March 1986, page 89, is wrong about how to nail siding. I am a side-waller and I do only wood siding, not vinyl or aluminum. The people who tell you to nail above the lap have never installed or repaired siding.

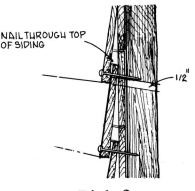

NAIL THROUGH TOP OF SIDING

1/2"

Right?

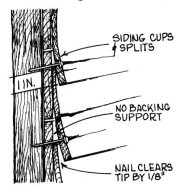

SIDING CUPS & SPLITS

1 IN.

NO BACKING SUPPORT

NAIL CLEARS TIP BY 1/8"

Wrong?

If you nail above the lap, you will force the clapboard into the small space between the two boards, resulting in a severe cup. In a year or less, all your siding will be cupped and probably split; ask any side-waller, or go and look at any old house with clapboards -- you'll see that the boards are nailed 1/2 inch up from the butt.

-- Stephen Winchester
Gilmanton, N.H.

[There seems to be a traditional divergence of opinion on which nailing method is correct. Both methods have their advantages and drawbacks, and each has its adherents. Many of those who recommend nailing above the lap do have considerable experience applying clapboard siding. Most architectural specifications we've seen, as well as government publications and Forest Products Laboratories, say to do it the way we showed in the March "Ask OHJ." Either way, there could be a splitting problem. Our minds are still open on this -- yours was one of three counterpoint letters we received on this debate. -- ed.]

Dear Editors:

I believe you are wrong about nailing 6-in. bevel siding above the clapboard underneath -- and not because I haven't tried it that way, or because my Daddy didn't do it that way.

(1) With modern bevel clapboards (as opposed to the old rectangular clapboards), the overlapping clapboard touches the underlying clapboard only at the bottom of the overlapping clapboard. The further up you nail from that point, the more likely it is that the nail will cup the clapboard, causing it to crack. 1/2 inch up is fine, but nailing 1-5/8 inch above the bottom edge means nailing where the clapboard is weak and has no firm backing. I realize that one shouldn't drive the nail "home," but you do want it flush, and that final tap frequently cracks the clapboard.

(2) The theory that only one nail in the clapboard allows the clapboard to expand

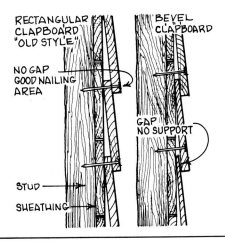

RECTANGULAR CLAPBOARD "OLD STYLE"

BEVEL CLAPBOARD

NO GAP GOOD NAILING AREA

GAP NO SUPPORT

STUD

SHEATHING

and contract with changing temperature and humidity is a nice theory. The reality is that one nail is not enough to hold a modern flat-sawn clapboard stable. It's even worse if there is rigid insulation behind the clapboards. There is not enough expansion and contraction in a 5-1/2-in. clapboard nailed 4 inches apart (above and below) to cause a problem. If the clapboard should split from expansion and contraction, it will split underneath the clapboard above, a harmless development.

I was passing by a nicely done addition to a local fine restaurant the other day, admiring the work. Then I saw where they nailed the clapboards (above the clapboard below), and many of the clapboards had 4- or 5-in. cracks right through the nail at the end of the clapboard.

The one project I did nailing clapboards this way was a nightmare of cracked clapboards. I don't recommend it.

On another subject, your new format looks great. Advertising may be a compromise, but it's also a good source of information for us builders.

-- Thomas F. Murray
Ashfield, Mass.

A Shellacking Miracle

Dear Patricia Poore,

In my joyous hobby of developing my 1910 Bungalow (I feel driven by the project!), I've discovered a true miracle.

Pigmented shellac, which can be purchased at any paint store, will: 1) cover and seal mildew (given resolution of the cause, of course); 2) seal mineral stains in old plaster and keep them from 'drifting' into new coats of paint; 3) prepare 'questionable' walls before hanging wallpaper!

It has been serving me for over 10 years on 'bleeding' plaster stains -- and all is well!

Thanks again for the great service you provide -- I truly feel that I could not have mentally survived my undertaking without your information -- and humor!

-- Michelle Burrill
Sacramento, Ca.

MIGRAINE CASTLE

by David Ferre

The Other Side of Old-House Living

WE'VE ALL SEEN the happy pictures: the wrecked house before, the renovated house after, with the proud owners/renovators standing before it. And we've read their stories of surprise, disaster, and ultimate triumph. We're told it was difficult, more time-consuming and expensive than they imagined, that they bit off more than they could chew, that they suffered, lived in unspeakable conditions with dirt, dust, inadequate plumbing, leaky roofs, cold winters, hot summers; battled animals, neighbors, governments small and large, and yet they stuck it out until they reached their goal.

MY STORY IS pretty similar, except for one thing: I failed. And measured in dollars, that failure cost $18,356.23.

WHEN WE STARTED searching for our "dream house" in June, 1981, my wife and I had been married for one year and had $10,000 saved. Although we'd always been fans of old houses, we weren't exactly looking for one to restore. We just wanted a safe, comfortable home, ideally a house with some "character."

WE PICKED A BAD TIME to go house-hunting (summer 1981). Mortgage interest rates were high, and homes in desirable areas were priced well out of our reach. After a few months of looking we realized we had two choices: buy something in an "adventurous" part of the city, or buy a place in the country. The city was out of the question. We didn't feel safe there and, well, this was supposed to be our dream home, and the urban neighborhoods we could afford just didn't fit the image.

SO WE FOCUSSED our efforts on the country. Since a suburban house would mean commuting to our jobs in the city, we wanted to live near an expressway. A new one, I-390, was scheduled to open in less than a year, so we decided to look at homes for sale in the villages along its route.

WE LIMITED OUR SEARCH to locations within an hour's commute. And we decided to "save" money by selecting a little village exactly one hour away -- where the houses were cheapest. It was going to be exit 3 on the new expressway, but for the time being it was 43 miles -- via country roads -- from work.

IN OCTOBER, 1981, we drove to our chosen spot to see if there were any houses for sale. There were. Dozens, in fact. And the prices! This one $17,900, that one $15,900, this one only $14,900. And look at _that_ one: an Italianate with a four-storey tower, arched windows, fireplace... and only $24,900?? Okay, I

know it needs work, it's carnation pink, it has ugly siding all over it, the floors tilt, but I'll fix it up, I'll renovate it, I'll restore! The owners accepted our offer of $22,000 and agreed to hold a $16,000 mortgage with a $6,000 down payment.

THE CLOSING WAS HELD in the morning of a cold day in February, 1982. It was snowing, and the trip to the village took almost two hours. I remember the sellers saying how much they appreciated us making the trip in such poor weather -- we were the only ones who realized the long trip would soon be a daily event for us. After the closing, we spent the rest of the day removing old carpeting and trash from the house. I had kind of an uneasy feeling that first day: The furnace never stopped running, and it wasn't only the floors that weren't level. The doorways, windows, in fact the whole place was not level. And did two people really need five bedrooms?

WE DECIDED we would move in after fixing up the bathroom, kitchen, parlor, and downstairs bedroom. The rest of the house -- four bedrooms, living room, and formal dining room -- could wait. We planned to do it all ourselves, but only on the weekends, since the trip was too long to be worthwhile on weeknights. We purchased tools and began.

ARRIVING ONE SATURDAY in March, 1982, we found that the furnace had gone off during the week and the heating system's water pipes were frozen. We had run out of fuel oil: 300 gallons in six weeks at a setting of 55 degrees! No water damage had occurred, because the pipes hadn't thawed out. We proceeded to remove the ancient hot-water furnace, the old radiators and their various pipes. We purchased a new furnace; it was delivered to the front porch.

WE SET OUT TO FIX the bathroom first. The floor tilted, we learned, because the beams underneath were rotted and the foundation severely damaged. In fact, the foundation fieldstones were nothing more than a loose stack. We purchased materials to fix the foundation and replace the rotted beams.

DURING A HEAVY RAIN in April, 1982, we noticed water dripping from the bathroom ceiling. A few tugs at the warped boards and the whole thing came crashing down. Clearly, the roof above the bathroom leaked. We purchased more materials, this time to fix the roof. There were no gutters, which explained the leaky bathroom roof -- runoff poured heavily on it each time it rained. We installed gutters.

AT THIS POINT my wife inquired, why was I putting in gutters when I promised to fix up the bathroom first?

BY THE TIME the new gutters were in place, the bathroom roof fixed, structural beams replaced, floor jacks inserted all over, and a new sub-floor put into the bathroom, it was June, 1982, and we ran out of savings.

I WAS ABLE TO ARRANGE for a $2,000 line of credit to enable us to continue. We stopped working on the bathroom and concentrated in-

Brenda Ferre used a paint roller dipped in hot water to loosen wallpaper from the ceiling. Messy, but looks like it works!

WHERE THE MONEY WENT

Total loss on sale (buy at $22,000, sell at $19,000) ...	$3000.00
Commissions/fees/mortgage/taxes	$5194.88
Bills (telephone, trash pickup, sewer, utilities)	$1295.80
Commuting (80 trips, 86 miles each, $.20)	$1376.00
Misc. (new furnace, insulation, ant killer, paving)	$1815.11
Tools (table saw, ladder, propane torch, etc.)	$1238.20
Plumbing (pipes, fittings, fixtures)	$964.96
Roofing, siding, and gutters.	$591.84
Foundation jack posts and mortar mix	$535.82
Doors & windows (including shades, glass, hardware) . . .	$534.51
Painting supplies (including caulking, primer, topcoat paint, varnish, brushes, rollers, masking tape, trays).	$500.08
Electrical supplies (fixtures, bulbs, wire, switches)	$479.67
Lumber (plywood, pressure-treated beams).	$412.98
Walls (dry-wall sheets, repair tape)	$130.04
General hardware	$91.10
Publications (*The OHJ Compendium* and *Catalog*, two-year subscription, *Century of Color*, architectural patterns). . .	$89.34
Cleaning (mops, sponges, trash bags).	$77.80
Film	$28.10
GRAND TOTAL.	**$18,356.23**

stead on the leakage problems throughout the house. The tower roof was replaced, the porch roof was fixed, siding repaired where water seeped into the house, and other general repairs were made wherever moisture was a problem. Then we found more foundation problems. We used up the line of credit in six weeks.

AT THE END OF JULY, 1982, we sat down to analyze our financial condition. We had zero savings, we had used up all available credit, plus we had payments to make for the line of credit, apartment rent, house mortgage, utility and telephone bills, Sears bills, as well as a car payment and commuting expenses. At this point our "dream house" didn't even have a working bathroom or central heat.

WE MADE THE PAINFUL realization that we'd made a big mistake in trying to restore this house, and the best thing to do was sell it. The house was listed with a local real-estate company in August, 1982. Asking price: $29,900. An ad was also placed in The Old-House Journal for the slightly higher price of $35,000.

WE HAD NO MONEY, so the only thing we could do to help sell the place was keep it as clean as possible. The real-estate agency was very generous. They listed the house as having a new furnace (even though the thing was sitting on the front porch and the radiators had been ripped out). During the three-month listing period only one person looked at it. No sale. One inquiry was received through The Old-House Journal. Again, no sale. The house was re-listed in October, 1982, for $19,900.

David Ferre dismantled a useless chimney and dropped it brick-by-brick down a stovepipe. Brenda sent it out the window via ramp.

BY DECEMBER, 1982, the unheated house was suffering. Walls were cracking everywhere. The first and only offer came in January, 1983. It was for $16,500. We negotiated with the prospective buyers and settled on a price of $19,000, with the stipulation that all the materials we had bought stayed with the house. The closing was completed in April, 1983. The dream-house nightmare was over.

What I Know Now

MY ERRORS FALL into eight general categories. I'll discuss each one below, in the form of advice.

1 REMEMBER, LOCATION, location, location. The three most important considerations in real estate apply to old houses too. I realize many good buys are located in "adventurous" and "progressive" neighborhoods, but if you have to answer "no" for any of the basic questions below, think again:

- Will you feel safe in the neighborhood?
- Is the house easily accessible from places of employment, shopping, good schools, diversions (movies, theatres, concert halls), parks/recreational areas, family, friends?
- Is the house situated in a reasonably quiet, residential neighborhood, preferably on a low-traffic street?
- Does the area have good street surfaces, sidewalks, and streetlights?
- Have property values been increasing in the area, i.e. is the house a sound investment?

2 LEARN EVERYTHING possible about the structural condition of the house. For this you need an engineer to give you a detailed, written inspection report. Relying on your own limited experience is not enough; you're no expert, and 'they don't make 'em like they used to' doesn't mean that every old house is naturally constructed better. The report costs about $200, and that could be the best money you've ever spent -- if at this point you're thinking, "I can't afford the $200," then you shouldn't be considering buying an old house in the first place! You can often track down a good engineer by calling the leading real-estate companies in your area and finding out who they recommend. (Don't necessarily take the recommendation of the agent trying to sell you the house.) And while the engineer is at the house, if at all possible, follow him/her around and tape-record all comments -- these might be prove useful later on.

3 CONSIDER THE SIZE of the house. Some old houses may be too small for your needs, but most often old houses are too big. Remember, everything multiplies with size -- like repair, maintenance, heat, and furnishing costs, not to mention taxes. Avoid the cavernous, drafty old barn of a house unless you plan to go into the bed-and-breakfast business.

4 MAKE A DETAILED time and money budget. The engineer's report will identify most of the problems. The next step is to figure out what you can do yourself, and what you'll need to hire professionals for -- and if you think you can do it all yourself, watch out! The old saying "if you want a job done right, do it yourself," doesn't always hold water when it comes to old houses. I've found that often professionals can do the job in far, far less time than the amateur, and usually at a reasonable cost; the only problem you might have is tracking down qualified people. Once you do, get an estimate from them in terms of both time and money, so that before you tackle the

"The bathroom ceiling collapsed! Quick, where's the camera?"

With a rusted foundation post like this one (center, surrounded by new jack posts), it's no wonder the living room sank two inches.

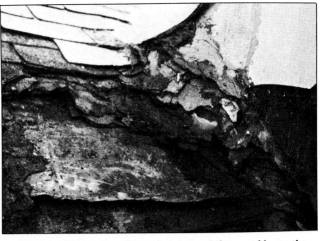

So many layers of roofing — but none of them could save the bathroom ceiling.

house you have a good sense of what it will cost and how long it will take. When you think you have the bottom line, multiply the figures by two and you should have something reasonably accurate. Then ask yourself, do I have adequate financial resources? Can I stand living in an unrestored house that long? Will the house be worth the expense?

5 WHEN BUYING, BE a good negotiator. I know, you love the house. It's loaded with potential, just the right size, and exactly what you've been looking for all these months. It just came on the market, it's in a great location, it's structurally sound, priced fairly, you can afford the repairs, and you have to have that house! Well, if that's the case, ignore my advice: Just pay the asking price. But if the place is anything less than perfect, you're probably in a position to haggle. Remember, everybody loves to look at old houses, but few are willing to take on the responsibility of actually fixing them -- so you usually won't have a lot of competition breathing down your neck. Watch out for pressure from the real-estate agent. Before you sign anything, talk to the neighbors and get the real story. Is this the sixth real-estate company to list the house, and has it been on the market for two years (meaning it's priced way too high)? Are there outstanding taxes or mortgage payments? And when negotiating the mortgage, 1) see if the owner will hold the mortgage and 2) make the least down payment possible, and get the largest and longest mortgage you can; try to make it assumable without approval -- this makes it easier to bail out on the project later.

6 BUY NOTHING until you need it. This rule applies with very few exceptions. Even if you see items on sale, and you're sure you'll need them, don't succumb. One purchasing mistake can eat up more savings than you make on all your other bargains. Decorating plans change along the way -- so who's going to buy your "used" pink bathtub, just because you decided you want a white bathroom instead?

7 TAKE ADVANTAGE of available discounts. At first it didn't occur to me I could walk into a plumbing wholesaler and buy at wholesale prices. I mean, it says on the door, "wholesale only," right? But you're not fool-

ing anybody: When you go into the business of repairing an old house, it really is just that, a business, so you're entitled to discounts. The first time I went to the plumbing wholesaler I found that just about everyone charges purchases to their account. When I tried to pay cash I was sent to the front office to explain who I was and what kind of discount I expected. I said I was in the business of renovating old houses, one at a time, and that I was new to the business. They gave me a full discount and an application for a contractor account, which opened a few days later. The amusing part came when an experienced plumber would walk up to the counter and order a "schedule 40 clip-lock clean-out, three-inch, 135-degree elbow," and I'd have to stand there muttering, "Gimme one of those bent things, about this big, with a cover on it, made out of the white stuff." Even the local hardware store gave me a flat 10% discount, simply because I asked for it.

8 KEEP CAREFUL RECORDS of events and expenses. From day one, write down everything that happens with your old house. Take lots of photographs, especially before you do any work. Keep a log of trips to the house, calls to contractors, phone numbers of suppliers, and any events or milestones. Good financial record-keeping is also essential, because should you ever sell the place, for tax purposes you may have to show exactly what you spent. Save every receipt. I organized mine in a spiral notebook, with a running tab of expenses in the right-hand margin. I used separate notebooks for "supplies" and "tools." The Internal Revenue Service, by the way, considers any tool with a life expectancy of less than one year a supply, so I did too. And don't forget bills like utilities and taxes, or mortgage payments.

Epilogue

IN OCTOBER, 1983, David and Brenda Ferre purchased a three-bedroom ranch house in "Mapledale Estates." The house needed only a fresh coat of interior paint. In 1985, upkeep expenses consisted of $20 worth of driveway sealer and a $3 furnace filter. David and Brenda are both very happy in their cozy tract house, but David muses, "I wonder, had we not gone through this, would we be as happy?"

Thoughts on Exterior Painting
Colorists Tell How To Get What You Want

James Martin
JAMES MARTIN
DENVER

. . . on what people really want

WE'RE IN THE THROES of a revisionist trend for older buildings. Whether you want to be a traditionalist or not is your choice. I will say that I've <u>never</u> had a client who, having come to me for a historic paint job, has upon seeing the authentic Victorian color palette and paint schemes, found that to be what he or she really wanted.

AN EXAMPLE IS ELLEN, who had a strong affection for things Victorian. She said she wanted the house to be absolutely authentic on the outside. I said, "Great, I've been eager to do an authentic one." So I brought over several books on period house colors, complete with color swatches, and showed her how the house should look if historically accurate.

ELLEN WAS DISAPPOINTED. "They look like the musty old house my grandmother lived in," she said. "I can't live with those kinds of colors." The way her house is painted today cer-

tainly tips its hat to authenticity, but we used shading and painted detailing unheard of 100 years ago. People come by and say, "That's the most authentic-looking Victorian I've ever seen!" But it's not.

WE LIVE SO FAST today we seem to need to have the fine detailing brought to our attention a little more than the Victorians did. A man told me in front of a newly painted building, "You know, I've walked by here for 25 years

Authentic? Not entirely . . . but colors and their placement have a historical basis.

and never noticed all the beautiful work on this building."

ONE THING I'M VERY opinionated about is the superiority of light-colored sash windows. Historically, windows were usually painted dark (the sash, almost always). I have found this makes a house look dark and closed up. A light sash gives a feeling of brightness and livability. Again, it's all your own choice, but spend some time comparing the windows of other buildings before you decide.

THINK ABOUT YOUR OWN color preferences. What's your interior like? Beside the general colors, think about the ambiance you've set. It's not essential that the <u>same</u> colors be used, but the exterior colors should complement the interior.

A color scheme has to relate to the "given" colors — in this case, the masonry provided a cue.

IF YOUR HOUSE SITS by itself, you have a free hand with the color. But if you live in a neighborhood, your house must fit in and <u>not</u> jump out. Even the most expertly decorated building may look like a street carnival if it is overtly unlike its neighbors.

A BUILDING MUST RETAIN its architectural integrity. It's very tempting to have a ball painting up details, but don't lose the feeling of wholeness: Too often, over-zealously "painted ladies" become more details than house, and the original proportions of the building are lost.

THE PORCHES, DORMERS, and bargeboards should not be allowed to "jump" off the main body of

Trim on this cottage is a medium value, but the sash itself is white. Light sash is preferred by many as more "inviting."

Dark brown trim and sash give this house a more "closed up" feeling. Light-colored curtains sometimes alleviate that.

the building. This will happen if the colors are not closely related or if the contrast between the parts and the whole is too great. Hue is the specific color used (red, blue, blue-green, etc.); value is the light-to-dark scale of the colors (black, dark gray, medium gray, light gray, etc.). Choose your palette so there is a·relationship of both hue and value running through all the colors.

. . . on getting started

TO START YOUR PLAN, make an elevation drawing of your house and get copies made. Since the front facade often shows all of the design elements in the house, you may need a drawing only of the front (or of the front and one side). Feel free to do all sides, if you want. If you're no artist, take B&W photos of each side and get 8x10 or larger prints made, then trace them. Making these drawings will give you a real familiarity with the building. You'll get a feel for the different areas, the size and distribution of trim, and how the detailing is layered and arranged.

LOOKING AT YOUR DRAWING, separate out the main areas: body, trim, windows, gables, repeating details, etc. Notice what stands out or what are your favorite parts. I don't recommend coloring your drawings. The reason for this is that there are about 30 colors at the art store and 1,600 colors at the paint store -- and since combining just the right shades is what makes a paint scheme great or only fair, color drawings are very misleading. Your house will never look like your drawing. Instead, I recommend shading the drawings in B&W with a lead pencil. Laying out your building in terms of value (the light-to-dark scale of color) will give you a better feeling for the balance and how to handle the details.

LIGHT COLORS SHADOW a lot and therefore show up imperfections. Dark colors will not show shadows as much and therefore can be used to play down or even cover problem areas that you may have to live with. In painting broad areas, get the most visual return for your money. For instance, areas with relief should always be painted a light color so that the natural shadowing enhances the relief -- you won't need an extra color to do so.

. . . on color choice

CHOOSE COLORS FROM paint sample chips of a good brand -- better paint will be truer to its chips. Cut a window in a sheet of white paper; use this to isolate colors on the chip.

PICK YOUR COLORS outside in open shade or under an overcast sky. The colors are truer in this light. The glare of sunlight inhibits your ability to see colors well and distinguish their subtleties (and you know what fluorescent lights do to color).

REFER BACK TO YOUR "given" colors -- stone, brick, roof shingles, etc. These are the colors your color scheme must be based on to give

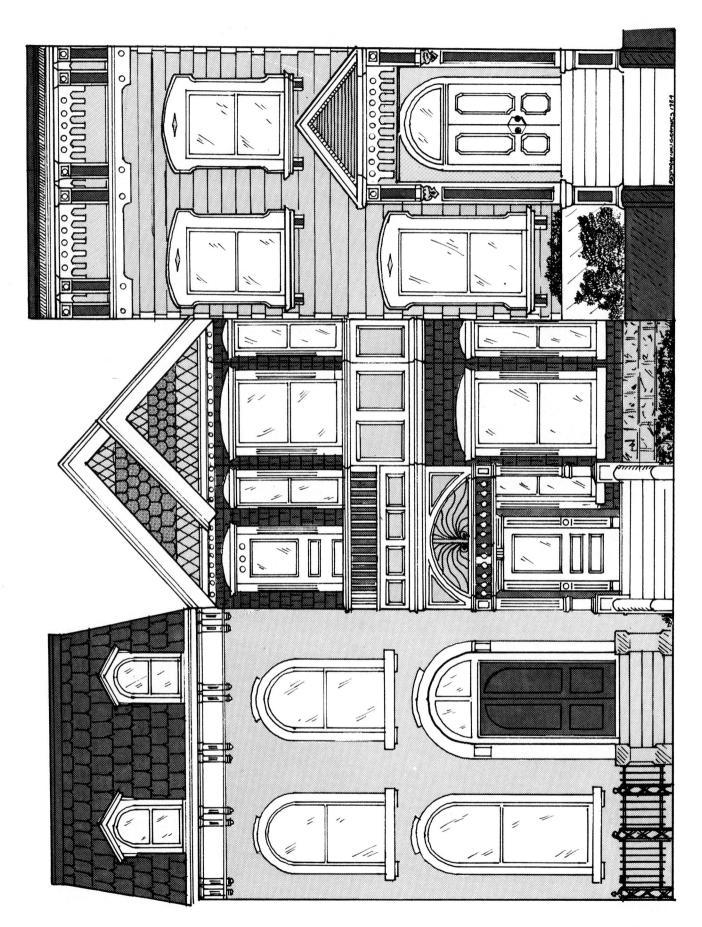

Shade drawings of your building in black and white — to lay out the paint scheme in terms of *value* (not hue), and to develop a sense of the details.

the house a whole feeling. Most colors can be adjusted to fit. If you're set on blue, make sure you use hues and shades of blue that work best with your given colors. Now, make sure the combinations of colors you choose go with each other as well. To do so, isolate them together on both a light and a dark background. Make adjustments as needed. When you've found the body color(s) you like, try different trim colors until one works. Then do the same for your accent colors. Make sure these colors correspond in value (darkness or lightness) with the B&W plans you have made.

WHEN YOU'RE CONFIDENT of your color selection, get sample paint mixed at a professional paint store (a store where the help knows how to mix colors). Get quarts. Now find a small, significant section of the building where all of the colors come together and paint it completely. Live with the painted sample for a few days. Look at it in every kind of light. Squint a lot. If one color seems to be wrong, modify or change it and put the new one up.

. . . on contractors

THERE ARE BASICALLY two types of painting contractors: production companies (who do large developments, rental properties, etc.), and custom painters. Start with custom painters. Call a few; if yours is a fancy job be sure they've done Victorians; make sure they sound "positive" about them. Cross out the ones who don't sound enthusiastic -- you have to love these buildings to paint them well.

ASK FOR REFERENCES and examples that you can look at. Go look and check the references. Then narrow your candidates down to three. Do let personality play a part in your final decision. If you relate well to the painter, if you like the cut of his jib, if talking to him is easy -- it augurs well.

CHOOSE SOMEONE WHO HAS been in business a while -- who has a reputation to protect. These people will do the job right (generally), because they do not want to come back and fix it if the paint peels in three years.

BE CAREFUL OF A LOW BID. An exceptionally low bid usually means that, halfway through the job, the painter will realize he's going to end up in the hole, and will finish up as quick-and-dirty as he can. You may not realize this for a year or so. If you have lots of time and knowledge so that you can supervise the job, it is possible to do alright with a cheap bid. But it's not a good situation when the person working for you knows he's losing money.

James R. Martin of The Color People is a graphic designer and restoration contractor. He does color consultation and exterior design nationwide, and offers a mail-order service. 1672 Madison St., Denver, CO 80206. (303) 388-8686.

Jill Pilaroscia
JILL PILAROSCIA
SAN FRANCISCO

. . . on approach

SELECTING COLORS can be intimidating. You're required to work with color on a grand scale. Your color selection is public and has a visual impact on your whole neighborhood.

AS A COLORIST I have watched tastes and color styles change, just as designs change in architecture and fashion. In California and elsewhere there are presently two schools of thought regarding exterior coloration for old buildings: the authentic, historical approach, and the contemporary approach sometimes referred to as the "boutique school."

TAKING THE HISTORIC approach, you'd work from color palettes documented in various books and archives of 19th-century exterior decoration. To be perfectly authentic, you'd take paint shavings from your building, analyze them under a microscope to determine what colors had been applied, and duplicate the original (or a subsequent) color scheme. In Century of Color, Roger Moss has written an excellent re-

In this example of the historic approach, Jill Pilaroscia collaborated with Bob Buckter to create a refined scheme in peachy-tan, rust, and burgundy-brown.

source for this approach. Numerous paint manufacturers have compiled "Historic Color" charts which do give you a start.

TAKING A MORE contemporary approach, you'd glean the best techniques from the past and combine them with imaginative solutions, such as exterior stencilling, trompe l'oeil, and faux finishing. You'd select a palette that primarily reflected your own personal color preferences. I feel both approaches are valid. A homeowner can look at both and then choose the more appropriate route.

. . . on use of colors

IN MY EXPERIENCE, I've found that four to six colors are the easiest to arrange on a building. Victorian architecture provides many planes for color. A two-color scheme may lack dimension and fight the complexity of the building; a three-color scheme is hard to arrange consistently. A four- (or more) color scheme lets you orchestrate the surface. Four colors does not have to appear overdone or busy. Four carefully coordinated colors will create a rich visual surface.

NOW, HOW DO YOU personally envision your building? Do you want a unique color statement which stands out from its surroundings? Do you wish to blend with your surroundings? Do you want to re-create a historically accurate color scheme? Do you want a more personal statement? Do you want continuity from interior to exterior colors?

LIGHT COLORS REFLECT ultraviolet light and heat, making them durable. They advance visually and make areas appear larger. They can outline shape, accentuate detail, and allow light and shadow to play. Dark colors absorb ultraviolet light and heat, making them susceptible to fading. They usually recede, make areas appear smaller. They create drama, weight, and mass. Some guidelines:

An example of "the boutique school" — five colors, and the giant engaged columns are whimsically marbleized.

INTENSITY: Color intensity increases as the volume and scale of the color increases. Select the grayed and muted hues. Exterior light greatly amplifies the intensity of color. What may look dull on a paint chip will become very lively on a large expanse.

BALANCE: Distribute color evenly over the building from its top or hat, to its middle or belt, and to its base or shoes. A building with a light-colored base and a dark-colored peak may feel top heavy and ungrounded. A well balanced color arrangement will have visual unity.

RHYTHM: Keep the same colors touching and interacting. Repetition of color juxtaposition will create a rhythm that pleases the eye.

DURABILITY: Select colors for major surfaces which are durable and neutral. Remember the sun will fade pure bright tones quickly.

ACCENT COLORS: Use strong colors only in small expanses so they will fade gracefully. Accents may be used on undersurfaces, such as soffits, to add an element of surprise and create surface texture. Don't overuse accent colors as they can cause visual chaos.

SKELETAL STRUCTURE: Use your trim to create a skeletal structure for the building. This technique will define and unify the architectural elements. Create a contrast in value between the body and the trim.

INTERACTION: White drains color from the color it is touching. Black accentuates the color it touches. Gray is a chameleon color. It makes whatever it touches resonate. If gray is touching red, it makes the red appear redder and it takes on a reddish cast itself.

. . . on picking a paint scheme

PHOTOGRAPH YOUR BUILDING with a 35 mm camera using color print film. Take some distance photos of the building in its setting, close-ups of window areas, entryway and front doors, ornamental details, and under-surfaces such as soffits. Shoot an entire roll. Have the film developed into 3"x5" glossy-finish prints.

COLLECT COLOR BOOKLETS and color chips. Buy or borrow a paint fan-deck, which contains all the colors the company makes. Cover a table surface with white paper to create a clean, neutral field on which to view your color samples. When possible, work in natural light. Place your developed house photos in front of you and have a list of "givens" for your building: its interesting -- and awkward -- features; its surroundings; the colors of its roof, stone, tile, landing, or stained glass; and its exposure and orientation.

LAY THE CHIPS on the white paper and see which colors appeal to you. Arrange the chips into groups indicating preference: first choice, second, etc. Select color(s) for the body, the building's largest surface. Once that's established, select a color for trim. Remember to refer to your list of given considerations, restrictions, and preferences. Next develop accent color(s).

AFTER YOU PAINT an actual sample on the house, you may decide to alter a color in the scheme. The addition of white, called tinting, lightens your color. The addition of black, called shading, darkens it. If two adjacent colors don't harmonize, try mixing some of color one into color two. This blending creates an "essence of one another" feeling; the colors become complementary. If you want to experiment with color mixing, I recommend buying a book on color theory; for example, Elements of Color by J. Itten. Get a color compass or color wheel by Grumbacher, too. 🏛

OHJ readers can write with questions — and for information on her mail-order color service — to Jill Pilaroscia, San Francisco Color Service, 855 Alvarado St., San Francisco, CA 94114. (415) 285-4544.

Paintbrushes

WE KNOW A PAINTER who gave a cheap brush to his helper to slap a coat of primer on a dirty, hastily-prepared closet. Left on his own, the helper went on to prime the trim in two large rooms with that same inferior brush. It took a long time, and the helper cursed the primer, which seemed to drag and covered poorly.

WHEN THE PAINTER returned to the job, he said, "Oh jeez, are you still using that garbage brush?! I didn't mean for you to use it in the rooms. Here, use a real brush." The helper shrugged and changed brushes. Now the primer flowed smoothly and covered well. The brush held a lot of paint, and he didn't have to dip it in the can very often. With the cheap brush, the job had been a frustrating struggle and the coverage poor. With the bigger, better brush, the job was almost a joy and the outcome neat.

THE HELPER still hasn't forgiven his boss for leaving him with that crappy brush.

WE'VE ALL USED brushes that don't seem to hold any paint, yet drip paint all over your arm the first time you paint over your head. This article will show you how to tell the difference between a quality brush and one that's second-rate. We'll also give you some tips on the proper use and care of your brushes.

What is a Good Brush?

RECOGNIZING a good paintbrush isn't always easy. The best paintbrushes are still hand-crafted by skilled brush-makers much as they have been for centuries. Consumer and bargain-grade brushes frequently are machine-made and less expensive, but you get what you pay for. The best way to see the differences between brushes is to compare a professional's brush side by side with the same size consumer model. Ask to see the manufacturer's catalog; it contains complete specifications. The characteristics of a quality paintbrush are the same whether it's a natural or synthetic brush. A good brush will have:

● Long, flexible bristles of varying lengths. Longer bristles allow the brush to hold more paint, and flexibility (softness) makes for smoother flowing of the finish.

● Flagged bristles. Flagging (splitting) at the ends of the bristles makes for fewer brush marks and more even application of the paint. In synthetic brushes, look for both flagged and tapered filaments.

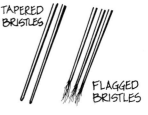

● Spread the bristles of a professional brush at the ferrule, and you will see a treated wood or aluminum spacer plug that holds the bristles in place and creates a void that allows the brush to hold more paint. Cheaper brushes will have cardboard spacer plugs.

● A wooden handle shaped to fit the hand. Cheap brushes often have a sharp-edged, un-contoured handle. Unfinished, smooth-sanded hardwood handles are the most comfortable. Varnished handles may cause blisters.

● A sturdy, corrosion-resistant ferrule (nickel-plated, stainless steel, copper or brass). Some cheap brushes will have an aluminum ferrule anodized to look like brass. The ferrule should be securely fastened to the handle -- if it wiggles now, it will eventually work loose.

● Bristles set securely in vulcanized rubber, epoxy, or chemically inert cements. Work the brush back and forth across your hand to see if it loses any bristles. A good brush will lose some bristles or filaments, but a cheaper brush will lose more, and they'll continue to fall out.

● The best brushes are built with a "cupped chisel" design (a filament-setting method). Check the manufacturer's catalog for this information.

● Good brushes feel smooth and silky when rubbed against your hand, not coarse or stiff. Look for brushes with bristle or filament that has a resilient spring to it (when pressed against your hand, the bristle should spring back into shape).

● Balance is hard to define, but all good paintbrushes have it. A balanced brush is comfortable to use all day.

SPECIALTY BRUSHES

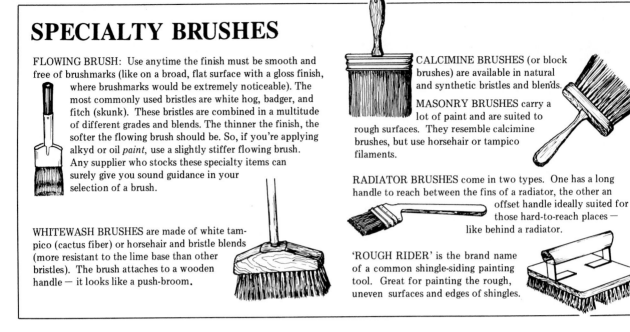

FLOWING BRUSH: Use anytime the finish must be smooth and free of brushmarks (like on a broad, flat surface with a gloss finish, where brushmarks would be extremely noticeable). The most commonly used bristles are white hog, badger, and fitch (skunk). These bristles are combined in a multitude of different grades and blends. The thinner the finish, the softer the flowing brush should be. So, if you're applying alkyd or oil *paint*, use a slightly stiffer flowing brush. Any supplier who stocks these specialty items can surely give you sound guidance in your selection of a brush.

WHITEWASH BRUSHES are made of white tampico (cactus fiber) or horsehair and bristle blends (more resistant to the lime base than other bristles). The brush attaches to a wooden handle — it looks like a push-broom.

CALCIMINE BRUSHES (or block brushes) are available in natural and synthetic bristles and blends.

MASONRY BRUSHES carry a lot of paint and are suited to rough surfaces. They resemble calcimine brushes, but use horsehair or tampico filaments.

RADIATOR BRUSHES come in two types. One has a long handle to reach between the fins of a radiator, the other an offset handle ideally suited for those hard-to-reach places — like behind a radiator.

'ROUGH RIDER' is the brand name of a common shingle-siding painting tool. Great for painting the rough, uneven surfaces and edges of shingles.

● Good brushes have a slight taper from the heel to the edge. Good brushes may have a "square edge" (for holding more paint and painting large, flat surfaces) or a "chisel edge" (for broader filament contact, more even application, and precise cutting in). Use a chisel-edged brush for inside corners and edges.

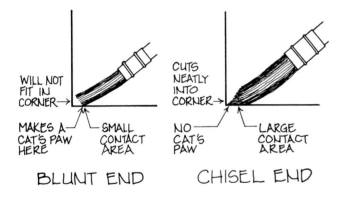

BECAUSE a blunt-end brush will not fit into a corner, it leaves a mark or thin spot near the corner (where the brush stroke starts) called a cat's paw. This occurs because you have to first push the brush into the corner and then pull it out. A tapered edge also allows you to see the edge as you are cutting in, whereas the blunt brush blocks your view of the edge.

Economy of Quality

PROFESSIONAL TOOLS cost more than consumer grades and are often available only at larger paint suppliers rather than hardware stores. But good-quality brushes pay for themselves through superior performance. Here's why:

● Your painting skills will never improve with inferior tools. If you want to work faster, neater, with better coverage, buy a good tool.

● Flexible filaments with well-flagged ends spread paint more smoothly, minimizing brush marks and holidays or thin spots. (A holiday is where the brush takes a vacation; a bare area.)

● A good brush cuts down on frustration (fewer holidays, easier to cut in, etc.) and time.

● More numerous bristles hold more paint, so the brush doesn't have to be dipped as often. Because the paint goes on faster, there is less chance of lap marks.

● A quality brush won't leave as many stray bristles for you to pick out of the finish.

● A well-made brush lasts longer and is worth the effort of cleaning it out.

Natural Bristle

"BRISTLE", to most of us, has become synonymous with "filament" (natural or synthetic). Bristle actually refers only to the hair of hogs. Hog bristle makes a good brush filament because of its natural flagging. Hog bristles are slightly oval and grow naturally to a taper. This gives them spring and elasticity and helps them maintain their shape.

BEWARE OF bristle brushes labelled China or ox hair blends. These cheaper brushes may contain as little as 1% China or ox-hair bristles. Reputable manufacturers clearly label their brushes with the percentage of bristle used (100% China bristle, for example).

CHINA BRISTLE is the most common natural bristle, and is best suited for non-water-soluble finishes (alkyds, oil enamels, oil-based stains, varnish, polyurethane, shellac, lacquer, etc.). If untreated natural bristles are used in a water-based finish, the bristles will absorb water and become limp. A limp brush is hard to control. Other types of natural fibers are used in specialty brushes.

Synthetic Filament

THE TWO MOST commonly used synthetics are nylon and polyester. Nylon (such as Dupont Tynex) is used in low- to medium-priced synthetic brushes. It can be used for oils, alkyds, latex paints, oil stains, varnish, and polyurethane. Nylon cannot be used for creosote, methyl- or ethyl-alcohol-based shellacs, or finishes containing ketones (like two-part epoxy finishes). Don't buy imported nylon (some get limp in water).

MEDIUM- TO HIGH-PRICED synthetic brushes are generally made of polyester or a nylon/polyester blend. Dupont Orel is one brand name. The longest wearing synthetic brushes are 100% polyester. It has higher solvent and temperature resistance than nylon, and better bend recovery. Polyester is also more resilient than nylon and can be used with any finish. Look for brushes with an even mixture of flagged and tapered filaments.

AVOID BRUSHES made of styrene unless they are for a single, crude job, and you plan to throw them away; they're not worth cleaning. (Polystyrene is a tough filament used mostly in wallpaper brushes.) Don't buy synthetic brushes with very coarse filaments. If the filaments stay bent when you pinch them with a fingernail, they're hollow -- not as durable, and likely to lose shape sooner.

The Right Size and Shape

IN ADDITION TO CHOOSING a quality paintbrush with the right kind of filaments, you have to make sure the size and shape of the brush suits the job. The proper size and shape can make the difference between a neat, fast job, and a sloppy, slow one.

BUY THE BRUSH to fit the job. The most common error in choosing brush size is buying one that's too small for the job. If you're investing in a quality brush, you can buy bigger. The more expensive brush will hold more paint, and still make it easier to cut in than a smaller, inexpensive brush. You won't have to work the brush back and forth over the edge to cover it.

WALL BRUSHES
3 to 5 inches

When you have no cutting in to worry about, the general rule of thumb is: the bigger, the better. Just keep in mind that if you're handling a full-bodied brush more than four-inches wide, your arm is going to start to ache after a couple of hours. If you're painting clapboards, match the width of the brush to the width of the clapboard.

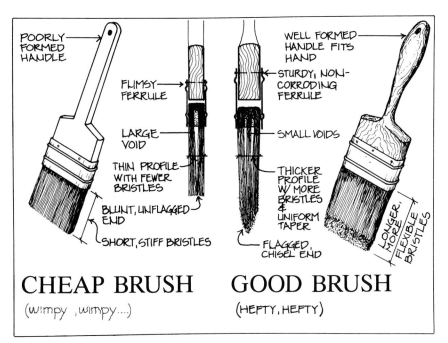

POORLY FORMED HANDLE
FLIMSY FERRULE
LARGE VOID
THIN PROFILE WITH FEWER BRISTLES
BLUNT, UNFLAGGED END
SHORT, STIFF BRISTLES

WELL FORMED HANDLE FITS HAND
STURDY, NON-CORRODING FERRULE
SMALL VOIDS
THICKER PROFILE W/ MORE BRISTLES & UNIFORM TAPER
FLAGGED, CHISEL END
LONGER, MORE FLEXIBLE BRISTLES

CHEAP BRUSH
(wimpy, wimpy....)

GOOD BRUSH
(HEFTY, HEFTY)

FLAT SASH & TRIM BRUSHES
1 to 4 inches

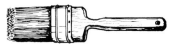

Chisel-edge trim brushes in this size range make easy work of window and door surrounds, baseboards, wall corners, etc. Brush width depends on the size of the trim you want to paint.

ANGLE SASH BRUSHES
1 to 3 inches

The long end of an angle sash brush helps for reaching into inside corners on window sash. Don't allow the angle alone to convince you this is the right brush -- a fine tapered edge is the most critical element of a sash brush.

SEMI-OVAL VARNISH & ENAMEL BRUSHES
1 to 4 inches

These tools have wider centers, longer filaments, and rounded edges. They carry a lot of paint, apply it smoothly, and make it easier to paint sharp edges. They usually have round handles.

ROUND OR OVAL SASH BRUSHES
even numbers 2—20

These brushes aren't very common, but they're excellent for fine work. Their dense bristles and thick profiles allow them to hold a lot of paint. They're compact and have a well-chiseled edge, so they make cutting in easy. They are especially appropriate for spindle work because they won't "splay out" as easily as flat brushes.

The technical information in this article comes from Stephen L. Wolf, proprietor of Wolf Paints and Wallpapers (771 Ninth Ave., New York City 10019.) Steve's an old friend of OHJ.

Cleaning & Maintaining Brushes

by Bill O'Donnell

Don't let this happen to your brushes — it's almost impossible to bring them back.

When you leave a neglected brush soaking in solvent, keep it suspended on a wire.

A GOOD BRUSH is expensive to replace; fortunately, proper cleaning and storage is easy. The secret to keeping a brush in good shape is to clean it immediately after each use. Cleanup is part of the job; consider it when making a work schedule.

YOUR QUALITY SASH BRUSH won't help you "cut in" neatly if it's spent the past few months at the bottom of a clutter-filled drawer in your workshop. Hang your brushes by their handles in a clean, dry place. Fold some kraft paper around them (or, if you can find them, use the protective envelopes they came in) to keep the bristles in shape. Never store a brush so that it rests on its bristles; they'll bend permanently.

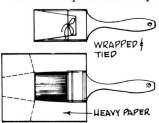

WRAPPED & TIED

HEAVY PAPER

Latex Cleanup

WATER IS ALL YOU NEED to remove latex paint. Don't bend the bristles down hard against the sink. Run warm, not hot, water on the face of the bristles only, not between the bristles with the brush upside down. Pat the brush sharply against the palm of your hand to bring the watered-down paint to the surface, and keep rinsing. Rinse until there's no hint of pigment. Be sure to work all of the paint out of the heel of the brush.

YOU CAN USE a little mild soap (Ivory Liquid) while rinsing the brush. The soap helps remove the paint and serves as a good gauge to judge when the brush is thoroughly rinsed -- when the soapy water lathers up easily, the brush is clean. Rinse the soap completely from the brush.

TO EXPEL EXCESS WATER, twirl the brush rapidly back and forth between the palms of your hands. If it's a good sash brush used for cutting in, just shake the water out; that way, you'll be less likely to cause permanent spreading of the bristles. Hang the brush from its handle until completely dry.

Oil/Alkyd Cleanup

BECAUSE OIL-BASED FINISHES repel water, paint will have to be rinsed out with solvent. The solvent to use is the same as the solvent that you'd use to thin the paint (check the label). For most oil-based paints and varnishes, mineral spirits (paint

thinner) will be all that is required; some will require turpentine. (For lacquer, use lacquer thinner; for shellac, denatured alcohol.)

FIRST, WORK THE BRUSH dry on kraft paper, newspapers, or paper towels. Don't distort the brush in the effort; just brush as you normally would until no more paint comes out. Fill a coffee can about half full with solvent, and work the brush up and down in the solvent for a few minutes. Save the solvent to use as a first rinse for all your brushes.

AFTER THE FIRST RINSE, pour fresh solvent in another coffee can. Use only as much solvent as needed to rinse the brush. Add the spent solvent to your "first-rinse" can. Three to five rinsings in fresh solvent is typical, although you may have to do more. Flex the brush gently against the bottom of the can to help squeeze out thinned paint. Be careful not to bend the bristles too far, and flex evenly -- one side, then the other. Seal the used solvent tightly. In a couple of days, the pigments will settle to the bottom, and the solvent can be reused for another brush.

IF THE BRUSH will be used for oil-based paint in the future, simply squeeze out the excess solvent, and store as usual. If it'll be used for latex, rinse the solvent out of the brush thoroughly with warm, soapy water.

Reviving a Dead Brush

IT IS POSSIBLE to restore natural bristle and some synthetic brushes that have hardened up. Sometimes it's relatively easy. For example, if the brush contains hardened shellac, an overnight bath in denatured alcohol may be all that's required. If paint has dried in the brush, soak it in paint stripper until soft, then comb the goop out of the bristles with a discarded wide-tooth comb. Follow with a rinse in the appropriate solvent.

SOME CHEAP BRUSHES will dissolve in paint stripper, others may lose their shape. Paint stripper is worth trying on an expensive, neglected brush -- as long as it dried in shape. If it dried with bent bristles, it will never be a good brush again. The trick is not to neglect a good brush in the first place -- clean it immediately after use.

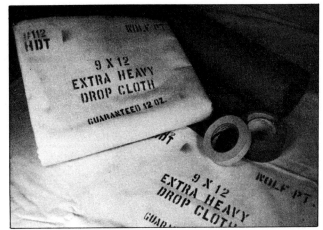

MASKING BEFORE PAINTING

by Bill O'Donnell

PAINT HAS A WAY of getting all over every-thing -- including surfaces that are al-ready finished. This article will help you keep paint where you want it: on the walls, not the woodwork. In an old house, you typically spend four to eight hours of preparation for every hour of painting. If a couple of additional hours are spent masking finished surfaces, you'll make the painting easier on yourself, you'll save time on clean-up, and your finished work will have a much neater appearance.

Floors

REGARDLESS OF WHAT PART of the room you're working on, the floor will have to be masked. Paint <u>will</u> splatter on the floor. If you've got much preparation to do before painting (plaster repair, etc.), the best and easiest masking method is to cover the entire floor with kraft paper.

MASKING TAPE won't adhere to a dirty surface. Vacuum the floor thoroughly, and wipe down any areas to receive masking tape with a rag.

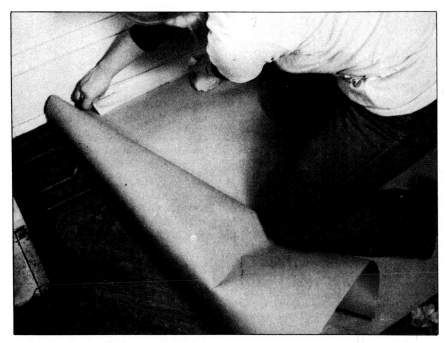

Kraft paper protects the floor throughout the project.

Tape the kraft paper right up against the shoe moulding with two-inch-wide masking tape. Burnish the tape down hard so paint can't seep under it. Overlap the lengths of kraft paper to minimize the amount of tape on the floor. That is, only tape to the floor around the perimeter of the room. Masking tape leaves a gummy residue and, if it's left down long enough, may damage the finish when removed.

IF ALL THE PREPARATION is complete, and the floor has to be protected from paint only, it's easier and more economical to simply lay down dropcloths to catch the paint. There are several kinds of dropcloths, and each has its advantages and drawbacks:

DISPOSABLE PLASTIC SHEETS -- Cheapest in the short run, but they tear easily, and they have to be taped down because they weigh so little. They don't provide good footing because the plastic is slippery -- they're especially dangerous on stairs. If you're going to paint one room in your whole life, a good dropcloth is not a necessary investment, so use one of these.

POLYPROPYLENE TARPS -- Gener-ally less expensive than can-vas, far more durable than thin-mil plastic. These tarps come in a variety of sizes, they repel water, and they're lightweight. They tend to bunch-up more than canvas, and are difficult to fold. If you have use for a dropcloth once every couple of years (and need a cover to keep your cordwood dry) they're a good buy.

CANVAS DROPCLOTHS -- Your best bet. A quality canvas drop-cloth lays flat, folds easily, and is virtually tear-proof. Although we've seen 9x12 drop-cloths for as much as $50, you should expect to pay between $20 and $30. It's a good long-term investment if you do most of your own painting. Bunch the cloth up at the edges so that it covers some of the baseboard. When it's time to paint the baseboard, pull the cloth back a few inches.

The Old-House Journal 175

Sheets of plastic are taped to the cove moulding to protect the wallpaper in this dining room. Note the well-masked floor.

WHATEVER DROPCLOTH you use, be sure to keep it tight against the walls at all times. If it bunches up, take a break from painting, and lay it flat again. Fix tears immediately. Paint has a way of spilling on the only unprotected spot on the floor.

Wood Trim

MAKE SURE THE WOOD is sealed before masking. If you just finished stripping the trim in the room, or if the old finish is deteriorated, be sure to refinish the woodwork before doing any painting on adjacent surfaces. If a little paint gets on finished wood, it can be removed relatively easily. If it gets on bare, open-pored wood, it will be very difficult to remove.

OF COURSE, you don't want paint to get on your woodwork at all, so even though it's sealed, you still have to mask it off. Tape kraft paper over the woodwork with masking tape. Press the tape to as little wood as possible. (The less tape you use, the less residue you'll leave on the finish.) Burnish the tape down hard along the edge.

IF YOU'VE GOT a large area to protect (an entire window and surround, for example), use thin-mil plastic dropcloths in lieu of kraft paper. The plastic folds around corners easier, and its light weight requires less masking tape to hold it in place.

ALSO MASK ANY HARDWARE or light fixtures that aren't easily removed to protect them from roller splatters or spray. It's easier to mask a doorknob than remove it. After you've finished using the roller, remove the masking to make cutting in with a brush easier.

Wallcoverings

WALLPAPER, especially if it's old, can be difficult to mask without damage. Any tape applied directly to it will almost certainly tear the paper when it's removed. You'll have to be crafty to cover the paper by attaching to adjacent trim. Look for:

1. Picture mouldings and plate rails -- When these features exist, they are usually at the uppermost edge of the wallpaper. You can drape plastic dropcloths down from this edge by taping to the top. Because there is a very small surface to tape to, tape alone may not hold up the sheets. Press a thumbtack through the tape here and there wherever you need some additional support. Nobody will ever see the small pin holes on the top surface of the moulding or rail.

2. Gaps behind loose pieces of trim -- If some pieces of woodwork that adjoin the wallpaper have worked loose, you can wedge a piece of thin cardboard into the crack. Pressure from the trim will hold the cardboard in place, giving you a surface to tape to.

COVERING THE WALLPAPER is most important if you're going to be spraying, or working on the ceiling with a roller. For cutting in around wallpaper when you're painting trim, a good brush and confidence are probably all you need. But if you're uncertain of the steadiness of your hand, work on a small area at a time while holding a 10- or 12-inch taping knife against the wallpaper. If you slip, the paint will hit the knife, not the wallpaper. Wipe the knife clean with a rag each time you reposition it to avoid smearing paint on the wall.

De-Masking

- REMOVE all masking tape as soon as possible after you finish painting. The sooner you pull the tape up, the less likely it will be to damage finishes or leave a gummy residue.

- CUT the paint film with a utility knife wherever it overlaps onto the masking tape. If you just rip the tape off, you'll chip some of the new paint.

- USE acetone and fine steel wool to remove any gummy residue left behind by the tape.

- FOLD the kraft paper up as you lift it. Not only will this make a neater pile to dispose of, but it will prevent dried chips of paint from falling on the floor.

What Masking Won't Do

A WELL-MASKED room is one in which any reasonably-likely mishap won't spell disaster for finished surfaces. It is possible to get carried away, though. If you're painting a baseboard, there's no need to mask the chandelier (unless you're especially clumsy).

YOU SHOULDN'T MASK window glass either (unless you're spray painting the window); you want a bead of paint to run from the sash slightly onto the glass to prevent condensation from soaking into the wood. If a little paint gets on the glass it can easily be scraped off with a razor blade once it's dry.

REMEMBER, MASKING should <u>save</u> you time, not preoccupy you from the task at hand (painting or stripping). Masking doesn't take the place of neat work habits, either. No matter how well you mask, finishes are bound to be damaged if you work sloppily.

MASKING BEFORE STRIPPING

Photos courtesy of BIX
Process Systems, Inc.

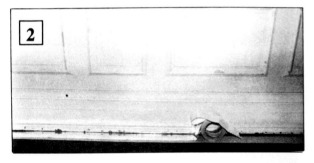

STRIPPING CHEMICALS and the dissolved paint they contain have complete disregard for kraft paper and masking tape. If you're going to strip, you'd better prepare the floor before the sludge starts running down the wall. Here's the procedure:

1. Lay down a strip of two-inch-wide masking tape about one-quarter inch away from the shoe moulding. Unless it's left down for a long time, masking tape usually won't damage the finish when it's removed.

2. Place aluminum tape (thinner, stickier, and more impervious than duct tape) over the masking tape. Butt the aluminum tape right up against the shoe moulding. Burnish the tape down forcefully. Aluminum tape will stick better than masking tape; solvents can't soak through it or seep under the edges. However, it will likely remove some of the floor's finish when you lift it — that's why you put masking tape down first, so that any damage will be limited to the quarter inch nearest the baseboard.

3. Put down standard polypropylene dropcloths. Tape the edge of the dropcloths up against the shoe moulding with duct tape.

4. Cut a width of particle board and lay it down at the edges of your dropcloths. Rip the particle board down to an 18-inch width; any wider and you may have difficulty reaching over the board without stepping on the slime you'll collect. Duct-tape the board directly to the shoe moulding. Burnish the tape down hard. If you plan to strip the shoe moulding, worry about it later — after the majority of the stripping is completed.

FINALLY, spread generous quantities of newspapers over the particle board. The newspapers are totally sacrificial — throw them away as they get wet.

THE IDEA is that your polypropylene dropcloths should never get dirty. All the effluent should be captured on the newspaper, or at least not seep beyond the particle board. If nothing spills onto your dropcloths, you can be sure that nothing is getting under them.

GLOSSARY OF HISTORIC PAINTS

compiled by Cole Gagne

THIS GLOSSARY concentrates on American paint from the 18th century through the mid-19th century, when the most common paints were either oil- or water-based. What they had in common in those years past was the use of coloring pigments (a subject surveyed below). The paints would be mixed on-site; the painters' recipes -- and results -- varied with the quality, availability, and price of materials in different regions of the country.

OIL-BASED PAINTS

POPULAR FOR EXTERIORS because they resisted weathering, oil-based paints had three primary ingredients: oil, white lead, and coloring pigments. Two of the principal types of oils were infrequently used: Animal-fat or fish oil took a long time to dry and tended to turn rancid with prolonged exposure to air; mineral oil was used mostly as a varnish thinner. It was the vegetable oils which were most common; poppy seeds and walnuts had their enthusiasts as oil sources, but linseed oil, plentiful and inexpensive, was by far the most frequently used. White lead was required for almost every job facing an 18th-century painter: puttying, priming, base coat, top coat. It retained its popularity throughout the 19th century (despite competition from zinc white).

SAND PAINT was a special variation on oil-based paints: While the applied paint was still wet, sand would be thrown into it or blown in with a bellows (or mixed in with the last coat of paint). The resulting texture created an effective illusion of stone. In 1850, tastemaker A.J. Downing wrote, "Nothing is more offensive to the eye than an avowed union of wood and stone in the same building." If you had a stone or brick house, this was the green light to use sand paint on its wooden architectural elements: decorative trim, door and window frames, the verandah or porch. (It was also commonly used on the cast-iron fences in front of city rowhouses.) Today's pre-mixed sand paints are hard to apply and don't really have the look of traditional sand paint. But you can still blow sand into wet paint -- try using a glitter gun, available from mason's suppliers.

WATER-BASED PAINTS

WHITEWASH was an inexpensive and popular water-based paint used throughout the country. It's essentially a liquid plaster made from slaked lime and water, but other materials were often added, including salt, sugar, glue, alum, and oyster shells. ("Treasury Department Whitewash," described in Dick's Encyclopedia Of Practical Receipts & Processes, included ground rice in the recipe.) Yellow ochre, charcoal dust, or brick dust could be thrown in for color. Virtually the only interior paint used in America prior to 1700, whitewash remained popular for both interior and exterior painting after the introduction of oil-based paint. By the 19th century, its use had become more specialized, centering on fences and the exteriors of cottages, barns, and outbuildings. If you try to buy it in a store today, they'll just sell you a package of lime, which is fine -- whitewash is still as easy to make and apply as it was 200 years ago (see the March 1985 OHJ, p. 49).

DISTEMPER PAINTS were made with a water-soluble adhesive or glue binder (and usually applied hot, as the glue thickened when cool). All the better animal glues were used, but isinglass, made from the air bladders of sturgeon, was especially popular. Other common binding agents were egg white, vegetable gums, and casein. The base was a whiting such as chalk or clay. Although distemper could be tinted by a compatible pigment, 18th-century painters used it primarily as a primer. By the 19th century, however, it was a popular interior finish, especially for plastered surfaces. The most frequently used distemper paints were calcimine and casein.

● **Calcimine** (or kalsomine) is the classic distemper paint: whiting, glue size, and water (maybe tinted with blue pigment). It was used on ceilings and walls throughout the 19th century, and was still being slapped on ceilings well into the 1930s (by the 20th century, a just-add-water-formula calcimine was commonly used). Nowadays homeowners seem more interested in removing it than applying it -- it creates peeling problems when latex paints are applied over it -- but the paint is still generally available. Besides its soft sheen, calcimine is advantageous because you wash it off before repainting; paint need never build up on plaster details.

● **Milk Paints** substituted skim milk for the water and binder. The milk was often curdled with rennet (an acid found in calves' stomachs) to form casein. Casein paints became popular for 19th-century walls and woodwork (furniture too) because they were inexpensive, dried quickly, and -- unlike oil-based paints -- didn't smell bad. For use as an exterior paint, linseed (or poppy or nut) oil was added to improve its weathering strength. Coloring pigments, berry juice, and/or animal blood were frequently mixed in to tint the paint, making it popular, especially in rural areas, as a stencilling paint. Milk paint is commercially available today, or you can make your own (see the Jan.-Feb. 1984 OHJ, p. 27).

THEIR ORGANIC MATERIALS -- blood, milk, berries -- tend to make the early paints very

hard to remove. Along with their permanent staining characteristics, they were thinner than modern versions, and so would soak into the substrate rather than simply form a film. Milk paint, for example, is a classic toughie to strip: Neither heat nor methylene chloride will phase it; ammonia gets out most of it, but a haze always remains unless you sand it away -- and the age along with it. That's the other factor which weighs against stripping these paints: They're often a primary characteristic of age, and add something unique to the patina of the woodwork or furniture on which they're found. Removing early paint from an antique can irreversibly change its appearance -- and lower its value.

LIVING COLOR

I T SEEMS THAT ALMOST ANYTHING -- animal, vegetable, or mineral -- that could impart color was used as a paint pigment at one time or another. Liquid dyes, derived principally from the first two categories, would be converted into a solid "lake pigment" which was added to the paint. Because they tended to become transparent when added to oil, they were commonly used in water-based distempers. The roots and trunks of trees yielded attractive, bright dyes in red (Brazilwood, logwood) and yellow (fustic), although many of these colors were fugitive and wouldn't stay bright; the yellows from buckthorn berries (Rhamnus infectorius) also were short-lived. More durable yellows came from turmeric and saffron; hardy red pigments such as carmine and madder lake were extracted from the bodies of dried insects. Most of the non-dye pigments were from mineral sources. (Unless otherwise noted, the examples below were used in oil-base paints.)

BLUE, a not-very-plentiful pigment, was prepared in several ways. Zaffre was made by grinding, washing, and roasting cobalt ore, and then adding pulverized flint. Smalt was zaffre fused into glass, cooled, and then pounded, washed, and dried; a coarse pigment, it was frequently strewn or thrown onto a paint base of white lead and clear oil, and then brushed into a uniform thickness with a feather. The popular Prussian blue, used in both oil and distemper, was made from the precipitate that resulted from combining prussic acid, copperas (ferrous sulfate), and alum. The bright blue ultramarine was prepared from the semi-precious stone lapus lazuli, which was very hard to grind into the required fine powder; its high cost kept it from widespread use in house painting.

BROWN pigments were usually mined from the ground. Brown ochre was an iron oxide pigment that ranged in shades from brown to orange; Cologne earth, used in distemper and oil, was made from lignite, or brown coal. Bistre, however, was a pigment made from wood soot (and used only in distemper).

GREEN was ordinarily made by mixing yellows and blues. The green pigments commonly available were made from copper dissolved in nitric acid (green verditer) or corroded with acetic acid (verdigrise). Terra verte was a natural blue-green ochre mined in Europe; its coarse texture restricted it to more common types of painting.

RED was available in many hues, and was especially useful as a tinting or toning color. Ordinarily it was made with iron: iron ore or clay with a high iron content (bole); iron oxide (Indian red), sometimes mixed with clay and silica (Red ochre). Burnt sienna was just that, a pigment made by heating the iron-and-manganese substance sienna. The iron-less realgar was an orange-red pigment made from sulphur and arsenic.

YELLOW was made from a variety of materials. Sulphur was commonly used, compounded with arsenic (king's yellow) or mercury (queen's yellow). The cheap, durable yellow ochre was a pigment from clay and hydrated ferric oxide. Raw sienna was an ochre used in oil (chiefly as a glazing color or stain) and distemper. Chrome yellow, massicot, and patent yellow were all lead-derived pigments. But for those who were into it, ground gall stones or the paste of evaporated bile yielded a golden yellow pigment.

WHITE coloring in oil-based paints was ordinarily obtained from their white-lead base; some pigments were derived by heating shells into a powder (pearl white, oystershell white). Distemper paints similarly relied on their base whitings of clay or chalk (materials which tended to darken and lose their lustre if used in oil-based paints).

BLACK pigments were made from carbons derived from burning organic materials. (An exception is asphaltum, from natural asphalts, used principally as a glazing color.) Vine stalks, peach pits (blue black), and wine lees (Frankfort black) were all thrown on the fire. Lamp black used the soot from burning resins or oils. Ivory black, from the burnt shavings of ivory or bone, was rather expensive, and its use as a house paint wasn't widespread -- but at least it could double as "tooth powder, and to decolorize syrups and other liquids"! 🏠

Although there are several suppliers of 'milk' paints, one firm which actually makes paint "using milk products and mineral fillers and pigments" is The Old-Fashioned Milk Paint Co., Box 222H, Dept. OHJ, Groton, MA 01450. (617) 448-6336. Send $.60 (stamps OK) for a brochure and color card.

If you're hunting down traditional calcimine paint, your best bet is Muralo Co., 148 East 5th Street, Dept. OHJ, Bayonne, NJ 07002. (201) 437-0770. Write them for the name of a distributor, or order the calcimine through Johnson Paint Co., 355 Newbury St., Dept. OHJ, Boston, MA 02115. (617) 536-4838. (Their minimum order is 25 lbs. of powder, which makes 12 to 15 quarts.)

The New York Times / Nancy Tutko

Uncovering Decorative Painting

by Julia Lichtblau

with Darla M. Olson

ARCHITECTURAL-ART CONSERVATOR

NATURE ABHORS A VACUUM and something in human nature abhors a bare expanse of wall. Along with eating, sleeping, and sex, the urge to paint decorations on walls must surely be one of mankind's most universal compulsions. From the earliest age, the sight of an unadorned wall -- be it in a cave, a cathedral, a subway train, or the living room -- makes us itch to fill it. Decorative wall paintings are found everywhere: in prehistoric caves in France, Spanish cathedrals, Tibetan monasteries, tiny roadside shrines in Italy, and on mud-walled mosques in dusty West African villages.

AMERICANS tend to assume that "the good stuff" exists only abroad, even though we have a long history of exuberantly painting buildings with folk talismans, portraits, geometric patterns, scenes, and illusory architectural details. Much of this work has been damaged or destroyed, but a substantial amount still survives -- sometimes visible, sometimes hidden by paint. If you own a pre-1920 house, especially one built between 1850 and 1900, you may have treasures waiting to be uncovered.

THIS ARTICLE will help you identify the paintings you have, and enable you to make an informed decision about what to do with them. It outlines techniques for uncovering and restoring decorative paintings, with an emphasis on paint removal and cleaning. The methods are those used by architectural-art conservator Darla M. Olson -- which puts some of them beyond the technical and artistic abilities of the amateur preservationist. But there's still a lot which you can do on your own, particularly preliminary research and discovery. And if you do decide to revive your paintings, an understanding of these techniques will help you work intelligently with a conservator.

Options

THESE RESTORATION PROCESSES are time-consuming, messy, and expensive. If there's damaged plaster, special techniques must be used to repair it without ruining the paintings. Also consider that decorated walls and ceilings can be overpowering -- they could

be a more-immutable part of your decor than you'd really care to have. But if you're game to proceed, there are several approaches to choose from:

● CLEANING & CONSERVATION: You need to clean exposed paintings and have the areas that have suffered paint loss "in-painted."

● STRIPPING & RECONSTRUCTION: Overpainting essentially destroys the paintings because they cannot be uncovered intact -- once you've stripped the later paint, you'll have to document the remnants and reconstruct the images.

● DOCUMENTATION: Through color analysis, drawings, and photos, you can create a historical record to guide future restoration. Isolated areas can be uncovered and left out for view beneath a shield of glass or plexiglass.

● COVERING UP: If restoration isn't feasible or desired, there are several ways you can protect and conceal paintings with drywall or panels. If the paintings are in good shape, they can be sealed with removable varnish and wallpaper. A drop ceiling could also be installed. (An architect can recommend an appropriate choice.)

BEFORE MAKING ANY DECISIONS, you may want to consult an architectural-painting conservator. (A college art history professor or museum conservator can also be helpful.) Your State Historic Preservation Officer (SHPO) may be able to refer you to someone. The conservator will examine the paintings (or the surfaces if they're covered), as well as any documentary evidence, and may remove a small area of overpainting. Then he or she will evaluate the condition of the paintings and estimate the documentation and restoration costs. Professional advice is essential for determining the value of the paintings.

IN AN ARCHITECT-DIRECTED RESTORATION, the conservator will probably locate the images and the areas of plaster damage on floor plans, interior elevations, and ceiling plans. If there's significant plaster damage, an architect or engineer should examine the structure; repairs must be done before anyone addresses the paintings.

Types Of Decorative Painting

STENCILLING — A design created by applying the paint to the surface through a template. A different template is used for each color. The technique produces a hard-edged image and precise repetitions.

POUNCING — A method for transferring an image onto a surface for painting. First, a drawing is made on tracing paper and the lines are pricked with a pounce wheel, which resembles a tracing wheel. The drawing is positioned on the surface, dusted with chalk, and removed, leaving a dotted-line tracing of the original to be painted in.

FREEHAND PAINTING — Work done without a pattern.

FAKE WOOD GRAINING OR MARBLEIZING — Also called "faux bois" or "faux marbre." Paint, glazes, and various methods of texturing are used to imitate wood or marble.

TROMPE L'OEIL — A painting technique that uses geometric perspective, light, and shadow to make painted images appear to be three-dimensional. Often used to simulate architectural details.

FRESCO PAINTING — Painting done on fresh, damp, lime plaster with water-based paints for which the lime acts as a binder. It is uncommon in the States, but the term is often used incorrectly to mean decorative wall painting.

This wall in Honolulu House showcases an array of decorative-painting techniques: stencilling, marbleizing, trompe l'oeil (the column is an illusion), & freehand painting.

Darla M. Olson

Research

THE FIRST STEP in restoring your paintings is historical research: if they're covered, to prove their existence and to locate them; if exposed, to learn when the paintings were done, by whom, and whether they're original or not. Documents describing local history and the history of the building (its function, original owner, etc.) may contain valuable data. Look for artists' or craftsmen's bills, letters, photographs, diaries, and newspaper articles in municipal or historical-society archives or in family records. For a big job (a mansion or public building), newspapers carried advertisements for "fresco artists."

ASK AROUND YOUR NEIGHBORHOOD. Elderly neighbors may remember your paintings before they were painted over or before the colors were "modernized." Clusters of decorative paintings sometimes exist in a given locale -- you may be able to identify the artist who did your paintings by comparing the style with others nearby. Localized economic booms encouraged such clusters: The newly wealthy often commissioned "dream houses" decorated in the height of fashion, and in the mid- to late 1800s, that meant decorative paintings.

Locating Images

AFTER RESEARCHING documentary evidence, look in the building itself. If your research has not revealed the locations of the paintings, explore areas where they were usually applied: above wainscotting, along cornice lines, in the corners and centers of ceilings. Sometimes you can slide an X-acto blade underneath blistering paint and peel away small areas. You should also look under anachronistic features, such as drop ceilings or light fixtures -- they may be hiding paintings.

OVERPAINTED IMAGES sometimes leave visible clues. Temperature differences in the paint layers can cause dirt to cling to the surface along the underlying pattern, creating a dark "ghost image" of the paintings, which usually can be seen under normal light. The extra paint thickness where a pattern has been applied over a field color can create a tiny ridge beneath the overpainting. This can be seen under "raking light": Standing two or three feet from the surface, shine a reflector-type light with a 300-watt bulb along the surface at an angle; the variations in the thicknesses may show up as shadows that trace the patterns.

Darla M. Olson

South Church, Nantucket, Mass.

Above: The pounced pattern on the tracing is dusted with chalk, leaving an image (visible at right) to be painted in.
Below: Bruce Lanehart in-paints the pounced design.

THESE VESTIGIAL IMAGES should be documented before any paint is removed. Using duct tape, cover each repeat of the ghost pattern with sheets of 5-mil acetate (available at art-supply stores). Tape the edges of the acetate so they don't tear, and trace the outlines carefully with acetate-marking pens.

DOCUMENT THE POSITION ON THE WALL of each part of the pattern as it's traced. Snap a 6-in. grid of chalk lines running the full height and width of the area to be documented, and identify them with numbers and letters like the locating grid on a map. Make corresponding marks on the acetate so it can be registered over the original spot for further documentation or re-creation. When large areas of paint are removed, leave the end points of the grid lines intact so they can be re-snapped, if necessary, to re-register the acetate.

Uncovering Paintings

OVERPAINTED IMAGES can seldom be resurrected intact, especially if the paint layers are firmly bonded together. Therefore, as each layer is removed, the patterns must be documented and paint samples taken for eventual reproduction. This is one of the trickiest processes and should definitely be left to a trained person.

A PASTE-TYPE PAINT REMOVER is usually required to remove overpainting, but mechanical methods are worth trying if the paint is chipping, extremely thick, or flaking off. This usually occurs where layers are incompatible, such as oil paint over a glaze. In that case, you may be able to "pop" it by working a sharp chisel or Number 18 X-acto chisel blade under the cracks at a shallow angle -- being careful not to scratch the substrate.

YOU CAN ALSO CHIP OFF THE PAINT by holding the chisel to the surface and gently tapping it with a small tack hammer. If the paint is thin and loose, you may be able to remove it by firmly pressing strips of duct tape on the paint and peeling it off -- in rare instances, this may leave the underlying paintings in good enough condition to be cleaned and retouched. If the overpainting is distemper, brush it off gently with very fine steel wool or sandpaper, taking care not to abrade the layer you want to save, especially if it's also distemper.

WHERE PAINT REMOVER is required, the process is a delicate one of timing and control. The materials needed for Darla's methods are:
● clear, non-flammable, heavy, paste-type paint remover (follow the safety guidelines on the label)
● a razor-blade-type scraper
● leather gloves
● goggles or a face mask
● an old pot or coffee can fitted with a handle (an old trowel handle will do)
● a 2-1/2-by-2-in., natural-bristle brush (synthetic will melt)
● a container for scrapings

FIRST DETERMINE the number of paint layers and how long each takes to melt. Hold the can of remover up to the surface and slide a layer of paste smoothly onto the wall in one direction in a swooping motion, moving the can with the brush to catch drips. Make a 2-ft.-square test patch and time each layer. The first layer often bubbles right off; scrape it into a container and reapply remover.

STUDY THE REACTIONS of the layers and note the patterns that emerge, down to the plaster. If you have distemper paintings, they were probably absorbed into the later oil and may leave only "ghost images" on the plaster or the first layer of overpainting. Darla says that once she's figured out the pattern in an area, she starts stripping a new one, "going down layer by layer, documenting as I go."

AS THE PAINTINGS start to appear, each layer must be recorded before it's stripped away. Usually the highlight colors and gilding penetrate and become visible in that first, oldest layer of overpainting. Before documenting, make sure any traces of stripper are dry. Lay the acetate over the design and trace it, noting the areas of color on the pattern. Remove the acetate, reapply stripper to expose the body of the design, scrape, and document.

MUCH DECORATIVE PAINTING consists of repeated and reversed patterns, so you don't have to keep on redocumenting the repeats as long as you've recorded where they begin. When the patterns have been traced and the colors noted, they should be redrawn on vellum, refined, and used to create stencils or pounce patterns for re-creating the paintings. Where sections have been destroyed, you may have to reinvent the design based on material appropriate to the building's period and style.

Exposed Paintings

JUST BECAUSE a painting is visible, that doesn't mean there's no work to be done. You may have to clean it, fill in cracked plaster, and/or in-paint damaged areas of the design. Paintings can be soiled from graffiti, repeated touching, old varnish, household dust, coal dust, and air pollution. Paint types and finishes determine which procedures and materials to use. But even in one building, there's no stock procedure for a given surface because of differences in the type of soil, paint chemistry, temperature, and humidity. When cleaning decorative paintings, the rule of thumb is to start with the most innocuous method and work up to stronger ones.

DISTEMPER PAINTINGS cannot be cleaned with liquid, nor do they withstand abrasion well. Test for distemper by rubbing a small, inconspicuous spot with a moistened finger -- if color comes off, it's distemper. Following the principle of Most Innocuous First, begin by vacuuming the surface <u>very</u> <u>lightly</u> with a soft-bristle-brush attachment.

NEXT, in a 1-ft.-square test area, determine how embedded the soil is by gently rubbing the paintings with green Eberhard erasers or the dry-cleaning pads that architects use to clean drawings (little cloth bags filled with a slightly gritty powder that picks up dirt -- available from art or drafting supply stores). As you work, keep checking the paintings for signs of abrasion. Repeat this procedure over the entire surface.

AS YOU CLEAN, you may find previous attempts to restore the paintings. If that overpainting was done badly or used incompatible paint, you'll probably need to scrape or strip those sections and in-paint with distemper.

Cleaning Matte-Oil Finishes

MATTE-OIL FINISHES are also hard to clean because they're porous and absorb dirt easily. But they can be cleaned with liquids and are more resistant to abrasion than distemper. Proceed as with distemper, starting with a soft brush or a vacuum cleaner, followed by dry-cleaning pads and erasers. Areas with complicated glazes, delicate brushwork, and metallic leafing are easily abraded and so require a light touch. Do as much as possible using the dry method.

IF THESE TACTICS DON'T WORK, begin testing the following series of liquid cleansers <u>in the order</u> listed:
● vinegar and hot water (1 cup/1 gallon)
● Soilax and water (1 oz./1 gallon)
● Murphy's Oil Soap and water (as indicated on label)
● concentrated Soilax solution (1 tbsp. Soilax /1 cup water)

Malcolm Krostue

A bad touch-up can be worse than no repair at all, as you can see from the peeling paint and unmatching colors in this photo.

● non-sudsy, clear ammonia or (in a pinch -- this is very dangerous to use) stronger ammonia and water (a few drops to a cup)

TEST IN 1-FT.-SQUARE PATCHES in different parts of the paintings. Patterned areas, field areas, and certain colors may all react differently -- cleaning methods that work in one area may not work in others. <u>Do as much as you can with the mildest method before going to the next.</u>

THE PROCEDURE FOR EACH CLEANSER is basically the same. Prepare three containers: a bucket of solution for refills (except when using the stronger ammonia -- a cupful is dangerous enough, to both the paintings and your lungs); a smaller container to work from; a third for rinse water. Always wear gloves and goggles (and for ceiling work, a face mask). Saturate a natural sponge or the finest grade steel wool in the solution, squeeze out the excess, and apply it gently (no scrubbing) to a 4- to 6-in.-square area. Clean the wall from the bottom up, and wipe off drips immediately with a damp, clean sponge. Usually, matte surfaces have to be cleaned twice.

IF SOIL is firmly bound into the paint, the last resort is a poultice of lime and plaster of paris (photo on the next page). The alkali in the plaster actually disintegrates a microscopic layer of paint that holds much of the soil. It's very effective but can also strip the paintings.

TO MAKE THE POULTICE, mix <u>dry</u> equal portions of regular plaster of paris and Ivoryclad Hydrated Finishing Lime. Sift into a bucket of water until the water can't absorb anymore; stir until smooth. Using a small (1-1/2-in.-by-4-in.) finishing trowel, apply 1/8- to 1/4-in.-thick test patches, in 1-1/2-in. squares, on different areas of the paintings. Time the plaster's reaction periods -- it usually takes around 45 to 60 minutes to lift the soil off the painting. But you must test each wall because plaster reacts differently on walls of different temperature and humidity (drying more slowly on an outside wall than an inside wall, for example). Don't leave it on beyond the tested time.

A plaster poultice is used to rescue the trompe l'oeil frieze border in one room of Connecticut's Lockwood-Matthews Mansion (Richard Bergmann, Restoration Architect). Louise Stoltz is applying the poultice. (Note the already-cleaned section of border to her right.)

Darla Olson removes the poultice — the surface seems as dirty as before, but . . .

. . . as Darla washes down the area with a hot-water-and-vinegar solution, the frieze returns to elegant life.

AFTER TESTING reaction times, apply plaster in small sections along a moulding or pattern area, leaving slits for inserting a trowel to break off the plaster. Plaster sets fast, so it's best to do this with two or three people: one to mix small batches of plaster and one or two to apply it. When you remove the plaster, be careful not to gouge the paintings with the trowel. In dryer areas, the plaster may fall off by itself. When it does, the paintings will still look dirty, but they'll come clean when washed with hot water and vinegar. This process blanches the surface, but after cleaning, plaster repair, and in-painting, the colors are varnished and become fully saturated again. This technique works best on busy pattern areas; the cracks between plaster patches leave unsightly lines of dirt on field areas.

Cleaning Glazed Oil Paintings

GLAZED OIL PAINTINGS are coated with varnish that may have yellowed over the years and become impregnated with soil. When cleaning them, you want to loosen the dirty layer with a solvent -- totally stripping the varnish removes the patina with it.

TRY THESE SOLVENTS in the order listed:
● pure mineral spirits (paint thinner)
● acetone and paint thinner (3/2)
● denatured alcohol and water (1/1)
● denatured alcohol, turpentine, and acetone (5/3/1/)

MIX EACH SOLUTION in a gallon can or jar, but work from a tuna can. Apply solvents with non-sterile household cotton. Soak a small wad of cotton in the solvent and wring out the excess. Working in 4- to 6-in. squares, rub the varnish in a circular motion. Keep turning the cotton inside out to get a clean surface, and check it frequently for color -- a sign that the varnish has been stripped. The solvents will blanch the paintings, but this disappears once fresh varnish is applied.

CAUTION: These solvents are volatile, flammable, and toxic. Make sure the space is well ventilated. Darla recommends wearing goggles, a toxic-fumes respirator, and two pairs of rubber gloves. The discarded cotton is a real fire hazard (spontaneous combustion); throw it in a covered container and remove it immediately to the outdoors after each work session.

Surface Preparation

IF YOU'RE VERY FORTUNATE, your newly cleaned paintings will need only light touch-ups and a coat of protective varnish. Even so, there will probably be small cracks in the plaster, 1/32 to 1/16 inch wide (wider ones are repaired before cleaning). These should be scraped out, filled, and in-painted to match. (Hairline cracks don't need filling.) Widen them a little by inserting a #18 X-acto chisel blade into the crack and tapping it lightly with a tack hammer. Rake out the loose

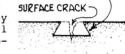

plaster underneath with the the blade or the point of a can opener, slightly undercutting the crack in an inverted "V."

USING A STANDARD MIX of slaked lime and plaster, fill in and smooth the crack following traditional plastering techniques. Take care not to let plaster sit on the adjacent paintings. Let it dry for several weeks. Test for dryness by striking a wooden match on the plaster -- if it's too damp, the match won't light. The plaster will shrink slightly, to about the depth of a paint layer. Level it with a thin layer of drywall compound applied with a palette knife; allow to dry overnight; and sand lightly without scratching the adjacent paintings.

In-Painting

BEFORE IN-PAINTING, paint the plaster with a penetrating oil-based primer/sealer that accepts acrylic emulsion. (Acrylics are preferable to oils for in-painting oil paintings because the colors are stable.) First, test the primer for adhesion by sticking a layer of duct tape to it and peeling it off after one hour. If more than a few flakes come off with it, the primer hasn't penetrated and must be stripped; the plaster may be wet, dirty, or greasy.

ONCE THE PAINTINGS ARE CLEANED, the colors can be matched. Always match colors under natural light or 3400-K photographic floodlights. Match a swatch of dry varnished acrylic emulsion to an area of dry varnished original. Determining the original colors of oil paint can be difficult, because they darken considerably when covered for long periods. Before matching, try bringing them back to their original brightness by exposing them to ultraviolet light from the sun or a UV lamp.

DISTEMPER COLORS that have been overpainted are difficult to restore accurately, because they'll have been distorted by the overlying paint's moisture -- and usually will have absorbed some of its color, too. But it's often possible to find little pockets of fresh color which are locked into porous areas of plaster. Once examined under a microscope, they can be matched easily. If the distemper wasn't overpainted, you can scrape away a patch of its surface to reveal a fresher color.

SAMPLES OF FRESH COLOR should be preserved as a permanent record of the original condition of the paintings; match them with Munsell System colors, and code them accordingly. The Munsell Color System is a universal system for documenting color; it's used by artists, architects, conservators, printers, and others who need a fixed, non-subjective color-reference system. Getting an exact match may be difficult, but a close Munsell match is still the best reference for recording purposes.

SAYS DARLA, "Color is difficult to determine because it is the nature of materials to constantly change. Realistically, the best you can do is create a very close interpretation. It is important not to rely exclusively on microscopic analysis to determine the original color scheme. You need to understand the artist's color concept to replicate what he did. Perhaps he used a cheaper color to cover a large area, saving the expensive color for the final coat. Or maybe he painted an undercoat of one color to give a certain character to

Dirty glaze is removed from a decorative painting in Michigan's Honolulu House (Hasbrouck Hunderman, Restoration Arch.).

The surface has been cleaned, the bad overpainting removed, and the plaster patched. Now the in-painting can begin.

the overpainting. It takes a combination of microscopic analysis, paint removal, and an artist's intuition."

AFTER DETERMINING the color scheme, the base or field coat is applied. The pattern is registered and transferred to the plaster; missing sections of the design are in-painted. With oil paintings, the final touch is to take a wide, soft brush and varnish with two coats of matte Soluvar (never polyurethane!), thinned with an equal part of mineral spirits. 🏛

New York-based architectural-art conservator Darla M. Olson has restored painted interiors throughout the U.S. Her projects include Wheeler Opera House (Aspen, Colo.), Ebenezer Maxwell House (Philadelphia, Pa.), Lockwood-Matthews Mansion (Norwalk, Conn.), South Church (Nantucket, Mass.). Her work has been featured in the New York Times, Architectural Record, and other periodicals.

Malcolm Krostue

POST-VICTORIAN HOUSES

PAINTING ADVICE from THE CRAFTSMAN

BETWEEN 1901 and 1916, a man named Gustav Stickley published a magazine entitled The Craftsman. In it he promoted a vision of how people should live: close to nature, untroubled by the frivolous trappings of commercial society, in houses made of natural materials and filled with handmade goods. Through house plans and articles on decorating, Stickley rigidly defined what should and shouldn't be in the ideal home. He was a tyrannical arbiter of taste; even so, his popularity was enormous. Craftsman philosophy and design affected almost every home built from the turn of the century through the 1920s. This article deals with some of Stickley's suggestions (more like commands) regarding painting.

STICKLEY MADE FEW compromises applying his philosophy, and using paint usually wasn't one of them. He considered paint an artifice that concealed the true nature of the material underneath. It seems he had trouble even uttering the word, using "tint" or "tone" instead.

This simple bedroom, designed for a bungalow, has intentionally mottled plaster framed by dark timbers.

NEVERTHELESS PAINT IS mentioned, albeit subtly, in many of his essays and descriptions. Its use was limited -- but could be dramatic, as in the murals that filled Craftsman friezes, or the earthy color schemes Stickley and friends advise.

A WORD ON THE EXTERIOR

CRAFTSMAN HOUSES MADE of rough stone and weathered shingles left little room for paint. Stucco could sometimes be "tinted"; it's not clear whether Stickley means with stain or paint, "brushed on irregularly, giving a general tone of green that yet is not a smooth color." Shutters, too, could be painted, sometimes in a different color on each storey of the house. Beams that decorated the exterior of a shingled house (see illustration, facing page) could be highlighted with cream-colored paint; this was not dishonest, in Stickley's view, because it served to accent the underlying structure.

PAINT WAS ALSO THE BEST option for coloring roof shingles deep red; in this case, Stickley says, stains are insufficient. And white paint appears on the classical posts that frequently support Craftsman porches or pergolas. This was rationalized as a way to emphasize the dark, natural woodwork behind the posts.

AND ON THE INTERIOR

STICKLEY LAID DOWN several strict decorating commandments. One: Never paint woodwork, lest its "friendliness" be destroyed by some "foreign color." Two: Bring art and nature into the home, especially in the form of stencils and murals. "Let us call in the artist, bid him leave his easel pictures, and paint on our walls and over the chimney corner landscapes and scenes ... which shall speak of nature ..., shall become part of the room." And three: Don't succumb to the vagaries of fashion. "Let us have rooms which once deco-

Two permissible uses of paint on Crafts-man house exteriors were decorative beams (above — a cream accent was recommended), and classically-inspired porch posts (right), painted pure white.

rated are always decorated...." The goal was to create a retreat, where the artwork was permanent and would never need "updating."

STICKLEY'S APPROACH to decorating was holis-tic, and began with the woodwork. To keep the decor harmonious, the plentiful woodwork had to determine the color scheme, simply because there was so much of it (wainscotting, built-in furniture, grilles, etcetera), and also be-cause of its near-religious significance in Craftsman philosophy. For example, if the woodwork were oak (Stickley was fond of this material because it ages well, which suits a house that will be decorated only once), it should be finished in a "rich nut-brown," which gives a "mellow sunny effect to the whole decorative scheme." Above that the plaster frieze would be done in a "warm tawny yellow," and from there the rest of the house's decorating scheme would follow.

OTHER PLASTER COLOR options included muted shades such as "dull green," gray, or biscuit, on rough- or sand-finished surfaces. The sug-gested method for applying these tones was to either leave the plaster in its natural state of gray (recommended almost invariably for ceilings), or treat it "with a coat of shellac or wax that carries the color desired," or "color" the surface (still no mention of the word paint) while it is still wet, "with a large flat brush, a process which incorporates the color in the plaster and gives it an agreeable texture, by reason of the markings make (sic) by the brush; the result being a beautiful tint of the color employed, free from the painty look so often seen in colored walls, and making the observer question the material." (Of course most homeowners won't have an opportunity to paint the plaster while it's fresh, unless you're replastering. Take comfort in knowing that, then as now, color was un-doubtedly more often applied to dry plaster.) A mottled effect was intentional. The Craftsman ideal when finishing either wood or plaster was to have them look exactly like what they were.

WHEN IT CAME TO PAINTING friezes, the Craftsmanite had freer reign. Stencils and mu-rals ranged in scope from repeating bands of simple, geometric, stylized flowers, to elaborate forest panoramas. Natural forms invariably pro-vided the subject matter.

ACCESSORIES PLAYED a central role in The Craftsman's uni-fied decorative schemes. Everything had to be coordi-nated: Rugs and curtains, for instance, repeated the pat-terns of the stained glass or of the stencils; these were pieces designed for the indi-vidual house and meant to re-main there. A whole room's tones could be based on one Japanese print (in harmony with the woodwork, of course).

There's clearly little need for paint here: Woodwork is natural, walls are covered in grasscloth or colored plaster, and the ceiling is unpainted plaster. The one use of paint — the mural in the frieze — steals the show.

Or a single choice "object" could balance a color scheme: If it "presents, by way of foil, its own complementary color," it prevents a room from becoming "dead and uninteresting."

THE WHOLE FIRST FLOOR was meant to be coordinated -- something else to keep in mind when choosing paint colors and placement. Often in Stickley's plans, halls and living and dining areas flow into one another. Ideally the three areas would have the same kind of woodwork, and in them the decorator would "treat the upper walls ... alike, as the object is to give a sense of space, dignity, and restfulness to the part of the house that is most lived in."

THE LIVING ROOM AND HALLWAY

THE CRAFTSMAN DESCRIBED in detail one exemplary home. Its living room had a fireplace tiled in blue-green tiles of varying shade, a

Though he told readers never to paint woodwork, Stickley was not unwilling to compromise on the bedroom walls.

hearth of dark red brick, woodwork fumed to a rich brown, walls tinted a "pale, sappy green," and the leather of the built-in seats and bookcase dyed a pale golden yellow. The floors were yellow, and the ceiling, of course, the gray of plaster. An open mesh linen hanging enlivened the "somewhat quiet scheme of color," a piece designed especially for this room. A Donegal rug and bookcase curtains repeated the main colors of the room; they too were intended to be permanent. Pictures on the walls were avoided, considered "superfluous and discordant."

THE HALLWAY "calls for a cheerful treatment that shall give a presage of the hospitality to be found beyond." Golden tones, "from a full dark orange to a pale lemon yellow," prevailed, and would be "contrasted at the extreme end of the hall by some object of pottery, or a fabric of a dull violet." The only other decorations were Japanese prints framed in dull ebony, "of a good period and by approved masters, hung at irregular intervals and heights."

THE DINING ROOM

"THE DINING ROOM, being used [only] at special periods, admits of a trifle stronger and more brilliant treatment. Here, the walls are a strong golden yellow, the ceiling the gray of the plaster, and the woodwork a rich olive green" [ed.'s note: this is probably stain and not paint]; "the visible wall in the alcove for the

The woodwork is stained light brown, the frieze is tawny yellow (ochre). The stencilled motif consists of white ribbons with deep green accents. Walls are mauve trimmed in sage green bands. The ceiling is pale gray, unpainted plaster, and the rugs and fireplace have subtle green backgrounds. The floor is dark, almost black.

sideboard is a dark, dull Indian red, and the floor a golden yellow, with a large moss-green rug in the center. Extending about the room is a small pseudo-frieze, which has for its color a bright Venetian red. The windows are hung with a fabric akin to India silk, whose color is, largely, a creamy white, old rose, and gold. The leaded window over the sideboard is framed with broad bands of blackened copper; while the martins in the designs are of a dark gray blue, with circles or halos about their heads of a bright yellow, and all against a background of cloudy, milk-colored opaque glass," with streaks of dull turquoise.

THE KITCHEN AND BATH

THE KITCHEN, "being one of the warmest rooms in the house," should have a color scheme "suggestive of coolness." The tiles lining the floor, of rubber or cement, should be in blues and greens and rise to form wainscot-

ting. The wallpaper above should be greenish gray, with a pale lemon yellow ceiling; all this "will remove from the kitchen its usual ugly and neglected appearance."

THE CRAFTSMAN CHOICE of bathroom colors will probably surprise the modern reader: yellow and red. "It is especially desired that the frigid white and blue decorations of the ordinary bathroom be avoided. If there is any one place in the house that should look as well as be comfortable, it is the bathroom."

THE BEDROOMS

THE DECORATION OF the bedrooms would depend upon how much sunlight they get. Northern rooms, presumably the cooler ones, "would seem to demand a coloration of yellows and orange, or reds and orange," and those on the south "schemes of green and blues." In a house Stickley designed and built at Craftsman Farms in 1911, there were two bedrooms, at opposite ends of the house: "One of them is furnished and decorated in yellow and seems aglow with sunshine; the other, a much larger room, is done in blue and gray with woodwork of dark gumwood. The walls are covered with gray Japanese grass-cloth, the hearth is of dull blue Grueby tiles with a brass hood, and the furniture is gray oak."

With its tile, wallpaper, and built-in cupboards, the kitchen called for paint only on its ceiling — a cheery yellow was suggested.

Checklist for Painting

ALTHOUGH LEVELS OF SKILL vary, everyone has some sense of how to paint. A novice painter can apply a smooth, lasting finish on a <u>well-prepared surface</u>, but even the most experienced painter can't do a <u>good</u> job on an inadequately-prepared one. Surface preparation is 90% of the job.

THIS CHECKLIST IS a guide to good preparation. An experienced restorer may find much of this list to be second-nature, by now. But no matter how many times you've prepared surfaces for painting, it helps to have a list of all the considerations involved -- just to make sure you didn't overlook anything. If you're going to hire a contractor to do the job, this will enable you to discuss the job. What we're presenting here is essentially a set of job specifications, written in layman's language.

by Jonathan Poore & Bill O'Donnell

g. Staining from knots, water, rust, etc.
h. Faded color
2. Open joints -- unsightly on the interior, and destructive on your building's exterior (permit water to enter)

C. LOOK FOR UNDERLYING PROBLEMS AND MISCELLANEOUS REPAIRS.

1. Moisture problems --
a. Rising damp
b. Leaking roof or gutters
c. Deteriorated flashing
d. Mold or mildew
e. Plumbing leaks
2. Carpentry repairs --
a. Doors and windows in proper working order
b. Miscellaneous carpentry (damaged or missing components, open joints, etc.)

I. Inspection

DON'T RUSH into a major project; look the job over carefully. A close inspection helps you decide whether to do the job yourself or hire it out, how long the job will take, and how much it will cost.

A. DON'T COMPLETELY REPAINT WHEN:

1. The existing paint is intact, but dirty. A thorough cleaning will freshen its appearance without adding unnecessary paint layers.
2. Cleaning and minor touch-ups will revive the finish. If the paint hasn't faded significantly, it will be fairly

easy to match the color and just touch-up where needed.
3. It would be more appropriate to strip the surface of existing paint. For example, hardwood trim with insensitive layers of paint, masonry that has only a few flecks of paint remaining, etc.

B. CONSIDER REPAINTING THE SURFACE (AFTER REPAIRS ARE MADE) WHEN YOU FIND:

1. Paint failure --
a. Flaking and peeling
b. Intercoat peeling
c. Cracking and alligatoring
d. Efflorescence
e. Chalking and streaking (check for interior calcimine)
f. Thick buildup that obscures detail

II. Planning

YOUR INSPECTION may have shown that painting should be postponed until repairs or reconstruction are completed. Now, devise a realistic plan, considering such things as:

A. TIMELINE:

1. If repairs and preparation are extensive, plan to do the work in phases. Will you do all the preparation, then all the painting? Or will you work on one room (or one side of the exterior) from start to finish? Determine logical breaks.
2. Do <u>not</u> leave any exterior surfaces bare -- prime even if finish painting has to wait.
3. If work will be contracted out, determine order so that tradespeople don't conflict. (The electricians should finish before the plasterers begin, for example.)

B. FINISH SYSTEM. WILL YOU USE:

1. Paint? -- No need to remove previous coatings if sound.
2. Stain? (semi-transparent or opaque) -- Previous paint layers must be totally removed.

Paint applied over obvious problems will fail again — unless inspection reveals the cause to be corrected first.

3. Canvas or wallcoverings?
-- Surface must be sound, but needn't be perfect. Consider time and skill necessary to install wallcovering.

C. ACCESS TO JOB. WILL YOU NEED:

1. Step ladder or extension ladders?
2. Ladder jacks?
3. Scaffolding?

D. DO-IT-YOURSELF VS. HIRING.

1. With what you know of scope of job, is it feasible to do it yourself?
2. If budget is low, you may have thought it would be cheaper to do the work yourself. But if work requires special tools/materials that you don't own, cost of these objects must be factored in.
3. Consider dividing job into d-i-y and contracted phases. Doing some phase of work yourself may save money or assure you of painstaking work where it counts.
4. Don't forget: "Time is money." Your time has value, too. If you're not as well equipped or experienced as a contractor, it will likely, take you much longer to do the same amount of work. Mistakes are expensive on large projects.

III. Setting Up

EITHER YOU or the contractor should first:

A. REMOVE ALL OBSTRUCTIONS:

1. Furnishings
2. Easily dismantled hardware or trim (light fixtures, wall plates, shutters, etc.)
3. Trim trees and shrubs so that they don't contact building. Tie back untrimmed vegetation for easy access and safety.
4. Remove vines and abandoned utility wires from the exterior. (Be sure the utility wires are in fact abandoned.)

B. PROTECT AND MASK:

1. Cover floors with kraft paper and/or dropcloths.
2. Cover pavement and ground with dropcloths.

3. Wrap remaining hardware and fixtures with kraft paper or plastic and tape securely.
4. Mask small pieces of hardware (like door hinges) with masking tape.
5. Protect adjacent surfaces not to be painted as needed. (See "Masking Before Painting," page 175.)
6. Cover nearby shrubs only as long as required.
7. Take additional care when masking area where paint will be mixed and poured.

C. CLEAN IT FIRST. CLEANING SURFACE IMPROVES PAINT ADHESION. PROCEDURE FOR:

1. Dirt -- Vacuum and wipe down with clear water on interior surfaces. Use a low-pressure water stream on the exterior -- pay careful attention to protected areas where rainwater doesn't cleanse. Stubborn areas may require mild detergent or ammonia added to wash water. Rinse with clear water. Don't use detergent on bare wood -- it may get trapped in open pores and interfere with paint adhesion.
2. Chalking -- Scrub with mild detergent and a stiff-bristle brush. Avoid "self-cleaning" and low-quality paints to prevent recurrence. For interior chalking, check for presence of calcimine paint. Wash clean if detected.

3. Mold and Mildew -- Use 50/50 mixture of bleach and warm water to kill fungi. Scrub the areas with a scrub brush and water (a little TSP -- tri-sodium phosphate -- speeds the cleanup). Determine cause of excess moisture and remedy as required to prevent recurrence.
4. Grease -- Scrub with detergent and warm water. If stain is stubborn (like crayon), cover with pigmented shellac before painting.
5. Oily residues on new galvanized metal -- Scrub off with TSP and water.
6. Efflorescence -- Wire-brush masonry to remove salts and loose paint. Correct moisture problem before repainting.

D. SCRAPE AND/OR STRIP:

1. Flaking, peeling or blistering paint. Scrape down to sound substrate, determine cause of failure, and remedy moisture conditions. Prime bare wood before repainting. Solve exterior moisture problems (leaky gutters, etc.). Exterior peeling or blistering may be caused by water migrating from interior. Ventilate high-humidity areas (kitchens and baths), and install a vapor barrier. Severe exterior paint buildup aggravates problem -- strip excessive paint layers.

Here, alligatored paint has failed down to bare wood, exposing the clapboard to weathering.

2. Excessive paint buildup that obscures architectural detail or shows signs of alligatoring. Adding another coat of paint to an alligatored surface will only compound the problem. Strip the existing paint, prime, and repaint.

E. REMOVE UNNECESSARY LAYERS:

1. Wallpaper should be removed before painting (especially with latex; water-based paint will loosen bond to wall). Vinyl wallcoverings can usually be pulled off. Most paper wallcoverings will succumb to hot water. Stubborn ones may require steaming. Thoroughly rinse size and paste residue, and prime with an oil/alkyd sealer or pigmented shellac before painting with latex.

2. Tapes, stickers and miscellaneous adhesives. Most are water-soluble and come off much like wallpaper. For others, test with mineral spirits or acetone. Acetone works well on bubble-gum.

3. Roofing tar will bleed through new finish and cause wrinkling and crazing of new coating. Scrape off as much as possible. Dry ice will embrittle it, making it easier to knock off. Scrub residue with mineral spirits.

F. REPAIRS:

1. Repair windows and doors so they are fully functional. Allow enough clearance between moving parts for paint-film thickness. Selectively strip areas of excessive buildup. Prime exposed wood on sash before reglazing.

2. Consolidate, patch, or replace all rotted or missing wood. Back-prime all exposed wood before installing new parts.

3. Back-prime all new galvanized sheet metal patches before installing.

4. Allow a minimum of 30 days before painting newly repointed or refaced masonry. Neutralize with dilute muriatic acid before painting.

5. Allow a minimum of 30 days before painting new plasterwork. Non-alkaline patching materials (like joint compound) may be painted immediately.

G. SANDING, FILLING, AND CAULKING:

1. Sand all glossy surfaces before painting. Wet-sand where a fine finish is important or dust is objectionable.

2. Prepare severely weathered wood before painting.
   a. Sand weathered wood.

b. Formula for bare, weathered wood: Mixture of boiled linseed oil and paint thinner brushed on in two or three applications (allow 24 hours between coats). Let dry for three days and prime with oil/alkyd sealer.

c. A WR (water repellent) or WRP (water repellent preservative) can be applied to bare, weathered wood on horizontal surfaces. (Sand <u>before</u> application.) Allow to dry thoroughly, and use compatible primer.

d. Rotted wood should be replaced with standard carpentry repairs. Minor rot or weathering can be consolidated and/or filled with exterior epoxies.

Inspection just might reveal the need for repairs that take precedence over painting.

3. Sand (feather) pocked areas where failed paint has been removed.

4. Knock bumps and pimples off plaster or existing finish with sharp paint scraper.

5. Remove all sanding dust and residue before painting.

6. Fill all open knots and nail holes (rigid fillers may be used only in masonry and plaster).

7. Exterior caulking:
   a. Caulk all cracks and joints where there is potential water penetration.
   b. Pack all joints wider than 1/4 inch with backer rods before caulking.
   c. Seal with paintable urethane caulk after priming.
   d. Apply silicone caulks after application of finish coats -- choose appropriate tint.
   e. Leave joints in protected areas open for ventilation of cavity wall (e.g., under clapboards).

8. Interior caulking:
   a. Caulk with paintable urethane or acrylic latex caulk after priming.
   b. Caulk all open joints -- especially around windows, doors, and other through-wall fittings which allow air infiltration.

Weathering is worst on exposed horizontal surfaces. This rail must be scraped, treated with a water repellent, and primed before painting.

IV. Application

A. TOOLS:

1. Brushes -- The most versatile paint-application tools. Buy high-quality brushes suited to the job. (See "Paintbrushes," page 171.) Use a paintbrush for:
   a. Trim, windows, and doors
   b. Corners and edges
   c. Clapboards
   d. Cutting in to adjacent surfaces

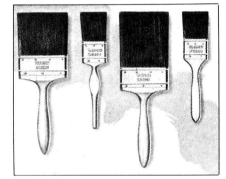

2. Rollers -- Best for covering a broad, flat area. Rollers produce a consistant textured finish, but this is not objectionable to most. Use a roller for:
   a. Ceilings and walls
   b. Brick, stucco, and other masonry (use a long nap roller)
3. Sprayers -- Fastest and best method for areas where brushing is likely to cause dripping and pooling. Sprayers should not be used for applying primer (the primer won't penetrate or adhere as well as it would with brushing or rolling). Consider using a sprayer for:
   a. Turnings or balusters
   b. Elaborate trim
   c. Radiators
   d. Shutters
   e. Single finish-coat application over a large area (there's only one cleanup)
4. Foam pads -- Nearly useless for all but the thinnest (most fluid) coatings. We have found them useful for applying penetrating-oil finishes (the oil runs out of a brush too fast).

B. PRIMING AND SEALING:

1. Spot-prime all bare wood, metal, and masonry before caulking and applying top coat(s).
2. When paint system is being changed (say, oil to latex), prime all surfaces. Use same brand of paint for primer and top coat(s).
3. Seal knots, water stains, and greasy or waxy stains with pigmented shellac (inside) or exterior-grade knot sealer before priming.
4. All surfaces previously covered with wall coverings, calcimine, or other water-soluble material must be primed with alkyd primer or pigmented shellac.

C. FINISH COAT(S):

1. Apply only one finish coat if paint buildup is a problem.
2. Selectively apply two finish coats to exterior surfaces where severe weathering is a problem.
3. Apply one finish coat to well-prepared interior surfaces unless coverage is a problem (as when going from a dark to light color).
4. Interior painting sequence:
   a. Ceiling
   b. Walls
   c. Windows (scrape old paint from glass before painting.
      (1) Mating surfaces of meeting rail
      (2) Muntins
      (3) Sash
      (4) Jamb
      (5) Trim
   d. Doors
      (1) Panel mouldings
      (2) Panels
      (3) Rails and stiles
   e. Baseboard and miscellaneous trim
5. Exterior painting sequence:
   a. Body (starting at top)
   b. Windows (same as above)
   c. Additional trim
   d. Doors (same as above)

D. TOUCH-UPS:

1. Selective touch-ups may be used instead of complete recoating when coverage is thin in some areas.
2. Large, flat interior surfaces with a semi-gloss or gloss finish cannot be touched up without becoming conspicuous -- recoat.

V. Cleanup

A. CLEANUP:

1. Clean all painting tools immediately with appropriate solvent.
2. Unmask immediately after paint is dry to prevent damaging surfaces with tape.
3. Clean tape residue with mineral spirits or acetone.
4. Remove drips and splatters before they harden.
5. Seal and label leftover paint (especially custom colors) for future touch-ups.

B. MAINTENANCE:

1. Inspect exterior annually. Look for moisture problems, clogged gutters, overgrown vegetation, etc.
2. Clean exterior annually, paying special attention to protected areas that collect dirt. Kill mold and mildew as soon as it appears.
3. Wash interior finishes as required. On flat-finish surfaces, vacuum rather than wash. (Washing may smear dirt into finish.)

Scraping and painting in Salt Lake City.

Restoration Products

Reviewed by Larry Jones

PAINTING TOOLS & SERVICES

Oval & Round Brushes

We first discovered Epifanes' outstanding line of Omega brushes at a wooden-boat show. These traditionally designed Italian brushes are made from natural, 100% black China bristle (each hair is split to produce the greatest softness). The bristles are hand set in vulcanized hard rubber, a process most brush manufacturers abandoned long ago for quicker and cheaper methods. Vulcanizing assures the longest possible brush life with minimal loss of bristles.

All Epifanes brushes come with quality, nickel-plated ferrules securely fastened to beautifully made, traditional hardwood handles. The brushes come in round, oval, and full (elliptical) shaped heels. The round brushes hold the most paint because of their volume of bristles. They come in 11 sizes from the #10 (3/8 inch, $8.45) to the #50 (2 inches, $33.70). The oval brushes release coatings more slowly, making them ideal for applying varnishes. These come in five sizes, from the #30 (1 inch, $10.30) to the #50 (2 inch, $33.70). The elliptical brushes resemble flat brushes except they have rounded edges for better control. These also come in five sizes, from the #50 (1-1/2 inch, $20.85) to the #75 (3 inch, $38.50). All of the brushes can be used with oil-based paints and varnishes.

If you haven't used one of these shapes of brushes before, you're in for a pleasant surprise: Not only do these shapes allow the brushes to hold the most paint, but they also improve the flow and control along edges. For more information contact Coastal Trade, Inc., Dept. OHJ, 601 S. Andrews Ave., Ft. Lauderdale, FL 33301. (305) 467-8325.

American Brush Co.

The American Brush Company of Claremont, New Hampshire, is one of the nation's largest makers of paintbrushes. They produce a variety of professional and consumer paintbrushes in five categories: Pro Edge, Worksaver, Timesaver, Odd Jobbers, and One Timers. Their Pro Edge brushes are hand-crafted with a choice of 100% Chinese double-boiled bristles, 100% tapered Tynex nylon filaments, or a blend of tapered Tynex nylon and tapered polyester filaments. The bristles are epoxy set with nickel ferrules, hand-formed chisel edges, sanded European hardwood handles, and uniform taper.

The Worksaver and Timesaver brush lines are machine-made tools designed for homeowner use. These high-quality tools, also with hardwood handles and epoxy-set bristles, offer the same bristle and filament options as the Pro Edge line and have similar painting characteristics. They come with a detailed sliding chart that explains how to clean them. Timesaver brushes are designed to be fully loaded with paint; they have a removable foam collar at the ferrule to keep paint from dripping or running down the handle.

For the name of a distributor near you, contact the American Brush Co., Dept. OHJ, Wellesley Office Park, 60 William St., Wellesley, MA 02181. (617) 235-5088.

Historic-Paint Research

Interesting facts about the history of every old house are recorded in its paint layers -- rich and varied paint-color schemes, fine varnishing, marbleizing, wood graining, decorative stencils, and even murals could be buried under the coats of paint on your old house. One of the best people for helping you uncover some of these mysteries is historic-paint-specialist Matthew Mosca. Using microscopic techniques and chemical analysis, Matt can determine original colors and finishes of the interior or exterior of a building, despite the changes wrought by age and the exposure to soiling and weather.

Matt has worked on projects for the Smithsonian Institute and the National Trust for Historic Preservation; recently, he's completed a project at Mt. Vernon, George Washington's Virginia home. But he's eager to work with homeowners and architects on more modest projects. He'll even show you how to carefully take samples yourself, which can then be mailed to him for examination. He charges $75 per sample (3-sample minimum) and will supply you with an accurate determination of the original finish and one later finish. Write describing your project and needs to Matthew J. Mosca, Dept. OHJ, 10 S. Gilmore St., Baltimore, MD 21223. (301) 566-9047.

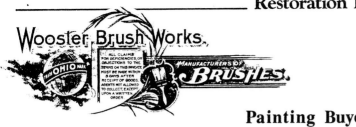

Founded in 1851, the Wooster
Brush Works is one of the
nation's oldest and largest
paintbrush manufacturers.
They offer a wide line of professional and consumer grade
brushes and other paint applicators. For all types of
paints and varnishes, they
sell Magikoter Professional
Brushes, available in nylon,
polyester, and nylon/polyester
combination. The
nylon/polyester Wooster-Pro
are handmade, professional
brushes with extra-fine
filaments for very smooth
finishes. Wooster invented
the Exploded-Tip filament
which gives their Super/Pro
brushes good paint pick-up and
release with fewer brushmarks.

Wooster's Black China and
White China bristle brushes
are a favorite for oil-based
coatings and varnish. Some of
the brushes in this line, such
as the White Semi-Oval Varnish
brush, haven't changed design
for over 50 years. For laying
on mirror-smooth, oil-based
coatings and varnish, they
make Brown Bristle/Ox brushes.
For a free catalog and a list
of dealers in your area, write
the Wooster Brush Co., Dept.
OHJ, P.O. Box B, Wooster, OH
44691. (216) 264-4440.

Painting Buyer's Guide

In September 1985, American
Painting Contractor Magazine
published their First Annual
Buyers' Guide which lists over
700 manufacturers and suppliers. It's become one of the
handiest catalogs in our
library. It lists not only
paints and coatings of all
kinds, plus all the tools and
equipment for applying them,
but also all the firms who
make these products. Of
course we would have liked a
listing of firms who offer
historic paint colors (perhaps
next year!). Single copies of
the guide are $2.50.

Other publications include:
Diagnosing Paint Problems and
Correcting Them ($4.75);
Refinishing Wood Furniture for
Profit ($4.75); Hanging Modern
Wallcoverings ($4.75); No
Molasses In The Wheat Paste, a
guide for professional and
amateur students of wallcover-
ing installation ($8.95). Add
$1.50 postage for all book or-
ders. American Paint Journal,
Book-Dept. OHJ, 2911 Washing-
ton Ave., St. Louis, MO 63103.
(314) 534-0301.

Historical Colors

Kyanize Paints has a Historical Color Collection consisting
of 72 colors, of which 36 are
listed Early American and 36
Victorian. They have fun
names, too, like Canal Boat
Red, Toll House Green, Charle-
ston Cream, and Alamo. The
Historical Color Collection
comes in both interior and
exterior grades of acrylic
latex, oil-based, and alkyd
enamel. Grant Doherty of
Kyanize spent over two years
scouring archives to develop
the paint line. He tells us
that the final colors chosen
for the collection (especially
the Victorian ones) are
slightly muted adaptations,
designed to appeal to modern
tastes. For a color card
write Kyanize Paints, Inc.,
Dept. OHJ, Second & Boston
Streets, Everett, MA 02149.
(617) 387-5000.

Clarification

Readers may have been confused
by our April 1986 write-up of
Silk Surplus Outlets in "Restoration Products" (page 138).
Regarding Scalamandre and ordering their fabrics by mail:
Scalamandre sells ONLY to the
trade. Silk Surplus Outlets
are retail stores with their
own line of fabrics; they are
also the exclusive outlets for
Scalamandre close-outs. For
more information, call Silk
Surplus at (212) 794-9373.

Special Painted Effects

Tromploy produces highly unusual and varied scenic wall
murals; faux-marble finishes
on floors, cornices, and man-
telpieces; skies on ceilings;
trompe-l'oeil finishes on all
sorts of surfaces; even wood-
graining for metal doors.
Owners Gary Finkel and Clyde
Wachsberger developed their
craft as professional scenic
artists working in theater and
television. Their painstaking
work produces finishes and
effects that can fool the eye
even from a few inches away.

The owners of a 1790 Long
Island house wanted a "naive
landscape" of their village
and surrounding farmland. A
commission such as this is
painted on canvas in the studio and then taken to the site

for installation. (Owners can
have them installed as permanently or temporarily as they
wish.) Other jobs are painted
directly on-site, such as the
application of wood-graining,
or marbleizing existing mouldings, doors, and floors. (A
recently completed faux-marble
finish applied to a new wood
floor took about ten days,
including the final protective
coatings.)

Tromploy's prices begin
around $10 per square foot.
Costs depend on how detailed
the project is; a 6-x-9-ft.
canvas painted and installed
could cost around $700 (in-
cluding installation). For a
kit which includes photos of a
variety of their projects,
send $5 to Tromploy Studio and
Gallery, Dept. OHJ, 400 Lafayette St., 5th Floor, New York,
NY 10003. (212) 420-1639.

Restoration Products

Arts & Crafts Fixtures

At last someone has come out with a line of high-quality, Mission/Prairie-style light fixtures. Stephen Kaniewski, of Brass Light Gallery, found the demand for his restored original fixtures far out-stripping the supply, so he's spent the past several years designing the Goldenrod Collection of reproduction Mission/Prairie-style lighting. The fixtures are solid brass with a polished finish (lacquer and antique finishes are available at additional cost).

The collection offers ten fixture designs to suit every need. Pictured at left is the Oak Park chandelier ($425) and above is the Sherman Park wall sconce ($135). Mr. Kaniewski brought prototypes of the new line to OHJ to let us take a look at them. We're impressed by his attention to detail. The fixtures' canopies are precise reproductions of original examples. The glass shades can be purchased separately. Brass Light is offering OHJ readers a 30% discount; buy one light or a houseful, but your orders must be postmarked by July 31, 1986. (This discount doesn't apply to shipping charges or sales tax.)

For a catalog, send $3 to Brass Light Gallery, Dept. OHJ, 719 South 5th Street, Milwaukee, WI 53204. (414) 383-0675.

Decorative Wood Lattice

Through old photographs, Pete and Marjory Holly found that the porches of their home were once graced with decorative lattice work. After they re-created their lattice, the Hollys decided to make custom-cut wood lattice available to other old-house owners. Their lattice (or vented-panel skirting) is different and more decorative than the usual diagonal lattice-stripped screens.

The Hollys also produce porch and balcony railings and scroll-cut inserts to order, as well as turned spindlework. For their brochure, write Marjory and Peter Holly, Dept. OHJ, 3111 2nd Avenue South, Minneapolis, MN 55408. (612) 824-2333.

Non-Rotting Lattice

Wood lattice looks great on a restored porch, but nothing is harder to keep painted or to protect from decay. We've found a product that may reduce this maintenance chore: PVC lattice manufactured by Cross Industries. Yes, we had the same first reaction: "Plastic lattice work? Oh, yuck!" But we're being open-minded about this one. The lattice is made of solid, foamed polyvinyl-chloride strips with a UV inhibitor. The strips are chemically welded into panels at the factory; the joints have no metal fasteners to get rusty. We inspected a 9-1/2-in.-square section of the lattice and found it solid, surprisingly heavy, and pretty darn convincing.

The lattice comes in six types. Type 2 (1-1/2-in. x 5/16-in.) is the closest match to the most common old-style lattice, which ran at a 45-degree diagonal and had spaces between the strips equal to the width of the strips. A 4-ft.-x-8-ft. panel of this type lattice sells for about $64 plus shipping. The lattice can be made and cut at the factory to suit your size requirements in either a diagonal or rectangular pattern.

We suggest you install it just as you would regular wood lattice, with the original kind of framing and trim work. It's easily cut with ordinary hand- and power-saws (with fine teeth); you can drive nails without predrilling. If any strips come loose, you can simply "weld" them with acetone. PVC expands and contracts more than wood, so you have to follow the directions on proper anchoring points. There's no fake woodgraining; it comes in eleven standard colors, including white. (It can also be painted with non-oil-based paint.) For a free color brochure, contact Cross Industries, Dept. OHJ, 5262 Peachtree Rd., Atlanta, GA 30341. (404) 451-4531.

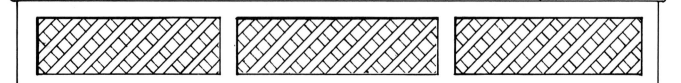

Ask OHJ

Covering Over Calcimine

Q: WE LIVE in a house built in 1843. The interior walls are plaster and were painted with calcimine in one room. The first coat of calcimine was sealed with a different type of paint, and then the wall was repainted with another layer of calcimine. Since the wall has only some minor plaster cracks, we'd prefer to canvas over the walls rather than apply paint. OHJ has warned us to remove calcimine before repainting, but you've never said anything about what to do with it before canvassing. There must be a way to canvas over calcimine, because we know of some houses where three layers of wallpaper are firmly affixed to old calcimine paint.
-- Mrs. W.G. Hudson, Selma, Ala.

A: MOST LINING-MATERIAL glues are water-based, which means there's a chance of the glue weakening the calcimine's bond to the wall. We're sure there are instances of people canvassing over calcimine without subsequent failure. But that would be small comfort if your ceiling should start peeling shortly after you've invested so much time in it. All you need to remove the calcimine is hot water -- a few tablespoonfuls of TSP will help speed the process. The task of removing the calcimine shouldn't take much more than an afternoon. Sure it's a messy, annoying job, but shortcuts during preparation almost always come back to haunt you.

Painting Kitchen Cabinets

Q: WE'RE STUMPED. We have large, white metal cabinets in our kitchen. The kitchen was probably remodeled in the late '40s or early '50s. The cabinets are in desperate need of care. The insides are fine, but the doors and drawfronts are chipped and show some rust. Is it possible to paint them? If so, with what? What kind of preparation will be necessary?

Please don't tell us to put in new cabinets. We've heard that suggestion before, but we'd rather save the money for other necessary restoration projects. Even though the cabinets may not be appropriate for our house, we'd like to save them. We've been told that they're the "Cadillac" of metal cabinetry.
-- Berta Lalomia, Jackson, Mich.

A: AS LONG AS YOUR METAL cabinets aren't rusted through, it shouldn't be too late to save them. The first thing to do is remove any loose paint, rust, grease, etc. Scraping and sanding will do most of this step. The important thing is to have a smooth, dirt-free surface to paint. Just before applying the paint, wipe the surface with a lint-free cloth dipped in a little mineral spirits (paint thinner).

Once you have the cabinets prepared for painting, apply a coat of alkyd primer specifically made for metal. Rustoleum brand sells one such primer. Whatever brand you choose,

use a topcoat from the same manufacturer as the primer. Two topcoats should be applied after the primer has thoroughly dried.

Colonial Revival Colors

Q: OUR COLONIAL REVIVAL HOME, built in 1903, is presently painted white. The shutters are dark green. The windows and storm windows are painted black (not the trim, mind you, just the windows). The house is huge,

approximately 9,500 square feet, and we're having a difficult time deciding what color to paint it. It needs paint desperately, as it is peeling badly. We are very much in love with our old house and want to keep it looking as it did in the old days. Can you give us some hints as to what colors would be appropriate for this type and size house?
-- Barbara A. Medina, Marinette, Wis.

A: COLONIAL REVIVAL HOUSES marked a return to pale colors: mostly white or cream, sometimes pale yellow, with white or cream trim -- a soft gray body, white trim and sash, and cream shutters would be very appropriate for your house. As you see, even within the boundaries of historical precedents, there are still a lot of color schemes available to you. Whatever you select, you're going to have to live with it, so we recommend that you do some research before making your decision. The Colonial Revival period has a large bibliography, so your local library is sure to have solid information on which to base your choice. We also recommend that you consult Century Of Color by Dr. Roger Moss. (See the Order Form in this issue.)

General interest questions from subscribers will be answered in print. The Editors can't promise to reply to all questions personally—but we try. Send your questions with sketches or photos to Questions Editor, The Old-House Journal, 69A Seventh Avenue, Brooklyn, NY 11217.

opinion...

Remuddling

Window Pains

JENNY LINN of Grand Rapids, Michigan, sent us these amazing photographs: "The landlord was trying to improve the value of his house by adding storm windows. He purchased odd-sized windows and fit them in wherever possible. The unused window space was filled with lumber. Then he painted the house white and the trim bright red, which really calls attention to the remuddled windows. One can only imagine how dark and grim the inside must be with the daylight cut off."

Vernacular Houses

A ubiquitous house type up and down the Pacific coast is this one-storey cottage with a hip roof and a porch across the front. The plan usually has four rooms flanking a central hall, but rear additions are common. Also variable is the height of the ground floor — which might be nearly at grade level, or raised as much as a half storey.

While this foursquare, pyramidal-roof house is an Eastern immigrant, it suited Western needs so well that it became one of the most commonplace 19th-century house types in California, Oregon, and Washington. Built from the 1860s into the 1900s, these houses reveal their specific time and place through decorative details on roof and porch brackets, and on door and window heads.

Earlier examples had minimal ornamentation and, in some cases, split porch columns. Earlier

West Coast Hipped Roof Cottage

houses like the one in the drawing are often more Classical or, as noted by the McAlesters,* in the vernacular Italianate mode. Later Victorian examples exhibit details such as the flat-sawn mill-work on the 1880s house in the photograph.

— *Sally Woodbridge, Berkeley, Calif.*

*A Field Guide to American Houses, *by Virginia and Lee McAlester, p. 218. Alfred A. Knopf, 1984.*

Photo: James C. Massey

Vernacular
Houses

The Virginia I House

The I House, a ubiquitous feature of the rural land-scape in the mid-Atlantic, southern and midwest-ern United States, is one American adaptation of England's Georgian center-hall house. From the 1750s right into the early 20th century, it was the farmhouse of choice in German, Scots-Irish, and English settlement areas. Its name refers not to its distinctive, tall, narrow shape, but to the states where cultural geographers first noticed it: Illinois, Indiana, and Iowa.

Whether brick or wood-frame, whatever its em-bellishments or additions, the I House profile is easily recognizable: two rooms high, two rooms wide, but only one room deep; side-gabled, usually with a chimney at each gable end and with three or five window bays (openings) in each storey across the front. Often a second I added to the rear forms an overall L or T shape.

This mid-century brick house in Millwood, Virginia, is of the three-opening type sometimes called "the Virginia I." (The classical I has five openings.)

— *James C. Massey and Shirley Maxwell*
Strasburg, Virginia

Vernacular
Houses

Norwegian Stone Houses In Texas

Here in Texas, it's hard to find better stone mason-ry work than that exhibited by the Norwegians of Bosque County. In a small triangle defined by the towns of Clifton, Meridian, and Cranfills Gap stand some two dozen stone Norwegian farmhouses built between 1855 and 1885. These are central-passage dwellings, with wide, dogtrot-like breezeways; hearths are set at either end of the house. They're related in form to traditional Scandinavian double-houses — a common type of residence for upper-middle-class landowners in all parts of Scandinavia by the mid-19th century. They also bear a resemblance to Southern dogtrot houses.

An imposing early example is the Jens and Kari Ringness house (lower left), built in the late 1850s. An old newspaper illustration indicates that the facade once had a small, intricately decorated porch.

Perhaps the best preserved example is the Olson-Arneson house (upper right), built around 1870. Note the typical central-passage plan and symmet-rical facade. The Bungalow-style porch is a later addition, replacing what was likely a highly decorated Victorian entryway.

— Kenneth A. Breisch
Texas Historical Commission
Austin, Texas

R.B. St. George

THE SALTBOX

Above: The Paine-Dodge house in Ipswich, Mass., dates from around 1702. The front door was improved in the 1840s with a Greek Revival frontispiece, but the house retains its traditional five-bay fenestration on the facade and the saltbox profile with an integral lean-to roofline.

Below: This 1725 house in Newington, N.H., has the characteristic five-bay facade, central entry and staircase in front of the chimney, and, of course, the classic saltbox profile.

R.M. Candee

Popularly known as the New England Saltbox, this vernacular house form was built throughout the region from the late 17th century through (and occasionally after) the Revolution. The basic form is a two-storey house with one room on either side of a central chimney. The identifying feature is the roofline, which extends over a one-storey range (row) of three rooms — usually a kitchen, pantry and unheated bedroom.

Earlier one-room-deep, central-chimney houses often had an added lean-to, with the pitch of the rear roofline broken at the level of the rear plate to provide greater

height in the addition. By the 1680s, however, a few prosperous yeomen and ministers in Massachusetts adopted the lean-to plan from the start. The rear roofline of the integral lean-to house is an unbroken line.

A symbol of prosperity in the 18th century, the Saltbox continued as an alternative vernacular form into the post Revolutionary building boom in New England.

— *Richard M. Candee*
Boston University

*Wynkoop house, circa 1740 and 1760, Saugerties
vicinity, Ulster County, New York.*

Dutch Stone Houses
of New York State

*Detail: Bevier-Elting house, built 1694,
(this section 1724), New Paltz, Ulster County.*

The Hudson Valley Dutch stone house is a distinct
American vernacular building type. It is identifiable by its low, rectangular, one-and-a-half storey
form, its gable roof, and an elongated, linear floor-
plan. Interior spaces are distinguished by massive
joists that span the depth of the house to create a
prominent ceiling. Chimneys are located on end
walls. Early fireplaces were jambless; later ones
were enclosed and panelled.

Interior layout followed a three-room pattern
typical of Northern European traditions: a best
parlor, a family living room or hall, and a utilitarian kitchen space. Garrets were unfinished and un-
inhabited.

Dutch houses grew in predictable stages; the
original was often a one-room house that grew to a
three- or four-room structure. As the Dutch community in New York State changed through three
centuries, the houses evolved stylistically, becoming more symmetrical and formalized externally,
and acquiring increasing levels of ornamentation on
the interior. The Dutch stone house is only one
variant of a polyglot array of ethnic masonry architecture in the Hudson Valley, which includes
German, Huguenot, and English traditions.

*— Neil Larson
Kinderhook, New York*

FACHWERK

Immigrants from northern Germany built hundreds of distinctive half-timber, or *Fachwerk*, structures in east-central Wisconsin. Developed in their homeland as a response to shortages of wood, this ancient building method incorporated a sturdy, braced framework of hewn timbers, nogged with mud and straw or brick. The walls were most often covered with weather-boards or plaster pargeting.

The houses were usually symmetrical. Inside, two rooms flanked each side of a central hall where separate stairways led to the second floor and basement. Wood-burning stoves provided heat, although some early houses had a huge, walk-in central fireplace, or *schwarze Küche*, used also for cooking, baking, and smoking meat.

The photo and floorplan show a house built by Friedrich Koepsell, a Prussian master carpenter and farmer, c. 1858. Now restored to its 1880 appearance, with a front porch (a subsequent addition), it is part of a German farmstead exhibit at Old World Wisconsin.

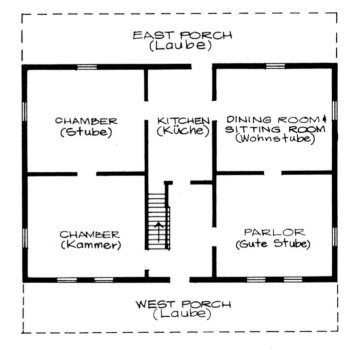

— *submitted by William H. Tishler*
Professor of Landscape Architecture
University of Wisconsin, Madison

Oechsner house
Walworth County
South Dakota

Campbell County, S.D.

The builders: *German-Russians settled throughout the Great Plains states (primarily the Dakotas). From southwestern Germany, they had migrated to western Russia, north of Odessa, before coming to America. Their building tradition encompassed timber-framed, log, and especially* fachwerk* *houses; out of necessity, their architecture adapted to the harsh environment and flat, treeless landscape of both western Russia and the Great Plains. Using skills acquired in Russia, they created a unique North American house type that is rapidly disappearing without much notice.*

* see FACHWERK, August 1986

GERMAN~RUSSIAN PLAINS HOUSE

Commonly mistaken for the ephemeral "soddy" of the Great Plains, the South Dakota German-Russian house was constructed of clay mixed with manure, straw, and water. Between 1873 and 1920, over 75 houses were built in an eight-county area in the southeastern /north-central part of the state. Ideally suited to the prairie where building materials were scarce, German-Russian houses used the earthen mixture in several construction techniques. Puddled clay, rammed earth, and hand-made bricks known as *batsa* formed load-bearing walls as well as interior partitions, loft floors, and massive center chimneys.

Rectangular, one-storey houses have a central or off-center entry leading to a kitchen flanked by a parlor and a storage or sleeping chamber. Some houses had a central, six-foot-square room known as a *schwarze Kuche* (black kitchen) for preparing and cooking food.

Most early German-Russian vernacular houses were eventually covered with clapboard siding. Later dwellings combined clay within a wood frame, but retained the traditional form.

— *Michael Koop*
Helena, Montana

Vernacular Houses

Small-town store/houses in the South

If vernacular houses are those that cannot be analyzed in the scholarly sense, because they're quirky, or regional, or remarkable only for how they fit into a context other than architectural ... then these humble buildings are vernacular. They housed such enterprises as general stores, hardware stores and fix-it shops, and at the same time were home to the people who ran the store. These two buildings, in Hampton and in Langley, South Carolina, are typical of early - 20th - century store / houses that were once universal in the South.

The first-storey plan was open to accommodate showcases, display racks, pickle barrels. Spans were supported by posts that were pressed into service as bulletin boards for hand-lettered signs advertising the Special of the Day or admonishing, "Please don't ask for credit." A back stair (or sometimes a covered outdoor stair) led to the second-storey living quarters, where room layouts varied. A common arrangement had the living room in front; a door led from living room to second-storey porch.

These buildings are notable not so much for their contribution to our architectural heritage as for their contribution to small-town life. These store/houses were quite literally the last stands of neighborhood shopkeepers who, though they were so frugal as to build house and store on the same foundation, were replaced (almost overnight it seems) by absentee retailers whose stores bear names with suffixes like "-A-Rama."

— *Walter Jowers, Nashville, Tenn.*
(formerly of Burnettown, S.C.)

Editor's Page

opinion...

Remuddling
...an update

When we devised the Remuddling Of The Month Award back in October 1981, we didn't realize we'd tapped into a vast reservoir of Americana. Thanks to our loyal readers, we've accumulated thousands of photos showing amazing, imaginative ways to mutilate old buildings.

We recognize that our Remuddling archive is of priceless value to scholars. So we engaged a team of cultural demographers, social histographers, and statistical psychographers to analyze, codify,

and interpret our collection.

After enormous expense, our crack team achieved an incredible breakthrough: They divided the Remuddling phenomenon into six sub-categories -- and identified the state of mind that causes each.

On this page, you're getting an exclusive preview of the research. Full results will be given in a 7-hour presentation at the annual meeting of the American Association for Cultural Determinism later this year. Don't miss it!

Cathy Anderson

CREATIVE CHAOS

The opposite of a Callous Conversion: The building becomes the vehicle for the owner's bold personal statement.

Donald Randazzo

MODERNIST MANIA

Businesspeople, particularly, suffer from this syndrome. Stuck with an old building? Do your level best to make it look brand new!

Allyn S. Feinberg

ASININE ADDITIONS

The Dictionary says "asinine" means "marked by an inexcusable failure to exercise intelligence or sound judgment." No further research needed.

Jackie Scarbrough

MEGA-BUCK MONOPOLY

Millions of dollars are spent each year on product ads with the dubious theme: "End maintenance headaches forever!" This is one unfortunate result.

Laurence Sommer

CALLOUS CONVERSIONS

Feeling no cultural responsibility or emotional attachment to the building, the owner does what's cheapest in the (very) short run.

Gerald R. Mosher

TECHNOLOGICAL TRASHING

When solar power was in vogue, old houses were breaking out in rashes of solar panels and trombe walls. Now it's satellite dishes.

Letters

Roslyn Restoration

Dear Editor:

The Roslyn Preservation Corporation is a small, not-for-profit, revolving restoration fund that operates in and around Roslyn, New York. Most of our projects have involved derelict buildings. I am enclosing two photos of the Roslyn House, which was built by John Warmuth in Roslyn Heights, ca. 1870. Following the adoption of the 18th Amendment, it was poorly maintained and was purchased by the Town of North Hempstead's office of Community Development Agency in 1974. The building was empty after 1979. (Its final occupants were a church and a beauty salon.)

During the period when it was unoccupied, it was extensively vandalized. It was bought by the Roslyn Preservation Corporation in October 1983. Ten days later, an arsonist set fire to the west front, doing considerable damage to that wall and to the roof. The first photo (below left) is of the east front, which was not damaged by the fire except for the roof. The second photo (below right) was taken in March 1985, when the restoration was complete but for landscaping.

Sometimes these restorations turn out pretty good. In this instance, the interior floor plan was also restored. The Roslyn House is now owned by an advertising agency that maintains its offices there.
-- Roger G. Gerry, D.M.D.
President
Roslyn Preservation Corp.
Roslyn, N.Y.

A Tile Tale

Dear OHJ:

The article on Victorian tile (March '86 OHJ) was very interesting for me, as I once salvaged some from a big Milwaukee home that was being demolished. I had to remove almost three feet of rubble that was in front of the fireplace to get at the tiles. There were 14 tiles in this set: Two were broken by rubble that had fallen against them, but the remaining 12 were perfect. They were embossed with a floral motif; the two corner tiles were a female profile with flowing hair. I framed them for a wall hanging. The tile cost me a six-pack.

I always did like The Old-House Journal, and it is even better now. I won't even miss the old "three-holer."
-- George W. Putz
Shawano, Wis.

Viva Vernacular

Dear Staff:

I own a vernacular, 1887 owner-built home and very much enjoy the new OHJ venture away from the classics. What about an article on period remodelling? There seems to be a pattern in it. These houses were never static. Appreciating the alterations that are part and parcel of their patina might be useful to those of us who have one bedroom and want two, etc.
-- Michael W. Conner
Bloomington, Ind.

A Sharp Old Saw

Dear OHJ:

I am somewhat amused by your "long-time readers" who bluster over your new look and threaten to cancel unless you get rid of the color cover and change back to the old format. They all claim to have been getting valuable information out of the magazine for years; if they cancel, where are they going to turn for the same high-quality articles and information? So far as I can tell, the contents haven't changed. Let's see, what was that old saw? "You can't tell a book by its cover..."
-- G. Kaye Holden
Jersey City, N.J.

A Helpful Company

Dear OHJ:

I wish to congratulate you on your new cover and advertising format. During your first month of advertising, I contacted one of the companies listed: Flueworks. I sent away for their literature and promptly received a reply. I immediately had an additional question which I sent them in a letter. A few days later the owner of the company phoned me back in the evening to answer my question; half an hour later, we were still chatting about the renovation of old houses. (My inquiry happened to concern a product that I wish to use in the construction of my new house.)
-- Joel Kroin
New York, N.Y.

The Roslyn House after the fire — December 1983.

The Roslyn House after restoration — March 1985.

Letters

Sort Of Grateful

Editors:

Having worn off the covers of The Old-House Journal Yearbooks, I find myself aware of problems I never knew existed in restoring old houses. Now, I tremble every time I think of my heavily tarred built-in porch gutter spewing water into the porch's innards. Yet when I bought the house, I was blissfully ignorant that such an animal as a built-in gutter could cause such devastation. I thought the peeling paint and "dry" rot on the porch stemmed from years of exposure to water on the outside -- not the inside -- of the porch. The solution will not be as simple as I first thought. For enlightening me, I can alternately thank you and damn you. However, my thanks weigh more heavily on the scale.

-- Marcus Woodward
Fort Smith, Ark.

In Defense Of YUPPIES

Dear OHJ:

First, let me commend you on your new look -- it's terrific! I'll be able to suffer through without holes in order to enjoy the benefits of the new format.

Second, I'd like to address those of your readers who equate the word YUPPIE with dastardly people. I refer specifically to the reader who, on seeing your new cover, said, "Oh no! They've gone YUPPIE! All is lost."

Please note that it is the vast number of YUPPIES who are revitalizing the abandoned and neglected older homes in our cities. YUPPIE money is financing the removal of horrendous remuddling and the ensuing expensive renovations. YUPPIES have made the commitment to live in the neighborhoods where their homes and cars are continuously vandalized, and where walking the dog after dark can earn you a graduate degree in street crime. It's the presence of YUPPIES which has brought excellent restaurants, live theater, and a variety of educational opportunities within commuting distance of suburbia; this helps keep the traffic, pollution, and population

problems out of these suburban neighborhoods. By expanding the tax base, YUPPIES can be credited with improving the available social services. How many CAT scanners can be purchased by hospitals serving 10,000 in population; how many training programs for the mentally handicapped can be supported by small suburban communities; how many drug treatment programs is Small-town, USA, willing to have next door to their homes?

YUPPIES aren't perfect, but neither are "hicks" or (gasp!) people who live in brand-new split-level ranches. The word YUPPIE shouldn't <u>automatically</u> be accompanied with a sneer. YUPPIE stands for young urban professional, not yucky, unattractive parasite. May I suggest that if you are less than 100 years of age, are hooked into a sewer system, and work (in the home or out of it), then <u>you</u> may be one of the dreaded YUPPIES.

-- Elizabeth A. Griffith
"A YUPPIE"
New Haven, Conn.

Aluminum Woes

Dear Old-House Journal:

Our museum was recently given a book entitled "The Kawneer Story"; it sheds some light on the 'alumi-siding' of Niles, Michigan ("Remuddling of the Month," Nov. '85 OHJ). The Kawneer Company was a pioneer in the design, production, and (unfortunately) <u>sales</u> of large aluminum-framed, plate-glass storefront windows. They also produced aluminum products such as the sheathing seen in your Remuddling photo.

Until recently, the Kawneer Company's headquarters was located in Niles, in the area served by our museum. This publication was a history written in 1956 by and for the company. Obviously, it attempts to shed the best light on Kawneer's accomplishments. In the eyes of a preservationist, however, the book is an amusing and, at times, sad view of the 20th century's attempt to cover up the past.

Particularly telling are the enclosed photos of two plates in the book. "Extreme ornamentation" is obviously a negative term in the company's mind; a problem to be "super-

seded by the strikingly simple design" of their line of architectural metal products.

Apparently the company convinced the Niles merchants of their point of view. We agree with The Old-House Journal and encourage Niles, as well as other towns, to make their Main Street true to its own character.

-- Jan H. House
Director
1839 Courthouse Museum
Berrien Springs, Mich.

Above: "A typical example of the extreme ornamentation of the pre-war storefront, which was superceded by the strikingly simple design brought about by the K-47 line." (*The Kawneer Story*, page 68).

Below: "Kawneer's new post-war line of architectural metal products once again brought a new look to Main Street, America" (*KS*, page 65).

Restorer's Notebook

D-I-Y Heat Deflector

PEOPLE HAVE CAUTIONED AGAINST using the heat gun to remove paint from slender window muntins, because of the possibility of the glass cracking from the intense heat. After several sad experiences with cracked panes, I devised the following tool; since I've been using it, I haven't cracked a pane. My solution is a heat deflector which I fabricated from scrap aluminum and wood. With it, I can strip muntins and even remove hardened putty.

By placing the deflector's aluminum blade on the glass at the edge of the putty or muntin, I keep the heat off the window pane and on the paint or putty. After the heat has done its work, I set down the deflector, take up a scraper or putty knife, and neatly remove all the softened material.

-- Joseph Patay
Toledo, Ohio

[Even with the deflector, the glazing points can get hot enough to crack a pane; we don't recommend this procedure for windows with valuable, antique glass -- ed.]

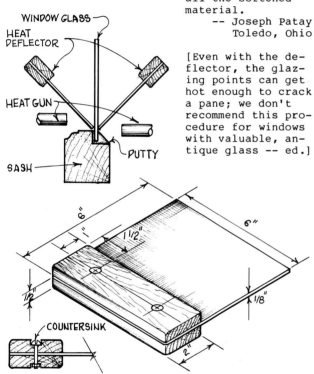

How To Paint Over Crayon

THANKS TO MY FOUR-YEAR-OLD NEPHEW, I've found an excellent material for hiding marks on the plaster walls of my Bungalow. On a recent visit to our house, little Godfrey decided to draw large kites on our parlor wall with his crayons. I tried everything to get the marks off, but had little success. I was about to repaint when a painter friend of mine said that the marks would probably come back to haunt me -- crayon stains can bleed through three or more coats of paint. He suggested I spot-prime the offensive areas with some white-pigmented shellac. I tried it, and it worked beautifully! The shellac sealed the area, and after the latex paint was applied,

there wasn't even a hint of those kites. (I'm told that this material is also good for sealing knots in softwoods.)

-- Sue Badham, Needles, Cal.

A Mouthwash House Wash

MY FRIENDS AND I are restoring an old house in Florida. After completing the exterior paint job, we discovered what appeared to be mold growing randomly on the house. We immediately scrubbed it off with Clorox, but after a few hours we found the growth thriving once again. We tried using a fungicide and an algicide, but they were disappointments, too.

We realized we were fighting not a mold but the bacteria from decaying seaweed. (The shore of a tidal river is just a half-block from our house.) Following the recommendation of a chemical company, we washed everything with hydrogen peroxide, but even this didn't stop the bacteria from returning.

In a flash of inspiration, our resident environmentalist said, "What about Listerine?" So we again scrubbed hydrogen peroxide over all the dark and damp places where the bacteria thrived (such as under the eaves), and then 'painted' the surface with Listerine. The problem ended then and there -- and this combination has had no effect on the paint, so unlike Clorox, we didn't have to rinse it off. Next fall, when the river is low again, we'll have to repeat this procedure. In the meantime, the house looks great!

-- Marceline Murphy, Melbourne, Fla.

"Steel Epoxy"

I'D LIKE TO SHARE a solution to a common problem I encountered while restoring my old windows. First, I tried plastic wood to fix a window sill that had some wood rot. Not long after, I noticed that the patch was crazing and working its way loose. I then removed the loose pieces and applied a product called "J.B. Weld." This is a two-part "steel epoxy" that has numerous uses. After patching the rotted areas, I purposely left it unpainted for a year just to see if it would hold up. To date there hasn't been a single crack or problem. It also made a great "weld" for a deteriorated area of my wrought iron fence.

-- Jim Petropulos, Wilmington, Cal.

Tips To Share? Do you have any hints or short cuts that might help other old-house owners? We'll pay $25 for any short how-to items that are used in this "Restorer's Notebook" column. Write to Notebook Editor, The Old-House Journal, 69A Seventh Avenue, Brooklyn, NY 11217.

Old~House Loving

by Marion Smith

THE FIRST TIME I saw the house it was a cold, desolate night in November, 1979. I had known Michael for a month. We were on our second date.

"WHERE are we going?" I inquired. "How would you like to see my cemetery?" "Cemetery? Nobody has their own cemetery." "Well, I do," he replied. And off we went.

HIS HOUSE STOOD abandoned in Jackson Heights, Queens, New York. It had been unoccupied for almost four years. It was known as the haunted house of the neighborhood and it had been repeatedly burglarized and raped.

AND HE REALLY did have his own cemetery, behind the house. It was the burial ground for the once prominent Riker family, among the first Dutch

"How would you like to see my cemetery?"

settlers in this area. They obtained a land grant in 1654 from Governor Peter Stuyvesant and, some decades later, built this house. The house faces Riker's Island, where the prison was later built. There was once a Riker homestead, too, but that burned to the ground in 1938. So this modest little farmhouse with its acre and family burial ground was the sole surviving property from this prominent family's history.

I STOOD SHIVERING in the middle of the neglected cemetery, surrounded by broken, toppled, and shattered headstones, shaking my head, not believing a place like this could still exist in New York City. The house itself was dark, cold, cluttered, and sagging; it seemed shrouded in mystery and ready to cry. The

This 1877 painting of the Smiths' house is now in the collection of the New-York Historical Society.

Here's how the same house looked around 1920. (Note what appears to be an outhouse at right in the photo.)

Marion Smith

The centuries seem to have barely touched the house, judging from this recent picture — only the snow is new!

electricity and hot water had been turned off; it was plain to see the house had died a mournful death. It was waiting for someone to bring it back to life. It was waiting for me.

AND SO we were married; Michael and I, that is. No sooner had he carried me over the threshold than I rolled up my sleeves and got to work. From the moment I met Michael, and saw that house, it was a labor of love.

THE FIRST PROJECT was the attic, where I fulfilled every little girl's fantasy -- sifting through an attic full of forgotten relics. Ours had not been cleaned in 100 years. The Riker family had rented out the house for years, and told tenants (among them my husband) that the attic was off limits. The estate's accountant later bought the place, continued to rent it, and stored all the family papers in the attic, some dating back to 1883: ledgers, wills, financial directories, diaries, photographs. My husband bought the place lock, stock, barrel, and contents of attic.

MICHAEL'S A RATHER TALL, robust man, not built for hoisting himself up through a tiny opening and then stooping under a low roof. He's been in the attic only twice during our five years in the house. (I'm up there every week.) It took me three months to read through the contents of the attic; it was such fun. The first time Michael came up, he looked around and grumbled, "It would take four men two weeks to clean this out." I rolled my sleeves up a little higher and did it in four days. Besides the books and papers, there were cartons of empty bottles, stacks of glass, piles of wood, a pot-belly stove, wooden Venetian blinds, old wooden cabinets, a set of 54 hardbound financial directories weighing six pounds each, and lots of dust. By the end of day three, as exhaustion was setting in from climbing up and down the attic to remove each item separately, I opened the attic window and, with wild abandon, started tossing the wood and other debris out.

THE CABINETS, stove, bottles, photos, and other useful items have all been incorporated into the house's decor. The papers we donated to a museum for a whopping tax deduction that staggered me more than had all that hoisting and carrying. My husband began to think I was worth my weight in gold, the house could breathe easier, and my hair was turning grey.

MEANWHILE WE WERE LUCKY ENOUGH to have a retired neighbor, Mr. Osso, sanding, painting, fixing, and stripping, stripping, stripping. I didn't mind hard work either, so he and I developed a great working arrangement. He did most of the stripping while I pushed, pulled, dug, scrubbed, crawled, and said goodbye to my fingernails. I may have found my prince, but I still felt like Cinderella, always down on my knees working while everyone else got to go to the ball.

MR. OSSO AND I made wonderful discoveries together. Under the '60s gold wall-to-wall carpeting in the living room, and under the tile in the library, we found 300-year-old, wide-plank floors. So we ripped up the carpet and nails, tile and tar, and when we reached black paint, we gave up and called in a professional floor sander. Our knees were red and sore for weeks. Mine turned black and blue. Mr. Osso kneeled on foam rubber padding from then on.

MR. OSSO ALSO HELPED us finish the kitchen. First we stripped the wainscotting of its many years of paint. Parts of the woodwork had been scorched by a fire in the 1950s, and though we managed to sand off some of the charring we had to leave some of it visible. When people first came to the house I was worried they would notice it; but no one seemed to see it, and I realized it just played a part in the history of this old house and actually added character.

THE KITCHEN HAD a Formica countertop and linoleum on the floor... poor house, so humiliated, so misunderstood. I took measurements for a new sink. I went to auctions every week. It took a couple of months to find a scrubbed-pine sideboard just the right size to convert. We took off its wood top, selected tiles for the surface, bought a stainless steel sink. Voila! Our piece de resistance.

"The boys" hard at it: Bill at a table saw in the Smiths' dining room; Pete sanding a door in the central hallway; Bill passing Pete a length of old pine flooring.

Above & Before: Mr. Osso points out a problem to Michael Smith in the unrestored kitchen.
Below & After: The kitchen is decorated with photos, boxes, and bottles found in the attic.

Ken Korotkin

The Smiths relax in the library. (Those big books in the foreground are the original ledgers of the Riker family, which Marion discovered in the attic.)

WHEN MR. OSSO MOVED AWAY, I was left alone to carry on, and I was terrified. I needed solace. I turned to my bible -- The Old-House Journal! I knew it would answer my questions, tell me where to find materials, and give me inspiration, encouragement, and the strength to continue. And it did.

THE FIRE IN THE '50s had done severe damage. The kitchen and dining room floors had been replaced with narrow oak boards, arranged haphazardly. The center hallway was floored with remnant wood. Tin patches and holes marked the places where pipes had once gone through. The hewn ceiling beams were badly charred and had been painted over by previous tenants.

OUR FIRST PRIORITY was to replace the destroyed floorboards with authentic replacements, which meant old, wide-plank, 11-to-12-inch boards. I called The Barnsider in Sugar Loaf, New York (about an hour and a half away). After Michael and I went to see their wood and made a deal, they sent down two old-fashioned country boys, Pete and Bill, to install the wood. I cleared the furniture out of three rooms and stored it, filling the attic and basement. "The boys" set up their big table-saw in the dining room. We worked in harmony; every day they arrived at 8 a.m., and I'd have a pot of coffee waiting. While they sawed and hammered, I vacuumed up sawdust and debris.

ONE DAY the plumber was there too, drilling a hole through the dining room floor to extend a pipe for the radiator. The drill, saw, hammer, radio, and vacuum were all going at once. I stopped the vacuum and wanted to run out from the house screaming. Instead I fled to the cellar; when I reached the bottom of the stairs, I saw how the plumber barely found space to run his extension cord along the cluttered floor to shine a light up through

the cellar ceiling to the dining room, and I just started laughing.

SO THIS IS HOW you renovate an old house. You laugh, you cry, you want to scream, you can't escape the dust, the debris, the clutter, the chaos. You wonder if you'll live long enough to see it finished. But you go on.

CAUGHT UP in the excitement of restoring this old house and wanting to do the best job possible, we even removed the wood mantel in the dining room to extend the new flooring under it. I hid my face in my hands as the boys pushed, pulled, and pried the mantel with a crowbar -- then all at once the piece came away from the wall, and we staggered with it out into the hallway. The only buried treasure we found lodged behind it was an old acorn, left by some long-gone squirrel.

HOW I WISHED I could go back in time to this very spot 300 years ago, and see the room as it was then! I knew that whoever was here then must have felt the same as we did now -- full of the excitement and expectation of finishing a room, creating a home. Pete and Bill told me that the beams in the dining room had originally come from a barn. This too filled me with images of those long-ago Rikers, razing a barn somewhere to begin the venture of building this homestead. Another missing piece to a puzzle, another bit of history retrieved.

AS THE OLD DOOR SADDLES in the hall were being ripped out, a lady's hairpin popped up, the kind that held braids and buns. I picked it up...so old and rusty. Who was this long-ago lady; did she labor over and love this house as I do? Did she spend the happiest days of her life here, as I am? Will someone find something of mine someday and wonder about me?

THE HOUSE IS LIKE a romance, no less exciting than my wonderful romance with Michael. Always something new to discover, wanting to be together, hating to leave. Returning to our house after being away is just like when Michael holds me in his arms. It's where I feel safe. It's where I want to be. It's home. That's what being in love is like. That's what being in this old house is like.

VALENTINE'S DAY arrived, no matter about the sawdust. So I baked heart-shaped cakes and cupcakes, complete with pink icing and red lettering (and wood shavings, I'm sure). I sent Pete and Bill back to Sugar Loaf with a few. Michael and I enjoyed ours that evening while planning the next job -- plastering!

WHEN THE PLASTERERS started hammering the lath to the ceiling, the mice in the attic got all upset. They decided to move downstairs with us. I briefly considered moving back to Brooklyn with my mother. And Jake the cat had his own problems, but it was every beast for himself....

Michael and Marion posed for this portrait at Christmastime, but the joy and good will last all year long, as their dream of 'Paradise Acre' comes nearer and nearer.

JAKE DIDN'T LIKE all the new smells the house had taken on, like mortar, plaster, and that icky red glue. He felt threatened. He peed in Michael's shoes, in the bedroom closet, on my new winter coat. The vacuum cleaner was not spared either. But then the strange odors made him gag, and he started vomiting. Worried he might die, I quickly forgave him all his sins, clutched him in my arms, and said six Hail Marys. I reassured him, and myself, that things would soon get back to "normal."

WELL, MAYBE NOT SOON. I decided to take a breather from the indoor work and start on the outside. Visions of a secret garden, a gazebo, and a circular porch danced in my head. A white picket fence around our entire acre: "Paradise Acre," that's what I'll call it. Just think, I would get to paint that fence every year ... on second thought, maybe every other year.

THE WINDOW BOXES will need planting. I'll continue the stencilling I started last spring. I'm going to rake, dig, chop down sumac trees. I'm going to lose five pounds. I can hardly wait. My loyal housekeeper, Mrs. Schaub, who helps clean, paint, sew drapes, and has a green thumb, is going to introduce me to the joys of our very own cutting garden. There is no end to the wonders that can and will take place here.

AS I LOOK BACK over the past six years, I realize only the house and I know what it really took to reach this plateau. The house and I share an intimacy, a bond so close even Michael doesn't know all our secrets.

Yet the house knows every step we take, hears our every utterance, feels our love.

AS I LOOK TO THE FUTURE and the work still ahead (I want to restore shutters to the windows and replace the aluminum sash with wood), I can't help but reminisce about our beginnings...like the first time I was up in the attic, and the sun was streaming through the tiny window. I opened it to discover a storybook view of the family cemetery below, surrounded by beautiful old trees. How peaceful it all was, to sit there and read through Riker memorabilia. Or the first time I cleaned the basement, untouched for years. I spotted a trunk fallen behind some debris. I opened it to behold a wedding gown, perfectly preserved. And then just last summer, when we opened our double-Dutch door to the local historical society for our first house tour. A lady came over to shake my hand and thank me "on behalf of Queens," for preserving this little bit of history.

I WOULDN'T HAVE missed a minute of it. But guess what? I'm not going to miss a minute of it, a hundred years from now, either: I'll be resting right out back in the family burial ground. I'm family now, and the house wouldn't want it any other way.

THAT'S MY CINDERELLA STORY. I found my prince. But instead of a glass slipper, he came bearing this jewel of a house. It suited me perfectly, but it needed a lot of polishing. It took the likes of me to do it.

I NEEDED SOMEONE to show me Paradise exists, and it took the likes of Michael to lead the way. Michael needed me to take his hand and follow him home. And we all lived happily ever after.

HOW TO FIX OLD DOORS

by Jonathan Poore

WHEN YOU START working on an old house, you're going to be lucky to find one or two doors that work properly. More often than not, doors will have fallen victim to building settlement, insensitive repairs, warping, paint buildup, or all of the above. Quite often, these problems are "solved" by indiscriminate planing to make the door shut. Planing a door is usually unnecessary and permanently damaging.

THE FIRST STEP in door repair is to understand how a door and jamb are constructed and how the parts should work together. Next, take a few moments to watch the door operate. Open and close it a few times, noting where it rubs against and where it clears the jamb.

A DOOR SHOULD never have to be slammed to close completely. Ideally, there should be a consistent gap of 1/16 to 1/8 inch between the door and jamb on all sides. A door should swing silently and effortlessly on its hinges and latch crisply. A closed door shouldn't rattle around between the latch and stops. Most doors in an old house don't fit this description....

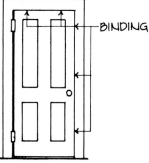

Door Binds Evenly Along Latch Side And Head

● PAINT BUILDUP -- the most common cause of binding. Remove excess paint with heat or chemical removers. If the paint is flaking off, you can simply pull a sharp paint scraper along the length of the mating surfaces. Be careful not to gouge or otherwise damage the door or jamb, especially if it may be worth stripping and refinishing.

● SEASONAL EXPANSION -- Humid weather will cause the door to swell, and make it difficult or impossible to close during these periods. If this is really the cause, it will be necessary to plane the door (see box). Wait for the peak of the humid season before planing, so you'll be certain to remove enough material.

Door Binds Along Top Of Latch Side And/Or On Floor

● LOOSE UPPER HINGE -- To check if the top hinge is loose, open the door part way and push the top in towards the jamb, while lifting up on the doorknob. If the hinge moves, it may be loose enough to allow the door to sag away enough to bind against the jamb or drag on the floor.

IF THE HINGE LEAVES move within their mortises, try tightening the screws. Usually, the screws got loose because they were pulled from the jamb or door, so the screw holes will probably be stripped. The leaf that contacts the door can be resecured with longer screws -- the stile is solid and will accommodate the extra length. The leaf that's mortised into the jamb will be a bit more difficult to secure. Because the jamb is normally only 3/4 inch thick, longer screws will merely extend into the hidden space between the jamb and framing. If the gap is small, a long-enough screw may catch the stud. More often, though, you'll have to drill out the screw holes in the jamb, plug them with (glue-coated) dowels, and redrill pilot holes for new screws.

WHEN YOU DRIVE the new screws, be sure they go in straight so the flat heads sit flush with the face of the hinge. (Be sure not to use a screw that's too big.) A protruding screw head will undo the repair you just made by acting as a fulcrum, causing the hinge to pull out of its mortise.

● LOOSE LOWER HINGE -- Very occasionally, the bottom hinge is the culprit. If the hinges have an unusually wide throw -- like those installed on an entry door to clear the deep trim profile -- sometimes the bottom hinge loosens. This causes the door to sag slightly (when closed, the door rests against the jamb on the hinge side).

LIFT AND PULL the bottom of the door away from the jamb to see if the lower hinge is loose. A loose bottom hinge causes trouble most when the door is being swung open or shut, and cannot rest against the jamb for support. The

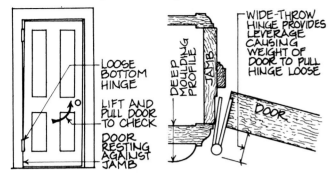

door may drag on the floor. Repair following the same procedures as above. But remember: An entry door is usually very heavy and wide-throw hinges provide a lot of leverage for the weight of the door to pull them loose. So be sure to make a strong, sound repair.

● WORN HINGE PIN -- If when you lift and push the door you see no movement of the hinge leaves in their mortises, but the knuckle moves or is misaligned, then the hinge pin is loose or worn. If the hinge pin is not set all the way into the hinge, try tapping it down into position. Often, unworn areas of the pin will tighten the sloppy fit. If the pin won't move, take it out and straighten it. Sometimes you'll have to remove the hinge to straighten bent knuckles.

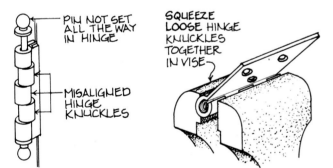

IF THE HINGE PIN is already set all the way and the knuckles are still loose and mis-aligned, you have to replace the pin or possibly the whole hinge. When the hinges are

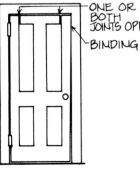

made of a malleable material such as brass or wrought iron, it may be that you can tighten the knuckles slightly by disassembling the hinge and squeezing the knuckles in a vise.

● OPEN JOINT BETWEEN UPPER RAIL AND STILE -- Look closely for this condition; the open joint may have been caulked or filled. This joint usually opens up because of the weight of the door, and will only worsen if not repaired. Less frequently, it's the result of

warping of the stile or rail. In either case, you're better off correcting it than trimming the door. It is possible to repair it with the door in place but a little easier if the door is removed.

REMOVE PAINT, filler, and caulk from the joint using standard paint-stripping practices. Now you can decipher the construction of the joint. If the door has a through tenon with a wedge, you'll be able to make a strong repair easily. Unfortunately, the rail tenon usually does <u>not</u> extend all the way through the stile. It is possible to repair such a joint, but you'll probably have to rely on fasteners to make it strong.

WITH A THROUGH-TENON joint, first remove the old wedges. Next, tug gently at the joint and push it closed a few times. Inject carpenter's glue into all exposed areas of the joint. Work as much glue as possible onto the broad sides of the tenon (as these are really the only effective gluing surfaces). Clamp the joint tight. Make new wedges (slightly longer than necessary), glue them, and drive them in snugly. Wipe up all excess glue. When the joint has dried, chisel wedges flush with the edge of the door.

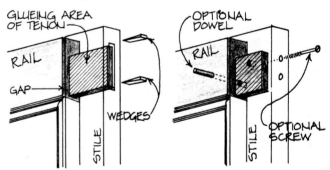

IF THE TENON reaches only part way through the stile, reglue as already described. If the joint opens back up, you may have to add a peg (dowel) or two through the stile and tenon as illustrated. If the door has or will get a clear finish, and seeing the pegs on the face of the door would be objectionable, you may want to screw the joint closed from the edge. Reglue the joint and clamp tight. Then countersink two long screws through the stile into the rail. Fill the holes with tinted filler or plug with wood and sand smooth. The repair will be hardly noticeable on the side of the stile.

Door Has Springy Resistance To Closing. Hinges Work Loose

● PAINT BUILDUP ON HINGE SIDE -- If, as the door reaches its closed position, you feel a

REMOVING A DOOR

ALWAYS START with the door in a closed position. Put a wedge under the door to take weight off the hinges or have a helper support the door. (The more stress on the hinges, the more difficult it will be to remove the pins, and the more likely you are to damage the hinges.)

TAP THE PINS gently up and out with a hammer and screwdriver. If they resist, try some penetrating oil. Check to see if paint buildup above the pin is interfering with removal. If you still can't remove the pins, try carefully grasping the finial or ball with a pair of locking pliers. Turn the pin slightly to break the bond; then try again. A really stubborn pin will probably come out if you remove the lower ball or finial and knock the pin up with a punch and hammer. Another alternative is to unscrew the hinges from the jamb — be sure to have a helper support the door in that case.

FREE UP ALL hinge pins before completely removing any of them. Remove pins from the bottom to the top — the top pin supports most of the load.

---

slight springy resistance and the hinges seem to be rocking in their mortises, most likely there is excess paint on the mating surfaces (of door and hinge side). Selectively or completely strip paint as previously discussed. Make sure the hinges are free of excess paint and screw heads are flush with face of hinge.

● HINGE MORTISE(S) TOO DEEP -- A previous, poorly-executed door repair may have resulted in more material being removed from the mortise than necessary. If the mortise is too deep, the hinge must be shimmed out flush with the jamb. The best way to achieve this is with a thin scrap of wood cut to the exact dimensions of the mortise. Another option is to use thin, plastic or metal prefabricated shims (available at most hardware stores). Avoid cardboard shims; they'll compress, and eventually decompose if exposed to moisture.

IF THE MORTISE on the door is too deep, the hinge can be shimmed as above. Or, if the door is a little tight in the opening, the hinge side can be planed enough to bring the hinges out flush with the edge of the door.

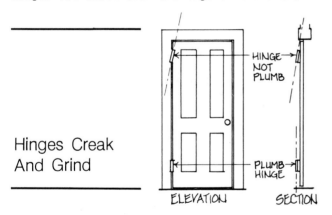

Hinges Creak And Grind

HINGE
NOT
PLUMB

PLUMB
HINGE

ELEVATION   SECTION

● HINGES NEED LUBRICANT -- Old hinges are bound to squeak and creak a bit. A couple drops of oil will usually silence them.

● HINGES ARE NOT PLUMB -- But if they continue to creak loudly and if there is even a slight feeling of resistance, the hinges are probably not plumb or in line with each other. Non-plumb hinges are not only noisy, but the extra friction on the knuckles will cause the hinge to wear out prematurely. Shim and/or remortise the hinges so they are plumb and in line with each other.

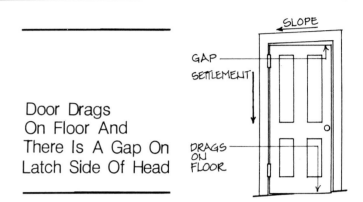

SLOPE

GAP

SETTLEMENT

DRAGS
ON
FLOOR

Door Drags On Floor And There Is A Gap On Latch Side Of Head

● BUILDING SETTLEMENT -- a common cause of the door dragging on the floor. This condition can be differentiated from simple loose hinges by a characteristic gap between the top of the door and the head. Check for squareness of door opening by putting a level on the head and along both sides of the jamb. An old building usually settles downward with only secondary lateral movement (leaning), so you'll probably see that the head is furthest out of alignment.

IF THE GAP at the top of the door is small enough that the door still meets the stop on the jamb head, it's not really worth rebuilding the jamb. Plane the bottom of the door instead. If, on the other hand, you can look right through the gap into the next room with the door closed, you should consider reframing the door.

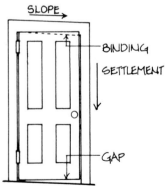

SLOPE

BINDING

SETTLEMENT

GAP

Door Binds On Latch Side Of Head And There Is A Gap At Floor

● AS WITH the previous condition, you're going to be faced with the decision to reframe the opening or simply plane the door. Keep in mind that the top rail of a door is usually narrower than the bottom and is more of a

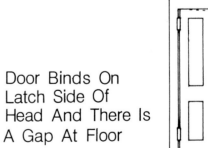

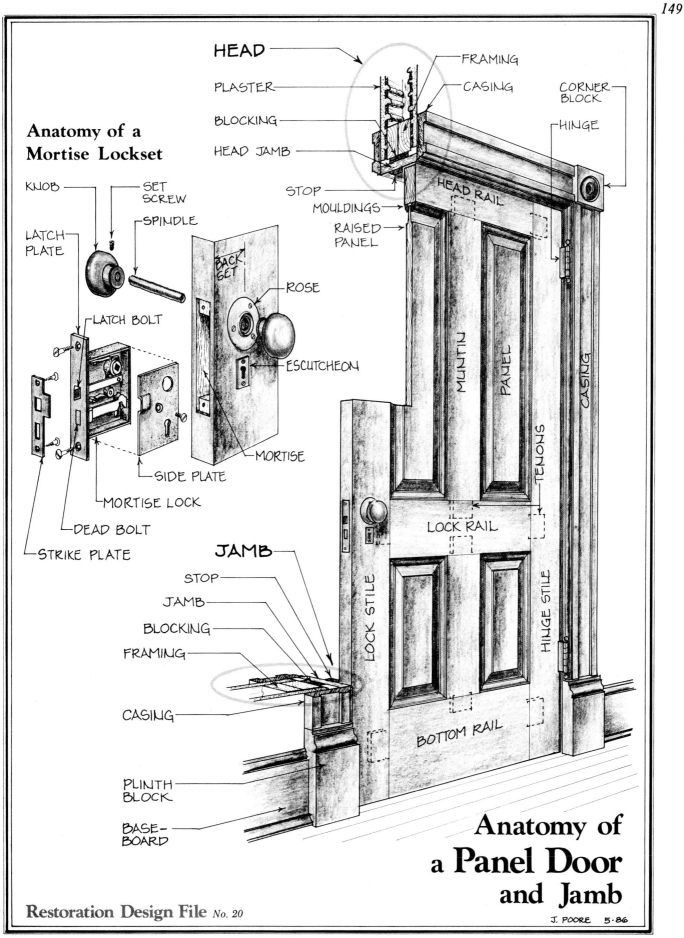

Anatomy of a Mortise Lockset

KNOB
SET SCREW
LATCH PLATE
SPINDLE
LATCH BOLT
STRIKE PLATE
DEAD BOLT
MORTISE LOCK
SIDE PLATE
MORTISE
BACK SET
ROSE
ESCUTCHEON

HEAD
PLASTER
BLOCKING
HEAD JAMB
FRAMING
CASING
CORNER BLOCK
HINGE
STOP
MOULDINGS
RAISED PANEL
HEAD RAIL
MUNTIN
PANEL
CASING
TENONS
LOCK RAIL
LOCK STILE
HINGE STILE
BOTTOM RAIL

JAMB
STOP
JAMB
BLOCKING
FRAMING
CASING
PLINTH BLOCK
BASE-BOARD

Anatomy of a **Panel Door** and **Jamb**

Restoration Design File *No. 20*

J. POORE 5·86

SOME TIPS ON
PLANING

● REMOVE PAINT from the surface to be planed. It's nearly impossible to plane through paint, and the blade will dull almost instantly. Set the blade for a shallow cut for maximum control and minimum tear-out.

● KEEP your tools sharp. A dull plane will not only make the work more difficult, but it will also damage the door. A sharp plane removes uniform ribbons of wood; a dull plane catches and slips, tearing out chunks of wood and rippling the surface.

● BEVEL the edge of the stile so that you don't produce a large gap when the door is closed. That is, remove more material from the side of the stile that passes the jamb first, and leave more material on the side that lines up with the jamb only when the door is completely closed.

● START at the corner on end grain (top and bottom of stile). Never run the plane off the end grain of the stile — you'll splinter the wood.

● TO AVOID knocking-off corners, bear down on the nose of the plane at the beginning of the cut and the back of the plane at the end of the cut. This is especially important when you're using a power plane; it can round off a corner in just one pass.

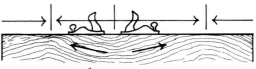

PLANE IN "UPHILL" DIRECTION

● IF THE GRAIN is wavy and the plane tears out wood in some places, try planing sections in alternate directions. If you're always planing "uphill," the plane can't dig in.

● AFTER planing, deepen hinge and lockset mortises as required to ensure hardware is flush with the edge of the door. Make sure spindle is centered in rose (see text).

focal point. Planing it to follow the slope of the head may leave it very unsightly and distorted. If a lot of material must be removed, you may even expose the tenon and weaken the door. This possibility creates a strong argument for reframing.

Door Binds Along Some Sections Of Jamb And Leaves Gaps In Other Areas

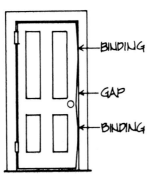

● DOOR HAS FALLEN VICTIM TO BAD OR UNNECESSARY PLANING -- Often this is quite obvious when you look at the edge of the door -- note unevenness, gouges, and torn wood grain. Check edge of door by holding a straight-edge against it.

IF THE DOOR is not straight (with a consistent bevel), swing the door against the edge of the jamb and mark the high spots to be planed. Plane these spots down even with the rest of the door (see planing box).

● JAMB IS NOT STRAIGHT -- If a straight-edge placed against the jamb shows that it bows or undulates, first check to see that the jamb is secure. Try pushing and twisting the jamb to see if it's properly secured. High spots

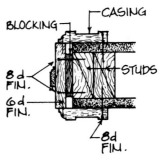

where the jamb is loose can be pulled back into line and secured with finishing nails. Use 8d finish nails where you must go through the jamb into the framing and 6d finish nails through the trim into the jamb.

IF THE JAMB cannot be forced back into position, remove the casing on the least conspicuous side. (Use a wide-blade putty knife to protect adjacent surfaces from the prybar. See "Removing Interior Woodwork", June 1985 OHJ, for more details.) On the opposite (most conspicuous) side, loosen the casing just enough to get a hacksaw blade behind it. Cut the nails that hold the casing to the jamb. This procedure allows you to free the jamb without completely removing the casings from both sides.

NOW YOU HAVE TO shim out the low spots in the jamb while cutting down the high ones until the jamb is plumb and correctly spaced from the door. To do this, drive some wedges between the jamb and blocking to shim out the low spots in the jamb. Chisel out existing blocking behind high spots and replace with smaller pieces of wood. (Sometimes there are small shims between the blocking and jamb. In that case, it's possible to simply remove the shims and renail.)

SOLID WOOD BLOCKING is better for shimming than wood shingles, because it won't compress or splinter, and it's less likely to split when nailed. Secure any new blocking with 8d finish nails driven through jamb, blocking, and stud. If you are working with fine woodwork with a clear finish, hide the finish nails by removing the stop before driving the nails. When the stop is resecured, the nail heads will be concealed.

AFTER the jamb is plumb and straight, reinstall the casing.

LATCHING PROBLEMS

NOW THAT ALL THE REPAIRS have been completed to make the door fit properly without binding, latching problems can be tackled.

Lockset Binds And Latch Doesn't Spring Back

IF THE DOORKNOB resists turning and doesn't spring back to position when you release it, try putting a few drops of oil into the latch. If that doesn't do the trick, look for a:

● PAINT-FILLED LOCKSET -- The most common problem with old, interior locksets is paint and dirt invading the mechanism and gumming up the works. Fortunately, old cast-iron or brass mortise locks are extremely durable and infinitely repairable.

REMOVE THE KNOBS and spindle. Unscrew the lockset and remove it from its mortise. If it resists, remove the excess paint that's holding it in position. Unscrew the side plate from the lockset to expose the mechanism. If you're lucky, you'll need only to scrape dirt and paint from the latch and its opening. At worst, you'll have to replace a broken part or two (parts can be salvaged from similar locksets). Be sure the return spring is intact and in the correct position. Oil all moving parts before reassembling.

● SPINDLE THAT'S NOT CENTERED IN ROSE -- If the spindle isn't centered in the rose (the metal plate that covers hole under knob), the knob may bind on the rose and prevent the latch from returning. This condition is likely if the door has previously been planed and the lockset mortise deepened.

SPINDLE NOT CENTERED IN ROSE

BE SURE the lockset is set all the way into its mortise so that it's flush with the edge of the door. Unscrew the rose or trimplate and shift its position so that the spindle will be centered when inserted. Rotate the rose a few degrees and redrill new holes so the screws don't split the wood alongside the abandoned screw holes. Remove any paint buildup from the mating surfaces between the knob and rose.

WHEN YOU REINSTALL the spindle and knobs, tighten them up, leaving only enough play so they don't bind against the rose. Tighten the set screws firmly against a flat surface in the spindle. If the screw doesn't bear squarely on the flat of the spindle, the screw will eventually loosen and the knob will fall off.

Lockset Functions Properly But Door Doesn't Latch

● PAINT BUILDUP ON STOP AND DOOR -- Thick paint on the latch side of the door will prevent the latch from reaching the strike plate. Remove as necessary.

● MISALIGNMENT OF LATCH WITH MORTISE IN STRIKE PLATE -- Look into the joint between the door and jamb to see if the latch and mortise line up vertically. If the joint is too small for you to see (and it ought to be), look for wear marks on the strike plate. Or, close the door and make a scratch on the outside of the strike at the top of the latch. Then open the door to see if the mark lines up with the mortise.

LATCH MISSES MORTISE IN STRIKE

IF THE MORTISE in the strike is just a bit high or low, the strike plate can be removed and filed to accommodate the latch. If the misalignment exceeds about 1/16 inch, it will be necessary to move the strike (assuming all other door repairs are complete). Extend the mortise for the strike with a chisel as required. Plug the old screw holes and refasten the strike in its new position. On extremely fine millwork, fill the exposed section of mortise with a thin piece of matching wood.

● DOOR IS WARPED -- If the latch lines up with the mortise, there's no paint buildup, and the door still refuses to latch, it may be warped. Sight across the face of the door or put a straight edge diagonally across the face to see if the door is twisted. Check along the face of the latch stile to see if _it's_ warped. It's impossible to unwarp a stile, and hard to take a twist out of a door. It's easy enough to remove the stops and reset _them_ so they conform. Renail stops with the door closed, so they can be bent slightly to follow the warp. There should be just enough space between the door and stops so the door closes easily without rattling.

Door Rattles Between Latch And Stops

● STOPS ARE TOO FAR FROM DOOR -- Remove the stops and renail them closer to the door as described previously.

● WORN LATCH -- Check to see if the latch is loose within the face plate of the lockset. If this is the case, you'll have no choice but to replace the lockset to eliminate rattling.

OCTAGONS

and Hexagons and Other Multi-Faceted Eccentricities

by James C. Massey & Shirley Maxwell

THE OCTAGON HOUSE is a mid-19th-century architectural curiosity that has had far greater impact on the imaginations of preservationists and architectural historians than on the American townscape. Still, several thousand of these eight-sided oddities (as well as other buildings with anywhere from six to sixteen sides) were built following the publication of Orson Squire Fowler's 1849 treatise <u>A Home For All</u>, which brought the octagon concept to national attention for the first time.

TRULY MORE A SHAPE THAN A STYLE, the octagon needs only one characteristic for absolutely certain identification: eight consecutively angled exterior walls. Decorative elements may be drawn from any mid-Victorian style; often, they were omitted altogether. Bracket-

ed eaves and Italianate door and window details are perhaps most common, although Stick Style is also frequently encountered. Roofs are usually hipped or pyramidal and are frequently topped by octagonal cupolas.

FOWLER was not the first American to be struck by the possibilities of the octagon and other multi-sided architectural forms. Williamsburg, Virginia, had an octagonal powder magazine, and Thomas Jefferson built a little octagonal summer home, Poplar Forest, in 1819. Hexagonal schools and churches were not unknown to Fowler, and circular jails enjoyed a certain vogue.

HOWEVER, IT WAS FOWLER -- theological graduate turned phrenologist, marriage counseler, lecturer, publisher, and inveterate giver of

It may still be known as "The Folly," but this 1863 octagon house built in Columbus, Georgia, today has the respectable status of a National Historic Landmark.

Opposite:
Among the several hundred octagon houses remaining today is this striking museum restoration: Longwood, built in Natchez, Mississippi, in 1862. The house is also notable for its exotic, onion-shaped dome and other Moorish-revival details.

socially uplifting advice -- who popularized the form for residential use. He would have preferred basing his ideal house on the circle, which he saw as the most natural, aesthetic, and economical way to enclose the greatest amount of interior space. Recognizing the limits of most builders' skills, however, he was willing to settle for a six-, eight-, or sixteen-cornered structure. He hoped the form would provide cheap, comfortable, durable housing for the working classes.

Materials

FOWLER IMAGINED that such dwellings could be constructed by the prospective occupants themselves, and he advocated the use of concrete as the cheapest, most permanent, and most readily available building material. In fact, his enlarged 1853 edition of A Home For All was subtitled "The Gravel Wall or Octagon Mode of Building." Although concrete construction was familiar to the ancient Romans, it hadn't been used in America, and Fowler was impressed when he came upon the concrete (or "grout") hexagonal house that Joseph Goodrich had built in Milton, Wisconsin. Goodrich concocted a sturdy mixture of lime, sand, and coarse gravel which Fowler pronounced "hard as stone."

GOODRICH'S HOUSE still stands today, but not all early-American concrete held up so well. In 1859, Daniel Harrison Jacques complained in another Fowler and Wells publication (The House: A Pocket Manual of Rural Architecture) that improperly mixed and cured walls often crumbled into dust within a couple of years. That fact, along with the unwieldiness of the material and the building public's unfamiliarity with the techniques for using it, probably accounted for its limited popularity. More octagons took shape in frame, vertical planking, brick, stone -- perhaps even cobblestone -- than in concrete.

Orson Squire Fowler's model for the use of concrete walls in a polygonal structure was the Joseph Goodrich House, built in Milton, Wisconsin, in 1844.

Fowler was no architect, but he was obviously fearless about following his own advice — he designed and built this gravel-wall house for his family in Fishkill, New York. Alas, the 60-room residence, completed in 1853, no longer exists.

A celebrated Washington, D.C., building, "The Octagon" isn't an octagon at all—it's really an irregular hexagon. Completed in 1800, the house sheltered James and Dolley Madison after they were burned out of the White House by British troops.

The John Richards House was built in Watertown, Wisconsin, in 1854. The largest octagon in the Midwest, it has 32 rooms and a central spiral staircase. (Note the octagonal cupola.)

The Armour-Stiner House, completed in 1860 in Irvington, New York, is a stunning blend of Gothic, Stick Style, Second Empire, and Eastlake details.

The Shape Of Things

ALTHOUGH OCTAGONAL HOUSES were constructed throughout the second half of the 19th century, their heyday came before the Civil War. They sprang up in modest numbers all across the United States, particularly in New York, New England, and the Midwest. The South had relatively few examples; the Southwest, very few or none.

IT MAY BE A TELLING COMMENT, both on the surface appeal of the design and on its practical shortcomings, that many small towns boasted one -- and only one -- octagon. The awkward interior arrangements fostered by multi-sided architecture must have discouraged many potential builders. Although Fowler and other pattern-book authors furnished simple floorplans, the layout of a polygonal house was seldom as space- and energy-efficient as it was advertised to be. Inserting conventional rectangular rooms within the octagon produced leftover triangles of hard-to-use space; wedge-shaped or irregular room designs filled out the perimeter of the house, but were often less convenient than traditional plans. Either way, it was hard to provide such essential amenities as logically placed windows, doors, and corridors. On the whole, the polygon seems to have been better suited to barns and outbuildings than to human habitation, and those utilitarian forms continued to be built well into the 20th century, especially circular barns.

"NATURE'S FORMS are mostly spherical. She makes 10,000 curvilinear forms to one square form. Then why not apply her forms to houses?"
— Orson Squire Fowler, "A Home For All" (1854)

Reading The Old House

Octagons, Hexagons, and other Multi-Faceted Eccentricities

BY JAMES C. MASSEY & SHIRLEY MAXWELL

SCROLL BRACKETS
WIDE, PLAIN EAVES
DENTIL CORNICE
PLAIN FRIEZE
BLIND OR FALSE WINDOWS

PAIRED OCTAGONAL CHIMNEYS
OCTAGONAL CUPOLA
PAIRED 6/6 LIGHT, DOUBLE-HUNG SASH

PORCH CORNICE ECHOES ROOF ON SMALLER SCALE — SCROLL BRACKETS AND DENTILS

DOUBLE SASH AND PANEL DOORS WITH RECTANGULAR TRANSOM

FEATURES: KEY FEATURE IS THE DISTINCTIVE OCTAGON SHAPE — ALONG WITH OCCASIONAL HEXAGONS. DESPITE FOWLER'S PLEA FOR CONCRETE WALLS, BRICK, STUCCO, AND FRAME WERE STANDARD. DETAILS WERE MOST COMMONLY ITALIANATE (AS THIS) OR STICK STYLE. ROOFS USUALLY PYRAMIDAL GABLES WITH CUPOLAS, AS THIS EXAMPLE, BUT MANSARDS AND DOMES MAY BE FOUND.

PLAN: DESPITE ATTRACTIVE OCTAGON SHAPE, IT WAS DIFFICULT TO LAY OUT AN EFFICIENT PLAN. WHATEVER APPROACH LEFT CORNER "CLOSETS" OR WEDGE-SHAPED ROOMS (AS HERE).

"VERANDA" WAS THE COMMONEST TERM FOR TODAY'S PORCH, WHICH THEN HAD A MORE UTILITARIAN CONNOTATION

SOURCE: O.S. FOWLER, "A HOME FOR ALL," 1854 EDITION

PANTRY
LIVING-ROOM
15 × 13
BED ROOM
16 × 16
CLOSET
CLOSET
PARLOR
5 × 3
HALL
6 6
STOOP
VERANDA
PLAN OF FIRST STORY

EXTERIOR STAINS

BY PATRICIA POORE AND BILL O'DONNELL

EXTERIOR STAINS come in so many different permutations -- oil and latex, semi-transparent and opaque, preservative and weathering -- that the whole subject seems complex. We sat down and read through all the manufacturers' literature we could get our hands on. After sorting it out and applying common sense (with a dash of experience), we've figured out it's not so complex after all. Here we'll give you a run-down of what's available and offer some tips specific to old buildings.

STAIN VS. PAINT

WHY USE a stain at all? They're gaining popularity in new wood construction because they are cheaper than paint and don't build up to a thick film. Maintenance is generally easier with stains: Preparing the surface before re-coating is easier. Also, modern tastes accept and even prefer that the wood texture show through the finish. Keep all this in mind if you're adding an outbuilding or a rear wing.

STAIN HAS less applicability for older houses that are already painted. You'll be able to switch to stain only if the paint film has weathered away to virtually nothing, or if you've stripped off all the paint to bare wood. The decision to switch will probably be based on your unwillingness to start the whole painting cycle over again. In harsh environments where paint regularly fails (such as on the seacoast), you might try a stain system instead. Stain must still be renewed, of course -- but preparation is easier, and stain weathers more gracefully than paint. (Opaque stain doesn't hold up as well as paint on exposed south-facing walls; recoat more often where degradation is apparent.)

STAIN CAN ALSO be used selectively. You could stay with paint (which has better hiding characteristics and color retention) on clapboards ... but switch to a semi-transparent stain on new or stripped rails and balustrades. Stain is excellent for use on these high-abrasion surfaces. (It's the only practical choice for a deck.)

OLD-HOUSE OWNERS might consider a stain finish for new wood shingle roofs. Nothing can "bring back" already-weathered shingles or shakes. But a new wood roof will look good longer (and maybe last longer) with a semi-transparent preservative stain on it. (Don't use paint or opaque stain on a roof; it won't hold up.)

TYPES OF STAIN

DESPITE ALL the different names used by manufacturers, most products fall into these categories:

(1) Semi-transparent -- allow some of the wood's color, plus its grain and texture, to show through.
(2) Solid-color or Opaque -- have greater opacity, giving a consistent color finish, but allow more texture to show than paint does.

MOST STAINS are oil-based, because the whole idea is that they penetrate the wood (rather than forming a surface film). An important departure are the relatively new latex opaque stains, which are a compromise between paint and stain. Because it is the only kind of stain that can be used over previously coated wood, it has a special usefulness for old buildings.

SOME PRODUCTS contain a wood preservative, commonly TBTO (tributyltin oxide), which is effective yet doesn't appear to have the human toxicity associated with bad actors like pentachlorophenol. Most contain a mildewcide such as Folpet (N-trichloromethylthio-phthalimide). The labels are usually obvious about active ingredients.

THERE ARE a few special-use stains, too. A popular one (for new wood only) is weathering stain. This imparts a soft grey finish on application, then chemically assists weathering to a natural silver grey in six to nine

The label will give you information on opacity and color, presence of water repellents or preservative chemicals, recommended uses, and application instructions. Major stain manufacturers also offer technical literature.

PRODUCTS \ FEATURES	FINISH	WATER REPELLENT	PRESERVA-TIVE	BASE	COLORS
CABOT'S Semi-Transparent	Semi-Transparent	Yes (non-paraffin)	TBTO & Folpet	Linseed Oil	28
CABOT'S O.V.T. Solid Color	Opaque	None	None	Linseed Oil	30
CABOT'S Acrylic Solid Color	Opaque	None	None	Acrylic Latex	15
CABOT'S Bleaching Stain	Clear	None	Folpet	Linseed Oil	Driftwood Grey
OLYMPIC Semi-Transparent	Semi-Transparent	None	None	Oil	36
OLYMPIC Solid Color	Opaque	None	None	Acrylic Latex or Linseed Oil	30
OLYMPIC Weather Screen	Opaque / Semi-Transparent	Yes	TBTO	Linseed Oil	30
OLYMPIC Natural Tones	Transparent / Semi-Transparent	Yes / None	Yes / None	Oil	3: Cedar, Fir, Redwood
MINWAX Ext. Wood Finish	Semi-Transparent	Paraffin	TBTO	Linseed Oil	8
MINWAX Solid Color Ext. Stain	Opaque	Paraffin	TBTO & iodine polyphase	Linseed Oil	8
BENJAMIN MOORE Moorwood Solid-C. Oil	Opaque	None	Folpet	Modified Linseed Alkyd	15 (+ custom)
BENJAMIN MOORE Moorwood Solid-C. Latex	Opaque	None	Yes	Acrylic Latex	15 (+ custom)
BENJAMIN MOORE Moorwood Semi-Trans.	Semi-Transparent	Yes	TBTO & Folpet	Modified Linseed Alkyd	20 (+ custom)
REZ (PPG) Oil-Based Stain	Semi-Transparent	Paraffin	TBTO	Oil / Alkyd	12
REZ (PPG) Solid-Color Latex	Opaque	None	None	Acrylic Latex	21
FLOOD CWF	Clear	Yes (non-paraffin)	Yes	Oil	Clear

FINISH \ USES	Weathered Wood	New Wood	Painted Wood	Freshly Stripped Wood	'Bleeder' Woods	Horizontal Surfaces	Shake Roofs	Masonry, Stucco, Metals
Clear or Transparent	Yes	Yes	No	Yes	Maybe*	Yes	Yes	No
Semi-Transparent	Yes	Yes	No	Yes	Maybe*	Yes	Yes	No
Opaque Oil	Finish Coat	Finish Coat	No	Yes	Yes	No	No	No
Opaque Latex	Finish Coat	Finish Coat	With Proper Preparation	Finish Coat	No	No	No	Yes
Paint	Finish Coat	Yes	Yes	Yes	Yes	Maybe*	No	Yes

*See product literature for instructions.

months. (Some companies call them "bleaching stains"; read the literature.) Another sub-group are the "natural stains." These keep the wood looking new. They do have pigment in them (the color of the raw redwood, cedar, or fir); a truly clear coating would allow ultraviolet light to penetrate and discolor the surface. Again, you'll find that the labels or literature are quite helpful.

WHAT TO USE WHEN

LET'S GO BACK to the beginning. Oil-base stains penetrate the wood; latex stains form a thin, flexible film. So if there is any paint whatsoever left on the house, your choice is limited to latex opaque stain. Prepare the surface as scrupulously as for painting -- there must be no loose paint, rough edges, dirt, mildew, etc.

HERE ARE some other situations when a latex opaque stain is best:
● To get a traditional, color-rich finish without using paint.
● To go from a semi-transparent or opaque oil finish to a lighter color. (To use a light-color latex stain on dark woods, you may have to prime with an undercoat product from the same manufacturer.)
● To cover over previous stain that contained creosote.
● To get an opaque-stain coating on new, bare Southern yellow pine, maple, and other close-pored, impervious wood species.
● When mildew is a recurring problem. (Latex stains are more mildew-resistant than oil.)
● When ease of application and cleanup is of utmost importance. (Latex is water-soluble.)

MOST STAINS are oil-based (penetrating) products. The most effective (and justifiably expensive) of these are chiefly linseed-oil-based (sometimes modified with a long-oil alkyd). For a semi-transparent finish, use only an oil-based product (not latex).

FOR WOOD that has weathered and is already showing signs of deterioration, it is possible to color with an oil-based, semi-transparent or solid stain, but only after careful prep-aration. First, the wood must be cleaned with a weak oxalic acid/water solution. All weath-ered wood must then be waterblasted or wire-brushed (use a non-iron brush) to remove loose and damaged wood fibers. You'll have to stick to dark colors if any greying or discoloration remains.

THE MANUFACTURERS of the preservative chemi-cals that are used to treat new lumber say that pressure-treated wood can be stained under certain conditions. For example, the Wolmanized brand can be stained with one coat of an oil-based, semi-transparent stain after the wood has been exposed to full weathering for at least two months. (Be aware that the green tinge in treated wood will affect the

color.) Do check with the manufacturer's technical literature or personnel.

USE OIL-BASED STAINS, not latex, on open-pored woods such as redwood, cedar, mahogany, and fir.

ON APPLICATION

MANY INEXPERIENCED APPLICATORS give up on the idea of semi-transparent or bleaching stain because they can't get even coverage. We've all been spoiled by the ease of application of high-quality latex paints, which are almost foolproof.

APPLYING STAIN does take a little more care, but it doesn't take any longer than painting. (And the next time, preparing a previously-stained surface will be easier than preparing a previously-painted one.) Here are some tips:

(1) Pour the top oils out and stir the pigment-rich contents. Then put the oils back in and stir thoroughly. It's best to pour two or three gallons into a five-gallon pail, and stir together for uniform color and pigment dispersion.

(2) You do have to box your stain; that is, mix one batch of stain into another to avoid pigment concentration and color differences. Never use the bottom third of a can; stir it into the next batch.

(3) Stir the stain often during application.

(4) To avoid lap marks, be very mindful to keep a wet edge. On clapboards, take a few courses and apply stain to a natural break such as a window or corner board. On vertical siding, start at the top of a few boards and work down. Don't stain in direct sun.

(5) A good brush is the best tool for staining. But if you're using a low-viscosity (very fluid) semi-transparent or bleaching stain and you find that it's running all over the place, switch to a foam-pad applicator.

(6) Follow directions on the label whenever possible. With latex stain: Don't apply when temperature is below 50 degrees (or will go below 50 within 24 hours). Doing so could actually affect the cure. (Applying oil-based products below recommended temperature will affect drying time, but not usually durability.) On hot, dry days, dampen the surface before applying latex stain. (Oil stain must be applied to a dry surface.)

(7) When possible, remove trim that's to be stained a different color from the body. It's almost impossible to cut-in with stain.

(8) On new work, pre-stain if possible. It's easier to control the finish when the clap-boards are laying across saw-horses in the shade. 🏛

OLYMPIC STAIN – 2233 112th Ave. NE, Bellevue, WA 98004. (800) 426-6306, (206) 453-1700. Free color cards and manual.
SAMUEL CABOT, INC. (Cabot Stains) – One Union St., Boston, MA 02108. (617) 723-7740. Free Technical Data Sheets; brochure.
REZ FINISHES (division PPG Industries) – One PPG Place, Pittsburgh, PA 15272. (412) 434-3131. R&D, (800) 441-9695. Free Rez Stains brochure.

MINWAX CO., INC. – 16 Cherry St., Clifton, NJ 07014. (201) 391-0253. Free literature and color card.
BENJAMIN MOORE – 51 Chestnut Ridge Rd., Montvale, NJ 07645. (201) 573-9600. (212) 925-4300. Free leaflet; specify ext. stains.
FLOOD COMPANY – PO Box 399, Hudson, OH 44236. (800) 321-3444. Free tech. brochure on clear preservative finishes.
Note: Other coatings companies also manufacture quality stains.

IVY IN VICTORIAN INTERIORS

by Ron Pilling

HENRY T. WILLIAMS, in his 1871 volume Window Gardening, called ivy the "poor man's vine," noting that it grew for almost anyone, green thumb notwithstanding. Everyone in the Western world must have agreed, because miles and miles of ivy were twined through parlors and draped over framed portraits of loved ones.

IT WAS TRAINED to climb columns and window frames, to crawl along cornices and surround doorways as if they were garden trellises. If ivy wouldn't grow in a particular place, housewives simply cut off some leaves, strung them like beads on wire, and nailed the "artistic" assemblage to the wall.

The American Woman's Home

Centered before this Victorian window is a shallow Wardian Case, appropriate for mosses, tiny ground covers, and short ferns. Ivy grows from two large pots placed on either side of the window; it may have crawled across the cornice, creating a "perpetual indoor summer."

THERE WASN'T MUCH TIME for "floral elegances" until the middle of the 19th century. Americans in the 1700s had a hard enough time just keeping body and soul together. But developments by the mid-1800s turned the attention of the Victorian homeowner to indoor gardening. In 1842, London physician Nathaniel Ward invented the "Wardian Case," what we now know as a terrarium. Plant collectors -- and there were plenty of them hunting the jungles of the world for tropical splendors -- sold plants that, without these glass cases, would never have survived the long voyage to shops in London, New York, and Philadelphia.

A GREAT CURIOSITY about indoor gardening developed. Magazines carried columns about propagating English Ivy, Climbing Ferns, Ivy-Leafed Toad Flax, and other vines. Readers were taught how to harvest houseplants in the wild and how to adapt them to Victorian interiors. There were hanging pots and huge jardinieres filled with various plants, but it was the climbing ivy that dominated indoor gardens, and it was ivy that tied the entire scheme together.

BY 1869, when Catherine E. Beecher and Harriet Beecher Stowe published The American Woman's Home, they were able to report that "The use of ivy in decorating a room is beginning to be generally acknowledged ... Ivy will live and thrive and wind about in a room, year in and year out, will grow around pictures, and do almost anything to oblige you." The use of ivy as an important decorative element reflected other mawkish Victorian sentimental ideas about nature. Natural forms, it was argued, taught lessons of patient endurance, meek submission, and innocent cheerfulness.

PARLOURS were routinely turned into ivy-laden jungles. In typical Victorian fashion, if a little ivy refreshed a room setting, yards of it were even better. No window was complete without it. The March 1868 issue of Hearth And Home showed a window garden "whose chief charm consists in the running vines that start from a longitudinal box at the bottom of the window, and thence clamber up and about the casing and across the rustic framework erected for its convenience."

The Joy Of Ivy

ENGLISH IVY was the most popular plant for parlour decoration. Its tendrils will grasp nearly anything that presents itself. Though a very common plant, English Ivy became living poetry for Victorian writers: "A single root has been known to wreath a bow window with thick garlands, and then strike off into lovely independent paths along picture cords

"Where adjoining rooms connect by folding-doors, the openings may be festooned with the vines in the most pleasing manner. [This illustration] shows part of such a doorway, there being a corresponding pot on the other side."

and above cornices, till the room seems all a-bud ... Wherever it goes it makes a green, perpetual indoor summer of life."

OTHER CLIMBING PLANTS breached the walls of parlours and drawing rooms. Irish Ivy was prized for its light-green foliage and its ability to grow in dimly lit rooms. German Ivy was especially fast-growing and could easily be propagated from cuttings. The purple stems and purple veins of Coliseum Ivy made the variety highly sought. One Victorian horticulturist noted that Coliseum Ivy grew in cracks of the wall of "the Grand Cathedral in Milan." Variegated ivy, with foliage of green, yellow, gold, and cream, was reserved for sunny rooms.

FOR LARGE GROWTH, the ivy was planted in heavy pots on the floor and then allowed to climb as the homeowner desired. Ivy is indeed a hardy plant, and will spread quickly with minimal care. Pots must be well drained and the soil must be rich. A Victorian recipe for ivy soil consisting of half composted leaf mold and half well-decayed manure is still a good formula. Commercial potting soil will also work well. Cover the bottom of the pot with an inch or so of gravel and then a thin layer of charcoal before filling with potting soil.

PART OF THE REASON for ivy's success in Victorian homes is that it isn't very sensitive to changes in temperature and does reasonably well in darkened areas. This made it ideal for hallways that may have been near a drafty entry or in heavily draped parlours with little natural light. Even an unevenly heated 1880 brownstone was an adequate environment, as long as the plants got a little warmth in the winter and a short daily dose of sunlight.

AS THE IVY spilled from its pot, it was trained on stakes or directly on interior architectural details. If limited to tall stakes securely anchored in the soil, the plant could be moved from window to window, and outdoors in spring and summer. It is more permanent, however, when climbing staircases, twined around balustrades, or framing entry arches (which was its favorite use). "Sometimes the whole side of a parlour is covered with it ... looped about brackets ... the most beautiful of all drawing-room plant decorations."

MORE ELABORATE TRAINING for large plants called for indoor trellises. A line drawing of the period to suggest designs for ivy shows a small sofa nestled inside a trellis that arches over its top (see illustration at left). The trellis ends are planted in two long boxes placed on either side of the sofa, from which the ivy grows. The climbing greenery obscures any activity on the sofa, creating a sort of natural inglenook when surrounded by tall pots of palm and plant stands with lush ferns.

By training ivy over a trellis, the Victorian homeowner could create a leafy 'inglenook.'

IVY GROWING in similar long planter boxes with a lattice screen attached to one long side of the box was used as room dividers. The ivy climbed the lattice, creating a leafy "wall" that could be used to divide large rooms into smaller, more intimate spaces.

VINES CAN ALSO BE GROWN by immersing their ends into vials of water. This was a popular way to train live ivy around "the portraits of father, mother, and cherished friends, who look forth smiling from the leafy environment." Each vial is attached to the back of the picture frame with a few small pieces of charcoal in the bottom to purify the water. Since Victorians hung their pictures and looking-glasses high on the wall, slanted downward from the top, a space at the top between the back of the picture and the wall was perfect for the water-filled vial. Plant shops sold tin or zinc containers with pointed bottoms, shaped to fit into this space. Care was taken to make sure all were kept filled with water.

THE IVY COULD THEN GROW around the frame and up the picture cords. If the picture were suspended from a picture moulding at ceiling level, the ivy often climbed from the cornice, down the wire, and around the frame. It was then gracefully draped from picture to picture, while that growing in the cornice served to border the room at the ceiling line.

GODEY'S LADY'S MAGAZINE, throughout the 1870s and '80s, described all manner of hanging pots, showing some with embroidered or beaded covers. Wall-mounted wicker baskets concealed pots of one sort of plant or another. Among the plants popular for such pots were the climbing varieties. "Here at home, it climbs and swings, and droops at will, thriving and twining until the arms of the basket are hidden in the dense verdure."

SOMETHING ABOUT GARDENING seemed to inspire plant-lovers a century ago with great poetic inspiration. Ivy, which "twined," "draped," and "rambled," represented all that was pure and forthright. The plant bent to its owners' wishes, served only to improve the environments of those around it, and willingly adapted to nearly any room.

"IT BECOMES AS ONE with the family. Wash its dusty leaves, and no child could look more gracefully in your face." Perhaps that's stretching the character of English Ivy a bit, but there's no denying that the dark green vine has a place in any newly restored row house or gothic cottage. 🏠

Right Above: This illustration "drops a hint as to how ivy may be concealed behind a mirror, with its graceful loops hanging down on each side, and a small portion just peeping into the glass."
Right Below: "At the side windows hang baskets filled with trailing plants ... good honest earthen pots that expect to be hidden, and usually are, by a luxuriant growth of verdure and bloom."

Ivy Suitable For Historic Interiors

• English Ivy (Hedera helix) was brought to America by our colonial ancestors, but grew wild by the mid-19th century. English Ivy grows well in full or partial shade and clings tenaciously to nearly anything. The leaves are shiny, leathery, dark green.

• Algerian Ivy, or Irish Ivy (Hedera canariensis), is distinctive for its wine-red twigs and stems. The large leaves (five to seven inches across) are bright green in summer and turn to bronze in winter.

• German Ivy (Senecio scandens) resembles its English counterpart. The leaves are smaller and lighter in color, and German Ivy grows much faster. It is also called Parlour Ivy.

• Coliseum Ivy (Linaria cymbalaria) has purple stems and small green leaves with purple veins. It has minute flowers of lilac, white, and yellow.

• Creeping Fig (Ficus pumila) has one-inch, heart-shaped leaves that grow very thick, and in time will form almost a solid mat.

• Swedish Ivy (Plectranthus australis) "grows so thick that it forms a living curtain." Tiny leaves are waxy green, with scalloped edges.

Our Homes And Their Adornaments, 1882

Home Interiors, 1878

POST VICTORIAN HOUSES

Better Homes, 1927

It may not look very porch-like, but the second-storey bedroom (that trio of windows, far right) is technically a sleeping porch — note the terminology in the floor plan (below right) for this 1927 Colonial Revival house.

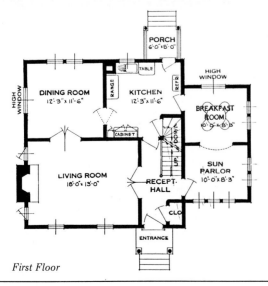

PORCH
6'-0" x 5'-0"

TABLE

RANGE

HIGH WINDOW

REFR

HIGH WINDOW

DINING ROOM
12'-3" x 11'-6"

KITCHEN
12'-3" x 11'-6"

BREAKFAST ROOM
6'-0" x 8'-5"

CABINET

UP DOWN

LIVING ROOM
18'-0" x 13'-0"

SUN PARLOR
10'-0" x 8'-3"

RECEPT. HALL

CLO

ENTRANCE

First Floor

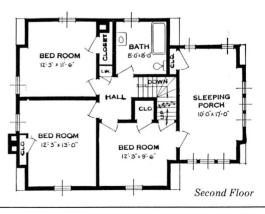

BED ROOM
12'-3" x 11'-6"

CLOSET

LIN.

BATH
8'-0" x 8'-0"

HALL

DOWN

CLO

BED ROOM
12'-3" x 13'-0"

CLO

SLEEPING PORCH
10'-0" x 17'-0"

BED ROOM
12'-3" x 9'-6"

Second Floor

SLEEPING PORCHES

by Eve Kahn and Walter Jowers

OT LONG AGO, sleeping in a closed bedroom was thought to be trouble. In the late 1800s, Harriet Beecher Stowe wrote of a child who "this morning sits up in bed with his hair bristling with crossness, strikes at his nurse and declares he won't say his prayers." She concluded: "The child, having slept in a close box of a room, his brain all night fed by poison, is in a mild state of moral insanity." Well, Harriet may have had a gift for hyperbole, but her ideas about stuffy sleeping quarters weren't too different from those of her contemporaries.

BY THE TURN of the century, much of American society had embraced the idea of open-air sleeping. From that time until around 1925, many families insisted that their new houses be built with that modern, health-giving amenity: the sleeping porch.

IF YOU WANT to restore the sleeping porch on your post-Victorian house to its original appearance or use, but you've had a hard time planning the project because your porch has been remuddled, this article should help. We'll give you some ideas about what these porches looked like, how they were used; and,

we hope, pass along a little bit of the special appreciation the original owners and builders had for these porches.

ARCHITECTS AND TASTEMAKERS of the era encouraged people to build and use sleeping porches. In 1914, architect Glenn Saxton wrote: "The secret is that you breathe the fresh pure air during your sleeping hours, which is worth more than any apothecary's pills in the world. A sleeping porch is one thing every house, little or big, should have."

AND MANY PERIOD HOUSES had them, usually on the second storey. The air up there was supposed to be better. People building one-storey houses figured that low fresh air was better than no fresh air, so they built sleeping porches, too. People with older houses that had no sleeping porch weren't about to risk the perils of sleeping indoors; they either hauled beds out onto whatever porches they had, or built additions. Sleeping porches usually adjoined bedrooms, though these bedrooms were often "demoted" to the role of mere dressing rooms, since all the sleeping was done out on the porch.

THESE PORCHES came in all forms. The most common type was the "wing," which generally

This circa 1920 interior is labeled a "sun room," but as it has a bed, it could easily have been used as a sleeping porch. The decor is typical of either room — wicker, rustic furniture, Native American rugs and blankets.

Representative California Homes, c. 1911.

Pennsylvania Homes, 1910

Inset: The "open-air roof garden" of this house would double as a sleeping porch.
Below Left: The tower sleeping porch of this Bungalow could catch breezes from all four sides.

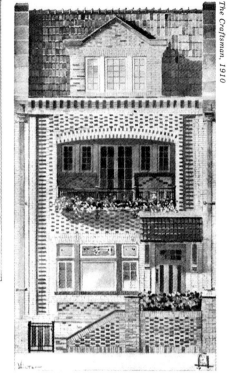

The Craftsman, 1910

Even city dwellers needed a chance to sleep outdoors, so architects obliged them with sleeping balconies.

The Craftsman, 1910

This cement house was fitted with a sleeping balcony — partly open for a better view on clear nights, partly covered in case of rain.

Craftsman Homes, 1909

A sleeping porch could simply be a room left open on two sides.

consisted of two storeys with a sunroom below and the sleeping porch above. (Sunshine was thought to be as healthful as the night air.) This wing would appear on either the side or back of the house. Sometimes the lower section was an open porch, while the upper section was closed in. Sleeping-porch wings were often built on the grander houses of the era -- Foursquares, larger neo-colonials and neo-Federals -- but they were not uncommon on smaller homes, and they were also used as additions to "update" older homes.

OTHER FORMS of the sleeping porch were less porch-like. The popularity of the movement was such that anything remotely resembling a generously windowed room was called a sleeping porch. If one bedroom had more windows than the others, that one was labeled "the sleeping porch" in the builder's plans. If a dormer had a row of windows, the room tucked underneath was called a sleeping porch. Sleeping balconies -- both roofed and roofless -- were also built, some even appearing on city townhouses. Sometimes a corner bedroom was left open to the elements on two sides, creating a "sleeping area." This was especially popular

The sun parlor / sleeping porch wing survived briefly in the post-post-Victorian world, as on this house — but eventually the garage and TV room supplanted it.

Baker's Book Of Homes, 1926

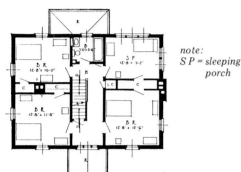

note:
S P = sleeping porch

SECOND FLOOR

Pennsylvania Homes, 1926

All that sets off the "sleeping porch" from other bedrooms is a double window, and a triple window that faces the backyard.

American Dwellings, 1914

This neo-Federal has a typical sun room / sleeping porch wing that's "all sashed in, in case it gets too cool or starts to rain."

on rustic vacation homes, where occasionally the entire second storey was left open.

THE SLEEPING PORCH reached its zenith with the sleeping tower. This rather rare structure (it was practical only in warmer climates) consists of a second-storey cap atop a one-storey bungalow. Inside were one or more bedrooms, with either open or screened windows.

THE SLEEPING PORCH'S POPULARITY was but brief (except Down South, where, before air conditioning, screened porches were a summer necessity). As people sought to balance their desire for fresh night air with their needs for comfort and privacy, the distinction between a sleeping porch and a merely well-ventilated room clouded. As screens went up to keep out summer bugs, curtains went up to keep out neighbors' gazes, and glazing and heaters were installed to keep out winter's cold, sleeping porches were gradually "absorbed" back into the bedrooms. And finally the noise and odor from increasingly car-infested roads, combined with growing skepticism of the sleeping porch as a cure-all, dealt the crushing blow to the sleeping porch fad.

Better-Built Homes, 1927

What makes one of the rooms under the dormer a sleeping porch, and the other a mere bedroom, is the unglazed window which is covered by only an awning.

Restoration Products

by Eve Kahn

To make our products section
more accessible, we'll be dividing it up
according to the general period for which
the products are appropriate.

for pre-1850 buildings

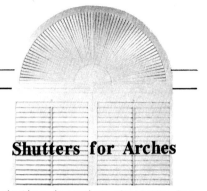

Classical Columns

For your Greek Revival or
Southern plantation home, the
Worthington Group makes attractive stock columns in
Ponderosa pine. They can be
fluted or left smooth; all are
tapered, and can be used inside or out depending upon the
preservatives applied. Prices
vary from $65.52 for a plain
8-ft. column to $1419 for a
20-ft. fluted column.

A wooden Doric capital
comes with each column. You
also have a choice of seven
capitals, made of fiber-rein-
forced plaster with a wooden,
load-bearing core. Styles
range from simple Ionic to
leafy Corinthian. Capitals
are sold separately, and their
prices depend upon their complexity and size; a 6-in.-wide
Ionic capital costs $67.20, a
24-in.-wide Corinthian capital
runs $960.

All columns are preserva-
tive-dipped. A limited number
of stock square columns is
available. Custom lengths,
diameters, and shapes including corner and wall pilasters
and non-tapered profiles can
also be ordered. (They sell
truncated versions of their
columns for use as table bases
or interior decoration.)
Worthington welcomes individual orders. They will ship
single pieces UPS, and can
arrange for trucks to deliver
large orders. Call or write
for free brochures, price
list, and order form (Visa and
Mastercard accepted).
Worthington Group Ltd., Dept.
OHJ, PO Box 53101, Atlanta, GA
30355. (404) 872-1608.

Quality Pierced Tin

Country Accents offers pierced
tin, copper, and brass panels,
both custom-made and in do-it-
yourself kits. There is a
wide variety of folk art
patterns and finishes; all are
suitable for pie safe and
jelly cupboard doors, kitchen
cabinets, bathroom cabinets,
plaques, screens, Revere lanterns, and even heat shields
for wood-burning stoves.
Country Accent's trademark,
"Museum Quality Pierced Tin,"
guarantees that the panels
have been handmade or custom
punched at their studio.

And if you don't have an
antique pie safe that needs
punched tin, Country Accents
offers complete plans so you
can build one; prices start at
$27.75 plus $3 shipping. For
$6.95 they will send you a set
of swatches showing all their
metal finishes, and for $7.95
you can get 8-by-10-in. sample
panels; get both for $13.50.
Their catalog also offers
tools for tin piercing; sheet
tin, zinc, copper, and brass;
plus an extensive array of
traditional pierced tin patterns. The informative catalog
sells for $3 from Country Ac-
cents, Dept. OHJ, R.D. 2 Box
293, Stockton, NJ 08559.
(201) 996-2885.

Shutters for Arches

Finding interior shutters for
an arched window can be a
problem, especially if you
can't afford custom work.
Pinecrest now offers interior
shutters for arched openings
in several formats; they come
in stock sizes and the price
tag is not overwhelming. One
version is a fan top whose
louvers form a sunburst. It
can be installed above standard shutters. Depending upon
size, fan tops cost from $168
to $1126. Widths range from
18 to 48 in., heights from 24
to 90 in.; larger sizes are
available, but the factory
does not guarantee them. Custom sizes can be ordered for a
$27.50 surcharge.

"Rake" designs are another
option. These consist of
standard rectangular shutters,
where the arched areas are
filled in with non-movable
louver panels. The cost is
$26 per panel, with a $93 minimum. A less expensive alternative features flat panels as
fill-ins; these cost $12 each,
$36 minimum.

Ponderosa pine is the standard material, though other
woods can be ordered at substantially higher prices (from
75% higher for red oak to 400%
for walnut). The price quotes
above represent unfinished
wood; standard stain or Glid-
den paint costs from 5% to 12%
more. Pinecrest sells only
through the trade; an architect, interior designer, home-
furnishing or wallpaper store,
or builder/contractor can obtain their catalogs and order
for you. Pinecrest, Dept.
OHJ, 2118 Blaisdell Ave.,
Minneapolis, MN 55404.
(612) 871-7071.

Marble Vanity Top

18th-C. House Parts

You don't have to own a pre-1850 house to make use of the services of the House Carpenters: They'll build you one from scratch! They also design and build barns; all you have to do is send a floor-plan sketch. For those who already have an early house, they produce a selection of accurate 18th-century house parts including storm windows, window frames and sash, hand-planed four-panel doors, as well as fireplace walls, wainscotting, interior shutters, and period moulding.

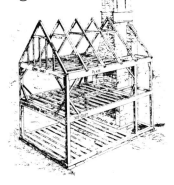

For more information, contact James Mizaur, The House Carpenters, Dept. OHJ, Box 217, Montague Rd., Shutesbury, MA 01072. (413) 259-1276.

You may already know about the excellent high-tank toilets, shower fittings, and copper sinks that Chris Rheinschild produces and sells. But we'll bet you haven't seen his latest and greatest reproduction: a marble vanity that's a dead ringer for those found in Victorian houses.

The marble used is called "Classic Venetian White"; it was actually quarried around the turn of the century and cut into large slabs, 1-1/4 in. thick (marble quarried today, by contrast, is only 3/4 in. thick). The top measures 30 in. wide by 20 in.

Colonial Mail-Order

Some restoration supply stores try to cover all bases by offering everything from Pennsylvania Dutch to Art Nouveau reproductions. These days, though, the market's getting so vast that specialty suppliers have been cropping up. For instance, Harry Kahn founded Colonial Restoration Products last January, after he'd fixed up a few colonial buildings and realized there was a need for a well-rounded source of authentic colonial reproductions.

Kahn's mail-order catalog (he plans to open a retail shop this fall) concentrates on exterior parts like hinges, doorknockers, and latches, along with interior accessories such as bookends, chandeliers, candleholders, and sconces. It also offers building materials like shingles, nails, clapboard, and window and door frames.

Some of the more unusual items: custom hand-moulded brick; a mortar-matching service -- for $10 (plus $11 to $14 per 70-pound mortar bag), the company will match a three-inch sample of your mortar with either soft mortar (for old brick) or hard mortar (for newer brick). The com-

pany also carries hard-to-find regional variations, like the Savannah, Boston, and Philadelphia versions of the bootscrape. Colonial Restoration Products, Dept. OHJ, 405 E. Walnut St., North Wales, PA 19454. (215) 699-3133.

Dutch Elbow Locks

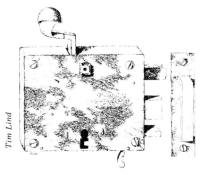

Tim Lind

When the Constitution was being signed in Philadelphia, Ball and Ball was making hardware right down the street. Still family owned, the firm is renowned for its quality reproduction hardware. They also carry originals, and they have a stock of antique Dutch elbow locks that they're offering to OHJ readers at special prices. So named because they can be knocked open with an elbow (in case your hands are full), these locks were first made by German settlers in 1780, and continued to be produced until about 1870. Some have decorated faces and levers, and on some the handle can be removed after the lock is bolted, leaving the house secure. All pieces are restored and ready to use. Ball and Ball, Dept. OHJ, 463 W. Lincoln Highway, Exton, PA 19341. (215) 363-7330.

deep and comes with a back splash that extends up the wall behind the faucets. The top has holes for faucets which you can enlarge to suit. What really makes these vanity tops special and duplicates the Victorian styling is the 3/16-in. recessed well that's hand-ground into the top around the basin; it keeps water from spilling.

The vanity comes with heavy metal mounting brackets (as did the originals) and a white basin (you supply the faucets and drain hardware). The entire unit sells for $610 plus shipping. There's no charge for crating, but you have to supply a deposit, which is refunded when you send the crate back. For details send $1 for the catalog to S. Chris Rheinschild, Dept. OHJ, 2220 Carlton Way, Santa Barbara, CA 93109. (805) 962-8598.

1886 Ceiling Fan

Hunter Fan company is 100 years old this year and they've chosen a fine way to commemorate their anniversary. They're producing a replica of a fan they originally made before the turn of the century. The Hunter 1886 Limited Edition ceiling fan has an ornate, ball-shaped motor housing, which is hand-cast in iron and has a burnished brass finish, just like the original. The original came with only two blades (two more were optional at extra cost), but the replica will have four wooden, wing-tipped blades and burnished brass blade irons. Unlike the original, the replica comes with a three-speed electrically reversible motor and a five-year limited motor parts warranty. The unit sells for $600 at local Hunter dealers. For a free brochure, contact the Hunter Fan Co., Dept. OHJ, P.O. Box 14775, Literature Dept., Memphis, TN 38114. (901) 745-9287.

The Antique Plumber

If you're planning any bathroom projects in your old house, you had better order a copy of Mac McIntire's new

Outdoor Cafe Furniture

You may have seen the beautiful cast-iron and enamel French parlor stoves made by Godin, one of Europe's oldest foundries (established in 1840). But you may not know about their Bistro line of outstanding reproduction enameled cast-iron furniture that's equally at home in a sidewalk cafe, your garden or living room. The enamel is fired on (as it is on kitchen ranges) which means it always looks good and won't rust.

The round Bistro table has a brass-bound marble top on an enameled iron base, 20 in. in diameter and 27 in. high; it sells for $250. (Base alone is $85.) The matching Bistro stool (27 in. high) with molded seat sells for $95.

Antique Plumbing Catalog. What started out as a retirement hobby of restoring antique plumbing fixtures has mushroomed into a booming business for Mac. Here are a few of the items you'll find in his catalog: one-size-fits-all replacement bathtub legs in heavy polished brass, an unusual porcelain tub spout with soap dish; a sink-mounted porcelain soap dish. Mac also offers all types of shower and tub faucets, enclosures, and accessories.

Besides new items, Mac maintains a large inventory of restored Victorian and a few Art Deco items such as pedestal sinks, lighting fixtures, and tubs (tell them what you need and for $2 they'll send you a photo of what they have). The handsome full-color catalog is $3. Write to Mac the Antique Plumber Inc., Dept. OHJ, 885 57th St., Sacramento, CA 95819. (916) 454-4507.

For comfortable garden seating, the enameled cast-iron bench has a sturdy middle support and red mahogany seat and back. It measures 65 in. long and sells for $100. All furniture is shipped freight collect. For a free flyer write to Stone Ledge, Dept. OHJ, 170 Washington St., Marblehead, MA 01945. (617) 631-8417.

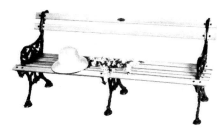

Lace-Trim Hammock

Roos International has a line of 100% cotton hammocks with handmade lace trim that has a decidedly Victorian look. Made in Brazil, the hammocks and pillows are fully washable and come in snow white, peach, emerald green, cardinal red, burgundy, cobalt blue, and goldenrod (all with white lace). There are three styles: the Deluxe Stretcher (62 in. by 95 in., $120), the Deluxe Traditional (62 in. by 95 in., $115), and the Three-Point (46 in. by 84 in., $110). The Stretcher and Three-Point models are held open with stretcher dowels at either end.

A hammock makes an ideal retreat from your restoration chores! These look great on porches, between trees, or in their own stands. Two metal stands are available: the Deluxe ($95) and the Three-Point ($35). With one of these your hammock can be placed in any location -- indoors. Write for a free catalog: The Roos Collection, Dept. OHJ, P.O. Box 20668, New York, NY 10025. (212) 799-1512.

_____ *for post-Victorian buildings* _____

Craftsman Borders

Those lovely scenes of meadows and forests that occupy the friezes in Craftsman homes are now available in a wallpaper border. The one shown left looks just like patterns of the period, and it's especially appropriate for a child's room, a most popular place for decorative friezes in Craftsman houses. The col-

ors are very light and pastel. In the version shown, the dog, trees, and fisherman in the foreground are medium-blue, the lake is pale blue and yellow, the houses and trees beyond the lake are pale green, and the sky is pale blue.

The company, Katrina Inc., makes several other traditional borders; all have complementary striped wallpaper to use as wainscotting. They are available through interior designers and some stores; contact the main office for the name of your nearest dealer: Katrina Inc., Dept. OHJ, 122 W. 74th St., New York, NY 10023. (212) 595-9779.

"Pump" Kitchen Faucet

This isn't a reproduction, but it got our attention as a compatible design for period-inspired kitchens. La France Imports offers this unusual, antique-style faucet that has the presence of a water pump. The De Dion French faucet comes in a variety of materials: polished copper with brass trim, aged copper, or brushed chrome. Of these aged copper has the most antique look. The unit alone costs $475 in polished copper, $530 in aged copper or chrome. With the optional matching spray attachment with wooden handle (pictured), the unit sells for $660 in polished copper, $715 in aged copper, and $770 in brushed chrome.

Besides this and other faucets, the firm also stocks copper sinks of all sizes and shapes. For a brochure, write La France Imports Inc., Dept. OHJ, 2008 Sepulveda Blvd., Los Angeles 90025. (213) 478-6009.

Modern Steel Windows

From the 1920s through the 1950s, steel casement windows were the windows of choice for American residences. They appear on most apartment houses of the era, especially Federally subsidized housing, and on many houses. Though they were stylish, they had drawbacks: They rusted easily and leaked air like crazy.

The Holford window, made by Henry Hope & Co., was among the most popular steel windows of the time. When other manufacturers stopped making these windows in the '60s, only Hope continued. Recently the company developed an updated version of the window, which they call the Landmark. It has the same look as the original, without its disadvantages. The Landmark has narrow muntins, like the original, along with state-of-the-art technological features like weatherstripping, double glazing, and gaskets (instead of the putty that was used on the originals). This cuts air and noise infiltration to a minimum. The Landmark resists rust with two baked-on finishes (epoxy followed by acrylic), which should last about 20 years; the window can also be dipped in zinc, a finish which can last up to 80 years. The window will need, as all windows do, minor maintenance and recaulking from time to time, but the days of the hard-to-keep-up, easy-to-rust, energy-gobbling steel window are gone.

Landmark windows are not cheap. They're designed especially for historic buildings, and all are custom made. Prices depend upon the amount of work needed for installation. Contact Hope's distributor/installer for details: Skyline Windows, Dept. OHJ, 625 W. 130th St., New York, NY 10027. (212) 491-3000.

This photograph comes from a 1926 advertisement for Hope's steel windows.

opinion...

Remuddling

THE LEGENDARY CONFLICT -- Remuddler Vs. Rowhouse -- rages on in Philadelphia. (All of these houses are on the same street within two blocks; remuddling, like mildew, can spread rapidly.)

TOP LEFT: One house is a rather sensitive restoration. Its neighbor lost its most important feature when the mansard roof was replaced with a brick wall extension.

TOP RIGHT: When is a mansard not a mansard? When it's hidden under a standard, "off-the-shelf," aluminum cover-up. Note the under-sized first-storey windows, with their heads blocked by the same sorry siding.

BOTTOM LEFT: This house is a litany of bad solutions to non-existent problems. Starting from the top: peeling asphalt instead of slate shingles; aluminum siding (two storeys' worth); fake wood siding (adding some vertical action to the horizontal siding above); inappropriate bay window and aluminum door (is there a "concept" to this remuddling?).

THANKS to subscriber Torben Jenk for the photographs of this unhappy Philadelphia story. -- Cole Gagne

Editor's Page

The Kitchen Question

PEOPLE WHO OWN eighteenth-century houses don't worry about doing a true period kitchen. A dirt-floored outbuilding with an open fire is unthinkable. People who own 1920s or '30s (or '50s) houses might be tempted, however. All of us wonder how a modern kitchen can be put sensitively into a period house.

FOR A LONG TIME, kitchens were exempted from restoration (bathrooms, too, before pedestal sinks and clawfoot tubs regained justifiable popularity). We've watched that assumption soften lately. (The New Yorker cartoonist noticed it, too.) This tentative but growing interest in period kitchen design led to the Sinks feature in this issue.

NOBODY WANTS to trade in the fridge for an ice box (the ice man doesn't come around anymore). But restorers are starting to have a better eye for period space planning and details. There's less phony Victorianizing and more low-key authenticity in kitchens these days. It may show up in a tongue-and-groove wainscot that's left alone during re-modelling. Maybe one good period piece -- a free-standing cabinet, an antique range -- is used in a simple modern kitchen.

I WAS NOT ONLY amused but also surprised when I saw this cartoon. I thought the trend toward period kitchens was an Old-House-Journal-reader phenomenon. Now that we know how to do parlors and bedrooms -- and even bathrooms -- the kitchen is the next frontier. And probably the most difficult challenge yet. It's a lot of fun to research and create a period kitchen -- but will you be able to live with the outcome? Worse, could it affect resale of the house?

WE'LL EXPLORE the period kitchen in a special issue next year. Here are some topics -- let me know if you can contribute:

● RESTORATION of an extant period kitchen; sensitive update.
● PRESERVATION of a later kitchen (example: preserving a well done 1940s kitchen in an 1895 house).
● INTEGRATION of a new kitchen in a pre-1860 house.
● DESIGN of a new kitchen (period-inspired or not) to go in an addition.
● RE-CREATION of an authentic kitchen -- say, a 1930s kitchen in a 1930s house.

PLEASE SEND some photos and a letter describing the work to KITCHENS, OHJ, 69A Seventh Ave., Brooklyn, NY 11217.

P. Poore

Drawing by W. Miller, © 1985 The New Yorker Magazine Inc.

"We just had the whole kitchen redone, Mom. Isn't it terrific?"

Letters

More On Mortar

Dear Patricia,

Regarding "Chinking, Daubing, & You" in the March 1986 "Ask OHJ," I suggest that Western log-cabin restorers who still have unanswered questions contact Greg Olson, Contractor and Architectural Conservator, 6872 Witzel Road SE, Salem, OR 97301.

Greg has restored several important log houses and has made detailed studies of their original daubing compositions. One in particular used whole milk in the basic lime-sand mixture because the cream content provided important water-repellent qualities -- useful folk knowledge. The use of portland cement in a daubing mix is decidedly modern and might not be appropriate for a historic building.

I wonder about Douglas Reed's recommendation that riverbed sands be used. While this may be a factor in matching sands in some parts of the country, in many others the "store bought" sand comes from the same riverbeds that the do-it-yourselfer might dig in. It may be the only difference is whether washed sand or "site run" (unwashed) sand is used. Sand-particle grading, sharpness, and mineral content may be factors in a mortar or daubing's strength, durability, and appearance, but to less of an extent than whether it is unwashed and contains a high percentage of silt and clays or organic matter. "Elasticity" as a factor of the sand is questionable, except as used to describe its dirtiness and bond with the cements.

-- Al Staehli, A.I.A.
Portland, Ore.

Thanks, OHJ

Dear Editor:

Just wanted to let you know how helpful your Journal has become! My firm has been doing restoration and rehab projects for years, and we use OHJ all the time. We found the recent issue on painting to be full of great information. I gave it to my spec writer for a job in progress. The level of detail in OHJ is impressive.

-- Bernard Rothzeid, F.A.I.A.
New York, N.Y.

Paint-Color Options

Dear Patricia,

Your special report on Exterior Painting (May 1986 OHJ) was very comprehensive and informative.

What it overlooked is how to choose colors which will not fade or have a minor fade factor over the years, what makes a color "cover," and sheen.

Do not select a color with an ultra-deep base which is "shot" by formula into a white base. If a deep and/or intensive color is sought, then at least start with a major paint company which has a factory-colored base closest to the color you wish to achieve.

However, for best results, "intermix" standard, factory-ground colors. For example, go to Fuller O'Brien and intermix two parts "Ultra Blue" with one part "Ultra Black" to achieve an oil or acrylic Navy Blue which won't appreciably fade for up to eight years.

Factory-ground colors of medium, light, or dark color values, or combinations thereof, and different color hues can be mixed together to get great, long-lasting results.

Correct, meticulous and (unfortunately) laborious surface preparation cannot be too strongly emphasized for long-term results.

A color which "covers" or takes one coat over almost any underlying color has "opacity" or opaqueness.

Choosing pretty pastels will almost surely end up in two or three coatings for solid coverage. This results in added material and labor expense, not to mention frustration or the feeling that you purchased an inferior-quality paint.

This pitfall can be avoided by choosing a color which has at least a small amount of raw umber, raw sienna, or lamp black. These are the most opaque colorants.

Four types of sheens that are available: Flat, satin, semi-gloss, and gloss. Various sheens, and even paint brands, may be intermixed, as long as they are stirred well, contrary to warnings on the directions (but remember to keep oil- and water-based materials separate!).

Variations on sheen contrast is an important dimension of a beautiful paint job. For example, satin on the main body, semi-gloss on the major trim, and flat in small, well balanced accent areas.

Gloss oil-based paints lose their sheen in one to three years, depending on the exposure.

Semi-gloss acrylic enamels will retain their sheens five to seven years, depending on the exposure.

-- Don & Bob Buckter
Color Consultants
S.F. and L.A., Cal.

The Burr/Otero House in Monrovia, California — Color Design: Bob Buckter

Letters

The Wheeler Opera House

Balthazar Korab Ltd.

Where Credit Is Due

Dear Ms. Poore,

In the May 1986 issue of The Old-House Journal, I read with interest the article on "Uncovering Decorative Painting." However, I was concerned with the crediting by Ms. Olson of the interior of Aspen's Wheeler Opera House as among the works undertaken by her studio.

Indeed, Ms. Olson assisted the architectural firm in preparing its specifications for the re-creation of the interior finishes, and her studio supplied three canvas pieces for installation. However, all major decorative finishes in the auditorium, i.e. the ceiling, coves, procenium, stage, and side boxes, were executed by The Grammar of Ornament, Inc.

These finishes include the graining and gilding of the auditorium's ceiling beams, opera boxes, procenium, and wainscotting. Similarly, all stencilled designs, striping, and gilding are the work of The Grammar of Ornament, Inc.

We request a clarification of this matter at the earliest possible opportunity in the OHJ.

We applaud your continuing publication of articles "demystifying" the craft of the ornamenter, and we look forward to your work in the future.

-- Ken Miller, President
The Grammar of Ornament
Denver, Col.

An Electro-Static Tip

Dear OHJ,

I thoroughly enjoyed the Painting issue (May 1986), especially as I am a painter. In your "Ask OHJ" column you answered a question dealing with the painting of metal kitchen cabinets. I agree with your response as far as it goes, but you failed to recommend a procedure for applying the Rustoleum. Our shop uses an electro-static sprayer for a number of metal surfaces, with beautiful results. The sprayer charges the paint and the metal, reducing the amount of overspray and increasing the chances of getting a great finish. A contractor using the gun may be very expensive, but renting the equipment may be possible.

Special preparations must also be made to the paint itself. The paint is usually thinned using naptha and ketone. The ketone (MEK or Methyl Ethyl Ketone) is used to enhance the paint's ability to hold the electro-static charge. The full directions for the process are somewhat complicated for a letter, but if rental is at all possible, I'm sure the agent can provide all the necessary information.

We use the electro-static sprayer for lockers, metal furniture, and the like, with excellent results. For something as nice as kitchen cabinets, the extra effort is definitely worthwhile.

-- Park Furlong
Painter-Prince
Laurel, Md.

The O.H.P. Understand

Dear Editor:

I have been enjoying the OHJ very much. Color cover looks good (miss the holes).

I especially like Ms. Poore's commentary on old-house living. I live in a construction site -- have been for three years and expect to for six more. Helps to know other people are doing it too. There's a need for an "Old-House Therapy Group" for venting frustrations of walls collapsing, etc. N.H.P (New-House People) just don't understand!

I now realize that if God wanted me to fix my roof, He wouldn't have invented plastic buckets.

-- Ellen Kardell
Victorian Glassworks
Washington, D.C.

========== Letters ==========

"Migraine" Responses

Dear Editors:

I awoke this morning to look up at the cracked, wrinkled, dingy moons and stars on my ceiling paper and felt that same "old-house depression" I've had off and on for about two years now. Up and out into the "gonna be beautiful" hall and open stairway, down past the "needs to be stripped" woodwork, into the country kitchen full of warped cupboards for my coffee. I sat at the table and looked up at "the beginning of the end" of the tongue-and-groove ceiling job, the bare plasterboard where my tile splashback "will be real soon" and at the uneven windows that "need to be done." My two-year-old is playing ball with himself: He rolls it out, the sloping floor rolls it back. Then I picked up my OHJ for my periodic dose of Old-House Vitamin B-12.

However, my "it'll get done one of these days" husband should have hidden it. Instead of finding "how I turned this dump into a mansion in five years and stayed married," I found "Migraine Castle." My first reaction was to call my husband at work and say "I told you so! Please, buy me a ranch house, something with no coal furnace to shovel into or out of. Something with storm windows, and thermostats, and doors that close, and, and, and...." But then I got hold of myself and peeked at "Remuddling," swept the newest batch of sawdust off the kitchen floor, and dreamed over a new wallpaper book. I got back into my "aren't we lucky to live in such a neat old house" frame of mind.

Keep up the good work -- but please, next month can't

we have another shot of B-12? I really need it!
-- Dolores Johnson
Logan Station, Penn.

Dear OHJ,

I just finished reading David and Brenda Ferre's "Migraine Castle," and feel compelled to write -- I want to help dispell any fears that may arise in the hearts of present or about-to-become old-house people.

I am an old-house owner myself and have been through many catastrophes of the type the Ferres experienced. I can readily sympathize. However, a lack of personal funds should not scare anyone away from an old beauty.

There are loan programs which every old-house person should know about. The two most readily available are Housing & Urban Development's (HUD) FHA 203(k) Rehabilitation Loan Program and the Federal National Mortgage Association's (FNMA) Rehabilitation loan. Both may be used to purchase or refinance homes that qualify as true rehabilitation projects. For single-family homes, the maximum mortgage allowed on FNMA's program is $133,250; HUD's maximum is $90,000. (The FHA loan limit differs around the country.) Higher amounts are available on multi-family dwellings of up to four units.

I am a Mortgage Banker and the head of my firm's Rehabilitation Loan Division. If anyone in the greater D.C. area would like more details, I'd be glad to be of service.
-- Ian R. McFarland
Account Executive
Ronzetti Mortgage
and Investment Corp.
10195 Main St., Suite A
Fairfax, Va. 22031
(703) 352-1360

Dear Ms. Poore:

We just received the May 1986 OHJ. I have finished reading the "Migraine Castle" article and am driven to write some comments on Mr. Ferre's essay.

It is obvious that the Ferres should never have been allowed away from a condo or housing development. One doesn't remove the furnace because it uses a lot of oil without arranging to install another one. If they were not planning on installing the furnace right away, they could have waited to buy it until they were ready to install (freeing working capital).

The thing in the article to which I objected most was that they listed the property with a local broker for $29,900 and with the OHJ for $35,000.

I do agree with one of his comments, that if one is not knowledgeable about structures one should hire someone who is to check out the place before buying.

I am not enchanted by articles like this and would not like to read any more of them.
-- Marilyn L. Sibley
Flemington, N.J.

Before & After

Dear OHJ:

Enclosed are before-&-after photos of my house. The first shows the structure when it was purchased and moved. In the second, the house has been set in place at its new site and is in the process of restoration.
-- Steve Lomske
Northville, Mich.

[For what NOT to do to an old house, see Mr. Lomske's photos in this issue's "Remuddling," page 312. -- ed.]

Ask OHJ

A Mantel Mystery

Q: MY HUSBAND AND I live in a stone house which we think was built in the late 1780s. In the house, we found an unassembled slate mantel that we want to restore. Two things puzzle us. On the back of each piece of the mantel are the identifying marks "J17:88G" -- could these signify the date (1788) and maybe the craftsman's initials (JG)? Secondly, the keystone and the two side

pieces were painted to look as though their centers were inlaid with marble. We're told that this marbleizing technique is Victorian, not colonial. Could the marbleizing be original to the mantel if it was indeed made in 1788? We'd like to restore the mantel to its original condition.
— Lorraine Dalrymple, Warminster, Pa.

A: WHAT A FIND! The "G" looks more like a "6" to us -- maybe it means June or July 6, 1788. Another possibility is that the mark was inscribed on June or July 17, 1886. We're not sure whether the mantel is a colonial-era piece. The design of it is similar to pieces we've seen from the mid- to late-19th century. The marbleizing is almost certainly not colonial; more likely it was done in Victorian times.
[If any of our readers can interpret the inscription and tell us more about the mantel, we'd love to hear from them.]

Combatting Silicone

Q: APPROXIMATELY three years ago, we had the paint stripped from the exterior of our brick townhouse. After the stripping, the brick was sprayed with silicone to provide a protective coating. Unfortunately, the silicone also coated the glass of our windows. We have tried household cleaners, alcohol, and paint stripper to remove the stuff, but to no avail. Can you make any suggestions?
— Lisa Heller, Jersey City, N.J.

A: OUR FIRST SUGGESTION is to get a hold of the people who sprayed the silicone and have it removed at their cost. Masking surfaces that were not to receive the spray must have been specified in the contract -- failing to protect the windows showed poor judgment and bad workmanship.
If this is impossible, you're left with two choices:
1) Scrape it off with a razor blade in a holder. If you keep changing the blades so you're always working with sharp ones, you can remove even the thinnest of coatings.
2) Apply a thin, watery-type paint stripper to soften the silicone, and then scrape it off. (The disadvantage is that the stripper will remove paint from the sash.)

The Stain That Wouldn't Die

Q: MY PLASTER CEILING is underneath a crawl space insulated with 3.5 inches of fiberglass. A leak in the roof has long been repaired, yet I still get cracked, chipped paint and water stains. The ceiling has twice been scraped and primed with BIN. Is it possible that the insulation has remained wet, and is causing the problem? Would venting the crawlspace remedy this situation?
— Virginia Zimmerman, Richmond Hill, N.Y.

A: YOU SAY THAT the leak was repaired, so it's doubtful that the insulation is still damp. If inadequate ventilation was the problem, you'd have more headaches than just a patch of peeling paint: The entire ceiling would be experiencing paint failure, and you'd have peeling paint on the exterior of the house outside the crawlspace, too.
Simple water stains would have been hidden under the shellac you used to seal the problem areas. It's likely that the plaster itself has been damaged by the leak, and so requires patching, not just sealing -- plaster loses its ability to hold paint after it's been exposed to water. Chances are you'll have to remove the bad plaster and patch it with Sheetrock or fresh plaster.

General interest questions from subscribers will be answered in print. The Editors can't promise to reply to all questions personally—but we try. Send your questions with sketches or photos to Questions Editor, The Old-House Journal, 69A Seventh Avenue, Brooklyn, NY 11217.

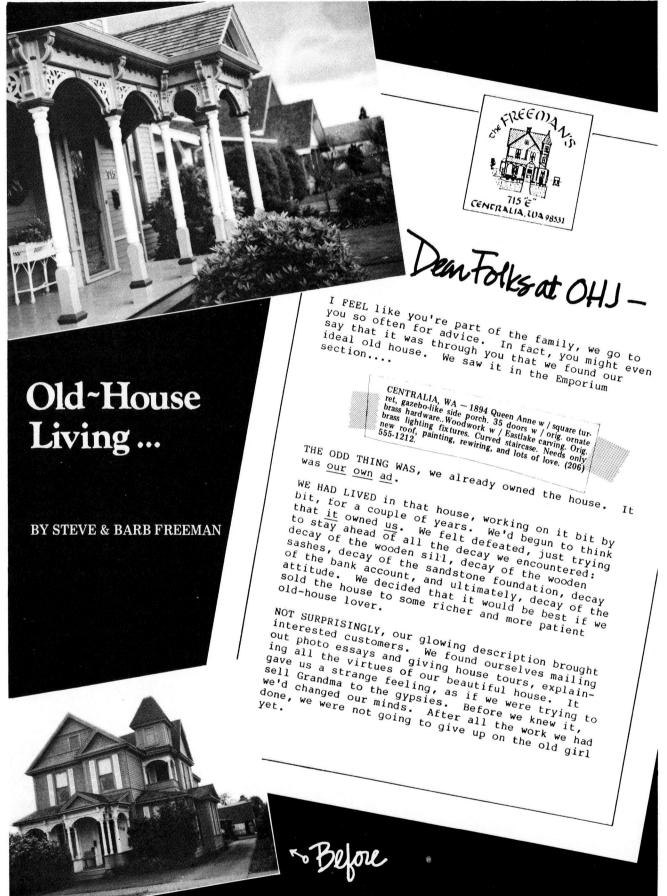

Old~House Living ...

BY STEVE & BARB FREEMAN

THE FREEMAN'S
715 "E"
CENTRALIA, WA 98531

Dear Folks at OHJ —

I FEEL like you're part of the family, we go to you so often for advice. In fact, you might even say that it was through you that we found our ideal old house. We saw it in the Emporium section....

CENTRALIA, WA — 1894 Queen Anne w / square turret, gazebo-like side porch. 35 doors w / orig. ornate brass hardware..Woodwork w / Eastlake carving. Orig. brass lighting fixtures. Curved staircase. Needs only new roof, painting, rewiring, and lots of love. (206) 555-1212.

THE ODD THING WAS, we already owned the house. It was <u>our</u> <u>own</u> <u>ad</u>.

WE HAD LIVED in that house, working on it bit by bit, for a couple of years. We'd begun to think that <u>it</u> owned <u>us</u>. We felt defeated, just trying to stay ahead of all the decay we encountered: decay of the wooden sill, decay of the wooden sashes, decay of the sandstone foundation, decay of the bank account, and ultimately, decay of the attitude. We decided that it would be best if we sold the house to some richer and more patient old-house lover.

NOT SURPRISINGLY, our glowing description brought interested customers. We found ourselves mailing out photo essays and giving house tours, explaining all the virtues of our beautiful house. It gave us a strange feeling, as if we were trying to sell Grandma to the gypsies. Before we knew it, we'd changed our minds. After all the work we had done, we were not going to give up on the old girl yet.

↳ *Before*

IT HAS BEEN sixteen years since my wife and I first noticed a big grey house looming behind some bushes in the rain. We were strongly attracted to it, but we had just bought a 1929 bungalow and so did not make an effort to find out more about it. A few years later, my wife and I decided we needed a bigger home. By then, there was only one person living in our house -- a wise old lady, full of memories of her many years in the house. We told her that we would like a chance to buy her house when she was ready. She said she would put us on her list.

THAT LIST was three pages long. But it mostly contained people who wanted to make the place into apartments; people who wanted to lower ceilings and panel walls. She even had people who wanted to put on aluminum siding. But, as I said, she was a wise lady, and she wanted to sell to someone who would preserve the house. A few months later, she phoned to tell us that it was ours if we still wanted it.

THAT WAS six years ago. In that time, we have experienced highs and lows beyond the comprehension of most of the "modern" world. It is, after all, very hard to get intimately involved with a mobile home or a pre-fab.

WHEN WE FIRST bought the house, we were full of ambition. We started by painting two of the rooms, which were an unappealing rose beige. Well, we did the two rooms, then kept on going into the entryway, along the stairs, and down the hall.... They were all connected! And it took as much paint and time to paint two rooms and a couple of halls as it had taken to paint our entire bungalow.

WITHIN THE FIRST WEEKS we developed a system for finding each other in the 13 rooms: "Stand still and start counting out loud, and I'll come find you!"

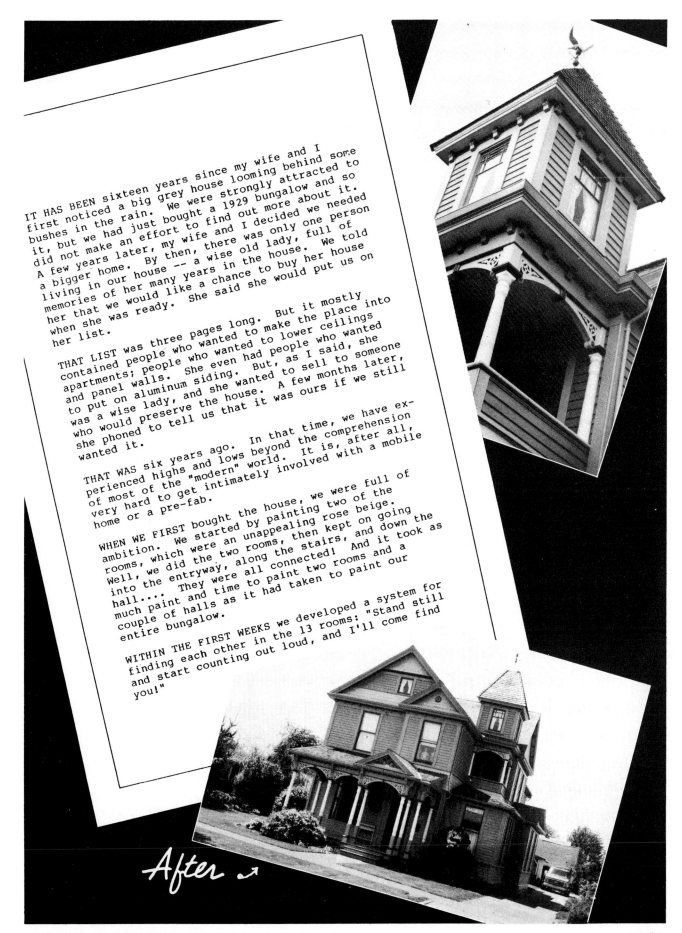

After ↗

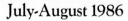

AFTER THE FIRST WINTER, we felt
like we'd made a heavy investment in a natural gas company. We installed a small
woodstove in the corner fireplace to keep us warm and closed
off most of the house.

BY SPRING, we knew we had to do something about
the leaky roof before the next winter. We should
have been forewarned when the guy whose Yellow
Pages ad said, "We make housecalls!" just drove by
and smiled. The only roofer who actually looked
at the job gave us a bid of $7500. Well, folks, I
hate to admit it, but it was at that point that we
decided we might as well just give up on the whole
project. (That's when we submitted the ad I told
you about. Fortunately, as you know, we were
saved by our own salesmanship.)

WITH A BETTER WOODSTOVE and some strategically
placed flashing, we survived the next winter in
fair shape. The following spring, our vigor
renewed by the sunshine and a newborn son, we were
ready to conquer the roof. We decided to do it
ourselves and invest our saving on labor in materials. Composition shingles wouldn't look right,
so cedar it would be.

MY NEIGHBOR is a retired master carpenter who
learned his trade from the men who built houses
like mine almost 60 years ago. He comes by periodically to check on my progress. He warned me
that I would not be able to find new cedar shingles that would last as long as the old ones did.
But OHJ would be proud of me. I searched around
for the best shingles and when
my carpenter friend checked
them out, he said he had
not seen such good, old-
growth shingles in years.

the fretwork
was fine ↗

the porch
wasn't ↘

edited by Julia Lichtblau

OUR MOST RECENT ENDEAVOR, the porch, is actually
what got me to sit down and write this letter.
This porch project started out to be relatively
simple -- replacing rotten floorboards. But,
while removing them, I realized the railing was
not original. Someone had converted the old
railing into a wall by inserting a nice fat two-
by-ten, which eventually caused the lower two feet
of the posts to rot. Fortunately, the carpenter
had used parts of the original rail for bracing
inside the new wall, so I had a model from which
to re-create the old one.

AND WE FINALLY bought a modern, gas-fired boiler
(just in time for a drop in gas prices). The old
one had been converted to sawdust, coal, and finally to just plain dollar-bills, it seemed. The
new one has cut our heating costs by 20%. We're
thrilled, of course, but it is discouraging to put
sooooo much money into things like boilers -- it's
hard to fit them into house tours.

WELL, folks at OHJ, I'm sure you'll be glad to
know that we're still making progress. We found a
company that re-made our sashes, complete with
lugs. I have another old woodworker-acquaintance
who has a large planer and a hoard of old-growth
fir. And before I start any job, I always check
to see if you have any advice that might help.
Thanks for all the help and encouragement so far!

Love from a devoted
family in Centralia,
Washington,

Steve & Barb

Steve and Barb
Freeman

← *the whole fan-damily*

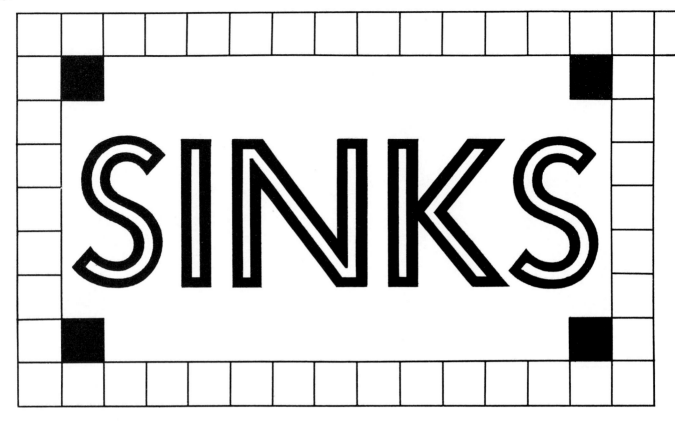

SINKS

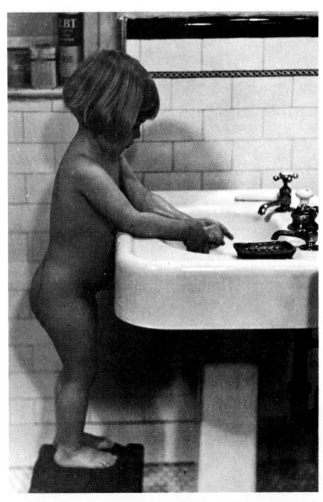

BY J. RANDALL COTTON

GETTING HOT AND COLD WATER from a kitchen or bathroom sink is taken for granted nowadays, yet as little as 100 years ago it was a pure luxury. As recently as 1930, less than one out of ten rural American homes had running water in a bathroom, and only 16% had piped-in water. In the 1920s, water systems were more common in the cities, yet one out of four homes didn't have a sink with running water, and only half had bathrooms as we now know them.

NO ONE RESTORING OR LIVING in an old house, however, would choose to be so "authentic" as to omit sinks, even though they may not be original to the house. Modern kitchen and bathroom sinks are concessions to today's way of life, even in the most meticulous restorations. Yet for those wishing to go an extra step, there are alternative solutions -- so-called "period" sinks can add to the particular flavor of your house. To understand what type of sink might be appropriate for you, a little background history is in order.

FOR THOUSANDS OF YEARS, water for washing, drinking, and cooking was hauled from a stream, spring, or well. (Occasionally, rainwater was collected in cisterns as a source of soft water, preferred for bathing and washing.) Only rarely did advanced cities, such as ancient Rome, have anything like a running-water system. Water was hand-carried in buckets from the nearest source into the house, where it was transferred to a variety of tubs and bowls; an arduous task by today's standards, but an accepted way of life worldwide (including pre-industrial America).

BUCKETS, TROUGHS, bowls, tubs, or anything else that held water were the forerunners of our modern sinks. These vessels were made of a variety of materials, including wood, stone, metal, or porcelain. In early America, food preparation and dishwashing were commonly done in a wooden tub that was usually set on a kitchen table. Water for bathing (an infrequent activity at best) was also put in bowls or small tubs. The whole concept of a bathroom was unheard of until the 1800s -- the 'great outdoors' served our forebears' needs for personal hygiene just fine.

IN THIS COUNTRY, it wasn't until the late 18th century that something resembling a bathroom sink came about: the washstand. Following English prototypes, washstands were simply small tables on which were placed pitcher-and-bowl sets; sometimes the bowl rested in a hole cut into the table top. Washstands reflected the popular furniture styles of the day -- Eastlake, Renaissance Revival, Hepplewhite, Chippendale, Empire, -- but regardless of their style, almost all had a backboard that served as a splashboard; many had shelves or small drawers for soap and other toiletries. During the 19th century, washstands became larger and bulkier, often with towel bars along the sides and a cupboard below to store the chamberpot (our first indoor toilets).

FROM ABOUT 1820 TO 1900, another piece of furniture -- the drysink -- was also commonly used in American homes. This was a low, wooden cabinet with a trough built into the top. This trough was often lined with zinc or lead sheets, and held bowls or buckets of water for use in food preparation or dishwashing. Like washstands, drysinks had back splashboards and shelves or drawers for cleaning supplies. But drysinks were usually very functional in design and only nominally reflected the prevailing furniture styles.

THUS, THE WASHSTAND was the precursor of the bathroom sink; the drysink, the forerunner of the kitchen sink. So it isn't surprising that, in their quest for authenticity, many house restorers have converted drysinks and washstands into perfectly usable sinks with running water. By introducing faucets through the splashboard and providing for a watertight basin with a drain, these furniture pieces offer attractive adaptive-reuse options (particularly appropriate for owners of houses that predate the last quarter of the 19th century). Victorian-era washstands can still be found at reasonable prices in many antique stores. (Converting a washstand or drysink into a sink with running water will destroy some of its value as an antique, so it's best to stick to

COURTESY OF THE BETTMANN ARCHIVE

This photograph was taken in the 1920s, but the kitchen, with its single-faucet drysink and turn-of-century stove, clearly recalls an earlier era.

the common factory-produced pieces rather than the high-quality formal examples.)

■ THE ERA OF RUNNING WATER

THE FIRST MUNICIPAL WATER SYSTEM in America was built in 1802 in Philadelphia. After an initial resistance to buying water, city dwellers accepted the idea, and by 1850, 83 American cities had their own systems. At first, they were steam-powered, with the water filtered through charcoal or sand. Early distribution networks consisted of cast-iron or wooden pipes.

DURING THE MID-1800S, the adoption of water and sewer systems, along with such advancements as central heating and balloon-framing techniques, changed the way the typical American house functioned and looked. Interior spaces became more specialized -- the living room, library, dressing room, dining room, laundry -- and the kitchen became less the all-purpose, live-in "family room" it was in colonial times. (The indoor bathroom was pretty much a new concept altogether.) After the Civil War, the "domestic science" movement, as espoused by Catherine Beecher, her sister Harriet Beecher Stowe, and others, did much to popularize efficient, labor-saving kitchen and bathroom designs.

DURING THESE FORMATIVE YEARS, sinks became a fixed and integral part of the house. Not surprisingly, these sinks resembled what they had replaced. In the illustrations of Stowe, Beecher, and A.J. Downing, the kitchen sinks are very similar to drysinks except for the addition of faucets and drains. The first bathroom sinks (also called "lavatories")

Here's "a convenient kitchen sink" of 1865, from *The American Agriculturist*. The wooden sink has storage space to its left and below; the work shelf at its right folds against the wall.

initially resembled a washstand; slick ceramic models came later.

WATER AND SEWER SYSTEMS may not have been available in many rural areas, yet the idea of a permanent sink took hold -- often with a hand pump attached to one end. Advancements in pump design and their mass production (which made them relatively inexpensive) brought indoor running water even to remote farmhouses. Hand pumps connected to sinks remained popular and were offered in Sears and Ward catalogs well into the 20th century.

DURING THIS TIME, hot water was generated in a small boiler that was usually connected to the

wood- or coal-fired kitchen stove. Later, boilers connected to the furnace supplied hot water throughout the house, including the bathroom sink and tub which eventually came to be seen as necessities.

■ THE SINK COMES INTO ITS OWN

MAJOR DEVELOPMENTS in sink designs came later in the 19th century, as the "sanitary movement" (as some contemporaries called it) became popular. Kitchen and bathroom designs were given a great deal of "scientific" thought regarding efficiency, motion study, and sanitation. The elements of the kitchen -- such as the stove, icebox, work areas, and sink -- were no longer thought of as individual free-standing pieces, but rather as a whole. This was the beginning of the "continuous work surface" concept, in which standardized table, stove, and sink heights, coupled with mass-produced kitchen components, eventually evolved into the modern kitchen.

WHITE, because of its association with sanitation, became the prevalent color for sinks and the other fixtures and surfaces in bathrooms and kitchens. This obsession with sterility led one observer to complain that when cutting up "a fowl in these kitchens one felt quite like a surgeon performing a major operation." White retained its dominance until the 1920s, when there was a return to color in wall coverings, floors, and even ceramic sinks.

THE HEYDAY OF SINK DESIGNS (approximately 1890 to 1930) saw a proliferation in materials and styles. The old metal-lined wooden sink gave way to models in cast iron, enamel, porcelain, china, stainless steel, galvanized iron, zinc, tin, soapstone, and even marble. In kitchens,

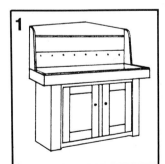

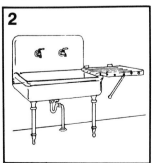

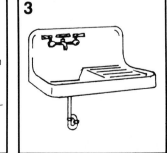

1) The 19th-century drysink was the precursor of the kitchen sink. With the introduction of hot and cold running-water faucets through the backboard and a drain into the zinc-lined trough, the age of the kitchen sink began.

2) The earliest kitchen sinks were free-standing, usually on cast-iron legs that were often painted white to match the enamel or porcelain.

3) A later development was the wall-mounted sink.

In this 1869 kitchen, the moulding board could be turned over and used as a preparation surface over the sink.

THE AMERICAN WOMAN'S HOME

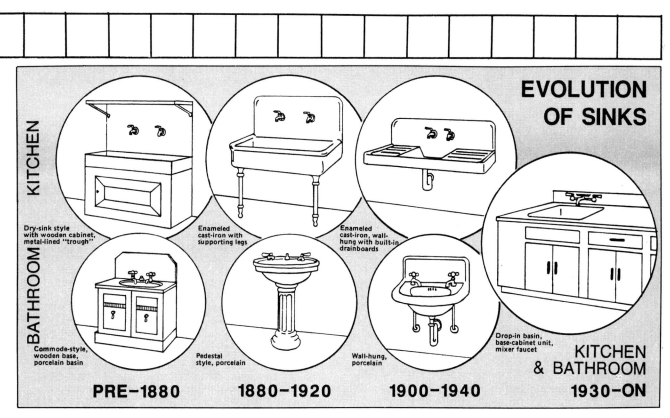

EVOLUTION OF SINKS

KITCHEN

BATHROOM

Dry-sink style with wooden cabinet, metal-lined "trough"

Enameled cast-iron with supporting legs

Enameled cast-iron, wall-hung with built-in drainboards

Commode-style, wooden base, porcelain basin

Pedestal style, porcelain

Wall-hung, porcelain

Drop-in basin, base-cabinet unit, mixer faucet

KITCHEN & BATHROOM

PRE-1880   **1880-1920**   **1900-1940**   **1930-ON**

enamel, metal, and soapstone sinks were the most popular because of their durability. China (porcelain) and marble sinks were popular for bathrooms, as they were considered more elegant.

ENAMELED SINKS, often referred to as "enamelware" or "whiteware," were manufactured as early as the 1870s. They were made by casting an iron sink, reheating it to a red-hot state, and then uniformly sprinkling ground glass over it; once cooled, the enamel surface was smooth and shiny. By 1900, enamelware had become the most popular type of kitchen sink.

SOAPSTONE, long used for a variety of items, was also a popular material for sinks. Its advocates praised soapstone because it didn't absorb acids or grease, as marble did; could be cleaned easily; and didn't chip like enamelware. Marble, a more delicate stone, was usually restricted to top-of-the-line bathroom sinks. (In 1855, a marble sink with silver-plated fixtures cost $50, a tidy sum in those days.) One-piece marble sinks were the most expensive, and so the basin and sink top were usually separate pieces. Often a marble top was combined with a porcelain bowl.

PORCELAIN, particularly popular for bathroom lavatories, was a vitreous material made from cast clay fired in a kiln and then coated with a glass-like glaze during a second firing. Because it was manufactured by a casting process, porcelain was produced in a wide array of elegant shapes. At the other end of the scale, cast-iron sinks were the cheapest but required periodic "oiling" to prevent rusting. Galvanized iron, and later stainless steel, eliminated this problem.

EARLY KITCHEN SINKS had basins of generous proportions, larger than today. Double side-by-side basins were common, especially for cast-iron enamelware. The earliest sinks were free-standing, like furniture, usually resting on cast-iron legs (often painted white to match the enamel or porcelain). The legs imitated table legs with fluting, ball or claw feet, and a variety of details simulating lathe-turning. Later, the back of the sink was hung on the wall, and the front was supported by large cast-iron brackets or a pair of legs. Kitchen sinks sold in early-20th-century Sears catalogs offered an option of either brackets or legs. For bathroom lavatories, the pedestal type was extremely popular.

1) This washstand, circa 1840, reflects popular furniture styles of its era. The hole in the top accommodated a porcelain wash bowl.
2) Side towel bars and a lower cupboard for storing the chamber pot characterize this Victorian-era washstand. The next evolutionary step would be...
3) ... the early bathroom lavatory. This typical example has the basin set in its top and attached running-water faucets.

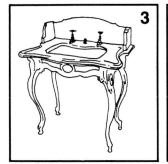

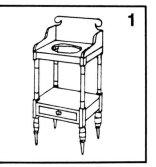

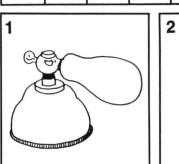

Three Types Of Faucets

1) A single-pronged, "lever" style, with handle and base of porcelain.

2) A four-pronged, "cross" (or spoke) style, with porcelain handle and chromed base.

3) "Cross" with chromed handle and base.

ARCHITECTURALLY, kitchen and bathroom sinks reflected the details of the times. In the late-Victorian era, sinks had routed, incised, carved, and turned designs, all imitatively cast into enamel or porcelain models. Scallop-shaped basins, angular bevel-edged tops and splashboards, even wooden Eastlake-styled cabinet bases appeared in bathroom lavatories.

AS THE NATION TURNED to the Colonial Revival, sinks became less elaborate, with cleaner, more refined lines. Classical elements showed up in the ogee-shaped edges of the splashboard, oval-shaped bowls, and particularly the pedestal bases which often looked like classical-order columns. Throughout the early 20th century, sink designs became even simpler -- almost all architectural detail was dropped and edges were rounded, giving them a unified sculptural look. This trend was in part due to the "sanitary" movement which viewed elaborate designs as providing a multitude of dirt-catching nooks and crannies. Simple lines, rolled rims, and streamlined design was the favored look of the 1920s and beyond.

CONTINUOUS COUNTERTOPS with drop-in sink basins, the kind we know today, first appeared during the 1930s. This development was partly due to progressive schools of architecture, such as the Bauhaus, which sought uniform solutions for house design. Countertops became a standard 36" high and 24-25" deep. Modern materials were used: linoleum and Formica for countertops, stainless steel for basins. Base cabinets, with drop-in sink and stove units, ran around the kitchen perimeter and were usually topped by continuous wall cabinets.

■ FAUCETS, DRAINS, ETC.

THE EARLIEST FAUCETS were merely water cocks in which a handle was directly connected to a valve in the water line. These were capable of functioning in only two positions: on and off. Although cocks are still occasionally used (as in line-shut-off valves, for example), by the late 1800s they were largely superseded by compression-valve faucets. In a compression valve, a rubber washer is attached to the end of a metal stem and is seated against the body of the faucet when fully closed. A compression-valve faucet allows for a continuous range of water flow from fully on to fully off.

INITIALLY, there were separate faucets for hot and cold water. They were usually made of iron, often nickel plated. Top-of-the-line faucets were brass or copper, but some were even gold or silver-plated. Chrome plating was introduced after the turn of the century. Faucet handles were also plated, but perhaps most commonly were made of porcelain. Two styles of handles were prevalent: a four-pronged knob ("cross" style) and a single prong ("lever" style, a type still popular in Europe). The words "HOT" and "COLD" were usually inscribed directly into the handle, or sometimes on porcelain buttons set into the top of the faucet.

SPOUTS WERE FIXED INITIALLY, but by this century swinging spouts were usual for kitchen

COURTESY OF THE BETTMANN ARCHIVE

This circa 1900 photograph shows a wall-mounted, double-basin sink. Work surfaces are provided by the cupboard at left and by the cutting board placed over the sink's right basin.

<table>
<tr><td></td><td></td><td></td><td></td><td></td><td></td><td></td><td></td><td></td><td></td><td></td><td></td><td></td><td></td></tr>
</table>

sinks. High, goose-neck spouts were an early type that is currently enjoying popularity again. Spray attachments on flexible hoses showed up as early as 1915 in some kitchens. "Mixers," in which the hot- and cold-water handles were connected to a single central spout, were a welcome development (as anyone who still has separate hot- and cold-water faucets can attest). By 1920, mixers were commonplace.

KITCHEN DRAINBOARDS evolved from simple, fold-back wooden shelves (hinged on the wall next to the sink) to metal shelves flanking the sink and permanently affixed by brackets. Metal drainboards usually had ribs pressed into their surface to direct the water back into the sink. By the 1920s, most kitchen enamelware sinks had integral drainboards incorporated into either side of a double-basin center.

OTHER SINK-RELATED INVENTIONS appeared in the early 20th century. Automatic dishwashers which connected to the kitchen faucet arrived in the '20s. In 1929, General Electric introduced the "electric sink," their term for an electric garbage disposal. Countertops adjacent to the kitchen sink, at first made of soapstone, slate, or zinc sheets, eventually were made of new products such as linoleum, asphalt tiles, or Formica. The "butcher-block" look, popular for countertops today, actually was used as early as 1917 when one-inch white maple strips were used.

IN THE BATHROOM, pedestal-base sinks remained popular. Amenities such as soap receptacles and towel bars were incorporated into sink designs. From 1900 on, mirrors, toothbrush holders, and drinking-glass niches were mounted into the wall above the sink.

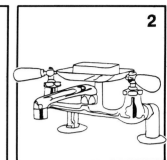
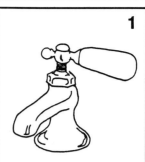

Three Types Of Spouts

1) Spout and faucet in one unit, with "lever" handle.

2) "Mixer" with hot- and cold-water handles visibly connecting into a single spout.

3) "Mixer" with goose-neck spout and hidden connection.

◼ LIVING WITH OLD-STYLED SINKS

IF YOU'D LIKE to include "period" sinks as part of your restoration, the first step is to decide on the type and style most appropriate to the era of your particular house. Finding the right sink isn't too difficult -- there are three primary sources: salvage, reproductions, and adaptive re-use.

ARCHITECTURAL SALVAGE DEALERS are excellent sources for finding old kitchen and bathroom sinks. Check your local Yellow Pages under "Salvage," "Junk Dealers," or "Plumbing Fixtures & Supplies," or refer to the list of salvage dealers in The Old-House Journal Buyer's Guide Catalog, to see if there's anyone near you. Here are some things to look for when selecting a sink from a salvager:

● BE SURE the sink will fit in the space you allot for it.

● CHECK THE BASIN for cracks and chips that can cause leaks -- fill the bowl with water, if possible. Cracks in the pedestal of a lavatory may present a structural problem, but minor chips and cracks are often only aesthetic flaws.

● CHECK THE FINISH -- worn or discolored enamel can be professionally repaired, but it can be expensive. Blemishes on the finishes shouldn't dissuade you from considering a sink you really like, however.

BUILDING WITH ASSURANCE

The illustration is from 1921, but the sink is comparatively old fashioned, being supported by legs. (Note, however, the built-in work surface in the right portion of the sink.)

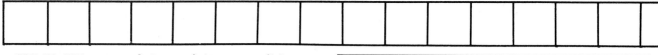

● TRY TO GET as complete a sink as possible, including all the original fixtures, fittings, etc. Fitting sizes have changed over the years, so it may be difficult to get new ones that will fit an old sink. Try to find an old sink which retains its connections, particularly the original supply stem nuts.

● BE SURE the mounting tabs on the back of wall-hung sinks are intact and sturdy.

■ USING SALVAGED SINKS

SEVERAL OHJ ARTICLES have covered the 'how-to' of installing old sinks: "About Old-House Plumbing," Aug.-Sept. '83; "Caring For Antique Plumbing Fixtures," April '77; "Restoring Marble Sinks," July '77. Another excellent reference is Salvaged Treasures by Michael Litchfield and Rosmarie Haucherr (New York: Van Nostrand Reinhold, 1983). Most of the procedures in installing old sinks fall within the range of common plumbing practices, but there are a few points to note:

● YOU'LL PROBABLY have to use a number of adaptors to make the fittings of the old sink

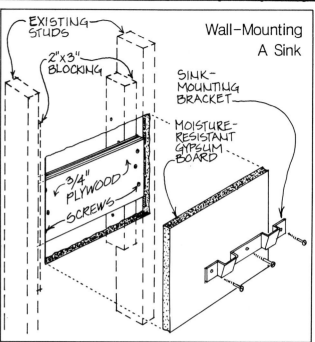

Wall-Mounting A Sink

EXISTING STUDS

2"X3" BLOCKING

SINK-MOUNTING BRACKET

MOISTURE-RESISTANT GYPSUM BOARD

3/4" PLYWOOD

SCREWS

connect to your modern plumbing system. Don't despair -- a well stocked plumbing-supply house should have a variety of them.

● OLD FAUCETS AND DRAINS, because of their age, may be leaky. Usually this is easily alleviated by replacing the gaskets. But remember how you disassemble an old faucet, because many vintage models are put together differently from modern faucets.

● DO-IT-YOURSELF PAINT TOUCH-UPS for enamel finishes are available, but they're generally inadequate. Color matching is very difficult and the patched areas quickly wear off under normal use. Unless you're prepared for a complete but expensive re-enamelling job by a professional, it's probably best to live with a worn enamel finish -- it makes no difference to the integrity of the sink. Many stains can be removed with common cleaning products.

● IF THE OLD SINK is wall mounted, it is very important to attach the mounting bracket to a sturdy wall surface. If you aren't mounting a sink where a previous one was hung, reinforce the wall by introducing a horizontal wood block that spans two adjacent wall studs. Cut the plaster and lath back to the inside edge of the adjacent studs. Fasten 2x3 blocking to the studs. (If possible, use a screw gun to prevent plaster damage from hammering.) Mount the blocking far enough back so that when you screw a piece of plywood to the blocking and gypsum board to the plywood, the gypsum board is flush with plaster. Fasten the sink bracket through the gypsum board into the plywood.

■ REPRODUCTION SINKS

MOST MAJOR SINK MANUFACTURERS now produce at least one "antique-style" design as part of

The smooth, gleaming surfaces of the wall-mounted sink match the simplicity and elegance of this turn-of-century bathroom.

Three Types Of Sink-Basin-Installation Cross Sections

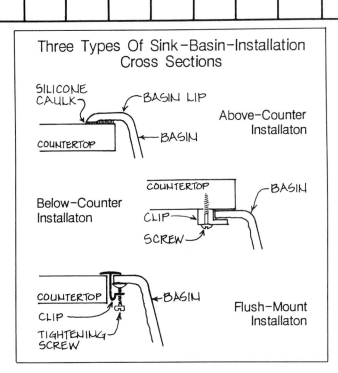

SILICONE CAULK

BASIN LIP

COUNTERTOP

BASIN

Above-Counter Installaton

Below-Counter Installaton

COUNTERTOP

BASIN

CLIP

SCREW

COUNTERTOP

CLIP

TIGHTENING SCREW

BASIN

Flush-Mount Installaton

architectural character of your house. For example, narrow, beaded tongue-and-groove "matchboards" were a popular material for wainscotting in kitchens and bathrooms from Victorian times into this century, and they're still available today. A custom-made base cabinet incorporating beaded boards as siding or in door panels would be an especially appropriate design. Other period details might include simple incised designs, glass knobs, panelled sides and doors, or natural wood finishes (especially oak). Look for design inspirations in the details of other antique furniture pieces such as Hoosier cabinets, old ice chests, pie safes, or linen chests.

EVEN A THOROUGHLY MODERN SINK can be made to appear more 'old-fashioned' by simply replacing the fixtures with period reproductions. A wide variety is available from the companies listed, ranging from very expensive, solid-brass fixture sets to less-expensive, chrome- or nickel-plated models.

J. RANDALL COTTON is a long-time OHJ subscriber and a frequent contributor to our pages. He's currently Project Manager for Middle States Preservation in Wayne, Pennsylvania.

their line; several smaller companies specialize solely in period designs. Page 278 offers a list of some of these suppliers and manufacturers, but any large plumbing-supply house should be able to order reproduction models for you. Remember to choose a design that's appropriate for your house -- many Victorian-era sinks would be too fancy for an early-20th-century house. The same is true for reproduction hardware (i.e., drains, knobs, faucets); earlier styles were more ornamental.

YOU'LL FIND A VARIETY of bathroom lavatory reproductions from which to choose, particularly attractive pedestal models. An even wider array of antique-style fixtures is available. However, very few old-style kitchen sink reproductions are available. Apparently, the more utilitarian look of an old kitchen sink has not yet found its way into our 'nostalgic' hearts. One source, the Vermont Soapstone Company, makes an attractive soapstone kitchen model complete with a side drainboard. (But perhaps your best source for old kitchen sinks will be salvage, not reproductions.)

■ SOME ADAPTIVE RE-USE IDEAS

AS PREVIOUSLY MENTIONED, old washstands and drysinks make good pieces for conversion to sinks. Fortunately, antique-style basins are readily available from many suppliers and come in a wide range of materials, including china, marble, enamel, copper, soapstone, cast iron, and stainless steel. The basins can be fitted into the top of a washstand in the same way as they would into a modern base cabinet.

SPEAKING OF BASE CABINETS, you don't have to settle for modern pre-fabricated designs. Anyone with reasonably competent skills can build custom base units which reflect the

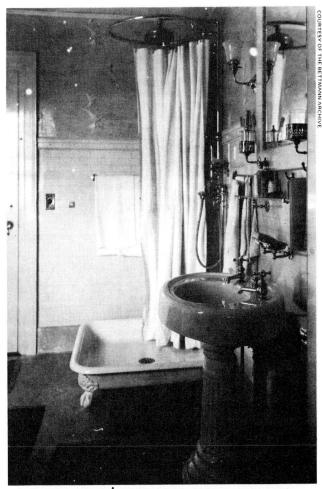

A beautiful pedestal sink highlights this well-appurtenanced, circa 1910 Massachusetts bathroom.

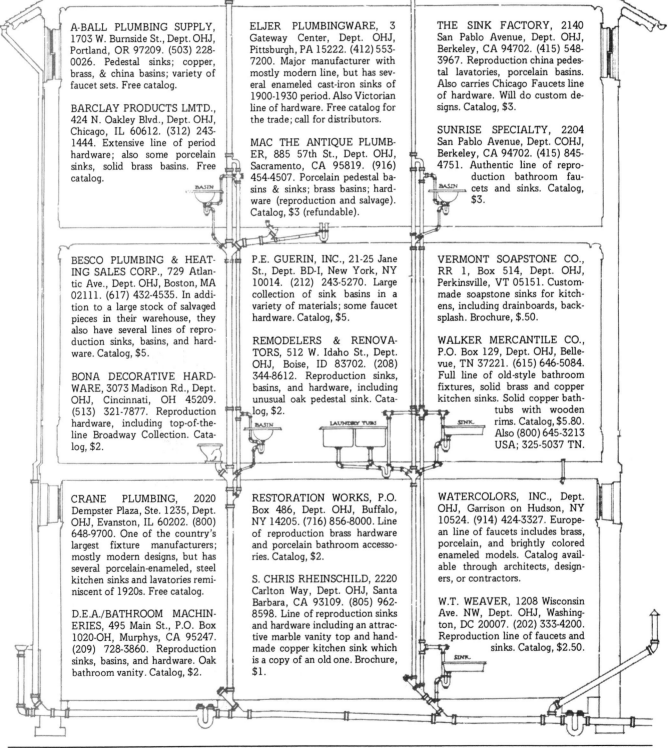

SINKS: SOURCES

A-BALL PLUMBING SUPPLY, 1703 W. Burnside St., Dept. OHJ, Portland, OR 97209. (503) 228-0026. Pedestal sinks; copper, brass, & china basins; variety of faucet sets. Free catalog.

BARCLAY PRODUCTS LMTD., 424 N. Oakley Blvd., Dept. OHJ, Chicago, IL 60612. (312) 243-1444. Extensive line of period hardware; also some porcelain sinks, solid brass basins. Free catalog.

BESCO PLUMBING & HEATING SALES CORP., 729 Atlantic Ave., Dept. OHJ, Boston, MA 02111. (617) 432-4535. In addition to a large stock of salvaged pieces in their warehouse, they also have several lines of reproduction sinks, basins, and hardware. Catalog, $5.

BONA DECORATIVE HARDWARE, 3073 Madison Rd., Dept. OHJ, Cincinnati, OH 45209. (513) 321-7877. Reproduction hardware, including top-of-the-line Broadway Collection. Catalog, $2.

CRANE PLUMBING, 2020 Dempster Plaza, Ste. 1235, Dept. OHJ, Evanston, IL 60202. (800) 648-9700. One of the country's largest fixture manufacturers; mostly modern designs, but has several porcelain-enameled, steel kitchen sinks and lavatories reminiscent of 1920s. Free catalog.

D.E.A./BATHROOM MACHINERIES, 495 Main St., P.O. Box 1020-OH, Murphys, CA 95247. (209) 728-3860. Reproduction sinks, basins, and hardware. Oak bathroom vanity. Catalog, $2.

ELJER PLUMBINGWARE, 3 Gateway Center, Dept. OHJ, Pittsburgh, PA 15222. (412) 553-7200. Major manufacturer with mostly modern line, but has several enameled cast-iron sinks of 1900-1930 period. Also Victorian line of hardware. Free catalog for the trade; call for distributors.

MAC THE ANTIQUE PLUMBER, 885 57th St., Dept. OHJ, Sacramento, CA 95819. (916) 454-4507. Porcelain pedestal basins & sinks; brass basins; hardware (reproduction and salvage). Catalog, $3 (refundable).

P.E. GUERIN, INC., 21-25 Jane St., Dept. BD-I, New York, NY 10014. (212) 243-5270. Large collection of sink basins in a variety of materials; some faucet hardware. Catalog, $5.

REMODELERS & RENOVATORS, 512 W. Idaho St., Dept. OHJ, Boise, ID 83702. (208) 344-8612. Reproduction sinks, basins, and hardware, including unusual oak pedestal sink. Catalog, $2.

RESTORATION WORKS, P.O. Box 486, Dept. OHJ, Buffalo, NY 14205. (716) 856-8000. Line of reproduction brass hardware and porcelain bathroom accessories. Catalog, $2.

S. CHRIS RHEINSCHILD, 2220 Carlton Way, Dept. OHJ, Santa Barbara, CA 93109. (805) 962-8598. Line of reproduction sinks and hardware including an attractive marble vanity top and handmade copper kitchen sink which is a copy of an old one. Brochure, $1.

THE SINK FACTORY, 2140 San Pablo Avenue, Dept. OHJ, Berkeley, CA 94702. (415) 548-3967. Reproduction china pedestal lavatories, porcelain basins. Also carries Chicago Faucets line of hardware. Will do custom designs. Catalog, $3.

SUNRISE SPECIALTY, 2204 San Pablo Avenue, Dept. COHJ, Berkeley, CA 94702. (415) 845-4751. Authentic line of reproduction bathroom faucets and sinks. Catalog, $3.

VERMONT SOAPSTONE CO., RR 1, Box 514, Dept. OHJ, Perkinsville, VT 05151. Custom-made soapstone sinks for kitchens, including drainboards, backsplash. Brochure, $.50.

WALKER MERCANTILE CO., P.O. Box 129, Dept. OHJ, Bellevue, TN 37221. (615) 646-5084. Full line of old-style bathroom fixtures, solid brass and copper kitchen sinks. Solid copper bathtubs with wooden rims. Catalog, $5.80. Also (800) 645-3213 USA; 325-5037 TN.

WATERCOLORS, INC., Dept. OHJ, Garrison on Hudson, NY 10524. (914) 424-3327. European line of faucets includes brass, porcelain, and brightly colored enameled models. Catalog available through architects, designers, or contractors.

W.T. WEAVER, 1208 Wisconsin Ave. NW, Dept. OHJ, Washington, DC 20007. (202) 333-4200. Reproduction line of faucets and sinks. Catalog, $2.50.

Flow~On Paint Stripping

A Good Compromise Between Hand~Stripping and Dip~Stripping

by Bill O'Donnell

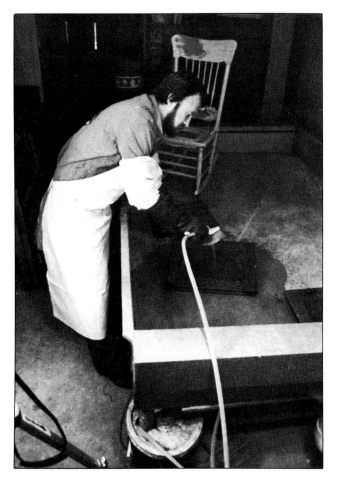

NO MATTER how large or small, fine or ordinary your paint-stripping job, you must first decide whether to strip it by hand or send it out to a local stripping shop. Stripping by hand is the most controllable way to strip wood, and the most likely to produce excellent results. It has significant drawbacks, though: It's time-consuming, messy, and irritating (to skin, eyes, nose, and temper). It's not surprising that many people would rather send the work out, even if that means dismantling woodwork. But there are disadvantages to the strip-shop option, too. Because hand-stripping is labor intensive and thus very expensive, most shops dip the piece in stripping chemicals. That can lead to raised, fuzzy grain, a greying of the wood, loosened glue joints, or bubbling veneer.

Hand-stripping assures excellent results. This photo demonstrates one of its drawbacks — the mess.

THERE EXISTS a third option: the flow-on or cold-tray method. This shop method saves you money over hand stripping, yet avoids many of the problems that occur when wood is dipped.

About Strip Shops

BEFORE WE DESCRIBE the flow-on method in more detail, let's review what usually happens to your furniture or woodwork at a strip shop. We've all heard horror stories about using dip stripping to remove paint. Yet there are many people who've had great luck with it, and who will never hand-strip again. Satisfactory results depend on the experience and care of the stripper, and the method used. When you take your wood to the shop, they'll introduce it to one (or more) of the following:

(1) A "cold tank" filled with a paint stripper based on methylene chloride.

(2) A "hot tank" containing a solution of lye or trisodium phosphate (TSP) in water. These tanks operate from 125 to 180 degrees F.

(3) A bleach tank containing oxalic acid. This tank neutralizes the caustic from the hot tank, and bleaches out any darkening of the wood that occurred in previous steps.

(4) A "cold tray" in which the piece will be coated (not immersed) with a methylene-chloride-based stripper. This is the equipment used in the flow-on method.

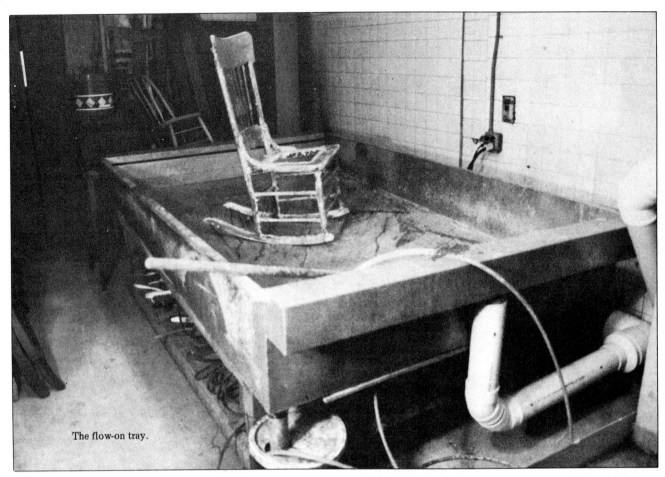

The flow-on tray.

MOST PROBLEMS OCCUR in the hot tank. Caustic strippers remove old finishes very effectively. But in the hands of a careless operator, caustic strippers will not only dissolve old glues, but will also attack the surface of the wood itself. And since it is a hot aqueous solution, you'll probably wind up with some raised grain.

OF COURSE, HOT TANKS do have some usefulness. We know some fine, reputable shops that have hot tanks. It is important for the customer (as well as the strip-shop operator) to recognize the difference between fine furniture or fine architectural trim, and run-of-the-mill woodwork. A quick dip in the hot tank might be fine for paint-encrusted baseboards, but it's likely to be a disaster for an oak dresser or walnut wainscotting.

COLD TANKS are less harsh than hot tanks. They are called "cold" because they operate at room temperature. They're filled with a methylene-chloride-based stripper. The cold tank avoids soaking wood in an aqueous solution; nonetheless, the wood is being completely immersed in a strong chemical. The wood will absorb some of the chemical; how much depends on how long it is soaked. So it is possible to get some swelling and raised grain.

Flow-On Stripping

THE COLD TRAY or "flow on" method is the gentlest of all. It's very similar to hand stripping in that the piece is not immersed in strong chemicals. Rather, a methylene-chloride-based stripper is pumped onto the piece through a nozzle. As the used chemical runs off the piece, it collects at one end of the tray. A coarse screen removes large pieces of stripped paint, and the chemical is recycled back onto the woodwork.

ONCE THE MAJORITY of the finish is loose, the cold-tray operator scrapes off the softened paint or varnish with a putty knife. More stripper is pumped back onto the piece to

The water-rinse booth.

Scraping off the softened paint.

Power rinsing the goop.

remove the remaining finish. Some especially intricate areas require hand cleanup with picks, small scrapers, or a brass brush.

THE STRIPPED PIECE is then transferred to a water-rinsing tray to remove the remaining chemical and dissolved paint. A small amount of water is sprayed onto the piece at high pressure to halt the stripping action of the chemical and remove all traces of the old finish.

THE WATER RINSE is the step most likely to cause problems. If a minimal amount of water is used, there should be no adverse effects. However, should the operator get carried away and drench the piece under a continuing stream, it may lift the veneer, raise the grain, or cause splitting or warping. There is no substitute for a knowledgeable and con-scientious strip-shop operator. No matter how gentle the techniques, a careless or inexperi-enced operator can damage the wood.

Advantages

LESS STRIPPER IS USED than with either hand-stripping or dip-stripping. As with hand-stripping, the chemicals are applied only where they're needed. Therefore, no chemical soaks into bare wood. Unlike hand-stripping, the chemical is reused. A five-gallon bucket of stripper is usually all that's required for an entire day's stripping.

LESS STRIPPER means less waste for the shop and lower cost to you. In many ways, flow-on stripping is less hazardous than other strip-ping methods. The flow-on trays used by BIX Process Systems, Inc.* (a nationwide distribu-tor of stripping equipment) feature an inte-gral ventilation system. Fumes from the stripping chemicals used are heavier than air and settle within the walls of the tray. Vents along the sides of the tray exhaust outdoors through a powerful fan.

Where Does It Go?

THE FLOW-ON METHOD is more ecologically sound than some other stripping methods. Because the stripping chemicals are recycled, less waste is produced. At the end of each day, the sludge is collected and stored. Once a drum has been filled, the solid wastes are disposed of in an approved site according to EPA standards.

LIQUID EFFLUENT produced in the water-rinsing tray goes through a 300-gallon filtration tank where it passes through three progressively finer filters that remove most of the solids. The water is then forced through an activated charcoal filter to remove the finest solids and much of the suspended solvent. Depending on state and local requirements, it is then introduced to the municipal sewerage system, leached into the soil, or contained for dis-posal in an approved landfill.

THE DISPOSITION OF
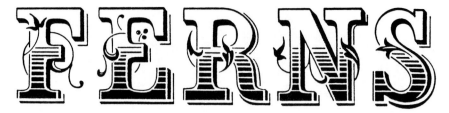

FERNS

by Ron Pilling

"NOT SO LONG as the woods are filled with beautiful ferns ... need you feel yourself an utterly disinherited child of nature, and deprived of its artistic use." Following these words of wisdom from the 1869 American Woman's Home, homemakers took to the forest to gather ferns for decorating drawing rooms and hallways. As indoor gardening became more popular after the Civil War, many other plants were picked from the wild and purchased from gardening shops, but the fern was still especially prized.

COMBINED with palms and flowering plants, framed with climbing ivy, ferns represented all that was best in nature. The lessons to be learned from a working relationship with things natural were held up as the epitome of virtue. In his 1871 book Window Gardening, Henry T. Williams praised indoor gardening as "a sign of healthy sentiment, for the presence of flowers always aids in the development of refinement and an elevated taste."

Ferns under glass.

THERE WERE practical reasons for the popularity of ferns in Victorian homes. They grow well in shady places or in rooms with heavily draped windows. They're easy to care for in hanging baskets and grow well from a variety of showy wall planters. Early directions for growing ferns emphasize that they need to be watered but twice a week, once in a "shower" that soaks the leaves and cleans any dust that has settled on the fronds.

SOME VARIETIES are very delicate and require a sheltered environment. The Wardian Case, invented in 1829, was the forerunner of today's terrarium, and made it possible to raise these less-hardy ferns in New York and London parlours. Some elaborate Wardian Cases featured ornate cast-iron frames into which plate glass was set. Unfortunately, few have survived; they're almost non-existent at antique shows and auctions. The smaller versions, however, were created a century ago from glass domes

An ornate, cast-iron stand could display a grouping of domed gardens.

that are easy to find today. Pedestal tables called "fern stands" were made especially for dome gardens. The plants-under-glass were placed on these high tables where they could easily be enjoyed.

FERNS WERE PLANTED in pottery bowls into which the dome fit securely. The gardener began with a thin layer of gravel on the bottom of the bowl for drainage. Then (according to a recipe from the 1869 American Woman's Home), the soil was prepared by mixing two parts of dark, rich forest soil with one part lighter meadow soil, one part sand, and a sprinkling of charcoal.

WHEN FERNS were planted in glass domes, the soil was generally covered with moss also gathered in the wild. The idea was to create a miniature forest inside the dome. Plants that grew wild were preferred not only for their economy but also because they brought the gardener a bit closer to nature. There was a certain enlightenment that could be experienced only by gathering plants in the forest rather than at the nurseryman's.

Pedestals called 'fern stands' highlighted the showiest ferns.

Ferns At Large

FERNS need not be planted under glass, however; Victorians displayed them in pots, implanted in sponges and baskets of moss, and used them as the centerpieces of large arrangements in flat dishes. Catherine Beecher and Harriet Beecher Stowe, in the aforementioned American Woman's Home, made some suggestions about "the disposition of ferns."

THEY ADVISED HOMEMAKERS to employ a tin pie pan condemned to the ash heap because of dents or holes. After painting the tin green and filling it with their recommended garden soil, "plant all sorts of ferns, together

A "fern brick" of terra cotta often rested in the front of the fireplace opening during the summer months. Putting potted plants in unused fireplaces was a century-old tradition by the mid-1800s.

"Rustic terra-cotta arbourettes" were sold in nurseries and by mail. The hollow interior was filled with potting soil, and the ferns often shared space with flowering bulbs.

with some few swamp grasses; and around the edge put a border of money plant or periwinkle to hang over. This will need to be watered twice a week, and will grow and thrive all summer long in a corner of your room. Should you prefer, you can suspend it from wires and make a hanging-basket."

ONCE AGAIN, the goal in combining various plants in the same container is to create a vignette of nature. It wasn't necessary for the plants to be ones found in close proximity in the wild, only that there be several types flourishing side-by-side in the pot. After all, the periwinkle that Beecher and Stowe talk about doesn't grow on shady forest floors near ferns; neither do their swamp grasses. But as the fern was the showiest forest plant available in most of North America, it was usually the focus of small indoor plantings.

On The Wall

A MONG the most interesting homes for ferns were those mounted to the wall. Again we will turn to the Beecher-Stowe book for an example: "Take a piece of flat board sawed out something like a shield, with a hole at the top for hanging it up. Upon the board nail an ox-muzzle flattened on one side; or make something of the kind with stiff wire. Line this with a sheet of close moss, which

A wall-mounted pot for hanging ferns could be fashioned from wire and filled with moss.

appears green behind the wire net-work. You can fill it with loose, spongy moss ... and plant therein great plumes of fern; they will continue to grow there and hang peacefully over."

THE HANGING POT was also a favorite fern container. Its popularity among today's amateur gardeners is nothing new -- pots were suspended from hooks all over Victorian homes. Because they were easily moved and easily tended, hanging pots were the favored container for many houseplants. But they were not the white plastic variety so common for today's Fuschia and Wandering Jew. Pots had to be decorated to be suitable for hanging in the drawing room, and here the 1880s home-decorating experts were full of suggestions.

MRS. C.S. JONES worked with the aforementioned Henry T. Williams on Household Elegancies, Suggestions In Household Art, published in 1875 (and now available in reprint).* Much of their sage advice concerned how to properly display houseplants from hanging containers. "A beautiful hanging basket ... is composed of a wooden bowl such is found in any kitchen, stained with a decoction ... of vinegar in which a few pieces of rusty iron have been placed for a few hours."

*Available from The American Life Foundation, Watkins Glen, NY 14891.

"EXOTIC GREENS"

A Choice Of Ferns For Victorian Window Gardens

"Their daily growth will afford you very interesting and pleasant study." Ferns need not have large, drooping fronds — some are quite delicate. The ones described here enjoyed a wide popularity a century ago.

Rabbit Foot's Fern (Polypodium aureum) grows from a furry stem. The root system is shallow, making the plant ideal for shallow dishes.

Licorice Fern (Polypodium glycyrrhiza) has one- to three-foot fronds with pointed leaflets. It was brought to eastern cities from the American West, where it grows wild.

Christmas Fern (Polystichum acrostichoides) is robust and forms symmetrical crowns of fronds. Victorians prized it for holiday decoration, hence the name. Its one- to three-foot fronds have rounded ends.

Maiden's Hair Fern (Adiantum) is said to have the power to restore, thicken, or curl hair. There are many varieties of this delicate, airy foliage. The Southern Maidenhair has elongated oval fronds that form lacy canopies as they droop from their pot. Variegated Maidenhair Fern has streaks of white on its tiny green leaves.

Staghorn Fern (Platycerium bifurcatum) is a perfect plant for wall-mounted planters (like the "ox-muzzle" arrangement described by Catherine E. Beecher and Harriet Beecher Stowe in *The American Woman's Home*). They are named for the shape of their fronds, which usually hang over a foot long.

Silver Fern (Pityrogramma calomelanos) is a member of a species that secretes a colored substance that gives the plant its name. The fragile fronds grow to three feet tall. Cousins of this delicate fern have leaves of gold, yellow, or pale orange.

Climbing Fern (Lygodium palmatum) sends out thin, wiry leaf stalks that wrap around nearby supports. It has hand-shaped leaflets, each a maximum of two inches across. Also called the Hartford Fern, it was the first plant ever protected by legislation: In 1869, the Connecticut legislature recognized that uncontrolled collection was threatening the fern.

YET ANOTHER HANGING BASKET is covered with pine cones, acorns, and a variety of nuts gathered in the forest. These bits of nature are sewn or pasted to brown paper which is then used to cover the plant container. Nut and seed work was all the rage in the 1880s, and this included using produce from the garden when possible. One hanging-pot variation called for stringing fresh, soft beans on wire. Large glass beads were interspersed with the beans. The wires would then be artistically bent and joined to cover the pot and the wires used to suspend it. When selecting the beans and beads, "care must be taken to produce a pleasing contrast or tasteful combinations."

FERNS THUS PLANTED in a hanging pot could be moved at the whim of the home gardener. Artistic arrangement of indoor plants was very important. In many interior photographs from the end of the 19th century, lush parlour gardens are placed at tall windows -- and ferns are always prominent. Huge pots of graceful ferns stand on marble-topped tables; others are scattered around the floor near the window, while more hang from hooks in the walls. And trails of ivy wander everywhere, tying the whole thing together.

THOSE WHO COULD AFFORD to add conservatories to their homes did so. Many were elaborate additions of wood and glass, some with direct entrances from the parlour or hallway. Houseplants could be brought into the conservatory for renewal after some days in a dark, airless corner. There was often artificial heat and large gasoliers with reflectors to provide light.

VICTORIANS took great satisfaction from the art of cultivating houseplants. Ferns aren't always easy to grow, but being lush and showy they suited the Victorian appreciation for grandeur and opulence. Also, as William Seale reminds us in his book The Tasteful Interlude, the Victorians attached a special meaning to their gardening acumen: "Healthy and well-maintained houseplants and flowers, besides being organic and thus aesthetically appealing, were the proud symbols of the vigilant housewife."

Glass beads and colored beans are strung alternately on wire for this hanging basket. The bowl is covered with oak leaves and stems.

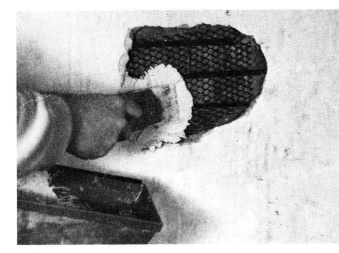

THREE~COAT PLASTER PATCHING

Whether it's the finish coat only or failure down to lath, this is the best way to patch.

by Walter Jowers

WHEN THE REALTOR first showed me through my new (1916) house, my first reaction was, "Awright! <u>Lots</u> of bad plaster!" Unprepared for this response, he asked what I was so happy about. "I'll be the only one to make an offer on this house," I told him. "Most people would sooner buy a house infested with rabid skunks than one with crumbly walls. They think the house is about to fall down."

WHILE IT'S TRUE that deteriorated plaster can be a sign of serious problems -- excessive settlement, plumbing leaks, roof or gutter leaks, or water penetration through exterior walls -- small areas of limited failure exist in virtually every old house. With some inexpensive tools and materials, and a little knowledge, it's easy to repair these minor blemishes.

YOU WILL NOT be transformed into a master plasterer simply by reading this article. We'll cover only patches (surrounded by sound plaster) that are no bigger than the length of a straight-edge. But you will (we hope) get the confidence to patch small holes in walls and ceilings.

What You'll Need

PATCHING WALLS is a skill that falls somewhere between the trades of plastering and drywall finishing. You'll need some tools from each trade:

Plastering Tools
- Hawk
- Slicker (flexible straight-edge)
- Plasterer's trowel
- Margin trowel
- Mortarboard and mudpan

Drywall Tools
- 6" taping knife
- 12" taping knife
- Joint tape (cloth mesh preferred)
- Stiff putty knife

Miscellaneous Tools
- Goggles, work gloves, and dust mask
- Hammer and cold chisel
- Needlenose pliers and wire cutter
- Screwgun and drill
- Spray bottle and dropcloths
- Tin snips

SOME of the following materials may not be found in your local hardware store or home center. A supply house that sells to contractors is the best source. If you have trouble finding these materials, call United States Gypsum.* USG will direct you to the nearest supplier of their products.

- Metal Lath -- Also called diamond mesh or expanded metal lath, it comes in bundles of ten 27x96-inch steets (equivalent to 20 square yards). Cost: $20-$25 per bundle.

- 18-Gauge Tie Wire; Drywall Nails -- You use these to secure the lath.

- Perlite Gypsum Plaster -- You use this for the scratch and brown coats (bottom two coats) of a patch. There are three types -- regular, which is what you want for patching interior walls and ceilings; masonry type, for use over highly absorbent surfaces; and Type S, for specific UL-listed assemblies (not something you're likely to need). I use USG Structo-Lite (regular). Cost: $7-$8 per 100-lb. bag.

- Gauging Plaster -- You mix this with finish lime for the final coat. Cost: $7-$9 per 100-lb. bag.

- Finish Lime -- I use USG Ivory autoclave (double-hydrated) finish lime. You can mix it instantly on-site. Single-hydrated finish limes must be slaked (soaked overnight) so you have to mix it the day before you use it. Some plasterers prefer the single-hydrated lime, claiming it has better workability. I find the two identical. Cost: $8-$9 per 50-lb. bag.

Removing The Loose Stuff

VERY OFTEN, only the top coat of plaster will be failing. Scrape off all loose finish coat with a putty knife. If water damage caused the finish coat to fail, you may find the underlying coats of plaster (although firmly keyed) are crumbly and soft. If this is the case, it too will have to be removed. To test, poke the corner of a putty knife into the brown coat. If it cuts through easily, the existing coat will not be able to hold new finish plaster. Remove it as described below.

---

* USG phone numbers — South: (404) 393-0770, East: (914) 332-0800, Central: (312) 321-4101, West: (818) 956-1882.

ON THOSE AREAS that have failed all the way to lath, make a three-coat repair. The first

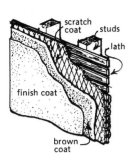

coat (scratch coat) stiffens the lath and provides a consistent base for the second (brown) coat. The brown coat is applied over the scratch coat and is built up to about 1/8 to 1/16 inch below the finished wall surface, providing a smooth, level base for the third (finish) coat. Complete failure of plaster that requires a three coat repair is usually localized around doors and windows, on stair soffits and, in a restoration project, wherever plumbers or electricians have been.

BEFORE YOU can make a patch, you have to cut out the bad plaster. Don't just start banging away with a hammer and chisel -- this indelicate approach is sure to loosen sound plaster and expand the area of damage. Wear a dust mask, goggles and gloves, and pull loose plaster from the walls with your hands. If the bad plaster is hard to pull away, a flat prybar will help bring it down. Be certain you have removed or resecured all loose plaster.

USE PLASTER WASHERS to resecure weakly-keyed areas of sound plaster to the wall or ceiling.

Plaster washers pull bowed areas back up tight to the lath or structural framing (an especially good idea if the bulging section includes ornamental plaster). You can order plaster washers from Charles Street Supply.*

SOMETIMES YOU MUST remove sound plaster (say, to add an electrical outlet or gain access to

plumbing). Drill holes in the line of your cut with a carbide drill bit, then carefully cut directly from hole to hole with a cold chisel. Hold the chisel at a shallow angle when you cut into the wall or ceiling. Don't just bash away at the face of the plaster -- the lath will bounce and loosen nearby plaster. Then cut the resulting plaster "island" free from the lath by chipping the keys from the side (again holding the chisel at a low angle).

NOW THAT YOU'VE exposed more wood lath, you'll probably find that some of it has pulled away from the studs. If necessary, cut the plaster back to the stud, and resecure the lath with drywall nails. Predrilling the old lath will lessen the chances of splitting it. If there are a few broken lath between the studs, don't worry about them; you'll be bridging over them with metal lath anyway. Knock any plaster that's stuck between the lath back into the

* Charles Street Supply Company, 54 Charles St., Dept. OHJ, Boston, MA 02114. (617) 367-9046.

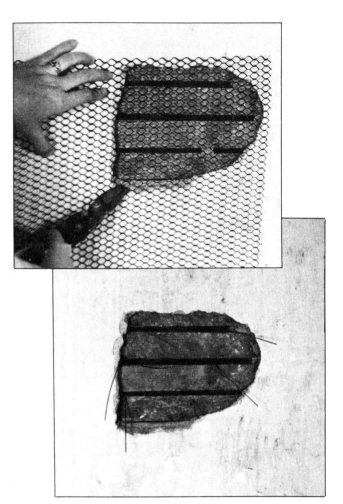

Cut the metal lath to the exact dimensions of the hole. Then use tie wires to secure it to the old wood lath.

wall cavity. Vacuum all dust, loose plaster, and other debris from the hole with a shop-vac (plaster dust will destroy a household vacuum), or sweep it out with an old paintbrush.

Lathing Up

TO ENSURE a durable patch, install metal lath over the wood lath. Metal lath provides better keying than wood lath and lessens the likelihood of cracking caused by the old wood lath drawing too much moisture out of the plaster.

DRIVE A FINISHING NAIL into an exposed stud or drill a hole in the lath and push a finishing nail in place. Take a piece of lath slightly bigger than the hole and hang it on the nail. This gives you a "third hand" to hold the lath in place while you cut it to conform to the hole. Cut the lath to shape with tin snips. For small holes, snip the ribs in the lath one at a time rather than using the tin snips like scissors -- it's easier on your hands, and you'll be able to cut a more precise pattern.

USE TIE WIRE to secure the metal lath over the wood lath. Bend a six-inch-long piece of wire into an elongated "U" and pull it around the old wood lath. Twist it tight with needlenose pliers and snip off the excess. Space the tie wires every six inches. To secure the lath at

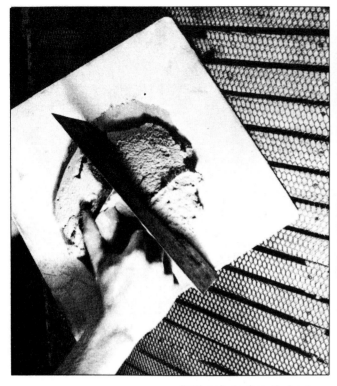

Cutting plaster from the hawk . . .   and applying it to the lath.

studs, drive 1" drywall screws between the lath into the stud. Always install the metal lath horizontally -- it'll hold the wet plaster better.

Mixing The Mud

WHEN YOU WORK with plaster, keeping your tools clean is all-important. Keep a bucket of water handy just to rinse your tools. Mix each type of plaster in a separate bucket and don't use the same scoop for different materials. When you finish a work session, clean and dry your tools immediately. Put waterproof dropcloths under the areas where you mix and apply plaster -- you'll drop a considerable amount.

FOR THE SCRATCH and brown coats, I use regular USG Structo-Lite. It's "instant" plaster; you just add it to water. The biggest trick for a novice plasterer is deciding how much to mix up. If you mix up more than you can use before it starts to stiffen -- about one hour -- you're going to have some waste. I find that I can use about half a five-gallon bucket in an hour. The professional plasterer that worked on my house could use about twice that amount. But it really depends on the type of plaster failure you have. You'll spend more time (and less material) repairing many little patches than you will filling a large area of failed plaster.

TO MIX MY customary half-bucketful, I pour about two quarts of cold, drinkable water into the bucket, then dump in about a third of a bucketful of plaster. Professionals normally mix plaster in a mortar pan with a hoe, but I prefer to mix it right in the bucket with a mixer attachment on my electric drill, then fine-tune the mix by adding a little more water or plaster until the consistency of the mix is right. The ideal mix is fairly stiff. To make sure the plaster cures properly, keep the room you're working in above 55 degrees F. until the plaster has set. Provide plenty of ventilation as the plaster cures.

● **The scratch coat**

THOROUGHLY MOISTEN the old wood lath with a spray bottle, so it won't draw moisture out of the wet plaster. To get the plaster from your hawk to your trowel, hold the hawk slanted about 45 degrees toward your body (you can only do this for a second or two -- any longer and you'll be wearing the plaster). Now cut into the plaster with your plasterer's trowel thumb side down. Bring the plaster directly to the wall with your plasterer's trowel. Apply it to the wall in an arcing motion (left to right for righthanders), making sure to work it well between the lath. Keep the hawk close to the wall under the trowel to catch falling plaster. Use a margin trowel to work the plaster into edges and corners. It's sometimes easier to throw plaster off the end of the margin trowel into the patch than pack it into hard-to-reach areas.

PROFESSIONAL PLASTERERS make it look easy when, with considerable elan and sleight of trowel, they bring the plaster from the mortarboard to the hawk and effortlessly sweep it onto the wall. You and I are a bit more clumsy, though, so make sure you've put down dropcloths: Until you get the hang of it, you'll spill a lot of plaster.

DON'T BUILD the scratch coat up any thicker than the old scratch coat (about 1/8 to 1/4 inch). As it starts to set, score shallow, random scratches in it diagonally about every inch or so to give the next coat something to grab. Let the scratch coat set for 48 hours.

Scratch-coating a fairly large area of failed plaster on a ceiling. Note the plaster washers securing the edges of the existing plaster.

● The brown coat

USE THE SAME plaster (Structo-Lite) for the brown coat that you used for the scratch coat. It's mixed the same way and applied in pretty much the same manner; the difference is that you want to make it smooth and level so that it will provide a solid, level base for the finish coat. To do this, run a slicker over the entire patch after you apply the coat. A slicker is nothing more than a long, flexible straight-edge; it's available where you buy other plastering tools. I use a two-foot-long straight-edge/paint guard that I bought at the hardware store as a slicker; some plasterers prefer a length of beveled siding.

KEEP THE BROWN COAT below the level of the surrounding finish coat by about 1/8 inch. When you're done "dressing" the brown coat, sponge or scrape the wet Structo-Lite off the surrounding finish coat. As the brown coat starts to set, knock off any high spots that you missed during your touch-ups. Plasterers use an angle plane (a specialized trowel with several sharp blades set at various angles) for this, but any sharp edge works well. Let the brown coat set for 48 hours before applying the finish coat.

● Mixing the finish coat

A LOT OF PEOPLE think applying the finish coat is going to be the toughest step. Not true. The real trick is to make a proper mix (the first time) and to work quickly, though not frantically. If it takes you 20 minutes to mix the plaster, it will be nearly set before you can get it on your hawk. You might want to practice the steps outlined below on the smallest patches before mixing up a large batch to do a big area. Once you gain confidence, finish coat work is easy -- providing your first two coats were properly applied.

THE STEPS OUTLINED below also apply to patching walls and ceilings where the scratch and brown coats are okay, but the finish coat has delaminated (a common condition in houses that have suffered slight water damage or have been left vacant without heating and cooling). If you're applying finish coat over an old brown coat, there's an important additional step: You must moisten the existing brown coat well before applying the finish coat (unnecessary on a newly-applied brown coat). The old plaster will absorb water faster, causing cracks in the finish coat as it starts to dry.

Smoothing the brown coat with a slicker.

MIXING PLASTER for the finish coat means working with lime. Lime is very caustic; it can damage your eyes, burn your lungs and nasal passages, and irritate your skin. Be sure to wear goggles, a dust mask (or better yet, a respirator), and latex gloves when you mix lime. Store it away from children and pets.

PLACE ABOUT TWO QUARTS of cold, drinkable water into a five-gallon plastic bucket, then scoop in autoclave finish lime until it starts to float, rather than sink into the water. (If you're using single-hydrated lime, you'll have to sift the lime into water the day before, and let it slake overnight before mixing.) Mix thoroughly with a mixer attachment on an electric drill, or by hand with a pointing trowel. Then, just as with gypsum plaster, fine-tune the mix by adding small amounts of water or lime as necessary, working for a mix in which all the lime is wet, and there are no lumps or standing water. This mixture of lime and water is called lime putty and should be about the consistency of joint compound.

NOW YOU'LL NEED a mortarboard, which is simply a board on which you'll mix the ingredients for the finish coat. It should be smooth enough not to splinter when you run a trowel across it. A scrap of plywood placed over a couple of sawhorses works nicely.

TOSS SOME LIME PUTTY onto the mortarboard. Use your margin trowel to form it into a ring. Now fill the center of the ring about two-thirds full with cold, clear water. Slowly sprinkle in gauging plaster until the water can't take up anymore. You want about one part gauging plaster to three parts lime putty. Mix the water and the plaster in the middle of the ring together -- it should be a bit stiffer than the lime putty. Then, fold in the lime putty, and mix until all of the ingredients are well acquainted. What's on your mortarboard now is finish plaster. Get to work: It sets up pretty quickly.

The lime putty ring on a mortarboard.

Why Not Sheetrock Patches?

MANY DO-IT-YOURSELF books and magazines, including OHJ (December 1983), discuss patching plaster using pieces of drywall (Sheetrock). To do this, you remove the damaged plaster back to two studs (so there's something substantial to screw the drywall into), cut the drywall to fit the opening, and tape the joints between the new drywall and existing plaster with tape and joint compound. This patching method does work, and has advantages for certain applications. But for filling small holes, it has some drawbacks:

● You have to cut the plaster back to the nearest studs or joists. Plaster isn't so accommodating as to fail on 16-in. centers. If a small area of plaster has failed between two studs, you'd have to cut away perfectly good plaster.

● You have to try to get the Sheetrock flush with the existing plaster. Plaster, because it was applied wet and worked by hand, is seldom of uniform thickness. It's usually 5/8" here, 9/16" there, etc. Drywall is uniform. Even if you fuss with shims, it's tough to get the patch flush with the old plaster. But your plaster patch can be made to match irregularities in thickness and surface texture.

● You have to make a neat hole in the old plaster to accommodate the drywall. After the patch is made, you're more likely to see the straight lines (and textural uniformity) of the drywall patch than you are to notice an asymmetrical plaster patch.

● **The finish coat**

USE YOUR PLASTERER'S TROWEL to pull the plaster onto your hawk. Then, using the motions described above for applying the scratch and brown coats, trowel it into the patch. It's not difficult to work the finish coat smooth -- for me, it's easier than working with spackling or joint compound. The finish plaster will stiffen as you level and smooth it; as it does, you can add little dabs of plaster to fill in hollows, and you can smooth out ridges. To get the finish coat really slick, spray a fine mist of water onto the plaster and make a few final passes with your trowel. Straighten edges or corners with your margin trowel.

ONCE THE FINISH plaster starts to set, discard any that you haven't used -- don't try to "retemper" it (extend its life by adding water). Retempering will not slow the chemical reaction; it will only weaken the resulting plaster. It's not hard to tell when the plaster has "gone off;" it becomes stiff and unworkable. You'll soon learn how much you can use before it starts to set; then you can adjust the sizes of your batches accordingly.

LET THE FINISH coat cure for about a week, then check for shrinkage. You may find a few spots where the new finish coat has shrunken away from the old one. Tape the cracks with cloth mesh tape and joint compound as you would tape any minor plaster cracks (see "What's Possible In Plaster Restoration" in the November 1983 OHJ). Large cracks should be chipped out and replastered.

Reaching High Places

Using Ladders and Scaffolds Indoors   by Patricia Poore

YOU'VE PROBABLY GOT two ladders around the house: a six-foot stepladder for odd jobs indoors, and an aluminum extension ladder to get at gutters outdoors. These ladders are versatile and nice to have around. But they are hardly the safest, most efficient, or most comfortable way to reach high places for many of the jobs you'll tackle.

WE COVERED THE BASICS of exterior scaffolding in an earlier article -- refer back to "A Scaffolding Primer," OHJ July 1985. The following article is a lot simpler and probably of use to more people. It will cover various ways to work at heights indoors. Although we'll start off with ladders, we'll concentrate more on simple scaffold arrangements.

Ladder Types

YOU CAN BUY everything from a step stool to an extension ladder that reaches 40 feet. For indoor use, a sturdy two-foot step stool and a high-quality six-foot stepladder are the basics. Aluminum ladders are good, as long as you don't buy the cheapest ones. Their advantage is their lighter weight -- a big advantage. You can move them with one hand, so you don't have to put down your hawk, paintbrush, or whatever every time you move the ladder a couple of feet. Aluminum ladders make un-

pleasant noises, and they leave black marks on your clothes and hands as well as scuffing the wall surface they're leaned against. They also conduct electricity, which is why we don't recommend aluminum extension ladders for use near electrical wires.

WOOD LADDERS are strong, a little cheaper, and less likely to mar the wall. They tend to get loose in the joints and a little wobbly with heavy use.

FIBERGLASS LADDERS are also available. Electricians often use them because they are lightweight, sturdy, and non-conductive. For a safe, medium-commercial-grade six-foot stepladder, expect to pay $55 for wood, $65 for aluminum, and $95 for (heavy-duty) fiberglass.

LADDERS COME in different grades as well as different materials. A light-duty ladder, more often called "homeowner grade," is rated at 200 lbs., and some of its construction details are lighter-duty than commercial-grade ladders. A medium commercial-grade ladder is rated at 225 lbs. for wood, 250 for aluminum. Industrial or heavy-duty ladders are rated at 250 or even 300 lbs. and take the most abuse.

LADDERS ARE REFERRED TO by their standing height when folded. You don't go up six feet with a six-foot ladder, because you can't stand above the second-to-top rung. Actually, your additional reach is a little under four feet with a six-foot stepladder.

A STEP STOOL (24 to 26 inches) is safe and convenient for jobs like hanging window coverings, wall-painting up to plate-rail or picture-rail height, or grouting bathroom tiles. At around $25, a step stool is such a low-cost item (compared to other ladders) that it only makes sense to buy a top-quality one. Be sure to get one with a safety grab bar.

YOU WON'T OFTEN NEED an extension ladder for indoor work. (About $100 for a good 20-foot one.) It'll come in handy for setting up a scaffold in a stairwell. We'll get to that.

Scaffolds

IF YOU'VE GOT some good ladders, why would you use a scaffold? Well, have you ever gotten a case of "rung feet"? It happens when you work from a ladder doing a task that takes hours and hours -- like paint stripping or decorative painting. Besides the foot pain, standing on a ladder is extremely fatiguing to the body. You have to balance carefully and hold on while you reach up or out. Because you can't reach too far, you have to move the ladder often, climbing up and down.

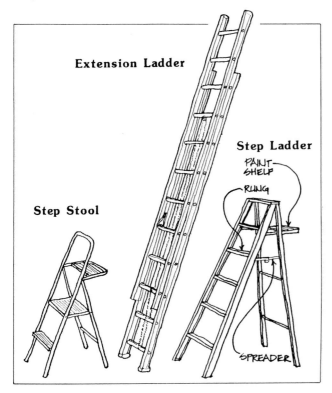

Extension Ladder

Step Ladder

PAINT-SHELF

RUNG

Step Stool

SPREADER

DOs and DON'Ts of LADDER SAFETY

WORKING FROM A LADDER is pretty straightforward — everybody does it. Yet falls from ladders are the most common cause of serious restoration-related injuries. Don't take safety for granted!

(1) DO use the right ladder for the job. If you use a ladder that's too short, you'll be tempted to stand on the top rung. If you use one that's too tall, you'll be uncomfortably far away from the wall when you're working at lower heights.

(2) DO make sure the spreaders are locked into position before you climb the ladder.

(3) DON'T stand on the highest step or top platform, and don't put any weight on the pail shelf — it will not support you.

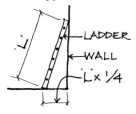

(4) DO follow the 25% rule — that is, 1/4 of ladder length away from the wall at the base. A ten-foot ladder would thus be set 2.5 feet away from the bottom of the wall.

(5) DON'T lean out over the side of a stepladder, because it will tip sideways.

(6) DON'T over-reach. Sure, it's a pain to get down off the ladder, move it, and climb back up. But it's worse to take a fall. If you're working on something that requires a long reach, set up scaffolding instead.

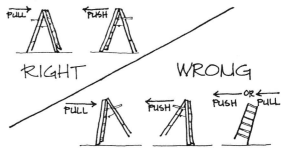

(7) DO position the ladder so it won't tip, if the job calls for you to pull or push on something.

(8) DO keep the door wide open — or close it and lock it — when you're working from a ladder near a doorway.

THIS IS WHERE scaffolds come in. If you know you'll be doing a job that requires many hours of working up high, a scaffold is more convenient, more comfortable, and SAFER than a ladder. A scaffold is better for stripping ceiling beams, stencilling a frieze, and running a plaster moulding. (I dare you to try running mouldings from a ladder!)

HERE ARE THE ADVANTAGES of scaffolding over ladders:

• A wider platform to stand on. It's a lot easier and safer to stand on a plank than on ladder rungs.

• Greater reach. You know how limited your reach is from a ladder. On a scaffold, you can walk perhaps eight feet across, bend down, or even sit on the platform.

• Access to tools. Ever walked up and down, up and down to bring various tools with you? Scaffolding can hold stencils, paint and brushes, or heat plate, putty knife and scraper (on shelves, not on the platform).

• Safety. For all the reasons above, carefully planned scaffolding is safer than a ladder. If you're working above five feet or if people will pass under the scaffold, you should also erect a safety rail and install toeboards.

Rented Scaffolding

THE REST OF THE ARTICLE will deal with inexpensive, homemade scaffolds that are built to suit the task. But first we should mention

rolling platform scaffolding, a useful type for indoor work, which is available for rental. It is welded-tube scaffolding, similar to the type covered in our previous article, but it is narrower and it rolls on casters (so it's easy to move). Wheels would be useless or dangerous on the uneven terrain outdoors, but they are relatively safe on interior floors. Even though the casters lock, we suggest that wheels always be chocked before you climb onto the platform.

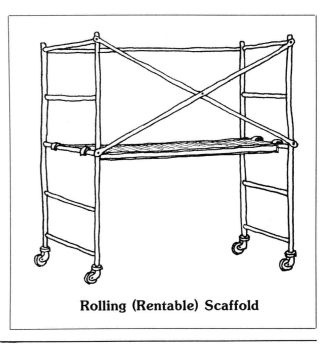

Rolling (Rentable) Scaffold

SCAFFOLD SAFETY

✍ Scaffolds 10 feet or higher

(Use these safety features above five *feet if you are nervous or clumsy.)*

● Guardrails should be installed. They should be of at least 2x4 stock, and 42 inches high.

● A midrail should be installed at the halfway point between guard rail and planks, and should be of 1x6 stock.

● Uprights should be installed no less than every eight feet.

● Toeboards with a minimum height of four inches should be installed on all sides (to keep objects from sliding off the scaffold).

● Wire mesh should be fastened between the toeboards and midrails if there is any chance of objects being dropped or if people are working underneath the scaffold.

✍ Horse Scaffolds

The lateral spread of the legs should be not less than two-thirds of the height of the horse.

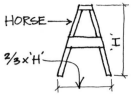

✍ General

● For scaffolding that utilizes a ladder as a support: Ladders must be placed or fastened to prevent the bottom of the ladder from kicking out.

● Platform planks must be scaffold-grade or equivalent, and at least two inches thick.

● The planks should extend over the bearing surfaces on each end by 12 inches to allow for board creep.

● On a span of eight feet, the walking surface must have a minimum width of 18 inches.

A ROLLING SCAFFOLD will cost no more than $75 to $95 a month to rent. Try the Yellow Pages under "Scaffolds-Rental". If you rent from an all-purpose rental place, be sure to check the condition of the scaffold. Reject bent tubing, casters that don't lock, and warped or knotty planks.

Scaffolding to Suit

THE TEXT AND ILLUSTRATIONS that follow describe home-built scaffolding suited to common restoration tasks.

BELOW is the simplest scaffold, good for raising you eighteen inches to three feet above the floor. The plank can also span between two stepladders. Be sure to overhang the plank six to 12 inches -- but don't stand at the end.

Horse to Stepladder Scaffold

ANOTHER USEFUL kind of step stool is the rolling library stool in the illustration below. We bought one specifically for reaching the high shelves in the kitchen, but it's become the favored "stepladder" for repair jobs. This kind of stool is tremendously convenient because it rolls freely until you stand on it -- your weight forces the rollers up inside and the stool grabs firmly. You can kick it here and there even with your hands full. Best of all, it cannot tip over. Because it takes up very little room, it's useful for tight spaces such as closets and vestibules. (The library stool costs about $30; some housewares stores have them now, and you can order one from an office supply store.)

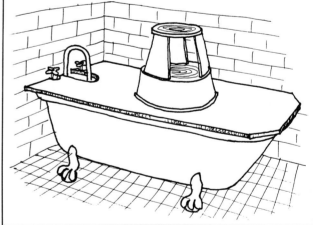

IN THE DRAWING, the library stool sits on a piece of 3/4-inch plywood, set over a bathtub. The plywood protects the tub from damage and also acts as a work platform. If you've ever fought with the legs of a stepladder around the fixtures in a small bathroom, you can appreciate this set-up.

THE PHOTO shows a scaffold, 10 feet long (8-foot working span), that was created for a ceiling-beam stripping project. The saw-horses have 2x6 legs with 2x4 cross-pieces (gussets are plywood scraps). The horses were put together with 2-inch drywall screws (not nails) for strength. A couple of hints: Build one horse a little narrower so they stack. If you use a screw gun, you can also back the screws out to disassemble the horses.

THE SCAFFOLD'S PLATFORM is 3/4-inch plywood, about 20 inches wide, screwed to continuous 2x4 ribs.

THE STAIR SCAFFOLD set-up shown at right stretches the limits of what you can work from safely without guardrails. Be sure the plank you use is sufficient to span between the ladders; you can rent safe aluminum scaffold planks. A cleat nailed to the floor keeps the legs of the leaning stepladder on the upper landing from kicking out. Clean rags wrapped around the tops of the ladder stiles keep them from marring the head wall.

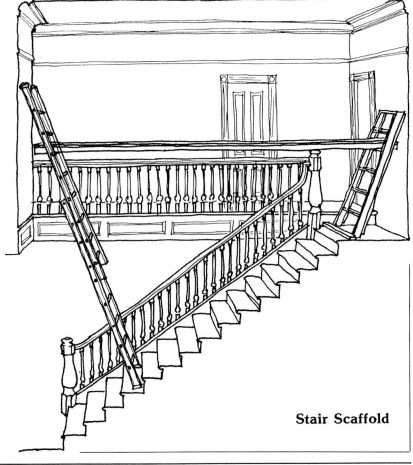

Stair Scaffold

POST-VICTORIAN HOUSES

TRELLISES

A PERGOLA ENTRY.

A Pergola Entry is the most stylish and expensive of the trellises pictured in this spread — a survivor from the pre-World War One Arts & Crafts movement. All that's required is a pair of store-bought Tuscan columns, some fancy scroll-sawing of beam

CORNER TRELLIS & FLOWER POT SHELF.

ends, and simple ladder trellis on a concrete slab covered with a decorative arrangement of plain tiles.

The *Corner Trellis & Flower Pot Shelf* is the oddity in this survey. It's tough to get vines to behave in corners, so this approach might work. The pot shelf would permit a changing

TRELLIS AND
SIDE WALL ORNAMENT.

variety of colorful bloom. But this should be used with caution: The function of the five other trellises is to mark and enliven a wall, an entrance, or a window; the function of this corner trellis is to obliterate the juncture of two walls and enlarge the perception of the two walls as one.

The *Trellis And Side Wall Ornament* brings life — metaphorically and literally — to a plain expanse of wall and its tiny window. Like the other

THE VICTORIANS said that the better house was the one that linked man with Nature, and since then there have been many ways to establish that prized bond — bay windows, conservatories, terrariums, flower boxes, hanging plants, herbacious borders, sinuous walks and roads, foundation plantings, climbing vines, arbors, gazebos, pergolas, and trellises. And it's worth recalling that Victorian porches, verandahs, and piazzas were often designed with lattice-like supports that provided a place on which vines and flowers could climb.

THIS DEEP-ROOTED NEED to link the house with Nature survived the demise of Victorian house styles. By the 1920s, the romantic points of reference were Ye Olde England and Ye Olde Colonial America. The former was driven by the cottage gardens of Gertrude Jekyll (author of such books as *Colour In The Garden* and *Gardens For Small Country Houses*); the latter, by the colored photographs of Wallace Nutting. At the popular level, six illustrations from William Radford's *Architectural Details* of 1921, seen on these two pages, show what the imaginative use of trellises can do to unite the post-Victorian home with Nature.

ARCH TRELLIS OVER
A WINDOW.

LATTICE ORNAMENT
FOR A WALL.

A TRELLIS AND
SEAT ENTRY.

examples shown, the object is to unite the house with nature without harming the structure. (If the vines were permitted to grow on the house itself, the siding inevitably would begin to rot.)

Arch Trellis Over A Window is an interesting placement of an ornamental device which is more commonly used over a gateway.

The *Lattice Ornament For A Wall* is so simple that it can be made in any size and any pattern.

A Trellis And Seat Entry would be perfect for a pair of French doors that served as an exit into the garden. The seat

ends can be easily band-sawn. The posts are 4x4s. (These days, the arch could be a pair of plastic tubes.) Adding this kind of trellis to the house does more than integrate one's home with the surrounding environment — it gives the homeowner what is essentially a miniature porch!

Restorer's Notebook

Making It Last

STORING PAINT for future touch-ups can be a real problem. Opening and resealing a can of paint every time you touch-up a few nicks will eventually distort the lid or get paint in the lip. In either case, a vapor-tight seal is impossible and the paint either forms a skin or dries out completely.

I avoid this problem by drilling a 1/8-inch hole in the lid and plugging the hole with a large self-tapping screw. Enough paint can easily be poured out through the hole for touch-up jobs. When the screw is replaced, the paint in its threads forms a very tight seal -- so tight that future stirring to remove a skin is unnecessary; vigorous shaking is sufficient. I've stored a quart of paint for nearly ten years this way, and it still flows easily.

-- Bill Walters, St. Augustine, Fla.

Simplifying Stripping

I RECOMMEND USING a simple kitchen tool, such as a large or small cake-frosting knife, when stripping layers of old paint from Victorian mouldings with a heat gun or heat plate. Its curved tip follows the contours of your moulding easily and quickly, removing the paint faster than a conventionally shaped putty knife -- and it won't scratch or mar the wood.

-- R.A. Mawhinney, Monroe, Wisc.

A Heat Shield Look-Alike

TWO OF THE TIPS I read in the June 1986 OHJ have prompted me to add my comments:

1. Joseph Patay recommends using a heat shield to protect glass when removing paint from window sash ("Restorer's Notebook"). It occurs to me that his homemade deflector is a "dead ringer" for my pastry scraper. So if you don't want to construct one, check your local kitchen supply store.

2. In his excellent door-repair article, Jonathan Poore recommends drilling and doweling stripped screw holes. I find it easier to fill the holes with ribbon epoxy. The stuff I use comes in two "ribbons," one blue and one yellow. Mix a piece of each together and blend until you get a uniform shade of green. Then just pack it into the hole. After it hardens, you can drill through it just like wood, and it holds the screws well. This method is especially well suited to holes near the edge of a piece of wood -- where driving a dowel might split the wood. I've had success using this technique in a number of patching projects.

-- Tom MacGregor, Plainfield, Vt.

Tape Those Tiles

MY HUSBAND AND I had no choice. The plaster in our second-floor bathroom was so bad simple patching wouldn't do. It all had to come down to make room for (sigh) water-resistant Sheetrock. The problem was, regardless of how carefully we chipped away at the old plaster, the tiles on the wall below kept working loose and falling to the floor. We broke four hard-to-replace tiles before a simple solution dawned on me.

I bought some two-inch masking tape and ran it horizontally across all of the tile joints in the first four courses. The tiles kept working loose, but they couldn't fall to the floor because they were all taped together. After the plaster demolition was complete, we carefully removed the loose tiles one at a time and marked the location of each tile on the back for later installation.

-- Joan Mezzina, Bayonne, N.J.

Defeating Knots

FACED WITH THE PROBLEM of knots in new pine boards and water stains on old plaster, which show through layers of shellac, primer, and paint, I finally came across a fantastic product: "Kilz" by Masterchem Industries (P.O. Box 2666, St. Louis, MO 63116). It's about $6 a quart at our local hardware store. One or two coats on the most persistent problem areas and the stains are gone forever (or in our case, 2-1/2 years with no bleed-through!). And it dries in only half an hour.

-- Elaine M. Czora, Ontario, N.Y.

Restoration Products

by Eve Kahn

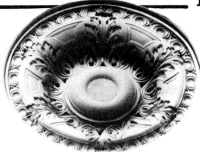

Moulding & Ornament

If you're looking for attractive ceiling ornaments and moulding, Nomaco offers two lines of products that look just like plaster but won't consume your decorating budget -- all cost substantially less than plaster or wood. The simpler line, Nomastyl, consists of extruded moulding and stamped ceiling ornaments made of polystyrene. There are nine moulding profiles available, and the ceiling medallions range from tiny two-inch rosettes to two-foot ceiling centers.

Arstyl, the more elaborate and expensive line, consists of eight types of crown moulding -- floral, egg-and-dart, denticulated -- plus framing with either curved or floral corners. The ceiling ornaments include stars, circles, and ovals, ranging in diameter from six inches to almost three feet. All are made of polyurethane, and details are reinforced with foil.

Installation of these pieces is simple. Since they're very light you don't have to worry about the burden on your plaster. All you need is filler adhesive or contact glue and a clean surface; a fine-tooth saw or even a sharp knife will suffice for trimming moulding.

You can order Nomaco products by mail, or write or call for a list of the distributors in your area. Nomaco Inc., Hershey Dr., Dept. OHJ, Ansonia, CT 06401. (203) 736-9231.

Period Clothing to Sew

Saundra Altman subtitles her company Past Patterns, "The Historical Pattern Company Devoted to Authenticity," and she means it. Her collection of pattern reproductions has two divisions. The first consists of exact duplicates of old patterns from 1830 to 1950. Dabblers beware: These replicas do not make for easy sewing. They do not come in modern dress sizes, and they retain the flaws of the originals: like oversize busts and wasp waists in the 1890s, or flattened bosoms in the flapper era.

Saundra also offers an easier collection. All of these have been adapted for modern, uncorseted sizes 10 to 20, but are otherwise strictly based on old designs.

The interesting and attractive catalogue includes sewing advice and tidbits from the history of fashion, and it even recommends appropriate underwear. The "adaptations" brochure runs $5. There are separate catalogs for the exact duplicates: 1901-1950 ($4.25), the 'teens and the '20s ($3 each), and the '30s and '40s ($.50 each). Past Patterns, PO Box 7587, Dept. OHJ, Grand Rapids, MI 49510. (616) 245-9456.

Peggy Powell

pre-1850

Colonial Lighting

If you're considering lighting for your pre-1850 house, whether it be chandeliers, lanterns, or sconces, you should invest $3 in Richard Scofield's Period Lighting Fixtures catalog. The catalog itself is a small primer on the history of early lighting; it will help you select the proper size and style of fixtures. There's a section on how to identify authentically re-created construction features. Where possible the origins and approximate dates of the fixtures are supplied.

The catalog comes with a little packet of samples to help you pick a color and finish; all have been antiqued with a patina. All fixtures are handcrafted and can be ordered either electrified or for use with candles. One thing that impressed us was the ingenious way Richard manages to hide the wires inside the hooks of his chandeliers. Richard offers what he believes is the largest and most historically accurate collection of wall sconces to be found in a catalog, and indeed the variety is impressive. Be prepared to order and wait, since each item is made to order. (These things take time!) Richard D. Scofield, Dept. OHJ., 1 Main St., Chester, CT 06412. (203) 526-3690.

──pre–1850── ─────── *for Victorian buildings*──

Heart-Pine Woodwork

The Joinery Company salvages heart pine from factories and warehouses that are being torn down, and remills it into flooring. Several grades are available; the most expensive ($5.31 per square foot) contains 97% heartwood and is completely free of knots. You can also get old heart-pine flooring; the edges and bottoms have been remilled for easier installation, but the patina of the surface is untouched.

The photos here show what else The Joinery offers: exquisite reproduction woodwork of the 18th and early 19th centuries. The cabinets, mantels, furniture, stair parts, and wainscoting are authentic and beautifully crafted. The company's nationwide clientele includes Colonial Williamsburg. Some pieces are in stock, like six-panel doors and Georgian newel posts. The company also does much custom work. Various types of wood, such as wormy chestnut, maho-

The Joinery Company made the woodwork and furniture for this room in Nashville, N.C.

The first ceiling fan, invented about 1889, had only two blades.

Antique Electric Fans

Ken Horan has always been fascinated by fans. In the 1960s, when fans went out of fashion, they were removed and discarded by the thousands: "You could buy truckloads for $5," Ken recalls. He started researching fans, which led inevitably to collecting. He now runs a company that buys, restores, and sells ceiling and desk fans of all eras, from the earliest two-bladers of the 1890s through Art Deco.

Prices depend upon the con-

dition, degree of ornament (the simpler ones are less expensive), and rarity. For example, a fairly common desk fan in as-is condition may cost $50; a restored desk fan from the early 1900s may cost $500. Ceiling fans range from $350 to $2500.

Ken strongly believes that old fans, restored to working order, are far superior in materials and craftsmanship to reproductions. He keeps several popular models in stock. He generally leaves fans unrestored until someone wants to buy them, because he offers all kinds of custom restoration work, like painting, plating, and replacing blades. His free flyer shows some of the models he typically has on hand, but there are many others to choose from. You can get the company's catalog of reproduction lighting for $3. M-H Lamp & Fan Co., 7231-1/2 N. Sheridan Rd., Dept. OHJ, Chicago, IL 60626. (312) 743-2225.

Doors, Gates, & More

Working out of a restored wagon factory dating back to the Civil War, the craftsmen at The Old Wagon Factory produce a fine collection of wooden screen doors, porch railings, garden gates, and planters in a variety of designs, suitable for Victorian or post-Victorian houses.

For porches, both open and screened, there's Victorian railing made of spruce. The scroll-sawn balusters have cut-out decorations; the 7-by-24-by-3/4-in. units come primed and sell for $20 each. Chippendale railing with diagonal stickwork also comes primed; it's 30 in. high and sells for $30 per ft. Another product we like is their Chippendale garden gate, custom-made to fit your opening. Sizes up to 38 in. wide sell for $185. There's lots more in the $2 catalog. The Old Wagon Factory, Dept. OHJ, 103 Russell St., P.O. Box 1427, Clarksville, VA 23927. (804) 374-5787.

gany, or walnut, and finishes can be ordered as well. You can obtain their portfolio, which comes with photos of some recent work, for $5. Their showroom is well worth a visit (make an appointment), for it's made entirely of recycled wood: floors, stairs, doors, even window sash and trim. The Joinery Company, PO Box 518, Dept. OHJ, Tarboro, NC 27886. (919) 823-3306.

300   **July-August 1986**

Victorian _for post–Victorian buildings_

New from Bradbury

Even the brochure for Bradbury & Bradbury's latest wallpaper collection is gorgeous. The Neo-Grec roomset (ceiling component shown above) is now available in five colorways: terra cotta, cream and gilt, jasper green, dove blue, and "ashes of rose." The brochure with color sheets costs $1, and samples can be purchased for $7. Also two new friezes have been produced. "Emelita's Frieze" is an exact reproduction of an existing frieze in an 1884 house. "Iris" is an adaptation of a Walter Crane frieze. Each comes in only one (exquisite) colorway; samples are $2.50. Bradbury & Bradbury, PO Box 155, Dept. OHJ, Benicia, CA 94510. (707) 746-1900.

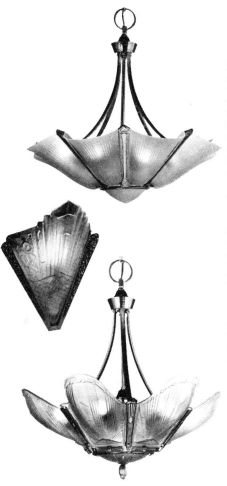

Saarinen Furniture

These beautiful pieces were designed by architect Eliel Saarinen between 1928 and 1930 for his own home. They're now being reproduced as part of Arkitektura's "Cranbrook Collection," named for the artists' colony and school where Saarinen lived. The collection also includes several adaptations of Saarinen's designs, along with several new pieces, like side tables, that fill in what Saarinen didn't provide. The prices are not cheap; they range from $1750 for a small cigarette table to $8100 for a spectacular round table with flared legs and intricate marquetry. The company does offer trade discounts, and they send out a handsome free information packet with photos of each piece and a price list. Arkitektura, PO Box 210, Dept. OHJ, Princeton, NJ 08540. (609) 683-9654.

Art Deco Lighting

If you've tried to find Art Deco fixtures in the antique stores recently, you know that they don't show up much, and when they do, they're swiftly snapped up. Fortunately Metropolitan Lighting Fixture Company supplies a collection of quality reproductions. Made in original moulds, with a little tarnish they'll be indistinguishable from their ancestors.

Both ceiling and wall fixtures come in polished brass or satin nickel (gold or silver color), and they're available through architects and interior designers only. The prices range from $2067 to $2721 for ceiling fixtures and $381 to $396 for wall fixtures (there's a 50% trade discount). The color brochure, which also contains the rest of the company's extensive line, is $5. Metropolitan Lighting Fixture Co. Inc., 1010 Third Avenue, Dept. OHJ, New York, NY 10021. (212) 838-2425.

On the inside of this hardwood cabinet's doors are Art Deco peacocks, inlaid in exotic veneers.

This solid maple chair has ebony and enamel ribs on both front and back.

opinion...

Remuddling

A fire was only the first misfortune to befall this Michigan Bungalow (above). The building was gutted, stripped of its exterior detail, and remodeled into a windowless expanse of vertical wood siding (top).

WE RECEIVED these photos from subscriber Steve Lomske of Northville, Michigan. In his letter, he explained how a proud but ailing Bungalow was reduced to a coffinlike box:

"I WAS DRIVING HOME from work when I passed this remodeling project. Being an architect and also a Bungalow restorer, I stopped and introduced myself to the builder. The inside of the house had suffered water damage due to a fire, which had ruined the oak floors. My first reaction was to restore the house, and I offered the builder my services. However, he had dreams of creating an 'expensive contemporary showplace' for future condo development. My opinion was if he was not going to restore, then he should save himself the money and time and simply bulldoze the structure in a day or so. Instead, the builder spent weeks tearing out the existing overhangs, oak floor, and ornate staircase; the house was stripped of history. As the 'after' photo [above] shows, the builder failed at both restoration and creating a 'contemporary showplace.' Another fine Bungalow bites the dust. The only identifiable item remaining is the chimney located toward the left of the roof."

My New Passion

I CAN'T GET OVER how many great old garages there are! It seems they weren't there last winter; now, all of a sudden, they're everywhere I go. I noticed them on a weekend bicycle ride: garages that used to be barns ... late Victorian carriage-house garages ... dozens of early suburban garages. On most, one door is missing and the other is sitting heavily in tall grass, long unopened.

I noticed them in Massachusetts when we visited family. In the village of Annisquam, on the grounds of a shingle-style home built in 1907: a vine-covered, two-bay garage with chauffeur quarters. A tiny one-bay garage in Pigeon Cove, freshly painted to match the house. And my favorite, the regional vernacular: granite garages that front directly on the street, growing out of the famous granite walls of Cape Ann.

Why didn't I ever notice them before?

YOU JUST don't notice something until you appreciate it. And you don't care enough to restore something until you can appreciate it. Thanks, Randy Cotton, for writing this month's article about garages. Learning to "see" things that were always there is the fun part of this old-house business.

Patricia Poore

Time Capsule

Why bother with these old places? Because you find yourself enjoying things like period garages . . . and being touched by history in a very personal way.

Mrs. Jones points to the wall that holds secrets. *Below*, the solid Foursquare.

Dear OHJ:

A 90-day project stretched into a year-and-a-half of headaches, backaches, and bellyaches with few inspiring moments. A ragged 80-year-old, our Foursquare house stands with the substantial dignity of one who is sure of a solid foundation and sound workmanship.

Originally, we had planned quaint touches that would relieve its severity, but the house would have none of them. It demanded straight-backed, eyes-ahead, no-nonsense attention from us.

But it held hidden secrets that it revealed in due time. We came upon the first one penciled on a bare living room wall after we stripped the wallpaper. Giant signatures of a former resident's children: The date was 1957 and they had written their ages and grades in school after each name. It was an unexpected "how do you do" from the recent past and we felt as if the house were choosing to let us see.

Not long after, while removing a beaverboard wall in the stairwell, we found a little tin box advertising colored pencils. Inside was a 3x5 card with a history of the house carefully printed on it, along with the names of the three teenaged boys in the family who had prepared the box and a description of the remodeling that was being done at that time -- 1939. They had cut pictures from LIFE magazine showing 1939 cars and the latest fashions. One of the boys wrote that the United States was threatened with war. He hoped for peace, although it looked as if there would not be peace. We've since learned that one of the boys became an engineer, another a musician. The third boy died in Italy during World War II, four years after they'd all fixed their tin-box time capsule.

It was time to seal the wall again. We placed the little box back in its buried vault between the studs and added a glass mayonnaise jar with our story in it: our names, the date, a remodeling outline, a few pictures. The carpenter's son dropped in two new pennies. Another chapter was added to the house's history.

Last Christmas we held a family dinner in the unfinished dining room. All 22 of us signed our names to the bare wall, along with birthdates and relationships to each other. A niece impulsively added, "This was a happy day." Surprise for the next people, 25 or 50 or 100 years down the line, when they take the paper off! And a silent message to say we love the house enough to acknowledge our presence, not with engraved brass plates or changes that violate, but in an unseen place only the house will know.

We're betting this old house will hide our messages until the new people respect its unpretentious, unabashedly upright character. Only then will it yield its secrets. By that time they too will understand that this is a structure which must be lived up to with integrity.

-- Frances Jones
Carthage, Missouri

Letters

Lane Hooven House

Our Octagon

Dear Ms. Poore:

I just finished reading the article about octagonal houses (June 1986). I thought your readers might enjoy seeing this community's version.

The photograph is of an octagonal house built in 1863, in the architectural style best classified as Victorian Gothic Revival. Very, very few octagonal houses were built in this style.

This house has undergone an eight-year restoration (often with the help of articles in The Old-House Journal). As with most restorations, it will never be complete; however, except for shutters, the exterior is virtually restored, and the interior has six of its nine main rooms restored. This house has an outstanding spiral staircase which ascends to the cupola. The original decoration in nine colors has been restored completely. The staircase alone is a sight to behold.

We were blessed at the outset of the restoration because the house had never been abused. It suffered only minor alterations at the hands of former occupants.

The building is now used as offices for its owner, The Hamilton Community Foundation, and a tenant, The Hamilton-Fairfield Arts Council. Some rooms are decorated as they would have been when the building was a residence, but other rooms, now used as offices, are being furnished as 1860-1890 offices.

Visitors are welcome weekdays (no charge) during normal office hours. An advance call is suggested for groups or if the visitor would like a special tour. The house is in The National Register of Historic Places. Across the street is the public library, also an octagon -- that one in the Romanesque Revival style.

The house is officially known as the Lane Hooven House, 319 N. Third St., Hamilton, OH 45011. The phone number is (513) 863-1389.
-- Thomas B. Rentschler
Hamilton, Ohio

Ivy Inquiry

To the editor:

The "Ivy" story (June 1986) was very enlightening. I'd never heard of this practice before. Was it, I wonder, something that the "taste-makers" of the era advocated, but that wasn't widely put into practice? The whole idea seems wrought with problems -- ivy and other vines are known to trap moisture, do damage to surfaces, and need constant attention. Their use on interiors would seem to invite staining and damage to walls, woodwork, paint, wallpaper, etc. In my opinion, some of the Victorian Tastemakers' ideas were intriguing, but there were good reasons why the ideas didn't take hold.
-- Randy Cotton
Wayne, Penna.

Painting Tips

Dear Editors:

I thoroughly enjoyed your comprehensive special report on painting featured in the May issue. I'd like to offer a couple of painting tips that I learned the hard way.

First, I agree that when doors are painted, all hardware, including hinges, should be removed for stripping, polishing, and lacquering before reinstallation on the freshly-painted door. When you remove hinges, I suggest you label the exact location of each leaf. Even steel hinges develop specific wear patterns over the decades, and failure to accommodate this "wearing-in" may result in squeaky or balky hinges. It's also a good idea to apply a thin coating of grease to the hinge pin before insertion.

Second, regarding masking: Regular masking tape will damage fragile surfaces (wallpaper, for example). For most applications, I prefer to use drafting tape. This low-tack tape is designed to hold down firmly, yet lift off easily. (It's available wherever drafting or blueprinting supplies are sold.) If you desire a razor-sharp paintline, a good choice is the specialized masking tape used by automobile paint shops. It's more resistant to paint solvents than household masking tape, so it's less likely that paint will seep under the edge. (Look for it at well-stocked automotive stores.)
-- Jim Coman
Asheville, N.C.

Some of your most helpful articles have been the ones on How to Cope With it All and Still Stay Sane. I've been at this extremely undercapitalized restoration for three years now, and I've weathered two major burn-out stages. Ms. Poore's excellent piece on walking barefoot (December 1985 OHJ) restored my sense of humor and helped me focus on How It Will Be (a.k.a. Someday...) instead of on Reality.
-- Ellen Kardell
Washington, D.C.

Ringness House, Texas

Olson-Arneson House, Texas

From Norway to Texas

Dear Ms. Poore:
I am writing regarding the Vernacular Houses page in your April 1986 issue (Norwegian stone houses in Texas). Last summer, I took this photo (top) of our "family" house in Skogn, Norway (near Frondheim). My cousin, Erik Ree, and his mother still live in the house. The house is nearly 300 years old, and has been occupied by my ancestors since it was built. It sits on a hill overlooking the Frondheim fjord and the tiny town of Skogn. The two end sections (each with four windows and one door) were added within the last 70 years, although they were designed with respect for the building.

The <u>original</u> slate roof was just replaced last year. Erik replaced the slate with a synthetic material that looks exactly like a clay tile roof. (If you look closely, you can see the curves.) The house was originally stone; the

timber siding was added later to retain heat.
The place is massive. The support beams of the roof are huge. Solid birch exists throughout. The Norwegians really do know how to build houses.
Our family church is one of only 30 remaining stave churches. It was built in 1150, and is still routinely used for services.
-- Clara J. Lyle
Chicago, Ill.

Aspiration Article

Dear OHJ:
I would be very interested in seeing an article comparing various industrial or commercial "dust collection systems" (i.e. vacuum cleaners that can handle restoration dirt). I burned out a shop-vac in about a month. A good product would have to be powerful, portable, and have good filters to keep the toxic dust down.

Won Over

Dear Patricia:
I must say that it took a few issues of your new format to win me over. Like many long-time subscribers, I was at first not 100% for the new look. But after setting aside my dislike for change in general, I must admit -- I LIKE IT! Keep up the great work.
-- Joe Scaduto
Lynnfield, Mass.

Dear OHJ:
I very much like the new format, and agree with G. Kaye Holden of Jersey City (June 1986) that your grouchy, "long-time readers" will look a long time elsewhere, to find another magazine with the helpfulness and quality articles your magazine delivers.
I also agree wholeheartedly with Elizabeth A. Griffith's letter, "In Defense of Yuppies" (same issue). It is the effort and respect of these young people that will restore the grand old neighborhoods, and the surburban areas, to their former glories.
I don't think I am too likely to undertake any old-house restorations, but I still enjoy the magazine very much. Keep up the good work!
-- Elizabeth M. Johnson
Los Angeles, Calif.

Dear Old-House Journal-ites:
I have been converted. When you first changed the format, I was immobilized. Change has never gone well with me. Now, I eagerly await each new edition of OHJ. A convert -- always hard for me to admit. I love this magazine, it's Number One. Bravo to all of you.
-- Happy Price
South Dartmouth, Mass.

Name That House

Q: CAN YOU IDENTIFY the house in this photo? I believe it to be of the "Gothic Revival Dormer" style, but I don't know for sure. The local real estate people call it a "Colonial." Of course, they label any pre-1930 structure as Colonial. The house was built in 1803 and is located on the waterfront in Mattapoisett, Mass. There are other examples of this style in the area, including several on the main street in Plymouth.
— Bob Whittier, Duxbury, Mass.

A: IF YOU'RE CERTAIN about the date of the house (1803), those dormers aren't original. It looks like a full Cape (Cape Cod house), to which gabled dormers were added, most likely during the Gothic Revival period — probably around 1860.

Heat Gun Hypothesis

Q: IF THIS QUESTION is as hopelessly ignorant as I suspect it might be, please don't use my name in print. I'd been stripping interior wood with a heat gun for some time before I read the relevant articles in back issues of OHJ. I notice that you advise against using the heat gun once you get down to the varnish level. Before I read that, I had been cheerfully using the heat gun on varnish with great success. Why do you recommend chemicals at this stage?
— Kay Denmark, New York, N.Y.

A: GOOD QUESTION. We've found that heat makes a gummy mess of varnish and is ineffective in removing it. That's why we recommend chemicals. If you're having success with the heat gun, great! We'll bet you still have to use some chemicals for the final cleanup, though.

Stripping In The Tub

Q: AT SOME TIME IN THE PAST, the bathroom wall tile in my house was painted over. What is the best way to remove the paint without damaging the tiles?
— M.C. Hennessy, Annapolis, Md.

A: YOU SHOULD USE a thick semi-paste paint remover such as BIX Tuff Job or Zip-Strip. Just flow it on and remove the sludge with <u>plastic</u> scrapers -- metal scrapers can scratch the tile. Use a plastic brush to scrub out the grout lines. Clorox will help whiten them. Unfortunately, the grout may never come back to its original color; you can dig it out and regrout. (See "Renewing Old Bathroom Tile," March 1984 OHJ.) Remember to wear a respirator and keep the bathroom well ventilated when you strip.

Substitute Shakes

Q: THE WOOD-SHINGLE ROOF on our dear old 1830 house is in pretty bad shape. While it's been patched and treated several times, replacement is inevitable. Problem is, there's a local ordinance against re-roofing with wood shingles because of the fire hazard. We've seen some fire-resistant substitute shingles that are supposed to look like wood, be we think they're poor imitations. Are there any "artificial" wood shingles that look like the real thing?
— John Sargent, Bronxville, N.Y.

A: NO SUBSTITUTE MATERIALS have been able to perfectly imitate the natural, textural variety of wood. However, fire-retardant wood shingles are available and are permitted by many municipalities (check this out locally). The best looking imitations were asbestos-cement shakes; unfortunately the company that manufactured them ceased production in the 1940s.

Perhaps the best product currently available is Ludowici-Celadon's clay tile shake. Their "Georgian" line has been used to imitate wood shakes in Colonial Williamsburg. From a distance, only the most astute observer will be suspicious. They do have the disadvantage of being heavy (1400 lbs./square) and quite expensive. For more information, write to Ludowici-Celadon, PO Box 69, Dept. OHJ, New Lexington, OH 43764. (614) 342-1995.

Hendricks Tile Manufacturing makes a steel-reinforced concrete "shingle" which is also heavy, but cheaper than the tile. It too is a pretty good facsimile of wood. Hendricks Tile Mfg., PO Box 34406, Dept. OHJ, Richmond, VA 23234. (804) 275-8926.

Your other option is to buy high-quality, composition (asphalt) shingles that don't seek to imitate wood, but are compatible in color and texture. Look to the top-of-the-line shingles -- they're only a little more expensive than average, and they look better and last longer. Additional advantages: They don't add weight, and it's easy to find a roofer to install them. (For additional information, see "Substitute Roofings," April 1983 OHJ).

General interest questions from subscribers will be answered in print. The Editors can't promise to reply to all questions personally—but we try. Send your questions with sketches or photos to Questions Editor, The Old-House Journal, 69A Seventh Avenue, Brooklyn, NY 11217.

1960

Before —

"At the beginning, you want to do it all in one year. Eventually, you learn."

by Eve Kahn

During...

1986

Old~
House
Living in
Upstate
New York

BRUCE AND ANNE CAMPBELL bought an old house in Carmel, New York, three years ago. It was nothing special, they thought. A pond in the backyard and a back stairway; other than that, it was just another house in need of lots of work. But the place started growing on them. Bruce found The Old-House Journal. Anne started getting crazy ideas, like should they tear off the aluminum siding? Bruce was inspired by old photos the sellers gave him, showing the house in pre-siding days. Tearing off siding was only the first step. Before they knew it, Bruce and Anne were in the midst of a full-scale restoration.

THIS IS NOT a "before-and-after" story. It's more like "before-and-during." If you have an old house "in process," you'll sympathize. Or if your project's nearing the end, you can reminisce about the days of grit and grunge.

WE -- MY MOTHER and I -- met Anne Campbell on a sunny Saturday afternoon at a Greek Revival mansion in Brewster, New York. She wanted us to see this grand house, once the home of town father Walter Brewster, because it is the town's most successful and challenging resto-ration project. The woman restoring the place, her hands covered in plaster, stopped working to show us around. The house had mar-ble fireplaces, a sweeping staircase, and many

sunny rooms, some with faux marbre and some already furnished in the high fashion of 1840. Anne kept protesting, modestly, "After this, our place is going to look like nothing."

WE FOLLOWED ANNE to the farmhouse where she and Bruce live with two cats and a dog. Her solid Volvo, and our rickety Cutlass, traveled down country roads, past the nearest signs of civilization (a bar and a Baptist church) to where the paved road turned to dirt. As we rounded a corner, a well-kept farmhouse, gleaming with new paint, the lawn recently mowed, came into view. My mother asked excitedly, "Is _that_ it? What a pretty house!" But Anne kept going, to a house a little less kempt, but to my eyes much more interesting.

THE DOG BOUNDED up to greet us, accompanied by Bruce. As our tour began, Bruce and Anne both talked about the house, often at the same time. They wanted to show us every inch of woodwork that they'd slaved over.

WE SLOWLY CIRCLED the house as they told its story. Though the sellers had said it was 100 years old, it actually began life as a farm-house around 1840. During the 1940s it lay abandoned for a few years, and then a family purchased it as a vacation house; Bruce and Anne bought it from them. No major remuddling: The family hadn't been around much; they'd even left the outhouse. But they had done some damage. The most visible and destructive change was the pale-green aluminum siding: "like putting a house in a tin can."

THE FRONT OF the house showed no trace of siding. Bruce and Anne had decided to finish one part of the house, to boost morale. Every last siding nail had been pulled out and the holes filled. Real wooden storms hung over the first-floor windows. Up above, re-created trim surrounded the blind eyebrow windows.

THE SIDE WALL was not yet as perfect as the front. There were still nails, siding remnants, and aluminum storms attached by rusting staples. The Campbells showed us their scars: The siding contractors had hacked off every bit of trim -- crown moulding, window frames, even drip edges. Bruce picked up the crown moulding he'd had custom milled for the porch, saying bitterly, "$110 worth of wood."

WE WANDERED TOWARDS the rear of the house, where there was an intriguing one-room addition. Its windows were smaller and lower than those on the house; its clapboards, narrower and flatter. It looked like an 18th-century building, hauled to the property perhaps in the late 1800s. Anne said that a friend who's active in preservation thinks so too. Inside, she explained, a tiny staircase leads to an attic crawlspace; was this once a small house?

STANDING NEAR the vegetable garden in the rear, we turned to face the house. From the

Shorn siding lay in heaps around the house.

"You do one thing, but you're never 'finished' because that one thing shows up the parts nearby that aren't done. It keeps you motivated."

Bruce's favorite part of the front porch is the band of red trim just under the roof.

Trim has since been restored to the blind eyebrow windows.

"The house keeps saying,
'Leave me alone, leave me alone,
live with me,' so we're starting
to say, 'OK, OK!'"

front it had looked like a standard farmhouse -- "the ranch house of the 1840s," said Anne. We'd seen several like it on the drive up. But from the rear it was a curious mixture of a 1920s garage, a 1950s shed, an 18th-century wing, all at various heights and angles.

WE ROUNDED the rear of the house. A pile of mangled siding lay next to it; Anne told horror stories of how many trips to the dump it took to remove the stuff; how they had to rent dumpsters when the dump closed. With weary familiarity she picked up a chunk of quarter-inch-thick foamboard -- "I've picked hundreds of these off my lawn," she explained. "These too," she added, stooping to snatch up a scrap of aluminum foil that blew past. (Foamboard and aluminum had lined the siding.) We examined the rear wall, studded with nails. "I've pulled hundreds of these out of my walls," said Bruce; his estimate seemed modest.

WE ENTERED the house by the front door. Sunlight streamed in. The living room was comfortable, though it still needed work. Anne showed us the "painting skills" of the previous owners: a two-foot-square spill of white on the oak floor. Still, she said, the floor "will finish nicely, someday."

THE DINING ROOM was even sunnier, with a bay window and yellow walls -- texture-finished, Anne said, but the texture washes off. We peered into Bruce's office, lined with shelves and file cabinets. Moulding and hardware catalogs were tacked up for easy reference.

The cat poses before the mantelpiece and texture-finished wall in the
dining room. At left is the Campbells' Art Nouveau glass-front cabinet.

THE REFRIGERATOR was vintage 1955, "and it'll go for 30 more years," said Bruce. Beyond the kitchen, a door led to the only completed part of the interior. Aided by a clever carpenter, the Campbells had gutted the 18th-century room (nothing salvageable was left) and turned it into an oversize bath/ laundry room, the only bath in the house. The walls and floor were polished wood; tub and toilet were separated by wood partitions. Only the old beaded ceiling still needed stripping. Anne showed us the tiny rear stairway, leading to the unused crawlspace; the door to it latched with a dusty Eastlake-style lock that didn't quite catch anymore, since the house had settled.

WHILE ANNE MADE tea, we looked through her scrapbook. First came the scraps of wallpaper she had carefully removed from the rear wall of the 18th-century wing. (She found layer after layer, and preserved them in the order in which she found them.) Then there was a note from an expert at Colonial Williamsburg, saying that the papers could indeed be from the 18th century. There were notes from friendly carpenters, copies of the old photos given by the previous family to Bruce and Anne, and then Anne's own photos: her family, her parents' Greek Revival in Maine, Bruce at work on the house; and the enormous wasp nest which turned up under the dropped porch ceiling that Bruce was so glad to rip down.

I ASKED the Campbells about their decorating plans. Anne said, "I'd love to do the dining room in a high style, like Art Nouveau" (to match the room's wood-inlaid cabinet) "but I don't think my taste is sophisticated enough." Bruce said he'd never noticed old houses before they started on this one, and now he

could see fixing up more than one ... they exchanged glances, and Anne looked dubious. "But we've got ten years of interior work here first," he added, to Anne's apparent relief.

THEY TOLD ABOUT the disastrous plumbing that had to be taken out and replaced from scratch -- and all before the first frost, though Bruce had a broken arm. They reminisced about the days before the siding came off, how it clanged like a subway train when it heated up, how people thought they were crazy to take it off -- and how aluminum-siding and storm-window salesmen still call (and Bruce hangs up).

WE SIPPED our tea in silence for a moment. My mother said, "You know, it's a happy house." Anne smiled. "That's what my mom said too, when we bought the place."

WE TOOK the back stairs up from the kitchen. A few odd shutters and a door leaned against a wall in the hallway. There were four bedrooms, plus a big closet that Anne said could be a second bath someday, if they ever figure out a way to get plumbing up there without destroying too much. She showed us the original hooks in a bedroom closet. I marvelled at the eye for detail that old-house people develop.

SHE TOOK ME to the attic last. The brick chimney was parged with cement and stained brown by leaking water. The Campbells can't find a mason who will work on it. Sunlight shone in the gap between chimney and roof. Anne put her hand on the stack, related the hellish logistics of relining or replacing it, and shook her head. "The house keeps saying, 'Leave me alone, leave me alone, live with me,' so we're starting to say, 'OK, OK!'" 🏠

WOOD WOES

Questions similar to the two below — both regarding wood technology — come from readers surprisingly often. The first relates to finishing problems with Southern Yellow Pine. The second question is from a reader who's had disappointing results using treated lumber. For the benefit of all, here's what we came up with.

by Larry Jones

Yellow Pine and the Red Caboose

OLD HOUSES and old train cars have a lot in common when it comes to restoration, as reader Don Plotkin of Champaign, Illinois, can attest. He purchased a thirty-foot, twenty-ton "fixer-upper" in the form of a 1929 B&O caboose, thinking it just needed a little paint. (Does this story sound familiar?)

MUCH TO his chagrin, Don found that everywhere the vertical V-groove, Yellow Pine siding hadn't been painted, the wood was rotten (for example, under the trim and in the tongue-and-groove joints). It's just that sort of deterioration on old houses that prompts us to advise treating and back-priming replacement lumber that will be exposed to harsh weather.

FACED WITH REPLACING virtually every piece of siding with new Yellow Pine, Don decided to dip-treat the new pieces for 24 hours in Woodlife II, a paintable preservative.

DON BRUSH-PRIMED the backs and then edges of the siding before installation. Unlike houses, where the siding is generally nailed on, the stresses and strains of caboose life require that the siding be installed with countersunk and plugged woodscrews -- about 750 of them per side. (Screw gun, anyone?)

TO FINISH the job, Don applied a high-quality, oil-base primer and high-gloss enamel that almost exactly matched the original caboose red. Well, things went well and then things went bad. About six months after it was painted, all of the paint began to come off right down to bare wood, not in little flakes but in giant pieces all over the car. The surface had been well sanded. The preservative was paintable, and was allowed plenty of time to dry. The preservative, primer, and top coats were compatible. So what was the problem? As Don discovered, the problem was Southern Yellow Pine. It doesn't hold paint well -- especially oil-based paint.

DON'S PROBLEM intrigued us, so we did some detective work. Our archives turned up a similar problem -- oddly enough, also from a reader in Illinois -- who had written to Building Age magazine way back in 1915. Their reader couldn't keep the Yellow Pine trim on his house painted. Here was their answer: "Yellow Pine is very sappy or resinous and whenever direct sun strikes the exposed painted surface it draws sap, which is bound to throw off paint. When pitch or sap is not plentiful and the wood well seasoned, coating it with shellac varnish before painting will usually hold back the sap."

THEY ALSO OFFERED a solution that's no longer legal today: using a mixture of equal parts (by weight) of white lead in oil (keg lead) and dry red lead, mixed with two parts (by measure) of pure raw linseed oil and one part turpentine. The mix was strained through a sieve and applied as a primer with the consistency of thin paint. If you didn't like the pink color, then you could add a little lampblack and follow with a thicker top coat of white lead and oil. Such paint finishes remain fairly soft and pliable for a long period, not unlike our latex paints today. But, as the lumber Don used was kiln dried, we really didn't suspect that sap was the culprit. So we looked further.

NEXT WE consulted an excellent little trade booklet about exterior wood finishes. It states, "The ability of lumber to retain and hold a finish is affected by species, by grain direction or how the piece was sawn, and by smoothness. The weight of wood varies tremendously among species. Some common construction woods such as Yellow Pine are dense and heavy with respect to lighter woods such as redwood and cedar. The weight of wood is important because heavy woods shrink and swell more than light ones. This dimensional change occurs as the wood gains and loses moisture. Excessive dimensional changes in wood consistently stresses a paint film and may result in early failure."

YELLOW PINE and some boards of Douglas Fir have dense, dark, wide bands called summerwood or latewood, to which paint will not stick well. These bands alternate between those of softer springwood or early wood, to which paint does stick well. That's why woods without wide summerwood bands (such as redwood and cedar) tend to hold paint better.

IT WAS BEGINNING to sound like there's no way to keep paint on Yellow Pine. Yet they managed to keep it on all those cabooses for all those years. To get to the bottom of this, we contacted Dr. William Feist, researcher at Forest Products Laboratory. Dr. Feist's advice: Don should strip the existing paint, treat the wood with a paintable water repellent or water-repellent preservative; then apply one coat of latex primer followed by two top coats of latex (all of the same system or brand). And the paint should be brushed, rather than sprayed.

PLYWOOD SOMETIMES has paint-adherence problems, too. Often, the problem is compounded because the wood also exhibits face-checking. So while we were at it, we contacted Harry Jorgensen of the American Plywood Association. Mr. Jorgensen and Richard A. Miller had carried out a 66-month test to determine the outdoor performance of various paint systems on both sanded and rough-sawn softwood plywood. Paint films were evaluated for check and crack resistance, flaking, and extractive staining. Their test results, published in 1983, showed that an all-acrylic-latex, stain-blocking primer with an all-acrylic-latex top-coat system gave the best performance, was the most flexible, and had the best crack resistance. (Incidentally, the poorest performers were vinyl-acetate latex primers and paints.)

FINALLY, we checked in with the technical staff at Sherwin-Williams. For Yellow Pine lumber (which normally doesn't face-check like plywood), they recommend using an alkyd exterior primer/undercoater, followed by two compatible acrylic-latex top coats. But for Yellow Pine plywood, they suggest using their Check-Guard latex primer, followed by two latex top coats.

BACK TO our friend Don. He wants the same high-gloss paint sheen that originally graced his caboose. Acrylic-latex paints are fairly glossy but they haven't yet matched the high gloss of enamels. Unfortunately, the high-gloss, oil-based enamels that Don would like to use were found (in U.S. Plywood tests) to become increasingly brittle and crack-prone with age. Perhaps it's better to sacrifice a little gloss for a lot less repainting. A latex-paint conditioner called Flotrol, made by Flood Chemical and widely available, makes the latex flow on smoother.

AN EPILOGUE: Besides finding Yellow Pine hard to keep painted, Don also discovered the wood is highly prone to warping and checking before installation. And he found it splits very easily if you nail too near the edges (use the old carpenter's trick of blunting the nail point before pounding it in). Finally, he found the wood was very difficult to sand without creating ridges, again due to the summerwood. All in all, Don notes, "If I had to start restoring the car all over again (and I hope that never happens), I think I'd leave the Yellow Pine at the lumberyard."

Bad Luck with Treated Wood

"**I** HAVE A PROBLEM using pressure-treated wood," begins an all-too-typical letter. "I bought Wolmanized 1x4-inch, tongue-and-groove lumber, and built two exterior cellar doors with it. After I assembled the doors, I allowed them to stay clamped and weighted down for seven days; they were flat and true at the time of installation.

"THE DAY after I installed the doors, they had warped so badly that they couldn't be opened. First they expanded, then a few days later the

boards started to cup, causing the width to shrink by 1/2 inch. Also the boards split lengthwise. I cross-braced the door with oak, glued and bolted in place, and attached angle-iron horizontal braces top and bottom. And within three days in the sun, the boards had warped to the point where all the glued tongues had split. I rebuilt the doors and the same thing happened! I've since built entirely new ones out of tongue-and-groove cedar and have had no problems.

"WHEN I went back to the lumberyard, they said, 'What do you expect when you bought treated white pine?' At the time of purchase, I wasn't told that I was purchasing white pine and I assumed that I was buying a good grade of wood. It certainly wasn't cheap. It turns out the wood was guaranteed against rot only, not against warpage. I plan to replace our tongue-and-groove porch floor next year and now I don't know what kind of lumber to use! Besides white pine, the only other treated lumber around this area is a poor grade of fir flooring that's not at all like the good Douglas Fir flooring I've seen. Please advise."

Misconceptions

MANY HOMEOWNERS buying pressure-treated lumber assume they're getting lumber that is rot resistant, mildewproof, water repellent, and paintable. There's also an assumption that wood which doesn't rot ALSO won't suffer the usual weathering problems of untreated wood -- shrinking, swelling, cupping, bowing, warping, or splitting -- even if it's left unpainted. This is not the case. Treated wood offers some protection against decay, but it is still wood and it behaves like wood.

TREATED WOOD is sometimes seen as the culprit in a failed project, when really the problem is poor detailing or some peculiarity in individual pieces of wood.

MOST FACTORY-PRESSURE-TREATED LUMBER available at the lumberyard is treated with CCA (Chromated Copper Arsenate). The lumber has a greenish color, is odor-free, and has a clean surface. The best known across the country is Wolmanized brand. Wolman preservative is a product of the Koppers Company, and Wolmanized wood is pressure-treated by licensed treaters.

FOR GUIDELINES, we contacted three good sources: the Koppers Company; Cox Wood Products, a licensed producer of Wolmanized lumber; and Dr. William Feist, Research Chemist at the U.S.D.A.'s Forest Products Laboratory. Compiled here are their comments and suggestions, plus a few of our own.

Thirteen tips for better luck

1 READ THE FINE PRINT. Most treated lumber is meant for weather-exposed applications where termite and fungal decay damage are likely. Some treated lumber can also be used indoors for beams, trusses, framing, flooring, and sills. (Check the specific manufacturer's product literature.) For residential use, Wolmanized lumber carries a 30-year warranty against termite and decay damage, but it does not cover warping, checking, or splitting.

2 BUY A BRAND-NAME PRODUCT from a well known, reputable dealer. He's the first guy you contact if you have trouble. You don't want to have to deal with the joker who tells you you should've known better. The brand should be stamped on the wood.

3 BE AWARE OF WOOD SPECIES. The type of wood that is treated or Wolmanized varies by region. The more common types are Southern Yellow Pine, Red Pine, Douglas Fir, Hemlock, Spruce, and White Pine. Before you buy, find out what types of treated wood are available in your area. Dr. Feist says to avoid buying lumber with uncommon names ("White Mountain Pine"). Woods like Yellow Pine are notorious for being dimensionally unstable and holding paint poorly, so save them for rough carpentry. Porch floors are best laid from good, hard, vertical-grain Douglas Fir, not soft pine. Don't settle for inappropriate lumber simply because it's available treated.

4 BUY DRY LUMBER. Moisture in pressure-treated lumber seems to be the main cause of trouble for our readers. Before it is pressure-treated, wood arrives at the treater kiln dried. After treatment, the wood is moist inside. Then it may be thoroughly kiln dried again, or it may be not-so-thoroughly kiln dried, or it may be thoroughly and properly air-dried, or it may be not-so-thoroughly or properly air dried. We favor buying kiln-dried, treated lumber. (Like buying prewashed and preshrunk jeans, you'll have some idea from the start of what you're getting.) Kiln-dried treated lumber is not available in all areas, and you can expect it to cost more. We think it's worth it for finish carpentry where a lot of movement would cause expensive problems.

Wolmanized wood that has been dried after treatment has that information stamped on it. The orange-labelled #1 grade is the best and most dimensionally stable.

Short of taking a moisture meter with you to the lumberyard, there's no way of telling how moist the treated lumber is, even if the wood has been kiln dried. Bundles of moist wood can come from the treating plant to the lumberyard and stay that way until you get it home and build something. Then the wood starts to dry and trouble begins. So if you have the dry space and the time, let the treated lumber sit for a few weeks (properly stacked for air drying, of course). It's good insurance.

5 PICK YOUR PIECES CAREFULLY when you buy treated lumber -- even at the risk of aggravating the lumberyard operator. The dimensional stability of wood depends on its species, grain pattern, and natural defects such as knots. Pick treated wood that is visibly clean and has no surface residue.

6 FINISH THE WOOD. Don't expect pressure-treated lumber to look very good if you leave it exposed to the weather with no protection (such as water repellent, water-repellent stain, or paint). Raw wood can be expected to soak up and give off moisture readily, causing excessive dimensional movement, which leads to cups, warps, shrinkage, and splits.

7 DECIDE WHAT FINISH you'll want before you buy. Consult the specifications of the lumber, and use only the types and brands of finishing products that they say are compatible.

Koppers advises using their RainCoat-brand water repellent to retard the movement of moisture into and out of the wood and to reduce dimensional change. If you intend to paint, we favor applying a paintable repellent before you prime. For wood exposed to harsh weathering, dip-soaking in water repellent is recommended. To stain, Koppers suggests alkyd-based solid or semi-transparent colors (ideally their own brand). They claim these have quicker drying times and better color retention than linseed-oil-based stains.

8 USE GOOD CONSTRUCTION DETAILING and methods, just as with untreated wood construction. Avoid open joints, seams, and exposed end-grain that allow moisture into the wood. (That will wreck a painted finish.) Designs that allow water to puddle on the surface are destined for trouble. Whenever possible, lay boards face up (bark side up -- the outside curve of the growth ring is the bark side).

9 AVOID LONG SPANS. The greater the distance between anchor or fastening points, the more force the wood develops as it's drying, and the more movement there will be. Avoid cantilevered beams and boards that aren't secured on one end.

10 DON'T USE LUMBER WIDER THAN 6 INCHES to form a flat outdoor surface. (Two 2x6s are better than one 2x12.) Moisture on wide boards makes them cup.

11 USE PROPER ANCHORS. With treated wood, use only hot-dipped, zinc-coated nails. Harsh environments (and perhaps even the preservative itself) can cause other ferrous fasteners to rust.

12 USE ENOUGH ANCHORS. For 2x4s, use two nails across; for 2x6s, use three nails across. For the greatest holding power, use ring-shank or spiral-shank nails or galvanized power-driven screws such as those made by Weather Challenger. Pre-drilling nail holes at the ends of boards helps reduce splitting.

13 USE IT SAFELY -- and only where necessary. Wolmanized woods are treated with an EPA-registered pesticide containing inorganic arsenic. Always wear gloves to avoid splinters. Wear a dust mask when cutting it. Don't use treated woods for countertops and cutting boards. Don't use scraps as firewood -- and don't dispose of the wood where someone else may pick it up for firewood.

F OR A LIST of government publications on various preservative treatments for wood, write to Forest Products Laboratory, Dept. OHJ, Publications Info., 1 Gifford Pinchot Drive, Madison, WI 53705. (608) 264-5657. Enclose a self-addressed, stamped envelope.
If you need more information on handling Wolmanized Pressure-Treated Wood, write to Koppers Co., Dept. OHJ, Pittsburgh, PA 15219.

THE GREAT AMERICAN GARAGE

PART ONE

by J. Randall Cotton

"**D**URING THE PAST ten years a new type of outbuilding has come into being," says an architect in 1912. "It is to be seen today about the grounds of most suburban and country homes, sometimes ornamental and more often not." What he is describing probably ranks as one of the most ubiquitous yet taken-for-granted of all building types: the garage.

THE GARAGE CAN range from a sophisticated architect-designed example (grand enough to be a house for most of us) on a large estate to the humbly functional little sheds that seem squeezed into every last bit of space along our urban alleyways.

IF YOU OWN an old house with an early garage, perhaps this article will give you a new appreciation for its history. Next month, we'll give guidelines for building or adapting a new garage to be appropriate for your old house.

The Auto House

FROM THE START, America has had a love affair with the automobile, and no single invention has changed the way we live and how our environment looks more than the "horseless carriage." Though in the 1890s the auto was a fad for the very rich, it soon became a "necessity" for moneyed businessmen and professionals, and eventually for the broad-based middle class as well. As more and more carriage manufacturers converted to automaking, the price of autos came down and by 1909 one manufacturer, Charles Duryea, said, "The novelty of owning an automobile has largely worn off. The neighbors have one. The whole family has become so accustomed to auto riding that some members generally prefer to remain behind while others go."

THE WIDESPREAD ACCEPTANCE of the automobile presented a host of problems, however, including the need for better roads, service and fuel stations and, not least, a place to store the contraption. Many an owner added insult to injury by putting his auto next to the soon-to-be-phased-out horse in an existing carriage house. In fact, the private garage is in many ways a result of a gradual evolution from the horse barn or another outbuilding. Even today we find many 19th-century carriage houses which were converted to garages many years ago. The carriage house itself was really a glorified barn which saw its heyday in the Victorian era. It was common practice at the time to mimic the architecture of the main house. Brackets, spindlework,

decorative wood shingles, fancy cupolas, and
multi-colored slate mansard roofs were common
appurtenances on Victorian carriage houses.

ALTHOUGH ADAPTING CARRIAGE houses for auto
storage remained popular in non-urban areas,
it was a different story in the city. Contrary to popular belief, earlier city dwellers
did not all own horses, but rather relied on
public transportation or walking to get
around. Because of the crowded city environment, along with the smell and filth associated with horses, urbanites who did own a
horse usually put it up at a livery stable.
Hence there was initially a lack of existing
space that could be converted to store the
new-fangled automobile.

THE FIRST SOLUTION for urban auto storage was
publicly and privately owned large-scale
garages, a natural outgrowth of the livery
stable. For $15 to $20 a month, an owner
could store his auto along with up to 100
others in a large, heated space where maintenance and cleaning services were provided.
But by 1910, automobile ownership was so widespread that a new building type had to be invented. Initially called auto houses or motor
houses, the first garages did not have the
objectionable characteristics of horse barn --
namely odor, waste, and germs. Hence the garage's "proximity to the house is an advantage
rather than a drawback," said one observer.

Variations on this simple, hipped-roof garage can be found in alleys
and backyards across America.

The Early Garage Is Refined

AS WITH ALL new building types (such as the
skyscraper or railroad depot), there was a
period of experimentation with the garage.
(The word, by the way, comes from the French
garer: to protect; now: to park.) How exactly
should it look? How should it function? What
are the best materials and construction method
to use? People disagreed. Some thought "a
garage is strictly for business. The utilitarian side must dominate." Others decried
what they saw as hideous little sheds "of a
mechanical nature" which are "apt to be ugly"
and called instead for "decorative utility."
Those who took the latter view suggested
garages follow the architecture of the house
much as Victorian carriage houses had.

A rather elegant garage from 1909 probably served affluent suburban-
ites; at right is the door to the chauffeur's quarters.

These are early commercial garages; their facades are updated versions of the typical urban livery.

Simply by repeating bays, the garage could be for one car or two.

ONE OF THE FIRST solutions was the so-called "portable" garage, available as early as 1908. These were really small, partially prefabricated structures consisting of wood or metal panels. They were manufactured by such companies as Hodgson Portable Homes, were available for $140, and could be put up in one or two days. They were relatively inexpensive, but they were flimsy and so a less than ideal solution; still, they remained popular throughout the first part of this century.

MORE SUBSTANTIAL prefabricated garages were also introduced. Most of the companies that produced "ready-built" homes also carried prefab garages. Sears, Roebuck was among the most successful in this endeavor and sold mail-order garage "kits" during the teens, '20s, and '30s.

LIKE PATTERN-BOOK HOUSES, pattern-book garages also proved popular. For example, the Home Builders Catalog Company of Chicago illustrated dozens of garages in their catalogs; complete blueprints could be purchased for $5. The Southern Cypress Manufacturers' Association offered a "pergola-garage" working drawing which, of course, espoused decay-resistant cypress as the best garage-building material. The true impact of pattern books is hard to estimate, but chances are that if you own a 1910-1930s garage, it owes its design to a published plan that the contractor followed.

SUBURBAN GARAGES WERE usually functional in appearance. The basic plan was rectangular (approximately 12 by 18 feet), large enough to accommodate one auto and not much else. Multi-car garages were built simply by repeat-

Wall construction is stucco on terra-cotta block; the pergola effect and trellises are wood. (1914)

A·M·GITHENS

ing this basic plan, with two or more bays side by side. The major distinguishing feature of these plain structures was their roof. While gabled roofs were the most common, flat, shed, gambrel, and hipped were popular, too.

BECAUSE OF THE FEAR of auto-related fires, garage-builders paid great deal of attention to "fireproof" construction. Vitrified brick, cast concrete, and hollow tile were considered

Pebble-dash

safe. When a frame garage was built, or an old carriage house converted, the framework was often covered with plaster, tin, or better yet, glazed tile (to retard fire). Frame garages had clapboard siding, of course, but stucco surfaces were also used, particularly with a coarse aggregate (sometimes called "pebble-dash"). Thin metal panels were sometimes used as siding; these had decorative pressed designs much like the metal ceilings of the day. Roofing materials were any of the standard fare including slate, metal, terra-cotta tiles, or shingles of asphalt, wood, or asbestos. Floors were sometimes simply gravel or cinder, but most consisted of poured concrete. Often the floor slanted down slightly toward the front, so that if all else failed, a little push could serve to start the car.

Windows and Doors

FROM THE BEGINNING, garages had windows to provide ventilation as well as light. These were mostly stock sash units similar to those used in houses. One window along each side was the usual arrangement, and garage doors almost invariably had several glazed panels.

NOT SURPRISINGLY, the first garage doors were identical to barn doors. Big double-leaf doors which swung out on heavy strap hinges were the most common. These had the disadvantage, though, of being both heavy and temporarily disabled by uncleared snow. Barn-like sliding doors were better, but not all garages were wide enough to allow the doors to be pushed to the sides on tracks.

SOON MANY NEW door types were developed just for garages. New sliding doors, divided into vertical sections, could slide around the inside of the garage. Bifold (or "accordion") doors were also popular, often used in combination with swinging doors. The sectionalized roll-up door, the most popular today, appeared soon after the turn of the century despite an early claim that "such doors as those that roll up after the fashion of the old-time roll-top desk have proved effective, but are not in widespread use, and probably never will be." So much for predictions.

ROLL-UP AND SWING-UP garage doors were spring-loaded for easy operation and early ads often showed a small boy lifting them. A smaller "wicket door" was sometimes incorporated into the main door so that one could enter the

The multiform garage could follow any house style. From top to bottom: Dutch Colonial Revival, Tudor Revival, Mediterranean Revival, or generic gable.

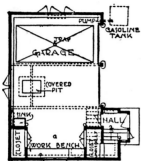

Built for a "suburban mansion," this circa 1912 garage offered a covered pit/work area, gas pump and tank, sink, work bench, and two closets.

garage without opening the entire door. Some garages provided doors at each end so that the car could enter one way and exit the other.

Amenities

BEFORE GAS STATIONS and repair shops were widely accessible, auto owners did much of their own servicing. Thus early garages were often better equipped than their modern-day counterparts. It was not unusual to find them outfitted with hoists, workbenches, repair pits, storage cabinets, electric lights, and washbasins. Many were heated by their own

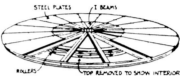

furnaces. Some even had a turntable built into the floor so that the car could be turned around. The turntable eliminated the need for backing out, which brought the risk, according to one contemporary, "of bowling someone over." Individual pumps and underground gas tanks, built in or near the garage, were also used in pre-gas-station days.

SOME CONVENIENCES we assume are modern were available early on. An overhead hose on a revolving arm was used for washing cars, like today's do-it-yourself car washes. Even the "modern" electric garage door opener was available in the 1920s. These devices were usually key-activated by a pole-mounted switch next to the driveway. A remote-control radio-signal unit, activated by a knob on the dashboard, was also introduced in the '20s.

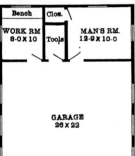

The 1909 garage above provides a generous 12'9" x 10' space in the rear for the chauffeur (see plan at left). There's also a closet, work room, and tool room.

The Heyday of the Garage

BY THE 1920S, automobiles were commonplace. In the cities, alleys originally intended as secondary roads for horse-drawn service vehicles and garbage removal were now lined with small garages. These were usually set on the rear corner of the narrow lots. Sometimes a

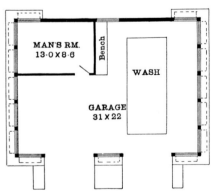

The Prairie-style garage at left appeared in a Radford plan book dated 1909. In its plan (above), the area marked 'Wash' probably denotes the reach of a car-wash hose.

wide multi-bay alleyway garage served several owners. In the post-Victorian suburbs -- whose development the automobile greatly encouraged -- individual freestanding garages with driveways to the street were the norm.

WHILE FANCY GARAGES had been built all along -- for the wealthy -- it was not until the 1920s and '30s that every automobile owner could choose from a variety of garage styles which matched his house. These decades can be considered the heyday of the freestanding American garage.

THE MEDITERRANEAN, French, Colonial Revival, and various English revival styles were all manifested in garage designs. The Craftsman school of architecture was especially adaptable to garages, as it extolled the virtues of wood shingles, openly expressed framework, wall lattice for vines, and attached pergolas. More than a few garages resembled Japanese buildings with wide kick eaves and upturned roof rafters. Spanish-influenced garages had tile roofs, smooth wall surfaces, and sometimes a Mission facade complete with a curvilinear parapet and an arched side portal leading to the garden.

THE GARAGE'S ROOF shape, siding, color, cornice detail, and material were often identical to those on the house. And the garage grew in size, too, to accommodate the larger automobiles. Many had finished attics or back rooms used as small chauffeur apartments for, as one observer put it, "chauffeurs, as we all know, rank infinitely higher

The two above, as well as the two in the upper right, are all suitable for Craftsman influenced houses or bungalows, with their natural materials and simple shape (all circa 1912).

With their horizontal lines and extended eaves, these garages have a definite Japanesque air.

This Georgian Revival house from the late '20s has a typical formal symmetry, the garage wing matched by the porch wing.

Pergolas, breezeways, and loggias increasingly linked the garage to the house, until it was absorbed into the main building.

The far wing of this provincial-style house, circa 1925, probably contained a garage. The architect was attempting to imitate gathered, walled-in outbuildings.

than grooms in the social classification of the household, and they may naturally expect quarters." (Such were the 1920s.)

The Garage Comes Home

AS THE AUTOMOBILE insinuated itself ever more strongly into our lives, it was inevitable that the car would come home to "live" with us, as it were. More and more, the once free-standing garage was connected to the house, eventually becoming an integral part. Beginning in the 1920s, garages were less frequently placed on the back of the lot. As they were drawn alongside the house, loose connections were made via covered walkways, pergolas, and breezeways. House and garage might be joined by a low wall which formed part of a courtyard. Here the garage played the part of the barn in the 1920s revival of picturesque English and French architecture, hearkening back to medieval walled compounds.

GARAGES BECAME DIRECTLY connected to houses when the initial fear of the incendiary nature of early autos was overcome. Still, for some time, fire walls were required between house and garage or else insurance companies would place higher rates on the whole house.

FOR COLONIAL REVIVAL houses, architects often emulated the rambling connected buildings of vernacular 19th-century New England farmsteads, and made the garage part of this complex. In a more formal arrangement, garages

This house, a circa 1930 forerunner of the raised ranch, boldly reveals its integral garage as part of the first floor.

became a side wing to Georgian Revival houses, balanced by porch wings on the other side.

FINALLY, THERE WAS complete integration of house and garage. For example, basement-level garages were built under the main living quarters -- this kind of garage was made accessible by a down-sloping driveway. In urban areas, the semi-raised basements of rowhouses were sometimes converted to garages. Particularly appealing was a two-storey wing with garage below and bedrooms or sleeping porch above; Tudor Revival houses, with their picturesque irregular massing, often had this arrangement. In all these early-20th-century examples, the visual impact of the garage was minimized. It was not until the birth of the split-level ranch after World War II that the broad, blank-faced garage door was openly and unabashedly displayed. It was no longer declasse to have the car live with us.

THERE YOU HAVE IT: From converted carriage houses to the stylized yet functional structures of the 1920s to the modern garage/house combination, the American garage has become an everyday part of our lives.

Randy Cotton is a contributing editor of OHJ. Next month we'll feature his article on designing a garage that's compatible with an old house: how to match garage with house; what roof configurations, details, doors, and windows are appropriate.

The irregular rooflines of Tudor Revival homes lent themselves to integral garages, as on this 1926 house.

This circa 1921 house contains a very early example of an integral garage; the plan book in which it appears calls the building "an interesting suburban home with a garage in the basement."

POST-VICTORIAN HOUSES

TILE FLOOR DESIGNS

Tile floors were popular features of houses built in the 1920s. William Radford's *Architectural Details* (1921) is a good guide to what was common then. His designs are based on three shapes: the full-size square, the ¼-square, and the rectangle made from two ¼-squares. Radford warned against using squares smaller than ¼ of the large square because "the pattern runs off at the side" and so lacks "repose."

When a four-unit square is made with joints in scale, the overall scale can be increased by separating the units with wider joints.

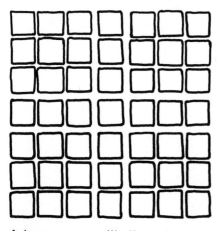

A larger room will allow nine-unit squares separated by bands of single squares; wider joints isolate the crossing bands.

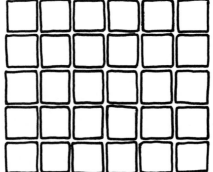

The simplest floor, with large square tiles, "is interesting if the joints are in scale."

 by

John Crosby Freeman

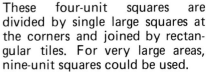

The overall scale can also be increased, and the design enlivened, by separating four-unit squares with ¼-squares. All joints are in scale.

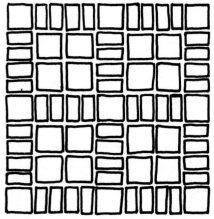

These four-unit squares are divided by single large squares at the corners and joined by rectangular tiles. For very large areas, nine-unit squares could be used.

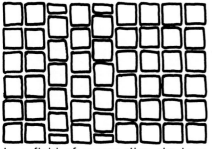

In a field of square tiles, the long lines for the border are provided by three rows with broken joints, which otherwise should be avoided in any field.

This classic herringbone is made solely of rectangular tiles. Notice the wide border also made of rectangular tiles.

A "windmill" effect is created by large squares arranged diagonally, with the resulting spaces filled with ¼-squares. At the perimeter or borderline, the field is finished with rectangular tiles.

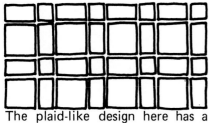

The plaid-like design here has a tighter "weave" than the pattern at right.

The next three illustrations demonstrate methods of creating borders:

A simple border for a diagonal pattern of squares laid parallel to the perimeter.

The last group of illustrations shows more decorative fields, beginning with three different varieties of "herringbone."

This design uses the same units in a more subtle herringbone design, in which straight diagonals subdue the zig-zag.

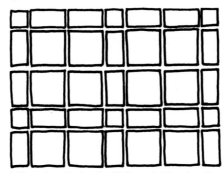

Like the "windmill" and "basket" above, this and the pattern below left evoke something other than tile: plaid cloth.

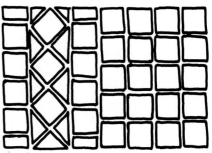

A decorative border can be enlarged by breaking the joints on either of its sides. This example features squares laid diagonally with triangles broken out of the squares.

This herringbone has a more complex pattern, using a combination of ¼-squares and rectangles.

A "basket pattern" results when rectangular tiles are laid as squares. Note how the joints have as much impact as the tiles.

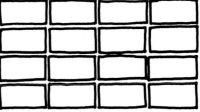

This straight marching band of rectangular tiles is recommended for corridors.

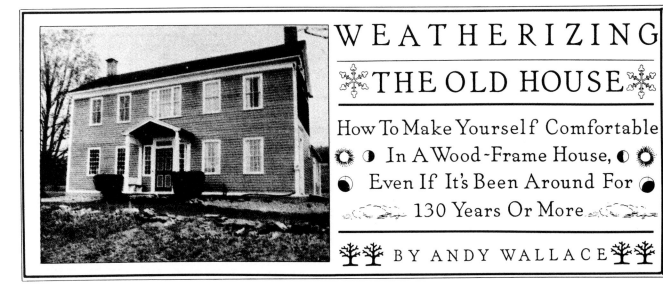

WEATHERIZING THE OLD HOUSE

How To Make Yourself Comfortable In A Wood-Frame House, Even If It's Been Around For 130 Years Or More

BY ANDY WALLACE

EVERY ONCE IN A WHILE I'll be digesting my latest issue of OHJ and come across a reference to resigning oneself to high fuel bills and some measure of discomfort if one suffers from a love of old houses.

AS I WRITE this I'm sitting in my 1797 farmhouse in cold Otsego County, New York. It's five degrees outside, with a brisk breeze, making for a wind-chill factor of thirty below. A year ago icicles would have been hanging from my nose and the drafts would have blown the cat out the crack under the door. I haven't had to take out a second mortgage or sell my firstborn to pay the fuel bill; I just spent a modest amount of cash and a lot of time on what's known as "weatherization."

WEATHERIZATION is a relatively new word, coined in the '70s, but the concept is one that the folks who built old houses were well aware of. After the early years of settlement, firewood was a scarce and expensive commodity. Houses were designed and built to use a minimum of it. Hence the compact, center-chimney saltboxes of New England with no north-facing windows, or the urban row housing of Boston or New York, with thick masonry party walls.

CONVERSELY, in warmer climates, homes were built to minimize solar gain from the summer sun. Exterior balconies, porches and wide roof overhangs, awnings, and shade trees were typical features of early Southern housing. Second floor living spaces to catch breezes and escape the radiant heat of the ground were also incorporated. Early Northern structures tended to have dark-hued exteriors to absorb the winter sun; those of the South were painted in light colors to reflect the summer sun. Old-house owners should understand these inherent energy-saving qualities and take advantage of them.

HERE, WE'LL REVIEW some of the ways to make your old house more comfortable and less expensive to heat and cool. (The Old-House Journal devoted two issues to this subject a few years ago -- September 1980 and September 1981. The information in them, both practical and technical, is invaluable.)

What To Look For

FOR STARTERS, arrange for an "energy audit." Many utilities offer this service at little or no cost -- and they can be worthwhile. Utility audits are no substitute, however, for your own detailed inspection. They're geared toward newer housing and emphasize heating systems, window replacements, and capital investments rather than the nitty-gritty sorts of things that are far more cost-effective.

HEAT IS LOST through two processes: infiltration and conduction. Infiltration is air movement through cracks and joints (drafts). Conduction is heat transfer through materials. The greatest heat loss through conduction occurs via window glass. Weatherstripping and caulking limits infiltration; insulating and installing storm windows slows conduction.

Limiting Infiltration

ANTI-INFILTRATION work is the heart and soul of weatherization. It's very time-consuming, picky work, and it requires a thorough knowledge of how your house is put together (it's a great way to learn). It has the best payback of any measure you can take. Caulking is the number one priority for stopping infiltration, both interior and exterior. Plan on using a couple of cases, maybe more, to do a thorough job. Buying by the case reduces the cost, too.

Andy Wallace has helped weatherize several hundred homes as Director of the Otsego County, N.Y., weatherization program. He's also restored three pre-1840 homes of his own.

EXTERIOR CAULKING will prevent water (more than air) infiltration, though it certainly cuts down on drafts. It's part of preparation for painting, and worth rechecking now unless you've painted very recently. Caulk around all window and door frames (but not under them), where clapboards or shingles meet edge trim, construction joints, and between dissimilar materials, such as brick and wood. Never caulk the spaces under clapboards or shingles; they allow the house to breathe and water vapor to escape from the walls.

WHILE WE'RE OUTSIDE, a word about the importance of pointing up foundations is in order:

In my neck of the woods, dry stone foundations were common during the nineteenth century (when most of the houses were built). An enormous amount of air (not to mention water) infiltrates through these foundations into basements and crawlspaces. A few hours spent with a trowel closing up these holes can make a big difference in comfort and fuel bills.

NOW FOR INSIDE: Thorough caulking on the interior is often overlooked. Yet is is the most effective way to stop air infiltration. (It also helps reduce moisture migration into the walls.) The best time to go sleuthing for drafts is in cold weather, preferably on a windy day. Take along a pad and pencil to note trouble spots and go over all surfaces at close range. No two houses will have exactly the same infiltration spots. But, in general, the following joints should be caulked on the indoor side of all exterior walls:

- Between window and door casings and walls, including tops and under sills.
- Joints in window jambs and casings, and the joint between window stop and jamb.
- Upper window sash, if stationary.
- Joints of baseboards and base mouldings.
- Corner joints and joints of boxed beams in post-and-beam construction.
- Ceiling-to-wall junctions, including crown moulding joints.
- Wall panelling joints (such as where wainscotting meets plaster).
- Around ceiling fixtures and penetrations (vent pipes, etc.) on the top floor.
- Insides of closets, cupboards, etc. These spots are often neglected and leak badly.

FOR AREAS that will not be painted over, use a clear, silicone-based caulk. The results will be virtually invisible if you run a neat bead.

For areas you plan to paint, use a high-quality, acrylic-latex caulk. Bargain-grade caulks are no bargain; they'll crack and shrink, and they won't last very long.

NEXT, SEAL AROUND electrical boxes. Turn off the circuit and remove the cover plate. If the box is tight to the wall, caulk around it and use a foam gasket under the cover plate. If there's a large gap, use spray foam to seal around the outside of the box.

Sealing Doors

MUCH OF THE AIR LEAKAGE in older homes occurs around and through doors and windows that have had better days. Often weathered, and usually out of square, they give an old house much of its character. Forget all the hype about shiny new, triple-glazed, vinyl-track, super energy-efficient replacement units. The payback on these babies runs to several generations, and what they take away from the house may never be returned. With a little time and care, you can preserve your old doors and windows and make them tight.

OLD DOORS require a lot of work to make them airtight, but it's worth the effort. First of all, the door itself must be in good shape. Getting it that way may involve removing the door, regluing and/or repinning loose joints, adjusting hardware, moving the stops, and finally, trimming the door to fit so that it latches snugly yet easily (see "How to Fix Old Doors," June 1986 OHJ).

INTEGRAL-METAL and spring-metal weatherstrip last the longest, but the materials are rather expensive. I prefer to use a good quality vinyl tube or flap weatherstrip. It's available set in either wood or metal.

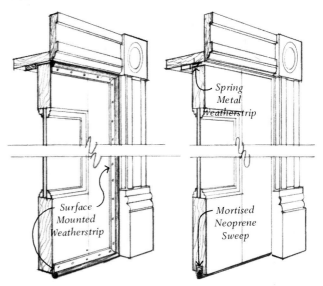

Spring Metal Weatherstrip

Surface Mounted Weatherstrip

Mortised Neoprene Sweep

SETTING THE WEATHERSTRIP requires precision. With the door closed, cut the top piece to length and set it so that it just touches the door surface. Tack it up with a couple of finish nails. Repeat this procedure with the hinge side and then the latch side, making sure the gasket is touching at all points. Don't drive the nails home -- yet. Now, measure the distance between the side pieces of weatherstrip and cut your door sweep to fit.

Don't Forget The Cellar

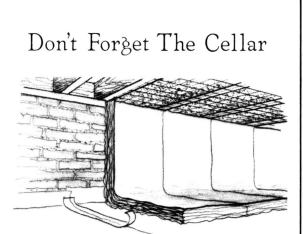

SPENDING THE DAY in the dingy confines of the cellar bumping your head on pipes and walking into cobwebs is no joy, but it is important. Cellars are often left neglected and can be real trouble spots of efficiency.

FIRST, SEAL air leaks. Caulk, spray-foam, or point cracks in the foundation, between sill and foundation, and where pipes, wires, etc. enter the house. Do this on a cold day so you can use your hand to feel for drafts. If you turn the lights off for a moment, you'll be able to spot miniscule cracks with daylight shining through them. Check windows for proper glazing and weatherstripping.

INSULATE ALL AROUND the perimeter with six-inch fiberglass, paper face showing. This will diminish infiltration — it's difficult to seal a cellar by caulking alone. Insulating between the joists with the vapor barrier up — towards the first floor — will keep your feet warm as you walk around the house. If you have an exterior door or hatchway, make sure it, too, is tight.

INSULATING your water heater (if it's more than five years old) and domestic water pipes is a good idea. Rather than buy one of those expensive water-heater jackets, wrap the heater with 3½-inch fiberglass and hold it on with wire. Don't wrap the top or bottom section where the pilot, controls, and vent outlet are. A fire or carbon monoxide poisoning could result.

THE BEST PIPE INSULATION is the extruded-foam kind that comes in 3-foot lengths with a slit down the middle. Duct-tape all seams for a tight seal. Insulating cold-water pipes won't save energy, but will prevent sweating in warm weather, if that's a problem for you.

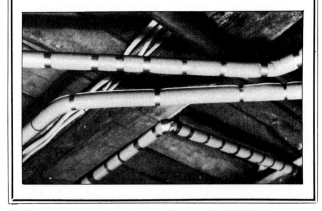

MANY PRODUCTS are available for sealing the bottom of the door, but for older houses, I prefer a quality neoprene sweep that attaches to a mortise in the door and can be adjusted to the slope of the threshold. Particularly useful are the sweeps that operate with a bushing and spring, closing down when the door is shut, and springing up when the door is open. This allows the sweep to clear a carpet or, heaven forbid, a sloping floor.

SET THE SWEEP so that it just touches the threshold with the door closed. Try the door several times to make sure it closes easily and the weatherstrip contacts all points. Make minor adjustments, resetting the weatherstrip as necessary. When the fit is just right, set the nails, and caulk the joints between jamb and stop and stop and weatherstrip.

DON'T FORGET THE DOOR to the basement, doors into unheated rooms, and the door or hatchway into the attic. Making a new attic hatch and adding a stop may be necessary to get a good seal. Don't neglect this: Heat rises in a chimney effect, and lots of it is lost through loose hatches.

Windows

ORIGINAL WINDOWS are one of the prime sources of energy loss, because they lose heat by both conduction through glass, and infiltration around edges and through joints.

HEAT LOSS THROUGH WINDOWS has been examined closely in recent years. What's come out of the studies is that taking the following measures will save energy:

- weatherstrip sash;
- install storm windows;
- caulk all joints between fixed parts;
- install pulley seals.

FIRST, YOUR WINDOWS must be good shape and properly glazed. If they're not, I suggest you refer to Bill O'Donnell's excellent and comprehensive article, "Troubleshooting Old Windows" (Jan./Feb. 1986 OHJ). Having just gone through the process he describes on 22 "12-over-12" original sash, I can attest to the fact that it's incredibly time-consuming, but well worth the effort.

IF YOUR WINDOWS are in bad enough shape to warrant removal and repair, you might consider installing spring metal or integral weatherstrip. Otherwise, it's not a cost- or time-effective measure. The materials are rather expensive, and rope clay (Mortite, for example) will accomplish the same thing at a fraction of the cost and time spent. If your house is pre-1840, as mine is, then the upper sash is probably stationary and can be caulked in place.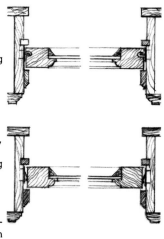

PULLEY SLOTS are a serious source of air leak-age. The Anderson Pulley Seal remedies the problem. Made of flexible plastic with a self-sealing surface, the pulley seal is unobtru-sive, installs easily, and doesn't interfere with operation of the window. It really works!

STORM WINDOWS are to my mind a necessity from a preservation standpoint. (See box.)

Old House Insulation

ATTIC OR CEILING insulation is a must. Fiberglass batts install easily if the attic is unfloored. Lay the batts, vapor barrier down, between the joists. Butt them tightly together. If the joist spacing is uneven or other than 16" or 24" on center, try using blown or poured insulation. It will provide more effective coverage than pieced-together batts. Dam around chimneys and electrical boxes (allow 3" clearance).

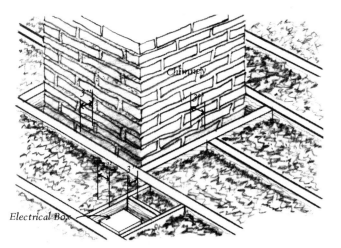

Chimney

Electrical Box

ATTIC VENTILATION (to allow water vapor to escape before it condenses) is usually pro-vided for at gable ends. Metal vents are readily available in a variety of shapes and sizes. But for a period house, it's much more sensitive to fashion a wooden-slat vent (screened on the inside to keep bugs out) that matches the existing trim.

METAL SOFFIT VENTS, ridge vents, and roof vents are easy to find, though I'd avoid using the latter on an old house. (They will alter the exterior appearance somewhat.) Adequate attic ventilation is a must, however, even if it means installing metal vents. Depending on conditions, requirements vary from 150 to 300 square feet of attic space per square foot of vent. Check this out locally.

Storm Windows

TRADITIONALLY, storm windows have been installed on the outside of a house to protect the prime win-dow from winter weather—rain, snow, wind, and sleet. Their energy-saving value is chiefly related to conduc-tion. They create a dead air space and slow heat loss through the main win-dow. They are not meant to be completely airtight; in fact, they have weep holes at the bottom to allow moisture to escape.

THE OLD-FASHIONED wood storm is more efficient than modern aluminum triple tracks — wood is a much better insulator than metal. Wood storms are less conven-ient, though; they are inoperable, and they have to be put up and taken down every year. While I prefer wood storms, aluminum storms will protect your windows and are perfectly acceptable for old houses according to the Secretary of the Interior's Preservation Guidelines. (They come anodized or enamelled in several colors now; so avoid the raw aluminum look.)

LATELY, I've become convinced that interior storms are the best bet for saving energy. I recommend them even if you already have storms on the outside. The product I'm most familiar with, having assembled and installed them on several hundred homes, consists of a rigid alumi-num frame, called Bailey or "C" sash, with pile weather-stripping, and either glass or .100 acrylic (a better insula-tor) in the gasketed frame. Corners can be mitered or square with plastic corners that press in. They're easy to make and can be mount-ed either on top of the window casing or recessed against the stop within the jamb.

WHEN properly installed, interior storms are com-pletely airtight. They elim-inate condensation (the pri-mary cause of window dete-rioration). They're easily removable, so you can take them down during warm-weather periods.

Heat-shrunk plastic sheet, or "poor man's storm."

Wall Insulation?

FEW WEATHERIZATION ISSUES cause as much debate as whether or not to blow insulation into the walls of a house without a vapor barrier. While there is no pat answer to this question (with success or failure depending on the construction of the house, the climate, how well the job is done, and other variables), on the whole, I'm a firm advocate of the process. I've seen dramatic differences in fuel bills and comfort with relatively few problems in hundreds of houses insulated in this way.

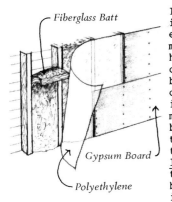

Fiberglass Batt

Gypsum Board

Polyethylene

IN COLD CLIMATES, wall insulation is a cost-effective weatherization measure. If your house has a wet basement or crawlspace, unvented bathroom or kitchen, a clothes dryer vented indoors, or exterior moisture problems caused by plants too close to the house, broken gutters, etc., don't insulate. Remedy all moisture problems before blowing the insulation in. After correcting these problems, paint interior surfaces (after caulking) with a vapor barrier paint followed by an oil-base primer or finish coat.

SEVERAL KINDS of blown-in insulation are available; fiberglass, rock wool, and cellulose are the most common. Cellulose is the most popular because of its lower cost, superior packing properties, and fire resistance (Class 1). It will retain moisture and lose some of its insulating value as a result, but if you've remedied all moisture problems, this will be a negligible factor.

BLOWING INSULATION is not a do-it-yourself project, even though you can rent blowing machines, buy bags of insulation, and attempt the job yourself. You're much better off hiring a reliable contractor, after getting several bids and checking out references, preferably on houses of similar age and framing construction as your own. Understanding framing makes for a good insulation job.

STANDARD PRACTICE calls for drilling holes (1-2" diameter) in each wall cavity every forty inches vertically. Insulation is blown into the holes, the holes are plugged, filled, and primed. If properly done, the work will be nearly invisible.

A BETTER METHOD on clapboard or shingle-sided homes is to carefully remove courses of siding and replace them after blowing. This enables the contractor to probe for hidden obstructions (knee braces, firestops, etc.), and makes for a better looking job. It also gives you an opportunity to check the work for voids and proper pack. Cellulose should be densely compacted in the wall so that there will be little settlement. If properly executed, the insulation will not fall out even if you remove the siding.

Another option: If there's a lot of plaster damage to be repaired, consider blowing in the insulation from the inside.

A Word Or Two About Retrofitting

ALL OF THIS ASSUMES that you are dealing with the original walls, ceilings, and exterior siding which, alas, is not always the case where neglected old houses are concerned. While wishing to preserve original material, it's often necessary to remove deteriorated plaster and lath or to replace hopelessly deteriorated siding. This makes it easy to insulate with fiberglass.

IF THE STUD SPACING is irregular, use unfaced fiberglass, tightly fitted (it's okay to compress it a bit) and install a polyethylene (plastic) vapor barrier over it (on the inside) taping all seams, including floor and ceiling, and electrical boxes with duct tape. Then install Sheetrock or rock lath.

IF YOU HAVE narrow stud cavities (many pre-1840 houses have less than three inches), or plank walls with no cavities, consider installing rigid foil-faced insulation, such as Thermax or Energy Shield, beneath the inside walls. If you have a narrow wall cavity, fill it with fiberglass batts first, then fasten the rigid insulation to the face of the studs with two-inch roofing nails. If you're installing it over plank walls, fir it 1 inch away from the wall to provide an air space. One caution: Rigid insulation releases toxic fumes when burned. Local codes may require it be covered with 5/8" Sheetrock.

Rigid insulation covered (partially) by Sheetrock.

RIGID INSULATION comes in several thicknesses from 1/2" to 2". With the seams properly taped, it forms a very effective vapor barrier (making plastic unnecessary). It has an R value of about 8 per inch, so it's ideal where space is limited. Although you may have to deepen your window jambs, it's worth the extra work in comfort and fuel savings. Do not, however, use it as exterior sheathing. It's a great vapor barrier and will trap moisture in your walls. If you're going to re-side, wrap the exterior in Tyvek, a tough, moisture-permeable sheeting that reduces air infiltration. Siding is simply nailed on top of it.

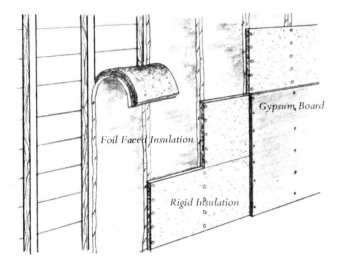

Foil Faced Insulation

Gypsum Board

Rigid Insulation

The Heating Plant

LAST, BUT FAR FROM LEAST, we come to the furnace itself. This is an area for a specialist, of course, and I can't pretend to be one. But there are a few observations I'd like to make.

ANNUAL CLEANING and tuning of your furnace or boiler saves fuel and headaches down the pike. When you have this done, request an efficiency test and have the technician explain the results to you. You may find the old monster worth replacing. If it's less than 75% efficient, investing in a new burner, (a Beckett, for example) could raise the efficiency to the 80-85% range, and pay for itself quickly in a large old house. If your furnace is on its last legs, you should look into the new generation of super-efficient (90-95%) heating plants that waste so little heat that they require only plastic (PVC) stacks (check local codes). They're more expensive than conventional units, but worth investigating.

IF YOU HAVE TAKEN any or several of the measures discussed in this article since your furnace was last tested, you may be able to have the nozzle size on your burner reduced (on oil-fired furnaces). Nozzles are rated in gallons per hour consumed, and a reduction in nozzle size of 1/2 gph after weatherization is common.

We wish to thank John Obed Curtis for his assistance in preparing this article. John directs the curatorial department at Old Sturbridge Village in Massachusetts.

The Wall-Insulation Controversy

THE PHONE RINGS one morning: a subscriber with a technical question. She explains, "Last year I had insulation blown into the wall cavities of my house. The local utility company helped arrange for the work. I've never had a problem with the exterior of my home, and it was just painted three years ago. Now, paint is blistering off the clapboards in several areas and some of the plugs that fill the holes they drilled have popped out. The utility company has been very sympathetic; they even offered to fix the problem. But they want me to tell them how to fix it. In the meantime, water is entering my house through the popped plugs."

WE'VE HEARD many similar stories. That's why we've always recommended against blown-in insulation as a first step in weatherization. Blown-in insulation will only be a cost-effective investment if you've taken all of the other steps outlined in this article. You have to ask yourself: "If I've done all I can to eliminate air infiltration; if I've tightened the windows and installed storms; if I've added attic insulation and bought a few nice sweaters, will it still be cost-effective to pay a contractor to insulate the wall cavities?" In harsh environments, the answer is probably "yes." The payback will take a while (but you'll be more comfortable in the meantime), and there is some risk involved.

ANDY WALLACE comes out as a strong advocate of blown-in insulation, especially for free-standing, wood-frame houses in harsh environments. (His own house is located in a wind-blown valley in Upstate New York.) But if you read closely, you'll see that he has the same concerns as OHJ.

ANDY POINTS OUT the importance of eliminating all moisture problems first, providing ventilation (particularly in kitchens and baths), using a vapor-barrier paint, caulking thoroughly, and hiring a qualified contractor.

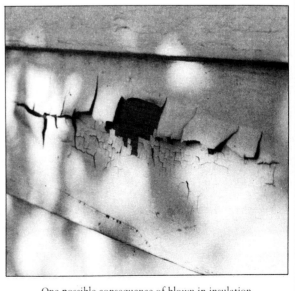

One possible consequence of blown-in insulation.

Restoration Products

Reviewed by Eve Kahn

Slate Look-Alike

There is a substitute for slate shingles: reinforced-cement shingles that approximate the look of slate, but are lighter and one-third the cost. (Even though the biggest cost in a major roofing job is <u>labor</u>, the saving in materials may be important.)

The manufacturer, Atlas International Building Products, claims that cement shingles can last "indefinitely," and they offer a 30-year guarantee (Vermont slate lasts 75 to 100 years or more). AIBP's asbestos-fiber cement shingles come in black, red, grey, and green, and cost around $400 per square, installed (or $165 to $180 loose). They won't curl; they

resist chipping, and weigh about half as much as real slate. Their colors are integral, which means that if one does chip, or is cut to fit a tight space, it shows the same color throughout.

AIBP provides a booklet with complete installation instructions. The small amount of asbestos in the shingles, by the way, is encapsulated and not considered a danger. AIBP sells through distributors (call for the location of the nearest dealer). Individual contractors can call and order the shingles, although they then pay shipping costs. If you're willing to wait until a full truckload of orders is going to your area, shipping

costs are much lower. For a free brochure, contact AIBP, 5600 Hochelaga St., Dept. OHJ, Montreal, Quebec, Canada H1N 1W1. (800) 361-4962.

Latex-Based Chinking

If you own a log home, you've undoubtedly experienced mortar or chinking failure. A low-maintenance alternative to real mortar is Perma-Chink, a latex-based sealant that hardens to a strong yet flexible consistency. It remains airtight, even if the logs settle; it's reasonably easy to apply, and you can apply it directly on top of failed mortar. It comes in two shades of grey plus white, beige, and tan, so you can approximate the color of your old mortar.

Perma-Chink costs $66 for a five-gallon pail, and the manufacturer also sells the tools you'll need to apply it: caulking guns, application bags (the material is applied like cake frosting), plus the Styrofoam-like backer board.

Purists should note: Once this stuff cures, it is difficult if not impossible to remove (it permeates the surrounding wood).

Perma-Chink Systems' free information packet includes application instructions and charts for estimating quantities and cost. The company sells both direct to consumers and through dealers. Perma-Chink Systems, 17455 NE 67th Ct., Dept. OHJ, Redmond, WA 98052. (206) 885-6050. Also, 1605 Prosser Rd., Dept. OHJ, Knoxville, TN 37914. (615) 524-7343.

Water & Crack Gauges

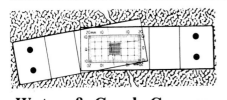

To keep track of your house's (expanding?) cracks, PRG sells a telltale called Avongard. It's an acrylic gauge that can be applied with screws, nails, or epoxy and left on the crack year-round. It has two halves that pivot around the center, which is positioned atop the crack's center. If the crack moves or expands, the two halves will move, and the center gauge will measure the extent of the movement. Avongard is accurate to one millimeter. Each unit costs $13, postpaid; you can buy ten or more at a discount.

PRG also makes a water detector called the Waterbug.

Its alarm sounds when the unit touches water, but it doesn't react to high humidity or surface dampness (which makes for fewer false alarms). It's especially useful for basements, where humidity isn't a concern but flooding is. Complete with batteries, the pocket-size Waterbug (about four inches long and an inch wide) costs $24.95 postpaid. PRG also sells many other useful gauges and measuring devices for old-house owners, and they send out free brochures and product bulletins. PRG, 5619 Southampton Dr., Dept. OHJ, Springfield, VA 22151. (703) 323-1407.

for Victorian buildings

Cast-Iron Cresting

To replace the iron roof cresting that some Victoriana-phobe tore off your roof, Robinson Iron offers a line of six stock crestings that are exact duplicates of originals. Or, if you know what yours actually looked like, Robinson can re-create it from either a fragment or a photo.

The minimum order of stock cresting is $150. The panels range in length from 16 to 28 inches, and in price from $21 to $41 each (so your minimum order is between four and seven feet, depending upon which model you choose). Two of the six patterns also have matching posts. If you need a specific length, Robinson can cut panels to fit (or you can have that done on site). Delivery time is four to six weeks; expect to wait up to eight weeks for custom work.

As for installation, most of the panels come with lugs at the bottom so that you can attach them with lag screws. If you have any questions

Cresting, far left, costs $35 for a 23-in.-wide panel, 18 in. high; below left, $28 for a 28¼-in.-wide panel, also 18 in. high. Right, the Oswego model comes in panels 28 in. wide, 25 in. high, for $41 each. Posts are $38.

about installation, Robinson will try to answer them over the phone (ask for Scott Howell), but it's best to ask also the advice of a roofer who's experienced with metals. The company sends out information with photos of the designs and a price list. Robinson Iron, Robinson Rd., Dept. OHJ, Alexander City, AL 35010. (205) 329-8484.

for post-Victorian buildings

Craftsman-esque Rug

This rug, with its border of oversized flowers, would fit well into any early 20th-century house, from Craftsman right through the 1930s. It's part of Couristan's "Symphony" line, and there are two color schemes available: shades of beige and shades of powder blue. There are three sizes: 4'1" x 5 1/2', 5 1/2' x 8', and 8'3" x 11'2". Suggested prices vary, but the average, for the 5-1/2'-x-8' rug, is $469 on the East Coast, $485 in the West. Contact the importer for the address of the nearest dealer: Couristan, 919 Third Ave., Dept. OHJ, New York, NY 10022. (212)371-4200.

Shoji Screens

The influence of Asia has persisted in American interior decoration ever since wealthy colonists covered their walls with Chinese wallpaper. In the 1870s and '80s, the Anglo-Japanese style interpreted Japanese motifs. But it was not until the early 20th century that entire interiors were done in an Oriental-influenced fashion. Owners of some Craftsman and most Japanesque bungalows, and architects like Frank Lloyd Wright, strove to imitate the uncluttered lines and simple, low furniture of Japan.

Shoji screens have come back in vogue, and they make very appropriate room dividers, doors, or freestanding screens for these Craftsman or Japanesque homes. Miya Shoji has been making Shoji screens for some 35 years. (Don't expect real rice paper; what you will get is fiberglass or laminated rice paper that has the irregular translucence of paper but not the fragility.) Frames are of basswood and, for an extra charge, they can be customized with any finish you like. Miya Shoji also sells frames and material separately so you can assemble the screen yourself. Prices range from $90 for a 24-by-36-inch frame with fiberglass to $360 for a 48-by-96-inch frame with laminated rice paper. Call or write for a free flyer: Miya Shoji & Interiors Inc., 107 W. 17th St., Dept. OHJ, New York, NY 10011. (212) 243-6774.

and any kind of custom work. The vanes are handmade by the old-fashioned <u>repousse</u> method, which involves hammering the metal over a concave block of wood. The results are three-dimensional copper pieces that can truly be considered sculpture. Tuck also engineers each piece so that it really points into the wind.

If you balk at the prices -- from $1200 to $2100 -- keep in mind that these not only took more than 40 hours each to create, but also that they'll become part of the legacy of

Copper Weathervanes

Travis Tuck's first weathervane, made in 1974, was in the shape of a great white shark. It was used, not surprisingly, in the movie "Jaws." (You can spot it atop the house of the shark hunter, Quint.) Since then Travis, trained as a sculptor, has branched out into weathervanes of all sorts, like sheep, whales, mice, osprey, geese, and old standards like weathercocks and arrows.

He offers six stock designs

your house. All vanes have bases with mounting brackets and the four points of the compass. And in case you love your vane too much to leave it outside, Travis sells an indoor display base for $150.

Packing, shipping, and insurance cost $55; or you can pick up your vane at the studio on Martha's Vineyard and get a chance to see the artist at work. He sends out a color brochure and price list for $1. Travis Tuck, Metal Sculptor, Box 1832H, Dept. OHJ, Martha's Vineyard, MA 02568. (617) 693-3914.

Colonial Kit Furniture

In 1949, Francis Hagerty had what was then a radical idea: selling kit furniture by mail. His goal was to offer quality reproductions of colonial furniture at reasonable prices. That's what Cohasset Colonials, the company he founded, still does; it's now run by Francis's son John. Some examples from the catalog: A bowback Windsor armchair sells for $198, a four-poster canopy bed kit for $435. Cohasset recently started offering its collection in finished, assembled

form, but the kits are still tempting -- the assembled pieces cost about twice as much, yet the kits require no more than three or four hours to put together.

Decorators will be pleased to know that the company has also branched out into selling lighting fixtures, fabrics, paints, stains, bed hangings,

curtains, and pewter accessories, though their specialty is still furniture. There's even a "Decorator Pack": coordinated fabric samples, paint chips, a catalog of room settings, and price charts. Cohasset also offers customers free decorating consultations by mail.

The colorful catalog ($2 for two years) shows several colonial room settings, and it names the museum where the originals of its reproductions can be found. The Decorator Pack costs $9, applicable toward fabric purchases of $35 or more. Cohasset Colonials, 646GX Ship St., Dept. OHJ, Cohasset Harbor, MA 02025. (617) 383-0110.

This birdcage Windsor armchair sells in kit form for $155 (assembly time: two hours) and pre-assembled for $324. The four-poster, queen-size bed is $459 in kit form, $819 pre-assembled (full: kit, $435; $798, pre-assembled).

The original of this Queen Anne porringer table ($239, kit; $459, pre-assembled) is in the Shelburne Museum, Shelburne, Vermont.

opinion... Remuddling

SOMETIMES, in an old gangster movie, you'll hear the heavy threaten to put someone "in a cement kimono" -- an excellent way to eliminate troublemakers. We don't know who was troubled by the house pictured left above, but it's been dealt with as ruthlessly as any B-movie stoolie: Its character has been virtually destroyed by that stucco straightjacket. It was probably the twin to the house pictured above right; both were constructed around 1900 by Fernando Nelson, San Francisco's most prolific Victorian-era builder. Of course, these houses are neighbors, and that's the worst news of all. As you can see from the picture at left, this remuddling has done more than eliminate the beauty of one old house; it's compromised an entire street. (Our thanks to Linda and Wolfgang Liebelt of San Francisco for sending us these photographs.) -- Cole Gagne

THE MUSHROOM FACTOR

PROBABLY YOU, like the rest of us, have fallen prey to one of the immutable laws of old-house living: The Mushroom Factor. But since OHJ has only recently identified TMF as a universal principle, you probably thought you were the lone victim.

THE MUSHROOM FACTOR always springs from a small, seemingly innocuous project. Then things... well, mushroom.

FOR EXAMPLE: You start out to change a light bulb. As you screw a new bulb into the porcelain ceiling fixture, however, you notice the fixture wobbles. You unscrew the fixture to investigate -- and discover the hanger bar in the electrical box is loose. As you begin tightening the hanger bar, you see the insulation on the electrical wires is dried and crumbling.

YOU'RE ALREADY 45 minutes into the bulb-changing project when you utter the fatal words: "While I'm at it, I might as well fix that insulation, too." So you find the electrical tape, figure out which circuit breaker controls that box, and start to tape up the bare wires. But as you're working, you discover the whole electrical box is moving.

FURTHER investigation reveals the box is just hanging on the lath and plaster -- and the weight has caused the lath nails to pull loose. Another decision point: Should you repair the plaster? You look at your watch: your weekend guests aren't due for another three hours. "As long as I'm at it, I might as well do the job right," you mutter.

OUT COME the electric drill, the carbide bit, the 2-in. screws, and the plaster washers. As you're drilling pilot holes for the screws, a 4-ft. by 4-ft. chunk of ceiling plaster lets go.

YOU EXAMINE the remaining plaster. Many of the plaster keys are broken, and the lath is definitely loose. "While I'm at it...," you think to yourself.

YOUR FRIENDS arrive just as the last chunk of ceiling yields to your pry bar. Alas, your triumphant pose atop the pile of broken plaster is barely discernible through the clouds of plaster dust still billowing through your house.

"WHAT ARE you doing?" your friends inquire incredulously. You begin to explain that you had originally set out to change a light bulb...but as you try to reconstruct the sequence, you realize an explanation is impossible. Instead, you shrug and offer them gin and tonic.

THANKS TO OHJ's new research, in the future you can offer a more satisfactory response. Allowing a world-weary smile to play lightly across your lips, explain simply that you were a victim of The Mushroom Factor. If they press for details, point out that The Mushroom Factor is the mysterious universal force that causes any old-house project to expand until the limits of time and budget are exceeded.

THE MUSHROOM FACTOR is not directly related to Murphy's Law (although that certainly applies to old-house living, too).

RATHER, our research indicates that TMF is a sub-category of Fred Allen's (less-well-known) Law. That bit of wisdom reads: "Everything is more complicated than anybody knows."

WE'RE STILL collecting case histories that illustrate the universality of The Mushroom Factor. You can contribute to the Advancement of Science -- and perhaps win a valuable prize -- by letting us know how The Mushroom Factor invaded your life. See box below for details.   -- C.L.

"I started out to fix a squeaky floorboard. Then I encountered ... THE MUSHROOM FACTOR!"

FABULOUS PRIZES

We hold The Mushroom Factor to be a Universal Law. But we need further documentation to prove the hypothesis. If you've had a firsthand encounter with TMF, we'd like to hear from you.

To the person who's experienced the greatest degree of unforeseen mushrooming, we'll award a complete set of OHJ Yearbooks. (Photos of before, during, or after your project will buttress the scientific evidence.) We'll also award 2nd and 3rd prizes of 3-year and 2-year renewals, each with a copy of the brand-new 1987 Catalog.

Send your experiences to The Mushroom Factor, Old-House Journal, 69A Seventh Ave., Brooklyn, NY 11217.

— Clem Labine

Letters

Wynkoop house, Ulster County, N.Y.

Dutch house with overhanging eaves, Bergen County, N.J.

Vernacular Ignorance?

Dear Editor:

Regarding "Dutch Stone Houses of New York State" (June 1986 OHJ): It's a pity that Neil Larson did not point out that the Wynkoop house in Ulster County has lost its probable wide-projecting eaves, which were characteristic of New York Dutch houses (see Riker house, p. 127 of the same issue). But he probably doesn't know. It's amazing how few people know what they're talking about, even in OHJ.

> -- Edward V. Lofstrom,
> Architect
> Minneapolis, Minn.

Neil Larson replies:

Wide-projecting eaves, while documented on some old Dutch houses, are not necessarily "characteristic" of New York Dutch houses. They seem to be characteristic of certain areas in certain periods. They are least characteristic in Ulster County stone houses (those pictured in OHJ).

They do appear fairly regularly on houses in southern New York and northern New Jersey. Based on survey work in Bergen County, N.J., these house forms date from the Revolutionary and Federal period almost exclusively. We have one example attributed to the 1760s in Dutchess County, but I am told that such an early example is rare.

You can pretty confidently assume the following:

● Colonial-era Dutch houses were characteristically gable-roofed, without overhanging eaves. Masonry construction was preferred.

● By 1750, the houses (in all areas) became more formalized architecturally. Houses (like the Wynkoop house) remained consistent in the linear form, but adopted center halls, balanced facades, and other "Georgian" patterns and details. Still, overhanging eaves cannot be said to have become characteristic at this point -- such early examples are rare.

● Sometime around the 1760s, the gambrel roof became a popular innovation up and down the Hudson Valley. It was about this time that the bell-cast roof (and gables with a "kick") first appeared in the lower valley. What also appeared was an overhang that created a porch. (Remember: Documented pre-Revolutionary examples of this house type are considered rare.) Ulster County houses did not adopt the gambrel-roof fad for some reason. The Wynkoop house definitely did not have eaves that overhang the walls.

I should have been more specific with my example and restricted the reference to Ulster County. It is impossible to characterize all the Dutch houses in the Hudson Valley, except with the most general attributes. Many people (at least one) assume that projecting eaves were a standard attribute. That assumption reflects more a twentieth-century antiquarian taste in architecture than an accurate understanding of the Dutch vernacular tradition.

> -- Neil Larson,
> N.Y.S. Historic Preservation
> Field Services Bureau

Historic Districtions

Dear People:

I am presently fighting with our local historic commission over the establishment of a historic district in my neighborhood. While we all seem to agree with the ideas and goals of a historic district, we are not willing to give up our rights, as property owners, to choose paint colors, type of roofing material, etc.

Do you know of any cities that have passed ordinances for the establishment of historic districts which are written such that the architecture is preserved, yet the rights of the property owners are not abridged?

> -- Lee LeClair
> Denton, Texas

[Historic district status can breed neighborhood pride, preserve character, and increase property values. Unfortunately, it can also be the perfect excuse for the most vocal (and perhaps least knowledgeable) residents to try and legislate "good taste." Taken to an extreme, such abuses can lead to homogenized streets that aren't even historically accurate. We'd like to hear from those of you who have found a happy medium. -- ed.]

Letters

Mrs. Crawford in her sitting room, 1912.

Looking Back

Dear OHJ:

I thought your readers might like a peek inside the interior of the home of a modest, working-class family as it appeared in 1912. The house was located in Aiken, Ohio. I don't know what became of this house after my great-grandparents (the Crawfords) passed away, but I do know a little bit about its history during the time these photos were taken.

When Mr. and Mrs. Crawford lived there, it was within walking distance of other focal points of family life -- the grocery store they kept, the Goodrich rubber factory many of them worked for, their beloved church, and the cemetery where, among others, Mr. Crawford's father (a Civil War veteran) is buried.

In both photos, Mrs. Crawford is reading, first in the sitting room, and then in an alcove opposite the sitting room. Mrs. Crawford, it was reported, kept a very tidy house. In the 1930s, her children bought her a clothes-washing machine. With it, Mrs. C. wrote shortly before her death at age 80, the washing was "no job at all."

If I ever go back to Aiken, I'll steel my nerves and look to see what's become of the house. In my fantasy, though, someone else reports back to me, "Guess what, they're restoring it."

-- Claire Packer
Plainfield, N.J.

Subscriber's Sleeping Balcony

Dear OHJ:

We read your "Sleeping Porches" article (June 1986 OHJ) with great interest. Our 1902 house (below) has an unusual second-floor porch that resembles the "sleeping balconies" in your article.

You enter this porch from a landing that's two steps down from the second-floor hallway. The porch has four windows -- one onto the stairwell, two onto the master bedroom, and one onto a smaller bedroom on the left. We've always wondered if it was intended for sleeping. It's very narrow; only two single cots can fit. Our children enjoy greeting friends from above and testing the weather as they decide what to wear, not to mention launching paper airplanes.

This photo was taken for Winchester Historical Society's forthcoming book on Winchester architecture. (The book was partially funded by two grants we have won in OHJ's revenue-sharing program.) We look forward to learning more about our house now that OHJ is including more post-Victorian articles.

-- Nancy Schrock
Winchester, Mass.

Ask OHJ

Aiming Your Moon

Q: WE'VE SURVIVED no heating system and no kitchen, having our hand-dug well run dry, a bat in the bedroom, snake in the family room, and a massive beehive in the bedroom wall. As the photo attests, though, our restoration of this magnificent structure is nearly complete. Our latest fun project has been to resurrect a dilapidated three-seater outhouse. Rotted timbers have been replaced, a new stone foundation has been built, a new cedar shake roof has been made, and a fresh coat of paint applied.

We do have a puzzling question regarding a finishing touch, though. Should the lunar insignia on the door point to the left or the right? I thought it should point to the left, but then I saw an oil painting of an outhouse that had it opening to the right. Our door handle is on the right, whereas the handle in the painting was on the left. Does that make any difference?
-- Patricia Williams, Saugerties, N.Y.

A: WE DID SOME RESEARCH, and found that the crescent moon was not a popular 19th-century motif at all. Chick Sale wrote a book in the 1920s called The Specialist. In it were humorous drawings of outhouses, all with crescent moons on the door. (The book is still available, for $5: The Specialist Publishing Co., 109 La Mesa Dr., Burlingame, CA 94010. (415) 344-4958.) It's pretty certain the motif was used on farmstead out-houses before his book (and possibly on cut-out shutters -- see page 392 in this issue). But after Sale's book was published, the motif came to be the instantly recognizable outhouse mark.

In the 19th century the outhouse was often a ramshackle affair, and little attention was paid to its construction. On fancier homes, the outhouse would be given details similar to the main house: For the Williams' house, for example, decorative bargeboards would be appropriate, with a panelled door, and perhaps a window.

The direction of the half moon remains controversial. Some people told us the crescent pointed to the left, others thought it should merely point away from the hinges, so the Williams' are going to have to take their best shot.

Readers Respond to Mantel Mystery

Q: ON THE BACK of each piece of our mantel are the identifying marks "J17:88G" [or "J17:886" -- ed.]. Could these signify the date (1788) and maybe the craftsman's initials?
-- Lorraine Dalrymple, Warminster, Penna.

[We turned this question over to our readers in "A Mantel Mystery," (July/August 1986 Ask OHJ). Following are some of the answers we received. -- ed.]

A: I USED TO LIVE in a Brooklyn apartment built in 1875. It had original slate fireplaces exactly like the one pictured in your column. The marbleizing on those mantels was original. I think OHJ is correct in the date being 1886, although the insignia could simply be a serial number. It could be the number (cumulative) of pieces J17 manufactured.
-- Amanda Husberg, Brooklyn, N.Y.

I AGREE with your appraisal that the mantel design is of the mid- to late-nineteenth century. Because it was manufactured in the midst of the industrial revolution, it was likely machine-made and ordered out of a catalog. The lettering appears on each piece of the mantel. This leads me to believe that their function is to ensure that all pieces of the same mantel are shipped out of the warehouse at the same time. It may be that the 886 would date the piece as 1888 or 1886 and be, therefore, part of the catalog number.
-- Robert W. Soulen, Architect Mansfield, Ohio

I AM SURE you know that the Europeans date things differently than we do. For instance, I as write this it is 30-7-86. Thirty the day, seven the month, and eighty-six the year. Could the markings indicate the seventeenth day of August, 1886?
-- Robert L. Dunn, Claremore, Okla.

General interest questions from subscribers will be answered in print. The Editors can't promise to reply to all questions personally—but we try. Send your questions with sketches or photos to Questions Editor, The Old-House Journal, 69A Seventh Avenue, Brooklyn, NY 11217.

Family Chronicle

of Old-House Living

BY JANE KIRKPATRICK

ON JULY 4, 1986, while most Americans were out celebrating Lady Liberty's centennial, Millie Moore of Moro, Oregon, was on a ladder in one of her bedrooms, celebrating her own piece of history.

"I COULD SEE something besides plaster through what I'd thought was the bottom layer of wallpaper," she recalls. "So I scraped, and there it was! The original wallpaper, 104 years old! It was already four years old when the Statue of Liberty arrived."

SUCH DISCOVERIES, for Millie and her husband David, are more than anonymous snatches of the past. In 1882 David's great-grandparents, John and Helen Moore, built this house in Oregon's wheat country. Millie is the fourth Mrs. Moore to live in it, and it has remained in the family since it was built. Each artifact David and Millie uncover means another piece of family history has been retrieved. The house itself, adapted over the years to suit changing needs and tastes, can be "read" like a family chronicle.

IN THE BEGINNING the Moores' house boasted seven rooms, front and back porches, hand-carved staircase, parlor and dining room, and four bedrooms. Each bedroom had a closet, an unusual feature in those days. There were two kitchens -- the summer kitchen stood out back in a separate building -- and two pantries. One pantry was kept dark to discourage weevils, supposedly attracted to light.

THE PARLOR WAS particularly elegant, as was the fashion, and used only on formal occasions. In fact Anna Moore, great-grandmother Helen's daughter-in-law, lived in the house six months before she saw the room. It was also the life-and-death room: Babies were born there, and wakes were held in it.

EVERY INTERIOR DOOR had a transom painted with a dark brown, spider-web design. All have been preserved. "Upstairs," recounts Millie, "Dortha Moore, my mother-in-law, found the signature of the artist above the door. I purposely did not touch that section when we redid the room, but the painters brushed right over it. I think it's lost forever now."

DESPITE THE HOUSE'S rich details, there were signs of frugality. "There is only one ceiling medallion -- in the entry," notes Millie. "and only one bay window. The floors are of soft fir (but this may have been due to the scarcity of hardwood). The doors are white pine, with redwood panels and painted grain-

---

ing. And shutters were used to cover the bay windows, instead of more fashionable (and expensive) drapes and curtains."

THAT WALLPAPER discovered on the fourth of July, however, appears to have been first class. It probably came by ship from San Francisco to Portland, and from there, overland to the Moore home. "The choice of wallpaper intrigues me," Millie says. "The first Mrs. Moore, Helen, had two boys, and we know one slept in this room and the other next door. So this was a boy's bedroom, yet the paper is gilded, with white flowers -- it looks like parlor paper.

"I HATE TO COVER it. I plan to frame a section of wall and have a plaque explaining it, to remember what the first Mrs. Moore chose."

HANGING ON to the past has become a full-time occupation for Millie. "When I first moved here in 1958, I wasn't paying attention to this old house, its details or character, or even the family stories. Then my mother-in-law found an old frame in the barn, had a mirror put in it, and gave it to me. From then on, saving the past became very important. I've been in every nook and cranny, piecing together what previous Moores thought and felt, living in and changing this house."

CHANGE IS PART of the house's tradition. The first major alteration occurred in the 1930s,

The neighbors rode by around 1900 to have their picture taken. The back porch visible at right was converted to a bath and later removed.

when David's father and uncle and their two families shared the house. A door was put up to separate the downstairs bedroom from the parlor, and that bedroom became the back kitchen. Today it contains the central furnace. The room still bears traces of original wallpaper.

A WALL WAS shifted to make the dining room bigger, and David's family lived in that part of the house. A pass-through from kitchen to dining room was closed; one pantry was made part of the kitchen. Part of the back porch was enclosed for a bathroom. And at some point, the summer kitchen was taken down. No

Millie Moore points to the wall and ceiling paper she uncovered on the fourth of July.

Every door in the house has a transom painted with a geometric design. This door, in the bay bedroom, also has its original painted grain.

one remembers what it looked like; only glimpses of it in old photos remain.

MILLIE learned all this from her mother-in-law, who has carried down family stories from earlier Mrs. Moores.

IN RESTORING the house, David and Millie have tried to respect their ancestors' tastes, although, Millie says with a laugh, "The first Mrs. Moore was the only one who had <u>everything</u> the way she wanted." In the parlor they removed the added door and kept the shutters. The plaster ornament, Millie says, "is different from the bay upstairs, and we wonder if it's original." (Some things about a house you never know, even if all the past occupants were family.)

THE OTHER restored room is the upstairs bay bedroom. The walnut bedroom set bought by the

Unlike the parlor, the bay bedroom has no ornamental brackets, just a simple moulded frame.

first Moores fills the room, and Helen Moore's tulip-pattern quilt covers the bed. "Only a few of the original pieces of furniture remain," Millie explains. "Most were loaned to a hotel which burned down in 1919." Unlike the rest of the house, this room still has original grained woodwork; elsewhere the graining has been painted over.

LIKE THOSE in the past, the current Moores have adapted the house to suit their needs. At the back of the house they built a wing with a dining room, hall, and two baths. "We removed the back porch, but I think our ancestors would understand," says Millie.

THEIR ANCESTORS would also understand their lives and loves. Family lore has it that Helen Moore loved cats. She had 35 of them.

The parlor has ornamental brackets around the bay window. Shutters, according to family stories, were the original window treatment.

The first Mrs. Moore, Helen, bought this bed and made the tulip-pattern quilt on top of it. That's Beauford, the Great Dane, sleeping at lower left.

Millie has considerably fewer, but dogs and cats are still at home here. Most Moore women have enjoyed handiwork, and Millie collects old linens.

THE MOORE MEN have all been ranchers. At first they were cattlemen. When the native prairie grass was gone, they became wheat ranchers like David. The wheat was harvested in late July, and Millie celebrated just as a past Mrs. Moore might have: She made curtains.

THE MOORES have planted trees around the house, to soften

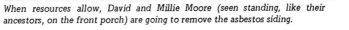

the rather barren landscape. Millie and David planted sunburst locusts -- one for each grandchild, one for the house's centennial. "The trees are our mark," says Millie.

THEY PLAN TO DO more for this old house. "If we had the resources, we'd first remove the

asbestos siding." They hope to repaint the windows and cornice next year, with several period colors, and rebuild the rotting front porch.

MOST IMPORTANTLY they hope they pass on their sense of history and appreciation of the house to their children, Julie and David John, and to David John's young children, who visit often. "They are interested in 'old things,'" explains Millie, "and we hope they'll want to preserve pieces of the past. Or those pieces will be lost.

When resources allow, David and Millie Moore (seen standing, like their ancestors, on the front porch) are going to remove the asbestos siding.

"BUT RIGHT NOW, I don't want to entrust the house's treasures to anyone else. You always think no one appreciates things as you do."

PROBABLY THE VERY sentiments of the first Mrs. Moore, as she admired her gold-and-white wallpaper, 104 years ago.

The worn carpet on the stairs is a last remnant of the house's original carpet. Note the brass dust corners, designed to make sweeping easier.

Millie Moore and friend Beauford stand before the front entry's ornate screen door and painted transom.

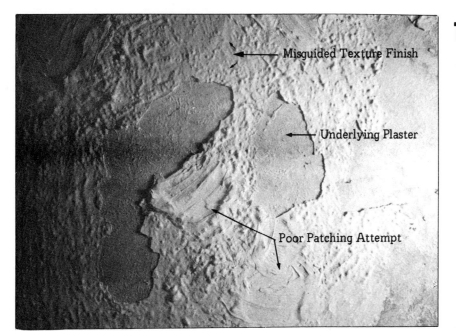

Misguided Texture Finish

Underlying Plaster

Poor Patching Attempt

UNWANTED TEXTURE FINISH

How To Get Rid Of It

by Bill O'Donnell

TEXTURE FINISHES have been around for centuries. In this country, they were most popular from the 'teens through the 1930s. In some parts of the country, the craze caught on to the point where splendid Victorian homes were slathered in a wall-to-wall coat of rough-textured finish -- decorative woodwork, ornamental plaster, and all. Worse, some homeowners were assured that a coat of texture finish would cure (hide) plaster failure. The extra weight only accelerated deterioration.

YOUR BUNGALOW, Tudor Revival house, or American Foursquare may have a perfectly appropriate, sound texture wall finish that you'll want to preserve. Alas, if not professionally applied to a well prepared surface, texture finish eventually fails. So even if you want to reapply a texture finish, it may be necessary to remove some or all of the existing finish.

What Is It?

THE FIRST THING to determine is what type of finish is on your walls. Before you can figure out how to take it off, it helps to know what it _is_. Victorian-era texture finishes were created simply by tooling the finish coat of plaster. It's not easy to texture the finish coat of plaster; a plasterer has to work fast and add lots of retarder to the mix. That's one reason why texture finishes were rare in the nineteenth century.

PLASTINT™ colored finishing plaster was a United States Gypsum product designed specifically for creating a rough, tinted finish. It had greater working time than conventional plasters. If the texture finish on your walls was produced by working the finish coat of plaster, it's going to be tough to remove. And even if you do remove it, you'll have to apply a new finish coat because only the brown coat will remain. Occasionally, a lime-based

product like Plastint was added over an existing finish coat. In that case, it will surely be weakly bonded, and may be removed using the steam method described below.

"PLASTIC PAINTS" BECAME POPULAR in the 'twenties. These formulations were essentially precursors to joint compound. They provided greater working time than finish plasters, and so required less skill on the part of the craftsman to impart the desired texture. The November 1922 issue of American Builder featured an article on this new and innovative wall finish. In it, the author said, "... a new plastic preparation is becoming increasing popular because of the unlimited variety of texture and color effects it offers. This material is neither a paint nor a plaster, but has the qualities of both.... The present day trend toward a permanent textured wall has brought a marked popularity to this product."

A texture finish — definitely unwanted!

IN THE YEARS that followed, several companies introduced their own "plastic paint" products. Perhaps the best known was United States Gypsum's Textone™ -- still available today. One caution: Many of these products contained asbestos. Morene Products Co., for example, described their wall finish as being "composed of Atlas white portland cement, sand, asbestos, oils and chemicals, all ingredients being so mixed and the oils so emulsified that they remain in solution."

TO BE SAFE, send a sample of your texture finish to a laboratory to test for the presence of asbestos. Any building inspector can tell you where to send a sample for testing in your area. Asbestos removal requires special procedures and precautions, the details of which will be the subject of an upcoming article.

Spending the day with a wall steamer and putty knife is no joy, but these simple tools will remove most texture finishes effectively.

"SAND PAINTS" were also used to create textured wall finishes. Sand paints had abrasive ingredients added to produce a stippled effect when applied with a brush or roller. Because they are in fact paints, they can be removed using standard paint removal procedures.

Removing the Texture

EXPERIMENTATION is the first step when you're trying to remove an unknown finish. But if you think you know what the finish is, there are some "best bets" you can try. If you experiment with all of the following techniques and still have no success, don't despair; you don't necessarily have to demolish all the plaster to remove the finish. You can cover over the finish by skim-coating with joint compound, laminating with gypsum board, or applying metal lath and replastering. We'll cover these "hide it" methods last.

The finish falls off in wet chunks — no dust is created.

Steaming It Off

MOST LIME-BASED and "plastic paint" texture coatings will succumb to steam. Albeit time-consuming, hot and sweaty, the procedure is uncomplicated. The trick is to work carefully so you don't damage the underlying plaster, and so that you get the majority of the texture finish off in the first pass.

WALL STEAMERS ARE AVAILABLE for rent at rental services, hardware stores, and building suppliers that rent equipment to contractors. They're most often used for removing wallpaper. A wall steamer is essentially a large electric teapot. A heating element boils water in a reservoir and the resultant steam is channeled through a hose to a perforated metal pan. Some of the steam condenses and collects in the pan, so keep a bucket handy to pour the condensate into -- even if you've thoroughly masked the floor.

WEAR HEAVY, gauntlet-type gloves when using the steamer. Let the steam do the work. Hold the pan tight to the wall until the finish is saturated. Move the pan down a couple of inches and scrape the loose finish above the pan away with a putty knife. (Use a file to round the corners of the putty knife -- that way it will be less likely to gouge the underlying plaster.) Keep the steamer pan against the next patch of the wall while you're scraping; there's no point wasting time and electricity.

CONTINUE SCRAPING the wall from the top down. You'll find that the finish will become increasingly easy to remove as you near the bottom of the wall. The condensed steam that runs down the wall softens the texture finish further down. Be thorough -- little blobs of remaining texture finish will come back to haunt you. It's easier to remove the stuff now, while it's soft, than it will be after the steamer is shut off.

Use a "combat chisel" on the remaining finish.

Wear a dust mask.

Use a taper's sanding stick for greater reach.

SOME ADDITIONAL WORK is needed after steaming. Go back over areas where texture finish remains with a "combat chisel." A combat chisel is one that's been retired from your fine woodworking toolbox but still is capable of holding a reasonably sharp edge. Hold the chisel at a flat angle to avoid digging into the wall. Most of the remaining finish should pop off the wall fairly easily.

NEXT, KNOCK OFF pimples and high spots with a quick sanding. Wet sanding is preferable to avoid creating a lot of irritating dust. Don't attempt a mirror-smooth surface; you're going to have to apply a skim coat of joint compound anyway. Just give the wall a quick once-over to remove the little bits of debris that are stuck to the wall. Rinse the wall thoroughly with plenty of clean water and a sponge to remove any chalky residue. Powdery traces of the old finish will interfere with the bond of joint compound or paint.

FINALLY, APPLY a couple of thin coats of joint compound over the wall with a 10- or 12-inch taping knife (as described on page 377). Joint compound fills in the nicks where the putty knife scarred the soft plaster surface, and covers over slight protrusions that remain adhered to the wall. If the wall didn't come as clean as you hoped, several coats of compound may be required. Tape cracks in the plaster with cloth mesh joint tape.

Removing Sand Paint

SAND PAINT can be removed from plaster by the same techniques used to remove any thick paint film from plaster. Because sand paint is applied in one or more <u>thick</u> coats, heat stripping works well. Just make sure to file the sharp edges off your putty knife, and scrape gently. After using the heat plate on plaster, chemical cleanup is usually not required. Any residual bits of melted paint can be easily knocked off the plaster with a putty knife or chisel.

Stripping Mouldings

UNVEILING TEXTURED or paint-encrusted plaster mouldings is a more difficult chore. Hardest of all is cast plaster: those elements that have sculptural detail, such as dentils, egg-and-dart moulding, medallions, etc. If you can take the mouldings off the wall or ceiling, the job is simplified somewhat, but there is always the danger of damaging the mouldings during disassembly. Unless you must remove the mouldings for another purpose, we recommend stripping them in place.

FOR LIME-BASED and "plastic paint" finishes, use a wall steamer. Disconnect the pan from the hose so you can point the steam from the hose directly where you need it. As the finish starts to soften, remove it carefully as described below.

FOR SAND-PAINT-encrusted mouldings, use chemical paint remover. Even when you buy paste-type removers, additional thickening is desirable. A good thickener is Cab-O-Sil, a fumed silica made by Cabot Corp. of Boston. (It's available at some art supply dealers and through epoxy distributors.) Fumed silica is extremely irritating to the respiratory tract. Be sure to use caution and wear a fine-particle mask when handling it. Less effective alternatives to Cab-O-Sil include cornstarch and whiting. Add thickener until the stripper is nearly the consistency of Jello.

COVER THE MOULDING with polyethylene sheeting after the stripper is applied. This will allow the stripper to work longer, permitting it to soften the sand paint even in the deepest grooves. Once the paint is soft, you've got to get it off -- this is the hard part. Experiment with small chisels, awls, sculptor's tools, dentil picks, and anything else you can think of to gently dig the slime out of the moulding's recesses. Soft bristle and polypropylene brushes also work well. Remember, the underlying plaster is easy to gouge or otherwise disfigure, so be patient.

All loose texture finish has been removed and the wall has been rinsed; now the first coat of joint compound can be applied.

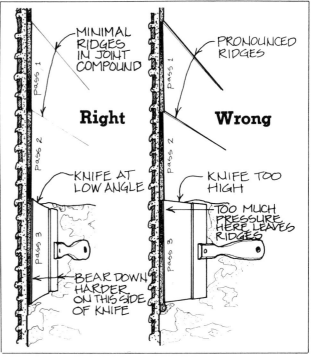

How to skim.

Covering It Up

IF YOU'VE TRIED STEAM, heat, chemical re-movers, and mechanical scraping, but you still can't remove the finish without damaging the plaster, you've got two choices: demolish the wall and replaster, or cover the finish with another material. Unless there's already substantial plaster failure, demolishing and replastering is to be avoided. It's only cost effective if fifty percent or more of the plaster is damaged.

THERE ARE SEVERAL WAYS to cover a texture finish. The least labor-intensive method is to laminate the walls with gypsum board (Sheetrock). Knock off the highest spots on the walls and screw the gypsum board into the studs right through the existing plaster. This method has the disadvantage of changing moulding profiles a bit and eliminating the hand-worked, wavy appearance of plaster. Both of these negative effects can be minimized by using 1/4" Sheetrock, though. Gypsum board of this thickness will flex enough to follow the undulations of the plaster somewhat. It will also alter moulding profiles less than thicker gypsum boards. If necessary, you can remove and reset baseboards, cap mouldings, and casings. It may be necessary to deepen window and door jambs to accommodate the extra wall thickness.

A BETTER WAY to cover most texture finishes is this: "Replaster" over the top of it with joint compound. This low-tech solution requires the least expensive materials, but is quite labor-intensive. Skim coating itself goes fast, but preparing the surface to accept and hold the joint compound is especially

time-consuming. The smallest area of badly-adhered texture finish will fail in very short order following the addition of a skim coat. So it's imperative that all poorly bonded texture finish be scraped clean with a combat chisel. The entire wall must also be tho-roughly washed to remove any chalky residue or dirt prior to skim coating.

FILL IN all the nicks and scratches first, using a six-inch taping knife. Joint compound must be completely dry before you can apply another coat. Apply the first skim coat horizontally working from the top of the wall down. Put pressure on the dry side of the knife (the lower edge) as you move across the wall. That way, the knife won't create ridges in the wet compound. Small overlap marks will be all that remains. Apply the second coat vertically, again bearing down on only one side of the knife. By putting each successive coat on perpendicular to the previous one, you'll eliminate the overlap marks, and make the wall flatter.

YOU CAN BUILD OUT joint compound to a thick-ness of about 1/4", so it can be used to cover even high-relief finishes. But you can only apply joint compound to a thickness of about 1/16" at a time -- any thicker and it will shrink and crack. Therefore, it's time-consuming to skim over an especially bumpy surface. Another option is to screw wire lath directly over the texture finish, and replas-ter on top of it. Plastering over the exist-ing surface will add quite a bit of thickness to the walls and drastically change moulding profiles, though. The only expense saved with this method is the cost of demolishing the existing plaster, which is relatively inexpensive, so you're better off starting from scratch.

"Where Do I Start?"

*A familiar question to anyone who has faced
the sheer volume of work to be done
and the complexity of sorting out priorities.
Whether you're a new owner paralyzed by indecision,
or well along in a restoration that could benefit
from others' experience, here's how to preserve
house, budget, and sanity.*

by Jonathan Poore and Patricia Poore

Setting your priorities and making a plan depends on budget, time available, occupancy of the building, and scope of work. The 'plan of attack' that follows presents not only the *when to*, but also the *why to.*

● Unless otherwise stated, the following guidelines assume that the house is occupied during renovation or restoration.

● To avoid expensive and frustrating work stoppage in mid-stream, obtain all necessary permits *before* starting work. Don't be unprepared when the building inspector pays a surprise visit.

● If the job involves more than cosmetic work, consider hiring an architect and/or a general contractor. They have more experience in sequencing a job, they know what permits are necessary and how to get them, and they know whom to hire. Having a professional run the job will certainly save you time and will probably save you money in the long run. An architect can help you plan your restoration even if you intend to do the work in phases. If major structural work is needed, consult an engineer.

one

STABILIZE, PROTECT, AND SECURE

against ongoing and potential property damage or personal injury. In other words: Protect your investment.

NOTE: Stop exterior deterioration before going on to the interior.

A. STABILIZE or REPAIR ongoing damage or deterioration.

1. "Stabilize" is quite different from "repair." To stabilize is to arrest deterioration. To repair is to eliminate previous damage. Decide in every case whether to stabilize only (stop further damage) and defer repair -- or whether it makes more sense to go ahead with a complete and proper repair.
    a. Inspect exterior for suspected water penetration -- the number one enemy. Exterior leaks eventually cause interior damage.
    b. Fix obvious leaks and water penetration, including downspout problems, etc.
    c. Inspect for and exterminate termites and other wood-destroying insects.

2. Be sure that a temporary repair does not cause more damage (long term) than it prevents (short term). If the temporary repair will be expensive -- or if it could cause additional damage -- it would be better to do a proper repair immediately. EXAMPLE: Leaking roof presents potential for continuing and more serious damage due to water penetration. Condition can be STABILIZED with temporary methods, such as removable caulking and cheap

aluminum or asphalt flashing. <u>But</u>: Roof cement on salvageable slates will ruin the slates, though it may temporarily stop the leak. A temporary repair should always be reversible.

B. PROTECT building elements and occupants from <u>potential</u> damage

---

1. Eliminate fire hazards:
   a. exposed or otherwise improper wiring
   b. overloaded electrical circuits
   c. any questions: have a thorough electrical inspection by a licensed electrician
   d. Inspect and repair boiler and chimney (to prevent carbon monoxide build-up, chimney fires, etc.)

2. Eliminate additional personal injury hazards such as:
   a. broken steps
   b. electrical shock hazards
   c. badly bowed or falling plaster; falling building elements
   d. immediate, blatant health hazards such as friable (loose, crumbly) asbestos, airborne lead dust from chipped paint

---

C. SECURE against the loss or damage of historic elements

---

1. Secure loose building parts such as stained glass panels, ornamental plaster

2. Secure building against break-in, vandalism, theft of architectural elements

3. Completely mask floors and unpainted woodwork before the dirty work starts

two

MAKE A RECORD AND CLEAN FIRST
before removing anything or making changes

A. DOCUMENT the entire building before you change anything

---

1. Take photographs of all exterior and interior conditions. Be sure to get all views of each facade and of each room.

2. Important: You will want a full account of all your work -- not only to look back on the job when it's done, but also for clues to reassembly, decoration, etc., during the course of the project.

3. Also, if you decide to nominate the building for listing in the National Register, this documentation will be required.

B. CLEAN everything before you make any decisions regarding what's "unsalvageable."

---

1. Cleaning takes care of the basic homeowner's need to "do something" to make the house your own -- without getting you into trouble. It is almost always a necessity. It's an excellent way to get intimate with the building -- to go over every inch and get to know the details.

2. Cleaning an object or area and its surroundings often changes your opinion about what should stay and what should go. Quite often, your initial reaction to a material or condition is colored by the dirt and disrepair you find it in. It's tempting to just "get rid of it." But once the area is clean and the general surroundings have been brought up to a consistent level of cleanliness and repair, what was once "old and dirty" becomes "old and interesting."

EXAMPLE: You've moved into a 1930s house with a mud room that has its original inlaid linoleum floor. Your first reaction is disgust, and the linoleum floor is a symbol of how dirty and out-of-date the room is. But don't tear out the floor yet! Sure, it looks dismal in the context of the crumbling, institutional green walls, the grease-stained, painted woodwork, the filthy windows. Nevertheless, mask the floor before you strip woodwork, patch and paint walls, and clean windows. Now uncover the floor -- it doesn't look nearly as bad. Remove the years of dirty, yellowed wax, scrub the floor, and give it a thin coat of a good wax. The old-fashioned, richly colored linoleum has a patina (almost like aged leather), and the inlaid border, you've learned, is a period detail that can't be reproduced today. Once you see the overall effect, you realize that this linoleum floor is exactly what should be in a 1930s mud room. And to think you almost got rid of it the week you moved in!

3. <u>Don't rush</u> and don't make any irreversible decisions until you've lived in the house a while. Learn what the house has to offer. See if your tastes begin to change.

4. Under no circumstances should you throw money at the house (by hiring a general contractor before planning, rushing to buy replacement materials, etc.). People strapped for money very often do a better restoration job because they have time to think.

three

MAKE A MASTER PLAN
now that you and the house are in no immediate peril -- and you've unearthed character from beneath the soot and filth.

● This is the single most important step; if you don't plan ahead, it will cost you to change your mind, you will regret your

---

early work on the house, you will waste time and money. Do not start in on a room or a project, no matter how limited it may seem, before you've got an overall plan.

● If you need help with the sequence/plan, design work, mechanical systems, structural problems, or finding and scheduling outside contractors, this is the time to hire an architect.

● The goal is to save money over the long haul, to be as efficient as possible about money and time.

NOTE: The following areas of work must all be considered in making a plan. They are interrelated and they overlap. For that reason, you must think through each phase of work before you can finalize the master plan and complete the work in a logical sequence.

A. STRUCTURAL WORK is high on the list of priorities:

---

1. It represents a relatively major cost.

2. It requires that conditions be open and quite often affects more than just the immediate area of work. Plaster, woodwork, door and window operation may be affected by jacking, sill replacement, footings, etc.

3. Repair of structural deficiency may also be important for personal safety.

4. Start with the foundation and sills and work your way up through the building, correcting structural conditions. Don't fix a structural problem at the roof and then jack the house up from the cellar -- everything will shift.

5. Structural work is hard to do in phases -- this is not recommended.

B. REDUCE OPERATING COSTS if you can get a substantial or fast return on your investment.

---

1. Energy savings
a. For old buildings, cost effective measures involve tightening envelope against infiltration: caulking, weatherstripping.
b. Deal with the old windows: repair, double-glazing, storms, night insulation? Replacement windows may be necessary, but consider their payback period (probably a long time) and aesthetic impact of replacements.
c. Evaluate heating plant and system. Upgrade or replace depending on efficiency and ongoing maintenance costs.
d. Evaluate domestic hot-water system.
e. Insulation may be cost effective (attic or roof surely; side walls and basement in some cases).

NOTE: Energy upgrading is difficult to do in phases (with exception of weatherstrip

and windows) because it involves whole systems, rather than individual pieces, and because it often requires opening up walls. Therefore, energy upgrading should be done early, and a good-size budget must be allowed.

2. Think ahead to maintenance cycles (especially for exterior materials):
a. Before making fundamental decisions such as to repaint the exterior, consider cost-effectiveness of waiting and changing the system: Instead of scraping and repainting a bad surface, would it be better to strip to bare wood and perhaps change to a heavy-bodied, non-peeling stain? If so, don't waste money painting now -- prime bare areas only.
b. Anticipate and avoid unnecessary future costs: If a slate roof is to be salvaged but the steel nails are rusting out, don't wait until the slates begin falling to the pavement. That adds material cost (new slates) to your renovation.
c. When replacing materials, match lifespans within a system. For example, don't use 10-year flashing with your 25-year roofing; don't fasten siding that could last 75 years with steel fasteners that last 15.

C. THE ROOF is primary protection from the weather:

---

1. Even if you made temporary stabilization repairs to stop leaks, deal with the roof permanently before going on to interior finishes.

2. Although the roof is expensive and not particularly glamourous, it will save you money and tremendous time in the long run to fix it first. One of Murphy's Old-House Laws is that an old roof <u>will</u> leak without warning as soon as you've completed interior plaster restoration.

3. Consider the time of year. If the roof starts leaking from an ice dam in the middle of winter, you can't do much about it till spring.

4. Sitework: While you fix the roof and related water-directing components (gutters etc.), attend to regrading, drainage, and foundation waterproofing as necessary.

D. MECHANICAL SYSTEMS -- plumbing, heating, and electrical are high on any priority list for several reasons:

---

1. They are central to the comfort and practicality of the house

2. Systems repair or replacement are high-ticket items which must be paid for early on, to help determine what's left in the budget for finishes

3. Work on these systems requires that walls, floors, and ceilings be opened up, so they must be tackled before any finish work. ("Finish work" means more than decorative finishes -- it means anything that covers the framing, including plaster.)

4. It is best not to work on mechanical systems in phases. It is often inefficient and adds cost for contractor call-backs. But if budget dictates, or if you are doing all work yourself, consider phasing it this way: Do all the roughing for mechanical systems first so that you can close up walls. Install plumbing and electrical risers in this first stage. Once the systems are in the walls, add bathrooms or kitchens (designed earlier, installed later) as budget allows.

EXAMPLE: Someday you'll want a small guest suite in the unused third floor. A bathroom up there will require a new plumbing riser to run up all three storeys, making a mess on all floors. Better to do it now, and close up the walls. The bathroom fittings and fixtures can then be installed at a later date without any disturbance in the rest of the house.

5. Think ahead to <u>lighting</u>. So often lighting is overlooked until the end of a project, when it is thought of as part of furnishing the room. It's important to consider placement of chandeliers and sconces before the plaster is repaired.

E. LIVABILITY, or Health, Safety, and Sanity ... crucial issues if you live in the house during renovation. In planning, consider measures that improve the livability of the house, even before demolition or repair begins on the inside.

---

1. Health
   a. Do whatever is required to avoid eating and sleeping in a dusty atmosphere.
      1) Do the work all at once to avoid prolonged exposure (rather than letting it drag on).
      2) Hire a contractor if necessary to expedite this work.
   b. Ditto to avoid chemical fumes such as paint strippers, paints, finishes, and cleansers.
   c. If the work cannot be finished quickly, then do whatever is required to isolate the work site from eating, sleeping, and active living areas. Hang heavy plastic tarps, tape up doors, build temporary partitions and hang temporary doors.
   d. If necessary, plan a phased approach that will allow you an undisturbed living area at all times.

2. Safety
   a. Any work which creates a new hazardous condition should be done quickly, especially if children are present. (For example: porch deck replacement, stair and rail reconstruction, window rehabilitation.)
   b. Build or provide temporary decking, safety rails, etc., required for safety.

3. Sanity

● Remember: You and other members of the household have to live through this renovation. Weigh priorities accordingly.

   a. Demolition: Try to complete demolition all at once as this is usually the dirtiest, dustiest, most physically disruptive, most psychologically disturbing part of any job. This is especially true for interior plaster demolition -- get it over with.
   b. First do those areas that are most important to you emotionally. Renovation always takes longer than you ever imagined, so don't set yourself up to "do without." If cooking at home is central in your life, do the kitchen first.

---

four

SEQUENCE FOR EXTERIOR RESTORATION

NOTE: Not all of the following will apply in every case, and there are exceptions to every general principle. But this list is the standard order for proceeding with work on the outside of the building -- after inspection, stabilization, and planning.

A. DEMOLITION and removal of debris

B. STABILIZATION of deterioration and repair of serious damage, including wood, masonry, and metal. (Stop further deterioration; see section I.)

C. STRUCTURAL WORK from the bottom to the top including chimneys and masonry. Insulate or waterproof as required while conditions are open.

D. SITEWORK including regrading, drainage, waterproofing

E. ROOF REPAIR OR REPLACEMENT; flashing, gutters, vents

F. PAINT STRIPPING: masonry, wood, metal

G. MASONRY repairs and repointing; large-scale wood and metal repairs and replacement

---

H. WINDOW, SASH, DOOR repairs

I. STAINING or priming

J. CAULKING, glazing, puttying

K. PAINTING

L. CLEAN-UP and labelling; storage of maintenance items

NEXT MONTH: These guidelines conclude with the sequence for *interior* renovation, and a discussion of phasing the job.

THE GREAT AMERICAN GARAGE

··PART TWO··

BY J. RANDALL COTTON

LAST MONTH'S article traced the development of the American garage. Here, we'll explore the detached garage in terms of overall shape, style, construction materials, and details. If you're about to undertake the major reconstruction of an old garage -- or if you intend to design and build a period garage to complement your old house -- this article offers food for thought.

YOU CAN, of course, go all the way and remodel an unattractive or dilapidated garage to be more in sympathy with the style of the house. But if the garage is in good shape and interesting in its own right -- even if it doesn't "match" your house -- consider just keying its paint colors to the house. Or, if its modern door is what looks most out of place, consider installing an old-fashioned one. If you have no garage at all and want to build one, you have several design options:

(1) The "carriage house" garage, which is appropriate only for houses that predate the automobile;
(2) The go-with-anything "utilitarian" garage;
(3) The "like house, like garage" approach, which takes its style cues from the house.

TO EDUCATE yourself on what's most appropriate, drive around. Take walks in neighborhoods with houses of the same vintage as yours. See what survives -- don't overlook alleys and side streets. Become aware of local use of materials, roof shapes, door styles, and ornamental details. If the local library or historical society keeps archival photos, go look at them. Check out the garage designs in antique builders' guides (like the ones pictured in the September issue of OHJ).

The Utilitarian Garage

THE "GENERIC" OR UTILITARIAN GARAGE was and is the most prevalent type. This is basic shelter for the automobile. Go for simplicity and functional design. Using traditional building materials and, if you like, an old-fashioned door will make the garage look timeless rather than obviously modern.

TO BE SURE, the garages on the grounds of turn-of-the-century estates were large and well equipped. They often housed a workshop,

a pit, a car-wash area, and an apartment for the caretaker/chauffeur. But in general, early garages were smaller than modern ones, which must accommodate larger cars and almost always provide storage space. Early garages were 10 to 12 feet wide (each bay), by 18 to 20 feet deep, with an 8-foot-high by 8-foot-wide door. If you can work within these guidelines, your new garage will have traditional proportions. If that's impractical, increase the depth, as this has less visual impact than if you were to change the width or height. For a multi-car garage, use separate doors for each bay, rather than the single, double-wide door common today.

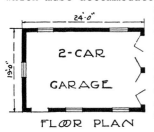

FLOOR PLAN

Like House, Like Garage

ANOTHER APPROACH is to build a garage that closely matches the main house. Because this approach requires more design skill and usually more money, style-conscious garages have never been as common as the utilitarian boxes. But many of the old garages that survive intact are the high-style type -- they undoubtedly survive precisely because they're special. This approach is certainly more fun.

FOR A VICTORIAN HOUSE, you might go a step further and make the garage look like a carriage house or other contemporary out-building. Such a design copies existing out-buildings that quietly changed function as time went on. It may seem strange to purposely construct a new garage that looks like a carriage house which outlived its original function. But this is the right approach for people who dislike anachronism.

AN APPEALING WAY to link the house and the garage -- visually as well as physically -- is with a connecting structure such as covered walkway, pergola, or wall. Breezeways were popular for Colonial Revival houses, pergolas for Bungalows and Spanish-style houses. (See April 1984 OHJ for notes on pergola construction.) Low walls create a "compound" reminiscent of medieval towns and were popular for Tudor and Norman Revival houses. Better to use an architect to design a sensitive connector between old house and new garage.

TO ASSURE a strong relationship between the house and a new garage, consider the possibilities of salvaged materials. Using old windows or doors, and even siding or roofing, gives a new building instant patina -- particularly important for a new structure that will be in close proximity to an old one. Old garages are (unfortunately) most often

The many intersecting gables on this Dutch Colonial Revival house...

...are mimicked on its garage.

A fancy Victorian carriage house has been converted into a multi-car garage. The row of small windows along the side once lit horse stalls.

The National Mill & Lumber Company offered this "roomy" 10x18 garage in 1915 for $115.

viewed as inadequate, beyond repair, even ugly -- so they are torn down and replaced. Be on the lookout for a soon-to-be-demolished garage and offer to take doors, windows, and hardware off the owner's hands. But don't expect to find garage parts at salvage dealers -- yet.

Construction Material

ALTHOUGH EARLY GARAGES commonly had load-bearing masonry walls of brick, stone, and concrete, balloon-framing was and still is more prevalent. Ordinary construction -- 2x4 stud walls on a concrete slab -- is the easy, economical choice. The walls can be clad in a variety of historical finishes such as clapboard, board-and-batten, stucco, metal panels,

The utilitarian garage can match any house, given similar body and trim colors.

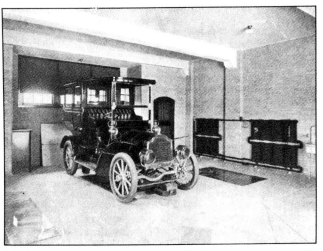

Early garages (this one dates from 1907) were equipped with plumbing, heating, lighting, and repair pits.

The garage is incorporated into this French Norman house's walled "compound," an imitation of medieval gathered outbuildings.

Classical pillars, tucked under the eaves, give this circa 1915 garage a Colonial Revival look, as does the coat of white paint.

wood shingles, or brick or stone veneers. Matching the wall finish of the house is the logical choice. Like houses, garages sometimes had a variety of siding materials; for example, clapboard or decorative concrete block at the base with wood shingles above window-sill height.

UTILITARIAN GARAGES were made of the common and inexpensive materials of the day. Particularly popular was concrete block and hollow tile (terra-cotta), both of which were frequently stuccoed. In fact, stucco (applied over metal or wood lath in frame construction) was one of the most common of all garage finishes and would be appropriate for old-fashioned garages today. Tinting the stucco was a common practice.

CONCRETE WAS a popular building material because it's fireproof. Both concrete block (stuccoed) and poured, reinforced concrete are traditional garage materials still used today. (A concrete mix recommended for garage walls in 1910: 1 part cement, 2-1/2 parts sand, 5 parts one-inch crushed stone.) Two other good materials, hollow terra-cotta block and pressed metal siding, aren't as common today as they used to be, but they are still available (see Sources on page 390). Pressed metal siding is stamped in imitation rock-face, brick, and shingle designs, is easy to work with, and can be painted.

Roofs

FROM GABLE TO MANSARD, all the popular roof shapes used for houses were used for garages. The more utilitarian garages had gable, hip, shed, or flat roofs. Fancier garages copied the roof of the house. Roof pitch was generally steeper than that of modern garages.

BY MIMICKING the main house's roof shape, pitch, and material, a new garage gains compatibility. Garage roofs were historically covered with standing-seam metal, clay tiles,

Gable front

Gable side

Hip

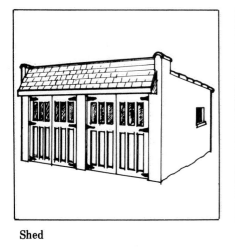

Shed

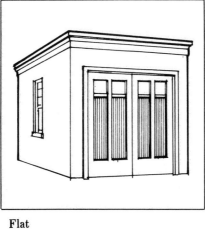

Flat

Gambrel

Folding doors like these are typical on 1920s garages. The inner doors swing out, the pairs of outer doors fold out.

Built into an embankment behind the house, the three-bay garage has cross-braced doors with matchboard panels.

or shingles made of asphalt, slate, wood, cement, or tin -- all still available.

EAVE DETAILS are very important. In the first 20 years of this century, utilitarian garages generally had open eaves with exposed rafter tails. Garages with more style had eaves and cornices finished in a manner similar to the architecture of the house. For example, a Colonial Revival garage might have a moulded box cornice, while one in the Prairie style would have a wide overhang with a finished soffit. Late Victorian carriage-houses-turned-garages often had bracketed eaves or bargeboards.

OTHER ROOF DETAILS to consider are dormers, cupolas, vents, cresting, and copings (for parapet-wall roofs). Where appropriate, any of the above could be used in remodelling a modern garage.

Details and Ornament

BESIDES ROOF and cornice details, period garages picked up other ornamentation from the main house. For example, Tudor Revival garages had false half-timbering in the gable over the door. Colonial Revival garages often had a semi-circular, round, or oval window in the gable, along with a boxed cornice and cornerboards. Vines grew on wall trellises or pergola-like canopies extending from the eaves of Craftsman-inspired garages.

COLOR IS the one way to get quick results. Simply put, even the most blatantly modern garage achieves a measure of compatibility if painted the same colors as the house. Whatever is historically appropriate (in terms of color and placement of colors) for the style and era of your house is also best for the garage.

Taking the "like house, like garage" approach to extremes, this Bungalow appears to have given birth. The garage is a scaled-down replica of the house.

A wing with bedroom and garage adds yet another gable to this Tudor Revival house's irregular roofline. Note the half-timbering that copies the house's main gable.

IF YOU'RE PLANNING a multi-color paint scheme, the various elements on the garage -- cornice, trim, window sash and frames -- should be picked out with a color that complements the body color. If the body of the garage is stucco, use light earth tones or pastels on the trim. A utilitarian material like concrete looks best in stone-y natural colors such as grey. Wood-shingle siding should be stained a natural color or painted dark green, brown, or grey. Half-timbering should be emphasized with light/dark color contrast. Colonial Revival garages were meant to be painted classical white, palest grey, or cream.

THE PANELS on the garage door were usually painted the body color, while the stiles, braces, etc., were given a complementary trim color. (For a quick fix, a modern door would benefit from such a paint scheme.)

Windows

A WORD ON WINDOWS before we describe old-fashioned garage doors: Use them. Windows provide light and ventilation and an easy way to "dress up" the garage in period style. Because you're not matching an existing window opening, inexpensive stock units are fine. Again, consider salvage materials too.

WINDOWS ALONG the side walls should be compatible with the age and style of the house. For example, casement windows are best for French- or English-inspired architecture. Use banded (horizontal) windows for a Prairie-style garage. For the simpler old-fashioned garage, the following do nicely: 4-, 6-, or 9-pane windows for rectangular fixed sash; 2/2, 4/4, 6/6 for double-hung sash ... or use 6, 4, or 2 panes in upper sash over a single lower pane.

The Garage Door

THE MOST IMPORTANT ELEMENT in garage design is the door. The door expresses the function of the structure, and it defines age and style. An old-fashioned door will make a garage look old. Modern doors just don't have the right look. Do be forewarned, though: An old-style door will not be as convenient and will require more maintenance. (Then again, some things are more important than practicality.)

EARLY GARAGE DOORS were made of wood. They usually had glass panels and they were no more than one bay wide. On multi-car garages, identical doors were placed side by side. The way the door opened has changed over the years. Before 1920, double-leaf swinging doors were the most common, but since then the advantages of sectionalized, overhead roll-up doors have made them the most popular.

SWINGING DOORS or simple board-and-batten or cross-braced construction are the easiest and cheapest to reproduce. There is still a wide range of appropriate barn-door type hardware available, including strap hinges. However, swinging doors are clumsy to operate (especially when there's snow on the ground) and they aren't very weathertight. Roll-up doors are easier to open and also offer better security. Although overhead door units are widely available today, finding one that has the right look is difficult; many are now aluminum or vinyl-clad. On page 390, we've listed a few sources of wooden overhead doors.

PERHAPS THE BEST SOLUTION is sliding or folding accordion doors, or a combination of both. These were very popular during the 'teens and '20s. The door units slide on tracks which can be built different ways to accommodate various widths; they can also be arranged to both slide and fold. Several companies still make these doors and the hardware for them.

Though this masonry garage is not high style, it befits the Dutch Colonial Revival house. A fanlight ornaments the gable.

Medieval-style diamond panes and a dark-and-light color scheme make a garage look Tudor. The driveway faces a side street around the corner from the house.

THE TYPICAL early garage door was panelled, regardless of how it opened. The top row or next-to-top row of panels were often glazed. Standard rectangular panes, as well as round-headed windows or diamond-patterned configurations, were used.

THE SOLID PANELS below the glass were sometimes recessed and flat, particularly after the 1920s. Earlier designs were more decorative. Raised panels befitted Colonial Revival garages and long, narrow panels looked at home on Craftsman and English types. Many garage doors had cross-braced ("barn door") panels.

TONGUE-AND-GROOVE WAINSCOT (also called matchboards or porch-ceiling lumber) was popular for door panels, too. Matchboards were usually applied vertically, but I've seen decorative, diagonally-laid matchboards as well. Cross-braces over the matchboard gives the barn-door appearance that was so popular on early garages. Today, a carpenter can build panels of exterior-grade matchboard lumber. Sold at many lumberyards, it's available with or without a beaded edge.

A MODERN GARAGE DOOR can be improved by adding mouldings to the panels. On a later door that has no glazing, you can replace a row of panels with window glass.

THIS ARTICLE and the previous one have described the evolution of the American garage, its styles and materials and its place in history. From the converted Queen Anne carriage house to the rock-faced concrete-block shed of the '30s, the sub-plot of the garage accompanies the greater story told through the changing architecture of our old houses.

WE HOPE you've gained an appreciation of those old garages that sit in rear alleys and on back lots -- and that you've gotten a good idea where to begin if you're designing a compatible garage today.

Swinging

Folding

Person-sized "wicket" door in folding door

Sectional overhead (roll-up)

Swing-up

Sliding door with diagonally-laid matchboard panels, designed to resemble a barn door.

ELEMENTS OF STYLE

HOUSE STYLE	ROOF SHAPE	ROOF MATERIAL	CONSTRUCTION MATERIALS	DETAILS & ORNAMENT	DOOR TYPES	COLOR SCHEMES
Colonial Revival (includes Dutch Col. Rev. & Georgian Rev.)	gable front gable side hip gambrel (for Dutch Col. Rev.)	slate wood or asphalt shingle	clapboard brick brick veneer stone wood shingle	boxed cornice, dormers, shutters, corner boards, pedimented gable, pilasters round, oval, or semi-circular windows in gable kick (flared) eaves (Dutch Col. Rev.)	raised or flat panels strap hinges multi-pane lights	Frame: white, pale yellow, ivory, silver grey Trim: white Shutters: dark green Shingles: natural, dark brown, grey
English period revivals (includes Tudor, English Cottage)	steep gable clipped gable hip with gable peak	slate wood shingle rolled asphalt ("thatch") shingle	stucco over hollow tile, concrete block, or lath wood shingle brick stone	half-timbering in gables tall, grouped casement windows on sides low walls adjoining house	vertical board construction, i.e., board and batten diamond-patterned lights decorated iron strap hinges	Stucco: off-white, buff Shingles: natural, dark brown Brick: dark red, brown Stone: grey, brown Trim: dark brown, grey
Spanish & Mediterranean revivals	flat shed low hip parapet	terra cotta or metal tile	rough stucco over hollow tile, block, or lath concrete	open eaves, curvilinear facade, parapets, side portals, pergolas, grillework arched windows and doors casement windows decorative tile insets	board-and-batten construction arched lights	Stucco: white or pastel Trim: dark, earth tones
French revivals (includes Norman, Chateau)	high hip pyramidal clipped gable	slate wood, asbestos, or cement shingle	stone brick stucco over tile, block, or lath	shallow, boxed eaves, sometimes flared low walls adjoining house casement windows	diamond-patterned lights panels	Stucco: cream, grey Brick, stone: natural Trim: dark brown, grey
Craftsman (Rustic, Bungalow, etc.)	low, broad gable hip	wood shingle tile	wood shingle stucco	open eaves with exposed rafter ends, sometimes upturned lattices, pergolas, window boxes, vines, eyebrow dormers	diagonally-laid matchboard in panels cross-bracing	Shingles: natural or stained grey or brown Stucco: earth tones
Prairie	low hip broad gable flat	asphalt shingle roll or built-up flat roof	smooth stucco on tile, block, or lath concrete Roman brick	wide, overhanging eaves with finished soffits; wide, flat cornice boards high, horizontally-banded windows horizontal bands of flat trim boards	flat panels diamond-shaped or rectangular lights	Stucco: cream, light grey Shingles: natural Trim: stained dark
Utilitarian	any; especially shed, gable, hip, or flat	any; especially asphalt shingle & metal	any; particularly hollow tile, stucco, ornamental concrete block, pressed metal, or asbestos shingle on frame	little if any ornament	Keep it simple.	Nothing flamboyant!

  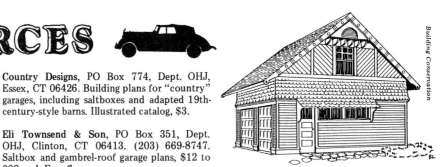

SOURCES

Building Conservation

GARAGE PLANS

Architectural Preservation Trust, 152 Old Clinton Rd., Dept. OHJ, Westbrook, CT 06498. (203) 669-1776. Kits for building two-and three-bay wagon-shed-style garages, including all timbers, pegs, roof boards, siding, instructions. Free flyer.

Building Conservation

Building Conservation, 2204 Luddington Ave., Dept. OHJ, Wauwatosa, WI 53226. Provides full blueprints of garage designs in Victorian and post-Victorian styles, including Queen Anne, Eastlake, Colonial Revival, and Italianate. Also plans for converting modern garages to Queen Anne. $18 for first set, $15 others. Brochure, $5. .

Country Designs

Colonial Garage/ Barn, Popular Mechanics, PO Box 1014, Dept. OHJ, Radio City Station, New York, NY 10101. Plans for a "country" garage which imitates small frame barn with second-storey loft, $30.

Country Designs, PO Box 774, Dept. OHJ, Essex, CT 06426. Building plans for "country" garages, including saltboxes and adapted 19th-century-style barns. Illustrated catalog, $3.

Eli Townsend & Son, PO Box 351, Dept. OHJ, Clinton, CT 06413. (203) 669-8747. Saltbox and gambrel-roof garage plans, $12 to $22 ppd. Free flyer.

Old Colony Crafts, PO Box 155, Dept. OHJ, Liberty, ME 04949. Plans for a two-car saltbox garage, $10.

Eli Townsend & Son

PRESSED METAL SIDING

W. F. Norman Corp., PO Box 323, Dept. OHJ, Nevada, MO 64772. (800) 641-4038. Galvanized steel panels stamped in pressed-brick, rock-faced brick, cluster-shingle, and pitch-faced stone designs. Catalog No. 350, $3.

HOLLOW TERRA-COTTA BLOCK

Gladding, McBean & Co., PO Box 97, Dept. OHJ, Lincoln, CA 95648. (916) 645-3341. Hollow terra-cotta blocks in sizes from 4x6 in. to 5x22 in. Through distributors. Free brochure.

Building Conservation

BEFORE

AFTER

Building Conservation

DOORS

The following companies have wood sectional overhead (roll-up) doors with several window and panel options. They do not sell directly to consumers; contact them for a list of local distributors.

Fimbel Door Corp., Coddington Rd., Dept. OHJ, Whitehouse, NJ 08888. (201) 534-4151. Can do custom work. No literature.

McKee Door, PO Box 1108, Dept. OHJ, Aurora, IL 60507. (312) 897-9600. Free brochure.

Plycraft Fabricating Corp., Barcol Overhead Door Division, 557 W. Main Rd., Dept. OHJ, Conneaut, OH 44030. (216) 593-5211. Free brochure.

Wayne-Dalton, Dept. OHJ, Mt. Hope, OH 44660. (216) 674-7015. Free brochure.

Swinging, Sliding, & Accordion

Richards-Wilcox Co., 174 Third St., PO Box 1407, Dept. OHJ, Aurora, IL 60507. (312) 897-6951. Particularly good designs are the "Sta-Rite" (no. 546) and "Superway" (no. 448) doors with matchboard panels; can be used as sliding, slide-fold, hinged, or vertical-lift doors. Also has wicket doors. Through distributors and some sales offices. Free catalog.

HARDWARE

The Macton Corp., On-the-Airport, Dept. OHJ, Danbury, CT 06810. (203) 744-6070. Makes an automobile turntable for garages. Free brochure.

Richards-Wilcox (see address above). Hardware and tracks for swinging, folding, and sliding doors.

F. L. Sainoman Co., 66 W. Colorado Ave., Dept. OHJ, Memphis, TN 38106. (901) 774-9025. Has a wide variety of sliding-track hardware including electrically-operated folding-door equipment. Through distributors. Free brochure.

Stanley Hardware, Dept. OHJ, New Britain, CT 06050. (203) 225-5111. Steel braces to plumb sagging garage doors, also hardware for sliding doors. Through distributors. Free brochures — specify interest.

Test Your Restoration~Products Awareness

If you find the how-to information in The Old-House Journal helpful, you're just the person who also needs the where-to information in the latest edition of our Buyer's Guide Catalog. The two complement each other and give you the whole story on restoring your old house. Preservation professionals -- architects, consultants, even real-estate agents -- can use the Catalog, too. It turns you into an instant expert. (We use it to answer reader questions every day!)

The OHJ Catalog took months of painstaking updating -- and was years in the making as the resource for the restoration market -- yet it's only $11.95 to subscribers ($14.95 to non-subscribers). To get a copy while it's still hot news, see the Order Form in this Yearbook.

Are you still resisting buying a copy of the Catalog? Then please take this test ... it may convince you.

---

1. IF THERE ARE NO RESTORATION SUPPLIERS LOCATED NEAR YOU,
(A) you'll never be able to restore your old house. Move to an apartment.
(B) don't worry: In the OHJ Catalog, you can find hundreds of sources, most of whom sell by mail order or through distributors nationwide.
(C) buy a truck, because you have some long-distance salvage-hauling to do.

2. HOW MANY COMPANIES ARE LISTED IN THE CURRENT OHJ CATALOG?
(A) 205
(B) 872
(C) 1,423

3. THE OHJ CATALOG IS A BUYER'S GUIDE. OUR BUYER'S GUIDE IS
(A) the floorwalker in Macy's wicker department.
(B) a tremendously helpful compilation that will save you money on fruitless phone calls and hundreds of frustrating hours hunting for hard-to-find old-house items.
(C) out of print.

4. A BUSY-BODY IS
(A) An old-fashioned exterior mirror that lets you see who's at the front door.
(B) A device for eavesdropping through old plaster walls.
(C) A 1926 movie starring Mary Pickford and Douglas Fairbanks.

5. THE OLD-HOUSE JOURNAL BUYER'S GUIDE CATALOG CONTAINS
(A) 110 pages.
(B) 240 pages.
(C) scratch-and-sniff ads.

6. THE CURRENT CATALOG IS
(A) last year's edition with a new cover.
(B) available to interior designers only.
(C) not only bigger than ever, but also redesigned to make it even easier to use,

with complete indexes up front and three separate sections inside.

7. YOU CAN GET PUSH-BUTTON LIGHT SWITCHES
(A) only by inheritance, because no one makes them any more.
(B) through antiques dealers who'll scalp you on the price.
(C) from a company that just started reproducing them (and is listed you-know-where!).

8. THE TWELFTH EDITION OF OHJ'S FAMOUS CATALOG LISTS RESTORATION PRODUCTS AND SERVICES
(A) only the rich could afford.
(B) for making every house look like a Victorian ice cream parlor.
(C) from wide-plank flooring to turn-of-the-century lamps, epoxy to wallpaper -- stuff appropriate for houses built between 1750 and 1940.

9. THIS IS THE COVER OF
(A) The OHJ Catalog
(B) the swimsuit issue of Sports Illustrated
(C) the redesigned IRS Standard Tax Forms booklet.

10. IF YOU WON'T SPEND YOUR LAST DIME TO REPLACE YOUR SLATE ROOF,
(A) you're a remuddler at heart. Admit it!
(B) don't despair: The OHJ Catalog tells you about a less expensive, good-looking substitute.
(C) you can kiss that roof good-bye.

ANSWERS: 1. B 2. C 3. B 4. A 5. B 6. C 7. C 8. C 9. A 10. B

SHUTTER CUT-OUTS

WRITTEN BY EVE KAHN

Illustrated by Bekka Lindstrom

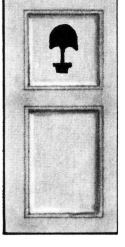

LOOK AROUND at the Dutch Colonial Revival houses in town — one of them will still have its old shutters, the kind with a diamond or a sailboat or a crescent moon cut out of a panel. Decorative shutters were immensely popular from about 1915 until World War II. If you own a colonial revival house of any sort, it probably had shutters, and those shutters probably had cut-outs.

Available through any millwork catalog, decorative wood shutters showed up even on post-Victorian Foursquares and Bungalows. But the historical precedent for decorative cut-outs is colonial.

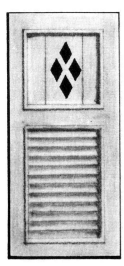
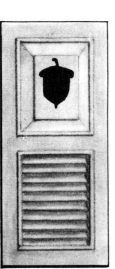
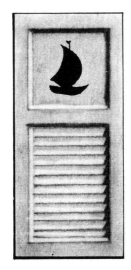
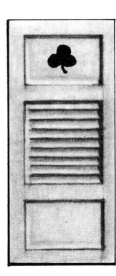
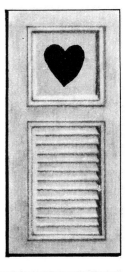

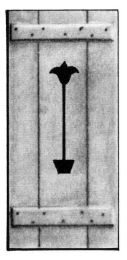

In the 18th century, shutters were kept closed all winter to protect windows and insulate. Cut-outs (usually crescent-shaped, sometimes star- or diamond-shaped) prevented condensation, let in some light, and gave inhabitants a peep hole (cut-outs usually fell at eye level).

Post-Victorian shutters were much less practical. Some were quite frankly decorative: Closed, they would not even cover the windows they surrounded. Architects adapted the three basic shutter types — panelled, louvered, and battened — for decorative panels. They often used different types of shutters on the same house. (This was a favorite technique of Aymar Embury II, noted Dutch Colonial Revival architect.) Panelled or battened shutters on first-floor windows, with louvered shutters on the second, was a popular combination.

The cut-outs shown here come from our collection of 20th-century catalogs and house plan books. You can't order the shutters from stock anymore; if you plan on making your own, why not use your imagination?

For panelled shutters with 1:3, 2:5, or custom proportions suited for cut-outs, contact Shuttercraft, 282 Stepstone Hill Rd., Guilford, CT 06437. (203) 453-1973. Thanks to Sara Chase of the Society for the Preservation of New England Antiquities for her helpful research.

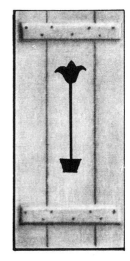

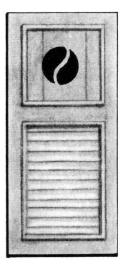

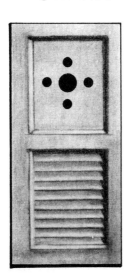

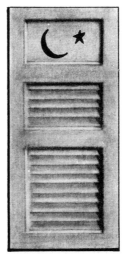

Restoration Products
Reviewed by Eve Kahn

Antique Hardware

When we examined Lee Valley Tools' catalog of antique hardware, we were rather surprised at the variety offered: everything from Eastlake door bolts to Art Deco door plates. But the real news is that none of these pieces is salvaged -- all are in new condition, unused! Lee Valley buys them in bulk from the basements and storerooms of hardware stores and factories across the U.S., where they've been stored, unwanted, sometimes for more than a century.

Sifting through the handsome, 79-page, color catalog is like digging in a box of treasures at a salvage yard -- except you don't get your hands dirty. You'll find hinges of every description, window hardware, hardware for cabinets, drawers, screen doors, plus latches, locks, and doorknobs. All pieces have been cleaned and are in working order. Some come in

sets, others in singles. There's more available than shown; contact the company if you don't see exactly what you want. Send $3 for the catalog to Lee Valley Tools Ltd., 2680 Queensview Dr., Dept. OHJ, Ottawa, Ont., Canada K2B 8H6. (613) 596-0350.

Colored Storm Windows

You don't have to ruin your house's color scheme with inappropriate black or silver storm windows. Another option is Elmont Manufacturing's line of colored, outside-mounting storm windows. They're made of aluminum, and they come in 15 shades: Wedgwood blue, barn red, bronze, avocado, yellow, gold, beige, charcoal grey, two shades of brown, mint green, mocha, dark green and, of course, black and white.

There are no stock sizes; all work is custom. The company can accommodate arched and oversize windows. The average price per window is $70. Doors begin at $300.

One caveat: Elmont sells through dealers only, and most of their dealers are in the East (as far west as Ohio). They will ship farther west, but it can be expensive. Elmont Manufacturing Co., Inc., 175 Kennedy Dr., Dept. OHJ, Hauppauge, NY 11788. (516) 231-7400.

Period Livestock

Some people take their restoration very seriously. Finished restoring a farmhouse? It's time to start on the pastures. Not the landscaping, but the livestock. The familiar mottled cows and fluffy white sheep dotting farms across the country don't necessarily look like the ones your farm had when it was new. Deep-red, solid-color cows and long-haired, grey sheep were the rule in some places 100 years ago. If you really want

an exact restoration, look into the many historic breeds still available; some of them closely resemble their 18th- and 19th-century ancestors.

The American Minor Breeds Conservancy (AMBC) and the Association for Living Historical Farms and Agricultural Museums (ALHFAM) are your two sources of information. The ALHFAM can help you determine what types of currently-available animals look like the breeds your farm probably had (if the ALHFAM doesn't know they can direct you to someone who does). Once you have a specific breed in mind, the

AMBC can put you in touch with the group concerned with preserving that breed, such as the American Milking Devon Association. (Once an extremely popular breed of cattle, Devons are deep red in color, friendly, and require little maintenance.) Terry Sharrer, ALHFAM, Room 5035, National Museum of American History, Smithsonian Institution, Washington, DC 20560. (202) 357-2813. AMBC, Box 477, Pittsboro, NC 27312. (919) 542-5704. American Milking Devon Association, c/o John Wheelock, Colchester, VT 05446.

for pre-1850 buildings

Low-E Colonial Sash

Low-emissivity glass, commonly known as low-e, has a fired-on, invisible coating which keeps in winter heat and blocks out summer sun. Recently Wes-Pine Millwork started offering low-e as a standard feature on their colonial-style, divided-lite windows. You can get both single windows and multiple units. Average prices, including storm windows, a preservative-treated Ponderosa pine sash, and weatherstripping, range from $300 for a single window to $1500 for a bay window. Costs are defrayed by the savings in heat and air conditioning and by the longer lives of carpets, upholstery, and wallpaper (low-e also blocks ultraviolet rays). Contact the company for a free brochure and the names of local dealers. Wes-Pine Millwork Inc., Dept. OHJ, W. Hanover, MA 02339. (617) 878-2102.

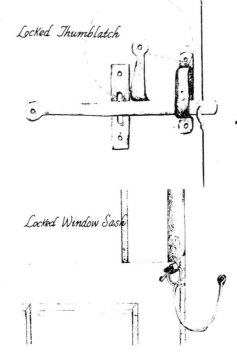

Locked Thumblatch

Locked Window Sash

Colonial-Style Security

Before thieves grew crafty and door locks became high tech, house security was a simple matter. Williamsburg Blacksmiths offers reproductions of several devices used in the 18th and 19th centuries to keep houses safe. One is a locking button ($3) for bar latches; when it's in place the bar can't be lifted. Also available are locking pins ($4.25) for thumblatches and window sash, cane bolts for double doors, slide bolts, and Dutch door quadrants. If your security standards are stricter, you can purchase Williamsburg's mortise locksets (from $89 to $193.50 single cylinder, $100 to $200 double) and disguise them with hand-forged iron collars ($2.60 each). The illustrated $3 catalog has many other items and includes a price list. Williamsburg Blacksmiths, Goshen Rd. (Rte. 9), Dept. OHJ, Williamsburg, MA 01096. (413) 268-7341.

for Victorian buildings

High-Style Ceilings

A flood destroyed Hosek Manufacturing's main facility in 1965, but old-house owners were in luck: All the company's models for plaster ornament were safely stored in the basement. That's why Hosek, now rebuilt and run by the fourth generation of the Hosek family, offers the same ornaments it has produced for some 50 years. Hosek created much of the ornament in Denver's civic buildings, theaters, and elegant homes; though the pieces date from the 20th century, they are ornate enough for any Victorian

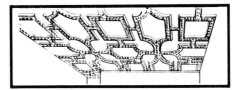

home. The ceilings shown here are of particular interest; there are floral, Tudor, Victorian, Louis XV, and Renaissance styles. You can buy panels, domes, or entire ceilings. Some panels come in 2'-x-2' squares (from $16 to $23 per panel), others in 4'-x-4' sections (from $5.50 to $8.50 per square foot; be sure to send room dimensions with your order). Domes designed to match the panels are 4' x 4' and cost $300 each. Full-ceiling prices are available upon request. The 44-page catalog ($3, refundable) has a wide array of items, from table bases to fireplaces to brackets and columns. And this, the Hoseks report, is just 5% of what was in that flooded building -- the other 95% has yet to be restored. Hosek Manufacturing Co. Inc., 4877 National Western Dr., Suite 205, Dept. OHJ, Denver, CO 80216. (303) 298-7010.

Victorian Mail-Order

While restoring a Victorian house, the McHenrys of Auburn, California piled up 50 catalogs from 50 suppliers. Then they realized: There must be a better way. So they started their own company, Victorian Warehouse. It's a one-stop source for Victorian reproductions; you can practically build a Victorian house from scratch using just the items the McHenrys sell. The $2.50, 40-page catalog features lighting fixtures, ceiling fans, lamps and shades, entry and screen doors, hardware, wood-burning and electric stoves, ceiling and wall ornament, stained glass, lace, panelling, moulding, custom drapery, and bath fixtures. Victorian Warehouse, 190 Grace St., Dept. OHJ, Auburn, CA 95603. (916) 823-0374.

Victorian _____ for post-Victorian buildings

Wall Ornament

Although Wallcraft moulds their unusual wall ornaments after pieces in 18th-century French chateaux, the results are often dead ringers for American Victoriana. Shown here are two of the possibilities; you can also get moulding, medallions, garlands, rosettes, capitals, and frame moulding. All are made of polyester resins which offer, the manufacturers say, the working characteristics of white pine; after being stained or painted, pieces are virtually indistinguishable from woodwork. The catalog costs $3 (free to the trade), refundable on orders over $100, and prices are reasonable. Wallcraft Inc., 2605 Waugh Dr., Dept. OHJ, Houston, TX 77006. (713) 522-1316.

Old-Style Lamp Cord

Even if you're not restoring a Tiffany lamp, you're sure to have uses for Bradford Consultants' Appolo Lamp Cord. It looks just like old cord: The two wires are intertwined, and the silk cover has a tarnished gold tone. The Appolo is appropriate for any pre-1940 lamp, clock, or radio.

Inside the silk cover are modern insulated wires. The cord is intended for use at less than 120 volts and for low-power loads not exceeding three amps or 360 watts of incandescent lamp load at 120 volts.

The cost is $1.95 per foot, with a $2 shipping charge on each order. The company sends out a free information sheet. Bradford Consultants, 16 E. Homestead Ave., Dept. OHJ, Collingswood, NJ 08108. (609) 854-1404.

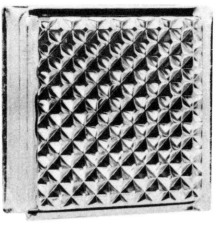

Glass Block

Homeowners have been building partitions, walls, and windows out of glass block ever since the product was introduced in the 1930s. Pittsburgh Corning, one of the first manufacturers, still makes glass block in smooth, wavy, and patterned styles suitable for Art Deco or International Style homes. The patterned blocks are useful for baths, since they admit light but maintain privacy. Blocks come in both squares and rectangles in sizes from 4" x 8" to 12" x 12". Prices range from about $3 to $10.50 per block, depending on size and pattern, or from $7 to $8 per square foot. Standard masonry mortar is all you need to build with the blocks. Contact the company for the names of local distributors. Pittsburgh Corning Corp., 800 Presque Isle Dr., Dept. OHJ, Pittsburgh, PA 15239. (412) 327-6100.

Craftsman Fixtures

Rejuvenation House Parts' Craftsman porch sconce is a compatible finishing touch for any Bungalow, Mission, Foursquare, or Craftsman home. You'll want two, of course, to flank your front door. The cast-iron sconces come painted black; with six-inch-wide glass shades, they cost $48.50 each plus $8 shipping. Inside the house you can install any of

the company's five interior lighting fixtures, all made of solid brass. Ceiling fixtures have one, two, or four arms. Wall sconces, which can be hung facing up or down, have one or two arms.

Jim Kelly, the manufacturer, also runs an antique store. Each Craftsman fixture is a faithful reproduction of a piece he's either had in his shop or seen in one of his old lighting catalogs. Only the walls of the tubing have been thickened for added strength.

A brochure describing the Craftsman fixtures is free; send $3 for a complete catalog of turn-of-the-century lighting. Rejuvenation House Parts, 901 N. Skidmore, Dept. OHJ, Portland, OR 97217. (503) 249-0774.

opinion... Remuddling

There are many ways to ruin a porch. A fragile architectural feature, particularly prone to decay, it is often the first to go. Shown here are two classic disaster examples. At left is a double-house in Cape May, New Jersey. Owners of its right half closed in both porches. Gone is the charm of sitting on a screened porch, watching the world go by. No more drying a bathing suit on the second-floor porch (the neighbors still can). The house is left with a split personality -- part Victorian seaside resort, part phony-colonial. Below, a porch in Dallas, Texas, was enclosed the cheap way. This short-sighted remuddling offers only one window, on one side of an otherwise blind box. On paint, though, no expense was spared: The "box" is striped in brilliant electric blue, as are the Corinthian columns (capitals are painted gold, a rather gaudy tribute to former elegance). Thanks goes to Signe Yanksley of Dallas for the Dallas photos, and to Michael J. Carmagnola, Jr., of Philadelphia for the Cape May picture.

-- E. Kahn

274

Landmark Burned by Fear

Camden (Maine) Herald

by Doug Hufnagel

They burned down the haunted house the other night. It stood on a bend in the road just south of my house. When giving directions I would always say, "It's about a third of a mile beyond the haunted house, down in the field," and everyone knew where that was; I didn't need to say much more. The house was probably the most famous house in Maine. . . .

When Charles and Vera owned the land there would often be cows milling about in front or on hot days drinking water from an old bathtub. But Vera died three winters ago, and Charles last winter; his heart gave out. It's safe to say the match was lit then. After all, the house was left untouched for somewhere between 50 and 70 years, and they had been on the farm for 45 years. It was built by man but shaped by time, and the seasons. Winter winds and summer sun could not bring it down. It eventually would have fallen to the elements, but it was enough to watch it slowly bend.

It was enough for Vera and Charles, who left the house the way it was because a relative long ago asked them not to touch the house but simply leave it. Just leave it, a simple request which they felt was right. It was enough for the hundred or so people from town who signed the petition asking the house be saved, and enough for the neighbors who loved the house. But it was not enough for the man from Massachusetts.

When I went to talk to him about the house, he told me it was an eyesore, or in legal terms "an attractive nuisance," which would invite people to it and open him up to a lawsuit if anyone were hurt there. He spoke about lawyers and insurance companies. He was ready with case after case of legal nightmares where people practically built moats around their attractive nuisances and still managed to be found guilty of negligence by a jury of their peers. I could see this guy was clearly afraid. There was a song a few years ago with a line, "Changes in latitudes, changes in attitudes." Well, I'm not sure of the latitude of Massachusetts but it doesn't sound like a very nice place.

Finally, when he told me the house represented everything that was wrong with Maine, I knew it was already on fire. It was too late. The latitude of fear was near. I tried for a while longer to explain that Maine looked at the world through different eyes. This is a safe place, we leave

Eliza McFadden

EVEN AS OHJ's October issue was being printed, this piece about the house pictured on its cover appeared in a Maine newspaper.

our doors open and our cars unlocked. When our kids go to school we know they will be home at night. We like to look at old houses crumbling into the earth and to stop and watch nature take its course. We live at a different latitude.

Whenever I passed the "falling-down house" I would think of the time-lapse photography which shows a flower opening or an orange decaying. By speeding up the film we are able to see the process of life by altering the rate at which it occurs. I could see the house in 50 years and 100 years from now. . . I would try to think about how it looked 15 years ago when I first saw it and if there were any detectable changes. Things were happening there for sure, but ever so slowly. I thought maybe I would take a picture of the house each year and then put them together in 20 years or so and make one of those hand-flip movies, just a short subject, but it would be interesting nonetheless.

Well, no need to consider that one anymore, the house is gone. The Northport Fire Department put the longest show in town to rest Monday evening at 6 p.m. But the torch of fear lit the fire. By Tuesday morning only the rock [sill] was visible as a thin column of smoke rose from a pile of ashes inside. My neighbor Judy, who lives just across the street, spoke about Vera and Charles and how they loved their farm. "It's not what they wanted. If they knew they would cry."

Tonight, when I drove by the field, I imagined Vera and Charles dressed in their ragged clothes standing in front of the house, holding on to each other, sobbing.

courtesy Camden Herald

The house was lost; local residents who understood its symbolism accepted that. But the structure had artistic and sentimental value to almost everyone who came upon it.

Almost everyone. The fear inspired by outrageous lawsuits and the disappearance of individual accountability clouded the vision for the new owner and his advisors. Even in Maine ... house, symbol, art, all suffering an ignominious death because of a legal concept hardly anyone would have comprehended at the time the house was built. Is a frog pond "an attractive nuisance"? Are the trees I climbed as a child "an attractive nuisance"? What the hell is going on here?

There is more to life than pragmatism and profit. If not, why do we feel sad? People who live in old houses are lucky; we have evidence of that intrinsic value.

Patricia F. Poore

Letters

Queen Of Garages

Dear OHJ:

The two articles on old-house garages looked terrific in print (September and October 1986). Did I really write that much?

I have to confess an oversight. I owe many thanks to Ms. Leslie Goat and the Vermont Division for Historic Preservation. Their excellent material -- and enthusiasm -- helped broaden the scope of the article.

-- J. Randall Cotton
Wayne, Penn.

Virtuoso Vacuum

Dear Ms. Poore:

Thank you for a most enjoyable issue (September 1986). I always read OHJ cover to cover, as the articles are interesting whether or not they are about my house's period or my problem-of-the-month. I know that if I haven't had to face the topics addressed in an issue's articles, I will, sooner or later!

Regarding the letter headed "Aspiration Article" on page 318, I just wanted to let you know that I have had excellent success with an Electrolux model commercial vacuum. It's not for wet work, but I've had it for about 14 years, and it has been through two house-restorations. It has swallowed absolutely everything which would go through the standard-size wand and hose (and a few things which got stuck along the way), and has never quit on me. It has a 4-gallon metal can on good sturdy casters, a two-stage filter (I don't know how it would rate on toxic particles), and a sufficiently powerful motor to suck up almost anything. When used on chimney (coal) dust or plaster dust, the cloth filter in the can needs to be tapped now and then, as dust cakes on it and reduces the suction; but for sawdust or anything coarser, it's fine. The vacuum has never had any repairs at all -- even the same tough plug is on the nice long power cord. I am on my second wand and set of tools (the hose is the original one, and of a generous length).

This machine was not cheap, but after an experience similar to your writer's with a most unsatisfactory and inconvenient 'cheapie,' I splurged on this machine, and I'm sure it has paid for itself many times over.

Thanks for the best magazine I get.

-- Walter Swoope
Philipsburg, Penn.

Glass–Block Moulds

Dear Patricia:

I'm involved with a project to get certain types of early-20th-century glass block into production again. The problem is locating the moulds. Possibly some loyal OHJ readers might now the whereabouts of the original moulds made by the American Luxfer Prism Co., Chicago. The firm went out of business many years ago.

Additionally, I'm interested in glass block (also called "window prisms") made by the American 3-Way Prism Co. of Philadelphia, and by the Mississippi Glass Block Co. of New York and St. Louis. These glass-block "prisms" ranged from under 3 inches to 13-in. square.

I'm afraid all of these moulds have been destroyed. But I'd be delighted to learn that I'm wrong.

-- Robert Hamilton
Marketing Consultant
Yorktown Heights, N.Y.

[We'd love to hear about this rare glass block, too. If you have a clue, please drop us a line. -- ed.]

14 different patterns from the Mississippi Glass Block Company, as pictured in the 1906 "Sweet's" Catalog.

Still Sappy

Dear Editor:

Since purchasing our 1726 Saltbox home two years ago, we've learned a great deal, not the least of which is the pleasure of being part of a continuous line of people, each contributing to the life of the house....

Your article "Wood Woes" (September 1986) had a sentence that grabbed my attention -- a quote from a 1915 edition of Building Age magazine. Regarding yellow pine, it stated, "When pitch or sap is not plentiful and the wood well seasoned...." When is yellow pine well seasoned? The yellow-pine floorboards in my attic have been in place for over 250 years. But a fresh saw-cut reveals sap that hasn't yet dried. (This also makes sanding difficult.) Cutting the wood produces a not-especially-pleasant odor.

But the beautiful color and graining makes for a warm, pleasing finish that we appreciate a great deal. We have not used any paint, so we encountered no problems.

-- Robert D. McNaughton
Cromwell, Conn.

The Real Clem Labine

Dear Editor:

We receive a number of "strange" questions from our readers, but the latest one in this category is beyond our considerable abilities to answer (and the question is for real). You are the only ones who can help.

"... is Clem Labine, the publisher of The Old-House Journal, the same Clem Labine who was a pitcher for the Brooklyn Dodgers in the '50s?"

-- Michael Reitz, Editor
New England Builder
Montpelier, Vermont

[Ms. Poore answers: No, he's not -- but he's thrown me a curve or two since we've met. Clem Labine of the Brooklyn Dodgers (the other Clem Labine) has moved to New England. Our Publisher (the famous Clem Labine) was born in New England and moved to Brooklyn. He may not be a Hall-of-Famer, but we consider him an All-Star.]

Letters

Wood Wise

Dear Ms. Poore:

I was particularly impressed by the article "Wood Woes" in the September issue.

For many years, I've used red metal primer in the bilges of my boats. It contains 47% pigment and thus covers a multitude of sins. It adheres well to all kinds of wood, even below the waterline. I've also carried on an affair with Sears "Weatherbeater" acrylic latex paint. It has been consistent in quality, reasonable in price, and has given good service.

For the past four years, I have been removing the paint from our turn-of-the-century Foursquare. All exterior wood on this house is Southern Yellow Pine. The species is virtually extinct (being called virgin Georgia Heart Pine). Many of the summer growth bands are 1/4-inch wide. I use your heat gun and heat plate to remove the paint, followed by a chemical stripper on the moulding. I then sand with around 100-grit paper. This is then followed by one coat of X-O Rust Red Metal Primer and two coats of Weatherbeater. All my colors are shades of brown, so strike-through isn't a problem.

The "Experts" would probably throw up their hands in horror at this system, but it works for me!

—Richard D. Hutchins
Crisfield, Maryland

A Must-Read

Dear OHJ:

What a refreshing surprise to read an article on door hardware and not find anything wrong with it. I am sure that "How To Fix Old Doors" by Jonathan Poore (June 1986) will be a MUST-READ-AGAIN article for many people over the coming years -- well done!

One trick that he did not cover was that on some hinges, you can turn them over to avoid the worn side of the knuckle. This will work on any 3- or 5-knuckle hinge. The purpose is to use the surface that was at the top and not worn.

-- W. Whitman Ball
Ball & Ball
Exton, Penn.

Octagon House

Dear Editor:

Two months ago, 20 non-artisan volunteers joined me in the effort to begin the restoration of our Octagon House in Camillus. Our goal is to rehabilitate it as a cultural center and a gracious place for community events.

Maxwell Memorial Library here has taken an OHJ subscription so we can pore over every article and advertisement while awaiting development of fund-raising plans and grants, and bids from restoration contractors.

In the meantime, there is water in the cellar, under the side where the stucco has come off below a second-storey window ... there too, the porch roof and floor have rotted out. Upon viewing the remarkably-good condition of the interior, everyone agrees the exterior should be worked on immediately.

Built by Ann and Isaiah Wilcox on their farm in 1856, our Octagon House of Camillus is now listed in the National Register. Our house looks as though it needs only a paint job and a little jacking up of its full-surround porch. But in actuality, it may require $100,000 to $200,000 to restore it, says the Syracuse architectural firm Crawford & Stearns.

The cobblestone-and-concrete walls are 22 inches thick at the base, rising to 17 inches thick, and faced with stucco. The original slate roof appears to be two colors. Not enough of the 1920 asbestos shingles covering it have yet been torn away by the elements to reveal any pattern.

A substantial, octagonal handrail follows the outer edge of a solid circular stair as it rises from the original cellar kitchen, up through the first and second floors, through the attic, and into the cupola.

The octagonal porch roof is board-bare in places -- open to the sky, no longer protecting the tongue-and-groove porch floor. Children who have been there have loved running around and around while their laughter echoes under that roof. We can hardly wait to see a carpenter or two repair it.

-- Betty Campbell
Camillus, N.Y.

[The Octagon House of Camillus Restoration Project Committee has asked for help "getting a leg up" on their long road ahead. Those with advice on fund-raising, technical matters, etc., can write to them at 1 Milton Avenue, Camillus, NY 13031. -- ed.]

This 130-year-old Octagon house in Camillus, New York, still 'needs some work' — to use a phrase which should be familiar to just about everyone who owns an old house. So Betty Campbell has formed a restoration-project committee. Maybe you can help....

─Old-House Living─

COMPATIBILITY

by Barbara Mayer

WHEN Loretta Fox and her husband Robert were house-hunting in Stamford, Conn., six years ago, they were looking for many things: like enough space for their four young sons and a convenient location. "If there was anything I did not want," recalls Loretta, "It was an old house."

BY CHANCE, Loretta was among the first prospective buyers to tour an 1890 house in Stamford's Shippan section, close to Long Island Sound. The house needed another bedroom and bath, a new kitchen, and a family dining area, but it was in a perfect locale, near bus lines and the train to New York. It also had a sound roof, storm and screen windows, a nearly-new furnace, and even an elevator. And, though Loretta didn't appreciate it at the time, it still had its original clapboards and Yankee gutters. She was smitten.

IT WAS CHANCE again that led the Foxes further into preservation. Listening to the local radio station, Loretta heard Renee Kahn, an active Stamford preservationist, talking about the value and importance of preserving the past. Soon after that Loretta read an article in another magazine about The Old-House Journal and its campaign against remuddling.

"WE ALREADY HAD an architect's plans for a totally modern kitchen which would have eliminated the pantry and its wonderful copper sink," she says. Instead of carrying out those plans, the Foxes abandoned them and called Renee Kahn for advice.

THE HISTORY

RENEE, director of a nonprofit preservation group, had compiled a registry of Stamford's historic houses, so she could tell the Foxes something about the history of theirs. One of the town's best-known builders had built it in 1890. Once it stood on a ten-plus-acre plot across the street and had a clear view of the Sound. The house was moved by the builder,'a man named Gurley, most

likely for his son. Gurley then built himself
an even grander home on the original site.

THE HOUSE STAYED in the Gurley family until
the late '20s, when a judge lived in the
house. He added a new kitchen, a library, and
a second-floor bedroom wing. It is believed
he installed the elevator to accommodate his
invalid mother.

THAT ELEVATOR was to become the bane of the
Fox family's existence. They decided to
extend it into the basement. But to do so,
workmen had to clear a mammoth granite boulder
out of the way, using a jackhammer. "For
eight or ten weeks, the workers kept at that
jackhammer. The dust, filth, and dirt was
indescribable. We just covered everything
with plastic sheets and tried to exist," says
Loretta with a shudder.

THE GAZEBO

THEN CAME the Foxes' biggest undertaking: the
dining wing. Renee came up with the idea of
adding an octagonal, gazebo-like wing to the
back of the house, which would contain a large
dining area but not conflict with the house's
Queen Anne features. She and set-designer
Steven Hirschberg worked out plans, and a
local builder contributed technical knowledge
and working drawings. The resulting space
comfortably fits a large round table and eight
chairs.

TO REMODEL the kitchen, the Foxes opted for
custom oak cabinets with glass fronts, which
match the woodwork in the pantry. Upstairs,
the attic was converted to two bedrooms and a
bath for the children.

RENEE KAHN also helped the Foxes find people
who knew how to work on early-20th-century
plumbing and late-19th-century woodwork.
Among them were general contractor Russ Cooper
of Darien, Conn., whose workers are craftsmen,
according to Loretta. "He would introduce
craftsmen by saying, 'I'd like you to meet the
best carpenter in Fairfield County.'" Others
who helped included a plumber who (after
others said it couldn't be done) fixed their
circa-1930 toilet by fashioning parts which
are no longer made. Loretta's father helped
too, by repairing the spindled fretwork above
the dining room entrance.

THE EAVES

HAPPY ACCIDENT again played a role in the
Foxes' finishing touch, the multi-color exterior paint scheme. Robert happened to read a
review of Painted Ladies, the well-known
volume about exuberantly colored wooden structures in San Francisco. After tracking down a
copy of the book, the Foxes discovered color
consultant Bob Buckter. They sent him some

*At right, the "gazebo" dining wing under construction. First an
octagonal hole was dug for the foundation. The poured-concrete
piers set up in the hole had to be done twice; getting the angles
just right proved tricky. Next, a frame of 2x4s was constructed
and sheathed in plywood.*

100 photos, showing the house at every possible angle, and he created a five-tone scheme appropriate for the house's original period. The body is beige; trim is cream; shutters are dark brown with rust louvers. The ornamentation, bull's eyes and fish-scale shingles, are also brown and rust. The dining wing has the same color scheme. Tucked under the eaves are gold highlights; Loretta says this gives the house a special glow on sunny days.

BUT THE HOUSE hardly needs those highlights to attract attention on the quiet, tree-lined street. Even on the cloudiest day, Loretta says, "people tell us they never noticed the house until we painted it."

Top: Lattice panels between piers, tiny brackets, and clapboard siding complete the dining wing's exterior. Above: The house's striking colors make it stand out even in the worst weather. The wing, under construction, is visible behind the house.

ADDING TO OLD HOUSES
BY RENEE KAHN

*S*everal years ago I was asked to give a talk on "good and bad additions." I rode around with a camera for days, found lots of bad examples, but no good ones. It became clear that good additions weren't noticeable; they blended seamlessly with the original building. The ones that jumped out at me as failures, on the other hand, made distinctive design statements which were incompatible with the original building.

I had trouble accepting this at first because, like everyone else who's taken an architecture course, I've been taught that additions, while respecting the general configuration of the original building, should be obviously modern. This works perfectly well in theory, but it looks dreadful in the real world.

The guidelines for preservation tax credits discourage any kind of "false historicism," such as additions that mimic the original building. In the government's view, this is "dishonest." Well, that is fine on a philosophical level — it is, in a sense, dishonest to copy a style that's not in line with current taste — but in practice it has led to some painful atrocities. They meet federal standards but offend the eye.

I wish that architects, rather than being doctrinaire, would let the building speak to them first, to see if it can tolerate a modern addition. Some buildings, like the Fox house, have such a distinctive style of their own that they fight anything modern tooth and nail. I've met architects who say, "The building is nothing special, so anything I do to it will be an improvement." What this usually means is that they're not well versed enough in architectural history to understand the building. (I'm told that architecture schools these days teach more history, and it's about time!) The other argument I hear — "you can't get the same materials today, so there's no point trying for a period look" — doesn't hold water anymore. Almost every old building material, from pressed-metal siding to beaded clapboard, is available somewhere. And substitutes — say, aluminum for cast iron or cement for terra cotta — are often appropriate.

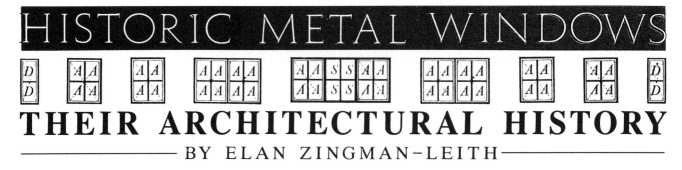

HISTORIC METAL WINDOWS
THEIR ARCHITECTURAL HISTORY
BY ELAN ZINGMAN-LEITH

THE HISTORY OF METAL WINDOWS in America begins in colonial New England, where early English colonists followed traditional European building practices. Their buildings were not medieval in character, with asymmetrical massing and numerous gables. Windows at first were merely holes in the walls covered with oiled paper. Later, glass was used, but as it was blown by mouth and had to be shipped from England, it was very expensive. Windows tended to be small not only because of the high cost of glass but also because of poor insulation and inefficient fireplaces in most colonial houses.

EARLY NEW ENGLAND WINDOWS were casements (which opened like a door, instead of sliding up and down). Glass (not yet manufactured in large pieces) was often cut in diamond-shaped panes held together by lead cames, a medieval tradition. Sash and frames were usually of wood, but could also be wrought iron. Along with nails and other luxury metal goods, metal sash were brought over from England.

BY THE 1720s, vertically sliding windows, usually of wood, supplanted casement windows. The double-hung window with large panes came into fashion with the grander classical homes of the Georgian era, made possible by fortunes amassed by New England shippers and Southern planters. With the new commercial money, woodworking reached new heights, and casements were entirely eclipsed by expensive, handmade, double-hung windows.

EARLY IN THE 19TH CENTURY, metal windows appeared on rural mills and factories. To admit maximum natural light in these pre-kerosene, whale-oil times, early factories had large windows. But dusts from cotton processing or flour milling, plus lamp flames, were already an explosive combination; wood window frames made the situation worse. So builders tried their best to eliminate exposed wood; usually by burying the window frames behind masonry walls, sometimes by making wrought-iron or steel imitations of double-hung wood windows.

AMERICAN BUILDING TECHNOLOGY completely changed in the mid-1800s, with the Industrial Revolution. As waves of immigrants crowded neighborhoods on the eastern seaboard, the cast-iron-fronted factories that employed them filled neighborhoods like New York's SoHo. First built in gargantuan imitations of Italian Renaissance pallazzi, then in every eclectic Victorian style imaginable, the structures were horrific firetraps. (Ironically, before the invention of modern fire-fighting

Precursor to metal casements: a 17th-century leaded window from Salem, Mass.

A sliding leaded window, still with wood sash, on a 19th-century Gothic Revival building.

The 20th century: cast-iron facade and metal casement windows, Boston.

companies, fire escapes, or strict building codes, designers of cast-iron buildings promoted fire safety as a major attraction.)

TO HELP MAKE the buildings fire-resistant, steel double-hung windows were substituted for the standard, immense, wooden double-hung windows. By the mid-1840s, French plate glass in large sizes was introduced; by the 1860s and '70s, they could be bought domestically. Windows became so large -- especially on the second floors of factories, where the showrooms often were -- that they couldn't slide up and down. Instead, vertically pivoting windows were installed, sometimes in iron or steel.

ON RESIDENCES, Romanticism encouraged the return of the metal casement window. This idealized longing for past simplicity led to Andrew Jackson Downing's irregular Gothic Revival cottages, St. Patrick's Cathedral, and Walpole's Strawberry Hill. Faux medieval buildings required faux medieval windows, and one of the recommended alternatives was a reprise of the diamond-paned casements we first encountered on early New England houses.

CASEMENT SASH on 1840s or 1870s Gothic Revival buildings were seldom metal, although they did have leaded panes. But they set the stage for the metal-sash, diamond-paned casements of the 20th-century Tudor Revival.

CITIES EXPANDED DRAMATICALLY in the last decades of the 19th century. At the same time, English steel casements were introduced. First the tenement, then the apartment building, used metal double-hung and casement windows. Metal-clad wood windows, called Kalamien windows, were developed as fire-resistant alternatives to wood. By the turn of the century, many window types and materials were readily available. The designers of Beaux Arts civic and commercial buildings even began to use bronze for windows and entrances. Wealthier civic and corporate clients had bronze windows made by the same companies that made steel windows.

FOR THE LARGE-SCALE production industries that dominated the economy after the turn of the century, factory sash were steel windows made by welding together standard sections (angles, T and Z bars) into frames, movable sash, and fixed windows. They were made to pivot horizontally, hinge at the top, hinge at the side (casement sash), or hinge at the bottom (hoppers). They differed from residential steel windows, which were always made from sections rolled to shape. Building up sections from angles was much cheaper, but left voids inside sash members that could not be painted or maintained, and so invited rust.

IN THE EARLY 20TH CENTURY, windows were one of the most prominent features of Beaux Arts apartments and hotels. The bulk of the fenestration was wood and double-hung, with French doors and oversize casement windows providing dramatic accents. The most elegant buildings had copper-clad sash, creating the green patina evident today on many urban windows.

DURING THE '20S AND '30S, the Georgian Revival and Art Deco (Moderne) styles predominated for apartment buildings. The Georgian Revival

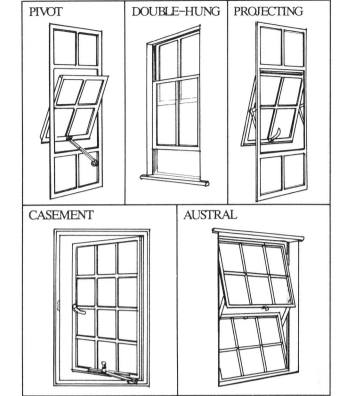

Metal windows and suburban romanticism: a typical, circa-1920 plan-book illustration.

Metal windows in the city: metal-clad Kalamien windows on an apartment building.

apartment building recalled the brick and limestone houses of 18th-century America and England, using multi-paned double-hung windows. But unlike old Georgian buildings, its windows were usually of rolled steel, factory-made, and inexpensive (and thus much larger).

THESE STEEL WINDOWS could be made with very slim muntins and stiles, imitating colonial models. The sash consisted of 12-to-16 gauge steel bolted around the glass. A simpler version without muntins became the standard for office buildings. (Campbell and Pomeroy were major manufacturers.) It peaked in popularity in the '30s and '40s; like all steel windows, it was eclipsed after World War II by the aluminum window, and now is no longer available.

ART DECO ARCHITECTURE (more correctly, Streamlined or Moderne) is associated with the steel casement window. The builders of the '30s, like the Puritans, got their metal casements from England (although major manufacturer Henry Hope & Sons eventually opened a factory in Jamestown, N.Y.). The popularity of steel casement windows zoomed after World War I, and made possible the horizontal "ribbon" windows of Art Deco skyscrapers. The casements were usually paired, and had a hopper below and a transom above. At their most popular, steel windows were available in five different weights, the lightest providing elegantly slim, one-inch members to hold the glass. The mullions' design was often coordinated with colored brick courses in the facade to emphasize the horizontality of the ribbon windows.

STEEL WINDOWS REPRESENTED modernity and technology in the city, but they stood for "olde England" in the suburbs. In the 'teens and '20s, railroad commuter suburbs grew quickly. Bronxville and Garden City for New York, Winnetka for Chicago, and Grosse Pointe for Detroit are familiar examples. The typical house in these communities was the rambling "stockbroker Tudor." Featuring asymmetrical massing, medieval ornament, with brick, stucco, or half-timber, the Tudor Revival house, like its Gothic Revival predecessor, used casement windows. But this time they were often steel, with multi-paned sash or (as in the 19th century) leaded glass.

BY THE 1940S, government-subsidized housing provided an enormous market for steel casements, the least expensive window of its time. After World War II, however, it was superseded by the aluminum window in the post-war housing boom. Aluminum windows are less expensive than steel, and because aluminum is extremely ductile it can be easily moulded into complicated shapes (steel is much harder to work with). Today, aluminum windows hold sophisticated weatherstripping and come with a variety of long-lasting finishes (anodic, acrylic, epoxy) that do not pit or corrode. Also, makers of aluminum casement windows are reproducing the slim profile of historic steel sash.

STEEL WINDOWS have been reborn, thanks to the growing interest in preserving the buildings of the 1920s-'40s. Most English manufacturers stopped making steel windows after World War II, except for Henry Hope & Sons. In the 1970s, Hope's Architectural Products (their corporate descendant), gave the windows heavier muntins and frames so thermal glass could be inserted. Putty was replaced by energy-efficient gaskets. The added double glazing and gaskets cut down on noise pollution as well (not an early-20th-century concern).

IN RECENT YEARS, pressure from several groups, including the New York Landmarks Commission, encouraged Hope's to produce an updated version of the steel casement window. The Landmark Window that Hope's now manufacturers has the same narrow shape and muntins as the original, but with modern weatherstripping, double glazing, gaskets, and two baked-on anti-rust finishes (epoxy followed by acrylic), which should last about 20 years; the window can also be dipped in zinc (not just electro-galvanized) so that it won't rust for some 80 years. This window is specifically for landmark buildings, and it's not cheap. Prices depend on the amount of work needed for installation. 🏠

ELAN ZINGMAN-LEITH is president of New York Preservation Specialists, a consultant to Skyline Windows, New York's largest installer of metal windows. He is former Deputy Director of Preservation of the New York City Landmarks Commission, where he drafted citywide guidelines on window preservation.

Elaborate diamond-paned metal windows in Dallas's Swiss Avenue Historic District.

Metal windows helped define the new architecture: here, steel casements in the Miami Beach Art Deco district.

HISTORIC METAL WINDOWS

MAINTENANCE & REPAIR
──── BY THE OHJ TECHNICAL STAFF ────

Hope's International Cotswold Casements, 1926

Projecting hinges to facilitate cleaning

B

All horizontal cames have Steel reinforcement

A

Bronze Two-point Handle with radial stop

Bronze Wedge →

Bronze non-projecting double bar sliding adjuster

Bronze Box & Turn

C

- presence and degree of corrosion (rust)
- condition of the paint film
- deterioration of metal –– bowed or bent segments, misaligned sash, etc.
- survival and condition of hardware (including screws, bolts, hinges)

ALSO INSPECT:
- condition of glass and glazing compound
- condition of masonry surrounding window
- need for corrective measures (from caulking to resetting slope of the sill)

STEEL RUSTS –– degree of corrosion determines the window's fate. Corrosion can be light –– flaking on the surface; medium –– a bubbled texture with rust penetrating the metal but without structural damage; or heavy –– structural damage such as exfoliation (bursting) or delamination (heavy peeling). As when inspecting punky wood, use a probe or ice pick to determine the extent of corrosion.

MOISTURE CAUSES RUST, so the source of water penetration or standing water has to be eliminated. Water can be coming from cracks in the masonry (repoint or caulk), from leaking gutters (clean and repair), from air conditioning condensate (rechannel), or from condensation on the interior (seal all joints; add interior storm glazing).

INTERIOR

REGLAZE AS REQ'D.

SEAL JOINT AGAINST CONDENSATE

CAULK

SILL

THEY LACK the stained glass and carved limestone hoods of Victorian windows, but metal windows are often the only facade decoration. Their proportion and scale, the rhythm of slender steel muntins, contribute to overall design. Metal casements, when open, project from the plane of the wall, adding a dimension. Inappropriate replacement, therefore, should be avoided.

LET'S BE STRAIGHT about this up front: Unlike wood windows, which are almost infinitely repairable, some steel windows are not practically salvageable. The reasons why will become apparent here. When preservation is possible, it will be cheaper than replacement with similar units and, of course, it ensures style integrity.

INSPECTION

METAL WINDOWS need maintenance. Your first task is to determine whether the deterioration is merely on the surface, or if corrosion has gone too far. If the window no longer latches, check for:

ROUTINE MAINTENANCE

BEFORE YOU CAN repaint (in fact, before you can adequately inspect), surface dirt and grease must be removed. Use a brush or vacuum cleaner, followed by a wipe-down with mineral spirits or denatured alcohol.

TO OVERHAUL salvageable windows:
(1) Remove light rust and built-up paint.
(2) Prime exposed metal with a rust-inhibiting primer.
(3) Replace cracked or broken glass.
(4) Replace missing screws or fasteners.
(5) Clean and lubricate hinges.
(6) Repaint all steel with two coats of finish paint, compatible with the primer.

Preservation Brief No. 13, written by Sharon Park for the National Park Service, was a major source of information-in-print for this article.

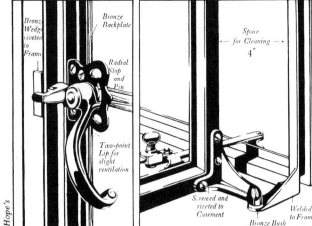

Solid Bronze Two-point Handle with Radial stop.

Projecting Hinge to facilitate Cleaning.

Hope's

Norma David

Cottage architecture in the 1920s: stucco walls, battened shutters, and metal casements.

(7) Caulk the masonry surround with a high-quality (expensive) elastomeric caulk (such as butyl or urethane).

TO REMOVE light rust, use a wire brush, aluminum-oxide sandpaper, or an electric wire or sanding wheel. Be sure to shield the adjacent areas, because all of these methods will scratch the glass. Besides mechanical methods, rust can be removed by chemicals. There are commercially available, anti-corrosive acid-based compounds that come as liquids or gels. Naval jelly is well known; it has a phosphoric acid base. Others contain ammonium citrate or oxalic acid.

DON'T USE hydrochloric or muriatic acid, which may leave a residue that will cause future deterioration. Wipe off chemical residue and dry immediately, preferably with a heat gun or industrial dryer. Do not use water in cleaning or rinsing. (Acids will attack both glass and masonry, so be sure to mask adequately using plastic sheets and waterproof tape.)

NOT RECOMMENDED are burning techniques such as torches and welding guns. Heat will distort metal and crack glazing. Also, flame methods operate at a temperature high enough to vaporize the lead undoubtedly contained in earlier coats of paint, releasing toxic fumes.

MOST OF THE METHODS that remove light to medium rust will also take off flaking paint. Additionally, you can use a solvent-rinsable chemical paint remover. A sound paint film is protecting the metal from rust and should be left alone unless it is thick enough to interfere with the operation of the window. Sand the paint and feather edges.

AS SOON AS you've uncovered bare metal, wipe it down with a solvent in preparation for an immediate coat of anti-corrosive primer. Rust will recur very quickly once the metal is exposed to air, so you may have to spot-prime as you go. Now that red lead is not readily available because of its toxicity, most metal primers are oil/alkyd-based preparations rich in zinc or zinc chromate. These are toxic to some degree too, so work in a well ventilated area and clean up immediately. Two coats of primer are strongly recommended.

IF CORROSION IS EXTENSIVE or metal sections are misaligned, the simple maintenance measures above won't be enough. Medium or even heavy corrosion that hasn't done structural damage can be removed chemically or by sandblasting. Use metal or plywood shields to protect masonry and glass. The Preservation Assistance Division of The National Park Service recommends low pressure (80-100 psi), and a grit size in the range of #10 to #45. A pencil-point nozzle allows the most control. It can even be used to remove dried putty after the glass has been removed.

AGAIN, as soon as bare metal is exposed, it should be primed, including the inside rabbet in the sash. If the municipal codes insist on wet blasting, the metal must be dried immediately with a gun. The fine particles blasted off almost surely contain lead.

METAL WINDOW SECTIONS may have bowed or bent due to an impact or expansion from corrosion. If the distortion is minor, you might be able to realign the metal in place. Remove the glass and apply pressure to the bent area. Use a protective wooden 2x4 behind the bent section. If the section is bent due to internal corrosion, cut the metal section to relieve pressure, then press back into shape and try a welded repair.

SMALL HOLES and uneven areas caused by rust can be filled and sanded smooth, not only for appearance but also to eliminate pools for water. Patching material made of epoxy with steel fibers is easy to use. It's available for industrial steel repair, or (in smaller quantities) as "plumber's epoxy."

FINISHING UP

TO COMPLETE deferred maintenance chores: (1) Replace cracked glass, deteriorated glazing compound, missing screws, and broken fasteners.

(2) Clean and lubricate hinges. Often brass or bronze, they can be cleaned with a cleaning solvent and fine bronze wool (try a marine supplier if you can't find it at a woodworkers' supply). Use a non-greasy lubricant

Late '20s English architecture, featuring stylized "half-timbering" and patterned brick "nogging."

formulated for metals, such as WD-40 or a graphite-based lock lubricant. Use spray-on lubricant from time to time on windows that are used often.

(3) Paint the windows and caulk the masonry surround. Paint on a dry day, and use a top coat compatible with the primer (from the same manufacturer -- read the label). Two coats are recommended if you started with bare metal. Bring the paint onto the glass slightly to give a weathertight seal. After the paint is dry, use a flexible exterior-grade caulk where the window and surrounding masonry meet. (paintable caulk after the first coat of paint, color-matched caulk after the second coat)

(4) If you must replace the glazing, retain all clips, glazing beads, and other fasteners that hold to glass (although reasonably similar replacements are available today). When bedding glass, be sure to use glazing compound formulated for metal windows.

WORKSHOP REPAIRS

WHEN DAMAGE IS SEVERE or many windows must be done all at once, the sash or entire unit may have to be taken to a shop for rust removal, metal alignment, welding or splicing, and reglazing. This is an expensive proposition, usually reserved for significant, irreplaceable windows.

THE SASH AND FRAME can usually be unhinged, then unbolted or unscrewed. But the subframe must be left in place; built into the masonry, it can only be cut out with a torch.

WITH GLASS OUT, rust is removed by chemical dipping or by sandblasting. Usually dipped in a phosphoric acid solution, medium rust will come off, but deep corrosion is more effectively removed by blasting. The paint will come off in either case. Primer follows. Serious bowing can sometimes be remedied by a combination of heat and pressure.

THE BOTTOM RAIL OF THE SASH and sill of the frame are usually the first to go. If you can <u>find</u> an ironworker willing to do the job, the bottom rail <u>could</u> be cut out with a torch, a

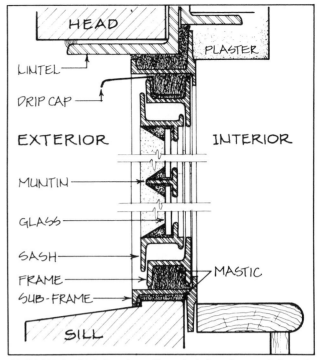

SECTION: Steel Window (Not all metal windows have a sub-frame.)

new rail welded in, the joints ground down, and the window primed, painted, and glazed. But two complications interfere. First, the rollings for light, light-intermediate, and intermediate casement windows are no longer available. The ironworker will probably make up the shape from standard angles -- which has disadvantages. Marrying of the sash and frame is what creates a tight seal against air and water. However, the built-up section is unlikely to match the old section very well and is, therefore, likely to leak. Second, spot-welding angles together often leaves internal voids between members (as in factory sash). The metal surrounding those voids cannot be maintained or painted and soon rust.

ONE SOURCE for replacement sections is from salvaged windows, maybe even from another part of the same building. If budget is unlimited, an ornamental-metal fabricator can weld flat plates into a built-up section, or a steel plant can mill bar steel to the right profile.

IF THE SILL has rusted out, this can theoretically be replaced as well. However, removing the old sill will require extensive plaster demolition. The same problems of poor match and internal voids pertain to sills.

SALVAGED WINDOWS are again the best source for replacement hardware. A metalworker can adapt ready-made modern counterparts by filling existing hardware holes with steel epoxy or plug welds, then tapping in new screw holes.

WEATHERIZATION

THE BLACKEST MARK on the reputation of metal windows is their energy loss. Not only the glass -- but also the metal frame -- lose a tremendous amount of heat through conduction. The cold surface also creates conduction currents (drafts) in the room. Condensation of interior water vapor on the cold surfaces is a familiar problem.

THEIR PERFORMANCE can be improved somewhat. Caulk will help with infiltration. Weather-stripping around the operable sash is sometimes suggested; practically speaking, it's not usually successful. Metal windows have close tolerances, leaving little room for the spring-metal or vinyl strips. (If you do weatherstrip, use the thinnest material that fills the gap. Too-thick weatherstrip can spring the hinges.) Besides, infiltration is not the issue -- conduction is.

FOR THE METAL CASEMENT that "leaks," a weatherstrip made from a caulk bead is worth a try. Clean the frame with solvent, and prime it. Then apply a neat bead of firm-setting ("low modulus") caulk or sealant such as silicone. Place a strip of bond-breaker tape on the operable sash, covering the metal where contact will occur. Close the window, tape in place, and let the caulk set for 2 to 7 days (depending on label directions and humidity). When you open the window, the bead will have taken the shape of the gap -- custom-fitted weatherstripping! Remove the tape.

TO OFFSET CONDUCTION LOSSES as well as infiltration, of course, you'll have to add another layer of glass. There are three possibilities; think of cost and aesthetics.

(1) Install a clear glazing (rigid acrylic or glass) over the original window. It can go inside or outside, and be permanently screwed in or removable. Depending on installation details, it may make the original sash inoperable.

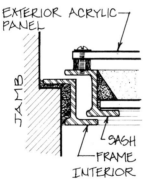

EXTERIOR ACRYLIC PANEL

JAMB

SASH
FRAME
INTERIOR

(2) Have storm windows made to fit. (Note that pivoting and austral windows, which when opened extend to both sides of the plane of the window, become inoperable when storm sash is added.) Obviously, the storm window should match the configuration of the prime window -- muntins should line up, and so on. Storm sash can be used on the inside or the outside, depending on operation of the window and appearance.

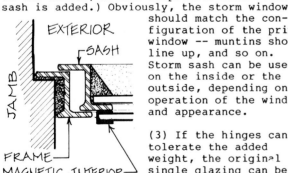

EXTERIOR

SASH

JAMB

FRAME
MAGNETIC INTERIOR
GLASS PANEL

(3) If the hinges can tolerate the added weight, the original single glazing can be replaced with thermal glass. As the rolled metal sections of steel windows are usually one to 1-1/2 inches thick, they can normally accommodate modern thermal glass which is 3/8 to 5/8 inch thick. Metal glazing beads reinforce the muntins. This way, the window keeps its appearance and is fully operational. This is the most expensive option.

AN EXPERT in such matters, Elan Zingman-Leith, sums up the rehabilitation prognosis this way: A steel casement window which works badly because of paint build-up or minor rusting is easy to repair. However, steel casements in which the structural members have rusted away can be repaired only at great cost, with just a moderate chance of your ending up with a window that performs well.

Steel windows can be replaced by new steel windows or aluminum windows. These companies have dealers nationwide:

HOPE'S ARCHITECTURAL PRODUCTS, 84 Hopkins Ave., Jamestown, NY 14701. (716) 665-5124. Make reproduction steel windows, but with modern improvements.

SKYLINE WINDOWS, 625. W. 130th St., New York, NY 10027. (212) 491-3000. An aluminum window similar to old steel windows, for now available only in quantity.

WAUSAU METALS CORP., PO Box 1746, Wausau, WI 54401. (715) 845-2161. An aluminum window that looks similar to some old steel casements.

KAWNEER, 555 Guthridge Ct., Norcross, GA 30092. (404) 449-5555. Variety of aluminum windows, including pivoting, top-hinged, projecting, and casement. Primarily commercial work; through contractor on residential projects.

Wesley Haynes, NYLC

Metal windows *vs.* remuddling: the repeating grid of slender muntins — and the integrity of the facade — lost to individual whim.

OLD-HOUSE SECURITY

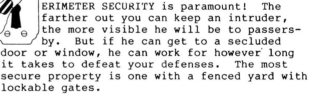

PART ONE – PERIMETER SECURITY

by David Swearingen

S A PROFESSIONAL LOCKSMITH living in a restoration area with one of the highest crime rates in Florida, I've learned about the problems of old-house security firsthand. I cringe when I see some of the security measures my neighbors, panicked by fear, have taken, locking up their homes like fortresses. All too often, their security measures are not only ineffective, but they also destroy the character of the house.

THIS ARTICLE is written for those of you who have enough aesthetic sense that you're unwilling to tack an incongruous assortment of modern security devices onto your house. In most cases, you can use homemade, antique, or reproduction security devices to gain a high degree of security. When modern devices must be used, there are ways to disguise them so they look old, or to hide them so they're nearly invisible.

LOCKS are a good example. The most secure lock in the world is a bit key, lever tumbler, rim or mortise lock. This is an old design, going back over 150 years. The same locks that were installed in Attica and Leavenworth when they were built are available for your house today. Alarms generally require modern components, but these may be completely hidden, or at least made very unobtrusive.

ALL OF THIS and more will be discussed here and in Part II. Let's start with security outside your home, and work our way indoors.

Assess Your Security Needs

THE FIRST STEP is to determine how much security you need. The number and type of security devices you require depends on your neighborhood, the local police, and yourself. Someone who lives in the inner city will obviously require greater security than someone who lives in a rural village.

WHEREVER YOU LIVE, you can reduce your chances of being a victim of crime in several ways -- without buying and installing any security

devices: Get to know your neighbors. If you develop a good relationship with your neighbors, they'll watch out for you. A befriended neighbor knows who belongs at your house, and who looks suspicious. Keep your guard up. Common sense is the most effective deterrent to crime. No security system will protect you if you forget to lock-up when you leave (even if you'll only be gone a few minutes). Make arrangements so that newspapers don't pile up while you're on vacation. Don't leave an open invitation to theft!

PERIMETER SECURITY

ERIMETER SECURITY is paramount! The farther out you can keep an intruder, the more visible he will be to passers-by. But if he can get to a secluded door or window, he can work for however long it takes to defeat your defenses. The most secure property is one with a fenced yard with lockable gates.

Fences

THE BEST FENCE for security purposes is an iron fence. Other types have serious disadvantages. Chain link is easy to climb, and totally out of character on an older house. Solid wood fences can be hard to climb, and are loved by homeowners for the privacy they afford -- but they are loved by burglars for the same reason.

CAST-IRON FENCING, however, is hard to climb, provides no hiding places for criminals, and is authentic for many older homes. The only drawback is the sky-high cost. I had my heart set on cast-iron fencing for my own home, but my heart broke when I found that it would cost three times as much for the fence as I paid for my house.

David Swearingen is the proprietor of D. S. Locksmithing in Jacksonville, Fla. In addition to securing his own old house, David has over 20 years' experience in the field.

INSTEAD, I DESIGNED and built a wooden fence that looks like a cast-iron fence. The materials cost me a fraction of what iron fencing would have. Each gate includes a built-in mortise lock that's nearly invisible unless you look closely. In the two years before we had the fence, we suffered four burglary attempts; in the three years with the fence, there has been only one. Quite a dramatic decrease. I'll plant daggerberry bushes inside the fence; that way, if anyone jumps over, they'll jump out again quick.

IF YOU HAVE a serious crime problem in your area, you may want an alarm on the fence to alert you if anyone tries to climb it. It takes a pretty sophisticated alarm to detect climbers while sifting out false alarms, though, so it's likely to be expensive. In most cases, such a device is unnecessary.

A securely fenced yard is your first line of defense. Not only is it another obstacle, it also makes it difficult for an intruder to explain what he's doing on your property.

Lighting

GOOD LIGHTING is one of the best deterrents to forced entry. Nobody wants to be in the limelight while committing felonious deeds. On the other hand, lighting up the entire property not only makes it look like a prison compound, it also puts you on a first-name

> 'Good lighting is one of the best deterrents to forced entry. Nobody wants to be in the limelight while committing felonious deeds.'

basis with the folks at the utility company. I've found the "Security Light Control" to be the perfect solution for most applications.

A SECURITY LIGHT CONTROL is an infra-red heat detector that can be connected to existing lighting. When someone passes near it, it activates the light. The beauty of this device is that it comes on only when needed, and it makes an intruder think that someone in the house has spotted him. Burglars get very uncomfortable when they think they're being watched. It's a good idea to use this device instead of leaving your porch light on. To most burglars, a lighted porch is a sign that says, "The residents are out -- will return later." A light that comes on automatically

may save you from being mugged at your door, too. Keep all your security lighting out of reach, and protected from breakage.

Garages & Common Sense

IF YOUR HOUSE has an attached garage, pay attention to securing both the garage and the door between garage and house. Garages are a weak spot, and once an intruder has broken in, he can spend all the time he needs to get in the house -- usually with your tools.

LARGE, NOISY DOGS also provide excellent security. Dogs are good at scaring intruders away before they damage antique doors and windows in their efforts to force entry. (Before buying a dog for this purpose, see "Guard Dogs" on page 434 of this issue.)

BASEMENT DOORS AND WINDOWS need to be especially well secured. They are more vulnerable to attack because they are so close to the ground and usually cloaked by shrubbery.

A BURGLAR'S BEST FRIENDS are seclusion and opportunity. Minimize seclusion by trimming shrubbery and increasing lighting to eliminate those hidden openings that invite intruders. Minimize opportunity by using common-sense practices that make it look like someone is always home, and by locking up all tools and ladders. Few burglars carry many tools with them -- too often, they can pick up whatever they need right on the job.

SECURING THE BUILDING ENVELOPE

Doors

ET'S HOPE your exterior doors are in good-enough condition that they won't have to be replaced. There are many suitable reproduction doors on the market, but a new set of old-style doors could cost you a fortune. Look for thin wood panels, glass, a poor fit between door and frame, a weak or flimsy frame, and inadequate door thickness. The presence of these conditions doesn't necessarily mandate door replacement. There are measures you can take to strengthen weak spots.

PRACTICALLY ALL DOORS have thin wood panels, large glass windows, or both. Because either can be easily broken, you may consider shatterproof glazing or high-security screening, or double-sided locks (all of which will be discussed later).

A LARGE GAP between the door and frame can be closed by adding blocking between the jamb and studs. Remove the interior casing to expose the studs and the jamb -- there's usually at least an inch between them. Add solid wood blocking between the studs and jamb to close the gap. It's wise to add blocking even if there isn't a large gap. Adding a few solid blocks will reduce springiness in the jamb and make it more difficult to jimmy the door.

DOUBLE DOORS are especially problematic. Neither door has a solid jamb to lock into; instead, an active door locks into the thin edge of an inactive door, which itself is locked at top and bottom. The thin edge of the inactive door provides virtually no resistance to kicking or prying.

"THE DOOR STIFFENER," by J.T. Security Products, solves this problem. The design is simple -- two heavy steel plates that clamp

> "Perimeter security is paramount! If an intruder can get to a secluded window or door, he can work for however long it takes to defeat your defenses."

onto each side of the door, providing tremendous reinforcement. It's available only through locksmiths. Adding steel plates isn't terribly sensitive, but it is less drastic than replacement.

New Doors

IF YOUR EXISTING DOOR is inappropriate, damaged beyond repair, or thin and weak, there are some things to consider about new doors:

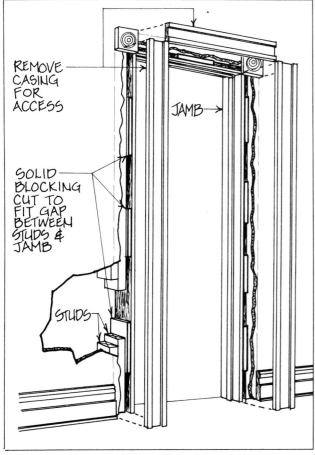

Strengthen weak door jambs by adding solid wood blocking between the studs and the jamb.

The door stiffener is sure to thwart this youthful intruder's attempts to gain forced entry.

● Stock door thicknesses at many retail outlets are usually 1-3/8" and 1-3/4". On <u>old</u> houses, you may find doors from of 1-1/8" to 2-1/4" or thicker, and everything in between. Large manufacturers and small shops that specialize in old-style doors are able to furnish 2-1/4"-thick or thicker doors on special order. It's a good idea to go with doors at least 2-1/4" thick even if it means repositioning the stops.

● Quality and construction of wood doors varies greatly. Consult your dealer and compare sample doors carefully before buying. Be sure panel construction is high quality with sturdy, well-secured panel stops.

Metal Doors

METAL DOORS and frames are stronger than wooden doors and frames, but they're usually not used in a restoration project for aesthetic reasons. Nevertheless, for a secluded opening (i.e., one that's not a focal point of the house), your best bet may be a metal door with a mortise lockset. If you do buy a metal door, you must demand heavy-gauge metal to gain an appreciable advantage over a wood door. Insist on 16-gauge <u>or thicker</u> metal for the door, and at least 14-gauge for the frame.

ONE DISADVANTAGE of steel doors is that they're normally available only as flush doors. Some of the available metal panel doors can be little more than tissue-thin sheet metal bonded to reinforced cardboard. In my neighborhood, the kids use them for dart boards. But if you shop around, you can find steel panel doors in 16- or 14-gauge thickness.

ANOTHER DISADVANTAGE is that they don't mimic wood. Applying a real wood veneer is the most attractive solution, but it's expensive. Steel panel doors can be grained by do-it-yourselfers, and two manufacturers (Steelcraft and Trusbilt) offer pre-grained steel doors.

> **"I had the only doors in town that hadn't been bored like Swiss cheese for a succession of night-latches and cheap deadbolts."**

High-Security Screen Doors

I HAD THE ONLY exterior doors in town that hadn't been bored like Swiss cheese for a succession of nightlatches and cheap deadbolts. And I wasn't about to violate those pristine doors. But we did have a security risk. All five exterior doors are thin, 1-3/8" panel doors. The front door is half glass. Any burglar could kick out the panels and crawl right in. But replacing all five doors with thicker, authentic-looking doors would have been prohibitively expensive.

WE OPTED TO KEEP our original doors, with original 1905 locks intact. One rear door was temporarily secured by an iron burglar-bar door. Ugly, but cheap, unobtrusive in that location, and easily replaced later. Three

The author's high-security screen door.

other rear doors were protected by constructing a steel latticework porch (see box).

THE FRONT DOOR was our biggest concern. It had to look authentic. A high-security screen door seemed the perfect solution. It provides a strong deterrent without replacing or completely hiding the entry door. Security screening is simply high-tensile strength stainless-steel screening that's custom fitted into a steel frame. All hardware and fittings are concealed. It's available from Kane Manufacturing (see suppliers box).

WE SPECIFIED a high-security screen door with four deadbolts that are thrown simultaneously, a close-fitting metal frame and, of course, a high-security lock with a huge, old-fashioned bit key. It has its own heavy metal frame and makes the front entryway virtually burglar-proof. We added some gingerbread and brass hardware so that it looks more appropriate. It cost over $500 four years ago, but the peace of mind it has provided has been worth many times the price. We're able to open our front door and talk to strangers without fear.

Windows

OLD WINDOWS are difficult to secure without compromising their appearance. A good way to secure them is to plant a spanish bayonet or large cactus directly beneath each window -- burglars will quickly get the point that they are unwelcome. Seriously, planting abrasive or irritating foliage provides an inexpensive deterrent that won't alter period details.

MANY INCONSPICUOUS, inexpensive locks are available. Window locks provide only limited security, though. If you live in a good neighborhood, and your windows are visible to neighbors, these locks are adequate. I recommend key-operated window locks. You have to weigh the hazard these locks may present in case of fire, but remember: any lock that's easily opened without a key is also easily

opened by a burglar, particularly one who's in your house searching for an unseen way to remove your belongings.

DOUBLE-HUNG WINDOWS are best locked with a security bolt that's mortised into the frame. This set-up allows the window to be locked even when it's partially open for ventilation. Another strong, inexpensive lock is a screw-type pin that screws the upper and lower sash together. This lock is slow and inconvenient to use, and could be an obstacle in a fire. Use it on seldom-used windows or to secure your windows before going away on vacation.

CASEMENT WINDOWS may also be locked. While there are some surface-mounted locks available, I feel that a simple, key-operated bolt mortised into the frame is best. It is inaccessible to burglars and so inconspicuous that it will not detract from the best restoration.

REGARDLESS of how you lock your windows, they will remain the most vulnerable points. So if you live in a high-crime area, you'll want to further secure them with one or more of the following security devices:

● WINDOW GRILLES (a euphemism for burglar bars) are perhaps the most common means of securing large openings. I've seen masterfully designed, exquisitely beautiful window grilles that fit right into the design of heavily-ornamented Victorian rowhouses, but these super-expensive creations are usually the exception. Most are downright ugly! I don't like them.

● UNBREAKABLE PLASTIC GLAZING is perhaps the most unobtrusive means of securing your windows. I strongly recommend Dupont's Lucite S-A-R™. It's about half the weight of glass, doesn't yellow with age, and is extremely scratch-resistant. Many banks use it instead of bullet-proof glass. (I have a photograph of a bullet disintegrating as it hits the surface of a Lucite panel.) High-security "stained glass" windows can be faked using Lucite panels with Stained Glass Overlay™. This is a patented process available through franchised craftspersons. The result is said to look identical to genuine stained glass.

● HIGH-SECURITY SCREENING provides perhaps the best protection for windows. Locks and Lucite won't do the job if a burglar is able to kick in the sash. Security screening is available in several wire and frame grades, giving you many levels of security to choose from. The screens are stainless steel, but can be purchased from Kane Manufacturing pre-enamelled in several neutral colors -- avoiding that "maximum security" look.

NEXT MONTH: How to choose locks and alarm systems that provide superior protection without detracting from your house's character.

STEEL LATTICE
An Example of Substitute Materials for Increased Security

OUR BACK PORCH was originally enclosed with latticework. It has a door that opens directly into the house, and a staircase that leads to two other porches, each with a door to the house. It's nice to leave these doors open for ventilation.

THE LATTICE turned out to be a weak spot in our defenses. A burglar pried off some pieces to gain entry, allowing himself out-of-sight access to all three doors (none of which was terribly secure). We were unable to find new lattice more than 1/4" thick — not sturdy enough to resist attack. Local "restorationists" advised enclosing the porch with plywood and a solid-core door. I used 1/4" by 2" steel instead of wood. Although I would have preferred diagonal lattice (I think it looks better), I settled for horizontal/vertical because of the difficulty in cutting steel plates diagonally. The original lattice was done this way, so at least it's appropriate.

THE MOST IMPORTANT consideration when working with steel is rust-proofing. Each piece was pickled with phosphoric acid to remove all traces of grease, then it was given a thick coat of zinc-chromate primer. This was followed by a top coat of enamel. Each piece was fastened to the framing with stainless-steel, tamperproof screws. All the pieces were joined with stainless-steel nuts and bolts wherever they intersected.

MY WIFE AND I designed a matching door, which we built ourselves. It is two inches thick, with steel lattice sandwiched between layers of through-bolted, rock-hard Georgia pine. The door is hung on massive ball-bearing hinges, framed with 4x4 timbers, and secured with a heavy-duty mortise lock. Houses come and houses go, but that latticework porch isn't going anywhere.

Addresses of Listed Companies
Kane Manufacturing, 515 N. Fraley St., Kane, PA 16735
(814) 837-6464

Steelcraft, 9017 Blue Ash Rd., Cincinnati, OH 45242
(513) 745-6400

Trusbuilt, 2575 Como Ave., St. Paul, MN 55108
(612) 646-7181

Dupont Lucite: See yellow pages under "plastics," or call
1 (800) 4LUCITE

Stained Glass Overlay, 151 Kalmus Drive, Costa Mesa, CA 92626
(714) 957-8188 or (800) 654-7666

J.T. Security Products, PO Box 368, Temple City, CA 91780
(818) 709-0857

BEWARE OF DOG

by Danielle Schultz

BETTER PROTECTION OR MORE PROBLEMS?

IF BUYING a big, tough dog sounds like a fine way to protect your house, think about it some more before visiting a kennel. We got our dog shortly after we purchased an old house in an inner-city neighborhood. We thought we needed protection and after all, one of the reasons we bought a house was to escape from a succession of landlords' "no-pets" rules. Within two months she cost us substantially more than our insurance deductible and did more damage than a gang of vandals could have. What follows are a few points I wish I'd known first.

SELECTING A BREED

IF YOU OWN a rambling farmhouse with a large tract of land, you can handle a dog that needs a lot of exercise. If, however, you live in a city row house, you will need to select very carefully. Dogs that need a lot of exercise can become stir-crazy house wreckers if not given daily, lengthy exercise. Do you really have time to run the dog for an hour per evening and every weekend? (Yes? Are you sure you're restoring an old house?) If you live in the city, chances are you'll want to avoid the sporting breeds (retrievers, setters, etc.) unless you're certain you have the time to properly work them.

MOST OF YOU who want to buy a dog for protection aren't interested in starting a guard dog company. So you want a dog you can handle safely without enrolling in a multitude of training classes. Simply put, you want your guard dog to be the family pet as well. Different breeds have different characteristics, and within a breed, each individual dog has a unique personality -- usually affected by training. Some breeds are inherently too friendly and trusting to be effective guard dogs. Others are too mean and unpredictable to leave alone with young children. You'll want to choose and train a dog that falls between these extremes.

THE BEST PLACE to educate yourself on the general characteristics of pure-bred dogs is at your local library or bookstore. THE COMPLETE DOG BOOK is the official publication of the American Kennel Club. It's an excellent reference for anyone who owns or is considering owning a dog. Once you've identified a breed you might be interested in, attend a couple of dog shows and talk to breeders and handlers. Most are more than willing to share their knowledge and can help you zero-in on a dog likely to have the characteristics you desire.

SELECT A DOG whose size you can manage, but big enough to do the job. Some people claim that a small, yappy dog is an effective watchdog. (The last person to tell me that had his Yorkshire Terrier stolen in a subsequent burglary.) To protect its territory convincingly, a dog needs to be a minimum of about forty pounds.

WHAT ABOUT A MUTT? When you buy a pure-bred dog, you're buying fairly predictable characteristics. My personal experience with mixed breeds leads me to believe that they're calmer and friendlier than pure-bred dogs. This makes the dog a good pet, but a poor guard dog. Also: Some dogs discourage intruders just by their appearance. It's hard to guess what a mutt will look like when it grows up.

PREPARE YOURSELF

THE YOUNGER A DOG is, the longer it will take to housebreak it. If you're accustomed to small dogs or cats, you may be surprised at how much more important early housebreaking is with a large-breed dog.

I MUST CONFESS that the only dog I had ever owned was a toy poodle, when I was a child. I was totally unprepared for the work of training and handling a large-breed pup. Sasha was six pounds when we bought her at six weeks. Within a few weeks, she was over twenty pounds. Her...let's say, output increased accordingly. We maintained a mop, bucket, and shovel on every floor of the house. We tried confining her to a smaller area -- she went berserk. She chewed a leg off the kitchen table, she ate a can of putty, she learned to open the freezer door and help herself. She screamed (as opposed to bark, cry, or whimper) anytime we were out of her sight. She ate woodwork, she ate part of a door.

SERIOUS TRAINING of your dog can't begin until at least six months. Oh sure, you can teach him a couple commands much earlier, but you can't truly rely on consistent behavior at such a young age. Be prepared for the tremendous strength large-breed puppies can have. And make provisions to keep them away from valuable objects.

WHEN YOU BUY a large dog, you're acquiring a potentially dangerous weapon. You must plan the time for obedience training for yourself and the puppy. Investigate the local obedience classes and enroll as soon as the dog is old enough to be accepted. You can't just send a dog off to school and expect it to come home trained; your participation is essential, so be sure you'll have the time.

THE VERDICT

IS IT WORTH THE TROUBLE? For us it was. But we were animal lovers to begin with, and although we went into it blind, we remained patient and learned as we proceeded. Of all the people on our block who are restoring houses, we're the only ones who own a guard dog. I don't think it's a coincidence that we're also the only ones who haven't been burglarized.

SASHA'S NOT TRAINED to attack, but I think she would if one of us were struggling with an intruder. Our heating contractor spent about ten minutes atop the fence when he walked into "her backyard" unexpectedly. She takes her job seriously, is very loyal and loving (to us), and she never complains about the mess we make as we restore our house. So if you're patient, and willing to take time to train and exercise the dog, you're likely to acquire an excellent protector and companion. Just remember to raise the puppy before you sand the floors!

BEWARE OF DYSPLASIA

HIP DYSPLASIA is a common condition in large-breed dogs. Hip dysplasia is an inherited condition that ranges in severity between individual dogs. The condition is marked by a deformity of the hip joint causing a poor fit of the femur in the hip socket. Even mildly affected dogs will experience pain and loss of mobility.

BECAUSE IT IS a congenital defect, you can pretty much assume that a dog will be free from the condition if its ancestors weren't afflicted. The condition can skip one or more generations, though, so just checking the dam and sire won't give reliable results.

THE ORTHOPEDIC FOUNDATION for Animals (OFA) tests the large-breed pups of licensed breeders and certifies them free of any signs of the disease. This certification isn't a guarantee that the puppy will not develop dysplasia, but the chances are significantly lower than for an uncertified pup. Insist on this certification when you buy a large-breed puppy. If you encounter problems, contact your local A.K.C. chapter or your local veterinarian.

A SAMPLING OF SUITABLE BREEDS*

German Shepherd

Perhaps the pre-eminent guard dog breed in this country, and with good reason. A properly trained German Shepherd exhibits aggressive behavior only under extreme conditions, as when its handler is being attacked. German Shepherds are extremely loyal and exercise good "judgment" in sounding an alarm (i.e., they won't keep you up all night barking at anything that moves).

Dalmatian

As a whole, Dalmatians are ideally suited for watchdog duty. The breed strikes a nice balance between friendliness toward strangers and a desire to protect its territory. This makes the dog a most reliable alarm. If a passerby stops to say "Hi" to the dog, he'll be responded to with curiosity or indifference. If an interloper starts to climb the fence, the Dalmatian will let you know.

Collie

Collies are a friendly, playful breed of dog. It is rare to find a vicious Collie. Nevertheless, they take seriously their role of family protector by discouraging trespass with a piercing bark. These characteristics make the Collie an ideal night sentry for families that include young children. Collies enjoy the company and attention of children as much as children are delighted with the dog.

Doberman Pinscher

Dobermans have received a lot of unwarranted bad press, being unfairly labelled as vicious. The breed does take well to aggressive training, and so has been used as an attack dog by police, the military, and security firms. Dogs that have been trained to attack should be supervised only by the most knowledgeable handlers. You do *not* need an attack dog to guard your property. Doberman Pinschers that have not undergone vigorous attack training are very affectionate and loyal. They make excellent companions and will display aggressive behavior to humans only when their "family" is in physical jeopardy.

Samoyed

Samoyeds are one of the most strikingly beautiful breeds. They also have a disposition that lends itself equally well to dependable watchdog or loving family pet. The Samoyeds are an old breed, and have worked for and protected man for many centuries. This association has created a modern animal that is adaptable to many roles and has unerring loyalty to its master. They too discriminate well between strangers who do or do not belong.

---

* This is by no means an exhaustive list of those breeds which make good family guards. Many other breeds have a temperament that strikes a fine balance between family pet and protector. Familiarize yourself with the breeds you have an interest in before investing in a pure-bred dog.

POST-VICTORIAN HOUSES

Right: The cabinet's semicircular doors slide apart to reveal the telephone. There's a fold-down compartment below for storing the telephone book. The ringer is mounted on the wall behind the book compartment. The unit measures 2 ft. 10 in. high, 1 ft. 7 in. wide, with an 11½-in. shelf. Below: The telephone book hangs from a rod behind the telephone.

Telephone Cabinets

BY EVE KAHN

Left: This typical telephone cabinet has a panel covering the ringer (perforated so that the sound isn't muffled) and a "tilting box" for the directory. The box doubles as a fold-down shelf for book or phone. The piece measures 3 ft. 9 in. high and 1 ft. 5½ in. wide. It fits a wall opening 3 ft. 6 in. high by 1 ft. 2 in. wide.

Right: Niches like this one, minus the bell-box panel, were also used to display sculpture or vases. It measures 3 ft. 1 in. high by 1 ft. 5½ in. wide. The wall opening should be 2 ft. 10 in. high and 1 ft. 2 in. wide.

The built-in telephone cabinet had a brief heyday, from 1920 to 1940. It appeared on the scene along with all sorts of built-in furniture, favored by post-Victorian builders as a way to save space and streamline interiors (smaller homes and apartments were popular, while Victorian clutter was not). It gave the telephone a home (the equipment was still an unfamiliar item, and people didn't know what to do with it). It covered the unattractive, wall-mounted box that held the telephone ringer (ringing mechanisms were separate units until the late '30s). And it usually had a convenient place to store the telephone directory.

Telephone cabinets were available from most millwork catalogs. The removable panel covering the bell was often perforated "to allow the sound of the bell to be heard." Some cabinets had semi-circular doors. The less expensive ones, actually simple niches, had bell-box panels but no book drawers. The most elaborate reached the floor and had a fold-down seat with backrest "for long conversations."

Cabinets were positioned on the wall high enough to make standing and talking comfortable. On some the book compartment, when folded down, created a lower shelf for sitting and talking — cords were shorter in those days.

When telephone technology improved, and built-in furniture went out of fashion, so went the telephone cabinet. The designs on these pages, taken from our collection of period millwork catalogs, should give you a good idea of what was available, in case you want to restore or build one. Approximate dimensions are provided where possible. If you're building one, be sure to take today's larger phones into consideration when determining the depth of the telephone shelf.

"Where Do I Start?"

In this conclusion to last month's priority list for starting a renovation, we examine working in phases, and give the proper sequence for interior work.

by Jonathan Poore and Patricia Poore

Renovation of the *interior* is difficult to plan and will cause headaches if not sequenced logically. Not only do you have to live in the midst of the work, but interior renovation is also more complicated and fussy than exterior. The exterior requires salvage of existing elements without damage to the materials and character of the building. In other words, you "fix it."

On the interior, decisions are more complex because they are interconnected. You may have to modify or update areas such as kitchens and baths, just to make them functional. In other words, you are faced with "changing it" while you "fix it."

In the real world of budget and time constraints, few people undertake a whole-house restoration all at once. Accepting that, we've included a discussion of *phasing* the project. But even if you're facing a one-room-at-a-time job, the master plan for the whole building must be scripted first — and adhered to. There's nothing worse (or more expensive) than going backward.

five
PHASED APPROACHES FOR INTERIOR RENOVATION

● You've come a long way: The building has been stabilized, water has been stopped, you've got a grip on an overall plan, and the exterior restoration is well under way.
  Before you can finalize the sequence for interior work, you must make a fundamental decision: Will you bring the entire building along in the most logical and efficient way, or will you break the work into phases in deference to livability or budget?
  (Exterior work can also be approached in phases, but decisions are less complex.)

A. UNOCCUPIED BUILDING

1. For an unoccupied building, the fastest and most cost-effective procedure is for each area to be brought along at the same rate. All the demolition, all the mechanical systems, all the replastering, all the stripping, all the painting, etc.

2. Although it is by far more efficient to work this way -- because there is virtually no contractor call-back and no steps backward and little time wasted on interim cleanup -- it means that the entire building will be in the same degree of mess. It is nearly impossible to live in a building that is undergoing this kind of restoration.

B. OCCUPIED BUILDING -- The Phased Job

● You will almost surely want to phase your restoration work if you are living in the building. Phasing is also necessary when there is not enough money in the budget to do everything at once. Some things, of course, are impossible to phase: You can't reroof this year and pay for flashings next year. But you can certainly tackle roofing one year and clapboards the next.

● Beware of grey areas that cost you extra in the long run. For example, it is possible to rebuild a chimney after the roof has been replaced. But there will probably be some damage to the new roof during the masonry work. If budget had allowed, it would have been better to have the mason come before the roofer.

● Always try to sequence the work so that there is minimal disruption to adjacent areas. Several approaches can help:

1. Living without finishes -- completing a room or area up to the point of livability but without any finishes or decoration. You can move into a room that has mechanical systems installed, sound plaster, and a fairly clean

floor. (Items that can be deferred: installation and finish on baseboard and most trim; light fixtures; final floor treatment; priming, painting, and wallpaper; all decorating.)
    a. Disadvantage is that you have to live without the aesthetic satisfaction of finishes, sometimes for quite a while. There is time wasted in moving into an area and then moving out again for final finishes, but this is almost unavoidable to some degree if you're living on a job site.
    b. Advantages of this approach
      1) The house will function fastest this way
      2) You don't have to commit to colors, furnishings, style, or decorating until the whole house is restored, at which point you'll have a better overview of its true character
      3) Any minor damage that occurs in the finished room when adjacent areas are being renovated will be easy to repair. For example, heavy work in the next room may cause hairline cracks in the already-patched plaster of the finished room. But if there is no paint or paper on the walls, it's quite easy to tape or patch later.
2. The "zone-by-zone" approach -- one suite of rooms, a floor, or a wing is brought up to a consistent level of finish before going on to the next area
    a. This won't work in a small house or one with an open floor plan. It requires a more flexible budget than the room-by-room approach below, because you'll be biting off more in each phase
    b. Logical breaks can often be made, but be sure that plumbing, heating, and electrical risers are brought to deferred areas before any finishing is done elsewhere. You don't want to break into a papered plaster wall in the parlor because you deferred <u>thinking</u> about the third floor mechanicals.

NOTE: Whenever a wall, ceiling, or floor is opened up, always think ahead and take advantage of the opportunity to get into the building's guts. Examples: If an exterior wall is opened up, consider installing insulation, electrical or plumbing risers, nailers for built-ins, etc. If a stair soffit is open, listen for squeaks: Tighten wedges, make repairs from below while you can.

3. The room-by-room approach
    a. The only advantage is a psychological one: You get to savor a truly finished room, which gives you a hiding place and the imagination to go on. (Some people elect to completely finish just the kitchen or a bedroom before tackling the rest of the house -- the bedroom is easier.)
    b. The disadvantages are obvious: You will undoubtedly mar or dirty finishes when work proceeds on each subsequent room. Also, it's a very difficult approach to budget.

NOTE: Do not procrastinate over major messes. It is tempting, but unreasonable,

to think you will "go backwards" and make a mess after some or all of the house has been finished. If you know that someday you'll want the hall wainscot stripped, don't succumb to battle fatigue and put it off until you "get over stripping the dining room." Once all the major work is done and you're into selecting wallpapers, you will <u>never</u> go back to stripping.

six
SEQUENCE FOR INTERIOR RENOVATION

• Some items will not apply and there are always exceptions. But what follows is the standard professional approach to job sequence, which can be applied to the entire interior -- or to one room.

A. DEMOLITION and removal of debris

B. STRUCTURAL WORK

C. FRAMING OR ALTERATION of partitions (non-bearing walls). Installation or closure of soffits, pipe chases. Sub-floor repair. Installation of nailers for built-ins, plumbing fixtures, chandeliers, etc.

D. PLUMBING and ELECTRICAL roughing

E. DRYWALL installation; lath and PLASTER repair or installation; taping and skimming

F. UNDERLAYMENT for new flooring or tile

G. CERAMIC TILE repair or installation

H. PLUMBING FIXTURES, radiators, electrical receptacles and fixtures set before any additional finishes are added; avoids damage to floors, walls, trim, etc., by outside contractors

I. FINISH FLOOR repair or installation

J. WOODWORK, WINDOW, DOOR repair or installation. Refinish if clear.

K. FINISH in appropriate sequence -- no matter which order you choose, there will be overlap and some touch-up will be needed:
    1) Install prefinished woodwork, trim, built-ins
    2) Prime, paint, and wallpaper
    3) Refinish floors (sand/stain/finish or scrub/wax)

L. TOUCH-UPS of paint and clear finishes

M. HARDWARE, electrical coverplates, etc. installed

N. CLEAN UP and wash windows

O. GLOAT: When alone, wander into finished rooms and stare happily into space.

INSTALLING A TIN-CEILING CORNICE

BY JONATHAN POORE

MAPPING OUT THE JOB and knowing where to nail makes installation go quickly. Cornices come in many sizes and styles. The size is indicated by depth and projection. To ensure solid nailing, measure the cornice before furring for the new metal ceiling. Measure the depth of the cornice (down from the new ceiling) at several points on the wall, and snap a chalkline along these marks as a guide. Deviations at the wall edge of the cornice will be more noticeable than at the ceiling, so make sure the cornice runs straight along the wall.

LOCATE AND MARK all of the studs in the wall before installing the cornice. Unless the cornice is small enough to nail right through the wall into the top plate, nails will have to be driven at the studs. Plan installation so that joints between pieces occur at the studs. If you can place a nail right at the joint, the joint will be tighter. If this isn't feasible with each joint, use a small sheet-metal screw to attach the two pieces.

DRIVE NAILS through the cornice's decorative buttons or bumps wherever possible. This is easy at the ceiling, because you're nailing into continuous furring. On the wall, it's not always possible. Don't set any nails until the entire cornice is up. If you can easily remove the nails, you can make minor adjustments without damaging the cornice.

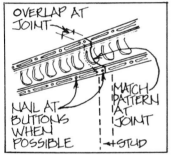

WHAT YOU'LL NEED

Cornice moulding — buy extra to allow for mistakes and waste
Wire Nails
Tin snips — sharp and in good repair
Tape measure
Chalkline
Hammer and large nailset
Heavy leather work gloves — Wear them! The pieces are razor-sharp.
Small block of wood
Indelible, fine-point magic marker

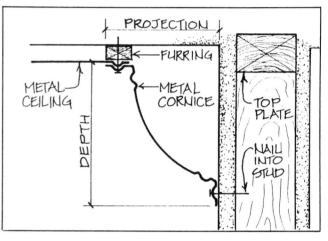

THE MOST DIFFICULT part of installing a metal cornice is fitting the inside and outside corners. Inside corners are coped (as with wood trim) and outside corners are mitered. Some manufacturers offer prefabricated pieces for both inside and outside corners. So before fussing with corners, check with your dealer — you could save a lot of work.

YOU CAN'T SIMPLY stick a piece of metal cornice in a miter box and cut it. You're going to have to fuss with making a template by freehand cutting and fitting scrap pieces of cornice by trial and error. But once you've successfully made your first mitre and coped joints on templates, you can make subsequent ones simply by tracing the pattern onto the cornice with your marker. Make sure the templates are positioned on the chalkline during trial fitting and cutting to ensure an accurate joint.

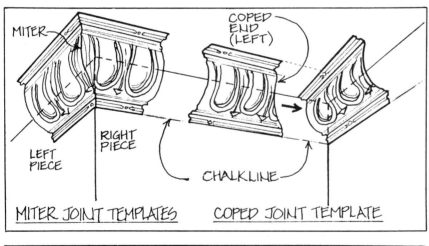

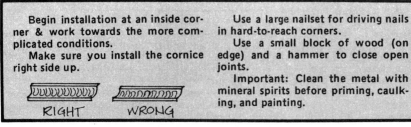

Begin installation at an inside corner & work towards the more complicated conditions.
Make sure you install the cornice right side up.

Use a large nailset for driving nails in hard-to-reach corners.
Use a small block of wood (on edge) and a hammer to close open joints.
Important: Clean the metal with mineral spirits before priming, caulking, and painting.

Restorer's Notebook

Safe Soldering

WHEN COPPER PLUMBING freezes and pops apart, the worst part of the repair problem is resoldering pipes in place -- it can be a real fire hazard, especially in older wooden houses. We found we could solder pipes close to the wall, without even scorching the paint, by using a protective pad of aluminum foil. Fold it at least six to eight layers thick (thicker if you're working with heavy pipes or large fittings), and don't squeeze the air out of the folds. Use tacks or brads to hold the pad in position behind the pipe (plastic-headed pins or tacks will melt). Be sure to let the foil cool before removing it.
-- Fred Mattfield
Long Beach, Wash.

Tripod Tip

WE THINK the handiest ladder for interior work is a short (six-foot), three-leg "orchard ladder." It's tall enough that it enables you reach most ceilings. With three rather than four legs, it's easier to work in corners and close to the wall in small rooms.
-- Elizabeth Mattfield
Long Beach, Wash.

[One manufacturer: Howard Manufacturing, P.O. Box 1188, Kent, Wash. 98032. (206) 852-0640]

Say "Ahhh"

AFTER THREE SUMMERS and autumns of stripping, scraping, and re-welding my circa 1878 cast-iron stoop, it was finally time for the finishing work -- filling in the weak spots and holes. I spent an entire weekend with a stiff putty knife, fast-drying auto body filler, and extremely short temper. Finally, my wife (a speech pathologist) handed me a box and said, "Try these." In the box were wooden tongue depressors, the kind used by doctors, nurses, and yes, speech pathologists. They worked great! They were flexible enough to reach even the most hard-to-get-to holes, and held just enough filler without spilling it all over the place. You won't find them in the hardware store, but they're available in most pharmacies.
-- J. Roginski
Brooklyn, N.Y.

Shining Sink

THE COST OF REGLAZING our old pedestal sink was just too high. The daily ritual of cleaning the porous surface was a real chore. I'd nearly resigned myself to permanent dishpan hands when I discovered Gel-Gloss. Gel-Gloss is a cleaner and polisher made for fiberglass, but I've found it works well on porcelain, too. It imparts a soft sheen and repels staining. It's not a one-time cure-all, but it has made my life easier. Gel-Gloss is made by TR Industries, P.O. Box 1533, Lynwood, CA 90262, but should be available at your local hardware store or marine-supply store.
-- Martee Whitehead-Kahn
Elgin, Ill.

Paint Touchups

IT'S NOT EASY to touch up an interior paint job without leaving noticeable inconsistencies in the paint film. But you don't want to continue slopping an extra coat of paint on the walls every couple of years. Try this: Go around the room with a small brush and dab paint onto all the nicks and scratches -- just enough to cover, no excess. Then, with a dry roller, simply roll over the wet paint. The roller stipples the wet paint to match the original "rolled" surface. You hardly notice the touchup, and you're not left with a soaked-through roller that requires lengthy cleanup.
-- Frank G. Council
Appleton, Wisc.

Tips To Share? Do you have any hints or short cuts that might help other old-house owners? We'll pay $25 for any short how-to items that are used in this "Restorer's Notebook" column. Write to Notebook Editor, The Old-House Journal, 69A Seventh Avenue, Brooklyn, NY 11217.

Restoration Products

Reviewed by Eve Kahn

Fancy Chimney Pots

With cool weather come toasty fires in the hearth, smoke drifting out chimneys into the night, and of course, chimney pots. Red Bank, a British company, made chimney pots in the '20s for English Revival homes. It's changed since then from a tiny pottery works to an automated factory, but it still produces an impressive array of pots, from simple cylinders to crenellated giants. Over 100 styles are available, in terra cotta, buff fireclay, or black slate. Heights range from six inches to six feet. Prices for stock designs are between $50 and $200. Custom work can cost between $350 and $600; expect at least a six-month wait.

The colorful, 24-page catalog ($3) includes all Red Bank's designs. The company's U.S. distributor, Clay Suppliers, sends out a free price list with drawings of pots currently on hand. To clear the warehouse, the company offers a 10% discount on their inventory until December 31. Clay Suppliers, 102 N. Windomere, Dept. OHJ, Dallas, TX 75208. (214) 942-4608.

Models pictured are, from top to bottom, Tee Can with Lid, Octagon Pot, Key Pattern Beehive, and Loose Ring Louvre.

Almost-Invisible Storm Windows

An effective -- and low-visual-impact -- storm window is Thermo-press Corp.'s interior insulating window. It's a sheet of 1/8-in. acrylic in a PVC frame; it attaches to the window frame with Velcro strips. The Velcro, gaskets, and a bulb seal at the bottom prevent air infiltration. Performance statistics in laboratory tests are impressive: Thermo-press windows let in as little as one-tenth the air leaked by magnetically-sealed interior storms; they resist up to three times as much condensation as a plain single-glazed window; and the Velcro seal remains tight even if winds reach 50 m.p.h.

Thermo-press windows are convenient, too, as they are lightweight and easy to remove for cleaning. They're practically invisible. The company will paint or stain the frame to your specifications. A strip of Velcro must be nailed to your window frame; the Velcro comes in a variety of colors (there may be a $25 to $50 charge if a color has to be specially ordered).

The cost, for an average window, is between $70 and $90 installed (less for large orders, more for oversize windows or odd shapes). If you install them yourself, the cost is about $3.50 per sq. ft. (less for quantity orders). Optional features include tinted, abrasion-resistant, or ultraviolet-filtering glazing. For all orders, Thermo-press gives free price quotes; they'll also help you figure out your payback period (usually two to four years). The company sends out a free brochure and technical information. On the East Coast, contact them for a dealer near you. They ship West Coast orders directly from their main office. Thermo-press Corp., 5406 Distributor Dr., Dept. OHJ, Richmond, VA 23225. (804) 231-2964.

Easy-to-Use Epoxies

Restoring rotted wood? Don't give up "the ship"! WEST SYSTEM™ resins and hardeners, the base components of a two-part epoxy system, were developed specifically for boats. They can prevent rot, peeling paint, swelling, warping, and many other problems with wood -- all nemeses of boats and old houses. Encapsulating wood with epoxy provides excellent moisture protection. To obtain the best moisture barrier, use two coats of resin on all wood surfaces (three if you plan to sand).

What we like about WEST SYSTEM™ epoxies is their simplicity. The basic system is a can of resin and a can of hardener. The squirt-pump tops measure out the exact amount you'll need; a full squirt of each component, a little stirring, and you're ready for work. Compatible fillers, solvent, and disposable gloves are also available. And the company bends over backward to help their customers. After you read their technical manual (free to OHJ subscribers) you'll feel like an epoxy expert. If you still have questions, they have a technical staff you can call. A mending kit, including everything down to gloves and hand cleaner, sells for $34.50, and all other products can be purchased individually. Gougeon Brothers, Inc., PO Box X908, Dept. OHJ, Bay City, MI 48707. (517) 684-7286.

Restoration Products

Books, Cards, & More

Saturn Press makes old-fashioned guest books, Christmas
cards, and menu cards with
old-fashioned designs -- Art
Deco, Art Nouveau, Arts and
Crafts, Eastlake -- and uses
an old-fashioned method:
letterpress. For $42 plus $3
shipping you can get a 400-
page, 9-by-14-inch guest book;
the cover is personalized in
gold-leaf letters. For $1.50
plus $.50 postage you can get
a packet of 12 high-style menu
cards, useful if you're host-

ing a party or running a B&B.
And for $1 each, you can buy
Saturn's black-on-buff holiday
cards.

James van Pernis and Jane
Goodrich started the Press in
January. Her interest is
architecture, his is printing;
hence the idea of printing for
old-house lovers. If you get
a chance to talk to them, be
sure to ask about the enormous
Shingle Style mansion Jane and
her husband Jim Beyor built
from scratch. Brochures are
free. Saturn Press, PO Box
368, Dept. OHJ, Swans Island,
ME 04685. (207) 526-4196.

for pre—1850 buildings

Greek Revival Wallpaper

In the past month we've heard
from two subscribers, both of
whom own Greek Revival houses,
and who complained we don't
feature enough Greek Revival
products. With that inspiration, we turned up the Millbrook collection of wallpaper
and fabrics. Not only do the
designs have classical styling
and colors, but they were in-

*Family Heir-Loom's
ingrain carpet sells
for $97 per yard.*

stalled in one of America's
most striking Greek Revival
homes, the Morris-Jumel
Mansion in Manhattan.

A range of some 100 wall-
papers ($12.99 to $14.99 per
roll) is available; all are
scrubbable, strippable, and
pre-pasted. Most have floral
motifs. The collection also
includes 29 all-cotton fabrics
($22.95 per yard) and 15 bor-
ders ($15.99 per yard), avail-
able in five-yard sections).
These prices are suggested
retail. The sample book is
worth a look: The photos depict the mansion's lovely
Palladian windows and arched
entrance hall.

Call the company's main
headquarters if your local
store doesn't carry Millbrook:
23645 Mercantile Rd., Dept.
OHJ, Cleveland, OH 44122.
(216) 464-3700.

Jacquard Textiles

Family Heir-Loom Weavers re-
produces two jacquard designs
from early-19th-century cover-
lets: One features a border of
colonial houses, the other a
bird-and-bush motif. Woven
into one corner is the buyer's
name and the date. A double
is $350; queen, $395; king,
$525; crib-size, $125. You
can also get table runners,
which are not personalized,
for $25 (37" x 16") or $55
(74" x 16").

Recently several museums,
including Abraham Lincoln's
Springfield home, asked the
company to reproduce 19th-cen-
tury ingrain carpet. Family
Heir-Loom now offers two ingrain carpet de-
signs, one for
$97 per yard,
the other for
slightly more.
The company
sends out a free
flyer. Family
Heir-Loom
Weavers, Meadow
View Dr., RD 3,
Box 59E, Dept.
OHJ, Red Lion,
PA 17356.
(717) 246-2431.

for Victorian buildings

Custom-Etched Glass

Great Panes Glassworks' claim
to fame is not their stock
sandblasted-glass designs,
which are lovely, but rather
their custom work. All you
have to do is send them a line
drawing, and they sandblast it
into glass using a
photo-stencilling technique.
It's a reasonably priced way
to replace broken or lost
etched glass.

Costs range between $20 and
$30 per square foot. The more
copies of a single design you
order, the cheaper the price
per foot; the major expense
comes from setting up the
stencil. Special types of
glass can be used for an added
charge. The company sends out
a free brochure depicting the
stock designs (some are shown
here). Send a sketch and
measurements for a price quote
on custom work. Great Panes
Glassworks, 2861 Walnut St.,
Dept. OHJ, Denver, CO 80205.
(303) 294-0927.

Ornate Wood/Coal Stove

E.F. Inc., a British stove
manufacturer, took all the
best parts from their collection of century-old stoves
-- intricate end castings,
decorated oven doors, fancy
trivets -- and assembled them
into the Enterprise Monarch.
The 132-year-old company calls
it "the most beautiful coal
and wood range we have had in
our history."

The Monarch burns both wood
and coal, which has its advantages -- especially if you're
furnishing a home in the backwoods where gas is not supplied. Unlike new stoves, the
Monarch has a warming closet
for keeping one dish warm
while another is in the oven.
The optional hot-water reservoir heats up to ten gallons
for bathing and shaving (handy
for the backwoods).

The stove comes with all
necessary tools (poker, ash
scraper, and the like).
Clean-up is easy, since a
drawer below the firebox
catches ashes. Other useful
features include a tempered-
glass window in the oven door,
a grate-level opening for
stoking the fire, and front,
top, and side doors for
loading the firebox.

The unit costs $2095 (with
reservoir, $2295). Freight is
not included. Lehman Hardware
& Appliances, one of E.F.'s
distributors, sends out free
flyers. For $2 you get an 88-
page catalog of non-electric
appliances and tools. Lehman
Hardware & Appliances, Box 41,
Dept. OHJ, Kidron, OH 44636.
(216) 857-5441.

for post-Victorian buildings

Casement Hardware

Speaking of casement windows:
These handsome stays and fasteners, copied from 18th-cen-
tury European models, are
appropriate for early-20th-
century, medieval-revival
casements. They're best to
use on wood sash, though they
can be retrofitted onto metal.
The fasteners cost between $10
and $12 in black iron; the
stays run $12 to $16. Expect
to pay double for brass. For
the stays many sizes are

available: from 6 to 18 inches
long. Fasteners come in only
one size. Transylvania Mountain Forge is a European company that's been around since
1860. Send $2 for a 30-page
catalog full of door and furniture hardware (knobs, locks,
hinges), brackets, hooks, mail
slots, and wall-hung lanterns,
most in medieval styles.
Transylvania Mountain Forge,
Graystone Manor, 2270 Cross
St., Dept. OHJ, LaCanada, CA
91011. (818) 248-7878.

1920s-Style Footscraper

Scottie footscrapers, just
like the one Virginia Metalcrafters is reproducing, were
popular in the 1920s. The
piece is cast iron, 9 in.
long, and 7 in. high. Suggested retail price is $17.
Contact the company for the
name of a local distributor.
Virginia Metalcrafters, 1010
E. Main St., Dept. OHJ,
Waynesboro, VA 22980.
(703) 949-8205.

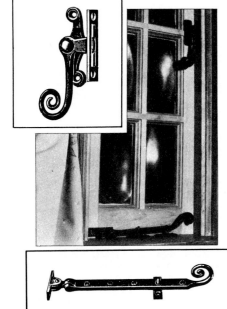

Remuddling

Above: The porch is marked as a later addition by its materials — concrete block and concrete columns.
Below: The addition is out of character in proportion as well as in architectural precedent.

When is Remuddling Remuddling?

Case in point: two once-identical houses in Fort Scott, Kansas. Neither one has stayed the same. On each the porch was remodeled -- updated -- around 1910.

So why do most architecturally-sensitive onlookers smile upon one and wince at the other?

Do we call any modification "remuddling," or only those changes that alter functions or degrade what we perceive as quality?

In the example above, the classically-inspired porch addition makes a big statement. But the workmanship is good, the details (dentils, pediment) are taken from the existing building; the grand scale of the original has not been compromised.

In the example at left, the worst sin is that the porch is no longer a porch. Instead of being a buffer between public and private spaces, an entry to the house, it's as solid and closed as can be. (This house is now a funeral parlor; behind that wall of brick is the casket showroom. A gross change in function from that of a porch....)

The classical addition above stems from the same architectural roots as the Italianate house. But the American Prairie references in the brick addition have no basis on the original structure. Maybe that, too, contributes to its jarring presence.

Thanks to Marilyn Loehr of Iola, Kansas, for the photos.

Editor's Page

LAST MONDAY Tricia came to work looking tired. But it wasn't the weekend's construction dirt or a surprise leak in the plumbing that had her down.

"WHY DON'T you write about managing kids?" she asked. "Maybe somebody will send in good suggestions on how to keep children happy without letting them wreck the house or kill themselves." (We detected mild exasperation.)

"WHEN they're babies, you worry about toxic dust. When they start crawling, you worry about nails and holes in the floor. But the real headache starts when they get old enough to want to 'help.' Willy took a keyhole saw to the porcelain bathtub yesterday. 'Just like Daddy,' he said. I told him Daddy saws wood, not tubs. Now I'm worried about the wainscot!"

(Actually, Tricia and John are great with the kids. Restoration is taking a little longer -- but it's entertaining.)

KIDS WANT to help, and they can. Willy hands nails to John. He puts joint compound on the hawk. (They lay a sacrificial dropcloth over the heavy one.) He holds one end of the measuring tape. He can even be convinced to just stick around and watch, as long as he gets to wear a painter's cap like his dad's.

THEY'RE SUBJECT TO a few rules and constraints, of course, that you wouldn't think of without having small-fry underfoot. Some safety rules:

● Gates in doorways become even more important when the blocked room is full of nails and power tools.

RESTOR -ATION KIDS

● Duct-taping a heavy plastic dropcloth or shower curtain as a barrier works amazingly well -- it makes whatever's beyond look forbidding.
● Keep the toolbox locked.
● Install high hooks to hang up the scary stuff (drill, Skil-saw) so you aren't always running to the basement to retrieve things.
● When you stack lumber against a wall, always tie it together and to the wall.

● Take the time to pull nails from woodwork you've removed.
● Cover up even dead electrical wires so children don't get used to touching them.
● Cover salvaged pieces that are likely to have lead paint.

THEN THERE ARE things that'll turn your kid into a real helper someday:
● Spend time explaining what you're doing and why. Teach respect for the work and the inherent dangers. Willy understood the danger of open stairwells and sharp tools as young as two.
● Establish a "help area" where your child can keep his or her own set of tools. Always clean up together.

THERE ARE times when it's better if the kids leave, however. Demolition is disturbing to many adults, and can be devastating to children. The noise and mess are real dangers -- and the feeling that "home" is being destroyed may be even worse.

TRICIA SAYS they learned that the hard way. When their front stoop was being demolished, three-year-old Willy screamed and cried -- and that was exterior demolition. In general, kids shouldn't be around during:
● demolition or extremely noisy activity
● major paint-stripping
● disruptive moving, such as clearing out a previously occupied room to prepare it for restoration.

A FINAL thought: Keep a sense of humor. You'll need it when your kid sees Mommy chipping out bad plaster, and decides to help . . . on a good wall. (Oh well, another story.)

[signature]

OHJ NEWS

WAY BACK WHEN, in the heyday of the IBM Correcting Selectric Typewriter, the editorial department at OHJ got hooked on "in-house typesetting." In essence, we already had that publishing luxury when we took typed copy and glued it directly to a layout board.

(Most other magazines send their typed manuscripts out to a typesetter, where it is coded and printed out as better-looking typeset copy.)

In the old days, we hated typing manuscripts a zillion times between edits, but we loved having control over the copy 'til the last minute.

Then came the micro and word processing. No more retyping long passages! But the output was still plain old Courier typewriter type. So, even though we'd entered the computer age, our type still looked a little funky. (Just like this, in fact.)

But now (trumpets please) we've got a laser printer that can make our type look better and more readable. In house!

You'll see our improved type in the next issue. We'll also be printing on a smoother, whiter paper stock to improve photo reproduction.

Letters

Illustration by Eric Sloane

His   Hers

The "Two-Hole" Variety

Dear OHJ:

I may have the answer to Patricia Williams' inquiry (October 1986 OHJ) concerning the outhouse on her property.

After reading her letter, I went straight to my bookshelf and pulled four books, all by the same author: historian, artist, antiquarian, early-Americana buff, and meteorologist Eric Sloane. In three of these books, Mr. Sloane points out that "the outhouse once meant <u>any</u> outbuilding on the early American farm," whereas the name for this particular structure was the "privy" or "private-house." Historian Sloane goes on to say that the privy was most often not only of the "two-hole" variety, but also of the two-door variety: one door for the ladies and one for the gentlemen. (This was certainly the case for the privy outside the town hall, school, church, and any other public building.)

On each door was an insignia, just as the town's shoe-maker, blacksmith, lawyer, or tavern owner had the appropriate insignia over his door. On the men's side of the privy was a carving of the sun (Sol, symbolizing man); on the women's side, a carving of the moon (Luna, symbolizing woman).

Antiquarian Sloane, I'm certain, did his homework and therefore dictated to Artist Sloane that the moon be "a waning moon in its final quarter" (i.e., the points go to the right). And believe me, Meteorologist Sloane knows his moons.

     -- Tom Flagg
     Jersey City, N.J.

A Fiery Fate

Dear Ms. Poore:

Thank you for the cover of the October issue: the picture of the old Greenlaw house in Northport, Maine. I grew up in a nearby community and will move back in November, after 45 years away. Over the years, people have watched the changes occur in the "haunted" house, have brought visitors to photograph it, and have checked it out after storms.

Unfortunately, the new owner ordered that it be burned.

In spite of many pleas to leave it alone, the old landmark experienced the ultimate in remuddling when it was torched. [See November 1986 editorial, p. 410. -- ed.]

No, there was no question of restoration -- it wouldn't have been worth it even before its back broke years ago. But it was doing no harm, and its deliberate destruction is resented.

     -- F. Eleanor Warner
     Lexington, Mass.

In Praise Of Cypress

Dear Editors:

I enjoyed your article "Wood Woes" in the September OHJ, and would like to see a follow-up about natural rot- and termite-resistant woods such as redwood, cedar, and cypress. I am a sawyer and dealer in old cypress (milled from old sunken logs). In southern Louisiana and Florida and other parts of the South, cypress has earned a reputation for holding up in jungle-like conditions where other woods fail very easily. No harmful chemicals are needed -- and it has a very pleasing grain pattern.

     -- Dan Kelley
     Franklin, La.

More Lumber Tips

Dear Patricia:

Larry Jones' article "Wood Woes" in the September OHJ was right on target.

As a professional home inspector, I am often asked for suggestions on working with pressure-treated lumber, especially for outdoor construction. It will be nice to refer clients to this article.

As an old carpenter, I'd like to offer two more "Tips For Better Luck" working with pressure-treated lumber:

1) PUT IT TOGETHER PROMPTLY. Lumber for small projects (6'-x-10' deck) will not stack with sufficient weight for air-drying. Removed from the larger stack at the lumber yard and left unused in your yard, it may warp to amusing and useless shapes in a very short time. Plan your work schedule so you can assemble the project promptly, using proper fasteners. If you must store lumber, keep it off the ground and out of the rain.

2) INSTALL DECK BOARDS "RIGHT SIDE UP." Place each board so that the curve formed by growth rings (visible at board-ends) has its arch pointing upwards. As boards dry, they usually cup in the same shape as this arch. Cupped deck boards with the arch-top facing down will hold rain/snow water, get slippery, and deteriorate even faster than boards installed as I suggest. If you don't believe this works, simply examine any deck which has some deteriorated boards -- the first ones to go are usually the ones installed "upside down."

I remain your greatest fan in Poughkeepsie.

     -- Dan Friedman
     Poughkeepsie, N.Y.

Letters

Discovering Cut-Outs

Dear Eve:

It was great fun digging out material to help you prepare your article, "Shutter Cut-Outs" (October 1986 OHJ). My eye has now gotten the knack of spotting a pierced shutter at 100 paces! In my ordinary daily rounds of Lexington, Waltham, and surrounding suburbs, I've found every one of the designs shown on this page from Brosco's 1935 Book of Designs catalog.

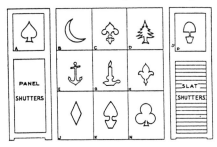

I thought your readers would also be interested in this patriotic "Minuteman" design (found on two different buildings in Lexington).

-- Sara B. Chase
Director, Conservation Center
Society for the Preservation
of New England Antiquities
Waltham, Mass.

Some Paint Comments

Dear Editors:

Your magazine is always fascinating. The May '86 issue, devoted almost entirely to painting, is outstanding -- it offers some excellent advice and tips. I would like to suggest a few additions:

1) The term "holiday" (page 172) applies to a discontinuity in a coating film, of which paint is one type. Holidays are not restricted to brush application, although they probably are more of a problem with low-quality brushes than with good ones. Holidays also occur with roller and spray application. Some of them are caused by small inclusions -- dust particles, small fibers, or bugs with kamikaze inclinations. If the inclusion occurs while applying the paint, it may be possible to remove it. If it occurs after application but before the paint sets, the best protection is a second coat of paint. (I refuse to comment on people who have the time to watch paint dry.) In

most cases, the best insurance against holidays is two (or more) coats of paint.

2) In cleaning a paint brush (page 174), a very handy implement is a pet-grooming comb. It is made of metal, with long, thin teeth that readily penetrate the brush; and with the handle at the end of the comb, your hands are less exposed to whatever solvent that's used for cleaning. (These combs are available quite reasonably at discount drug and variety stores that have pet supplies.)

-- V.I. Montenyohl
Aiken, S.C.

Stain Experience

To the Editor:

My experience with solid-color oil-based stains has proved that they are much more versatile than your article "Exterior Stains" (June 1986) states. In the past 10 years, I've used them (Olympic and Benjamin Moore) on wood with heavy coatings of paint and stain; on bare, new galvanized steel; on bare aluminum; and on baked-enamel finishes. All these applications have proven to be very durable, with not one failure having occurred.

The most important aspect of any coating project is preparation. All surfaces must be clean and dry. I am

convinced that solid-color, oil-based stain will perform well on any properly-prepared surface, even glass.

On question about latex stains: How do they qualify as stains if they don't penetrate the surface being treated? Could it be that they're essentially thin latex paints?

-- Roger T. Panek
Architect
Dover, Mass.

Antique Apples

Dear Editor:

The brief article "Period Livestock" in the October OHJ prompted me to write this letter. Can you or any of your readers direct me to a source for old apple-tree stock? I am seeking Red Ashokean and Pearman's Apple Stock. (Botanical gardens, libraries, and historic preservation organizations have been to no avail.) I know vegetables are fairly easy to find and many flowers are still available. But fruits are hard to locate.

-- Dr. Clark S. Marlor
Brooklyn, N.Y.

[Southmeadow Fruit Gardens has all sorts of rare, early fruit varieties -- including the apple-tree stocks you're searching for. Their address is Lakeside, Michigan 49116; or phone (616) 469-2865. -- ed.]

Caveat Emptor

Dear Editors:
A word of caution on low-e glass (October 1986 OHJ, page 396). It took a lot of effort to find a sample of this glass, and then more time to have my five large windows made -- few people would work with it. Everything looked great, but when the first one was installed, I went outside to admire it. Ugh!

Low-e glass looks good from the inside looking out (and from some angles on the outside). BUT standing directly in front of my 1874 Chicago Cottage in our National Register Historic District (The Old Town Triangle), the glass looked more like a green-and-blue mirror -- it was definitely out of character with the house. It also cleans like cellophane and scratches. Neither the sash-maker nor the installer will ever work with it again.

I replaced it all with regular, double-strength glass and weatherstripping. This was a nightmare -- an expen-

sive lesson of several hundred dollars!

-- Leigh Sills
Chicago, Ill.

He Can't Help Himself

Dear Pat and Clem:
I don't often write to magazine editors, but in this case I can't help myself. The crisp, clear copy and well-designed layout enhance the always-interesting articles. Each issue has some interesting tidbit or handy tip that I can use in my own renovation. Keep up the fine work!

Michael H. Baribeau
Manager/REALTOR
Bath, Maine

Geography Lesson

Dear Ms. Poore:
I am an Old-House Journal subscriber. And I'm deeply offended!

On the back page of the October 1986 issue, you've got misinformation about German-Russian Plains Houses. For

your information, the "Russians" who migrated from "western Russia, north of Odessa," were UKRAINIANS.

Odessa is in the Ukraine -- not Russia. Ukrainians emigrated to the Great Plains in the late-19th and early-20th centuries because the terrain and agricultural attributes of the region reminded them of their motherland.

-- Bohdan Zachary
Los Angeles, Cal.

[Actually, they were neither Ukrainians nor Russians; they were German nationals. But Odessa _is_ in the Ukraine. We regret any offense this oversight may have caused. -- ed.]

A German-_Ukrainian_ Plains House

Old-House Living

IT'S WORTH IT...

IF YOU LEARN TO LAUGH

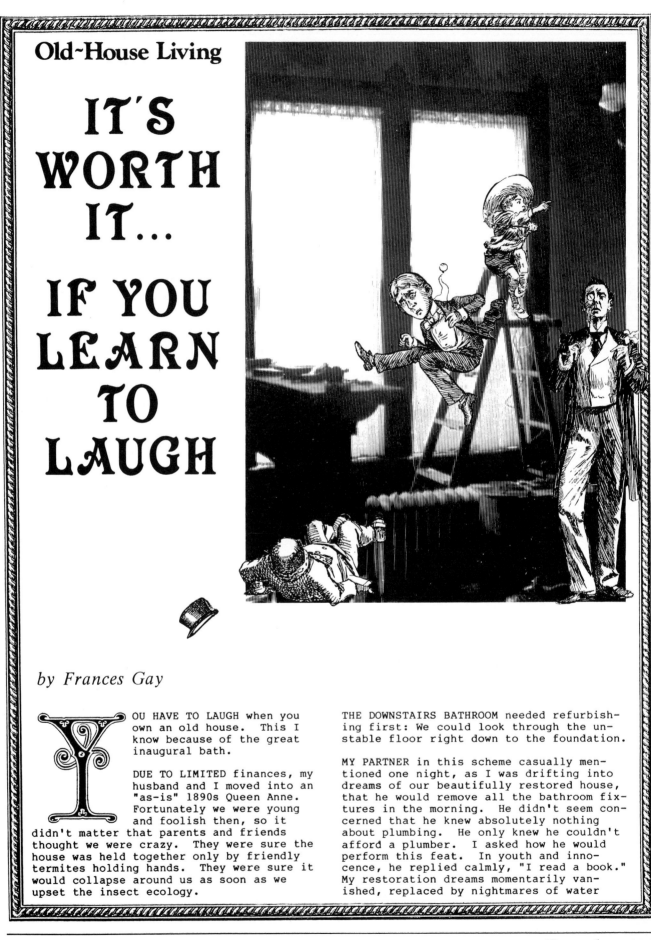

by Frances Gay

YOU HAVE TO LAUGH when you own an old house. This I know because of the great inaugural bath.

DUE TO LIMITED finances, my husband and I moved into an "as-is" 1890s Queen Anne. Fortunately we were young and foolish then, so it didn't matter that parents and friends thought we were crazy. They were sure the house was held together only by friendly termites holding hands. They were sure it would collapse around us as soon as we upset the insect ecology.

THE DOWNSTAIRS BATHROOM needed refurbishing first: We could look through the unstable floor right down to the foundation.

MY PARTNER in this scheme casually mentioned one night, as I was drifting into dreams of our beautifully restored house, that he would remove all the bathroom fixtures in the morning. He didn't seem concerned that he knew absolutely nothing about plumbing. He only knew he couldn't afford a plumber. I asked how he would perform this feat. In youth and innocence, he replied calmly, "I read a book." My restoration dreams momentarily vanished, replaced by nightmares of water pouring throughout the house.

THE NEXT DAY I <u>gladly</u> departed for work. ("Are you sure you want to tackle this?" "Oh sure, nothing to it! See you later, dear!") I whispered a little prayer, "Oh God, please protect Victoria (our nickname for the house)" and left. Not once that day did I have the nerve to call to ask how work was progressing. Maybe all would go well; in any case, it was better not to know.

WHEN I RETURNED, I was surprised to find no flooded floors or spraying geysers. All the fixtures, safely removed, stood majestically in an adjoining room, which was to become our beautiful bedroom. Nothing was broken or chipped, and my proud partner insisted the project had been easy. "Absolutely nothing to it!"

WORK CONTINUED smoothly for days. Walls and woodwork were painted, floors repaired, and fixtures re-installed with equal confidence. Then the bedroom was complete and, with great excitement, we moved back in, happy to stop sleeping with paint cans, ladders, and other tools of the trade. We reminisced about the horrible pink paint we'd found in the house, and about how we didn't know to prime before painting, and so the walls have five coats of paint. (After the first coat, the walls had looked like road maps, because of all the patched plaster. Remember, we were novices, and this was years ago in the pre-Old-House-Journal era.)

NOW WE WERE ready to enjoy living in our newly decorated suite. All the doomsayers had been wrong! I went to take my first bath in the restored bathroom. Our white miniature poodle Dixie followed me. She loved my nightly bath; her favorite treat at the end of a day was to lick a soapy hand. We were having a marvelous time when suddenly the tub tilted backward and the geyser, no longer expected, rose from

The dining room walls called for much plaster repair.

the foot of the tub. Dixie barked with delight as I screamed for help. Help didn't come, because he was soaking in the upstairs tub, gloating over his successful plumbing job, imagining how pleasant and memorable my first bath would be. Memorable all right, for both of us; clad only in a towel, he had to race downstairs and go out in the cold to enter the basement and shut off the water.

IT SEEMED THE SCREWS bolting the claw feet to the tub weren't tight enough, so the legs gave way. To this day, two large paint cans sit under the tub, just in case the feet decide to move again. (No one sees them, but they give me a sense of security.) For a long time Dixie would peer around the bathroom door to check weather conditions before entering. She wasn't taking any chances of an unscheduled shower!

ONLY AFTER ALL these years can we look back and laugh. And there are more stories, mostly about our naivete. When we bought Victoria, we asked the realtor if the roof leaked. "Absolutely not," was the reply. One thunderstorm later, we were running around in the attic from

The library's spectacular fireplace, complete with embossed tiles, was carefully stripped of a coat of white paint.

rafter to rafter with pans to catch the water. Still, with the optimistic enthusiasm of an old-house lover, I reassured my partner not to fear. I suggested, as a joke, that we ask God to drop a limb on the leaking section so we could then have it repaired.... Don't ever do that, unless you're serious! Two weeks later, in another storm, a limb crashed exactly on the leaking portion of the slate roof. After some lengthy discussions, the insurance company agreed to replace the damaged roof -- but cancelled our policy. Later we found a more understanding insurer, who likes old houses, too.

AS IF THAT is not enough to make you pack your possessions and head for a tract house.... Still we stayed to see what new challenge would arise. After all, life was getting interesting. We were the historic preservation pioneers of Charlotte. Articles appeared in the local newspapers about our beautiful project. People knocked on the door on Sunday to ask for tours. Our house offered about as much privacy as a fishbowl.

THE FIRST WINTER we thought we would freeze to death; it snowed every Wednesday for a month. We began to suspect that all

Antique paintings hang near a well-stocked buffet.

Beautiful details, like the parlor fretwork, remained sound.

the people who doubted our sanity were right; our brains, more than likely, had frozen. Because the kitchen was unheated, we drew straws in the morning to see who would get served breakfast in bed. The second winter I devised a way to guarantee I always drew the right straw. I was served coffee, juice, and the rest as any Victorian lady should be. The next summer we painted and caulked, insulated the attic, and had the radiators overhauled. Today the house is toasty warm (more or less) in the winter.

OUR NEXT EPISODE revolved around my affinity for little furry creatures. I usually give them names, homes, and food. But sometimes I draw the line, as in the case of the midnight appearance of a flying squirrel on our landing. He provided a show that would have put the man on the flying trapeze to shame, flying from staircase to gasolier to table and back again. To catch him we closed off doors after each swing, and then placed a trap, baited with a tasty entree, in the entrance hall. We waited to hear the trap door close. After what seemed hours it banged shut, and we took our friend outside and freed him. The next day we

The restored library is a Victorian showplace.

curators of Charlotte's most opulent Victorian landmark. We had spent seven-and-a-half years in military-base housing, plus one year in a new house, and there wasn't much to occupy our time. Victoria certainly took care of that problem. We often wondered if there would ever be enough hours to do everything. But eventually we reached a point where we could relax and begin showing off the results of our hard work. Sharing makes it all worthwhile.

SO DON'T WORRY if people think you're slightly daffy. After all, can they tell stories about their new houses? Have they had as much fun as you have lately -- come on, it is fun, if you learn to laugh a little. Your house, like mine, has been around a long time, and with your tender loving care it will survive. And so will you!

Frances Gay, an active preservationist, has taught restoration courses and served on the Mecklenburg Historic Properties Commission. She is currently Director of Development at Architectural and Engineering Concepts, P.A., a restoration architecture firm.

investigated and closed off all access to the interior for friends with furry coats (Dixie excepted).

THE ONLY TENANTS we still have are little bandits. Although we live minutes from the heart of the city in an early street-car suburb, we are blessed with lots of wild animals. For years we heard bumps in the night on the roof but were too sleepy to investigate. About eight o'clock one night, my curiosity finally won and I crept upstairs to a window where I could see the roof. There stood a raccoon, as surprised to see me as I was to see her. That was the beginning of a long relationship. Since then, a family of raccoons has occupied one or more of our unused chimneys. As it is impossible to tell them apart I never know whether I'm conversing with mother, daughter, granddaughter, or great-granddaughter, but we do have babies each spring. The mother comes down nightly to eat her ration of dog food. Sometimes we visit; she eats out of my hand or sits atop the back porch lattice, taking a rest from motherhood.

SIXTEEN YEARS have passed, and while I reminisced for this article, the question arose: "Was it worth it?" Well, at first we were only looking for an old house to refurbish, and not planning to become

"Victoria" stands proud, painted yellow with white trim.

WEATHERSTRIPPING ENTRY DOORS

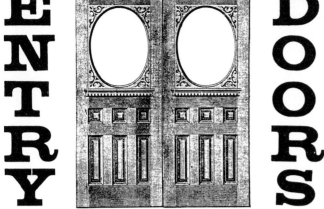

by Jonathan Poore

THE PRIMARY PURPOSE of door weatherstripping is to limit air infiltration. Take a look at the fit of the door in the jamb. If the door binds or if there are large gaps between the door and jamb or stops, repair before weatherstripping. (See "How to Fix Old Doors," June 1986 OHJ.) It's a waste of time to weatherstrip a door that doesn't fit well.

CHOOSE a type of weatherstrip by these four criteria:
1. Effectiveness -- Why bother otherwise?
2. Aesthetics -- Exterior doors are quite visible.
3. Durability -- Will it last long enough to warrant the time it takes to install it?
4. Ease of installation -- This affects cost if it must be carpenter installed. The cost of materials is minor by comparison.

EFFECTIVENESS is an obvious consideration. Don't install cheap "hardware-store variety" vinyl or vinyl-and-aluminum weatherstrip on

VINYL AND ALUMINUM WEATHERSTRIP NOT RECOMMENDED

doors. The cheap vinyl type is usually self-stick -- and doesn't adhere well to old, rough woodwork, regardless of how well you wash it. Cheap vinyl weatherstrip gets brittle and may crack as it ages or when it gets cold. The inexpensive vinyl-bead weatherstrip that's set in a strip of soft aluminum (it usually comes on a roll) is just as ineffective. The aluminum is so flexible and the vinyl so rigid that you can't fasten it in enough places to make even contact.

WEATHERSTRIPPING is effective only if you can still shut the door easily after it's installed. Let's face it: A weatherstripped door accidentally left ajar is less effective than a closed, unweatherstripped door. Most of the hardware-store variety, self-adhesive foam (polyurethane or PVC) presents this problem. The joint you're trying to seal usually varies in width. The manufacturer's instructions will tell you to layer the foam in the widest part of the gap. But that means increasing

1/8" thickness at a time. The extra thickness makes the door hard to shut because there's too much foam to compress.

AESTHETICS cannot be overlooked when you're working on an entry door. Avoid cluttering the door with a lot of surface-mounted weatherstripping. The least offensive location for surface-mounted weatherstripping is a sweep at the bottom of the door. It's away from eye level, away from any decorative hardware or details.

DURABILITY means cost effectiveness. You don't want to have to re-weatherstrip your door every year. Therefore:
● Avoid vinyl beads on the threshold. They wear out quickly when you walk on them.
● Avoid cheap vinyl as previously discussed.
● Avoid foam weatherstripping. It decomposes (gets crumbly) in a year or two.
● Avoid anything vulnerable. The edges of a door receive a tremendous amount of abuse, so make sure your weatherstrip is up to it, or locate it in a protected spot -- such as mortised into the door edge, or tucked in next to the stop.

EASE OF INSTALLATION is important but... if you spend a little extra time putting in well-designed, high-quality weatherstripping now, you won't have to do it again for a long time. Interlocking (or integral) weatherstripping will last many decades if properly installed.

TYPES OF WEATHERSTRIP

USUALLY the same type of weatherstrip is used at the head, hinge jamb, and lock jamb. A different type is used at the sill.

THERE ARE TWO major categories of weatherstripping: interlocking and resilient. The advantage of interlocking is that once installed it becomes an integral part of the door (even visually). It also allows the door to close and latch completely unimpeded. The disadvantage is that it requires carpentry skills to install. The edge of the door must be rabbeted with a router to receive the weatherstrip, and the two pieces (on the door and jamb) must mate accurately. It could be argued that interlocking weatherstrip does not seal as well as resilient because it doesn't provide continuous contact. The longevity and ease of operation of interlocking weatherstrip outweighs the disadvantage, though.

RESILIENT WEATHERSTRIPPING is that kind which flexes, bends, or compresses somehow as contact is made, thereby sealing the joint. The

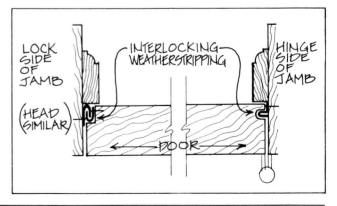

LOCK SIDE OF JAMB (HEAD SIMILAR) — INTERLOCKING WEATHERSTRIPPING — HINGE SIDE OF JAMB — DOOR —

contact part of the strip must "give" enough
to allow the door to shut, yet must be durable. There are six materials to choose from:

1. Silicone
2. EPDM rubber
3. Neoprene
4. Vinyl
5. Wool pile (or synthetic pile)
6. Spring metal

SILICONE AND EPDM have the best "memory."
That is, they don't permanently compress; they
will always return to their original shape.
Silicone and EPDM also remain flexible at low
temperature.

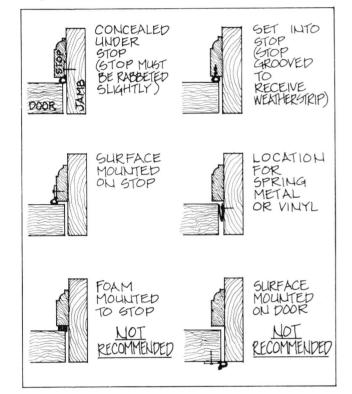

NEOPRENE has similar characteristics but is
less expensive and less durable. Vinyl is
less durable, ages sooner, and becomes less
flexible when cold.

WOOL OR SYNTHETIC PILE weatherstrips are
better suited for door sweeps than for the
jambs because they can span a large gap. For
less money, you can buy wool or synthetic
felt -- less resilient than pile.

SPRING METAL is very durable but can create
friction, making the door a little harder to
close.

DOOR BOTTOM SEALS / SWEEPS

ALL BOTTOM SEALS or sweeps should close
against a threshold so they don't have to
drag across the floor. There are three basic
types of door bottom seals or sweeps: interlocking; resilient; and automatic (drop down).

INTERLOCKING is always a good choice for
reasons previously discussed. It does, however, necessitate in-
stalling a compatible
threshold to receive the
hook on the door.
Thresholds and hooks are
available in bronze or
aluminum so they will
match your existing door
hardware.

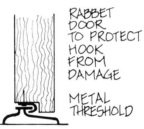

RESILIENT sweeps or bot-
tom seals are available
in all of the same mate-
rials as resilient head/
jamb weatherstrips. In
the box above are some available configurations. Many different design variations exist;
these are most typical.

AUTOMATIC door bottoms are the high-tech
solution to weatherstripping. They are the
most expensive and most difficult to keep
properly adjusted. When they are correctly
installed and adjusted, they work very nicely.
But if they're maladjusted, they can make the
door bind, or fail to form a good seal. As
you shut the door, a button hits the hinge
side of the jamb, causing the seal to drop
down snugly against the threshold.

Accurate Metal Weatherstrip Co. Inc., 725 S. Fulton Ave., Mount
Vernon, NY 10550. (914) 668-6042. Interlocking, EPDM rubber,
neoprene, vinyl, wool/synthetic pile, bronze and zinc spring-metal.

Pemko Co., Box 3780, Ventura, CA 93006. (805) 642-2600. Interlocking, silicone, EPDM rubber, neoprene, vinyl, wool and
synthetic pile, spring-metal.

Resource Conservation Technology Inc., 2633 N. Calvert St.,
Baltimore, MD 21218. (301) 366-1146. Silicone, EPDM rubber.

Schlegel Corp., Retroseal Division, PO Box 23197, Rochester,
NY 14692. (716) 427-7200. Wool-and-synthetic-blend pile.

Zero International, 415 Concord Ave., Bronx, NY 10455. (212)
585-3230. Interlocking, silicone, neoprene, wool pile, spring-metal.

PART TWO

Locks & Alarms

HOUSE SECURITY

by David Swearingen

A COMMON old-house security error is installation of unauthentic locks on entry doors. The front door is a focal point of any building, and contributes greatly to that all-important "first impression." The glossary on page 475 chronicles the development of various types of locks. This will give you a clear idea what styles are authentic for the period of your house.

BOTH RIM AND MORTISE locks have simple, large mechanisms housed in heavy metal cases. The mechanisms are easily accessible, so the lock will function for many years without breaking, and if a part does wear out, it can be replaced easily. Some rim locks made over 400 years ago are still in service.

RIM AND MORTISE LOCKS have been made somewhat obsolete in recent years by cylindrical and tubular locks. Not because modern locks are better, but because they are easier and faster for builders to install. Mortise locks are frequently specified for commercial and government buildings. Reproductions of solid brass Colonial rim locks are available, but they are very expensive ($250-$350) and do not offer much security unless furnished with an unauthentic pin tumbler cylinder.

KEY-IN-KNOB LOCKSETS are grossly unauthentic and offer virtually no security. Likewise, the average tubular deadbolt is no obstacle to a determined thief. Even if the cylinder is encased in a solid hardened ring, the entire unit can be popped right off the door instantly by forcing a crowbar or claw hammer under the cylinder housing. Many burglars slip an awl around the housing and flip back the deadbolt so quickly and silently, it looks like they're using the key.

THERE IS an inherent weakness in any tubular installed on a wood door that opens inward. Even the best tubulars leave only 1/4 to 3/8" of wood around the tube, and any force applied to the door is concentrated on that thin slice of wood. With one swift kick, the tube breaks right through the door.

A RECENT IMPROVEMENT over the old tubular deadbolt is the cylindrical deadbolt. This is an exceedingly durable lock, yet the mechanism is so simple that malfunctions are rare, and

repair is inexpensive. The most notable manufacturer of such a lock is the Lori Corporation. It's a very good security lock.

COMPARING TYPES

GENERALLY SPEAKING, mortise locks are the most secure and durable locks, but rim locks are best for thin doors because none of the door needs to be cut away. While a pin-tumbler mortise lock does have an exposed cylinder, it projects less than tubular cylinders. It is much less obtrusive, and more secure. The cylinder is the weakest point of a mortise lock; it must have a hardened slip ring.

MORTISE LOCKS require a pocket be cut out of the door. Because so much material is removed, it may seem that a door with a mortise lock can be kicked in more easily than one with a tubular lock. This is not the case. Only a very narrow band of wood need be broken to kick in a door with a tubular or cylindrical lock. Conversely, the large case of a mortise lock spreads the force out over a big area, so it takes more force to break through the door.

CASE IN POINT: A week after I installed a mortise lock in the door pictured at right, it was attacked by burglars. This door opens off a narrow corridor, so the burglars set up a jack across the hallway. With the bottom of the jack against the opposite wall, they started tightening it. This put more pressure on the door than anyone could by kicking it. When the door began to crack, the cracks ran up and down the length of the door rather than straight through it. Such extreme force was applied that the jack finally collapsed into the corridor wall, foiling their scheme.

JIMMY RESISTANCE

MOST ANTIQUE LOCKS had only one-half inch throw bolts as opposed to the one-inch throws available today. Longer bolts are better, but their advantages are overrated considering the weaknesses previously detailed. Old-time locks had short throws for two reasons:

1. Because of the nature of bit key operation, bolt throw was generally equal to the length of the key bit. One-inch throw bolts were

available, but required turning the key two complete turns. They were secure, but never very popular because of the inconvenience.

2. There was less need for longer throws years ago. Doors and frames were made from solid wood and closely fitted by carpenters who took pride in their work. A one-half-inch throw on those doors provided better security than a one-inch throw on today's pulpy wood doors that have big gaps between door and frame.

THE "TOGLOCK" by Almet Manufacturing prevents jimmying by interlocking the door and frame with expanding claw bolts. Lock-smiths have hailed this "revolutionary new invention" as being "a generation ahead in dead-bolt security." While Almet does have a good product, it's hardly "revolutionary." Similar claw bolts were available in bit key mortise locks nearly a century ago. If you look hard enough, you can still find old-fashioned lever locks with jimmy-resistant claw bolts.

SALVAGING ORIGINALS

 IF YOU'RE LUCKY, the original locks are intact on your house, or you'll be able to find some nice antiques from other sources. In either case, you'll want to restore them. Locks can be complicated, and so are probably best left to an experienced locksmith. Most locksmiths won't be interested in working on old locks; they'd rather sell you a new one. You'll likely have to fix them yourself.

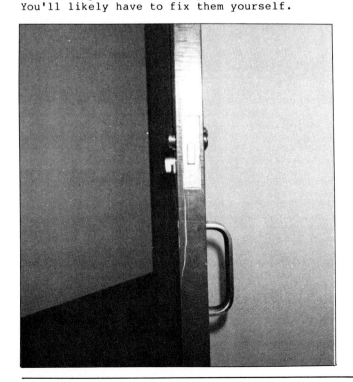

FIRST, REMOVE the knobs. A small screw in the shank of the inside knob holds the knob fast to the spindle. Remove any paint buildup in the slot of the screw to avoid "stripping" the screw -- replacements aren't easy to find. Loosen the screw, and the knob will either pull straight off or will screw off. Then pull the outer knob and spindle straight out.

RIM LOCKS are usually attached by four screws, one at each corner. Mortise locks are secured with two screws in the edge of the door. After removing these screws, pull the lock out by yanking on the latch or deadbolt. You may have to pry gently through the knob holes and around the front of the lock. Some locks will be very stubborn, but work patiently so you don't damage the door.

TO EXPOSE the internal mechanism, remove the one or two screws that hold the cover on the case. Remove the cover carefully so you don't lose any springs or other small parts that may fall out. Ideally, you'll have another lock that you can leave open, undisturbed, to serve as a model. If your lock has multiple levers, be very careful to keep track of the order you remove them in.

CLEAN EVERY PART thoroughly. This may involve degreasing, wire brushing to remove rust, and paint removal from the front plate, latch, and deadbolt. Often, one or two of the springs will be broken. Hardware stores carry a large assortment of replacement springs; locksmiths, too, should have replacements. Have a lock-smith replace broken lever springs. If the post the levers are pivoted on is loose, use a small hammer to "rivet" the fixed end into the case more solidly.

REPAIR BROKEN PARTS by brazing. Solder is inadequate for most lock repairs. If the cast-iron case is cracked or broken, weld the outside of the case. The bolt may be bent (it's likely made of soft brass or bronze). You can straighten it in a vise, but do so carefully and slowly.

AFTER EVERY PART has been cleaned and re-paired, reassemble the lock with great care to ensure that each part is where it belongs. The slightest deviation may keep the lock from functioning properly. After the lock is reassembled, lubricate all moving parts with a very thin oil -- 3-in-1 Oil, or sewing machine or gun oil is appropriate. Spray lubricants like Tri-flow and LPS are also good. Lubricants make the lock work more smoothly, and prevent rust.

IF YOU NEED a key for your lock, see a lock-smith. Aside from the skill required to cut a key accurately, you may need a PhD in key making just to locate the proper key blank. Around the turn of the century, lock makers were producing thousands of different key blanks for their locks. Using the proper blank makes a big difference in how well the key will work.

REATTACHING THE LOCK to the door is basically a matter of reversing what you did to get it off. When you put the knobs back on your door, be careful not to screw the knob onto the spindle too far, or the knobs will bind. If it's too loose, there will be excessive rattling.

N ALARM SYSTEM can be a very worthwhile investment. Not only does it
give you a second line of defense
against intrusion, but it can also
incorporate other important safety
features such as fire and medical
protection. An alarm system is an especially
good idea for houses that are isolated, in
high-crime areas, difficult to secure, or full
of priceless belongings.

IMITED SPACE precludes us from describing all available alarm systems and
their various components. We can introduce you to some of the most important
features and limitations, though. If
you decide that an alarm system is for
you, pick up a copy of The Burglar
Alarm Book by Doug Kirkpatrick*. This
excellent and comprehensive text demystifies
alarm systems without assuming that the reader
has an advanced degree in electronics theory.

LARM SYSTEMS can generally be divided
into three types: hard-wired, line
carrier, and wireless. Some systems use a combination of these
three types. Hard-wired means that
the alarm components are physically
connected with wires (just like your lights,
switches, and outlets are). Line carriers use
your existing electrical circuit. Wireless
transmitters use radio waves.

EPUTABLE alarm installers will tell
you hard wiring is obsolete; wireless is the only way to go. I dis-
agree. I think they say that because hard-wired installation
requires care, patience, and hard
work -- now that's the part that is
obsolete today. Although wireless technology
is advancing, I still believe that hard-wired
systems provide the most reliable protection
in most situations.

ANY HOMEOWNERS have been scared
away from hard-wired systems
because of the high cost. The
components are actually cheaper
than those of wireless systems.
The extra cost is the labor
that's involved in installing
the system. This can be a real boon to the
do-it-yourselfer. You could install a hard-
wired system yourself for half the price of a
good wireless system.

YSTEMS THAT USE wireless transmitters
do have their advantages, especially
in an old house. If you have a lot of
ornamental plaster and fine woodwork,
the last thing you want to do is fish
wires through the house. In that
case a wireless system like that made available by Premier Communications is the way to go.

BURGLAR ALARM SYSTEMS provide two types of
protection: perimeter and interior. The
cheapest alarms provide only one or the other.
You really need both types, and they should be
on two separate circuits. Here's why:

● If a burglar circumvents or defeats the
perimeter circuit, he'll be detected by the

---

interior circuit.
● If one system fails, you're still covered.
● Separate circuits allow you to turn off the
interior circuit when you are at home, while
still keeping the perimeter circuit armed to
protect your family from intruders. (They're
often called day and night circuits.)
● Separate circuits enable your system to
provide a different response to an attempted
break-in than to a successful break-in.

ERIMETER PROTECTION, also called
"point of entry" protection, is your
first line of defense in a home
security system. It can be kept on
when you are at home. This, and the
fact that perimeter protection can be
completely hidden, are the biggest
advantages, particularly for old-house
owners.

IDEALLY, you'll have an alarm on your fence
and an alarm on the grounds around your house
to detect prowlers. In most cases this is
impractical. Install wired window screens and
alarms on your screen doors. This is an especially good practice for old-house owners. An
alarm that goes off when a burglar breaks down
your door is fine for summoning help and
scaring him off. But it didn't help your
hand-carved, leaded glass door that was just
destroyed. An alarm that sounds an ear-
splitting whelp the instant he penetrates the
screen door is likely to scare him away before
he damages irreplaceable doors and windows.

IN ADDITION to screen alarms, you should have
sensors on your doors and windows themselves.
Preserve the pristine appearance of your
vintage doors and windows by using recessed
(concealed) magnetic switches or plunger
switches. Foil tape on windows is terribly
unauthentic and totally unnecessary. If you
feel you must detect glass breakage, there are
better ways -- like using a wireless sensor.

NTERIOR PROTECTION is provided by a
variety of devices which detect an
intruder inside your house. Although
more prone to false alarms than perimeter sensors, interior detectors are
also harder to defeat. Thieves broke
into a Fanny Mae house (just three
blocks from my own home) by sawing a
hole through the floor. No perimeter system
would have stopped them, but an interior alarm
certainly would have.

THE INTERIOR ALARM system should activate a
"repel system." Once an intruder has forced
his way into your house, you want to get him
out as quickly as possible. This is best done
by installing a number of "speakers" (a technical term for noisemakers) throughout the
house in hidden places like return-air ducts.
Install the very loudest speakers you can buy.
Atlas' Q3 speaker, powered by a Moose JDS100
driver, can turn the toughest thug into
quivering jelly. Never mind if you actually
deafen him; he'll get his hearing back when he
goes before the judge.

---

* Baker Publishing, 9348 Monogram Ave., Sepulveda, Calif. 91343.

A COMPLETE SECURITY system includes a number of safety features in addition to the two types of intrusion protection already described. Safety protection requires a third circuit, known as a "24-hour circuit." It has no "on/off" switch, as it must be on continuous alert to provide "other protections": smoke and heat detectors, emergency panic buttons, calls for medical help, poisonous gas detectors, flood detectors, freezer failures, or just about anything else that you want to continuously monitor.

Atlas' Q3 speaker, powered by a Moose JDS100 driver, can turn the toughest thug into quivering jelly. Never mind if you deafen him; he'll get his hearing back when he goes before the judge.

ALL OF YOUR ALARM components will be connected into a central unit called the control box. Be sure it features an auto shut-off to satisfy legal requirements that are in effect in most cities. And of course, auto reset so that it will automatically re-arm itself after it shuts down. The best control boxes contain batteries that are continuously recharged, so your system will always have power even if the house current fails. Permanent gel-cells provide the best battery power.

MOUNT ALL exterior speakers, sirens, and bells out of reach. Ideally, they'll be in a tamperproof box, or mounted behind louvers in your attic to protect them from the weather and from being sabotaged by intruders. A strobe light high on the exterior of your house will enable emergency vehicles to find your house much faster.

ALTHOUGH ALL ALARM SYSTEMS can be turned on and off at the control box, you will find it more convenient to install one or more remote on/off switches at convenient locations. Place the control box in an out-of-the-way, secure spot.

REMOTE SWITCHES may be either key-operated or digital pads (which use a push-button combination). Many systems are controlled by a switch located outside the front door; if you choose this location, it can be concealed behind a hinged mailbox to maintain the integrity of your restoration.

Addresses of Listed Companies

Almet Manufacturing, 9166 Viau Boulevard, Montreal, Quebec, Can. H1R 2V8. (514) 326-9780

Lori Corporation, Old Turnpike Road, PO Box 490, Southington, Conn. 06489. (203) 621-3601

Premier Communications, Box 1513, Dept. OHJ, High Point, N.C. 27261. (919) 841-4355

The Evolution of Locks

RIM LOCK – BIT KEY
The earliest locks were self-contained in a large, rectangular box that was mounted on the rim (surface) of the door. Used on residential and commercial buildings through the early 20th century.

MORTISE LOCK – BIT KEY
In 1835, a new type of lock was invented that was mounted entirely within the door. It was installed in a pocket that had been mortised out, hence the name. Commonly used on buildings from 1850 to 1950.

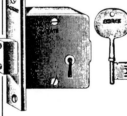

MORTISE LOCK
Mortise locks using pin tumblers were invented in 1865, but very few were actually produced prior to 1900. These locks were used on fine residences and commercial buildings from the '20s to the '40s. Still used on commercial properties, but seldom on residences due to high cost.

AUXILIARY DEADBOLT – BIT KEY
The complete locksets described above consisted of a lock case containing both a latch and a deadbolt. Small bit key deadbolts were often used in conjunction with locksets to provide additional security.

CYLINDRICAL KEY-IN-KNOB
Invented about 1925, the cylindrical lockset was slow to gain acceptance. It derives its name from the cylinder-like housing that contains its mechanism. Inherently insecure and expensive to repair.

TUBULAR KEY-IN-KNOB
This lock is similar to the cylindrical K-I-K described above, but a cheaper version. Consists of little more than a latch tube and two knobs. Provides minimum security, yet has been used on 95% of post-1950 houses.

TUBULAR DEADBOLT
Invented in 1932, this is a small auxiliary deadlock consisting of little more than a tube and one or two cylinders. Inherently weak and insecure.

CYLINDRICAL DEADBOLT
Invented in 1971, this lock looks just like a tubular deadbolt, but the construction is entirely different. Much more secure than a tubular. Can be used authentically on houses dating back to the 1930s.

REPRODUCING EMBOSSED TILE

This tile, with its simple design and high relief, is relatively easy to reproduce.

In the March 1986 OHJ, we published an article on collecting Victorian embossed tiles. It prompted David and Lorma Wiebe of Kearney, Nebraska, to write and tell us their uncomplicated method for reproducing these scarce tiles. We sent the Wiebes' information to two experts: Susan Warren Lanman, author of the original article and an avid collector; and Susan Tindall, a specialist in the preservation of architectural ceramics. "Could reproducing embossed tiles really be this simple?" we asked. The answer was yes — if you aren't looking for a perfect match and if you have luck on your side. For this article, we've incorporated Ms. Lanman's and Ms. Tindall's comments into the Wiebes' text.

THIRTEEN YEARS AGO, we bought our 1888 house and were delighted to find it had three original fireplaces. Two were in perfect condition and surrounded by intact embossed tiles. The one in the dining room, however, had been heavily used and hadn't fared as well. Many of its tiles were loose, and about 15 were cracked or broken.

WE DECIDED to reproduce the ruined tiles ourselves; working with a ceramist who lives nearby, we developed a method that gives quite satisfactory results. And the first step is to find a good ceramist -- someone to fire the tiles and experiment with glazes for you (unless you have your own firing facilities and some experience in this kind of work).

MAKE A FLAT WOODEN BOX of 1/2-in. plywood. It should be large enough to extend some 4" beyond the tile on all sides, and about 2" deep. Seal it with shellac so the wood won't draw moisture out of the plaster. The box has to be tight enough to keep the plaster from leaking out, so seal all the joints with clay or silicone caulk.

CAREFULLY REMOVE the tile you wish to copy. Thinly coat it with a mould-release agent such as tincture of green soap (available at art- or sculpture-supply stores and at some building-supply dealers). Use clay to affix the tile to the bottom of the box -- be sure no plaster can get underneath the tile, or you'll never get it out of the box. Mix plaster of

paris (or even better, number-two moulding plaster, available at some art-supply stores and most masonry or sculpture suppliers) according to the directions and pour it into the box. Tap and stir it gently to remove air bubbles.

THE PLASTER will become warm to the touch as it hardens; let it cool down again, and then knock the box apart and gently pry the tile loose. Don't wait too long or it will be impossible to remove. Let the mould dry for about two weeks. Use plaster to fill in any air holes in the finished mould.

YOU CAN'T EXPECT the finished tile to look exactly like its neighbors. You'll be using "slip" (liquid clay) to make the reproduction, and slip will shrink about 20% as it dries -- an 8" slip-cast tile turns into a 6-1/2" tile. But there are ways to compensate for shrinkage. The ceramist can press modeling clay into the mould, which leads to only 3-6% shrinkage and less warping. Or you can enlarge the mould by stretching the pattern at the edges, and deepening and accentuating the design with common, inexpensive sculpting tools. (Make sure it's 20% thicker, too.)

THE CRITICAL THING is that the overall length and width of the tile match that of its neighbors. So enlarge the dimensions of the mould by 20% at this stage. If the pattern doesn't match exactly, it won't be too noticeable. But if the replacement tile is too small, the grout lines around it will be fatter -- and that's really noticeable. (Likewise, if you overcompensate and make a tile that's too big, it won't fit! Better test-fire one to check its size before you order a dozen.)

KEEP IN MIND: The image in the mould is reversed, so look at the tile in a mirror while you work on the mould. Simple designs with heavily raised surfaces are easier to reproduce than tiles with complex patterns and low

The complicated, low-relief pattern of this tile makes reproduction more difficult.

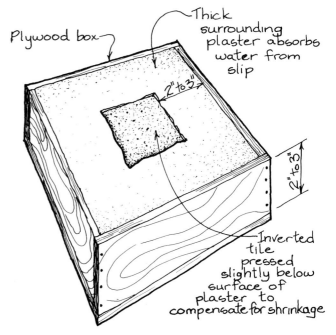

relief (use extra care if yours is one of the latter).

ANOTHER METHOD is to make a 20%-enlarged photocopy of the tile and place it over plasticine, which is available at art- or sculpture-supply stores. (If your local stores don't carry it, you can always buy those kits for kids with packages of multi-colored plasticine -- you'll end up paying about $15 for enough to make your tile.) Trace around the photocopy with either a razor blade or a pattern-marking wheel, and then carve an exact replica of the tile out of the plasticine, using the photocopy as a guide. Seal the replica with shellac (to keep the plasticine oils from leaking into the plaster) and cast it in the box as you would a tile. Plasticine is much easier to remove from plaster than tile, so you'll have to perform only minor touch-ups on your mould.

ONCE THE MOULD IS READY, take it to the ceramist to have the tiles made. Touch up any imperfections before they're fired. You'll want to obtain a good matching color, so have the ceramist experiment with the under-glaze and glaze. Of course, the original glaze formulas were carefully guarded information; your ceramist may find the colors difficult to match, which means you might have to settle for an approximation. Also, try to have the glaze "pool" in the valleys of the design, as the original tile-makers did.

AS FOR CONE SETTING, your ceramist will undoubtedly have some advice here. Cone 06 is the most frequently used temperature firing point, and most readily-available commercial glazes use this setting. Cone 04 may make the tiles more durable. Consider having a couple of experimental tiles cast and fired, to see which cone setting works best.

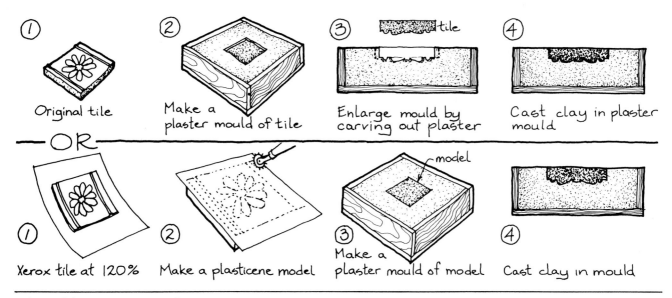

NOW

THEN

BY EVE KAHN

FINDING LINOLE

WE GET WEEKLY calls from people trying to locate linoleum. The real thing — linseed oil, wood dust, cork, resins — isn't made in the U.S. anymore. Major manufacturers stopped making it around 1974. (See OHJ January, 1982 for a complete history of the linoleum industry.) We offer several solutions: You can purchase the real thing from distributors of European and Canadian linoleum. You can buy vinyl-tile "rugs" that look like linoleum. Or you can buy standard vinyl tiles, some of which look like old-fashioned linoleum. Beware: Unlike linoleum, most vinyl has a textured surface.

THEN

WE COMPARED old linoleum catalogs to current vinyl-tile catalogs of Armstrong and Congoleum. Both have new patterns that recall the old: marble, parquet, and cork imitations; irregularly arranged rectangles; old-style figures. Armstrong's

THEN

NOW

JM

NOW

ALL "THEN" DESIGNS shown are from our c. 1930 linoleum catalogs. The designs labelled "now" are vinyl, except where noted (see pages 480 and 481). Listed below are linoleum distributors and one manufacturer of linoleum-style vinyl rugs.

¶ Domco Industries Ltd. manufactures sheet linoleum in eight marble-like tones. Average prices are $2 to $2.25 per sq.ft. Contact the company for a distributor near you. Domco Indust. Ltd., 1001, Yamaska, E., Dept. OHJ, Farnham, Que. J2N 2R4 Canada. (514) 866-5461.

¶ Gerbert Ltd. distributes Nairn linoleum, made in Scotland. It's the only importer we found who will deal directly with consumers. Their Armourtile 90 (3.2 mm thick, eight colors) and Armourtile 200 (2.0 mm thick, ten colors) linoleum tiles are 30 by 30 cm (about 1 sq.ft.), have old-style swirls, and come in boxes of 50. Armourtile 90 sells for about $100 per box ($2 per sq.ft.); Armourtile 200, $75 per box ($1.50 per sq.ft.). Flooring contractors receive a 25% discount. Gerbert Ltd., Box 4944, Dept. OHJ, Lancaster, PA 17604. (717) 299-5035 or 299-5083.

THEN

NOW

funkiest designs — martini glasses or fedoras with gloves, for example — are tile inserts that look straight out of the 1940s. (You get custom colors, even Art Deco letters.) Armstrong and Congoleum are available at most floor-covering stores, where you'll probably turn up other vinyl flooring that resembles linoleum.

WE ALSO FOUND linoleum makers in Europe and Canada. Their flooring has the marble-like swirls and mottled tones of old linoleum (the more colorful the swirl, the more old-fashioned the look). Nobody has re-created the tiny-tile or floral designs of yesteryear. Linoleum today comes in 6-ft.-wide sheets and 1- or 2-sq.ft. tiles. To make small, period-style pieces, cut the linoleum with a mat knife, or find a professional who has a cutting machine. Companies listed on these pages provide literature, samples, and instructions for maintaining linoleum.

¶ Forbo N.A. makes the "Linoflex" tiles shown at right. (Superimposed is a similar pattern from 1930.) The tiles measure 30 by 30 cm (approx. 1 sq.ft.) and 2.5 mm thick. They come in ten grainy colors, including red, blue, orange, ivory, black, brown, grey, coral, green, and white. Forbo also makes "Marmoleum," a sheet linoleum, in some 30 colors. Marmoleum looks a bit more like old linoleum, but Linoflex comes in a more manageable size. Both cost between $2.25 and $3 per sq.ft. Forbo N.A., Suite A, 218 W. Orange St., Dept. OHJ, Lancaster, PA 17603. (717) 291-5874 or (800) 233-0475.

¶ Linoleum City is a supplier of Hollywood props that sells all kinds of linoleum: tile and sheet, solid-color and imitation marble. They also have pieces of old linoleum on hand. No literature; write with your specific needs. Linoleum City, 5657 Santa Monica Blvd., Dept. OHJ, Hollywood, CA 90038. (213) 463-1729.

(linoleum)

At left is an inlaid-tile linoleum pattern from 1930. Nobody sells borders like this anymore, but it's easy enough to create your own. To make the trim, cut strips of solid-color linoleum; called battleship linoleum, it's available from Forbo N.A. and Linoleum City (addresses listed above left).

¶ Believe it or not, the single tiles shown at right and on page 481, top left, come from Armstrong's 1986 catalog. The castle (enlarged, page 481), though, is from a 1930 linoleum brochure entitled, "New Ideas in Home Decoration." Armstrong's tiles are all made to order; they come in 18-, 27-, 36-, and 63-in. squares. You get custom colors on all tiles and custom lettering on initial tiles. Expect to wait at least four weeks for delivery. For more information, call the company's toll-free number: (800) 233-3823.

¶ A2Z makes "hard rugs" out of pieces of ¼-in. vinyl tile. "Navajoleum," shown at right with its c. 1930 ancestor, recalls Native American designs and comes in three colorways. "Classic Quilt" looks like a diamond-patterned quilt (one colorway: grey, black, and white). The four sizes, as shown, range from 2-½'x4' to 3'x8' or 4'x6'. Prices range from $350 to $700. The company will do custom work in vinyl or linoleum (prices upon request) and they will also ship pieces of vinyl tile so that you can create your own arrangements. A2Z, 5526 W. Pico Blvd., Dept. OHJ, Los Angeles, CA 90019. (213) 937-2072.

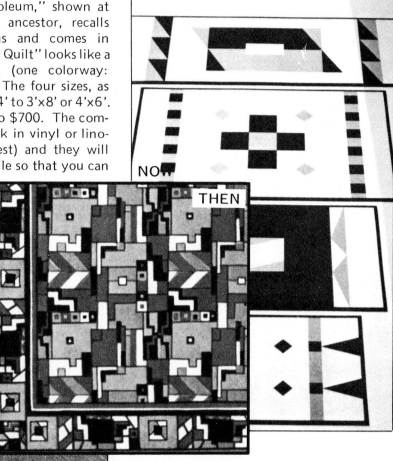

NOW

THEN

THEN

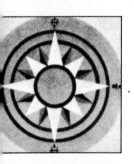

¶ DLW stands for Deutsche Linoleum Werke AG, founded in Germany in 1926. They offer 46 shades and thicknesses of linoleum, all handsome and similar to old linoleum. Prices of between $1.60 and $2.50 per sq.ft. include estimated installation. Shown at left is DLW's "jaspe"-pattern sheet linoleum, popular since 1930 (inset, left). DLW also sells PVC tiles that measure about 2 sq.ft. each and have the matte surface and marble-like swirls of old linoleum. PVC tiles cost between $2.30 and $2.75 per sq.ft. installed. Call for the name of your distributor. DLW Flooring, Anderson, Dewald & Assocs., 2750 Northaven, Ste. 210, Dept. OHJ, Dallas, TX 75229. (214) 247-4955.

NOW

THEN

(linoleum)

A COMPATIBLE GARAGE

To follow up October's article on designing old-house garages, here's a successful case history by architect Richard Bergmann.

PROBLEM: My squat, 1950s, two-car garage was drastically out of proportion with my 1836 Greek Revival home. Making the two buildings more compatible offered several benefits: I could make the garage look like a carriage house, which a house of this vintage would once have had. I'd get much-needed space on the second floor for a workshop. The surrounding historic district would be served: The 1950s garage had no appeal, and detracted from an otherwise consistent neighborhood (the district nomination forms called it a non-contributing building).

AS I'M A RESTORATION architect, I was able to draw up plans myself. I opted to raise the roof on the dated little garage, rather than tear it down. A local house-moving firm, The Monroe Company of Norwalk, Conn., provided the necessary services. Fortunately the garage had approximately the same roof pitch as the house, so all we did was raise the roof to create a second storey.

THE PHOTOS ABOVE show the roof being lifted. The house movers jacked up the roof and supported it with cribbing (railroad ties). Then carpenters put down new floor joists and walls. The roof was lowered onto the new walls, the cribbing removed, and the floor completed.

I INSTALLED three basement-size windows on the side facade, and two salvaged double-hung windows in the rear gable. In the main gable I put a pair of louvered doors;

they open to move machinery in and out, close up tight in winter, and complement the shutters on the main house. Above them projects an old mahogany beam; in the past beams like this were used to hoist hay, but they work on modern machinery and supplies just as well. I replaced the garage-door glazing with Masonite panels, to make the doors look more like true carriage-house doors. Finally, I added corner boards and moulding -- simpler versions of those on the house -- along the roof and around doors and windows.

I THINK THIS sympathetic approach improves properties where the garage is unrelated, unremarkable, and detached -- where the garage was a design afterthought. 🏠

The garage as it relates to the house: Note similar shutters, moulding.

Ask OHJ

Muddled Main Street

Q: OUR MAIN STREET has been terribly remuddled. We need guidance to help restore the storefronts in our small town. The buildings were built between 1880 and 1920. We've found very little published material on how to successfully rehabilitate business districts. We've seen pretty before-and-after pictures, but with little explanation of how the changes were implemented.

Not long ago, two out-of-state motorists pulled to a fast halt and got out to take photos of the worst examples of Permastone and vertical cedar siding. I live in dread that they'll submit the pictures to The Old-House Journal for "Remuddling of the Month." Please help us!

-- Deanna Cooper, Auxvasse, Mo.

A: THE OLD-HOUSE JOURNAL is currently gathering information for a future article on storefront restoration. (Examples of successful business-district rehabilitations are eagerly sought.) In the meantime, contact the Main Street Program of the National Trust for Historic Preservation for more information: 1785 Massachusetts Ave. N.W., Washington, D.C. 20036. They'll be a tremendous help to you.

Out, Damp Spot

Q: THE PLASTER WALL in our foyer becomes wet periodically. The affected area is from the baseboard upward, approximately 2-1/2 feet. There is also sporadic dampness in an isolated area about halfway up the stairs. We've had our tin roof checked and repaired where seams had split open. The plaster was applied directly over brick with no air space. The wall has wallpaper on it and can look perfectly dry, but if the humidity goes up, it will be soaked in a matter of hours -- even on days when there has been no rain. We're considering furring out the wall, insulating, and finishing with gypsum board. Are we on the right track?

-- Susan Yeingst, Carlisle, Penn.

A: FURRING OUT THE WALLS may alleviate your moisture problems as long as you provide a vapor barrier. But chances are you needn't rip out all that plaster. Your problem is isolated in a couple of small areas, so it sounds like faulty mortar joints are to blame. The bricks on your home's exterior may need repointing. When you run your air conditioner, water vapor between the bricks condenses where it touches the relatively cool plaster. Also, check the soil around your foyer; if it's abnormally damp, it surely is contributing to your problem.

Before you repair the damaged areas of plaster, use a cementitious product such as Thoroseal™ to waterproof the inside surface of the bricks. This will help ensure that the problem won't recur. It makes more sense to isolate and solve the problem and patch the damaged plaster then it does to demolish the plaster and build new walls.

Insulation Dilemma

Q: I AM INVOLVED in the renovation of a small miner's cottage in Virginia City, Nevada, which was built in 1875. The house is based on a barn-type construction method, and has no wall studs. Can you point me in the right direction on how to insulate such a house?

As you can see from the photograph of the kitchen, all there is is wallpaper over a building paper of some sort of muslin ("Cabot A"), and then long wooden planks. Between the cracks of those planks you can see the exterior or clapboard -- and sunlight. (Note how the electrical cable and switch box cannot be recessed because there is no stud-wall cavity.) If we erect stud-wall framing on all exterior walls, we'll reduce the dimension of the very small rooms by critical inches -- one room is already not quite 8' x 8'. Also, adding plaster board will destroy the wonderful depth of the window-frame moulding.

-- Kathleen E. McCarthy, Concord, Calif.

A: UNFORTUNATELY, any means you use to insulate the house will involve a compromise: Something will have to change, be it room size, exterior covering, or moulding profiles. The best approach is to frame out the stud walls and stuff them with fiberglass-batt insulation. A four- to six-inch space would provide the best insulation, but you can always cheat it down to save floor space (although this will reduce R-value). As far as the window-trim profiles are concerned, you can always remove the casings and block them out away from the window frame. Of course, you'll have to rip a wide jamb to reach the casings, thereby increasing the depth of the window pocket.

Restorer's Notebook

Wrap It Up

I RECENTLY STRIPPED several lengths of delicately carved, soft pine mouldings. The mouldings had deep recesses that made it difficult to remove paint without damaging the pieces. I carefully removed the moulding and placed each piece on a length of aluminum foil that was slightly longer than the longest length of pine. I then applied a liberal coat of paste-type paint remover and wrapped the foil securely around the woodwork. I returned several hours later and wiped the moulding clean with a piece of burlap. A quick and easy mineral spirit rinse completely the relatively painless process.

The aluminum foil inhibits evaporation, and so allows the stripper to work longer -- softening the paint in even the deepest grooves. I saved money, time, and didn't mar the wood in the least.

-- Nate Bekemeier
New Bedford, Mass.

Top Rung

LADDERS ARE GREAT for reaching high places. But they don't help you much once you're up

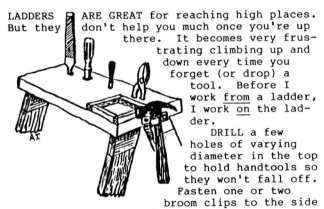

there. It becomes very frustrating climbing up and down every time you forget (or drop) a tool. Before I work from a ladder, I work on the ladder.

DRILL a few holes of varying diameter in the top to hold handtools so they won't fall off. Fasten one or two broom clips to the side of the ladder -- they're great for holding hammers and the like. Finally, tack some scrap lumber to the ladder in the shape of a square to make a spill-proof place to keep small nails and screws.

-- Douglas Anderson
Ontario, Canada

Be Good To Yourself

AFTER A MESSY DAY of battling to restore your old house, you're likely to find yourself covered with paint, grease, or other goo. Most folks reach for a container of mineral spirits to clean their skin. Try cold cream instead. Although it's not as powerful a solvent (it'll take a little longer), it's a lot kinder to your skin -- and it leaves you smelling better, too.

-- Rosalie Friend
Brooklyn, N.Y.

Drywall Tip

IN YOUR OCTOBER ISSUE, you mentioned covering texture finishs with gypsum wallboard ("Unwanted Texture Finish"). I recently laminated a cracked, roughly-textured ceiling with 1/4" Sheetrock. The uneven surface made it difficult to screw the Sheetrock in place without tearing the paper. I could push the board in place with one hand, but when I let go, the screw would pull through the Sheetrock. Solution: Plaster washers. I used two or three plaster washers with drywall screws to pull the Sheetrock up tight to the ceiling. They dimpled (but didn't tear) the paper. Two coats of joint compound concealed them completely.

-- George Foley
Green Bay, Wisc.

Card Shark

I SPENT a recent Saturday sanding several hundred feet of just-stripped oak cove moulding. It was tedious work. I planned to get together with some friends for a game of poker that evening. Looking forward to cutting the cards gave me an idea: I wrapped my fine sandpaper around about twenty playing cards, and used them as a sanding block. The edge of the cards conformed perfectly to the shape of the moulding and spared me many splinters.

-- Charlie Wilson
Kansas City, Mo.

Backside Brazing

I LEARNED THE HARD WAY that cast iron is very brittle: I was tapping on a stubborn hinge pin and my fancy Victorian door hinge broke. After overcoming my sickness, I began to think of ways to repair this accident. I concluded that welding was my only chance; however, I didn't want any weld to show on the outside of the hinge. A retired machinist neighbor repaired my hinge by grinding away part of the back of the hinge to leave room for the weld so it wouldn't be visible on the face of the hinge. Excess weld on the back was all right, because the mortise on the door could be deepened slightly in that spot to accommodate the weld. (Check your Yellow Pages for a welding shop in your area.)

-- Dan Miller
Elgin, Ill.

Tips To Share? Do you have any hints or short cuts that might help other old-house owners? We'll pay $25 for any short how-to items that are used in this "Restorer's Notebook" column. Write to Notebook Editor, The Old-House Journal, 69A Seventh Avenue, Brooklyn, NY 11217.

Restoration Products

Reviewed by Eve Kahn

Greek Revival & Japanesque Wallpaper

From the 18th through the 19th centuries, imitation-stone wallpaper was stock-in-trade at wallpaper stores. The paper that Thibaut is reproducing comes from a c. 1830 Greek Revival house in Connecticut. Thibaut offers it in the original gold on ecru and three other colorways, for $14.95 per roll. It's well suited for any Greek Revival or Federal house.

Thibaut also found a wonderful c. 1881 Japanesque paper to reproduce. It looks Japanese at first glance, but upon closer examination the turkey motif in the border reveals American origins. The paper costs $20.95 per roll, the border $7 per yard. Thibaut offers the original mauve and cream on silver plus three other colorways. All papers, part of the company's Historic Homes of America collection, are pre-pasted, strippable, and vinyl-coated. Richard E. Thibaut Inc., 706 S. 21st St., Dept. OHJ, Irvington, NJ 07111. (201) 399-7888.

Drop-In Sinks

Above, a Japanesque sink; right, a blue pinstripe sink suitable for colonial and Colonial Revival homes.

Stove-Part Supplier

The world of stove parts is extremely complicated. Literally hundreds of types of wood- and coal-burning stoves have been produced. Kenneth Spahr, owner of Washington Stove Parts, has been in the business for 20 years and still, he says, "I don't know it all, not by a long shot."

If your stove is missing parts, Kenneth has thousands of replacements on hand, from door handles to fireboxes. What he doesn't have he can usually get or have cast. His specialty is New England-made parts, but he has sources for other brands as well.

Delivery for pieces on hand is one to two weeks; for castings, four to six weeks.

Kenneth guarantees fit and quality: "I do not send parts that are not correct." (The subscriber who recommended him told us, "He works diligently to accommodate customer inquiries.") Kenneth asks customers to be very specific about their needs and to send cash up front; stove grates, for example, cost between $65 and $100, depending on size, complexity, and scarcity. A free information sheet describes frequently-requested parts. Washington Stove Parts, Box 206, Dept. OHJ, Washington, ME 04574. (207) 845-2263.

Norstad Pottery offers some 20 styles of drop-in sinks; several are appropriate for old houses. All are handmade of high-fire vitreous stoneware, and Norstad guarantees them against cracking and chipping.

Six sizes are available, from 13-1/2 to 20-1/2 in. in diameter. Prices range from $165 to $295, FOB Richmond, California (shipped UPS). Custom work can be ordered (there's an additional charge and a longer delivery time). A color brochure depicting all styles is free. Norstad Pottery, 253 S. 25th St., Dept. OHJ, Richmond, CA 94804. (415) 620-0200. Showroom: 1201 Bridgeway, Sausalito, CA 94965. (415) 332-5306.

Restoration Products

Waxing & Polishing at My House

I waxed a table with Renaissance™ micro-crystalline wax a few weeks ago. I felt a little funny applying $1.50-an-ounce wax to a $3 table, but it was easy, and the piece looks great: It has a soft sheen, and I used only a tablespoon of wax.

Renaissance™ is the same wax the British Museum has used, and the manufacturer says the product works as well on marble, metal, and leather. The coating protects from liquids, heat, and finger marks. It retards moisture penetration, oxidation, and tarnish, and doesn't have to be re-applied often. It's also clear, colorless, and easy to apply (you just dab a small amount on a rag and buff; I can verify that).

An eight-ounce can costs $11.95, FOB Hastings-on-Hudson, New York. Cereus Inc., 184 Warburton Ave., Dept. OHJ, Hastings-on-Hudson, NY 10706. (914) 693-8698.

After I waxed the table, I was on a roll, so I decided to polish a dusty, tarnished bronze lamp. I squeezed out a drop of Simichrome, let it work on the lamp for a few seconds, and -- this is a true story -- when I wiped away the excess, the spot I'd polished was gleaming. I'd never suspected such a pretty lamp lay underneath the dirt!

Simichrome is a powerful yet gentle metal polish that's been around for a long time. It's been most popular for use on motorcycles (every man over age 30 who walked by my desk this week said, "Great stuff! I used to use it on my motor-cycle"). You can find it in antique shops, motorcycle- and car-supply stores, as well as home centers and hardware stores. A 50-gram tube (approx. 2 ozs.) costs $3.80;

for the serious polisher Simichrome also comes in 250-gram cans (about 9 ozs.) for $11.10. Contact the company if you can't find a distributor near you. Competition Chemicals Inc., PO Box 820, 715 Railroad St., Dept. OHJ, Iowa Falls, IA 50126-0820. (515) 648-5121.

New-Old Cookstoves

From the outside, Elmira's Model 6000 electric range looks just like a c. 1910-25 stove. But inside are hidden practical modern features like a built-in exhaust fan and switches that turn off burners left on too long. All controls are cleverly disguised. The unit is rather wide -- four feet -- but that leaves room for storing utensils, pots and pans. And it has four square feet of stove-top work space!

Model 6000 costs $2495. Elmira also manufactures wood- and coal-burning stoves in two traditional styles. The "Oval" has an open area under

Malleable Moulding

Installing moulding on bumpy, bulging, or curved old plaster can be a problem. No matter how you manipulate the strip of moulding, you end up with gaps between it and the wall. Flex Moulding offers a solution: polyester moulding, flexible enough to conform to the most irregular surfaces.

Flex does both custom reproductions and stock designs. Stock pieces range from simplest classical to elaborate Japanesque. Along with moulding, Flex makes furniture parts, wall ornament, rosettes, columns, and plaques. There's no minimum order, and

the resin can be mixed to any consistency you want -- floppy (for moulding) or solid (for supporting columns).

Moulding costs between $.75 and $8 per foot, depending on complexity. Other pieces are equally inexpensive, especially in comparison with plaster and wood. Flex moulding is also lighter, something else to consider when you're installing it on old plaster.

A full catalog is free. Flex Moulding Inc., 16 E. Lafayette St., Dept. OHJ, Hackensack, NJ 07601. (201) 487-8080.

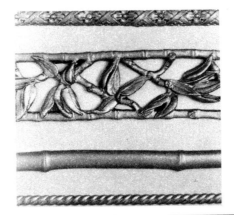

the oven and costs $2295. The "Sweetheart", with a solid base, costs $1695. Optional hot-water reservoirs are $200.

There are Elmira dealers around the U.S.; contact the main office for a free brochure and the name of a dealer near you. Elmira Stove Works, 22 Church St. W., Dept. OHJ, Elmira, Ontario, Canada N3B 1M3. (519) 669-5103.

———— *for post-Victorian buildings* ————

Craftsman Stencils

Here's a source of Craftsman-inspired floral stencils: Rasa Arbas, a West-Coast designer, has created seven designs that would make great decorative friezes. You have a choice of alpine-strawberry, crocus, ficus, lily-of-the-valley, jasmine, violet, or long-stemmed-rose motifs. Each pattern is $5, payable in check or money order, and comes with easy-to-follow instructions (no special skills or materials

needed). Be sure to send a self-addressed, stamped, #10 envelope with your order. Rasa Arbas, 306 22nd St., Dept. OHJ, Santa Monica, CA 90402. (213) 395-5529.

Canadian Source

Getting old-house parts hasn't been easy in Canada. But the situation is improving, we're told, thanks in part to Steptoe's Old House Store. This one-stop source has almost anything a restorer could want: cast-iron Victorian staircases, tin ceilings, architectural details, Victorian wallpapers, embossed wall-coverings, lighting, furniture, and more. The company has just moved into an 11,000-sq.ft. warehouse/showroom, which, they report, is "rapidly filling with new products." Steptoe's Old House Store Ltd., 322 Geary Ave., Dept. OHJ, Toronto, Ont., Canada M6H 2C7. (416) 537-5772.

Stand-Up Desks

We liked the name right off: The Stand-Up Desk Company. It brought visions of a mom-and-pop factory of yesteryear. And yes, that's all they make: stand-up desks, with spare styling that would look great in any Bungalow, Prairie, Mission, or Craftsman house.

The company claims many famous people did their best work at stand-up desks, like Thomas Jefferson, Virginia Woolf, and Ernest Hemingway. It's also said that working while standing, with one foot slightly elevated, is beneficial for bad backs. The desks are crafted in a choice of red ($1000) or white ($1100) oak, walnut ($1175), or mahogany ($1275). Matching stools cost $310 (·$375 for mahogany). Each desk comes with a brass foot rest, storage compartments, a pen-and-pencil groove in the front, and a flat area in the back (handy for the telephone or a mug of coffee). Optional features include brass trim, casters, a storage rack between stretchers, and gold

tooling on the leather writing surface. Best of all, desks are made for your height.

Shipping costs between $35 (Washington, D.C. area) and $250 (Pacific region). Stools cost $35 to ship (free in the

Washington area). The Stand-Up Desk Co., 5207 Baltimore Ave., Dept. OHJ, Bethesda, MD 20816. (301) 657-3630.

Terra Cotta Reborn

Used on many storefronts and some houses in the early 20th century, decorative terra cotta practically disappeared by the 1950s. But it's now making a comeback. The National Building Museum's recent exhibit, "Ornamental Architecture Reborn: A New Terra Cotta Vocabulary," featured winners of a terra-cotta design contest. Ludowici Celadon is reproducing each design.

The pieces range from the serious to the silly, and from $400 for a hand-painted plaque to $4 for the pigeon bracket at left. Custom sizes and colors can be ordered. The company provides a brochure

showing all designs. Ludowici Celadon, 4757 Tile Plant Rd., Dept. OHJ, New Lexington, OH 43764. (614) 342-1995.

opinion...

Remuddling

The house today (above, front view; left, rear view). Below, the house in 1892.

The Mystery House

 ENEE KAHN, an architectural historian in Stamford, Connecticut, had shaken her head over this eyesore (above and left) more than once. What had it been like? She could begin to guess, but the harsh reality of the Permastone box stopped imagination dead.

NOT TOO LONG AGO, Renee came upon this old photo (lower left) in an 1892 book about Stamford. "The Larches, estate of Warren Roosevelt, engineer," read the caption. The structure was long gone, she was sure -- certainly, she'd have noticed such a house! As she turned the page, though, the dormers caught her eye; they looked ominously familiar. Later she drove by the ugly building and confirmed her worst suspicions. That featureless box, unrecognizable but for its dormers, was once The Larches.

"I WISH they'd torn the house down," laments Renee. "Then the old photo would be a pleasant view of what had been, rather than a painful reminder of today's errors."
                      -- Eve Kahn

INDEX 1986

(L) = Letter

(P) = Product Listing

(RN) = Short Item (Restorer's Notebook, Ask OHJ, etc.)

 **ORDER FORM**

The Old-House Journal

Our magazine — published six times per year — is the only how-to-do-it periodical in America for old-house people. Filled with money-saving, mistake-saving ideas and techniques, *The Old-House Journal* will help you restore, maintain, and decorate your pre-1939 house. Every issue is packed with practical advice, and generously illustrated with drawings, photos, and step-by-step diagrams.

☐ New Subscription   ☐ Renewal (Enclose Current Mailing Label)

☐ 1 Year — $18   ☐ 2 Years — $32   ☐ 3 Years — $42

Bound Back Issues
The OHJ Yearbooks

We keep back issues in print, bound in sturdy, softcover books. Our set of 'Yearbooks' is like a Restoration Encyclopedia: the biggest, most complete, most authoritative reference on old-house restoration available anywhere. Over 2,000 pages in all!

700 ☐ The 1970s Set — $39.00
1976-1979 at 77% the price. You save $17!

806 ☐ The 1980s Set — $79.00
1980-1986 at 63% the price. You save $47!

700-806 INDEX ☐ The Full Set — $118.00
All 11 Yearbooks at 65% the price — plus a FREE Cumulative Index. You save $74!

Individual Yearbooks are also available:

76 ☐ 1976 — $14   79 ☐ 1979 — $14   82 ☐ 1982 — $18   85 ☐ 1985 — $18
77 ☐ 1977 — $14   80 ☐ 1980 — $18   83 ☐ 1983 — $18   86 ☐ 1986 — $18
78 ☐ 1978 — $14   81 ☐ 1981 — $18   84 ☐ 1984 — $18   **INDEX** ☐ OHJ Cumulative Index — $9.95
Your key to all the information that has appeared in OHJ since 1973!

Paint-Stripping Tools

OHJ's staff has tried just about every paint-stripping method known, and these tools are the best at their respective tasks. *The Master Heavy-Duty Heat Gun* is the finest tool around for stripping paint from interior woodwork — mouldings, corners, recesses, turned wood. *The HYDElectric Heat Plate* is the best tool for large jobs such as exterior clapboards, shingles, and flush doors. Both are backed with the OHJ Guarantee: If the tool fails for any reason within 60 days, we'll take it back and replace it.

☐ Master Heavy-Duty Heat Gun — $77.95
11

☐ HYDElectric Heat Plate — $41.95
10

All prices postpaid, and include fast UPS shipping.

Send My Order To:

Name _____

Address _____

City _____ State _____ Zip _____

Amount enclosed: $ _____
YBK86   *NY State residents please add applicable sales tax.*

NOTE: If your order includes books or merchandise, you must give us a STREET ADDRESS — not a P.O. Box number. We ship via United Parcel Service (UPS), and they will not deliver to a P.O. Box.

Please clip this page and mail together with check payable to The Old-House Journal to THE OLD-HOUSE JOURNAL, 69A Seventh Avenue, Brooklyn, NY 11217.

Prices valid until Sept. 1, 1987

The OHJ Catalog

☐ Please send me _____ copies
12 of this invaluable sourcebook, which lists companies supplying almost 10,000 products & services for pre-1939 houses. *The OHJ Buyer's Guide Catalog* is fully cross-referenced & indexed for easy use, so I can find whatever I need to repair, restore, or decorate my old house. ($11.95 ppd. for current OHJ subscribers; $14.95 ppd. for non-subscribers.)

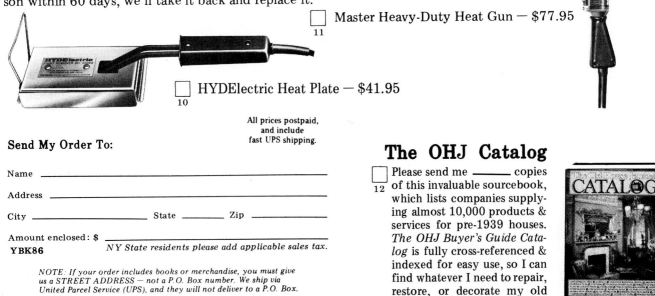
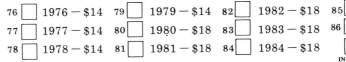
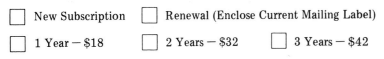